'Conducts us through [Kipling's] life and times with authority, dispassion and clarity. This is an excellent biography, with everything in its place' Lawrence James, *Literary Review*

'Well researched and finely written ... Anyone who wants to learn about this curious figure in our culture could do no better than to start here' Simon Heffer, *Country Life*

'This meticulous new biography ... numerous telling asides ... Lycett is strong on Kipling's physical sense of himself ... and of the immediate world around him' Adrian Poole, *Times Literary Supplement*

'A solid and valuable book ... The judgements are measured, intelligent and nearly always right' David Gilmour, *Financial Times*

'Tells the fascinating story unobtrusively and convincingly' Philip Hensher, *Spectator*

'Thorough, painstaking, conscientious and his scholarship cannot be faulted ... indispensable ... We should be grateful to Lycett for the effects he has triumphantly brought off' Frank McLynn, *Glasgow Herald*

'Thoughtful and thorough ... Lycett gives us a warts-and-all Kipling, yet manages to retain our sympathy' Tony Gould, *Independent*

'Does full justice to every stage in Kipling's career' David Goodall, *The Tablet*

'Kipling emerges far more clearly and, it must be said, far more unpleasantly, than from any of the previous biographies' Humphrey Carpenter, *Sunday Times*

EX LIBRIS

RUDYARD KIPLING

Born in Stamford, Lincolnshire, Andrew Lycett spent his childhood in East Africa. After reading history at Oxford University, he worked as a journalist and foreign correspondent. His previous books include a study of the Libyan leader Colonel Qadaffi and a well-received biography of Ian Fleming, the creator of James Bond. Now living in north London, he is on the Council of the Kipling Society.

Rudyard Kipling

ANDREW LYCETT

PHŒNIX

A PHOENIX PAPERBACK

First published in Great Britain
by Weidenfeld & Nicolson in 1999
This paperback edition published in 2000 by Phoenix,
an imprint of Orion Books Ltd,
Orion House, 5 Upper St Martin's Lane,
London WC2H 9EA

A CIP catalogue record for this book
is available from the British Library.

ISBN 0 75381 085 9

Typeset by Selwood Systems, Midsomer Norton

Printed in Great Britain by
The Guernsey Press Co. Ltd, Guernsey, C.I.

Contents

Book Four

Book Five

Illustrations

Rudyard with the Bishop of Perpignan and Field Marshal Lord
    Roberts and Lady Roberts, Perpignan, 1911
Colleagues (H. A. Gwynne, Perceval Landon and Julian Ralph) on *The
    Friend*, Bloemfontein, March 1900
John Kipling with fellow members of the Irish Guards, Warley, 1915
Rudyard at a recruiting rally in Southport, 1915
War correspondent in Rheims, August 1915[8]
Rudyard with Perceval Landon and Captain F. Monroe, France,
    August 1915
Cousins: Sir Philip Burne-Jones, Rudyard, Carrie, Stanley Baldwin,
    Margot Baldwin, Diana Baldwin, Elsie Kipling[9]
Rudyard and Carrie in the garden at Bateman's with dog (probably
    Mike), 1930s
Rudyard's installation as Rector of St. Andrews University, 1923, with
    Stanley Baldwin
George and Elsie Bambridge, marriage at St Margaret's, Westminster,
    1924
George and Elsie Bambridge, with dogs, Paris, early 1930s
Rudyard Kipling, 1924[6]

In addition the part titles of the five books of this biography are
illustrated by drawings that come from the Berg Collection, New York
Public Library (books three and five), the Kipling papers at Sussex
University (books two and four), and the Weidenfeld & Nicolson
archives (book one).

The author and publishers are grateful to the following for permission
to reproduce the following illustrations. Unless otherwise credited, the
pictures come from the Kipling Papers at Sussex University and are
copyright The National Trust for Places of Historic Interest or Natural
Beauty.

[1] Kipling Society
[2] Susan Eastmond
[3] British Library
[4] Robin Egerton
[5] Wolcott Dunham Jr
[6] National Portrait Gallery
[7] Stowe C. Phelps
[8] Weidenfeld & Nicolson Archives
[9] Lord Baldwin of Bewdley
[10] Berg Collection, New York Public Library
[11] Mark Samuels Lasner and the Estate of Max Beerbohm
[12] Michael Smith

O Ye who tread the Narrow Way
By Tophet-flare to Judgment Day,
Be gentle when 'the heathen' pray
To Buddha at Kamakura!

The Kiplings and the Macdonalds: Family Tree

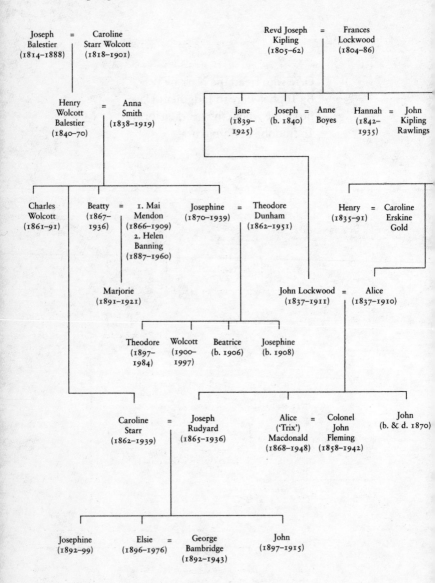

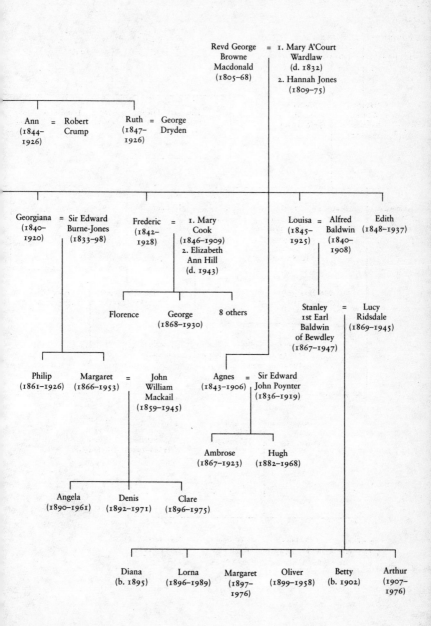

Introduction

I did not read Kipling at first. He was read to me. At the age of three, I loved hearing the story of Rikki-Tikki-Tavi, the darting mongoose who protected a family in India against the attacks of a vicious cobra. As a child in tropical Africa, I recognised Kipling's vivid descriptions of the garden, the bungalow and the heat. Somehow I was aware of a moral tale, and applauded the bravery of this small animal, acting as a sort of St George figure in an archetypal myth.

Later Kipling disappeared from my life. As a teenager, I was impervious to the raucous, mannered antics of the Stalky stories. I appreciated *Kim*, but knew little of the author's poetry, beyond obvious, often tub-thumping, verses such as 'If–', and nothing of his later tortured and sophisticated short stories. The trouble was the man and his image. To a colonially reared child of the sixties, Kipling was the epitome of all the superior and reactionary Anglo-Saxon attitudes that I naively believed I was rebelling against.

Now I realise that he was this stereotype figure, and, more interestingly, he was not. And in that ambivalence lies the man's fascination.

When I came back to reading Kipling, I was attracted, as a journalist, to someone who had put in his 'seven years' hard', re-writing copy and later reporting for the *Civil and Military Gazette* in Lahore and for the *Pioneer* in Allahabad. What struck me was his professionalism – his reporter's eye for colour and his genius for verbal expression. This carried over into his most accessible 'grown-up' stories, the *Plain Tales from the Hills*, with their cynical anatomy of the machinations and human foibles behind the haughty image of the Raj. It was also clear in his non-fiction writings, such as his underestimated (not least for their humour) collections of travel articles, *Letters of Marque*, *From Sea to Sea* and, later, *Egypt of the Magicians*.

I appreciated Kipling's work for its historical insights into the closed society of British India. I was not initially aware of the extent of his personal involvement in the matter of history. Here was a man whose three aunts (on his mother's Macdonald side) had married Edward Burne-Jones, the eminent pre-Raphaelite painter, Edward Poynter, the President of the Royal Academy, and Alfred, businessman father of Stanley Baldwin, later the Conservative Prime Minister.

When I started to consider Kipling as a subject for a biography, I was intrigued by the prospect of his life providing a panorama of Britain's intellectual, cultural and social history. It offered everything from high-minded tittle-tattle at Burne-Jones's open house in London in the 1870s and 1880s – where Browning might be found one day, Leslie Stephen, or even Oscar Wilde another – through the gruff military men and their strategies of high imperialism either side of the Boer war, to the critical political adjustments of the 1920s when Stanley Baldwin, with his cousin's help, tried to reposition Conservatism in the face of the grim advances of the dictators. Kipling could not have straddled the nineteenth and twentieth centuries more skilfully if he had tried. Born in 1865, he died in 1936, aged seventy. He is therefore a vital figure if one wants to understand how Victorian turned into Edwardian England and came to terms with the modern age.

Investigating more closely, I was curious to discover why a figure once so popular, even iconic, had fallen so rapidly into disfavour, and wondered what this could tell us about ourselves and our age. I found that his history had been approached primarily from a literary perspective, and vast areas were under-

Germany. He was clear
rehearsal for a conflict i

Back in England, wit
the countryside, with i
history. When, in the 19
needed to appeal to th
democracy, Kipling he
of conservatism that er
realistically, England's)
inherent good sense of
contribution to this m
enabled Britain to with

Kipling would have
about civilisation being
brance'. He had a good s
He celebrated the fact tl
streak that encouraged
tion Francis Drake to
not militaristic in the
strong instincts for free
though his attachment
Stalky schoolboy tales.
was the mentor and ch

He had little time for
institutions he loved.
Noel Annan on 'Kipli
Waugh noted that Kipl
believed civilisation to
was only precariously
fully manned and he
them gullible and fee
man and ready to abai
qualms.'

Perhaps Kipling wa
hybrid. His parents an

researched. I convinced myself (and my publisher) that it would
not be useless to examine Rudyard Kipling's life and times again.

As I warmed to the project, I enjoyed unravelling the details of
his personal life – the fraught period at the 'House of Desolation'
in Southsea, which left him wary about the nature of his mother's
love; his pragmatic coming to terms with the realities of teeming
India and the demands of the Raj; his unease on his return to fin
de siècle London, and his precipitate marriage to the sister of
Wolcott Balestier, his American publisher friend, who died unexpectedly; his efforts to make this unlikely union work, and his
willingness to allow his wife to run his day-to-day existence while
he attended to the calls of his imagination and of his adopted
imperialistic ideal; his love of his children and his distress when
two of them died; his late efforts to find some accommodation
between his views of science, religion and society.

On the way there were important biographical discoveries:
detailing the background of his early love, the pioneer female
artist 'Flo' (or Violet) Garrard, who came from the wealthy family
of the Crown Jewellers; throwing new light on his school days
through original correspondence between his parents and his
headmaster 'Crom' Price: alighting on an unknown cache of
letters to Isabella Burton, his mentor in India, and the original of
his waspish character Mrs Hauksbee; fleshing out his wife's family,
a mixture of immigrant, established New England and frontier
stock; finding how Max Aitken (later Lord Beaverbrook) helped
set up Kipling's fortune; or unravelling the tale of Kipling's fraught
relations with the cinema, including a banned 'sexploitation'
movie and his role (about which he tried to suppress all mention)
in a disastrous feature film.

On another level, I was making a voyage into the mind of a
conservative – a process that involved the shedding of several
personal prejudices. At one stage Rudyard might have been a
William Morris type socialist like his aunt Georgiana Burne-
Jones. He appeared to be going in that direction during his teenage
years when he quoted Gladstone as his favourite politician.

In India someth
found himself in a ı
were rulers of a vast
by Russian encroac
agitation on the su
With his ring-side v
tribal attitude to s
maya (or illusion)
edifice; temporal p
survived enjoyed or
shared belief or re
professional expatr
soldiers – who brou
to India. He was c
and worthwhile, ar
role.

When he return
vapidity and egoce
the wake of his un
identity, he took o
empire. A period o
his political ideas.
he was fearful of
democracy withou
home convinced h
with its hierarchy ʑ

His idealism fo
Rhodes in 1897. Hɛ
empire, he was inje
the *mission civilisɛ*
Anglo-Saxon valu
interested in Afric
compromises of
developing a gut fɛ
life he loved came

born in India and spent his formative years there. As a result, as he put it, he gained 'two sides to my head' and saw the world from both an Oriental and a Western perspective.

Keeping the balance between these two often conflicting tendencies provided the ambivalent dynamic to Kipling's life. At one moment he could be full of energy, an engaging extrovert; the next, he was plunged into depression and prey to fanciful notions. He rejected Hinduism as a hotchpotch of scheming Gods and stood out in favour of monotheism, but he took his own religion from a buffet of Islam, Christianity, Buddhism, Mithraism, Freemasonry, anything he laid his hands on – and he later advocated the need for an elemental spirituality. He seemed the epitome of the crusty reactionary, yet he understood the importance of his ability to get inside people's skins and he applauded the ability of his late hero, St Paul, to be 'all things to all men' – the theme of his poem 'At His Execution'.

On the one hand he was a strong advocate of technology (in paeans to the machine, the car and the airship); on the other, he set his stall against modernity (refusing to have a telephone in his house). Despite the abundance of literary references in his work, his favourite entertainment was the light musical. He appreciated pomp and ceremony (and was a friend of King George V), yet he declined all state honours and preferred to let his writing speak for itself. He was gruff and obtuse, kindly and direct. Even his sex life was ambiguous: his Sussex neighbour, the playwright Enid Bagnold, thought he was gay, yet Peggy Ramsay, her agent, used to say (however unlikely) that Kipling had been one of Bagnold's lovers.

Crucially, he advocated the law, but celebrated the quirky individual, such as Stalky, who often flouted petty conventions. He glorified pack life, but was not part of it. He was Won-Tolla, the outlier or outsider, who brought news of the marauding Red Dogs in *The Second Jungle Book*. In thinking of Kipling, Nirad Chaudhuri, the Indian writer who also rejected the Hindu pantheon, was reminded of Chateaubriand's comment on Byron – that there were 'deux hommes distincts ... l'homme de la nature et l'homme de système'.

It was a difficult, often neurotic position to adopt – one that sometimes threatened to topple over into insanity. This was familiar enough territory for Kipling: as a young man in India, he had been confronted by the struggle between reason and irrationality – nowhere recorded more graphically than in his story 'The Strange Ride of Morrowbie Jukes'. His sense of the void that can open up in the space beneath these two contradictory forces gives his writing an often exciting modernity. (His appreciation of this point was given added poignancy by the regular mental breakdowns of his sister, Trix.) As he grew older, he looked for bridges to straddle the gap, and himself dabbled with religion, Freemasonry, science, art and other forms of psychic healing – the stuff of his later stories. He realised the fine line he was treading. Towards the end of his life he advised his friend Michael Mason to 'stay a little mad'. That way he himself kept in touch with his creativity – through the 'daemon', or writing muse, he acknowledged in his autobiography.

Throughout, Kipling was a consummate craftsman – precise in his use of words, ambitious in his subject matter, acute in his thinking, always readable. The most persistent criticism of his writing is its 'vulgarity' – in the sense of being both flashy and incapable of portraying the subtler feelings of life. Certainly he could be overexuberant, lacking the sensibilities of his friend Henry James. But Virginia Woolf was wrong to complain that he had no spark of the woman in him or that he lacked the power of suggestion. She might have taken note of his story 'The Wish House', for example. Three modern women have attested to his importance in their lives – Maya Angelou, the American author, has told how 'If–' gave her strength as a teenage single mother in San Francisco; Arundhati Roy, the Indian novelist, noted *The Jungle Book* as one of her greatest literary influences (and this is evident in her best-selling *The God of Small Things*); while Aung San Suu Kyi, the Burmese opposition leader and Nobel peace prize winner, has written of her fondness for *Kim*, and how, when she re-read the book during long periods of house arrest, she found in it the Buddhist concept of 'metta' or loving-kindness.

That said, what about the man himself? I am often asked if I would like to have met Kipling. The young writer would have been stimulating company – original, full of ideas, open to all influences. His older self poses more problems. He could be prickly and lugubrious; even making due allowance for the mores of his day, his dismissive stereotyping of whole groups of people was silly.

However, the prejudices seething beneath his rational mind only confirmed him in his role as 'everyman'. He was not always brave. He could be banal. He often flinched from people (particularly when they came en masse, mouthing mantras of democracy). At least he was painfully familiar with the broad range of human emotions. There is no point in wishing he had shown more compassion. (It is there in his writings, if you want it.) Anything else, and he would not have been the quirky, inventive character of this book – like Rikki-Tikki-Tavi, a 'restless companion', maybe, but an intrepid slayer of cobras when required. Remarkably, this buttoned up Englishman can still speak across generations and cultures. According to André Maurois, Kipling had 'a permanent natural contact with the oldest and deepest layers of human consciousness'. To find out how he managed this, I have chipped away at the accumulated debris and unearthed a life that is also a history of establishment English attitudes in the latter years of Empire.

London, February 1999

Book One

There are nine and sixty ways of constructing tribal lays,
And – every – single – one – of – them – is – right!

One

Hair of the Dog

TO 1865

Rudyard Kipling kicked and shoved his way into the world. That would have been typical. Or else, he wilfully held himself back from life. That, for some people, might explain all they need to know. From a medical view, however, neither of these popular images of birth is correct. Babies have no input into when, how, or even whether they are born. In Rudyard's case, he was simply late, and the process a struggle.

He had been expected on Christmas Day 1865. But he held aloof for five days as his mother Alice went through a lengthy confinement that has usually been described as labour. She and her husband Lockwood had only recently moved into a house on the Esplanade, on Bombay's eastern shoreline. The servants were so concerned at their mistress's perinatal exertions that they sacrificed a goat to the Goddess Kali to help ease her pain and bring her to term. Some time after the chubby infant made his entrance at ten o'clock on the evening of 30 December, Alice commented, with the sharp wit she was known for, that even God's creation of the world had taken no longer.

Two months earlier, Lord Palmerston had died in London, and with him an era of brinkmanship in British foreign policy passed. Also in October the suppression of a so-called rebellion in Jamaica had revived memories of the 1857 Indian Mutiny and sparked renewed debate on the purpose of empire. A more sophisticated theory and practice of imperialism was beginning to evolve. As a member of the Indian civil service, Lockwood Kipling, Rudyard's father, certainly had a role in this process. But his posting as an art teacher was ungraded, without statutory pension rights, and therefore lowly in both the imperial scheme of things and – an important factor in Bombay – the social pecking order. Baby Rudyard's birth was duly announced without fanfare in the 'Domestic Occurrences' column of *The Times of India*.

Later, when he wrote his autobiography, Rudyard chose to play up the differences between the two sides of his family: 'My Father with his sage Yorkshire outlook and wisdom; my Mother, all Celt and three-parts fire'. His characteristic emphasis on racial stereotypes hinted at a truth, while glossing over a more basic reality: both his grandfathers had been Methodist ministers, and his parents had striven to get away from their non-conformist background. (Another of Alice's celebrated remarks was her cry: 'See! A hair of the dog that bit us', when she came across a lock from the hair of John Wesley, the founder of Methodism, in a family cupboard. And she threw it into the fire.)

In a sense both sides of Rudyard's family were warriors and outsiders. On the one hand, Alice's proud forebears, the Macdonalds, could trace their line to Somerled, the fearsome half-Scots, half-Norse 'King of the Isles', who in the tenth century tried to drive his close Viking relatives from the Irish Sea. On the other, the Kiplings were descended from these same Vikings, who raided widely in the North of England. Ironically, Somerled's campaigns encouraged the Vikings to seek new landing places in Lancashire and Cumbria, whence they migrated over the Pennines into Northern Yorkshire.

The name Kipling is found in places as Kypeling in the eleventh century and Kippelinge in the thirteenth. By the late Middle Ages, there were Kiplings around the River Swale, close to modern-day Richmond. The nearby village of Kiplin was the original home of the Baltimores who sailed to America to found the East-coast settlement that bears their name. Their seat, Kiplin Hall, designed by Inigo Jones, dated from 1600, a little later than the first reference (in 1513) to the Kiplin Cotes, one of the most gruelling horse races in the world, run over four miles of the windswept Yorkshire Wolds.

During the eighteenth century the Kiplings moved across Yorkshire to farms on the bleak, windswept moors west of Whitby, where Rudyard's immediate ancestors were to be found in the village of Lythe. His great-grandfather, John Kipling, gravitated towards the relatively new religion of Methodism, which seemed to offer down-trodden labourers some hope of a better life, both now and in the hereafter. His sympathies wavered slightly when his son Joseph expressed a wish to become a Methodist minister. John was annoyed because this would mean the loss of an able-bodied hand on the family farm. Joseph persevered, confirming his resolve by overcoming the normal Methodist reluctance for its ministers to marry out of the religion. He had fallen in love with Frances Lockwood, the Anglican daughter of a builder who lived slightly north-west of his own family in Skelton-in-Cleveland, on the edge of the Whitby Moors. Frances's mother Ruth was the daughter of Peter Merry who, as a steward on Lord Mulgrave's nearby estate, had featured in David Wilkie's once well-known picture, *The Rent Day*, painted in 1807.

Following their marriage in 1836, Joseph and Frances Kipling settled temporarily in a cottage in Pickering where, in July the following year, their son John, the first of six surviving children, was born. (Until his late twenties, this boy was known as John. Thereafter he adopted his mother's maiden name, Lockwood, which, to avoid confusion, is how he will be designated throughout this book.) Usefully for a preacher, Joseph possessed what was described as a 'voice of rare sweetness'.[1] His grandson Rudyard never knew him, but as a boy he sometimes stayed with his grandmother and his Yorkshire aunts, from whom he learnt enough about Joseph to portray him in his story 'On Greenhow Hill'. Joseph appears as the preacher, the Reverend Amos Barraclough, 'a little white-faced chap, wi' a voice as 'ud wile a bird off an a bush, and a way o' layin' hold of folks as made them think they'd never had a live man for a friend before'.

One year older than her husband, Frances Kipling had unusual Mediterranean looks, with striking dark eyes, black hair and bushy eyebrows, a Merry family trait that Rudyard was to inherit. Frances's offspring were said to 'alternate between "Spanish" brunettes and apple-blossom blondes'. This gave rise to a family myth that an ancestor had been a Spaniard who was rescued from a wreck of the Armada.

When he was still a few weeks short of his eighth birthday, Lockwood was sent to Woodhouse Grove Academy, sixty miles across the county at Apperley Bridge on the River Aire near Bradford. As a boarding establishment, run on a shoe-string, it had been set up in 1812 specifically to cater for the sons of itinerant Methodist ministers. Schooling was free, but it was spartan and there was virtually no contact with the outside world. A contemporary, W. F. Moulton, recalled, 'A newspaper seldom reached us, and the [1848] French Revolution was little more than a rumour.' Beating was rife, one master prefacing his assaults on Lockwood Kipling with the words that he was only doing this 'out of high regard for your father'. The headmaster also flogged the boy for so-called 'stoical apathy', a reaction hardly surprising in the circumstances. As a result, Lockwood showed scant enthusiasm for his father's religion and no desire to follow him into the ministry. In 1851, at the age of fourteen, he had a magpie intelligence and obvious artistic abilities, but little idea of the direction his life might take.

If – exaggerating slightly – Rudyard Kipling could later claim of his father's family, 'I believe that, in a humble way, few stocks carry back cleaner Yorkshire blood for a longer time,'[2] his mother's forebears, the Macdonalds, were more hybrid.

Looking back to the mighty Somerled, they had once been the most powerful clan on the west coast of Scotland, guardians of 25,000 square miles of territory and fifty castles. With his 10,000 followers, the Donald chieftain Angus Og had turned the battle of Bannockburn against the English. Rudyard's maternal line was part of the Sleat branch of the clan. Jacobite in sympathy, it had supported Bonnie Prince Charlie in his struggle to regain the Crowns of England and Scotland in 1745. Following his defeat by the Duke of Cumberland on the bloody fields of Culloden, the Prince famously sailed 'over the sea to Skye' in the company of young Flora Macdonald, a distant cousin in the Sleat house.

In the ensuing diaspora, Rudyard's ancestors sought to join relatives in North America. But, like the Lithuanian Jews who landed in Newcastle rather than New York at the end of the following century, James Macdonald's family only made it as far as Northern Ireland where, after hearing John Wesley preach in 1783, he also was inspired to become a Methodist minister. After moving back to England he was followed into the priesthood by his younger son, George, who, thirty years before Lockwood Kipling, became one of the first pupils to attend Woodhouse Grove Academy, the school for Methodist ministers' sons.[3] While he was there, the headmaster's good-looking niece, Maria Branwell, married a local curate, Patrick Brontë, a union which produced celebrated daughters in Charlotte, Emily and Anne.

The harshness of early nineteenth-century life was once more demonstrated when George's first wife Mary Wardlaw died young of tuberculosis. He married again in 1833, this time to Hannah Jones, the daughter of a Welsh grocer who had prospered as a wholesaler in Manchester. She was not always happy with her husband's peripatetic existence, particularly during an uneasy period in Birmingham at the height of the Chartist riots from 1839 to 1842, when he was hardly ever at home. 'There's no luck about the house when my good man's away,' she wrote in her diary.[4] Her dissatisfaction was not mitigated by her conviction that marriage had led to a drop in her social status.

It was as well that her energies were channelled into running a large family. Over sixteen years from 1834 to 1850, as she and her husband made their way round England on a cycle of three-year-long circuits, she gave birth to eleven children, seven of whom survived into adulthood. They ran an unstuffy household, with a typical non-conformist respect for learning. When George returned to Birmingham a second time in 1850 he ensured that his eldest son, Harry, found a place at the local King Edward's School which, as well as being first-rate academically, had the advantage of being free of charge.

Until then, Harry had been educated at a Wesleyan establishment in Sheffield and was considered something of a prig. But at King Edward's he blossomed in the company of a brilliant circle of schoolboys who included Wilfred Heeley, Cormell Price and Edward Jones (later better known, with a hyphen, as the painter Burne-Jones). The witty Heeley, who was to go up to Cambridge, was the son of Hannah Macdonald's best friend. He and his friends frequented the Macdonalds' house in Nursery Terrace, Handsworth, where they met Harry's spirited sisters, Alice and Georgiana, who were thirteen and ten in 1850. (Another sister, Caroline, aged twelve, had recently contracted tuberculosis and died four years later.) For the time being, the younger Macdonald children – Fred, eight, Agnes, seven, Louisa, five, and Edith, two – kept a respectful distance.

By all accounts, Alice was the most 'Irish' of the family. Her sister Edith described her as of medium height, with

slender, pale complexion, dark brown hair and grey eyes with black lashes, and delicately pencilled eyebrows. In those eyes lay the chief fascination of her face, so expressive were they that they seemed to deepen or pale in colour according to passing emotion. The Irish blood ... seemed to take effect in Alice; she had the ready wit and power of repartee, the sentiment, and I may say the unexpectedness which one associates with that race. It was impossible to predict how she would act at any given point. There was a certain fascination in this, and fascinating she certainly was.

Alice wrote fine sonnets, sang beautifully and helped her mother around the house. But her streak of rebelliousness would sometimes out; not for nothing did she name Thackeray's minx-like Becky Sharp as her favourite fictional character. As she developed through her teenage years, her brother's former school friends and their associates gravitated towards her and her daintier, equally intelligent sister Georgiana, known as Georgie. While Georgie cultivated the contemplative, artistic Jones, whom she was later to marry, Alice went for the more bookish types. William Fulford, a great friend of Heeley from King Edward's (though of a slightly earlier vintage) was reading Divinity at Oxford. He often invited Alice and Georgie to visit him there, introducing them to the secular intellectual currents of the day (the High Anglicanism of the Oxford Movement was making way for the mature mid-Victorian humanism of Ruskin in the arts, Carlyle in ideas, Tennyson in poetry and Darwin in science). He also helped expand their knowledge of verse. For although nothing was banned in the Macdonald household, poets as established as Keats and Shelley were considered avant-garde.

So close did Alice and Fulford become that, when the Macdonalds moved to London in 1853 (to a plush living in Walpole Street, Chelsea), Hannah asked the young man to state his intentions towards her daughter. It was resolved that they would marry once he was ordained, even though he was a High Church Anglican. But the prospect of becoming a vicar's wife held few attractions for the precocious teenage Alice and she broke off the engagement.

The reasons are easy to understand, for her interests were taking her in a different direction. Fulford had been followed at Oxford by her brother Harry and his friend Burne-Jones. While Harry pursued a conventional career towards the Indian Civil Service, the pasty-faced Burne-Jones, who had once seemed destined for the Church, became obsessed with atavistic ideas about society and art. Although his native Birmingham had been transformed into the workshop of the world (where Joseph Chamberlain, the future apostle of imperialism, had just entered the family screw-manufacturing business, prior to taking up municipal politics), he himself rejected technological progress and, with the encouragement of William Morris, a wealthier fellow undergraduate, harked back to the integrity and beauty of a pre-industrial, medieval way of life. Together, he and Morris expanded on the concept of a Pre-Raphaelite Brotherhood, as had been suggested in the sensuous paintings of Dante Gabriel Rossetti and commended by John Ruskin in *The Times* in 1851.

Neither Burne-Jones, who had decided to become a painter rather than a priest, nor Morris, who was interested in design and craftsmanship, bothered to obtain more than a pass degree at Oxford. As soon as possible, they decamped to London where, with the help of Rossetti, they apprenticed themselves as art students, based in Red Lion Square near Holborn. Initially, not knowing many people in the capital, Burne-Jones spent long periods of his free time with the Macdonalds in Chelsea. Before long, he and Morris had been assimilated into Rossetti's vast network of friends, which included original Pre-Raphaelite painters such as Ford Madox Brown and William Holman Hunt, as well as poets of the stature of Robert Browning, Algernon Charles Swinburne and William Allingham. And at the centre of this expanded second-generation Brotherhood was the charismatic Rossetti, giving the young Oxford men a heady taste of Bohemianism, with his bevy of mistresses, including the anguished laudanum addict Lizzie Siddall, later to be his wife.

Soon Alice and Georgie were clamouring to take part in these gatherings, albeit for different reasons. Red Lion Square (and, later, after Morris's marriage to Jane Burden, Burne-Jones's rooms in Russell Place) happened to be on the omnibus route between Chelsea and Islington where their aunt, Alice Pullein, lived. (Aunt Alice was Hannah's sister, and her husband Edward was a partner in a firm of city accountants that young Fred Macdonald joined for a short period in 1857, before following his father into the Methodist ministry. A couple of years later, when George Macdonald moved to a new ministry in Manchester, Alice and Georgie stayed behind at the Pulleins'.) Georgie became a regular Pre-Raphaelite camp follower since, after taking a course at the government-run School of Design, she was more conventionally interested in art than her sister. She regularly accompanied Burne-Jones to galleries and it was no great surprise when the two became engaged in 1856 (though they waited until 1860 to marry – on the anniversary, Ned lugubriously insisted, of the death of his ideal woman, Dante's heroine Beatrice).

Alice attended Pre-Raphaelite parties in the hope of meeting literary figures. She had some success for, in the early 1860s, Dickens's raffish friend, Edmund Yates, printed several of her stories and poems in his magazine, *Temple Bar*. On a personal level, however, she was unrequited. While her dependable sister found herself a husband, the headstrong Alice ran through a succession of unfulfilling relationships. Following her liaison with Fulford, another short engagement to an anonymous schoolmaster was abruptly broken. History repeated itself in October 1862 when she agreed to marry the Anglo-Irish poet William Allingham, whose *Day and Night Songs*, as illustrated by Rossetti, had inspired young Ned. With his day-time job as a Customs Officer, Allingham seemed a respectable match. Now best remembered for his earlier poem, 'The Fairies', which begins, 'Up the airy mountain, down the rushy glen', he has been described as 'a presentable mid-Victorian version of a poet'[5] – the antithesis of another member of the Pre-Raphaelite circle, the fiery, complicated young Swinburne. But, despite setting several of her fiancé's ballads to music, Alice's latest betrothal lasted only one month. Her father seemed to think that her problem was her flightiness, for he was heard to admonish her for being a flirt. 'P-h-l-u-r-t,' she spelled out, 'Phlurt: what is that?' – a reply which seemed to confirm the charge as stated. Clearly, a certain wilfulness was part of her nature. But this was offset by a strand of equally Celtic melancholy that ran in the Macdonald family. As she wrote in 'Love's Grave', one of her poems for *Temple Bar*:

> Love that was born a year ago
> We buried to-day with weeping;
> We laid him low in the winter snow
> Where when Springtime comes the flowers will blow
> And the pale primrose and violet grow,
> A sad sweet place of sleeping.

The two families – the Kiplings and Macdonalds – came together in the early 1860s. A decade earlier, in the summer of 1851, the problem of Lockwood's career had been solved when he travelled to London on one of Thomas Cook's early cheap railway excursions and visited the Great Exhibition. Unlike his future brother-in-law Burne-Jones, who saw only 'a length of cheerless monotony, iron and glass, glass and iron',[6] Lockwood was thrilled by this showcase for the best in mid-nineteenth-century engineering, arts and crafts. He was quick to appreciate the Exhibition as a monument to the spirit of an age where industry was beginning to work on mankind's behalf. As the Poet Laureate, Alfred, Lord Tennyson, wrote in the ode sung at its opening:

> From growing commerce loose her latest chain,
> And let the fair, white-wing'd peacemaker fly
> To happy havens under all the sky,
> Till each man work in noble brotherhood . . .

In time, Lockwood came to understand one of the more specialist reasons for staging the event. The Exhibition was also intended to meet the concerns of early-Victorian artists about the deterioration in British design, which had drifted away from basic principles in its enthusiasm for 'illusionist' motifs in the wake of the Industrial Revolution. One influential display (much admired by the author Gustave Flaubert, who was visiting from France) was the East India Company's collection of Oriental arts and crafts. Many observers, including the leader writer of *The Times*, suggested that the simplicity and vitality of Indian design offered a viable alternative to Western shoddiness.

Even at this stage Lockwood might have had to follow his father into the ministry. Employment opportunities were scarce for a boy of his background. However one stand at the Exhibition had particularly fired his imagination – the display of decorative porcelain by the Minton company of Stoke-on-Trent. Having already shown an aptitude for handicrafts – once making a pair of ice skates, with tapes instead of straps, and blades fashioned out of an old school slate – he opted for a career moulding pottery figures. Fortuitously his father was able to call on the Methodist 'old boy network' to help out. Eight years earlier, in 1843, Edward Pinder, a former pupil of Woodhouse Grove, had taken up a living at Hornsea on the same circuit as Joseph Kipling's Howden. Like Joseph, Pinder had followed his father into the ministry. But his brother Thomas, who had been at the same school in the 1820s, had gone into a family business making basic earthenware in Burslem, in the smoky heart of the Staffordshire 'Potteries'.

In 1851 Thomas Pinder had expanded into a partnership, Pinder, Bourne and Hope, and taken on a disused pottery, the Fountain Place Works. It was arranged that Lockwood should join this firm as an apprentice, while at the same time broadening his horizons as a part-time student at the newly opened Stoke Art School. It was not long before he was prospering in this dual role. On behalf of Pinder's company, Lockwood acted as designer and modeller, providing artistic input into a traditional crafts industry keen to improve its products in a new consumer age. (As well as inspiring new ideas about design, the Great Exhibition played a useful role in educating the public's taste.) At the Art School, Lockwood came under the influence of two able French-born teachers, both of whom worked at various times for Minton – Albert Carrier de Belleuse, a medallist who became director of the French national porcelain factory at Sèvres, and Hugues Protat, a sculptor. Together they inculcated in him a passion for Gallic culture that he passed on to his son.

A far cry from the Enlightenment that he imagined prevailed on the other side of the Channel, Burslem's spirit was the dour nonconformity portrayed in the novels of Arnold Bennett. Work was the focus of the community and Lockwood knuckled down, showing his promise by winning at least two prizes – a local medal in 1855 and a National Medallion three years later. After seven years in this apprenticeship, Lockwood moved to London in search of greater opportunities. He found employment as an assistant to John Birnie Philip, a jobbing sculptor whose main business was executing designs for the distinguished architect George Gilbert Scott. Philip was later responsible for the frieze on the podium of Scott's Albert Memorial. In 1858 he was assisting Scott in the design of four vast statues of the Evangelists which adorn the tower of St Michael's, Cornhill. Lockwood helped Philip with this project, and, later, with some modelling for the chapel of Exeter College, Oxford; and for All Souls, a new church in Halifax. He also worked for John Thomas, another sculptor much in demand at the time, who had assisted Sir Charles Barry with the decorations for the Houses of Parliament. Through this experience Lockwood developed a feeling for working in bas-relief, which was later one of his specialities.

In 1860 he swapped the insecurity of this freelance existence for a more settled job in the government's new Department of Science and Art, which had been formed specifically to implement the Great Exhibition's lessons about integrating good design with industrial innovation. Its leading light, as with the Exhibition, was Henry Cole, epitome of the high-minded mid-Victorian intellectual who, nurtured on a mixture of utilitarianism, evangelicalism and general prosperity, wished to spread sweetness and light by means of official diktat. As part of his mission to raise design standards, Cole had persuaded Queen Victoria in 1853 to set aside forty rooms in London's Marlborough House for him to establish a Museum of Manufactures, for which he purchased part of the East India Company's collection, and a linked Metropolitan School of Ornamental Art. This establishment later transferred to South Kensington where Cole had purchased land from the proceeds of the 1851 Exhibition. The South Kensington Museum became, *inter alia*, the headquarters of the design tsars of the Department of Science and Art.

While studying in Stoke, Lockwood Kipling had almost certainly come under the influence of the School of Ornamental Art (soon to be called the National Art Training School and later the Royal College of Art).Within the wider remit of Cole's Department, this school sought to change the focus of art teaching throughout the country and establish a national curriculum, which stressed South Kensington principles of 'scientific' drawing, or copying directly from examples of 'good' design, including those from India.

In London, as an employee of the Department of Science and Art, Lockwood flourished in an environment where his own values of decoration and practicality were prized. Being more of a craftsman than an ideologue, he worked alongside Geoffrey Sykes, formerly of Sheffield Art School, who had inspired a revival in the use of terracotta (baked earth) in architectural decoration. Lockwood Kipling adopted this type of hard, unglazed pottery which, in the context of building, was considered to be more resistant than bricks to the growing problem of industrial pollution. Quite what he did is unclear, since the Department's records are annoyingly scarce, but he certainly played a role in the construction of the South Kensington Museum, for visitors to the quadrangle of the present-day Victoria and Albert Museum can see Sykes's own terracotta plaque, commemorating the completion of its earlier incarnation and showing some of the people involved – among them Cole, the first Director, Redgrave, officially the Department's art superintendent, and Lockwood Kipling, unmistakable with his flowing beard and stocky (5 foot 3 inch) Yorkshire physique.

Lockwood might have stayed in London and worked his way up through the ranks of the Victorian arts establishment, but for the premature death of his father in January 1862. He decided to resign his position at the Department and return to Burslem in order to earn enough money to support his widowed mother and four unmarried sisters. Perhaps he knew that there had been a change in the fortunes of Thomas Pinder's pottery. After a series of financial difficulties in the 1850s (which may have spurred Lockwood to seek his fortune elsewhere in the first place), the business was at last beginning to prosper. Under the name Pinder Bourne it was producing an acceptable standard of earthenware tableware, vases, jugs, bowls and jardinières. Pinder again showed Methodist solidarity by offering Lockwood his old job back as modeller and designer. Before long the young man was also working on plans for Burslem's new Wedgwood Institute.

Lockwood's return to Staffordshire was to have momentous consequences for him personally. For in that same year of 1862 the Wesleyan Conference made two crucial appointments. First, it transferred the Reverend George Macdonald from Manchester to Wolverhampton; second, it sent his son Frederic to embark on the first ministry of his career at Swan Bank Wesleyan Chapel in Burslem. Before long Fred had not only met Lockwood Kipling but also introduced him to his sisters, including the forceful but so far unfulfilled Alice.

The following summer the Pinders held a picnic at Lake Rudyard, some six miles from Burslem, to which both Lockwood Kipling and the Macdonald sisters were invited. Like the Potteries themselves, the 164-acre lake was a testament to the energy and ingenuity of the age. Until 1849, it had been a man-made reservoir, providing water for the Leek and the Trent and Mersey canals. When its natural beauty attracted interest, an enterprising company connected it with a railway line, purchased the local inn and staged gala events, such as regattas.

Lockwood was initially unaware which of the Macdonald sisters would attend the picnic. This did not concern him much, since he found them all attractive and later said, 'If I had not married my wife, I should have liked no-one so well as one of her sisters.' His fate was sealed, however, when he looked across at 'a beauteous creature, pensively eating salad',[7] and she was twenty-six-year-old Alice.

During a post-prandial stroll, he and she came across a bedraggled grey horse, which inspired Lockwood to quote from Robert Browning's poem 'Childe Roland to the Dark Tower Came': 'Thrust out past service from the Devil's stud', and Alice murmured a later line, 'He must be wicked to deserve such pain!' Although there was no obvious romance in this exchange, Lockwood turned to her in delight, with the words, 'You read Browning.' As Alice later told her friend Edith Plowden, 'It was done in that moment.'

Poetry, which 'moved him like music others',[8] also provided the bond when they stole their first kiss. The couple were reading some of his favourite verse when he had the urge to bend down and kiss her, and she responded 'with simplicity and gentleness'. When he subsequently travelled to Wolverhampton to ask her father's permission to marry her, Alice for some reason had failed to inform her parents and the earnest, rather shy Lockwood arrived at the Macdonald house just as the family was gathered for prayers. George Macdonald was starting to read from the first chapter of St John's Gospel: 'There was a man sent from God whose name was John,' and they all burst out laughing because that was the name by which the young man was known to them.

The prospect of matrimony forced Lockwood Kipling to think again about his career. His wedding to Alice had to be delayed until he found another job capable of supporting not only her but in time, they hoped, a family. His future only became clearer after he had met Claud Erskine, a High Court Judge in Bombay, who had been asked, while on leave in Britain, to recruit a teacher for his adopted city's School of Art and Industry, an institution endowed on 'South Kensington principles' in March 1857 by Sir Jamsetjee Jeejeebhoy, an enlightened Parsee merchant who had made a fortune earlier in the century in shipping, grain and, while it lasted, the opium trade between India and China.

At the time Bombay was enjoying an unprecedented economic

boom, largely as a result of the special opportunities afforded by the American Civil War. After cotton from the Confederacy ports of the South was denied to Britain by the Northern naval blockade, Lancashire mill owners turned to India for their raw supplies. As luck would have it, Bombay had just been linked by railway to the main cotton-growing areas of the Deccan. Over the course of the war from 1861 to 1865, cotton exports from Bombay to Britain grew fourfold, some seventy million pounds' worth of revenue was generated and in the process further fortunes were made. With this surplus wealth, Sir Bartle Frere, who became Governor in 1862, set about building a modern city that combined the imperial magnificence of Baron Haussmann's Paris with the practical infrastructure that utilitarian reformers were bringing to Britain's provincial towns. Such a construction programme required skilled artisans and teachers to train them.

Armed with a glowing reference from Philip Cunliffe-Owen, Assistant Director of the South Kensington Museum, Lockwood impressed Erskine, the President of the School, who reported back to Bombay in December 1864 on his good fortune in securing the young man's services as an architectural sculptor. Lockwood was employed on a salary of 400 rupees a month (roughly £400 a year), plus whatever he could earn from private tuition. This was a sizeable income for the son and daughter of two country ministers who had never earned anything like that in their lives. Lockwood seemed to feel his new-found status required a certain gravitas, for the agreement sealing the deal six weeks later was the first instance of his incorporating his mother's maiden name into his own and signing himself John Lockwood Kipling.

The wedding of Alice Macdonald and Lockwood Kipling finally took place in St Mary Abbots Church, Kensington, on a bitterly cold day in March 1865. The absence of her parents through George Macdonald's ill health was partially offset by the attendance of Lockwood's mother Frances, who travelled from Yorkshire with two of his sisters. Lockwood himself won the approval of Aggie Macdonald for not being 'spoony', or sentimental. She was not so sure about his best man, Henry Longden, a friend from the nearby Department of Science and Art, who was dubbed 'The Undertaker'. Once again her new brother-in-law saw fit to sign himself John Lockwood Kipling, with a decorative twirl of the 'J', adding in the register that he was an 'artist' and 'of full age'.

The wedding party provided a clue why he might have needed to embellish his name. After the ceremony the guests repaired across the High Street to Kensington Square, where Georgie and Ned Burne-Jones had recently set up home – complete with blue and green serge 'Pomegranate' wallpaper from William Morris's firm, and a set of Dürer prints which had been a present from Ruskin. Several of Ned's long-haired artist friends were present, including Rossetti, Swinburne and Ford Madox Brown, who amused the assembled company by referring to the bridegroom as 'John Gilpin', the 'linen-draper bold' in William Cowper's ballad. For all his skill as an architectural sculptor, Lockwood must have felt little more than a jobbing civil servant among these colourful quasi-Bohemians, with their rich patrons. As was to become clearer in India, he adhered to the official South Kensington diktat on design, which was different from the sensuous sweep of Burne-Jones, or his friends Morris and Ruskin.

Observing the scene – the main source for the event in her letters home to Wolverhampton – was Aggie Macdonald, the most attractive and uncomplicated of the sisters, whom Lockwood described as 'tyrannously pretty' with a conversation like 'champagne'.[9] But Aggie only had eyes for another artist, the prim Edward Poynter, who had moved into 62 Great Russell Street where the Burne-Joneses had once lived. He had studied in Paris, where his friendship with the American artist James Whistler and the satirist George du Maurier was to be celebrated in the latter's 1894 novel *Trilby*. On this occasion, he endeared himself to Aggie by staying behind to help clean the silver.

On the eve of his departure to India, Lockwood still needed to convince his in-laws, the Macdonalds, that their daughter Alice would be safe at his side. They were worried about both the health risks – Wilfred Heeley's wife had recently died there – and the political uncertainties that still affected the country eight years after the Mutiny. The combination had caused Harry Macdonald to decide against joining his friend Heeley in the Indian Civil Service and to opt instead to seek his fortune in the United States. So, for their honeymoon, Lockwood and Alice spent the next month visiting and reassuring their immediate families in Skipton and Wolverhampton. Lockwood had to return to London for a leaving party with his South Kensington friends beside the River Thames at Putney, while Alice remained rather glumly at her sisters'. Then, on 12 April, a bright spring day, the newly married Kiplings made their way down to Southampton where they joined a paddle-steamer, the s.s. *Ripon*, for the voyage to Alexandria. From there they travelled overland to Suez (the Canal across the desert had yet to be built) and thence onwards by sea to Bombay.

Two

Of No Mean City

1865–1877

The 'tents' were up on the Esplanade when Lockwood and Alice
Kipling first stepped ashore at Bombay's Apollo Pier in May 1865.
Officially, these colourful *ad hoc* buildings, cobbled together from
plaster and bamboo, should not have been there, as they had been
banned in the wake of the Mutiny by an anxious government
wanting to preserve a clear field of fire if the (originally) seven
islands of Bombay were ever attacked from the west. But the city
itself had been little troubled by the 1857 revolt. So, in the euphoria
of the cotton boom, these temporary summer cottages, festooned
with bunting, had become essential features of expatriate community life – retreats where *le tout* Bombay went to bask in the
cool breezes off the Back Bay when the main residential area
around the Fort became too hot.

Although immediately struck by the 'blazing beauty' of the
place, with its rustling palm trees, darting dhows and dazzling
blue sky, Lockwood was not prepared for the turmoil he found.
The immediate symptom was that neither the Art School nor the
house which went with his job was ready for occupation. So, for
a short while, as the thermometer inched its way up towards the
start of the monsoon season, the Kiplings had to make their home
in one of these rudimentary *banglás* (the Hindustani word from
which we derive 'bungalow').

He soon learnt that Bombay was in the middle of a severe local
economic crisis. Shortly before he and Alice arrived, the city's

bubble had burst: inflation had already been rising dangerously, when the Back Bay Company, an ambitious investors' scheme to reclaim 1500 acres of land from the sea, failed in 1864. Then, in May 1865, the month the Kiplings reached India, came news of the North's final victory over the rebel South in the United States. Within a year, after Britain again started importing American cotton, Bombay was reeling from the effects: several leading businesses went bankrupt, including the Bank of Bombay, which had defied London by committing the funds of the local government, one of its shareholders, to the controversial land reclamation project.

At the same time British India was still struggling to come to terms with the aftermath of the Mutiny. One immediate effect had been the ending of the last remnants of political power enjoyed by the East India Company. The 1858 Government of India Act put the country under the control of a viceroy, responsible to a secretary of state and ultimately to Parliament in London. Less obviously, a new post-revolt attitude towards Britain's imperial responsibilities was evolving. Until now, the utilitarian principles which inspired most Victorian institutional reforms at home and abroad had been interpreted paternalistically to require the greatest good for the greatest number of all India's inhabitants. Thus the ritual burning of widows, known as sati, had been banned, and thuggees, or religiously motivated brigands, suppressed. Although English had been adopted as India's official language of instruction as a result of the historian Thomas Macaulay's uncompromising 1835 minute, the underlying liberal assumption was that education would enable the British and Indian middle classes to work together, leading one day to the sub-continent's self-rule.

But the Mutiny led to a rethinking of this approach, even if the full effects were not felt until the 1870s when conservatives with impeccably utilitarian pedigrees such as John Strachey, who was on the Viceroy's Executive Council from 1868, and James Fitzjames Stephen, the Law Member from 1869 to 1873, held sway.

The new mood, already apparent in 1865, was that earlier reforms had helped precipitate the Mutiny by introducing inappropriate Western models of social change and so undermining the authority of the Indian ruling classes who were the Raj's natural allies. The British administration now became more conventionally 'Orientalist', emphasising the timelessness and traditions of the East. Although, at one level, this approach did at least require the new 'competition-wallahs' now entering the Civil Service to try to understand Indian culture better, more generally it reinforced racial stereotypes about the backwardness of native customs and encouraged a more distant and authoritarian style of rule.[1]

Lockwood Kipling discovered an interesting variation on this debate in the rarified world of the Indian art establishment. Though recruited to help with Bombay's municipal construction programme, he owed his presence in India, in more general terms, to a late flowering of old-style liberal utilitarianism. Fearing that the artisanal skills which had so impressed Henry Cole at the Great Exhibition were already being destroyed by cheap imports from the West, Macaulay's brother-in-law, Sir Charles Trevelyan, had set out the basic guidelines for the introduction of art education in India in a typically high-minded report to the House of Lords in June 1853. Without the luxury of the English distinction between fine arts, as taught by the Royal Academy, and decorative arts, as inculcated by the recently established School of Ornamental Art, the new schools in India had to pretend to perform both functions (thus the name, the Sir Jamsetjee Jeejeebhoy School of Art and Industry).

But, by the time Lockwood arrived in Bombay, this unsatisfactory compromise was already foundering. Only the previous year the School had been taken under the wing of the Department of Public Instruction, making it an anonymous arm of a disinterested bureaucracy. More tellingly, any faint suggestion that India's art was more than mere skilled decoration and that its painting and sculpture might have inherent qualities had been dealt a near fatal blow by the Mutiny which, for critics such as

John Ruskin, who believed in the inextricable link between art and moral behaviour, only proved the barbarity of Indian sensibility. Perhaps Lockwood attended the seminal lecture at the Museum of Ornamental Art in 1859 (shortly after he first came to London) when Ruskin railed about the artistic lessons to be learnt from the 'bestial ... acts of the Indian race in the year that has just passed by'. Certainly, throughout his career, Lockwood stuck firmly to Ruskin's line that Indians were incapable of 'higher' forms of art (or, indeed, of intellectual maturity at all). At the same time he remained powerfully committed to the development of Indian artisanal skills – a telling illustration of the two-tier 'Orientalist' mentality now emerging in the Raj and soon to exert a powerful influence on his son.

Such was the unsettled environment into which Rudyard Kipling was born on 30 December 1865. The date suggests that Alice had conceived while still in England – possibly during her honeymoon. At an early stage in the pregnancy, her sister Louie must have put forward Rudyard – after the Kiplings' meeting place in Staffordshire – as the new baby's name, for in October Lockwood had written to ask her if, as a putative godmother, she minded the established Kipling Christian name, Joseph, also being used. (Her fellow godparents were to be her brother Fred and a colleague of Lockwood at the Art School, John Griffiths.[2]) Although clearly hoping for a boy, Lockwood was worldly enough to realise that Alice might have a girl, for whom the matrilineal names Margaret Macdonald were reserved.

Given his mother's lengthy confinement, Rudyard did well to arrive in the coolest period of the year. Later, he remembered the breezes blowing through the palm trees and the ocean-going liners waiting out to sea, and was proud to have been born in a cosmopolitan 'island city' which enjoyed the same relationship to the rest of India as New York to the United States. (His father wrote that old Anglo-Indians were apt to regard it 'as a very un-Indian, cockney sort of place'.[3]) Whenever, as a young adult,

Rudyard found himself 'under an alien sky', he comforted himself with the thought, 'Of no mean city am I'.[4]

After his christening at St Thomas's Cathedral on 22 January 1866, he returned to the Kipling compound and to the care of a Goan ayah. A plumpish baby with golden hair, he was generally good-humoured and observant, though he had a marked belligerent streak – possibly a result of his wait to come into the world. When he was just six months old his mother reported home in glowing terms: 'He notices everything he sees, and when he is not sitting up in his ayah's arms, he turns round to follow things with his eyes very comically.'[5] A photograph shows what were to become well-known Kipling features: a broad forehead and deeply cleft chin. He is asleep, guarded by his ayah, which caused his uncle Fred Macdonald to jest, 'Dear me, how dark Alice has become!' Apart from his ayah, Rudyard's favourite playmates were the family's three dogs, who used to sit around, watching him intently, as he ate his meals in the relative cool of the veranda. Occasionally he would lash out impotently at them, shouting and gurgling. His father felt the child was 'a great lark'.[6]

Every morning Rudyard would be taken out in his pram by his ayah. Sometimes they went to the Crawford market behind the railway station where they bought mangoes, papaya and other exotic fruit that he was subsequently disappointed to find were not universally available. In the late afternoon they might stroll in the other direction – towards the green parkland of the *maidan*. As dusk fell with tropical suddenness, the wind would rise and often they had to move quickly to avoid coconuts falling off trees. The 'menacing darkness of tropical eventides' remained another of Rudyard's abiding memories.[7]

Theoretically, the Kiplings enjoyed limited status. As *Thacker's Directory* baldly put it, Lockwood was an employee in the Art School's 'Practical Department'. So he and his wife had reluctantly (since neither was particularly religious) to make their initial contacts through the Church. Once in their own house, their social life picked up. In December 1866 Lockwood was telling his

sister-in-law Edith how Alice had been parading her attractive
singing voice before Lady Frere, the Governor's wife, at an evening
soirée. Lockwood himself had discovered the pleasures – and
potential dangers – of messing about in boats along Bombay's
beautiful coastline. 'A friend of ours has a yacht and we go a-
sailing and a-sketching sometimes. Only the last time we sailed
some 20 miles out to the mouth of the harbour, where is a dangerous island, and the black rib bones of unlucky ships wrecked
last season stand stark out of the water, and the wind against us
coming back, so that at 1.30 a.m. I found Alice a trifle funky . . .'[8]

Before long, Lockwood's professional skills were also in
demand. The city might be in economic straits, but a massive
construction programme had been initiated earlier in the decade
and the Governor, Sir Bartle Frere, an enlightened administrator
of the old school, had a personal interest in ensuring that Bombay
did not lag behind Leeds or Birmingham for municipal finery or
infrastructure. In the early 1840s he had been Private Secretary to
the governor, Sir George Arthur, whose daughter Catherine he
had married. So a healthy combination of family tradition and
rivalry inspired him to embellish his city. He frequently visited
the new art school to talk to the instructors, including Lockwood
Kipling. And so insistent was he on good drainage that even
Florence Nightingale was impressed, writing to him only half
jokingly that Bombay would soon surpass London in 'the sanitary
race' and that people would go there for the sake of their health.

Through the governor, Lockwood met a clutch of administrators who tended to be of a type: they came from a narrow
range of families with a history of illustrious service to the Raj
and they took an educated interest in Indian art and society.
Typical was Harry Rivett-Carnac, charming but indolent scion
of a clan of colonial administrators, the sort, Rudyard noted
admiringly in his 1897 story 'The Tomb of his Ancestors', who
'serve India generation after generation as dolphins follow in line
across the open sea'. Both his uncle and grandfather having been
Governors of Bombay, Rivett-Carnac, in keeping with family

custom, was making his way effortlessly up through the Civil Service, largely by virtue of his connections rather than any innate talent. As a youngish man, in 1866, he was appointed Cotton Commissioner in the Central Provinces, where his more experienced cousin, Sir Richard Temple, was Governor. A couple of years later he married Marion, daughter of Sir Henry Durand, who had heroically blown open the gates of Ghazni during the British advance on Kabul in the first Afghan War in 1839 and who later became Governor of the Punjab in 1870. His best man was Charlie MacGregor, an army officer who became India's leading expert on the 'Great Game' being played out with Russia for control of Central Asia. MacGregor shortly married another of Durand's daughters, becoming chief of staff to Sir Frederick Roberts during the Afghan campaign of 1878–80, Quartermaster-General of the Indian Army and head of its fledgling intelligence service. Durand's own son Mortimer was Foreign Secretary of the Indian government at the height of the 'Great Game' conflict with Russia in the mid-1880s. Such was the élite administrative caste with which the Kiplings came in contact.

Rivett-Carnac himself was generally more interested in ideas and art than matters of state. He claimed to be an 'intimate' friend of Virginia Woolf's uncle, Sir James Fitzjames Stephen, soon to be the hardline Law Member of the Viceroy's Council.[9] He acted as an occasional correspondent for both *The Times* and the *Manchester Guardian*. He swapped poems with Alfred Lyall, a highly literate administrator who became Governor of the North-West Provinces in the 1880s. Like Temple, Lyall was later an author: he wrote a life of the Viceroy, Lord Dufferin and Ava, and was himself the subject of a biography by Sir Mortimer Durand. Lyall was also a Trustee of the British Museum, which must have pleased Rivett-Carnac whose greatest pride was his collection of Indian artefacts, particularly his coins. Whenever the young Cotton Commissioner's job took him down to Bombay, which was often, he stayed with Frere and met both Dr George Birdwood, the Curator of the Museum, and the newly arrived Lockwood Kipling. (We know this because Rivett-Carnac recorded in his autobiography that the Art School was still in 'wigwams', prior to the construction of a permanent building.)

For all his family and friends, Rivett-Carnac was an absurd character, and the Kiplings regarded him so: 'Trivet-Claptrap', he was later nicknamed by their daughter Trix, who described him as 'absolutely patronising'. There was rather more truth in her jest than she imagined: as a patron, Rivett-Carnac introduced Lockwood to an extraordinarily powerful network. To take one more example, his cousin, Sir Richard Temple, was an admirer and former colleague of the then Viceroy Sir John Lawrence. Temple had made a smooth transition from old-style paternalism (as Commissioner of Lahore) to new-style authoritarianism (he stated cheerfully in his autobiography that his period in the Central Provinces was known as 'Temple's Raj'). As Finance Member of the Viceroy's Council, he became the most unpopular man in India when he introduced income tax. For relaxation, however, he liked to paint and in his various official jobs he did his best to promote Indian art. But there was no denying his uncompromising 'Orientalist' position: he wanted the Bombay art school to teach Indians 'one thing, which through all the preceding ages they have never learnt, namely drawing objects correctly, whether figures, landscape or architecture. Such drawing tends to rectify some of their mental faults, to intensify their powers of observation, and to make them understand analytically those glories of nature which they love so well.' Ruskin could not have put it better.

Rudyard was only two years old when, in February 1868, he had to kiss his father goodbye and return to England with his mother. Alice was pregnant again and, fearing the pain and difficulties of her first child's birth, was determined this time to be in the bosom of her family where she could come under the skilled care of Dr Charles Radcliffe, the son of a ministerial colleague of Lockwood's father. Dr Radcliffe, a graduate of the University of Paris, had so impressed her sister Georgie when her husband and their young son Philip had been ill the previous year that Ned had given him a drawing called *The Mother of Healing*. This showed the Virgin Mary with the Christ-child on her knee; in the background a sick child (Philip) lay in bed, while at her feet the same child, clearly fully recovered, played happily.

While Alice was abroad, there had been a flurry of activity in the Macdonald family. In August 1866 two of her young sisters, Aggie and Louie, had married on the same day – the former to Edward Poynter, who was beginning to make a mark as an academic painter, and the latter to Alfred Baldwin, scion of a wealthy iron-making family which had until recently (before taking to Anglicanism) been a pillar of the Methodist community in Worcestershire. A couple of days later Fred Macdonald had pledged his troth in Burslem. In the autumn Georgie had moved with Ned Burne-Jones to a larger London house, The Grange, in North End Road, Fulham. Then, at the end of the year, the failing health of Alice's father George dictated that he could no longer continue his ministerial duties. So he retired, with Hannah and their remaining unmarried daughter Edith, to the peaceful village of Bewdley, just up the road from the Baldwins, who lived at Wilden, near Stourport, in Worcestershire.

On reaching England, Rudyard was parked at his grandparents' red-brick Georgian house, backing on the River Severn, while Alice completed her pregnancy with her sister Georgie at The Grange. It did not take long for his truculent nature to assert itself. He had to share a bed with his Aunt Edie, which was uncomfortable for both. He strayed into his grandparents' bedroom, only to return and announce, 'They've gone and tooken the best rooms for themselves.' Sometimes his exasperation became too much: he would dash out of this geriatric household and march down Bewdley High Street exclaiming, 'Ruddy is coming; Ruddy is coming!' And when on at least one occasion someone had the audacity to get in his way, the refrain became more threatening: 'An angry Ruddy is coming.'

For nearly five months, from late March until early August,

Rudyard made his presence felt as he explored this 'dark land'[10] with its all-encroaching mud and its rain. He quickly learnt the ways of the countryside: after trapping his fingers in a farm gate, he howled with pain. But it clearly made an impression, for when he saw a chicken bearing in the same direction, he advised compassionately, 'Hen, don't put your fingers in the gate.' Used to the company of Indian servants, he was happy to spend time with a new friend, the Baldwins' coachman Reuben, from whom he picked up a broad Worcestershire accent. When in mid-July his mother, having survived another difficult birth, returned to Bewdley with her month-old baby,[11] also called Alice, and someone remarked, 'She is like a little Rubens baby,' Rudyard piped up gruffly, 'Ah, 'ur be very like Reuben.'

In mid-August Rudyard, with his mother and tiny sister, left Bewdley and went to stay for a couple of months in Yorkshire with his other grandmother. They returned to Worcestershire for a further month, and then were off to India. Rudyard's pious grandmother Hannah could not hide her sense of relief. The young boy 'screamed horribly' as he was leaving. She confided to her diary, 'I cannot think how his poor mother will bear the voyage to Bombay with an infant, and that self willed rebel. I hope his father will train him better.'[12]

Within a fortnight of Rudyard's departure George Macdonald was dead – hastened to his grave by his wailing grandson, or so Aunt Edie felt. Louisa Baldwin seemed to agree: 'Dear old Alice left us on Monday . . .', she had written to her sister Agnes Poynter. 'Sorry as we were to lose her personally, her children turned the house into such a bear garden, and Ruddy's screaming tempers made Papa so ill we were thankful to see them on their way. The wretched disturbances one ill ordered child can make is a lesson for all time to me.'[13]

Rudyard must have felt unsettled in England: removed abruptly from his father and (for a time) his mother, living in a strange country, among elderly people, and now with a sister to contend with. Back in Bombay that winter of 1868 he rediscovered the city's easy rhythms. The India of famine, disease and hardship was on his doorstep, but he was unaware of it. Under the watchful eye of Dunnoo, the syce, he rode his dumpy pony Dapple Grey around the huge pink oleanders at the bottom of the garden. Sometimes he strayed on to the nearby park, where he loved the green parrots. He watched fascinatedly as huge white bullocks in blindfolds described endless circles round a well, lifting up water in red pots. Occasionally this 'little friend of all the world', a sturdy lad with long, straight, fair hair, 'eyes like violets' and few inhibitions,[14] would wander across the road to his father's studio, where he was allowed to play with the modelling clay, taking in the powerful aromas of paint and oils. An instructor, a Parsee called Pestonjee Bomonjee, later recalled the child flinging lumps of clay into classrooms. (Young Rudyard so liked this name that he used it for his *Just So* story, 'How the Rhinoceros Got His Skin', in 1895.)

Lockwood and Alice Kipling were now much in demand on the Bombay social circuit. According to their friend Harry Rivett-Carnac, they could both 'see persons and events from the humorous side and were the most excellent company'. In the clipped style of his autobiography, Rudyard recalled how his mother 'sang wonderful songs at a black piano and would go out to Big Dinners'. On the down side, Sir Bartle Frere had retired as Governor of Bombay in March 1867 and his successor, Sir William Fitzgerald, showed little interest in either municipal decoration or art education. The Sir Jamsetjee Jeejeebhoy School's uneasy compromise between academic and practical functions meant that it appealed more to Bombay bourgeois with vague aspirations to painting in Western style than to craftsmen immersed in the Indian design traditions Lockwood Kipling valued. In his architectural ornamentation work on various official buildings, both in Bombay and nearby Poona, Lockwood did his best to encourage indigenous artistic traditions, materials and methods. But he was frustrated by the standard of workmanship: 'a Hindoo makes a shot at the right thing & he hits or misses by chance so that no one thing is quite right – no masonry is square, no railings are straight, no roads are level, no dishes taste quite like what they should … One lives as in a dream where things are just coming about but never *quite* happen.'[15] And he was finding that the economic recession was at last hurting and his official commissions were drying up. Often, when the Public Works Department did require sculptural or architectural adornments it simply plagiarised his work. To make matters worse, when his original three-year contract came up for renewal in April 1868, one of his perks – his concession that he could charge extra for his students' private tuition – was removed. Well might Lockwood complain that he could only provide a bare subsistence for his family.[16]

Harry Rivett-Carnac did his best to help out. He had recently been appointed the Government of India's Commissioner for Cotton and Commerce, based in Allahabad, a fast-growing railway town and business centre, which was capital of the confusingly named North-West Provinces. In this capacity he arranged for Lockwood, an excellent draughtsman, to spend some time in the autumn of 1870 sketching native craftsmen. Lockwood's drawings were so good that they were sent back as exhibits to the South Kensington Museum where Dr George Birdwood, now 'Art Referee' of the Indian Section, later arranged for them to be published in magnificent photolitho facsimile.

Rivett-Carnac also used his connections in Allahabad to find Lockwood an additional part-time job in journalism. On 2 January 1865 the first issue of a new English-language newspaper, the *Pioneer*, had been published in the town. Its proprietor was George Allen, who ran a successful family trading business, with branches as far away as Lahore and Simla.[17] During the Mutiny, Allen had been in Delhi where he had unearthed an old printing press and started a daily broadsheet. Having discovered a penchant for journalism, he launched the *Pioneer* eight years later, as a mouthpiece for conservative and business opinion. In 1870, when the *Pioneer* had expanded enough to become a daily rather than a bi-weekly newspaper, Allen was looking for a correspondent in Bombay and Rivett-Carnac recommended his friend Lockwood Kipling, whose first authenticated column is dated April 1870. Along with his sober commentaries on city affairs, Lockwood liked to keep *Pioneer* readers apprised of the latest gossip, such as, 'Mrs Lennon's "conversion" to Mahommedanism has ended, as such cases usually do – disgracefully; and her paramour who is said to be a fine-looking Pathan, was yesterday sentenced to six months' imprisonment for adultery. The punishment seems heavy for the offence.'[18]

With his parents often otherwise occupied, Rudyard was left in the charge of the servants. On one level this made for an interestingly ecumenical existence. When they were out together his ayah, a Roman Catholic, would stop at the wayside to pray to the Virgin Mary. From the evidence of his story 'Baa Baa Black Sheep', she also took him to the Roman Catholic church, close to the Botanical Gardens at Parel. She had now been joined by a Surti bearer called Meeta who made toys out of oranges and nuts, and in whose company Rudyard went to Hindu temples, where he gazed with interest at 'dimly-seen friendly Gods'. These two servants would recount local folk-tales and teach him Indian songs. Rudyard particularly liked a story about a Ranee from Delhi who turned into a tiger: at the appropriate moment Meeta, in red-and-gold turban, would grab hold of a tiger-skin rug, throw it over his head and make savage jungle noises – often, inadvertently, scaring baby Alice out of her wits. (She was now known as 'Trix', a nickname given by her father because of her 'tricksy' ways.) There came a point when kitchen Hindustani was so much the lad's first tongue that he had to be reminded to speak English when he was presented to his parents in the early evenings. Rudyard was drawing on memory when in 'Tods' Amendment', the precocious, eponymous child delivered 'solemn and serious aphorisms, translated from the vernacular into the English, that made his Mamma jump and vow that Tods *must* go Home next hot weather.'

Rudyard's multi-cultural influences were extended during the Kiplings' summer holidays. When the temperature on the coast

became too stifling, the family took the train to Nassik, a hill
station 120 miles inland in the Western Ghats. There they stayed
in a big house on the escarpment overlooking the River Godavari,
which they shared with Lockwood's friend Proctor Sims, Public
Works Councillor in the native state of Bhaunagar. When his
schoolfriend Lionel Dunsterville visited Nassik in 1886, Rudyard
described it unimaginatively as 'a lovely spot'. From this, he might
seem to have been referring to a dozy hill station for weary
Bombay residents. In fact, Nassik was (and is) one of the leading
places of pilgrimage in the Hindu religion. Every twelve years, as
part of the Kumbh Mela festival, millions of devotees descend on
the town where they immerse themselves in the purifying waters
of the River Godavari. According to the holy Hindu text, the
Ramayana, Nassik was where Rama (the God Vishnu in human
form) lived, with his brother Lakshmana and his wife Sita, during
their exile from Ayodhya. When the demoness Surpanakha spied
the two brothers, she lusted after them and jealously tried to
devour Sita. However, Lakshmana intervened and cut off the evil
intruder's nose (nasika in Sanskrit).

Rudyard later acknowledged this religious dimension to
Nassik in his story 'The Potted Princess' for the American children's magazine *St Nicholas* in January 1893. He referred to the
'nungapunga', or naked holy men, on the mountain there, and
how 'they showed me their little Gods and I burned stuff
that smelt in a pot before them all, and they said I was a Hindu,
and—'[19]

That abrupt ending reflected his ambivalence about the experience. Despite these influences, he held little brief for Hindu mythology, as is clear from the secular tones of *The Jungle Book*. The
reason was that he grew up in a household that was wary of
Hinduism. Despite his respect for Indian craftsmanship, Lockwood Kipling subscribed to the Ruskin school of thought that
dismissed the Hindu pantheon as barbaric. As a child, Rudyard
had to view – and struggle to understand – these colourful images
through a filter of paternal disapproval. Consequently, he was

condemned to the classic expatriate's limbo of being neither part of the indigenous culture nor out of it.

The cerebral nature of the Kiplings' retreats in Nassik was better reflected in the high Brahmin Bostonian figure of one of their visitors, Charles Eliot Norton, a Harvard professor who had got to know Burne-Jones and the Pre-Raphaelites in London. On an earlier trip to India in 1850, Norton had befriended Sir Jamsetjee Jejeebhoy, about whom he penned a flattering profile in the *North American Review*.[20] This time, Norton noted the small Rudyard walking hand-in-hand with a Nassik farmer and calling back to his mother in Hindustani, 'Goodbye, this is my brother.'[21] Somehow, this cute image persisted. During their 1870 stay in Nassik, both Rudyard and his father fell sick with a fever. The young boy was revived with his favourite treat, a mixture of honey and jam, which he found so delightful that Lockwood could not resist making a charming drawing of his son, looking fat and cherubic, entitled *Ruddy's Idea of Heaven*.

For all its enchantment, this upbringing was idle and spoilt. From time to time the 'other' more aggressive Rudyard would surface and he would pull his ayah's hair (once he bit her to avenge some imagined wrong to Trix), or he would throw stones at the chokra, or youngest in the retinue of eight servants. Even his doting father had to admit that Anglo-Indian children's lives were so pampered that they needed regular chastising. He had his own spurious rationale: 'We are willing slaves to our small emperors, feeling that the best we can give them is but poor compensation for the loss of their birthright of English air.'[22]

So, in April 1871, when Lockwood Kipling's contract again came up for renewal, he decided to follow his instincts and take an offer of six months' leave. Even without a plague of rats, the previous year had been hard. In April 1870 Alice had lost her third child, another son called John, who survived only a few days. Unlike her sister Georgie, who had suffered the same devastating experience six years earlier, Alice received no consoling letter from the poet Swinburne to boost her morale. For Rudyard, too, this had been a disturbing event: one that he buried deep in his unconscious and never mentioned. As a result, along with its vibrancy, he retained an image of Bombay as a place of death. In his auto-biography he noted his mother's distress when she found a child's hand at the bottom of the garden and told him explicitly not to ask about it – a prohibition his ayah was happy to disregard. A sense of India as a country built on dead men, ghosts and illusions became a feature of his subsequent writings.

Like many Anglo-Indians, Lockwood felt unsettled by news of the Franco-Prussian War, which brought out (in one of his early columns for the *Pioneer*) a latent anti-Germanism that his son was to inherit. 'I don't seem to want many things German,' wrote Lockwood, courting the displeasure of his patron Harry Rivett-Carnac, who was a fervent Germanophile, 'neither her high (and dry) Art, nor her tobacco, nor her cigars, nor anything that is hers.' When the Prussians occupied Paris, Lockwood thought this 'the saddest and most terrible story in the civilised world'.

On their journey homewards in a P & O steamship, the Kiplings were able to travel through the Suez Canal, which had opened to great fanfare in November 1869. Back in 'Blighty', as Rudyard's soldier heroes would call it (from the Hindustani *bilayati*, meaning foreign), Lockwood decided to treat his family to a traditional English seaside holiday. The Burne-Joneses had rec-ommended the Sussex coastal town of Littlehampton as an excel-lent place for small children. (Quite why is not clear, since their visit in 1864 had led both Philip and Georgie Burne-Jones to contract scarlet fever, causing her to lose her second son Christopher.) This July it rained incessantly but, unperturbed, the Kiplings sallied forth from their rented house at every oppor-tunity and made for the beach where Rudyard's first attempts at building a sandcastle had an appropriate literary model – a plan from an illustrated edition of Harrison Ainsworth's novel *The Tower of London*, which he read (or was read) around this time. Rudyard rode donkeys, watched acrobats and even played 'elem-entary cricket'. There were forays to nearby towns, including

Arundel and Chichester, and, in early August, as far afield as Winchester, Salisbury and Stonehenge. In a series of five articles for the *Pioneer* entitled 'Loafing', Lockwood could not avoid sounding bored with the whole exercise. But he was delighted at Rudyard's enjoyment and his affection shone through his description of his son at play:

> A good plan for getting a small boy well wet is to shape for him in the sand an elaborate Rob Roy canoe with a deep hole in the centre in which he can sit, and a trench all round. The tide rises and the happy child sees his boat being gradually surrounded by water; he splashes his spade right and left, proud of the mimic paddling of his own canoe, till a big wave sweeps in, deluging him as he sits, and filling his pocket, shoes, and knicker-bockers with sand and water, and his youthful mind with deep contentment.

It was all the more strange when, on 1 October, the family made the thirty-three-mile journey along the south coast from Little-hampton to Southsea, a once elegant resort adjoining the great seafaring town of Portsmouth. With its views across the Solent to the Isle of Wight, Southsea was a favoured dormitory for genteel folk with naval or military connections. Ellen Ternan, Dickens's mistress, lived there towards the end of her life and Arthur Conan Doyle tried unsuccessfully to practise as a doctor in the town during the 1880s. Even before then, it had become down at heel: a place that attracted 'that kind of officer who lived in cheap lodgings at Southsea ... good men all, but not well-off'.[23]

The Kiplings were not in Southsea for its recuperative powers or its tourist attractions. They came because they had read a newspaper advertisement placed by a local couple offering to look after children whose parents were stationed in India. Lockwood soon had to return to India and Alice was determined to accompany him. So references were taken up, feelings of guilt bottled up and, thinking hygienically of the 'birthright of English air', they decided to leave their tender-aged son and daughter in the care of these foster-parents.

With apparently no warning, five-year-old Rudyard and his three-year-old sister were taken that autumn morning to a bow-windowed house on the edge of the town and left there. The name Lorne Lodge was prominently displayed on the gate. Rudyard later recalled how he had disliked the place the minute he set foot in it. With his usual self-assurance, however, he talked contentedly to its inhabitants and expected, as had always happened on visits before, that he would soon be leaving. Only this time there was no respite, no going home. Instead, he found that he and his sister had been delivered into the hands of Captain Pryse Holloway, a tall, spindly man with a limp, and his wife Sarah, a sinister apparition in black. Lurking in the background was the third person in the household, the Holloways' twelve-year-old son Henry (known as Harry), who had black hair and an oily complexion.

Rudyard did not know it, but he would come to hate this 'House of Desolation'. In three main literary works – his extended story 'Baa Baa Black Sheep', published in 1888, the novel *The Light that Failed* (1890–1) and his autobiography *Something of Myself* (1936), he gave vent to the loathing which built up during six years at Lorne Lodge. 'I had never heard of Hell, so I was introduced to it in all its terrors,' he wrote in the last of these accounts, when his anger might have been expected to have subsided.

By everything his parents had to go on, Lorne Lodge was not a bad place for their children. It was situated in a smart new residential district, Havelock Park. The house had just been built: it did not even appear on the census returns in 1871, that very same year. And the neighbourhood had impeccable Anglo-Indian connotations: the man who gave his name to the road was Sir Colin Campbell, Palmerston's commander-in-chief of the Indian Army, and the park was called after General Sir Henry Havelock, whose forces had relieved both Cawnpore and Lucknow during the Indian Mutiny. (Possibly, news of this link had been reported in the *Pioneer*, where the Kiplings first read of the place.)

Captain Holloway came from a respectable Oxfordshire family. Among his brothers were a solicitor, a university don, a clergyman and a distinguished soldier – General Sir Thomas Holloway, who had served at the siege of Sebastopol in the Crimean War, and lived in style nearby at West Lodge, Havant. The Captain's early career in the Royal Navy had come to an abrupt end in 1827 when, as a volunteer aboard HMS *Brisk*, he was wounded at the Battle of Navarino, fighting the Turks in the Greek war of independence. Invalided out as a midshipman two years later, he joined the merchant service and gained his officer's rank as commander of an Arctic whaling vessel (stories of which sparked Rudyard's interest in polar exploration). In 1855, aged 45, he switched to dry land and worked in relative comfort on the east coast of England as Chief Officer of the Coastguards at Sizewell in Suffolk.

All told, the Captain was not a bad cove – much the most agreeable of the three members of the household as far as Rudyard was concerned. The first of several 'father figures' in the boy's life, the old salt told stories about Navarino, where the sound of gunfire was so deafening that no-one could hear anything for three days afterwards. Young Rudyard wanted to ask about the wound that had caused his limp but, such was the stuffy atmosphere of the place, did not think it appropriate or wise.

Every three months the Captain would wend his way along the sea front to an office in the Portsmouth dockyards where he would collect his minimal coastguard's pension of £31 12s 8d a year.[24] Rudyard often accompanied him on his walks: sometimes, amid the smell of seaweed and the sound of swirling gulls, the old sailor would take the lad to see the little training brigs outside Southsea Castle; on other occasions they would visit Admiral Nelson's original flagship, HMS *Victory*. Alongside this mooring were huge booms of floating timber, which Rudyard noted in his autobiography were still used in the naval dockyards, despite moves to ironclad vessels. According to John Keegan in *Battle at Sea*, 'After 1865, all the Royal Navy's new ships were built of iron; the most modern of the old were cut down and ironclad.'[25] But, even on these timber was still incorporated in the construction of decks and armour.

Not all Rudyard's recollections were quite so accurate. For example, he claimed he and the Captain saw the Arctic exploration vessels HMS *Alert* and HMS *Discovery* in Portsmouth harbour after their historic Polar expedition. But the ships did not sail until May 1875 and returned the following year, two years after the Captain's death. While this does not mean that his memories of Mrs Holloway, the mistress of the house, are wrong, it requires them to be treated with discretion. According to Rudyard's accounts, she and her oleaginous son Harry gave Lorne Lodge its hateful character and they were the people Rudyard detested.

Of Mrs Holloway's past, little is known except that she was born Sarah Slatter in 1823, the daughter of an Oxford High Street tailor. She was thirty-six when she married in August 1859, and her son Harry was born in Sizewell in June the following year. Both she and her husband were well beyond the usual mid-Victorian age for marrying (he was forty-nine). This suggests that, after four years as a coastguard, the Captain was lonely and returned to his Oxfordshire roots to find himself a wife – perhaps a trusted family retainer or a 'spinster of this parish' who had long given up hope of marriage. At one stage the Captain appears to have been thinking of becoming a publican, for he took a tenancy on a pub, the Rose and Crown in Charlbury, his local Oxfordshire village, in 1866, four years before he retired. But nothing came of that initiative, and the Holloways found themselves in Southsea, running a boarding house.

This background would explain the frustrated nature of the Sarah Holloway who emerges in Rudyard's accounts. On the one hand she was a pillar of her local church, who – ironically, the beleaguered Kipling children thought – lent her support to a petition for the ending of solitary confinement in prisons. This was the woman who charmed the Kipling parents and who continued to placate any relative who came to visit Rudyard and Trix.

On the other hand, she was a stern Evangelical disciplinarian, whose sweet voice was only ever heard when the vicar paid one of his regular visits. This was the zealous tartar who chastised Rudyard and made his life intolerable. In India the little boy had had minimal experience of organised religion. But this woman had a direct line to 'an abstraction called God'.[26] When Rudyard told Trix a version of the Creation story which drew heavily on his recollection of Indian fairy-tales, she was furious. Rudyard's regular punishment was to be banished to the attic room he shared with Harry where he was forced to learn Collects. The time was put to good use: it helped nurture a deep and abiding knowledge of the Bible.

Rudyard and Trix were mystified why their parents should have left them in this dark, forbidding place. Although newly built, Lorne Lodge had a dank atmosphere, epitomised by the basement play-room where toys turned blue with mildew after just three days in the cupboards. But when the children asked for an explanation, Mrs Holloway replied it was because they were 'so tiresome'[27] and she had only taken them in out of pity. And then, when her fury was aroused, she would say she had 'secret orders' that Rudyard in particular was to be beaten.

When brother and sister drew closer in adversity, speaking a secret kitchen-Hindustani, 'Aunty', as she liked to be called, tried to prise them apart. With no daughter of her own, she reserved her occasional shows of affection for Trix, with whom she shared a bedroom hung with grim grey wallpaper. While Rudyard went on regular visits to relations, such as the Burne-Joneses, Trix always stayed with Aunty, even going with her to spend Christmas in Brighton. She was encouraged to believe that, if she behaved herself, she might one day win Harry's hand in marriage.

Unused to rejection, Rudyard turned in on himself, becoming increasingly morose. This brought out a tendency to clumsiness that hitherto had been masked by natural good humour. Inevitably, spilling things led to more recrimination and more punishment. Rudyard could expect no let-up at night when he crept under the red wadded quilt in his attic bedroom. For Harry was a natural bully who had been primed by his mother to keep up the torture. He was 'at once spy, practical joker, inquisitor, and Aunty Rosa's deputy executioner' (Aunty Rosa being the name Rudyard gave Mrs Holloway in 'Baa Baa Black Sheep').

Rudyard's way of coping was to retreat further into books. This was a new experience for him. He only learnt to read while at Lorne Lodge and at first he found it difficult. Trix liked to recall that, although two years younger, she was quicker to master this skill than her brother. He ungallantly told her, 'That's because you're so little you have much less brain to see the hard things about reading.'[28] His own backwardness, however, was clearly an indication of his poor eyesight.

Soon he was devouring everything he could lay his hands on. He enjoyed a thrilling moment of self-recognition when, in an 1872 volume of *Aunt Judy's Magazine*, he read Mrs Ewing's story 'From Six to Sixteen', about a couple of Anglo-Indian sisters sent home to England. He discovered poetry through the children's fantasies of Elizabeth Anna Hart, a distant cousin of Lewis Carroll. A letter to Bombay requesting 'all the books in the world' brought *Grimm's Fairy Tales* and a volume by Hans Andersen. Soon he had graduated to more adult fare, such as the novels of Walter Scott, and the poetry of Wordsworth and Tennyson, which he found in *Sharpe's Magazine*, another of the improving periodicals lying around the house. When his uncle, Alfred Baldwin, sent a copy of *Robinson Crusoe*, Rudyard developed an elaborate game: behind a protective cordon of a trunk, a packing case and a coconut shell strung on a red wire, he imagined himself as a trader on an island of savages. He later came to see this particular type of play-acting as a form of 'natural magic' by which he kept his real-life surroundings at bay. He elaborated on the idea in his own tales such as 'The Story of Muhammad Din', and was fascinated, when he read Edmund Gosse's autobiography *Father and Son* in 1907, to find that another author had honed his creativity in much the same way.[29]

This private initiative did not please Aunty at all. She redoubled her accusations that he was 'showing off', particularly when he asked visitors to explain things he had read and did not understand. In his various writings on the period, Rudyard throws interesting light on how he progressed from being told he was a show-off to being branded a liar. In an attempt to wean him off books (again, shades of the more fundamentalist Plymouth Brethren household of his later associate Edmund Gosse), Aunty sent him to play, 'and be sure that I hear you doing it'. The ingenious child devised a ploy where he mounted three legs of a table on toy bricks and crashed the fourth periodically to the floor. He managed to perfect a system whereby he could do this and read at the same time. But one day, inevitably, he was found out. He was told he was 'acting a lie' and, since he was old enough to do this, he was mature enough to be beaten. (At this stage Aunty's light cane was introduced to the proceedings.) No sooner had this happened than Harry developed the regular habit of calling him a liar.

So long as the Captain was alive he protected Ruddy from the worst of these ravages. When Harry stole Ruddy's paintbox without asking, his father clipped him round the ear, causing Aunty to abuse the old man for cruelty to his own flesh and blood. Jealous of the relationship between Rudyard and the Captain, she complained that the young visitor was always 'showing off'. Harry no doubt read the signals and redoubled his persecution of his room-mate. Once when Rudyard and the Captain visited the cemetery behind Havelock Park, the old sea-dog pointed to a gravestone and said, 'I shall lie there soon' and then, as if to confirm their complicity, he added, 'You needn't tell Aunty.'[30]

Captain Holloway's death in September 1874 removed any last constraints on Aunty. As a gold-digger of lower class than her husband, she was devastated the following year when his brother, the General in Havant, also died and she was left without an expected legacy. In less than twelve months she had lost not only her husband's pension, but also any hope of a comfortable retirement. As a result, Harry was forced to leave his school, Hope House, in Somerset Place, Southsea, and find employment in a bank. There were advantages for Rudyard: at the end of a working day Harry was often too tired to vent his frustrations. But there were exceptions to this rule and the young paying guest learnt to know Harry's mood – and what was to come afterwards – from the sound of his footsteps as he approached the house.

For a short time the two boys had attended the same school together. The headmaster, T. H. Vickery, offered 'a sound Classical, Mathematical, and General Education' and, if required, would prepare pupils for the 'Examinations for entry into the Royal Navy'. Given Trix's emphasis on her brother's sailor suit, with its man-o'-war blouse, lanyard and whistle, in her accounts of Southsea, it is possible that Rudyard (like his son, later) was earmarked for a naval career. (This may explain why he used the headmaster's name, Vickery, for the naval gunner in his elliptical story, 'Mrs Bathurst'.)

Rudyard liked school little better than Lorne Lodge. He found that, thanks to Harry, a false reputation for deceitfulness had preceded him. Rudyard's reaction was interesting because it showed that, for all the apparent ease of race relations in his Bombay nursery, he had managed to ingest a typical colonialist's prejudices about class and caste. (Indeed, his antipathy to Mrs Holloway may have arisen partly from his sense that she was not 'one of us'. When she screamed at him, he was shocked because, in his experience, only the untouchables in the bazaar raised their voices in this manner.) Among Hope House's small complement of pupils (twenty-six in 1871) were two Jews and, also, a dark boy who, because of his behaviour and appearance, must, Rudyard reasoned to himself, be a 'hubshi' or negro. He decided to keep quiet at home about his amazing piece of detective work, in case he was accused of showing off. But, goaded by Harry, he could not prevent himself telling Aunty that normally he would not speak to such children: their fathers worked in shops. He was told that he ought to be grateful that anyone talked to him at all: 'It isn't every school that takes little liars.'

Rudyard's reaction was to become a liar. With a child's logic, he said to himself that when he told the truth he was called a liar, so why not fib a bit and see if he could get away with it? As a result, he told Aunty he was doing well at school when he was not. She found out and, after a ritual beating, paraded him through the streets of Southsea wearing a sign on his back that announced to the world 'LIAR'.

At least that is the gist of the story as Rudyard told it and it was confirmed in most essentials by Trix. In assessing the story a number of questions arise, such as why the Kipling children were sent to this hell-hole in the first place and why they were allowed to remain there so long. They could have stayed with any number of aunts, uncles and, more to the point, cousins of their own age, in London, Yorkshire and Worcestershire.

Unfortunately there were difficulties with all of these options. The children's most obvious home from home, The Grange, was temporarily unavailable because, in the summer of 1871 when the Kiplings returned from India, the Burne-Joneses, who lived there, were experiencing severe domestic upheavals – with repercussions for the rest of the family.

On one level, this was the result of the sexual intensity that affected the Pre-Raphaelite circle as much as the Bloomsbury group half a century later. Often finding it difficult to keep his hands off his models, the irrepressible, often impossible Ned Burne-Jones had fallen deeply in love with the exotic, flame-haired Mary Zambaco (née Cassavetti), a married woman related to the Ionides, a prominent Anglo-Greek merchant family, who were important patrons of his. Georgie's evident misery had attracted the sympathy and, it seems, the love of the normally sexless William Morris, whose wife Janey was enjoying an affair with Rossetti.

As a result, both Ned and Georgie were plunged into a gloom which, in his case, had been worsened in the summer of 1870 by a row over his painting of *Phyllis and Demophoon*, in which the naked female had the head of his mistress, Mary Zambaco. The Old Water Colour Society declined to show the work, forcing him to resign. His general good humour was not improved by a down-turn in critical favour, the temporary loss of important patrons and the consequences of trying to end his affair with Mary, who broke down and increased her consumption of laudanum after he rejected her. Georgie had already started living a semi-detached existence, taking the children on holidays with the novelist George Eliot and developing a close friendship with Rosalind Howard, the Countess of Carlisle. But when, in a fit of despair, Ned suddenly decamped to Italy in September 1871, she had had enough. Money was becoming a problem and she had made herself ill by her stoicism in the face of her husband's affair. So she closed down The Grange and took her two children, Philip and Margaret, now nine and five, to stay with her sister Louie Baldwin in Worcestershire.

Alice Kipling did not consider Yorkshire an option. She had noticed the ease with which Rudyard had picked up a Worcester accent and she did not want him speaking broad Yorkshire. Trix later expressed disappointment that they did not spend time with their grandmother who 'had a nice little house in Skipton, and Aunts Jenny and Ruth were both with her then, and I know they would have been kind to us'.[31]

The Kipling children's other grandmother, old Mrs Hannah Macdonald at Bewdley, offered to look after them, but Alice was wary of leaving them there too. As she told a friend[32] a few years later, she only saw this leading to 'complications' and anyway 'the children were quite happy ... and she was able to be with [Lockwood] and help him with his work'. Perhaps she remembered the bad odour little Rudyard had left three years earlier. Perhaps, also, she was showing her selfish, socially ambitious side, which allowed her, with little sense of remorse, to disregard her children's feelings and dump them on a strange couple. This would explain her failure to inform Rudyard and Trix about their fate. The children's vague realisation of this treachery only increased their sense of bewilderment at their abandonment. (The boy Harry understood this weakness and exploited it cruelly.)

Alice did, however, make sure that her Macdonald relations were ready and willing to act *in loco parentis*. In late August and early September 1872, just under a year after the two children first came to Lorne Lodge, Hannah Macdonald, three of her daughters (Aggie, Georgie and Louie) and various of their offspring spent a couple of weeks in Southsea. Although they had difficulty finding rooms over the Bank Holiday, representatives of three generations of the family – Hannah, Aggie Poynter and her five-year-old son Ambrose – visited Rudyard and Trix as soon as they arrived in the town and found them 'well and happy'.[33] In general, the young Kiplings were 'much improved in manners ... They seem to be attached to Mrs H., and she seems very fond of them.' Various outings ensued, and on at least two occasions the Holloways and their son joined them all at the beach. At the end of the visit Captain Holloway accompanied Rudyard by train to Reading so the young boy could join the Baldwins – his Uncle Alfred and Aunt Louie – on their journey back to Worcestershire, where he was able to spend four weeks in the company of his five-year-old cousin Stanley.

If they all seemed curiously blind to what was going on, the Macdonalds would again have recalled Rudyard's antics at Bewdley in 1868 and sympathised with Mrs Holloway's plight in trying to socialise him. Indeed, for all her loyalty to her brother, Trix, with her sharp and intuitive Macdonald temperament, later admitted as much to Stanley Baldwin:

Between ourselves I think that in some ways 'Auntie' [Holloway] saved [Rud's] soul alive. He was about as spoilt as he could be when we came home in 1871. Six and a half years old and he had never been taught to read! I don't know what the parents were thinking of – and how he escaped learning – He and I were taught together by Auntie – and I learnt first – age four! And he was not naughty or wilful at lessons – when he saw the point of it he lapped it up eagerly – but he hadn't been taught!

Mother had a very strong will, but there were curious streaks of sand in her marble.[34]

By the following Christmas (1873) the Burne-Joneses had pulled through the worst of their matrimonial difficulties and Rudyard was able to go to a revitalised The Grange for the first of at least four successive annual visits at this time of year. Doubtless, underlying tensions persisted, but they did not concern a seven-year-old boy. He was determined to enjoy himself – from the moment he arrived at the gate and, looking like 'a burly little sea captain in a pilot coat and cap, with a carpet bag for luggage',[35] reached up to the open-work iron bell-pull. (He so liked this object that, later in life, after the Burne-Joneses had left The Grange, he acquired it for his own house in Sussex 'in the hope that other children might also feel happy when they rang it'.[36])

In contrast to Lorne Lodge, The Grange pulsated with energy and excitement. During the day, while visitors flitted in and out to see Uncle Ned, Rudyard amused himself with his cousins Phil and Margaret. Phil, now twelve, was about to go away to boarding-school at William Morris's alma mater, Marlborough. The three children made the most of their unchaperoned play, whether shinning up the huge mulberry tree, their 'conference centre' in the garden, or making a toboggan slide out of a tilted table in the nursery.

Towards the end of the afternoon, looking to be useful in the bustle of a working studio, Rudyard found jobs to occupy himself, such as working the bellows of an organ for Aunt Georgie as she played for her husband while he painted. When finished, Uncle Ned would relax and play games with the children. They had draped a chair with rugs to serve as their oracle, 'Norna of the Fitful Head' (the character in their favourite Walter Scott novel *The Pirate*). He would go behind it and answer their questions 'in a voice deeper than all the boots in the world'.

That first Christmas, Aunt Georgie 'gathered together such grown-up friends as were not claimed elsewhere, and who could if needed still romp with a will'.[37] So the party included 'Uncle Topsy', Ned's unworldly business partner William Morris, and his long-suffering wife Janey. The Poynters came with their son Ambrose, and also present were the painters William de Morgan and Frederic Burton, and a couple of Ned's university friends, Charlie Faulkner and William Allingham. Georgie later recalled how Burton's 'beautiful face beamed on the scene'.[38] Knowing him was to have interesting repercussions for Rudyard in India a decade or so later. At this stage the Irish-born Burton was simply an amiable antiquarian cum middle-ranking painter in his mid-fifties. He had helped found the Archaeological Society of Ireland in 1840 and had made one of the few surviving portraits of George Eliot. He was also one of those artists (like Rudyard's Uncle Edward Poynter) who naturally become part of 'the great and the good'. Shortly to be appointed Director of the National Gallery, Frederic had endeared himself to the Burne-Jones household by resigning from the Old (later Royal) Water Colour Society in sympathy with Ned in 1870, following the dispute over the latter's painting *Phyllis and Demophoön*. In the wider context he was also the uncle of Francis Burton, an Indian Army officer whose wife Isabella became the model for one of Rudyard's most intriguing and alluring fictional characters, Mrs Hauksbee, the witty Queen of Simla.

Even with Uncle Ned on best behaviour, young Rudyard could not avoid the heady whiff of high Bohemianism and bookish intellectualism that exuded from the members of this Burne-Jones circle. On the one hand, their tortured lives complemented their mannered aesthetics, offering a foretaste of the decadence of the 1890s. Ned himself might have halted his amorous liaisons, but he still enjoyed the company of actresses such as the pert cockney Katie Vaughan, whom he liked to watch performing her daring 'skirt dance' at the music-halls – Rudyard's first experience of this particular form of entertainment. The tragic shadow of Rossetti and his drug-taking models would not go away, and some scandal always needed hushing up (Simeon Solomon, the homosexual painter, had been arrested for indecency in a public lavatory earlier that year).

On the other hand, Ned had a mid-Victorian's thirst for knowledge. He relished the company of literate friends such as Morris, Ruskin and the American academic Charles Eliot Norton. Faced with painting a challenging new subject, he made research trips to the British Museum (or further afield, to see the works of the masters in Italy). In his quest for cultural syncretism in a post-Darwinian age, he delved into topics as varied as Assyrian writing and Celtic mythology. Having been alerted by Swinburne to Edward Fitzgerald's translation of the *Rubáiyát* of Omar Khayyám, Ned acquired a taste for Persian literature: only the previous month he had been trying to find a copy of Firdausi's epic *Shah Náma*. From his youngest days, therefore, Rudyard had access to an eclectic range of literature – from the obvious *Arabian Nights*, through *Sidonia the Sorceress* (a disturbing German tale, which was intriguing both for its subject matter – about a typically 'gifted, ferocious'[39] Pre-Raphaelite female, who used her beauty for evil ends – and for its provenance – it had been translated in 1849 by Oscar Wilde's mother Jane, or 'Speranza'), to the poetry of Robert Browning. As the artist Val Prinsep, an associate of Burne-Jones, noted, Pre-Raphaelitism's main requirements, apart from trying to catch Dante Gabriel Rossetti's intonation, 'were to read Sidonia and Browning'.

These influences made their mark on Rudyard, though what really mattered to him at this stage was that his uncle and aunt's friends also had time for games (the only exception, he recalled, being the elderly Robert Browning). At night the children would go to bed, passing along passages where Uncle Ned had placed his unfinished cartoons (the eyes were often painted first which gave a particularly eerie effect). And then, when they were supposed to be asleep, they would crawl to the top landing where they could hang over the stairs and 'listen to the loveliest sound in the world – deep-voiced men laughing together over dinner'.[40]

Strangely, neither Ned nor Georgie noticed anything troubled or untoward in Rudyard's behaviour during his visits from South-sea. Nor did the boy seek to inform his aunt and uncle about the injury that was being done to him. He later tried to shrug this off with the explanation, 'Children tell little more than animals, for what comes to them they accept as eternally established. Also, badly-treated children have a clear notion of what they are likely to get if they betray the secrets of the prison-house before they are clear of it.' But this told only part of the story: if, as is likely, Rudyard felt abandoned by his mother, he experienced it so deeply that it was impossible to reveal.

During Rudyard's annual visit to The Grange in December 1876, however, Aunt Georgie was forced to pay attention when she caught him striking out at a tree at the bottom of her garden. Questioned as to what he was doing, he said he thought the tree was Grandma, and he had to hit it to make sure. Georgie realised that the boy was in distress and asked a family friend, Jonathan Inverarity, an elderly Bombay lawyer who had known him from birth, to go to Southsea to discover the causes. Rudyard was diagnosed to be suffering from astigmatism and was fitted with glasses. However, the problem proved more intractable than the usual 'poor eyesight'. As with Dowse, the lighthouse keeper in his story 'A Disturber of Traffic', Rudyard's hallucinations were linked to a form of mental instability. Even in his reticent autobiography he admitted that he had been having 'some sort of a nervous breakdown' in which he imagined he was seeing 'shadows and things that were not there, and they worried me more than the Woman' (i.e. Mrs Holloway).

Alerted by her sister Georgie, Alice Kipling now saw fit in March 1877 to return to England to visit the children she had last been with more than half a decade before. She had been expected a couple of years earlier but, at the start of 1875, her life – and her husband's – had taken a different tack. That spring, shortly before his thirty-eighth birthday, Lockwood Kipling had been offered a new post as head of the Mayo School of Industrial Art in Lahore, capital of the Punjab. Once again the ubiquitous Rivett-Carnac claims to have played a role in supporting Lockwood's application, for his father-in-law Sir Henry Durand had recently been made Lieutenant Governor of the province. Lockwood was attracted because the Bombay School, his current employer, was moving further and further away from its aim (which Lockwood held dear) of training artisans. In becoming more of a traditional fine arts establishment, it had, two years earlier, dropped the word 'industry' from its official title, Sir Jamsetjee Jeejeebhoy School of Art and Industry. Lockwood's mind was made up because the headship of the Mayo School came with another job which appealed to the methodical, encylopaedist side of his nature: he would also be Curator of Lahore's Museum which, although dating back to 1856, had grown substantially after taking the pick of the collections made for the 1864 Punjab Exhibition of Arts and Industry.[41]

Alice, ambitious for herself and her husband, felt she should accompany Lockwood and he expected nothing else than for her to be at his side. The Kiplings found themselves in a frontier garrison town: the Punjab had only been brought under British control in 1848. Indeed the School's name was a constant reminder of India's potentially volatile political situation, since it commemorated Lord Mayo, the Viceroy who was assassinated by a Pathan convict in February 1872 while on a visit to Port Blair, capital of the penal colony, the Andaman Islands.

Lockwood was happy to escape the day-to-day frustrations of Bombay. With its emphasis on architectural drawing and design, the Mayo School of Industrial Art was much more suited to his interests. Like many Englishmen in the Raj, he found the local Sikhs and Moslems easier to communicate with than Hindus (though, in Bombay, he had liked the Parsees who figured strongly at the administrative level). Since the British community in Lahore was so small (no more than seventy civilians), his professional skills were much in demand for jobs such as redecorating Montgomery Hall, the town's social centre, in advance of the

Prince of Wales's visit at the end of the year. The Hall was covered with a teak floor, which allowed both dancing and 'rinking', as the latest sport of roller-skating was known. Lockwood wrote approvingly in the *Pioneer* that this pastime not only 'had the advantage of bringing you into closer and more intimate contact with the fair sex than any other diversion going'[42] but also broke through class distinctions. Lockwood never met the Prince, however, because for three months from November 1875 he was laid low with typhoid, which left him in his own words 'grey, feeble and fat'.

Unexpectedly, Lockwood soon found himself on the receiving end of regular attacks in the local paper, the *Indian Public Opinion*, which was owned and edited by Dr Gotlieb Leitner, a mysterious, brilliant and dogmatic Hungarian who monopolised the intellectual life of Lahore. Born in Budapest in 1840, Leitner had, as a young teenager, been chief interpreter to Her Majesty's Commissariat in the Crimean War (1854–6) – with the rank, it was reported, of Colonel. Having attended the Moslem Theological College in Constantinople, he became Professor of Arabic and Muhammadan Law at King's College, London, in 1861 at the still tender age of twenty-one. Appointed principal of the Government College in Lahore in 1864, he published widely on the languages of the North-West Frontier and Kashmir. At a time of post-Mutiny conservative reaction elsewhere, he and his newspaper provided a progressive voice in the Punjab. As founder of the Anjuman-i-Punjab (the Association of the Punjab), he worked for the setting up of a full university in the Province and for the introduction of native languages as the medium of instruction. This radical proposal, more than anything, brought out the conservative in Lockwood Kipling, who considered Macaulay's 1835 minute on the use of English – and all the utilitarian measures that flowed from it – as gospel. The two men traded regular *ad hominem* attacks in the pages of the *Pioneer* and *Indian Public Opinion*. When in May 1876, Leitner sought to be made Law Professor at Lahore's University College, Lockwood pointed out that he had already accumulated so many official positions in the Punjab education system that he was in danger, 'in the homely Yankee phrase, [of becoming] "the whole team, and the dog under the wagon besides".[43] There was a thinly veiled touch of anti-Semitism in Lockwood's comment that Dr Leitner was 'hardly to be judged by the rigid official standards of etiquette or the frigid social canon of Britannic self-restraint and conventional modesty'. When Leitner postponed a trip to Europe because of anti-Jewish pogroms, Alice commented uncharitably that she would like to start a pogrom to rid Lahore of Dr Leitner. This small-town feud between its museum chief and leading educationist was to rumble on for years.

Towards the end of 1876, Lockwood was on hand when Lord Lytton, the new Viceroy, passed through Lahore *en route* to the North-West Frontier town of Rawalpindi, where he was going to be briefed first-hand on the growing threat from Russia in Central Asia. The son of the novelist and MP Edward Bulwer-Lytton, the Viceroy was an aristocratic roué who, in his youth, before becoming a diplomat, had written poetry under the name Owen Meredith. During his very first season in Simla, the Punjabi hill station to which the Imperial court retired from Calcutta during the heat of the summer, he put his Bohemian stamp on the place, encouraging amateur theatricals and the arts. Given his weakness for flirtatious affairs with the wives of subordinates, Lytton was often dismissed as a playboy. (One of his *tendresses* was for Mrs Trevor Plowden, who was married to Assam's Inspector General of Police, and who once scandalised Calcutta society when she was seen to be wearing no underwear after her dress split while she was curtsying.) In fact, as a conservative pragmatist who drew on his lifelong friendship with James Fitzjames Stephen, the Viceroy was a more effective operator than he seemed.

While in Lahore, he raised the Kiplings' social standing by remarking to Alice how surprised he was to meet his old friend Burne-Jones's sister-in-law in such a place and she, with her sharp wit, retorted that she had not expected to come across Owen

Meredith. Already Lytton had called on Lockwood Kipling to help him with another important project. As a show of political resolution, he had decided to proclaim Queen Victoria Empress of India at a special Imperial Assemblage of all India's Princes on 1 January 1877. 'The further East you go, the greater becomes the importance of a bit of bunting,' he once patronisingly said.[44] So he asked Lockwood to advise on overall presentation and, in particular, to work on embroidered insignia for each Maharaja present. With his interest in heraldry, Lockwood enjoyed design-ing over seventy banners in Chinese satin, which were expertly stitched – this was a joint effort – by Alice and a team of 'dirzies' or native needlemen. He was rewarded for his services in staging this set piece of political theatre with a silver medal and the gift of 500 rupees, which helped pay his wife's passage when she needed to return to England later that year.

On a personal level Lockwood Kipling now had kudos and influence, and was prepared to enjoy them. His kindly manner, diverting conversation and general Yorkshire bluntness made for a magnetic personality that was attractive to women. One pretty young girl who fell for his charms was Edith Plowden who, having just left school, was staying in Lahore with her brother, a local judge (and member of the respected Anglo-Indian family to which the Viceroy's mistress belonged). Alice was going through a dowdy stage: at the dinner where they first met, Edith Plowden noted that 'Mrs Kipling's dress was severely plain and her arms bare of ornament, the pose she thought of an artist's wife'.[45] But Lockwood, 'with his fine head, beneficent expression and grey beard' was a different proposition. He delighted in the young newcomer's company, teaching her about Shakespeare and Browning, and flirting so openly that, although she first called him 'Socrates', she later changed this name to 'Chaucer' when she realised 'his intense interest in the world of men and nature'. Although it is clear from Edith's innocent report that this liaison was not physical, that did not stop Alice, on the eve of her depart-ure for England, from advising Edith, with rather more edge than her jocular manner suggested, that she and Lockwood were 'to be as much together as is consistent with propriety'. Lockwood took the hint: once his wife left, he selected a bust of Venus from his Museum and took her as his companion to live with him in the Club. And when, as soon as Alice's back was turned, an old Bombay flame wrote to suggest a rendezvous, he claimed he burned the letter immediately.

A suspicion of sexual infidelity was in the air, however, for on her voyage home Alice, coquettish Alice, allowed herself to get close enough to a man for him to try to kiss her. She too protested her innocence, later saying she created such a fuss that her unfortunate suitor was put off the boat at Suez. But such incidents do not happen without some encouragement and the concurrence of events suggests there were problems in the Kiplings' twelve-year-old marriage.

Immediately she arrived in England, Alice made her way to Southsea where her children greeted her in contrasting styles. Rudyard was overjoyed to see her, as she 'fluttered with tender excitement', looking 'young, frivolously young, and beautiful, with delicately flushed cheeks, [and] eyes that shone like stars'.[46] But still he was afraid that any show of affection would be construed as 'showing off'. Trix had no inhibitions on this last score, but she had succumbed to the 'Stockholm syndrome' experienced by siege hostages who take on the views of their captors. Mrs Holloway had convinced her that Alice intended to remove her from Southsea. And, incredibly, given that this was the only life she knew, the suggestible eight-year-old Trix believed this story.

When, at the end of the day, Alice went upstairs to say good-night to Rudyard, she found him in bed. As soon as she entered his room he instinctively flung up his right arm as if to ward off the blow that he felt, from bitter experience, must surely follow. This incident, recounted in 'Baa Baa Black Sheep', may have been little more than symbolic, but it powerfully evoked the terror of a little boy cringing at every strange apparition. For Alice, it was also too much. 'Oh, my son – my little, little son!' she cried. 'It was my fault – *my* fault, darling – and yet how could we help it? Forgive me.'

Rudyard seemed happy to assent, but his feeling of abandonment remained. In a classic case of denial, he tried to mask his hostility by adopting an idealised picture of his parents. (Psychologist Melanie Klein called this phenomenon 'splitting'. Psychiatrist Anthony Storr noted something similar in Winston Churchill's life.[47]) The result was an unresolved relationship, particularly with Alice, whom Rudyard blamed for depositing him in Southsea. This was to trouble him throughout his life. When, eleven years later, he wrote 'Baa Baa Black Sheep', he directed his negativity towards Mrs Holloway. But his parents understood that he was giving voice to his hidden resentment and, according to Trix, were devastated.

For the time being, however, everything was fine. Alice took her children away from Mrs Holloway for the summer – though, as further indication that Lorne Lodge was not quite as bad as it seemed, Trix returned there for two more years. Indeed, shortly after the death of the Captain, Alice had tried to find Aunty a couple more lodgers from India.

First Alice had to pay her respects to Lockwood's erstwhile employers, the Pinders, in Burslem. It would have been entirely in Lockwood's style to keep in touch with his former colleagues, swapping ideas about new pottery glazes and so on. But as far as Trix was concerned, old Thomas Pinder was only a 'tiresomely faithful friend of Father' who reeked of stale tobacco. His daughter, Jenny Owen, was more fun: as a young woman, she had travelled in the South Seas, lived in New Zealand and crossed 'From San Francisco to New York' (the title of her first book in 1869). After a ship wreck off Cape Finistere in 1882 (the subject of another book), she took to writing about natural history. Under the pseudonym 'A Son of the Marshes', she enjoyed popular success. In 1894 Lockwood succumbed to her repeated entreaties and designed an attractive decorative cover for her *The Country Month by Month*.

While in Staffordshire Rudyard 'tried to make cups and plates, and drove a coal cart',[48] though one of the Pinders remembered him being clammed-up, like an 'oyster'. The lad did not begin to open up until he and his sister reached their next destination, their home for over six months from May to early December – a small farmhouse at Golding's Hill, near Loughton, on the edge of Epping Forest in Essex. They were joined part of the time by ten-year-old Stanley Baldwin who demonstrated his more conventional childhood by bringing his cricket bag and hoping to educate his cousins in the mysteries of the game.

The Kiplings were not interested in such gentlemanly pursuits. Their mother wanted them 'to forget Aunty [Holloway] and her influence as soon as possible', recalled Trix.[49] So, as part of an energetic, outdoors regime, they threw themselves into work on the farm, helping 'Jarge', the hand, with all his regular jobs, such as milking. They became familiar with the local fauna and flora on donkey rides deep into the Forest with Savile, a mysterious half-gypsy. Often they could be found rolling their iron hoops, the fashionable toy of the moment, down the public highway. Reading was positively not encouraged.

At one stage the demands of these noble savages proved too much for Alice, who succumbed to shingles and had to summon her sister Edie Macdonald from Bewdley to take charge. Edie found the gang no easier to control than Alice: on her first day, when she served fish, all three children ran from the room, holding their noses and saying they could not stand the smell. In her desire to assuage her guilt, Alice was overcompensating and allowing too much licence. Indeed, her own temporary affliction was as much psychological as physical.

In early December the Kiplings moved back to a foggy, wintry London where they found rooms on the Brompton Road, in a pleasant flat-fronted cottage owned by a bewhiskered ex-butler and his wife. Rudyard and Trix used to amuse themselves by wrapping useless objects in neat parcels and leaving them on the pavement outside the house. From a window, they watched as respectable citizens would spy a promising-looking bundle, look surreptitiously left and right, and pocket it as a Christmas gift.

Here, for the first time, as Rudyard put it, 'it happened that the night got into my head'. As he found in Lahore six years later and again in London on his return in 1889–90, he liked to roam around the city in the early mornings, just before daybreak. His 'fortunate hour', he thought, was 'on the turn of the sunrise, with a sou'west breeze afoot'.[50]

Because of the foul weather, Alice used her contacts to arrange 'students' tickets' at the South Kensington Museum where Lockwood had worked. In next to no time, the guards were saluting and Rudyard felt he owned the place: 'from the big Buddha with the little door in his back, to the towering dull-gilt ancient coaches and carven chariots in long corridors'. This was a new experience: a larger, more stimulating version of Uncle Ned's picture-lined studio. After the intellectual restrictions of Southsea, his mind began to stretch itself once more. He was encouraged to read, sampling more mature fare, such as the work of two Americans – the poet Ralph Waldo Emerson and the novelist Bret Harte. As well as introducing Rudyard to the United States, the latter's fiction gave him a taste for frontier life and psychology that was to bear fruit in his own tales about India.

Sometimes he picked up his pen and wrote what came into his head. No-one accused him of 'showing off'. And this was no bad thing, for, the following month, Rudyard was due to go away again – this time to the United Services College, in Devon. His few months in the care of his mother had been vital in helping him regain his confidence.

Later Rudyard was able to look back on his experiences and comment, rather too tritely, that his period at Lorne Lodge provided useful training for his future career 'in that it demanded constant wariness, the habit of observation, and attendance on moods and tempers; the noting of discrepancies between speech and action; a certain reserve of demeanour; and automatic suspicion of sudden favours'. He compared himself to Browning's

Fra Lippo Lippi who, as a penniless waif, roaming the streets
before he became a monk, discovered

> Why, soul and sense of him grow sharp alike,
> He learns the look of things, and none the less
> For admonition from the hunger-pinch.

While correctly emphasising how his years at Southsea had honed
his skills of observation and deduction, Rudyard failed to note
how they had also taught him the advantages of evasiveness and
dissimulation. Why did he make so much of his experience of
being branded as a liar? Because he understood that lying was at
the heart not just of social relations but also of story telling. In
'Thrown Away', one of the *Plain Tales from the Hills*, the narrator
is called upon to cover up the suicide of a pathetically raw army
recruit who had recently arrived in India after a sheltered life at
home. In order to soothe the feelings of 'The Boy's' family, he has
to concoct 'a big, written lie' about the lad's heroic life and death,
and the bigger lie, the better: 'it was no time for little lies'. A few
years later Rudyard wrote 'A Matter of Fact', a quasi-horror story
about three journalists on a voyage from Cape Town to Southampton who, after an earthquake, witness the appearance of an
extraordinary sea monster and his mate. They soon realise they
cannot write this tale as a true story: no-one would believe them.
As one of them says, 'Truth is a naked lady, and if by accident she
is drawn up from the bottom of the sea, it behoves a gentleman
either to give her a print petticoat or to turn his face to the wall
and vow he did not see.' In other words, truth is sometimes too
precious and dangerous to be viewed directly: it needs to be robed
and presented as fiction.

Appropriately this story was collected in a book titled *Many
Inventions*.

Three

Dusky Crew

1878–1882

When twelve-year-old Rudyard arrived in the weather-beaten
North Devon resort of Westward Ho! in January 1878, it was the
middle of winter and 'the Coll' must have looked even bleaker
and more 'hefty damp' than in his story, 'Stalky': 'The smoking
vapours of the Atlantic drove in wreaths above the boys' heads.
Out of the mist to the windward, beyond the grey bar of the Pebble
Ridge, came the unceasing roar of mile-long Atlantic rollers. To
leeward, a few stray ponies and cattle, the property of the Northam
potwallopers ... showed through the haze.'

Westward Ho!, named after Charles Kingsley's 1855 novel, was
a forlorn outpost of the Victorian leisure industry on Bideford
Bay. In the distance, over the rolling waves, one could see Lundy
Island with its puffins, and, further afield, the Shutter Rock where,
in Kingsley's fiercely patriotic book about the Armada, Don Guz-
man's *Santa Catherina* galleon evaded his rival, the vengeful
Amyas Leigh. But the village's efforts to cash in on its moment of
literary fame never succeeded and the speculators who had built
a block of twelve lodging houses half-way up the hillside overlooking the sea were happy when a group of investors representing
the United Services Proprietary College Ltd offered to buy the
place in 1874. The purchasers, all with service backgrounds, added
a gymnasium, which doubled as chapel and assembly hall, and
not much else. Their rudimentary public school was ready for

business that autumn, offering a sound education for boys intending to enter the army.

The United Services College (USC), as it was generally known, was filling a gap in the caste-based English education system. Following the ban on the purchase of commissions in the Army in 1871, there had been a frenzy of competition among public schools to prepare pupils for the army training academies at Sandhurst and Woolwich. In the process, one school, Wellington College, which was supposed to cater exclusively for boys preparing for the Army, priced itself out of the market. So a cheaper alternative was needed – one that catered particularly for the sons of serving army and navy officers.

Rudyard was hardly an obvious candidate for such a place. By now confirmed as a bookish child, his interest in the services was limited to the Navy – if at all. However, his ambitious mother had known the amiable headmaster, Cormell Price, as a friend of her brother Harry at King Edward's School, Birmingham, in the early 1850s. At Oxford University, Price had been a member of the proto-monastic Brotherhood which evolved round Edward (Burne-) Jones, another King Edward's old boy, and the rich and gifted William Morris. The Brotherhood sought to maintain the High Anglican tradition of Pusey and (until he converted to Rome) Cardinal Newman. Its adherents read the poetry of Tennyson, followed the Christian Socialist principles of (appropriately enough) Charles Kingsley and admired the writings of the intellectual sensation of the time, John Ruskin, whose attacks on the distinction between designer and workman struck a particularly strong chord. Price, who was at Brasenose College, assisted Burne-Jones and Morris with the preparation for their Arthurian-inspired murals in the university's Union building and with the production of their short-lived *Oxford and Cambridge Magazine*. After graduating he declined to follow them into their chosen careers as artists, but opted instead for the more settled profession of medicine. When this did not suit him, he tried his hand as a private tutor to an aristocratic family in Russia, where he adopted some of Muscovy's fashionable Francophilia as well as gaining a taste for European literature. Returning to England in 1863, he at last found his *métier* as a schoolmaster at Haileybury, another breeding ground for imperial rulers, where he ran the 'modern' (i.e. non-classical) side of the school. When the USC was set up, he was offered the job of headmaster. The school, with its motto 'Fear God Honour the King' was intended to have 200 pupils, accommodated in four houses, but when it opened for the autumn term of 1874 there were fifty-eight boys, five of whom came with Price from Haileybury. The fees were sixty guineas a year for the nominated sons of officers, seventy guineas for unnominated sons and eighty guineas for the sons of civilians.

This gradation (and its financial repercussions) was on Alice Kipling's mind when, writing from Bombay in July 1874, even before the school opened, she first approached Price about Rudyard's education. Not having been in touch for the best part of two decades, she apologised if, in addressing him as 'Crom', she was using an old nickname. She had seen an advertisement for the United Services College in the *Pioneer*. In telling him about Rudyard, she wondered if entry to the School was open to the son of a gazetted officer in the Bombay Education Department, or if, perhaps, this 'privilege is reserved for the Military and the "Heaven-born"'.

Crom clearly provided satisfactory answers because when she came to England in 1877, she followed up her initial inquiry, saying she was thinking of sending her son to Westward Ho! (as the USC was also known) as a day-boy and taking lodgings in the vicinity. At the same time she provided a progress report: 'Ruddy is eleven years old – has gone through the first four books of Euclid and 12 rules of Algebra – and is in the second book of Caesar – is that pretty well for a child of his age?' She told of Rudyard's interest in the Navy, 'born of his propinquity to the Dockyard at Portsmouth', but, indicative of the boy's darting intelligence and limited attention span, she added, 'But it soon changed to something else and we should never have entertained it.'[1]

Price was a curious choice to run a military orientated establishment such as the USC. For a start he was not a clergyman, something that Rudyard was to find a great advantage: 'as soon as a boy begins to think in the misty way boys do, he gets suspicious of a man who punishes him one day and preaches at him the next.' More unusually he was a typical Gladstonian liberal, with a pacifist attitude to foreign affairs (in January 1878, the month Rudyard went to the school, Price had helped Burne-Jones and Morris organise the Workmen's Neutrality Demonstrations in London, in protest against Prime Minister Benjamin Disraeli's intervention in the Russo-Turkish war) and with moderately progressive ideas about education. He was not, for example, obsessed with classical studies: in practice, his teaching was dictated by a curriculum geared to the needs of the Army (and, to an extent, Civil Service) examinations, which emphasised practical 'modern' subjects, such as English, languages, science and mathematics, over traditional skills of textual exegesis, as required by the classicist.

Preparing boys for 'the big race that led into the English Army' remained the primary aim of the school. But 'the Head' was determined to introduce his pupils to other influences – ranging from acting to zoology. As Rudyard recalled, Price's style (and lasting gift) was to teach 'us hosts of things that we never found out we knew till afterwards'.[2]

In the event the Kiplings decided their son should attend Westward Ho! as a boarder. The conditions might have been spartan (with no doors to the bare, windy dormitories, for example) and the food atrocious (something for which Rudyard later took Price to task) but the place had a primitive, boisterous energy and that was its 'unique selling point'. As a result of Price's influence, it was not bowed with the weight of tradition, nor, to a great extent, was it beset with pettifogging rules: there was no fagging as such and, unlike in regular 'public' schools, senior boys in the 'army class' were allowed to smoke, though this may have been another marketing ploy to enable 'the Coll' to compete with the large number of 'crammers' for the military academies at Sandhurst and Woolwich that permitted this practice. Despite the evidence of 'In Ambush', the archetypal *Stalky* story about a hideaway hut in the woods, there were few restrictions on bounds. Pupils were free to roam the country lanes and wander into the nearby market towns of Appledore and Bideford.

In his autobiography Rudyard noted Price's aim was to 'send us to bed dead tired' and, in part, this was intended as a 'prophylactic against certain unclean microbes'. Writing in the mid-1930s, long after authors such as Robert Graves and Alec Waugh had suggested that homosexuality was rife in English public schools, Rudyard seemed a trifle over-eager to emphasise that the Coll was 'clean with a cleanliness that I have never heard of in any other school'.[3]

He did, however, admit the extent of bullying, particularly in his early years. This mindless activity was probably no worse than in other schools, but there were Westward Ho! specialities, such as the game of 'hanging', which involved some unfortunate being taken to the top of a stairwell, sentenced to 'death', blindfolded and bound with a rope, and lowered slowly from that height until, at an unspecified and dangerously arbitrary distance from the bottom, the rope was let go.

As a result, in his first week at the USC, Rudyard was plunged back into the torment of Southsea. The memory of the previous few months, relaxing in Epping and in London, was forgotten. To add to the unfairness, he had been looking forward to his new school with keen anticipation. In a letter to her friend Mary Wyndham, on 14 January, Margaret Burne-Jones painted an affecting picture of him preparing for his new term: 'My cousin goes to boarding school ... on Thursday and is greatly set up – he is marking all his clothes with a huge 264 which is his school number.'[4] (Mary Wyndham, who married Lord Elcho in 1883, was the daughter of Percy and Madeline

Wyndham, friends and patrons of Ned Burne-Jones.)

Within days of hanging up his neatly numbered coat on his new peg, however, Rudyard was bombarding his mother and Trix with a succession of miserable, tear-stained letters. Although Aunt Georgie assured her sister that her own son Phil had settled at Marlborough after a similar start, Alice could not refrain from writing to Crom Price on 22 January informing him that Rudyard was very homesick '– and will be – from what I know of him – till he finds a chum of some kind – or gets a pet rabbit or hedgehog or what not. For old time's sake, don't laugh at me for a spoon as I write this – but the boy is different from most boys – and I can't stop worrying.' At the time Rudyard had been away from home for only a week, but Alice was determined that he would not suffer as at Mrs Holloway's – and that she should not be saddled with the blame. The following day, she had received four further letters from Rudyard, and they all seemed to tell the same story of bullying: 'It is the roughness of the lads he seems to feel most', she told Price on 24 January. He doesn't grumble to me – but he is lonely and down.'[5] The number of Rudyard's letters did not worry her: in the Kipling family, scribbling things down was as much an accepted way of communicating as talking. But, referring for the first time to the complex psychology of her son, she pleaded for her old friend to keep a special look-out: 'The lad has a great deal that is feminine in his nature and a little sympathy – from any quarter – will reconcile him to his changed life more than anything.'

Concerned at his wife's reports of Rudyard's unhappiness, Lockwood hurried to arrange his affairs so he could return to England on leave at the end of March. In his haste, he failed to complete a commission for the design of a satin dress for Mrs Halsey, the wife of a Lahore-based army colonel and friend of the Allens who owned the *Pioneer*, and had to write from his ship at Suez to apologise.[6] As evidence of his position as artistic factotum in Lahore, he later sent her a Venetian design he recalled from a cassone in the South Kensington Museum, which required a mixture of white and gold satin, together with black velvet and black silk embroidery. Unfortunately he had learnt by telegram – he went to great lengths to satisfy his customers – that he only had four yards of gold satin left in Lahore, though there were also twenty-six yards of white Chinese satin. Lockwood's drawings for Mrs Halsey may have been more important than appeared, for her daughter Sibyl was to become one of England's leading interior designers under her married name Sibyl Colefax, with her own firm, Colefax and Fowler.

Lockwood was well suited for designing women's dresses, because he clearly liked female company, as two other incidents demonstrated. Before departing from Lahore he could not resist trying to plant a farewell kiss on Edith Plowden's cheek and she was forced to rebuff him. Then, back home, visiting the Essex farmhouse where Alice had stayed with the children the previous summer, he made the point – witnessed by his daughter Trix – of asking where his wife had slept and extravagantly kissing the pillow.

Unable to tear himself from his work, Lockwood was already committed to attending that year's Paris Universal Exhibition. The Indian Hall, which he was to oversee, had ill-advisedly been given over to showing off the gaudy trinkets collected by the Prince of Wales during his visit to the sub-continent two years earlier. This gave Dr George Birdwood, the former Bombay Museum curator who now oversaw the Indian Section at the South Kensington Museum, an opportunity to loose off on a favourite theme: the shapes 'of the Bombay School of Art pottery are detestable,' he wrote, 'taken from neither Scinde nor Western India, but from Chinese sugar jars, Japanese vases, and English jam and pickle pots'.[7] Birdwood had made this sort of charge before, accusing Indian art schools of subverting indigenous taste and techniques, and while Lockwood agreed with much of this overall thesis, he had felt the need to defend his own Mayo School, which he said was attempting 'to revive crafts now half forgotten, and to discourage as much as possible the crude attempts at

reproduction of the worst features of Birmingham and Manchester work now so common among natives'.[8] To prove his
point, he brought examples of Mooltan and Peshawar
pottery and Kashmir metal work (and Harry Rivett-Carnac's
wife Marion provided 6000 pieces from her extensive
collection of Indian peasant jewellery). But general artistic
opinion sided with Birdwood that there had been a sad
decline in Indian design since the 1850s when it was held up as
a model.

For Lockwood, visiting the Paris Exhibition, France's answer
to the Great Exhibition that had been such a seminal event in his
youth, was a labour of love. Since Rudyard had had to stay at
the USC over the Easter holiday (his mother had gone to meet
Lockwood – with his crates of artefacts – off an Italian ship at
Genoa),[9] he was allowed time off in lieu to join his father, whom
he had not seen for seven years, for the opening of the Exhibition
in the French capital in late April. The two Kiplings shared a
bright, sunny pension at the back of the Parc de Monceau. Waking
up every morning to the 'divine' smell of coffee roasting
downstairs and to the sharp call of the *marchands d'habits*
outside, Rudyard's heart would leap with excitement at the
range of possibilities the day would bring. Usually he accompanied his father on the one-mile walk to the exhibition site:
in fact, two 'halls' facing each other across the Pont d'Iéna on
either side of the River Seine. The structure on the left-bank
Champ de Mars was later flattened to make way for the Eiffel
Tower, the highlight of the 1889 exhibition, also attended by
Rudyard.

While Lockwood was marvelling at 'the wit, order, sense and
practical power of a great nation set forth with exquisite clear-
ness',[10] Rudyard found himself some holiday playmates – two
English boys who were staying in his pension. Little is known
about them except that they attended Christ's Hospital and provided a curious spectacle walking about Paris in their school
uniform of blue gowns and yellow stockings. These three young

friends would hang around the exhibition hall and then, having exhausted their elementary French on the workmen, would venture further afield. Wheeling through the Bois de Boulogne, they startled the locals by laying a proper paper-chase (the latest craze among children at home). At Lockwood's suggestion, they visited shops, art galleries and even the revered Salon, where Rudyard's glimpse of Pascal Dagnan-Bouvert's painting of the death of Manon Lescaut proved a lasting influence.

When Rudyard returned to the Coll in the summer, he had fond memories of France, but still needed to feel more secure in Devon. His mother had noted an improvement in his general attitude but he was not yet fully adjusted to boarding school life. Part of the problem may well have been his parents' over-protectiveness. Now that they were both at hand they were determined to make sure he knew he was loved and cared for. But the effect might well have been to make him more hypochondriac and self-conscious. For a while he was excused all punishments. In May Lockwood saw fit to write to Crom Price: 'I am afraid, indeed I am sure, Ruddy inherits a sensitiveness of liver which makes cold bathing of any kind dangerous.' Rudyard's own confusion was clear from his father's additional comments to Price in June: 'I find Ruddy a delightfully amiable chap, but the way in which he only half apprehends the common facts and necessities of daily life is surprising. Vagueness and inaccuracy I fear will always bother him and they take curious forms. He couldn't give me a straightforward detailed account of school routine for a day, breaking down under a most gentle questioning like a hysterical woman under cross-examination by an Old Bailey barrister. And yet a few hours later, talking of some little play that had interested him, he wrote from memory a scene or two – evidently remembering the thing accurately – for the French idioms of the original showed through.' Not for the last time, Lockwood believed his son needed some routine: 'If there is anything in him at all, the steady stress of daily work in which exactness is required should pull his mind together a little. But I should think he will always be inclined to shirk the collar and to interest himself in out of the way things.'

Although still not thirteen years old, Rudyard looked much older, with the outline of a black-haired moustache discernible on his notably dark-coloured face. His most obvious feature was his spectacles – with thick pebble lenses and blue steel frames. This gave rise to one of his nicknames, Gigger (or Gigs, short for Gig-lamps), though he was also known to friends as Beetle because of his stooped shoulders, short neck and 'habit of walking about with his elbows held forward and his hands in his pockets'.[11] His friend George Beresford vividly recalled Rudyard's odd Neanderthal-like quality: 'His skull appeared of moderate size in relation to his rather large face; his forehead retreated sharply from a heavy browline – in fact, so sharp was the set-back from the massive eyebrow ridges that he appeared almost "cave-boy". His lower jaw was massive, protruding and strong; the chin had a deep central cleft or dimple that at once attracted attention. Owing to its width, his face appeared rather Mongolian...'[12]

Rudyard's continuing unease at the Coll was reflected in the 'very troublesome boils' he suffered in the autumn term. Luckily, as his mother had forecast, he found solace in an odd assortment of birds, invertebrates and small furry creatures. This at least gave him an opportunity to show off his nascent powers of observation, remarking to his cousin Stanley Baldwin on his fellow pupils' practice of keeping young jackdaws, which they boarded out 'like dogs' with a local farmer. Some children owned magpies, hawks and blackbirds, and Rudyard had been experimenting with traps to catch tits and finches. However, an unfortunate thrush had tangled itself in his snare, damaging it beyond repair. Rudyard had tried to keep moles and mice, but found that, like squirrels, they took 'a great deal of looking after'. Touchingly, in view of his own indifferent sight, the creatures Rudyard liked best were his blind-worms, which required minimal care and looked 'very pretty if you have a lot of them'. He offered to send his cousin some samples.

Since his parents were in England for most of the following year (1879), Rudyard was able to spend his holidays with them. Annoyingly, there is little record of the Kiplings' movements while they were together at this crucial stage in Rudyard's development. We know that Lockwood introduced his son to several of his own friends, including the architect John Tavenor Perry and his wife Mary, and Jenny Owen, the writer and editor who was part of the Pinder family from Burslem. Rudyard used to write to both these women after he returned to school.

We know, also, that under the watchful eye of Lockwood and Alice, who had both dabbled in journalism, Rudyard was writing screeds of poetry, which he illustrated with sketches in a distinctive thin black ink. A favourite caricature featured a menacing little devil which, while clearly based on the 'bogeys' his uncle drew, also reflected his own sense of being haunted by outside powers.[13] (This image included something of his warped recollection of Hindu demi-gods.) Entering into the spirit, some time that year, Lockwood Kipling made a delightful sepia drawing as a frontispiece to a marble-backed manuscript book of his son's verse. This showed a bright-eyed tousle-haired young Rudyard, pen and copybook in hand, waiting to join a procession of great poets, including Shakespeare and Browning. Lockwood must have drawn this in 1879 (before sailing for Lahore that October), because he did not then see his son for another three years, and in the meantime Rudyard presented the same book of verse, complete with his father's sketch, to Edith Plowden. Rudyard later retrieved the book and destroyed it, but not before he had cut out and retained the drawing.

Lockwood enjoyed this short period of family bonding. On his return to Lahore in the autumn, he told Edith disconsolately that Rudyard had been 'the best companion I ever had'. Surprisingly Alice, once always at her husband's side, was not there to console him. She could not be induced to leave Trix (at least, that was what Lockwood told Edith) and she had decided to stay in England for another year. Perhaps her decision was affected by the unsettled situation on the Punjab's borders. For, following renewed Russian threats in Central Asia, the Afghans had murdered Sir Louis Cavagnari, the British resident in Kabul, in September 1879, forcing General Sir Frederick Roberts VC (another friend of the businessman and newspaper proprietor George Allen) to march through the Khyber Pass to sack first Kabul and then put down a dangerous revolt in the south of the country, near Kandahar (the name he later took for his earldom). As a result, by the time Alice returned to the Punjab in November 1880 she had been away nearly four years. Her relationship with Lockwood was clearly going through a more difficult patch than has been imagined.

While she remained in London, Alice had important business to attend to. She and Lockwood had decided that, so long as they were living in India, their children needed a base in England which they could call 'home'. So she arranged for Rudyard and Trix to stay in an old-fashioned bookish house in West London. Situated at the 'wrong' end of Kensington High Street, 26 Warwick Gardens stood at an intersection of three circles in Alice's life – India, Pre-Raphaelitism and Methodism. In this way, it highlighted how different aspects of Rudyard's background overlapped.

Most obviously, this was the house of Hannah Winnard, the unmarried sister-in-law of George Hooper, a distinguished journalist who had been one of the Kiplings' limited circle of literary friends during their early days in India. As a young man in England, Hooper had founded a lively political weekly, *The Leader*, with Leigh Hunt's son, Thornton Hunt, and George Eliot's paramour, G. H. Lewes. He had edited the popular London evening paper *The Globe* in its Liberal heyday in the 1860s. For three years from 1868 he was at the helm of the *Bombay Gazette* (which published Alice Kipling's social columns from Simla in 1871), before being summoned home to write leaders for the *Daily Telegraph* by Edwin Arnold, another old India hand and now one of the paper's editors. (At that very moment in 1879, Arnold was enjoying minor celebrity status following the publication of *The Light of Asia*, his epic poem about the Buddha.)

Miss Winnard lived there with two cousins, Mary and Georgiana Craik. Together, these were the 'three dear ladies' Rudyard acknowledged with affection in his autobiography. The Craik sisters were daughters of a professor of English Literature and History at Queen's College, Belfast, who, at an earlier stage of his life, had hobnobbed in London as part of a distinguished literary circle that included Carlyle and Leigh Hunt. The sisters were also related to Dinah Mulock, best-selling author of *John Halifax, Gentleman*, who had married their cousin, George Lillie Craik, a partner in Macmillan, the publisher. Georgiana Craik herself was a prolific author of romances and children's books, with thirty-six titles to her credit in the British Library catalogue.[14] She was the lady who, young Rudyard noted, 'wrote novels on her knee, by the fireside, sitting just outside the edge of conversation, beneath two clay pipes tied with black ribbon, which once Carlyle had smoked'.[15]

Warwick Gardens was also close to The Grange, which allowed Rudyard and Trix to see their Burne-Jones cousins regularly during the holidays. The 'dear ladies' provided a cultured, if old-maidish, alternative to the freneticism of The Grange. The poets Jean Ingelow and Christina Rossetti were friends, though Rudyard did not meet them. He did, however, encounter the potter William de Morgan and his sister Mary, who wrote fairy stories and later became an enthusiastic seamstress for (William) Morris & Co. De Morgan must already have been familiar from The Grange: not only was he one of the privileged Burne-Jones family friends who were there over Christmas 1873 when Rudyard came up from Southsea, but also he was responsible for the observation that the Macdonald sisters never started a sentence without knowing how it was going to end. His presence at Warwick Gardens emphasises its position as an outpost of second-generation Pre-Raphaelitism (albeit that his sister sounds a likelier candidate than he as a friend of the 'dear ladies').

Hitherto unremarked, Alice had another connection in the
same street. From 1876 to 1879, the Methodist chapel in Warwick
Gardens was the site of her brother Fred's latest ministry. Rudyard
would have met his Macdonald cousins, including George, who
was just three years younger than himself and about to go to
Clifton College. Of them, however, there was no mention in
Rudyard's autobiography. In keeping with the muted nature of
that book he chose instead to emphasise the literary advantages
of living with the 'dear ladies' – and, in particular, his access to
their fine library, which ranged from the novels of Wilkie Collins
to various volumes of the Duke of Wellington's despatches from
India.

Once Alice returned to India, 26 Warwick Gardens came into
its own as Rudyard's home from home. The 'dear ladies' provided
an element of emotional stability: he wrote to them dutifully from
school, enclosing copies of his latest verses. However, it was not
all plain sailing, as Lockwood acknowledged to Edith Plowden:
'[Miss] Winnard is such a fidget, and we are anxious to see how
Ruddy, who can be as suddenly rough as he is usually gentle, will
bear fidgetting. He is very likely to blaze out and be unpar-
liamentary. Trixie will do her best to act as a buffer but, after all,
a schoolboy of his age wants perhaps more loose rope than so
very fidgetty a person as she appears to be will be inclined to allow.'
Indeed, Rudyard used to complain of his boredom at Warwick
Gardens – between the lines – in his letters to Mary Tavenor Perry.

Back at school, Rudyard's life had improved considerably during
his second year. He had been glad to see the back of his original
housemaster, the Reverend J. C. (Belly) Campbell. A cold-hearted
cleric who never fitted in with the ethos of the place, Campbell
was described by one of his pupils as 'a very peppery individual,
who endeavoured to rule by fear. ... I can never recall his face
without an expression of ferocity on it, nor his hand without a
cane in it.' His successor, M. H. Pugh, who featured in Rudyard's
book *Stalky & Co.* as 'Prout', was better. People respected his bluff

integrity, though Rudyard never liked him. His barbed comments in his autobiography about Pugh's 'pure and excessive goodness' masked irritation at his housemaster's unctuousness and overly suspicious nature.

Rudyard's acclimatisation was helped rather more when he made two firm friends, both of whom were oddballs in a school of Army aspirants. Lionel Dunsterville came from the right martial stock, as the son and grandson of career officers who rose to become major-generals in the Indian Army. He too had been brought up by a guardian (though a kindly one) and he had already shown his distaste for institutional life by running away. In Rudyard's eyes, Dunsterville incorporated all the skills of cunning, daring and surprise needed to outwit the blundering oppression of adult schoolmasters. In school slang, this quality was known as 'Stalkyism'; so Rudyard nicknamed Dunsterville 'Stalky'. His other friend, George Beresford, was also the son of a military man, albeit a wealthy cousin of the Marquess of Waterford, with a quick Irish wit and aristocratic hauteur to match. He was called 'Turkey' or 'M'Turk', after the Maumturks, a remote mountain range in County Galway – therefore implying 'wild Irishman'.

Although 'Stalky' Dunsterville was the same age as Rudyard or 'Beetle', he had been at the Coll two years longer. His school number of 10 seemed to suggest even greater seniority, but this reflected his father's prescience in putting his name down for the USC as soon as this venture was announced.

Initially, Rudyard and 'M'Turk' Beresford shared with others in a five-person study. But by the summer term of 1879 they were already in cahoots with Dunsterville. That is the evidence of Rudyard's poem 'The Dusky Crew', which was offered for publication to *St Nicholas Magazine*, the popular American children's monthly, in August.[16] This told of the exploits of 'Me and the Other Two' who roamed 'in parks and grounds far out of bounds'. It was originally composed, probably during the summer holidays, for the *Scribbler*, a handwritten magazine produced by his cousins, Philip and Margaret Burne-Jones, and their friends,

William Morris's daughters Jenny and May. Then someone sent
it to the *St Nicholas*, stating it described 'an episode in last term'.
Although the accompanying letter was signed J. R. Kipling,
Rudyard later said it was not from him and probably came from
his father.[17] (His mother is a much more likely candidate.)
However, the editor, Mary Mapes Dodge, could find no merit in
the verses of an unknown English schoolboy and rejected them.
Such was the fate of Rudyard's first submission to an outside
journal.

When a smaller room for three became available that autumn
term (this seems the probable date, though it might have been
early 1880), the 'dusky crew' was able to consolidate in Number
Five study in Pugh's house. In recreating the daily life of this
command centre one must differentiate between their riotous
behaviour as presented in the fictional account *Stalky & Co.* and
what actually happened. In the book this 'resourceful' three-
some – 'Me and the Other Two' – are crypto-anarchists who,
when not smoking in their hut on the edge of school bounds, or
ragging unfortunate members of the non-academic staff such as
'Foxy', the school sergeant, are meting out their own brand of
rough justice – whether rescuing friends in trouble with local
farmers ('Stalky') or turning tables on the House bullies ('The
Moral Reformers'). True to the tradition of Stalkyism, they are
forever twitting authority – causing the unpopular master 'King'
to be pelted with stones after he had offended them in 'Slaves of
the Lamp', or leaving a dead cat under the floorboards of King's
house after he had implied that they – and their fellow members
of Prout's house – were casual and unclean ('An Unsavoury
Interlude'). They disdain normal team sports like cricket and opt
instead for shooting rabbits, playing marbles, or bathing (so long
as they can avoid some regular activity this way). They create
havoc wherever they go (as in 'The Impressionists'), but always
try to ensure they have a reasonable alibi. Their adolescent lout-
ishness is highlighted when Stalky casually spits on the back of a
rabbit in the middle of an otherwise lyrical passage about the

beauties of Devon's natural environment in 'In Ambush'.

In 1935, when he wrote his autobiography, Rudyard reinforced this Stalky myth, talking of their world of 'raids, reprisals and retreats'. However, Beresford told General Sidney Powell – a former USC pupil who, like many of his fellows, rose to the top in the Indian Army – that, in this respect at least, *Something of Myself* was 'as full of misstatement and absurdities as *Stalky & Co.* which is undoubtedly farce'. According to Beresford, 'the quiet denizens of No. 5 study never raised a hand or foot against anyone'. He thought Rudyard had become 'rather "gaga"', wanting to portray himself as 'a hearty, hefty, athletic person to match his propaganda of imperialism and jingoism, instead of what he was – a podgy, spectacled highbrow'. But, by then, Beresford had his own axe to grind: following personal and professional set-backs, his wit had taken on a cynical edge that not even his professed socialism could mask.[18]

Realistically, the three different personalities in Number Five study made for an unusual place, even if it was not quite the 'variegated insanity' of 'Slaves of the Lamp', or, indeed, the communist cell that Rudyard intimated in his 1893 memoir, 'An English School', where 'everyone is good . . . their possessions were in common, absolutely'. Dunsterville had a lot of Stalky in him – as his skeleton army unit, 'Dunsterforce', showed in early 1918 when, by dint of chutzpah, it convinced the Turks not to advance into the Southern Caucasus in the wake of demoralised (post-revolution) Bolsheviks. Never an intellectual, Dunsterville's high-spirited cunning reflected his favourite reading – the adventures of Ned Kelly, the Ironclad Bushranger, the Red Indian stories of James Fenimore Cooper and, in Rudyard's fictional Stalky, the 'sporting' novels of R. S. Surtees. The madcap escapades of Surtees's huntsman John Jorrocks are as close as one can get to Dunsterville's eighteenth-century spirit.

The characters of the other two study occupants were also reflected in their literary tastes. Having read Carlyle and Ruskin, the languid Beresford considered himself an aesthete and used to quote the latter on the improving nature of art. He was left to oversee the design of the study, which had a basic olive-green colour scheme. Aiming for a full Pre-Raphaelite effect, he added a dado, cretonne hangings and some smart stencils in grey-blue paint. Any vacant spaces were tastefully filled with decorative oak carvings (retrieved from Bideford Church when, to Beresford's Ruskin-inspired disgust, it was being restored), old prints and a variety of chipped but otherwise fine china, acquired from the Bideford antique shops. As M'Turk remarked in 'Slaves of the Lamp', if the other two had been responsible for this adornment, they would have 'stuck up brackets and Christmas cards'. Rudyard came to enjoy the group's unofficial hobby of curio hunting and was thrilled whenever he happened upon something interesting, such as the century-old liqueur glass he bought in January 1882.[19]

In that 'socialization of educational opportunities', Rudyard nominally traded his knowledge of French and English literature for Dunsterville's mathematical insights and Beresford's skills in Latin. As the study swot, he could be relied on to know the arguments for Francis Bacon's authorship of Shakespeare, which brought such welcome fictional results in 'The Propagation of Knowledge'. But his real value was as a cultural lightning conductor. Whenever Rudyard returned to school from his holidays, he was sure to be familiar with the latest arty gossip. His reports from London were eagerly seized on in Study Five – an unwonted form of popularity for an ungainly bespectacled youth who had suffered the ostracism of a colonial child. One can imagine him escaping Warwick Gardens for the brighter atmosphere of The Grange where – to take an obvious example – he would have learnt about the libel action taken out in November 1878 by the American artist James Whistler against the Pre-Raphaelite hero (and study favourite) John Ruskin, who had dared to suggest that his painting *Nocturne in Black and Gold* was a 'wilful imposture'. With the natural exuberance of youth, Rudyard would have noted signs of his uncle's Pre-Raphaelitism coming under challenge from the more refined aestheticism of Walter Pater and, in particular, the emerging figure of Oscar Wilde. At Oxford University in the mid-1870s, Wilde had decorated his walls with cherished reproductions by his artistic hero, Burne-Jones, and when in 1878 he moved to London, where he was a neighbour of Whistler, he came to know the Burne-Joneses (who remembered his mother's spirited translation of *Sidonia the Sorceress*).

One of Wilde's first pieces of journalism in April 1877 was about the opening of the Grosvenor Gallery, Sir Coutts Lindsay's lavish new show-case for the Aesthetes, the latest incarnation of the Pre-Raphaelite ideal. By 1881 the 'greenery-yallery' Aesthetes, with their P. B. (Passionate Brompton or Professional Beauty) attendants such as the actress Lillie Langtry, were celebrated enough to be parodied in George du Maurier's drawings in *Punch* and in Gilbert and Sullivan's operetta *Patience*. Since du Maurier had shared a studio in Paris with Whistler and Rudyard's Uncle Edward Poynter, Gigger was uniquely well informed on the '*Patience* epidemic'[20] which swept the USC that year. (He was also doubtless aware that, in the incestuous metropolitan world of art, Whistler had married Beatrice, daughter of Lockwood Kipling's old artistic mentor, John Birnie Philip.)

For someone so obviously 'brainy', Rudyard wore his learning lightly. He revelled in elaborate literary jokes – such as the study's shared disdain for Dean Farrar's prissy school tale, *Eric, or Little by Little*. With his anarchic streak, he annoyed his teachers by 'dumbing down' and showing his familiarity with the latest *Punch* cartoons, the *Boy's Own Paper* or the doggerel of Hans Breitmann. And when, in 1882, a craze for the Uncle Remus stories of Joel Chandler Harris swept the school, Rudyard, with the fine ear that later became a valuable professional tool, amused his friends with his ability to quote Uncle Remus's cod black American dialect, such as 'Too much ticklee, him bust'. Since his teachers were seldom privy to this secret language, they were infuriated.

Rudyard's life at the Coll was not all neatly packaged and referenced with literature and art. One problem with authors' lives is that, with hindsight, the details of their reading assume too much importance, especially with a character like Rudyard whose autobiography was dedicated to showing how he came to write as he did – and to not much else. Rudyard's real-life existence was full of mundane details such as food. Number Five study prided itself on its well-stocked cupboard. In a letter to Mrs Tavenor Perry, Rudyard listed the three members' requirements for a month: 30 lbs sugar must; 6 tins condensed milk; 3 lbs coffee; 2 lbs cocoa; 2 lbs oatmeal; 7 lbs biscuit. And that was just their staple: on top of that, lashings of 'lobster, cream, pilchards and cake'[21] all helped stop the gaps in their stomachs caused by an otherwise dreary communal diet.

Much of their time was spent out of doors, away from the cramped room. Price later chided Rudyard, 'I expect you were healthy because you lived in the open almost as much as Dartmoor ponies.'[22] Like their fictional alter egos, the three friends had a bolt-hole, a hut in a thicket of furze bushes, where they went to smoke, read and relax. From there, on the edge of 'bounds', Rudyard could look along the coast, past the short-lived Kingsley College, designed for children of Anglo-Irish families threatened by Fenians, and out to sea. During winter he was struck by the number of wrecks, but both his descriptive powers and his humanitarian instincts were lacking when he witnessed the bodies of some drowned sailors being brought ashore in Bideford. 'One old fellow in a jersey was terribly upset. I never saw anything so strange in my life. He was as grey in the face as the river and shaking like a leaf.'[23]

In winter, when the hut became too cold and damp, Rudyard and his friends rented a room, little more than a pigsty, from a drunken yokel. For all his apparently cloistered existence in a traditional public school, Rudyard enjoyed considerable contact with local people, whether he was ragging the farmers, fighting the Northam lads, or joking with tradesmen in Appledore. In Charles Kingsley's *Yeast* (quoted as one of Rudyard's favourite novels in a family questionnaire around 1880), the protagonist is converted to radicalism after witnessing the poverty of rural Cornwall. This did not happen with Rudyard, but Angus Wilson may have had a point when he suggested that Rudyard learnt some of his respect for principled law-breakers such as English poachers and Afghan warriors from the smugglers who still operated around Westward Ho!.

Rudyard's exploration of the countryside was helped because, as he extravagantly claimed in that same questionnaire, his favourite pastimes were the outdoor pursuits of fishing, pistol practice and walking. He also enjoyed swimming, which he had learnt at the hands of Sergeant-Major George Schofield, the school gym instructor, in the long salt-water Nassau baths by the sea-shore. Rudyard's cry of anguish as he lost his glasses in the water became a familiar sound to Schofield, who was known as 'The Weasel' at Westward Ho! and 'Foxy' in *Stalky & Co.* Team sports held no interest for Rudyard: he really was scornful of 'the flannelled fools at the wicket or the muddied oafs at the goals'.[24] In his later evocation of 'An English School', he pretended that cricket and football had once meant something to him. But this was false: he did his best to avoid these games, which were played on the Burrows, an expanse of tufted grass between the school and the sea. His usual excuse was his poor eyesight, but, as C. H. Aukland, son of the school doctor, recalled, Rudyard was 'very fond of going into the Sick House'.[25] The inference was that this otherwise hearty lad was a hypochondriac – a charge borne out by the number of afflictions he claimed in his letters to suffer, including chicken-pox, a hernia, a severe cold and a swollen gland in his neck.

The only communal activity to which Rudyard admitted was singing in the choir. However, this also was a struggle: in a letter to a family friend, Rudyard complained that, in preparation for a concert, he was forced to attend choir practice for an hour every Thursday, Friday and Sunday. 'The constant la-la-la-la-la-la-la-la-la-la-la-la-la-la brings out all sorts of queer notes. I can't make out where I get 'em from.'[26] Perhaps fortunately, Rudyard's singing career came to a premature end when a marble dropped from his cassock and he was asked to leave.

Inside the classroom his teachers were a motley band of bachelor misfits with respectable university degrees. Herbert Evans, a self-effacing graduate of Balliol, oversaw Rudyard's early enquiries into the world of nature. In *Stalky & Co.*, he is caricatured as Hartopp, whose Natural History Society is popular only for the opportunities it provides for extended bounds. But from Dunsterville's account, Evans (known in real life as 'Punch' because of his large, curved nose) was a careful teacher who inspired his pupils to real feats of taxonomy. Their reports on the first flowerings of plants and new arrivals of birds were meticulously forwarded to the relevant learned societies in London. Even Rudyard, the lover of blind-worms, was inspired to read a paper on 'Insect Life' in July 1880. If Evans's field trips did indeed provide cover for poaching missions, they also gave his charges some early training in ballistics – as they fled the grapeshot from the barrels of irate gamekeepers.

On a personal level, Rudyard warmed more to the Reverend George Willes, who succeeded the dreaded 'Belly' Campbell as school parson. Dunsterville remembered Willes as 'a genial, robust type, popular with both masters and boys, and possessed of uncommon common sense that enabled him to settle many feuds by friendly arbitration or by kindly hints'. A product of Christ Church, Oxford, Willes featured in *Stalky & Co.* as the Padre, the Reverend John Gillett. To Rudyard as Beetle, he was 'emphatically a gentleman', who not only bothered to knock at a study door before entering, but also 'never carried over into the official life the confidences of idle hours'.[27] In other words, Rudyard could talk to Willes, not only on theological issues (the theme of man's creation surfaced in a poem in 1881)[28] but also on more personal matters, such as his tentative relations with the opposite sex.

Pugh, the Number Five housemaster, inevitably played an important part in Rudyard's development, as did W. C. Crofts

('King', or at least part of him, in *Stalky & Co.*), the eccentric English and Classics teacher. Like Crom Price, Crofts was a scholar of Brasenose, though of slightly younger vintage. A fine rower who had twice won the Diamond Sculls at Henley, Crofts enjoyed winter holidays in Norway, where he liked to show off his physique skiing cross-country in the buff. At school, during term-time, his exercise was limited to swimming on Pebble Ridge with the boys, who were naked. According to his pupil General Sidney Powell, 'A scorner of the opposite sex, [Crofts] revelled in any classical allusions which were uncomplimentary to women.'

Today Crofts's bullying, histrionic classroom style would not be tolerated. He once hurled a copy of Browning's *Men and Women* at Rudyard, who calmly picked it up and began reading 'Fra Lippo Lippi', a poem with which he strongly identified, about a young monk who breaks out of his cloisters to become a leading Renaissance artist. Unlike his fellows, Rudyard enjoyed his 'year-in year-out form-room bickerings' with Crofts. Once, when Crofts asked his students to name their favourite poet, he was given the usual, obvious answers – Browning, Tennyson and Swinburne.[29] Amid stifled giggles, someone had the temerity to blurt out, 'Kipling, sir.' Provocatively, Rudyard plumped for the American Walt Whitman, causing Crofts to explode, 'Really! Walt Whitman! So that's the latest thing among your London friends, Kipling. A little mutual admiration society – you scratch my back and I scratch yours.' And he proceeded to read out some of Whitman's worst poetry – a turgid list of country pursuits. Rudyard was not put out by his master's childish pique, which was merely a form of jealousy at his pupil's access to London literati. He described Crofts's temper as 'no disadvantage in handling boys used to direct speech' and added, 'One learns more from a good scholar in a rage than from a score of lucid and laborious drudges.'

Crofts did indeed introduce Rudyard to hitherto undiscovered areas of English literature, giving the boy the run of his personal library to explore a number of poets he did not know so well, such as the raw, emotional Swinburne. Rudyard was so carried away by Swinburne's powerful rhythms that he used the poet's verse drama *Atalanta in Calydon* as an aid to learning to swim. He also derived his appreciation of Latin literature from Crofts. As Rudyard put it, this martinet of a schoolmaster 'taught me to loathe Horace for two years; to forget him for twenty, and then to love him for the rest of my days and through many sleepless nights'.[30]

The most important influence on Rudyard's young life, however, was the thoughtful encouragement of the Head. Far from being the stern whacker of *Stalky & Co.*, Crom Price was often accused by his staff of not being firm enough. Rather negating his own theory that a headmaster should not be a parson, Rudyard benefited hugely from the fact that Price was, at one and the same time, both the ultimate source of authority and a friend of the family – the 'lean, slow-spoken, bearded, Arab-complexioned' man he had known at The Grange as 'Uncle Crom'.

At one stage in the autumn of 1880, Rudyard's school work began to suffer because he was writing (and illustrating) too much poetry. Despite receiving regular outpourings of fine youthful verse (at one stage he complained jokingly he was being 'literally pelt[ed] with poems'), Lockwood Kipling became alarmed at his son's school report (Rudyard was consistently at or near the bottom of the mathematics class) and wrote to give him a 'wigging' ('I confess every word a two edged sword – the sharpest one in my soul,'[31] he told Edith Plowden). Undeterred, the benevolent Price knew exactly what to do. Having noticed Rudyard's facility for expressing himself in the English language, he excused him from his maths classes and put him in the library, ostensibly to do French translation. As the Head hoped, Rudyard availed himself of the surrounding books – traditional English classics from Chaucer to Matthew Arnold, as well as unusual items such as Isaac d'Israeli's *Curiosities of Literature*, which provided further material to regale his study mates,[32] and Walter Savage Landor's *Imaginary Conversations of Literary Men and Statesmen*, which introduced Rudyard to the art of satire.[33] Rudyard tried to emulate Landor's style, but his efforts – long-lost libels on his teachers, no doubt – were considered too close to the bone. Not that Crom panicked; he saw this as an opportunity to take Rudyard closer under his wing for private tutoring in Russian. Their shared joke was that Rudyard would be able to make himself understood if he were sent to Siberia for lampooning the authorities. Possibly, a career beckoned in India, where a smattering of Russian would be a useful tool in the Great Game being played out for control of Central Asia.

This individual tuition gave the boy access to the Head's personal library, with its esoteric mixture of English dramatists and travel writers – Marco Polo, Hakluyt and 'thick brown books of voyages told in language like the ringing of bells'. Rudyard particularly loved it when Crom sat back, cigar in hand and, in his soft Birmingham drawl, would reminisce about his times in Russia or, even better, his Oxford experiences, when the Head mixed with Morris, Swinburne and Rossetti, and helped them write articles for a variety of journals.

Such talk led to the idea of reviving the school magazine, the *Chronicle*, which had not been published for a couple of years. Nominally, Rudyard shared the editor's job with Price, but from the first issue of this new series, in June 1881, the schoolboy ran the *Chronicle*, taking its responsibilities very seriously. As well as his poems, he injected an element of social realism into the magazine, turning a sceptical, journalistic eye on aspects of school life, such as the bestial habits of Lower School members who grilled half-plucked blackbirds on rusty pen-nibs in front of their gas fires. This report made him particularly unpopular, but he had his reward: as he later noted, he learned 'how sweet and good and profitable it is – and how nice it looks on the page – to make fun of people in actual print'.[34]

Not content with ensuring a regular flow of copy, he took a keen interest in all stages of the *Chronicle*'s production. Like Beetle in 'The Last Term', he 'saw himself already controlling *The Times*'.

As press day approached, he spent most of his free time at the printer's in Bideford, where the paper would be locked in 'formes' on a stone-topped table. In the absence of intelligent help, he often set or adjusted the type himself. Not for the world would he 'have corrected from the mere proof. With a mallet and a pair of tweezers, he knocked out mysterious wedges of wood that released the forme, picked a letter here and inserted a letter there, reading as he went along and stopping much to chuckle over his own contributions.' Conditions were basic: the gas-driven printing machine once fell through the floor into the cellar below, where it continued to operate. As a back-up, Rudyard looked into obtaining a modern lithograph machine. He badgered London friends for subscriptions (at three shillings per annum). And still he could produce occasional articles for the *Bideford Gazette*. Indeed, in his last year at the USC, with the connivance of the Head, his literary output took precedence over all else. He was up to his eyes in work, he complained or, rather, boasted in May 1882 – 'articles for local newspapers and gas and sewerage comments, poems, schoolwork, Russian, *Chronicle*, and stories flying through my head like a railway train'.[35]

Despite this pressing schedule, he had time for further extra-curricular activities, as the pages of the *Chronicle* make clear. At the Literary and Debating Society, where he was Secretary, he proposed the motion that 'the advance of the Russians in Central Asia is hostile to the British power', demonstrating his familiarity with continuing tensions on the Afghan border and giving notice of political opinions he was later to hold. He also started on a long career in amateur dramatics. 'Kipling's "Sir Anthony" was a capital performance, somewhat marred unfortunately by an obvious catarrh and a voice too slender,'[36] the *Chronicle* reported with admirable objectivity on his role in the school's Christmas 1881 production of Sheridan's *The Rivals*. When the precocious Number Five study staged its own version of *Aladdin, or the Wonderful Scamp*, Rudyard (who insisted on the pronunciation Allah-deen) was cast as the Widow Twanky. He looked magnificent in 'an elaborate brocaded gown covered with gold lace ... with a huge chin projecting underneath a grey horsehair wig and a pair of spectacles'. Sadly, when this outfit came to be returned, it was found to be ripped and Rudyard had to employ his best epistolary talents to appease the London costumiers, Nathan's.

But, for all Rudyard's literary knowledge and for all his willingness to involve himself in school activities, he was conscious of something missing in his life. He was not clear what this was, though one of his best youthful poems, 'From the Wings', approaches it. In this verse an actor bemoans the artifice and deceit of his trade and longs for a real taste of the love he is portraying: 'I believe you – only kiss me! This forced passion's dreary stuff!'[37] Like most teenagers, Rudyard was looking for some fiery romantic experience to give meaning to his life.

Over four years in this educational environment, Rudyard's inhibitions steadily fell away, as he grew into an intellectually confident young man. A series of contemporary drawings by Beresford show Rudyard's development from an apprehensive (though physically mature) new boy into a self-satisfied teenager, with the trace of a 'public school' sneer on his lips. A common complaint throughout his life was his 'knowingness', or his not always attractive quality of parading his superior intelligence. This is exactly how he appears in one of Beresford's sketches – even down to the caption, 'Gigger knows his way about'. A photograph from around this time has an element of this, showing a chubbier boy, with a friendly, robust energy, but caught in limbo between childhood and maturity, as he twiddles his moustache, with his school cap still perched comically on the top of his head.[38]

One area of human activity where Rudyard liked to express superior knowledge was sex. In his memoirs Beresford noted this, but wondered how much of Rudyard's awareness of 'that baffling entity, Woman' came from personal experience and how much from second-hand gleanings from his vast reading. Rudyard later claimed that he had been sexually initiated by the fish-girls of Appledore.[39] Curiously, at the time (three and a bit years after leaving school), he was complaining to Crofts that he had just learnt that his housemaster Pugh suspected him of homosexual activities and this was why he had once been asked to move dormitories. Rudyard was furious at this implication. But the fact that Pugh imagined these goings-on at all and the note about the masters' 'steady policing' of the dormitories in *Stalky & Co.* rather undermine Rudyard's claims that the Coll was a 'clean' school.

Most of Rudyard's references to women during his time at the USC suggest a confused boarding-schoolboy's mixture of angst and braggadocio. In *Stalky & Co.* there is an innocent, adolescent misogyny in the boys' concern that their masters do not marry ('it rots up everything') and in their efforts to bribe Mary, the 'fair-haired, blue eyed and apple cheeked' assistant in Mother Yeo's shop in Bideford, to kiss the unpopular prefect Tulke. In real life, Mary was Polly Hopkins, née Westway, a local farmer's daughter. When, much later, Dunsterville met her again, Rudyard wanted him to send her his love, adding, 'we all loved her in those days, from the Lower Third upwards.' Rudyard also liked to catch sight of Sarah Hopper, the teenaged daughter of the Head's house-keeper, whose neat figure was always enhanced by a tight dress. (She was known as the 'Pricienne', partly because of her Parisian fashion sense and partly because of her closeness to Price, which was confirmed when she later became the Head's wife.)

Something of Rudyard's direct approach to women was caught by Edith Plowden when she first met him at Warwick Gardens in 1880. Rudyard was taller than she expected, with a rough head of brown hair. He told her brusquely, 'Mother's out; I know who you are, and all about you.'[40] She replied that she knew about him too, and his love of Browning. Within five minutes they were sitting on a cushioned window seat, talking of this poet (now his favourite, along with Whittier, Emerson, Tennyson and Poe, according to the questionnaire he filled in around this time). Of Browning's works, he still liked 'Fra Lippo Lippi' the best, claiming that the monk had no choice but to rebel. 'He said so himself,' Rudyard argued. 'He would have been all right if they had given him his chance.' To Edith, writing much later, this epitomised Rudyard's general philosophy. He 'insisted always on personal freedom, but you had to pay for it. You were responsible for yourself.'

A darker side to Rudyard's personality still surfaced from time to time. Once, as he admitted to Crofts,[41] he attacked members of his dormitory with a 'small' penknife, an act of petulant anger that looked back to the spoilt baby from Bombay and the rejected child in Southsea. This raw emotion could erupt unexpectedly, as his cousin Florence Macdonald recalled. Some time in 1880, while still at school, Rudyard went to visit her family. He was in an odd, uncommunicative mood and his behaviour became even stranger when he started to roll about in a fury on the nursery floor. The reason, it emerged, was that a porter at the station had boxed his ears – apparently in retaliation for an insult. Rudyard's mood perked up, however, when he decided to return to the station and hurl more abuse at the man.

With his combination of general truculence and vivid imagination, the boy was no longer satisfied with ogling or even occasionally kissing the fish-girls of Appledore. By the age of fourteen, Rudyard was searching for a Browning-type romance to match his literary fancies. That same year of 1880 (we can assume it was the summer), he thought he had found it when, while visiting Trix (still at Southsea), he met another of Aunty's paying guests with whom he immediately became infatuated.

Florence Violet Garrard was a frail, enigmatic beauty, almost a year older than Rudyard. She had been born within familiar Burne-Jones territory in Victoria Road, Kensington on 31 January 1865. But her upbringing was far from typical. Her grandfather was Robert Garrard, whose family business R. S. Garrard and Co. had, since 1830, been Crown Goldsmith and then Crown Jeweller. The firm's most famous commissions were the America's Cup, first competed for in 1851, and the Koh-i-Noor diamond, cut the following year. With his regular output of candelabra for royalty, wine coolers for aristocrats and trophies for race meetings, Robert became wealthy and acquired a country house, East Heath Lodge, in Wokingham, a small Berkshire town where the local squires were the Walter family who owned *The Times*. He had four brothers, two of whom, James and Sebastian, worked with him, while another, Stephen, was a London solicitor, and the youngest, Henry, emigrated to Australia in 1838.

Robert Garrard's eldest son, Florence's father, who was also called Robert, looked set to join the family business and was elected as a Liveryman of the Goldsmiths' Guild in 1853. But with the start of the Crimean War the following year, he opted to join the Army, becoming a lieutenant in the 95th (The Derbyshire) Regiment of Foot. After being wounded at the Battle of Alma in September 1854, he returned home and was awarded the Crimean War Medal, which, unusually, was presented to him personally by Queen Victoria on Horse Guards Parade in May 1855. Subsequently, seeking promotion to the rank of captain, he joined the 5th (The Princess Charlotte of Wales's) Regiment of Dragoon Guards. Having also seen service in the Crimea, this cavalry unit was sent to perform the usual round of tedious peacetime duties which, as its official history notes, meant it was 'frequently employed in aid of civil power'. Quelling Fenian disturbances from a base at the Curragh barracks in County Kildare was not what this Robert Garrard joined the Army for. So he made what seems to have been a dynastic marriage to Fanny Mortlock, whose family ran William Mortlock, the Regent Street china and glass store which held a warrant of appointment to Queen Victoria and the Prince of Wales, and, shortly after the birth of their daughter Florence, he opted on 1 September 1865 to retire from the Army on half-pay. (This amounted to the princely sum of 7s. a day, or £125 per annum, which he opted to have drawn for him by the established agents, Cox and Company.[42])

For some reason his re-entry into civilian life did not proceed as intended. His uncles' children had control of the family firm, and the ascendancy of Sebastian's line had been confirmed when he adopted the three eldest children of Henry, his brother who had emigrated to Australia in 1838. (Henry and his wife Mary still had seven children in Australia.) The younger Robert Garrard moved across London from Florence's birthplace in Kensington to Victoria. But he did not find his *métier* and, in July 1872, opted to have his pension commuted, for which he was paid £1691. 16s. 0d. With this sum of money he took himself and his immediate family to live in France, where his son, another Robert, was working as a banker in Paris at the time of his marriage in 1877. Florence herself seems to have lived a peripatetic existence, often in hotel rooms.

Rudyard later provided a fictional portrait of Florence Garrard as Maisie, the cool heroine of his novel *The Light that Failed*. The real-life Florence (known as Flo) was the spitting image of the 'long-haired, grey-eyed little atom' in that book. Like Maisie, Flo was self-contained, owned a much-loved goat and measured out her life in letters from lawyers who acted as her guardians. ('I shall write to my lawyer-peoples and tell them you are a very bad woman,' Maisie tells Mrs Jennett, the Aunty Holloway character in the novel.) According to one not necessarily reliable newspaper report, Flo even had a revolver with which she liked to fire at a snowman at the bottom of her garden.[43]

Mrs Holloway's in Southsea was exactly the sort of place a girl such as Flo would have attended during her peripatetic upbringing. Her sister Maud was there for a while too and Flo was visited by one of her two brothers, whom Trix remembered as tall, dark and distinguished-looking. (It seems likely that there was a blood relationship between the Garrards and the Holloways. Flo's grandmother, Esther, the wife of old Robert Garrard, was a member of a prominent Oxfordshire family, the Whippys, and Esther's brother Benjamin had married Captain Holloway's sister Jane and acquired the Holloway seat, Lee Place in Charlbury.)

Since Rudyard never wrote a description of Flo (save his fictionalised version in *The Light that Failed* and several idealised portraits in verse), his sister Trix's sharp-eyed observations more than suffice. Trix was almost as entranced as her brother, recalling Flo's 'beautiful ivory face, the straight slenderness of her figure, and the wonder of her long hair when she brushed it at night'.[44] Flo's grey eyes – 'clotted with black lashes' – were large in proportion to the rest of her slight face. Her svelte figure allowed her to wear old Holland frocks she should have long discarded: 'she was like the Princess disguised in the shepherd's cottage,'[45] noted Trix. Most of Flo's dress allowance actually went on her sister. (Trix was appalled by this, finding Maud – and her desire for adornment – common.) 'It keeps her happy,' Flo used to say with a shrug, 'and I hate fuss and feathers; if I had a best hat, Becquot [her pet goat] would eat it and perhaps die.'

Flo's personality was a 'curious blend of simplicity and sophistication, wisdom and ignorance. A gift of natural refinement stood in the place of religion and of home training.'[46] As a companion, she was friendly and amusing, with an acute eye for what was happening around her. Trix taught her to recite poetry and recalled the charming way she would repeat, 'Ho, pretty page with the dimpled chin'. But Flo's general education had suffered from her wanderings. Although she went to language classes and practised the piano attentively, she showed little interest in drawing at that stage and she hardly read a thing. Trix was most disappointed when she found that her new friend was unable to write a decent letter: 'A scrawl about the weather, the fact that she had one of her tiresome headaches, "I took Becquot over the common and round the castle today. She sends you her love and a lock of hair from her tail. I'm sorry you had to go away. Flo."'

No such simple missives survive from Flo to Rudyard, or vice versa. If they did, they would tell the enthralling but melancholy story of his growing attachment and her cool rejection of him. In the absence of this direct evidence his poems have to fill the gaps. In a letter to Edith Plowden in October 1880, Lockwood Kipling wrote that his son, now rising fifteen, had sent him a copy of some verses called 'The Lesson' 'which might be to the address of Miss

Flora [*sic*] Garrard or possibly to you. In any case they are prettily turned and show that he has started on a round of spoors which he will follow up till his death.'[47]

This poem speaks of a love affair between a naïve young 'boy-lover' and his more mature and knowing paramour. He wonders if a meeting that had been so exciting to him was actually so 'utterly novel' to her. For she is 'so womanly wise' and, he implies, blasé about his romancing. Although Rudyard liked to flirt with older women (perhaps Oedipally hoping to supplant his father in pretty Edith Plowden's affections), the verses were certainly directed to Flo, whose nomadic existence (including time in Rudyard's favourite country of France) imbued her with a heady exoticism.

From now, for the next couple of years, Flo Garrard's hazy image hangs tantalisingly over all Rudyard's poetic output. Occasionally, he is passionate about her, as in the undated 'Parting', which starts intently:

> Hot kisses on red lips that burn –
> A silence – Then some loving word.[48]

More often, he laments his failure to win her affections, as in 'Discovery', in May 1882, which tells of two people finding a lifeless corpse in the woods. He was annoyed when Miss Winnard, one of the three 'dear ladies', imagined this referred to a dead canary, rather than the decomposing remains of his love.

In the absence of a positive response from Flo, he cast around and became intrigued by the business of buying love, as his September 1881 verses, 'Venus Meretrix', show:

> This much am I to you –
> If I departed out of your house
> Coming no more at all –
> You would wait a while 'tis true
> You would lift your voice – You would call –

> You would take some Lover into your house
> And be to him all in all.[49]

Perhaps this was when Rudyard found solace in the arms of the fish-girls of Appledore. His poem 'Overheard', written in that year, dealt with the same subject of prostitution in realistic terms which suggested at least familiarity with contemporary French literature, if not with the physical experience of making love. In it, a whore laments:

> Failed, lost money, undone;
> Took to the streets for a life.
>   Entre nous,
> It's a terrible uphill strife,
> Like all professions – too filled.[50]

The passionate phase of Rudyard's romance for Flo lasted roughly a year. At one stage he speaks of it enduring for 'three hundred days'.[51] It is likely that their initial meeting in the summer of 1880 was fleeting and the 'affair' only developed the following summer. In a letter to Edith Plowden in August 1881 he was still concerned because he had lost a photograph of Flo. But by May the following year he was telling Mrs Tavenor Perry that 'everything that has ever existed between myself and the fair F.G. is entirely at an end'.[52] Flo's grandfather Robert's death, and her father's inheritance of £40,000 in lieu of any share in the family jewellery business, may well have given her an exalted idea of her place in the world. The final rupture came, one surmises, around the time of a raw poem, dated 11 April 1882, undoubtedly addressed to Flo and titled, unambiguously, 'An Ending':

> By the trouble and pains we endured together.
> By the council and the help, and the strength which
>   you gave me.

> By the influence of your soul over my soul.
> By year long vigils watched out together
> By the great tie that is between us
>   Yours and yours only.[53]

Such adolescent love poems were not for general consumption. They were kept in what Beresford described as 'Russia-leather, gilt-edged, cream-laid MS books' and were strictly private. No echo of these innermost thoughts was heard in the poetry or prose Rudyard produced in the classroom or for the *Chronicle*. There he stuck to more traditional schoolboy material, such as 'The Pillow Fight', 'Told in the Dormitory', or 'A Legend of Devonshire' – with their self-explanatory titles.

One rendering in this genre suggested more than meets the eye. 'Ave Imperatrix!', Rudyard's forthright hymn of thanks for Queen Victoria's survival from an assassination attempt in March 1882, was – *pace* T. S. Eliot who included it in his 1941 anthology *A Choice of Kipling's Verse* – a modest piece of verse journalism, notable, if anything, as an early attempt to deal with the theme of patriotism. Years later, after becoming a photographer, Beresford shocked Dunsterville, by then a major-general, by suggesting Rudyard had written these traditional verses with tongue in cheek. But Beresford is unlikely to have understood how much they were an 'in' family joke. For Oscar Wilde had published a poem of the same name the previous year, around the time that Rudyard's cousin Phil Burne-Jones, a newly arrived Oxford undergraduate, had begun to correspond with the Irish extrovert.[54] Wilde shared a solicitor, George Lewis, with the Burne-Joneses, and when he set out on a promotional tour of the United States in early 1882 he carried a letter of introduction from Ned to his friend Charles Eliot Norton in Boston. (On this trip Wilde is supposed – apocryphally, according to his biographer Richard Ellman – to have told the United States Customs, 'I have nothing to declare but my genius.')

While Wilde's 'Ave Imperatrix' was quietly Republican,

celebrating the circumstances but questioning the value of any deaths overseas in the service of the Queen, Rudyard's lines were unambiguously tub-thumping – a reflection of the new aggressive mood of imperialism which was found in sources as varied as the *Boy's Own Paper*, the novels of G. A. Henty and, in 1883, John Seeley's influential tract *The Expansion of England*, which called for Englishmen to take up their natural role of Empire. In fact, Seeley was only expanding on John Ruskin's vision in his 1870 inaugural lecture at Oxford: 'There is a destiny now possible to us, the highest ever set before a nation to be accepted or refused. Will you youth of England make your country again a royal throne of kings, a sceptred isle, for all the world a source of light, a centre of peace and mistress of learning and of the Arts, faithful guardian of time tried principles?' For all his world-weariness, George Beresford, the Ruskin enthusiast, may well have read this speech (an inspiration to Cecil Rhodes) to Number Five study.

Rudyard's separation of private and public poetry reflected the growing conflict he felt – and which the Flo Garrard affair served to bring into focus – between two sides of his personality. In his poem 'Two Lives', dated March 1882, he expressed something of this split:

> One life is strange and full of hot red days,
>   Strong Love, that checked at naught, wild hope, mad sin;
> But in the other there are beaten ways
>   I traverse steadfastly nor fail therein . . .[55]

These became his most widely disseminated verses yet, because he submitted them to *The World* which, though publication was delayed until November, sent him the princely fee of one guinea. When he used this windfall to buy chocolate and other delicacies for the study, his two friends were surprised to find that poetry could be profitable. Perhaps they did not realise the element of nepotism involved. Not for the last time, Rudyard had used his parents' wide circle of friends to his advantage. For Yates, the editor of *The World*, had once published early work by Alice Kipling. Son of the famous actor Frederick Yates, he was one of the most colourful journalists of the nineteenth century. A close friend of Charles Dickens, he fell out with another author, William Makepeace Thackeray, after lampooning him in a profile that the latter protested could only have resulted from a conversation within the hallowed portals of the Garrick Club. Yates was undeterred at being expelled from the Garrick: a muck-raker by instinct, he went on to edit the literary magazine *Temple Bar*, which was where he published Alice. For a short while he was London correspondent for James Gordon Bennett's mould-breaking *New York Herald*. Then in 1874 he founded *The World*, a self-styled 'journal for men and women', that combined the aspirations of a serious newspaper with the output of a scandal sheet. One of his protégés, whom he published in the early 1880s, was Oscar Wilde and he later helped bring George Bernard Shaw to the attention of the British public.

Rudyard's last poem at school was 'The Battle of Assaye', his prize-winning entry for the school poetry competition in the summer of 1882. Although similar in tone to 'Ave Imperatrix!', the verse style was more sophisticated, with a metre copied from his 'latest "infection"', the American 'frontier poet' Joaquin Miller. The finished product was not much good, but it did not matter: there were no other entries, the whole concept of a poetry prize having been devised by Crom to cater for Rudyard's special needs.

For, after a year's correspondence between India and Westward Ho!, the boy's future had just been finalised. His parents had concluded that they could not afford to send him to Oxford. Instead, they felt that Rudyard was slightly too precocious (Aunt Georgie had told Alice that he was 'seeing too much of life about town'[56] during his holidays) and needed a period of sorting out in the bosom of his family. Lockwood told Price damningly, 'I must confess from what I have seen of Ruddy, it is the moral side I dread a break out on. I don't think he is the stuff to resist temptation'. Alice had her own reasons for wanting the boy home.

She made little secret of the fact that her husband was 'getting dreadfully absorbed in things' and was no longer 'the conversational companion he used to be'. As a result, she told Edith Plowden: 'To me the companionship of these bright young creatures would be new life.'[57]

Since Lockwood had begun to see journalism as a possible career to engage Rudyard's general interest, he turned to his friend George Allen, the proprietor of the *Pioneer*. Over the course of more than a dozen years this newspaper had flourished: it was not only a commercial success but also so clearly the voice of informed conservative opinion that often it appeared to be an official mouthpiece. Its success had encouraged Allen to help finance a similar paper in Lahore. The *Civil and Military Gazette* (*CMG*) had originally been started four years earlier as a weekly paper in Simla. In 1873 it was acquired by James Walker, an Allen-like figure, the son of a policeman who, having made a fortune in the grain trade in the Punjab, had set up the Alliance Bank in Simla, and by William Rattigan, an illegitimate Irishman who had forged a distinguished career at the Lahore bar. Their stated manifesto was to act as 'a faithful and conscientious advocate of the true interests of the services, civil and military, in India, watching all that affects these interests for good or evil'. In 1876 they needed additional capital to buy the Agra-based *Mofussilite*, the leading English-language paper in the provinces, and to relaunch the *Civil and Military Gazette* as a daily based in Lahore where, for good measure, they acquired Dr Leitner's *Indian Public Opinion* the following year. This was when Allen made his capital injection. Thereafter the *Pioneer* and the *Civil and Military Gazette* were run as separate and often competing arms of the same newspaper group.

At the same time Allen's other interests were prospering. In 1876 he and four other businessmen had set up the Cawnpore Woollen Mills, largely to manufacture army blankets. With the Afghan War of 1878–80, the Mills had done well. In 1880 Allen and one of his partners, William Cooper, had set up a separate company, Cooper Allen, to act as agents for the purchase of raw materials for the factory. Looking for further opportunities, they started a tannery in Cawnpore and began lobbying to supply the Army with boots. In January 1881 they were rewarded with a seven-year contract for 25,000 pairs of boots per annum.

Having learnt of Lockwood Kipling's wish for his son to work in Lahore, Allen arranged for Stephen Wheeler, editor of the *Civil and Military Gazette*, to interview the boy in London. Allen also saw Rudyard and offered him a job on the paper at an initial salary of 150 rupees a month, or £150 a year, with a promise of regular increments. Rudyard seems to have been surprised by the suddenness of this move. 'Then came a day when he [Uncle Crom] told me that a fortnight after the close of the summer holidays of '82, I would go to India to work on a paper in Lahore,' he wrote blandly and perhaps disingenuously in his autobiography. Even in May 1882 he did not seem to be aware what his future held and was telling Mrs Tavenor Perry he was looking forward to getting out of England on 'the German scheme' – possibly another initiative of Rivett-Carnac who had once studied German at a private tutor's in Bonn where he had befriended Crown Prince Frederick William; possibly simply a teaching job such as Uncle Crom had done in Russia. There had also been talk of his becoming a doctor and he had done a short internship at the Middlesex Hospital. Inspired, no doubt, by his headmaster and by leftist-leaning talk at The Grange, Rudyard had a youth's social conscience and, Trix recalled, he regarded medicine 'from the noble point of view as an ideal profession'. However, the sight of a body on an operating table literally made him sick and he decided not to become a doctor. He still retained his interest in medicine: drugs, doctors and healing were essential points of reference throughout his career.

Having himself trained as a doctor, Crom was convinced Rudyard had made the right decision and was destined to write: his whole relaxed style of teaching had been geared to this end. So when the decision about Rudyard's career was made, Crom held the poetry competition as a form of celebration. The Battle of Assaye was an important victory by Arthur Wellesley, later Duke of Wellington, against the Mahratta army in 1803. Not only would Rudyard have read about this conflict in the volumes of Wellington's despatches in the library at Warwick Gardens, but also it would have been impressed upon his consciousness when he was in Bombay. The Mahrattas were the fierce indigenous peoples of the area surrounding his birthplace, and Assaye could be easily reached from the Kiplings' summer retreat at Nassik. The poetry competition was rigged, of course: there being no other entrants, Rudyard was awarded the prize, a copy of Sir George Trevelyan's slightly dated *The Competition Wallah*, which was deemed appropriate both for its title (which related to Rudyard) and its subject matter (a brisk survey of post-Mutiny India, written from a liberal standpoint that would have appealed to Crom Price).

Although he was still only sixteen, Rudyard's character had blossomed under Price's avuncular eye. Some things about him would never change. That wilful, obstinate streak – the fractious schoolboy in his make-up – would not go away. He was still fearfully clumsy and the lack of co-ordination in his limbs ensured that he would never be a sportsman. But the makings of the mature man could now be discerned. Rudyard enjoyed a confidence in his own intellectual abilities that would serve him well in the sapping heat of India. An unrequited first love affair had accelerated his emotional development. There had even been a hint of ambivalence between Rudyard's 'two lives', which would surface in different ways in the future.

Later, he would look back on his schooldays and come up with the *Stalky* stories – those 'tracts or parables on the education of the young',[58] which had such an ability to get up people's noses. 'Only the spoiled child of an utterly brutalised public could possibly have written *Stalky & Co.*,' wrote Robert Buchanan, a consistent contemporary critic of Rudyard. 'The vulgarity, the brutality, the savagery ... reeks on every page.'[59]

Unpleasantness does exist in these stories: it is found in the beatings, the bullying and the masochistic idea that there is any advantage in masters who 'Daily beat us on with rods, / For the love they bore us'. But, like Crofts, this part of the tale is an anachronism. Looking beyond it, one finds Rudyard putting forward a recognisably modern educational philosophy whose basic tenet can be summarised: the best way to bring up children is to allow them some freedom to test authority, devise their own ways of coping and so arrive at a sense of their own individuality. Of course, they will behave like hooligans at times. But this way they will develop their own 'law', based on 'God's Own Common Sense', leading to a social cohesiveness that will serve them well in future life.

The United Services College, for all its Victorian infrastructure, was not unlike that. While it was certainly an imperial forcing house, it was an academy for the second phase of imperialism. An earlier era had required its young men to die for their country in distant lands; these were heroes fêted in the poetry of Henry Newbolt. Now a different approach was needed, one that called for intelligence, cunning and Stalkyism, as inculcated by liberal-minded schoolmasters such as Crom Price.

As a result, there was little inherently imperialistic about Rudyard at this stage. Asked in his family questionnaire to name his favourite politicians, he chose Gladstone, the Liberal party leader, and Bismarck, the architect of German unity (and strength), a reply that would be anathema to him only fifteen years later. His – and his school's – values were accurately portrayed in 'The Flag of their Country', the *Stalky* tale about the fat, self-satisfied MP who visited the Coll to lecture the boys about their futures as army officers and the 'hope of Honour and the dream of Glory'. But no-one had any idea what he was talking about. In order to draw at least some applause, the Head had to give an outrageous pantomime wink as he thanked the speaker for 'the most enjoyable address he has given us'. The boys retired to their dormitories, called the MP 'a Flopshus Cad, an Outrageous

Stinker, a Jelly-bellied Flag-flapper (this was Stalky's contribution), and several other things which it is not seemly to put down'. One of Rudyard's more enduring legacies from Westward Ho! (and Stalkyism) was an ability to see through claptrap.

Book Two

As it was in the beginning
Is today official sinning,
    And shall be for evermore

Four

Punjab Sahib

1882–1884

All his life, Rudyard enjoyed the liberating sensation of travel. Now, as he boarded the s.s. *Brindisi* to begin his career in India, he celebrated his independence by letting his sideburns grow. His last few days in England had been spent with the Burne-Joneses at their new retreat, North End House, in Rottingdean on the Sussex coast, close to Brighton. Typical of that family's blend of Victorian respectability and radicalism, his baggage contained the recently signed life insurance policy he had taken out with the Union Assurance company. This promised his dependants £500 plus a bonus £135, in return for his modest premium of five guineas per annum. At the same time, he had his prize copy of *The Competition Wallah*, which adopted a line he was soon to discover was not popular in Lahore: that Indian civilisation had developed 'while Fortnum and Mason were driving a bouncing trade in acorns, and Swan and Edgar were doing a good thing in woad'.[1]

His voyage out was not without interest. Although he later claimed 'one only sees mirage in the putrid ditch falsely hight the Suez Canal',[2] he must have noticed signs of his country's latest imperial adventure. Only weeks earlier, after a prolonged period of political unrest, Egypt had been taken under British administrative control. Indian troops had served in the related military campaign, which was designed to protect that vital lifeline, the sea route to India. Ironically, their involvement was well received in Britain, thus encouraging advocates of greater self-government for the sub-continent.

On reaching Bombay on 18 October 1882, residual thoughts of Flo Garrard – and he was clearly harking back to her in his jaunty verses 'Les Amours de Voyage', about a fanciful shipboard romance – were at least temporarily banished as he was over-whelmed by the sensory avalanche of familiar sights, sounds and smells, when he stepped ashore on the Apollo Pier in his native city. He realised he was back home, when all his old kitchen Hindustani flowed back on to the tip of his tongue. Before he could relax, however, he still had a three-day journey by train to his new home. The railway service was patchy and the main bridge joining the Punjab and the rest of India across the great River Sutlej was not to be completed for four more years. When he finally pulled into Lahore station, the fort-like structure, built by the British in 1864 to be 'totally defensible',[3] provided stark evi-dence of the military strength that necessarily underpinned imperial rule. Then, back in the bosom of his family, he found that 'my English years fell away, nor ever, I think, came back in full strength'.

Until the annexation of the Punjab, following the defeat of the Sikhs at the battle of Chilianwala in January 1849, Lahore had been beyond the pale, a predominantly Moslem city situated in what the India Office knew for a while as Trans-Sutlej Territory. Thirty-three years later this ancient but, in British terms, frontier town had been transformed into a thriving provincial centre of the post-Mutiny Raj – important both as the crucible for a new, efficient 'Punjab style' of administration and as the platform for military expeditions setting off to defend the boundaries of empire against Russian advances in Central Asia.

Under its first Chief Commissioner John Lawrence (later the Viceroy), the Punjab's civil servants took a different approach to their duties from the bloated nabobs and box-wallahs of Bengal, living in luxury around the imperial capital of Calcutta. Drawing strength from Evangelical roots set down in early Victorian

England, they had interpreted the ideas of Bentham and Macaulay in robust frontier style, working to bring new roads and new water schemes to the province, asserting the rights of the Punjab peasant against greedy Sikh landlords and so helping ensure that this latest geographical addition to the Raj was spared the ravages of the Mutiny. Even now, with the rest of the country suffering a post-revolt reaction, Punjab administrators still managed to be confident and a bit different.

The Punjab's sense of its worth was heightened because it was a vital buffer between the heartland of India and areas of continuing unrest beyond its north-west frontier. As Rudyard had argued in his Westward Ho! debate only the previous year, the Russians in Central Asia harassed British interests by threatening to occupy Afghanistan. Though the sack of Kabul by General Roberts in October 1879 had eased the situation, consolidating the rule of the generally pro-British Amir Abdurrahman, newspaper reports of 'atrocities' during the cold-blooded execution of this expedition had shocked the British public, leading to a change of both government (from Disraeli's Conservatives to Gladstone's Liberals) and Viceroy (from Lytton to the more conciliatory Lord Ripon). Though opinion in the Punjab was less censorious and tended to approve a 'forward policy' of the kind associated with Roberts, it realised it could not be complacent and needed to carry the machinery of imperial power, including Westminster, with it. Indeed, one of the *Civil and Military Gazette*'s objectives was subtly to promote the cause of reactionary politicking.

Lahore was really several towns, as Rudyard soon discovered. Two hundred thousand Punjabis lived cheek by jowl amid the hubbub of the old walled city, with its twisting cobbled alleys and imposing Mughal monuments, ranging from Emperor Akbar's sixteenth-century fort to the revered Mosque of Wazir Khan. A sizeable population of Eurasians, or Indians of mixed race, worked in the railway workshops, Lahore's main industry, alongside the station, in the northern suburb of Naulakha (a significant name in the Kipling canon). Slightly to the south, the British had built an

orderly administrative centre, with a typical broad thoroughfare
known as The Mall, flanked with municipal and other important
buildings in favoured imperial 'Mughal-Gothic' style. The
expatriate community lived in shady streets off The Mall, in an
area known as Donald Town, within easy access of custom-made
leisure facilities, such as the popular Lawrence Gardens and the
adjoining Lawrence and Montgomery Halls – the former basically
an assembly room; the latter, the community social centre with
its 'rinking' facilities. Then, east of the town, five miles down a
straight, dusty road across the Bari Boab canal, lay Mian Mir, the
military cantonment, where an infantry battalion and artillery
battery were always in residence.

The Kiplings had a large, rambling house, set in its own compound, on the Mozang Road, close to The Mall, behind the
Museum where Lockwood worked. Lockwood liked the location,
partly because it was close to the 'office' and partly because he
had an aversion to being surrounded with trees,[4] believing, eccentrically, like Mellish in Rudyard's later story 'A Germ-Destroyer',
that greenery attracted unwanted carriers of disease – in his
case, in particular, mosquitoes. As Alice often complained, their
fourteen-room bungalow was therefore a dust trap, a point not
lost on the Kiplings' friends who called it Bikanir House, after
the great Indian Desert. Walter Lawrence, a Punjabi civil servant
who was later private secretary to the Viceroy Lord Curzon,
simply found the place 'as gloomy as its inhabitants were gay'.[5]

Rudyard has chosen to portray his return to Lahore in positive
terms: 'that was a joyous homecoming' and so on. However,
other evidence suggests that the Kipling household was more
emotionally fraught than he made out. No sooner had Rudyard
stepped across the threshold than his mother was asserting her
authority. Within an hour of his arrival she demanded that he
remove the rebellious whiskers, which had sprouted from his late-
adolescent face. His response to being so effectively reduced to
the status of a child was to voice his own complaints. While at
school, he had discovered that, without his permission and against

her husband's advice, she had gathered together the various poems he had sent back to his parents and had published a selection in Lahore in a limited edition under the name *Schoolboy Lyrics*. Alice, the socially ambitious wife and mother, had been up to her tricks again. (One recipient had probably been the man who hired him, George Allen. Another, via the mediation of Aunt Georgie, was the poet Swinburne, who pronounced non-committally that there were 'clever and promising touches, I think, here and there – and some things not so promising'.) While it is unlikely that Rudyard was wholly ignorant of his mother's initiative, we have Trix's usually reliable word that he only saw a copy of *Schoolboy Lyrics* on his return to Lahore and was very annoyed. He told his mother 'that she had taken and made use of something he needed and valued, and sulked for two days'.[6] So perhaps Alice had a point when she treated him as a child.

Rudyard must soon have discovered that his parents' marriage was not running smoothly. As Alice had intimated to Edith Plowden, her husband was no longer the companion he had once been. And Lockwood had told the same woman, who played a curious intermediary role in their relationship, 'Mrs Kipling is not at all bright and at times I think I was a brute to bring her out. If I could have a deputy wife it might be arranged somehow, but the state of society is not yet sufficiently advanced.'[7] In his avuncular manner, Lockwood was still trying to seduce young Edith.

One recurring niggle in the older Kiplings' domestic arrangements was Alice's acute awareness that she was marginally older than her husband. Trix noticed how, when her father used to tell her 'You can easily remember my age – for I was 30 the year you were born, and I shall always be 30 years older than you are', her mother would pipe up, 'I wish I could say that.'[8] Later, when asked their respective ages, Lockwood learned to say, 'My birthday is in July and Mrs Kipling's is in April' and to leave it at that. In fact, both Lockwood's statements were true: for Trix had indeed been born in June 1868, when Alice had just turned thirty-one and he was still only thirty. Somehow, this fact rankled with Alice, even though everyone said she kept her looks well. Certainly she appeared much younger than her husband, whose beard had turned grey and whose face had become more gaunt after his bout of typhoid in 1875–6.

Alice's good humour was not helped by her aversion to the heat and dust of Lahore. Having recently spent four years in England, she could not wait to return, informing Edith Plowden that her house was 'inconvenient' and badly situated, declaring that the other European women in the city were stupid and asking rhetorically, 'How I am going to exist here God knows – I can't imagine.' It seems likely that this spirited, talented woman was struggling with depression. 'I am home-sick worse than I ever was in my life – I *cannot* care for this country,' she wrote, and, 'I have never been cheerful except by excited spurts ever since I came out last, and I often wonder if this dull depressed woman can be the same she was in England.'[9]

While Alice found Bikanir House 'ugly . . . in spite of a wooden floor to the drawing room',[10] Rudyard liked the unpretentious whitewashed rooms and wide verandas. In the drawing-room his father had embellished the conventional Ruskin-style décor with Oriental details: richly woven Persian and Kashmiri rugs on the floors and above the dado, with its bright Punjabi panelled design, a Rubens engraving and some black-framed nursery rhyme illustrations by Walter Crane. Rudyard's own bedroom was more basic, with regulation white walls, some bookshelves and rush matting on the floor. He introduced his own touches, such as the polo ball on the mantelpiece. Later, having been given a small partitioned space in the entrance hall as his office, he inscribed the door in mock heroic style, 'Respect the apartments of the great'.

For a short while, as a form of familiarisation, Rudyard helped his father in the Museum, which was on The Mall next to the Central Post Office. At the time (it later moved) the Museum was housed in a shambling building originally constructed for the

Punjab Exhibition of 1864. Outside, on a raised platform, stood Zam-Zammah, the giant gun which had been cast in Lahore in 1757 for the Afghani warrior king Ahmad Shah Abdali (the name meant 'lion's roar', referring to its noise when it was fired). Inside, in what the local people called the Aja'ib Ghar, or Wonder House, Lockwood had already assembled a fine collection of artefacts, ranging from run-of-the-mill Punjabi copperware to fine Graeco-Buddhist sculptures from the Afghan city of Gandhara. (The cultural commissars Lockwood knew considered Buddhist – and particularly Graeco-Buddhist – art superior to Hindu, because it was more naturalistic.) Lockwood had a way of coaxing these items from the local peasantry. As Trix recalled, 'Many of them Father literally "took" from confiding young civilians who appeared to think that because they had been present when some priceless fragment . . . was unearthed they had the right to dispose of it.' They would consult the omniscient 'Mr Kiplin' about their loot and he would make sure it was acquired for the Museum.[11]

In November Rudyard was ready to report for his new job at the *CMG*'s offices a couple of hundred yards down The Mall from the Museum. He was immediately plunged into the thick of it. Apart from Stephen Wheeler who turned out to be a prickly and demanding character, he was the only member of the 'editorial staff'. And, as he soon found out, 'a daily paper comes out every day of the year even if fifty per cent of the staff have fever'. Initially, as *de facto* chief copy-taster and rewrite specialist, he was responsible for the contents of all but two of the pages. Every morning he had to sift through thirty local papers, which included abusive scandal sheets, 'literary journals written by Babus in the style of Addison', self-important trade magazines and tedious official reports. Their contents were précised and served up for *CMG* readers. He had to sub-edit all the reports that came in from accredited correspondents. Finally, he had to ensure that the paper received a regular flow of civic information – about forthcoming polo matches, garden parties and other social events.

Technically his working day lasted from 10 o'clock in the

morning to around 4.15 in the afternoon, or, as he told his old
friend Willes, the padre at Westward Ho!, 'earlier if I can manage
it'.[12] But often – particularly after he became more experienced –
he had to return to oversee the running of the presses until the
early hours of the morning. Although he claimed to have 'seventy
men to bully and hector as I please', that did not make the work
any easier. The Punjabi compositors managed to set copy without
knowing a word of English, but that sometimes led to glorious
misunderstandings. The proof-readers, who were characterised
by Rudyard's favourite adjective 'seedy', tended to be the worse
for drink. As a result, he claimed in his autobiography, 'I never
worked less than ten hours and seldom more than fifteen per
diem.'[13] And, in the circumstances, there was seldom time for any
creative writing.

Towards the end of the year, Rudyard began to venture out as
a reporter. Generally, he had steered clear of politics, as he sought
to find his own middle path between the liberalism of *The Competition Wallah* and the robust conservatism of his commercially
minded newspaper. But one of his first forays, in mid-November,
provided a sharp introduction to the emotion that could be generated by local issues. The occasion was the inauguration of the
new Punjab University by the new Viceroy, Lord Ripon. This was
a triumph for Dr Gotlieb Leitner, the radical lawyer, who had
long promoted university education as a means towards the social
and political emancipation of local Indians. Lockwood Kipling
had taken a different view, arguing that schooling should halt at
a technical and crafts stage. At the core of the debate were the
related questions of whether Indians were mature enough to
benefit from a Western education and whether they would use it
to agitate for a greater political voice. The aspirations of the Indian
Association (formed in 1878, a forerunner of the Indian National
Congress) already alarmed more people than Lockwood. A
common Anglo-Indian (i.e. British) reaction was to ridicule the
manners of the educated Indians, the 'babus', who were usually
Bengalis. 'I can imagine no more terrible future for India than

being governed by Competition Baboos,' Lord Salisbury had observed from a healthy distance when he was still Foreign Secretary in 1879. As the son of his father, Rudyard quickly picked up on this prejudice, observing, in this instance, the 'killing effect' of seeing 'a brown legged son of the east in the red and black gown of an M.A.'.[14]

Then, on Christmas Eve, just as he was looking forward to his only day off until Easter, he was pitched into running the newspaper on his own, after learning that Wheeler had had a riding accident and was concussed. So Rudyard had to spend Christmas Day at the office: he cancelled an appearance at the Club Ball on 27 December and attended the Masonic Banquet the following day when, in the absence of anyone else, he delivered a speech of thanks on behalf of the press. At that stage he was still (for two more days) aged only sixteen.

A couple of poems from these early times provide a wry view of his working life. In 'The Pious Sub's Creed', dated 26 January 1883, he tries to convince himself that he enjoys topping and tailing stories about Afghan frontier wars and that his sub-editor's scissors are 'the world's most sure foundation / And pasting paragraphs by far the finest occupation'. (This poem reiterates his second-hand prejudice against the pretensions of the babu dressed in English clothes.) The other poem, from later that summer, was sent to the padre at Westward Ho!, presumably for inclusion in the *Chronicle*, though there is no record of its appearing. In Rudyard's best light-hearted tones, it contrasts his hard life on the *CMG* with the soft existence he once led at school:

> Grimmer than any 'thousand lines',
>   The lines that I must read,
> More crabbed than Euclid's worst designs
>   A correspondent's screed.[15]

Slowly, Rudyard adapted to the rhythm of a job on an Indian newspaper. During the winter months, the *CMG* premises were agreeably sociable. Rudyard's day was interrupted by welcome calls from supplicants needing a journalist's services – anyone from a renegade army officer keen to ditch a colleague in an anonymous article, to a pretty woman in a rustling dress who wanted her cards printed *immediately*.

With the spring, Rudyard began to get out of the office, though his social life was limited to the odd dance and a taste of the amateur theatrical productions that were to occupy him in the years to come. Lockwood was happy that Lahore offered his son nothing more exciting, telling Edith Plowden, 'I am sure [Rudyard] is better here than anywhere else where there are no music-hall ditties to pick up, no young persons to philander about with ... For all that makes Lahore so profoundly dull makes it safe for young people.'[16] However, Alice, with her keener antennae, recognised her son was bored and, as a result, could be 'very trying in his moods – being subject to sudden fits of the blues'.[17]

And that, as Rudyard wrote in 'The Man Who Would Be King', was 'the amusing part of the year'. As summer drew on and the thermometer inched higher (86 degrees Fahrenheit in the shade with the water-cooled punkah flapping, 108 degrees without it, and 167 degrees in the sun, Rudyard noted one sticky, late-April day), life became unbearable. The printing presses turned red-hot, social amusements ground to a halt and friends sickened with one of a predictable series of illnesses – heat-stroke, fever, dysentery or cholera. Gradually most people departed to the hills to frivol and recuperate and, by July, the city – or at least the European section – was almost deserted.

Towards the end of May, Stephen Wheeler duly broke down with a fever and Rudyard was again left to run the paper. The full weight of this responsibility only became clear when he was called on to deliver the paper's editorial line on the controversial Ilbert Bill. This was no easy matter, particularly for a young man still feeling his way in a strange country. Under instructions from Prime Minister Gladstone, the new Viceroy, Lord Ripon, had been trying to halt the post-Mutiny political impasse and to rekindle an earlier spirit of benevolent co-operation between the British and native Indian élites. He had revoked his predecessor Lord Lytton's Vernacular Press Act, which tried to limit the scope of Indian-language newspapers, and he had put forward proposals for greater municipal self-government. His most controversial innovation, however, was to encourage his Legal Member, Courtenay Ilbert, to introduce a bill allowing Indian judges to try Europeans who, until then (February 1883), had enjoyed the privilege of coming before benches of their own race. Ilbert's draft legislation caused a furore among planters in the more rural areas of Bengal and Assam. In Calcutta an Anglo-Indian Defence Association was formed and, amid the prejudice about 'jumped-up-babus', there was talk of a secessionist Anglo-Indian state. Rudyard was alarmed enough to write to Crom Price asking his opinion about these developments. As he told his old headmaster, 'I can't trust myself to write calmly about that "Bill". Old stagers say that race feeling has never been so high since the Mutiny.'[18] Price's reply has been lost, but is likely to have favoured the Bill, and this indeed was the line Rudyard took in his editorial of 2 June.

When the young journalist poked his head round the door at the Punjab Club, he was bewildered to find people hissing at him. Only the intervention of an army officer silenced the din: 'Stop that! The boy's only doing what he's paid to do.' This at least was how Rudyard reported the event in his autobiography, where he tried to shift the blame on to the paper's proprietors and show them in collusion with the government. (He was right insofar that Allen's business interests were greatly dependent on government contracts.) But the real lesson for Rudyard was more visceral: the extent of anti-Indian prejudice was abruptly brought home to him and not even the liberal nostrums of Crom Price could help.

He expected to stay in Lahore throughout the summer until, in July, as a gesture of thanks for his stepping into the editorial breach, he was invited to join one of the paper's owners, James Walker, and his family at Kelvin Grove, their luxurious holiday

home in Simla. Situated at over 7000 feet in the western Himalayas, Simla was India's premier hill station, the place where the
entire imperial administration, Governor-General included,
repaired when Calcutta, the capital, became too hot. As Rudyard
was to portray in his *Plain Tales from the Hills*, all the Raj's social
climbers, office seekers and hucksters who could afford it came
too. On this occasion, however, Rudyard had little thought but to
enjoy himself. He explored the cool of the surrounding slopes,
took part in the usual 'round of picnics, dances, theatricals and
so on',[19] and flirted with Miss O'Meara, the bold, black-eyed
daughter of the local dentist (himself the nephew of the Emperor
Napoleon's one-time personal doctor). His assessment of the dramatic potential of the place had to wait.

Returning to Lahore in mid-August, he found himself in the
dog-days of summer. There was no one at Bikanir House: his
father was still in the mountains and his mother had gone back
to England to collect fifteen-year-old Trix, who was completing
her education in London at Notting Hill High School, an academic girls' day school which Margaret Burne-Jones and Jenny
and May Morris had also attended. Indeed, there was hardly
anybody in the city. Rudyard was one of only eleven people (nine
men and two women) still 'on station'. He spent most of his free
time at the Club which, at this time of year, practically ground to
a halt. The members had to be chivvied by the secretary to change
for dinner; they snapped at each other and refused to pass the
newspapers; a game of billiards or whist was the height of both
exertion and entertainment. In better times Rudyard grew to like
the casual camaraderie. Sitting in the Club, whisky and soda in
hand, he heard from professional men, passing through town
from remote spots, how India really functioned. And he came to
admire the dedication to the service of Empire of these administrators, doctors, soldiers and engineers.

Outside the Club Rudyard started to investigate the town and
its environs – largely as a way of coping with the general tedium.
Until then he had risen each morning in a leisurely, even decadent,

manner – allowing his hawk-faced Moslem bearer, Noor Ali, to shave him as he lay in bed, sometimes while he was still asleep. His routine changed when his father gave him an old roan stallion called Joe, who had seen service with the 19th Bengal Lancers. Now he instructed his man to wake him earlier, before sunrise. '*Kutch perwanne hum* "damn" *bolta* [Never mind if I say damn],' he told Noor Ali. Astride his horse, Rudyard would trot through the park where, just before first light, night animals such as jackals still scurried around. Breaking into a canter, he might make his way down to the Ravee river where once, as he recalled in a poem, he watched a hungry alligator wrestling with the body of a dead Hindu who, according to the rites of his religion, had been cremated on the ghats but had not yet fully decomposed. Observing the practical consequences of the Indian philosophy of reincarnation (even if he mocked them in his irreverent lines about the Indian 'Who stank and sank beneath the tide / Then rose and stank anew'), Rudyard felt a sense of exhilaration as the sun came up and a new day began. 'Oh! a ride in an Indian dawn, there's no such pleasure in life!' he exclaimed in a poem to his Aunt Edith. At this stage, however, there could be no hanging around: Rudyard knew he had to be home by seven o'clock; otherwise the heat became too intense.

Entering his second year at the *CMG*, he still had office politics to contend with. As a journalist of the old school, the editor, Wheeler, thought his assistant was too literary and tried to make him knuckle down to the more mundane reporter's jobs, such as turning the turgid reports of official government inquiries, known as Blue Books, into readable English prose. (Perhaps he had been briefed by Lockwood to knock some of the stuffing out of the young man.) He also made sure that Rudyard was occupied in works of translation, though, no doubt unintentionally, this proved more interesting: the French-language papers, *Journal de St Petersbourg* and *Novoie Vremya* (published in Moscow) introduced the youngster to first-hand Russian accounts of the Great Game. Among the memoirs he translated were the war diaries of the Russian adventurer Lieutenant Ali Khan (known as Alikhanoff), who in February 1884 had scared Anglo-Indians by annexing the strategic town of Merv in Turkmenistan. In Lahore, and elsewhere, this was again interpreted as a direct threat to British interests in India and if Gladstone's Liberal government had not been pre-occupied with a war in the Sudan it might have reacted more combatively to an incident that only encouraged Moscow to probe further Britain's resolve in Central Asia.

This way, at least, Rudyard began to understand some of the external pressures that Anglo-Indians felt, along with their domestic concerns. Alikhanoff's encroachment impressed itself so deeply on him personally that, fifteen years later, when he suffered an attack of pneumonia in New York and was close to death, he had a vivid nightmare about leading a cavalry unit over vast, desolate steppes and stopping at the various camps that Alikhanoff had meticulously recorded in his account. At each halt in his dream he would see the name of the place 'heaving up over the edge of the planet' – a surreal image which indicated both his political paranoia and his powerful imagination.

As a gesture of solidarity with his fellow citizens against the dark threats in the north-west, Rudyard decided, with the tentativeness of a new boy, to join the 1st Punjab Volunteer Rifles. However, he spent little time drilling with the unit, particularly after mocking his fellow recruits' shooting skills in a light-hearted poem,[20] which told of his experience of being peppered with bullets while walking down The Mall – on to which the Volunteers' rifle range backed. (The range was moved soon afterwards: built for muzzle-loading Enfield and breech-loading Snider rifles, it was too short for 'modern' Martini-Henry guns, introduced in 1871 – and now widely available in India.)

Rudyard's appreciative employers gave him a pay rise, on his first anniversary in the job, to £300 a year – a reasonable salary for someone his age, living with his parents. They encouraged him, when possible, to escape Wheeler's leash and get out of the office. Within Lahore, there were details of personal tragedies to be revealed from the divorce courts, and municipal scandals to be uncovered, such as the lack of hygiene (and, he claimed, the large number of lepers) in the city's meat trade.[21] With his energy and ''satiable curtiosity', he steadily familiarised himself with the mundane realities of British India.

He did not take long to discover the extent of local corruption. In February 1884 a rich Afghan noble, who was held under house arrest after a long career of fighting the British, considered the man-boy Rudyard already influential enough to offer him a series of attractive bribes for favourable coverage of his own plight. Rudyard refused 16,000 rupees (£1200 at the time), telling the old man 'the years had impaired his eyesight and I wasn't a Bunnoochi or a Baluchi (two races the most covetous on earth) but an English Sahib'.[22] Unimpressed, and muttering that all Englishmen were fools, the Afghan then tempted Rudyard with a gorgeous young Kashmiri girl. When that too failed, he tried something he was sure would work: Rudyard could take his pick of seven of the most handsome horses he had ever seen. As Rudyard felt his resolution wavering he was forced to leave. Even then, under Joe's saddle, he found a small bag of uncut sapphires and emeralds which he disposed of by throwing them as far as he could into a nearby building. Leaving the teeming Old City, he rode back into what he described to his Aunt Edith as 'our peaceful little station' where everyone was just coming out of church. A seminal experience: the contrast between the two places could not have been greater. As he told Aunt Edith, 'Verily India is a strange land, and its people are still stranger.'[23]

Nevertheless, as at Westward Ho!, Rudyard's second year in Lahore was already proving a marked improvement on the first. Each time he ventured out, he learnt more about a country that was, by turns, exciting, dangerous and unfathomable. A couple of months later, in April, he accompanied the Viceroy on an official visit to the Sikh princedom of Patiala, some 150 miles south-east of Lahore. Such 'native states' were an anachronism – satrapies that, for the most part, continued their feudal ways with the barest interference from the British 'resident'. Rudyard was both fascinated and appalled by the mixture of ostentation, wealth and decadence – 'albums in Russian leather, malachite, ivory, mother-of-pearl, silver, onyx, and agate ... riding whips, sausage-machines, champagne-tweezers, candle-sticks ... and a flock of India-rubber decoy ducks'.[24] When his favourable journalistic coverage was sought through the time-honoured gesture of leaving a wad of 500-rupee notes at the bottom of his fruit bowl, Rudyard complained so vocally that his bearer Noor Ali feared for his life and ordered him to refrain from further food or drink. (Wrongly, in his autobiography, he remembered this as the first attempt to bribe him.)

Rudyard's sense that he was somewhere weird and impenetrable was enhanced when, wandering around the palace, he came across five old men discussing what he thought were affairs of state. In a surreal moment, they shooed him away and he was given to believe he had strayed too near the ladies. His sense of relief when he 'managed to rejoin modern civilisation in the shape of the barouche'[25] provided by the authorities was palpable. Later, in an effort to steal a march on his newspaper rivals, Rudyard made a sixteen-mile dash on horseback to ensure his copy caught the 10.30 p.m. train to Lahore. After reaching his destination (Rajpura railway station), Rudyard's horse was too tired to continue. So, swapping the beast for a similar animal tied up beside a sleeping soldier, he rode back across the desert to Patiala – the whole journey, under a canopy of stars, having taken him less than two and a half hours. He was to draw on this experience when writing the novel The Naulahka with his friend Wolcott Balestier in 1891.

Reunited with Joe in Lahore, Rudyard began to explore the shrines to Mughal potentates and Sufi saints that lay just outside the boundaries of the city. Several of these memorials were situated in tranquil gardens where local people liked to congregate on feast days. One of the loveliest, six miles into the countryside, was the Shalimar (Abode of Love) Gardens, with five hundred fountains, built by the Emperor Shah Jehan in 1637. Often, in the evenings, Rudyard would join some friends there for a romantic moonlit picnic. (There is no evidence of a man proposing to the wrong woman, as happened in the dust storm at the 'Great Pop Picnic' in his story 'False Dawn', but there is no doubt where the idea came from.) As he began to find out more about Lahore's Mughal heritage, Rudyard was inspired to delve further into local history and culture. He hired a native teacher to give him an hour's Urdu lesson each morning and, under the guidance of his father, he began to study Persian.

At Christmas 1883 his mother and sister returned from England, and this heralded the start of a period of intense family bonding. Trix had grown into an attractive teenager – witty, literate and pretty. In addition, she seemed to have inherited her mother's (and the Macdonald females') gift of 'second sight'. Under Alice's formidable influence, the Kiplings consolidated into what they called the 'family square' – a term that suggested not only a cohesive unit but also a solid defence against the outside world. During long winter evenings at Bikanir House they created their own private domain, with shared secret language, jokes and insults (the unfortunate Stephen Wheeler was dubbed 'the amber toad', for example). Surrounded by a growing menagerie (Rudyard had a bull terrier called 'Buz', Trix a Persian cat and fox terrier puppy, while Lockwood made great play of tending a pair of crows), Alice softened in her long-standing dislike of animals and was even to be found petting the cat. She revelled in her *mater familias* role – with herself sewing, Lockwood reading, and her children occupied with pencil and paper, composing the clever parodies of famous poets that would be published in volume form in Lahore that summer under the title *Echoes*.

Prodded by his mother, Rudyard now devoted more time to his non-newspaper writing. In addition to his poems, he claimed in mid-February to have started a novel, though this project was, for the time being, stillborn and he made no further mention of it for more than a year. In April he was due to play Chrysal, the hero in W. S. Gilbert's melodrama *The Palace of Truth*, which was staged by the Lahore Amateurs in the Railway Theatre. However, he was prevented by illness from appearing and it was left to his leading lady, Miss Coxen, to carry the show in her role as the scorned Palmis. Having had little opportunity to meet women except on strictly social occasions, Rudyard sought out her company and took her riding. Though in no way committed, he sent her, as a token of his affection, a Valentine card with the rubric 'Constant and True' and, when she left town in June, he wrote a poem expressing his sadness, nominally from his horse Joe.

That summer Alice and Trix escaped to the hills earlier than expected. Since Trix was still only sixteen, the Kipling parents decided she was too young for the sophistication of Simla and opted instead to take their vacation in the smaller, less expensive resort of Dalhousie. Trix was unimpressed: she called it Dullhouses. When Rudyard joined them in August he arranged for his beloved Joe to accompany him. But his holiday turned sour when, owing to the carelessness of a groom, the horse fell and broke his back, and had to be put down.

Earlier, as the thermometer again began to rise in Lahore, Rudyard had, for the first time in India, been troubled by ill health. Before travelling to Dalhousie he had suffered a bout of fever (perhaps malaria) which, when linked to problems with his eyes, led to a recurrence of the same sort of hallucinations he had experienced at The Grange the day he had hit a tree to see if it was Grandmother. He found that only by increasing his already onerous workload to sixteen hours a day (an incredible undertaking at the height of a Lahore summer) could he ward off what he called his 'blue devils'.[26] Significantly, this attack coincided with his renewed communication with Flo Garrard. Although their relationship had, to all intents and purposes, ended two years earlier, the distance of 6000 miles had had a marked aphrodisiac effect. As he wrote in his story 'On the Strength of a Likeness', an unrequited attachment can be a comforting accoutrement – like a well-smoked pipe – for a young man in India. 'It makes him feel important and business-like, and *blasé*, and cynical; and whenever he has a touch of liver, or suffers from want of exercise, he can mourn his lost love, and be very happy in a tender, twilight fashion.' But no sooner had he been in touch with Flo than, in July 1884, she had rejected him again. And even two years later, when he told Margaret Burne-Jones, he admitted that the memory still hurt.

After he returned from Dalhousie, a different malaise took hold: on 16 September he had excruciating stomach cramps, which left him rolling on the floor in agony. This time he was only saved by his servant preparing an opium pipe and insisting that Rudyard should smoke as much as possible. Before long he found the pains in his body subsiding, and 'a minute or two later it seemed to me that I fell through the floor'. Next morning, as he brought Rudyard a glass of milk, a smiling Noor Ali seemed satisfied with his ministrations. The patient himself was not so sure: he felt dull-headed and people in the office later thought he had been drinking. Noor Ali claimed he had cured his master from a fever that was raging through the Old City. In relating the details of his unusual medicine to his Aunt Edith (and begging her not to tell his mother who, he pleaded, would fret and possibly curtail her holiday in Dalhousie if she heard), he said that it 'certainly cut short a spell of the acutest pain I have ever experienced in my life and no woman could have tended me more carefully than he through those three terrible hours between eleven and two'.[27]

Initially opium, one of the oldest analgesics in the Indian pharmacopoeia, helped ease the combined effects of fever, stomach cramps, even love sickness, and a demanding mother (he confessed he did not play polo when she was in town because she thought it was too dangerous). Rudyard must have known about the Pre-Raphaelites' use of laudanum, an opium derivative, and perhaps, after reading his father's colleague, now Sir George

Birdwood, in *The Times* a couple of years earlier, had wanted to try it. According to Birdwood, opium was 'almost as harmless an indulgence as twiddling the thumbs and other silly-looking methods for concentrating the jaded mind'. Certainly Rudyard was remarkably unperturbed about use of the raw drug – 'an excellent thing in itself and in moderation about as harmful as tobacco', he later told his Uncle Alfred, adding an argument that is still heard from the pro-drugs lobby: 'I *know* that the opium habit in India is nothing compared to the ordinary effects of liquor in a town full of white Christians but you see I can't prove it.'

Opium also had an unexpected psychic effect, giving Rudyard a subtle new perspective on his surroundings. No longer was he viewing India as a naïve foreigner, but he had taken on something of the accumulated experience of an inhabitant of Lahore's Old City. The neophyte, who until recently had been writing clever parodies of the great poets, was freed to step out of his own cultural and intellectual environment and make something more substantial of his immediate experience.

Hitherto, like the hero of 'The Conversion of Aurelian McGoggin', Rudyard had been too 'intellectually "beany"' and, while not subscribing to McGoggin's positivism, he had worked too hard and paid the price. He had been finding what old-timers already knew: that it is difficult to be too dogmatic in an India 'where you really see humanity – raw, brown, naked humanity – with nothing between it and the blazing sky, and only the used-up, over-handed earth underfoot'. India had its own rhythms and ways, and one had to learn to adapt. Certainly, as with McGoggin, Rudyard had discovered that 'no man can toil eighteen annas in the rupee in June without suffering'. As the doctor in that story put it, in treating McGoggin (significantly a man whose grandfathers on both sides were Wesleyan preachers), 'There are a good many things you can't understand; and, by the time you have put in my length of service, you'll know exactly how much a man dare call his own in this world.'

Opium was one way Rudyard found of dealing with the vast mystery of India. Although he distanced himself from the drug by telling his aunt it was 'infernal', he showed his continuing interest by using it as the subject for an important early story for the *CMG* – the first in a series that would later be collected under the name *Plain Tales from the Hills*. Taking advantage of the absence of Stephen Wheeler, Rudyard squeezed 'The Gate of the Hundred Sorrows' into the *CMG* on 26 September. Under the guise of fiction, the piece is an objective report on the workings of an opium den, near the Mosque of Wazir Khan in the Old City. Rudyard does his best to keep aloof from the action: in the *CMG*, the story appeared under the byline 'By the Janitor' and was prefaced with a disclaimer that 'this is no work of mine', but was spoken by his friend, the half-caste Gabral Misquitta, six weeks before his death. He further removes himself by stressing the difficulties of finding the place: 'I defy [anyone] to find the Gate, however well he may think he knows the City. You might even go through the very gully it stands in a hundred times, and be none the wiser.'[28] Like India itself, this secret place is hidden and virtually unattainable. But, so the underlying message goes, someone of Rudyard's curiosity perseveres. Eventually, he alights upon The Gate of the Hundred Sorrows, run by an old Chinese bootmaker Fung-Tching, who was 'the handiest man at rolling black pills' ever seen. As Rudyard, the narrator first sampled the drug in his own house to see what it was like. He took to it more seriously when his wife died (or, in Rudyard's terms, when his relationship with Flo finally floundered). However, unlike Rudyard, Misquitta was an addict. 'At the end of one's third pipe the dragons used to move about and fight. I've watched 'em many and many a night through. I used to regulate my Smoke that way, and now it takes a dozen pipes to make 'em stir.'

Curiously, when he wrote to Edith Macdonald on 17 September, the day after his nocturnal agonies, he stated that this story, which was not published in the *CMG* until nine days later, had 'stirred up the easy-going clericals here to state of virtuous horror'. This

suggests either wishful thinking (the eighteen-year-old was trying
to shock) or that Rudyard had completed 'The Gate of the
Hundred Sorrows' before this experience and was already familiar
with the Old City's opium dens.

Even now, Flo Garrard preyed on his mind, like a recurring
hallucination in an opium reverie. Among several inscribed
copies of *Echoes* that he sent back to England was one to her,
dated September 1884, with lines reading in part:

> And should my foolish songs discover
> Some traces of your girlhood's lover
> Forgive me – two long years apart
> Still leaves you mistress of my heart.

Although Rudyard admitted that their relationship had changed
from the heady days 'when I was yours, and you were mine', he
asked that Flo should now accept him as a 'friend'. Following her
great-great uncle, the animal painter George Garrard, she was
pursuing a career as an artist and had that very autumn started a
course in Fine Art at the Slade School in London. Initially she
commuted to her studies from suburban Beckenham where she
was living with the Vineys, the family of her banker brother
Robert's wife, Ellen.

Back in Lahore, an added concern for Rudyard was that George
Allen, the forceful businessman behind the *CMG*'s success, was
talking of transferring him to Allahabad, 800 miles away, to work
on the group's other paper, the more prestigious *Pioneer*.
Although Rudyard's salary would rise to £500 per annum and no
move was expected for a year, he was uncertain whether he wanted
to be uprooted from the 'family square'. With Wheeler's regular
absences from the *CMG*, he told his aunt, he had the opportunity
to shape his own newspaper, while on the *Pioneer* he would be an
office junior again. In a gesture that, paradoxically, both celebrated his independence and showed how his own views were
merging with his proprietors', he knocked off a poem, published

in the *CMG* on 15 September, which welcomed the premature resignation of the ineffectual Lord Ripon as Viceroy.[29] In the style of Tennyson, Rudyard mocked the fact that Ripon had been defeated by India's inertia – a valid view that the stuffier *Pioneer* had managed to ignore.

In the event, Rudyard stayed in Lahore for another three years. Quite likely, his parents wished to keep an eye on him at a crucial stage in his personal development. For the evidence of one extraordinary story he wrote in November 1884 was that, having experienced something of the weird timelessness of India, he was growing up fast and beginning to understand the terrible personal compromises that were required if a man were to succeed as a coloniser in a boundless, unforgiving land. On 21 November, he noted jauntily to his Aunt Edie, 'I've been writing a story in my leisure. It has only taken me three months and is only six pages long but I've never fallen in love with any tale of my own fashioning so much – not that it has any merit.'[30]

The last six words were typical self-deprecation: 'The Dream of Duncan Parrenness', published in the *CMG* on Christmas Day 1884 a few days before his nineteenth birthday, is vivid and mature. It provides astounding evidence of that rare phenomenon, a precocious talent managing to articulate thoughts that he had not even begun to understand on a conscious level. Later, he would talk of his 'daemon', a creative force he submitted to when he wrote. This story shows that energy at work. In stark puritanical terms, it tells of the eponymous Parrenness, 'Writer in the service of the [East India] Company and afraid of no man', who has left his fiancée Kitty Somerset in England and come to Calcutta to seek his fortune. Within three months of his arrival, however, she jilts him for another man. As a form of consolation, he begins to pay court to a notorious local man-eater – a pale, pretty woman with violet eyes called Mrs Vansuythen.

The main body of the tale takes place in what is described as a drunken stupor, but could equally well have been an opium dream. Trying to get Mrs Vansuythen out of his mind, Parrenness chastises himself: 'I saw how the one year that I had lived in this land had so burnt and seared my mind with the flames of a thousand bad passions and desires, that I had aged ten months for each one in the Devil's school.' He attempts to make his peace with his mother, but her face metamorphoses into that of Kitty and Mrs Vansuythen. Subsequently he is confronted by his *doppelgänger* – an image of himself as a much older man, which also oscillates with that of the Governor-General and his dead father. As his own features grow whiter and more drawn, he is told that he must pay his price if he is to be spared these haunting visions. At this stage, Duncan Parrenness, who was once 'afraid of no man', becomes a quivering wreck. To regain his equilibrium and be rid of his intruder, he is told he must give up, first, his faith in man and, second, his faith in women. Thinking of his lying, bragging colleagues, and the women who have betrayed and ensnared him, he reluctantly agrees to these two conditions and his *alter ego* slowly disappears, growing 'pale and thin against the white light in the east, as my mother used to tell me is the custom of ghosts and devils and the like'. In the process, the 'certain goodness' in his heart is replaced by a 'deadly coldness'. Parrenness (no great ingenuity is required to decipher his name as a play on 'drunken barrenness') is left to contemplate his position: 'There be certain times in a young man's life, when, through great sorrow or sin, all the boy in him is burnt and seared away so that he passes at one step to the more sorrowful state of manhood: as our staring Indian day changes into night with never so much as the grey of twilight to temper the two extremes.'

With its echoes of Flo and the Kipling family, this account of a young man's initiation into adulthood also deals with his loss of innocence, and the fears surrounding this loss.[31] Parrenness understands that if he is to make his way in a masculine society, he needs to compromise and give up his youthful idealism. (In a later story, Kim is faced with much the same dilemma in different circumstances.) With a modern twist, Parrenness realises his decision is ultimately meaningless. For when his *alter ego*, his devil, departs, he leaves a gift (in return for the two crucial trusts the narrator has given up) and this turns out to be nothing more than a little piece of dry bread.

Such subject matter did not mean Rudyard was suffering from any overt depression. He was talking of taking two months off to travel by sea to Ceylon and Madras. (In fact, this voyage never materialised.) But he was experiencing a significant turning point in his attitude to India. For two years he had sampled different aspects of the country – from the tedium of the office and comradeship of the Club, to the mysteries of princely states and the recesses of the Old City. Now, with his fine intelligence – sensitised, to some extent, by opium – he became aware that, if he was to make headway, he needed to abandon his adolescent ways and fantasies (including his longing for Flo) and approach the business of living in India in what he imagined to be a more mature manner.

One response was to redouble his efforts to understand India. Ever since that period in London around Christmas 1877, shortly before first going to Westward Ho!, he had known how the night could 'get into' his head. Now in Lahore, he 'would wander till dawn in all manner of odd places – liquor-shops, gambling- and opium-dens, which are not a bit mysterious, wayside entertainments such as puppet-shows, native dances; or in and about the narrow gullies under the Mosque of Wazir Khan for the sheer sake of looking'.

He described one of his nocturnal prowls[32] in 'The City of Dreadful Night', another article he liked so much that he recycled it in a later volume of fiction, *Life's Handicap*. As with his earlier 'The Gate of the Hundred Sorrows', this story is crammed with powerful images. On first entering the Old City through the Delhi Gate, he cannot avoid the mass of men sleeping 'like sheeted corpses' in the open air and he is almost overwhelmed by the baking-hot, dry midnight air.

It is a compound of all evil savours, animal and vegetable, that

a walled city can brew in a day and a night ... The high house-
walls are still radiating heat savagely, and from obscure side
gullies fetid breezes eddy that ought to poison a buffalo ... On
one of the roofs a hookah is in full blast; and the men are talking
softly as the pipe gutters.

With a mixture of incredulity and affection, Rudyard describes
the various manifestations of this restless, over-heated city, with
its suffocating sense of life and death so closely intertwined. As
he rightly says, Doré might have drawn it, or Zola described it.
And then suddenly, as dawn breaks, the air is rent by the muezzin's
cry, 'Allah ho Akbar. Allah ho Akbar (God is Great)'. For a moment
a promising freshness pervades the air, but then, almost as quickly,
it disappears, and as Rudyard leaves the city, it disgorges its secret
of death: a woman who died in the night is brought out to be
buried.

Like so many visitors before and after, Rudyard became
obsessed with the paradoxes of India, where colour and vitality
coexist with death and destruction. Babus who aped the West
held little interest. But the ordinary people's efforts to cope with
their existence proved endlessly fascinating. The only trouble was,
the more he understood the country, the more appalled Rudyard
was by her inherent anarchy. By the time he came to write 'The
Man Who Was' in 1890, he had come to the conclusion, 'Asia is
not going to be civilized after the methods of the West. She is too
much Asia and she is too old. You cannot reform a lady of many
lovers, and Asia had been insatiable in her flirtations aforetime.
She will never attend Sunday school or learn to vote save with
swords for tickets.' But that was five years into the future: for the
time being his own attitude was still being formed.

Rudyard's movements around this time can be charted with more
confidence than usual because his 1885 diary has survived. Normally he would have made sure that such a document was
destroyed. But he left this in his office at the *CMG* where it was

later discovered and sold to the Houghton Library of Harvard University. Most of the diary is mundane, dealing with his writings, freelance journalistic income and output for the paper. He completed a 'scrap' or short report here, 'fudged up' some notes there, frequently felt 'seedy' or had a headache, and called on his father (a constant support) to help 'spin out a watery sort of special to close upon three columns. Kept me up till 1. of the night.' Rudyard met several lowish-level officials and, significantly, noted Russian incursions in Tibet and Korea.

One day's entry shows both the range and, often, triviality of his journalism. Thus, on 19 January: 'Wrote Jellalabad horse fair from notes; notice of the Gaiety Company, par on Luker's *Press Guide for India* (a good biz.) wrote notes for a week in Lahore, doctored scrap of the Pater's on E. About, and was generally very busy over small jobs.' Rudyard's interest in French writers continued unabated: in his family questionnaire five years earlier he had mentioned Edmond About as one of his four favourite authors. Emile Zola, whom he quoted liberally in his investigations into the Lahore underworld, was one of the others. In February, when the Rosa Towers Company staged *Drink* (an adaptation from Zola's *L'Assommoir*) at the Railway Theatre, Rudyard gave it a stinking review. It probably failed to match a London production of the late 1870s, after which he had astonished his school friends with his masterful acting out of the final scene of delirium tremens.

The diary is guarded about his private life. It suggests he had regular liaisons with unnamed women: 'usual philander in gardens',[33] runs a typical entry, and, on one occasion, he was afraid he had picked up a venereal infection. He saw such sexual encounters as therapeutic: as he wrote to a colleague the following year, he could no sooner give up his literary activities (and so concentrate on his journalism) than he could 'put aside the occasional woman which is good for health and the softening of ferocious manners'. When he felt the need to be particularly cagey, Rudyard uses symbols to denote his movements, as in early February:

'Mem. eris cum [symbol] Thursd. [symbol] a bundobast. My task
is to lie low and wait.' The next Thursday the letters W.R.W.M.
are followed by another symbol and the comment 'a thoroughly
satisfactory conclusion'. The first entry can be read in Latin,
'Remember, you will be with [an unknown acquaintance] Thursday.' Since bundobast is a Hindustani word for a settlement, this
indicates a dispute in which he was involved.

Then suddenly, on 7 March, Rudyard noted, 'The idea of
"Mother Maturin" dawned on me today.' Within a short time this
idea had developed into a fully fledged novel – possibly the one
he had been thinking of the previous year. By the end of July he
was writing to his Aunt Edith informing her that his novel, *Mother
Maturin*, had grown 'like Topsy' and now covered 237 foolscap
pages. 'It's not one bit nice or proper but it carries a grim sort of
a moral with it and tries to deal with the unutterable horrors of
a lower-class Eurasian and native life as they exist outside the
reports.'[34] He said he had not yet shown it to his father, but
Trix thought it was 'awfully horrid' and his mother 'nasty but
powerful'. He claimed that he had been wondering whether to
publish it in England or in India and had decided on the latter,
possibly because he had already received an offer for the book
from an unnamed Indian paper.

Mother Maturin was Rudyard's often mentioned but never
published novel. He referred to it off and on as 'work in progress'
for most of the next two decades. Although 237 pages long at this
stage, it developed into a much weightier tome. According to Mrs
Edmonia Hill, an American woman who befriended Rudyard
when he moved to Allahabad in 1887, it dealt with exactly the sort
of subject matter that was occupying him at this time: it was, she
said, 'the story of an old Irish woman who kept an opium den in
Lahore but sent her daughter to be educated in England. She
marries a civilian and comes to live in Lahore – hence a story –
how Govt. Secrets came to be known in the bazar and vice versa.'[35]

Clearly this was an absorbing tale: how the convent-educated
daughter of a flophouse 'madam' became a double agent in British

India. Sadly, the manuscript has been lost, believed destroyed. As Trix and Alice Kipling's comments suggested, such subject matter was not popular within the family square. Eventually, it seems, Rudyard bowed to various pressures to abandon the book, but not before he had milked it for several stories and, in particular, for his 1901 novel *Kim*, whose hero, originally Kim O'Rishti (or 'of the Irish'), emerged from its low-life background.

So *Mother Maturin* remained 'the novel that is always being written and yet gets no furrader'.[36] For the time being, at least, it gave Rudyard an excuse to continue his research into 'that wonderful, dirty, mysterious anthill' that was Lahore. He told a friend he knew the city blindfold and liked to wander through it 'like Haroun Al-Raschid in search of strange things'. But he now understood he was more than a mere reporter seeking flashes of colourful exoticism. As a writer and artist, he had begun to pursue a greater ambition – and that was no less than explaining the strange phenomenon of the British presence in India.

Five

Special Correspondent

1885

Away from the oppressive heat of the Old City, the weather was wet and windy, and Rudyard had difficulty stopping his teeth chattering, as dawn broke on the morning of 29 March 1885. He was in the far North-West Frontier town of Jamrud, waiting for His Highness the Amir Abdurrahman of Afghanistan to make his way over the Khyber Pass. Having acquitted himself well in his 'specials' from the Amritsar Fair the previous October, Rudyard had been sent by the *CMG* to the Afghan border to report on the much-trumpeted meeting between the Amir and the new Viceroy, Lord Dufferin. The encounter, which had been elevated to the status of a durbar, with all the trappings of court ritual, was considered a necessary act of diplomacy. With the Russians ever threatening in Central Asia, the British felt that the Amir, who had been encouraged to return from exile to take over his country following General Roberts's sack of Kabul in 1879, needed cosseting – and confirming in his generally pro-British 'neutrality' – with a magnificent show of imperial pomp and ceremony.

After Lord Ripon's mood of compromise in both domestic and foreign policies, Anglo-Indians expected more resolution from their cultured new Viceroy. The owner of extensive estates in Ulster, Dufferin had already served as Governor-General of Canada and Ambassador to both Moscow and Constantinople, where his diplomatic skills were credited with improving relations with the Porte after the British occupation of Egypt, nominally part of the Ottoman Empire. Although a Liberal by upbringing, he had been specifically requested by his friend, the Secretary of State for India the Earl of Kimberley, to restore a measure of stability in the sub-continent so that the London government could pay more attention to imperial matters elsewhere. Rudyard later wrote of the Indian sub-continent's shock at hearing of Britain's inability to defend Sudan around the time of General Gordon's death in Khartoum in January.[1] Lockwood Kipling reflected Lahore opinion when he told Edith Plowden, 'If Lord Dufferin had not come, I think poor Anglo-India would have gone crazy with vexation and apprehension, but we have no end of confidence in the new man.'[2]

Out in the field it was a different story: the Amir and his 800-strong bodyguard cum household were making painfully slow progress from Kabul and the Viceroy had been left kicking his heels in Rawalpindi, the venue for the durbar. As a frozen Rudyard looked through the mist towards the rugged jaws of the Khyber Pass two miles away and strained to make out if the Amir was among the ant-like line of 'camels, yaboos, coolies and loud-voiced donkeys'[3] in view, he felt depressed and, at times, frightened. When, showing his usual curiosity, he ventured a few yards nearer the Pass, he was met with a volley of stones from a young boy who did not like the look of him – an incident that made such a lasting and unpleasant impression on him that, half a century later in his autobiography, he erroneously remembered having been shot at.[4]

The far north-west had none of the familiar routine of even Lahore, as Rudyard had discovered two days earlier when he ventured out into the muddy streets of nearby Peshawar where, with his junior-reporter status, he was billeted in a down-at-heel guest-house, with a motley assortment of second-raters, whom he later detailed with some distaste – 'a dentist, a photographer who had been to Nepal, an American from San Francisco, a British officer recruiting for a native regiment, and a nondescript who got piously drunk at sundown, and in that condition wept bitterly'.[5] Everything seemed to be going wrong: his hat had been destroyed, after being cut to pieces by three-inch-long hailstones, and 'then the Khansamah's [butler's] horse came into my bedroom and wanted to sleep with me'.

As he reported in his colour piece for the *CMG*, he found Peshawar chilling and alien. With none of Lahore's familiar landmarks, nor the Club as a retreat at the end of the day, this frontier town seemed like the Inferno – 'unlovely even beneath dark sunshine, and when set off with heavy slime under foot, dark skies, and rolling thunder overhead, and driving scotch mist, everywhere repellent to every sense'.[6] Amid the din and congestion of the bazaar, the local people – Pathans and Afghanis, camel drivers and ghee salesmen – were a human menagerie; their 'faces of dogs, swine, weazles and goats, all the more hideous for being set on human bodies, and lighted with human intelligence'. If he or any other Englishman passed, these 'magnificent scoundrels and handsome ruffians ... will turn to scowl upon him, and in many cases to spit fluently on the ground after he had passed'. Returning to his dak bungalow that night – he did not put this in his *CMG* piece – his nerve was further tested when, forgetting there was a curfew, he failed to answer a challenge from a native night patrol and was terrified when its two members raised their carbines at him. 'The little incident was over in a flash but it seemed to last for hours and hours, and by the time the night patrol had passed I felt that I had been through Austerlitz, Marengo, Waterloo, Maiwand and *all* the glacis of St Privat. Yah!' he wrote nearly three years later. 'It makes me sweat now when I think of it.'[7]

For his *CMG* readers he needed a more uplifting conclusion. So he suggested these frontier savages were at least prevented from cutting one another's throats by the presence of British-trained police and from contracting far worse diseases by the government's foresight in building 'the magnificent drain and water main which run through the main streets'.[8] France might have brought cafés and Russia firmer authority, but only England could have kept Peshawar 'reservoired, watered, drained and policed in the face of all opposition'.

Here, then, was one solution to the issues that had troubled Rudyard since he first started probing Lahore's mysterious underbelly: what India needed, what Britain could give, what might provide meaning to the chaos that sometimes threatened to engulf him, was a sense of municipal orderliness. If this essential insight seems trite, it was in keeping with the mid-Victorian spirit of utilitarianism, which was at the root of the 'Punjab style' of administration. And it was reinforced in a different way the following week when, after sloshing around in the mud of Peshawar, Rudyard found himself in a much brighter Rawalpindi, standing on the parade ground of the King's Dragoon Guards, about a mile from the city's main fort.

The Amir and his cohorts of wild, unshaven Afghanis had now completed their tortuous journey from Kabul and were ready to experience the full pomp of the British Empire. For the major formal event, a march-past of massed regiments on Easter Monday, the Amir was dressed in the traditional Afghan gown of duffel grey, 'with a gold embroidered black belt, long boots and the Tartar cap of grey Astrakhan fur'.[9] Sitting beside him, taking the salute, was the Viceroy, looking less ornate, in a plain uniform with a single star to his breast. Before the ceremony, Rudyard noticed in the distance the 33rd Regiment preparing itself below the Fort. As they made their way forward, its soldiers initially appeared as 'little red specks, which shuffle and agglomerate themselves, until they finally assume the shape of two red bars, and moving on, are lost to view behind the trees of the Jhelum road'. Eventually, keeping time to one of several bands, the 33rd reached the platform where the two potentates were seated. Behind them followed a relentless line of battle-scarred soldiery: the Royal Irish (admired as 'a strong regiment in every respect' by Rudyard); a variety of swaggering British and native units, from the Highland Light Infantry to the 4th and 5th Gurkhas; and, finally, the cavalry and artillery.

Mesmerised by the colour and synchronisation of 'an infinity of booted feet coming down and taking up, with the exactness of a machine', Rudyard titillated his Bank Holiday readers with another gush of imperial nostalgia.

Even an Englishman, accustomed as he is to talk of the degeneracy of our armed forces in these days, has, for once, to let such idle cavilling be, and content himself with wonder, pure and simple, at the harvest of the dragon's teeth, which we garner within our borders. Dublin and the Deccan, Paisley and the Punjab, Nepal and Lancashire, one might continue the antitheses indefinitely, have all contributed to the crop of armed men ready for war, and it may be that the grey clad figure in the fur cap is reading, marking and inwardly digesting the lesson.[10]

Rudyard's upbeat martial mood may have owed something to the presence of no less than seventeen old boys of the United Services College in and around Rawalpindi. ('We met and drank some drinks,' he later nonchalantly stated.[11]) Other friends there included Harry Rivett-Carnac who was temporarily ADC to Sir Donald Stewart, the Commander-in-Chief of the Indian Army, and who doubtless introduced Rudyard to his brother-in-law Mortimer Durand. During a lull in proceedings, Durand was appointed Dufferin's Foreign Secretary at what – for India – was the youthful age of thirty-five. Unfortunately for Rudyard, these contacts failed to provide him with immediate news when, even while the Amir was in Rawalpindi, the Russians took over the disputed town of Pandjeh, close to the eastern Afghani city of Herāt. (Rudyard later claimed Donald Mackenzie Wallace, Dufferin's Private Secretary, kept him 'dancing on the mat for half a day refusing me news'.[12]) As a result, full-scale war between Britain and Russia loomed for much of 1885. In the event, the show of pomp and arms at the durbar did its trick. The Amir ('a sensual brutal savage – a sort of Afghan Henry the VIIIth',[13] recalled Durand) stuck by his British alliance and the Russians realised they had to back off. Before long, wiser counsels prevailed and the immediate crisis was averted.

The parade stayed in Rudyard's mind too. It had given him an insight into another 'grown-up' truth – the link between the flash of steel and the success of Empire. Nearly a decade later he used it as the backdrop for a story in *The Jungle Books*. When, in 'Servants of the Queen', an old Central Asian chieftain marvels at the orderliness of the animals in the march-past, a native officer informs him that this comes from having an effective chain of command and the Amir might well learn something by starting to obey the Viceroy.

All in all, a chastened and weary young reporter returned to Lahore in the middle of the second week of April. The realities of frontier life had been rather more than he bargained for. And they left him with renewed respect not only for the soldiers who kept the Queen's peace, but also the large numbers of anonymous administrators who lived out their lives in distant parts of India, away from the comforts and diversions of metropolitan existence.

One reason he might have been stoned during his fleeting visit to the Khyber Pass was that he was wearing tribal dress. He had adopted this all-enveloping garb because it hid his 'Lahore sore' – an unsightly red blemish on his cheek that he originally thought was an ant-bite. It had not responded to his doctor's prescription of cocaine in February, and with good reason. Now known as Leishmania, this affliction comes from a parasite transmitted by sandflies. Common to dry, dusty areas, it is easily curable. But in the 1880s no treatment was available and its effects could be embarrassing.

Back in Lahore, Rudyard's paper decided to spare him the discomfort of the fast approaching summer. He had acquitted himself well on the North-West Frontier and perhaps his facial lesion suggested he needed a rest-cure. So the *CMG* decided to send him to Simla as its correspondent for the entire four-month-long season. This was a make-or-break appointment: the hill station could be either a journalistic graveyard or an opportunity for an ambitious reporter to shine.

The new Viceroy Lord Dufferin had yet to show his hand but, if recent trends were anything to go by, Simla was set to play an increasingly important role in the machinery of government. Since 1879 it had been the base for the Army's influential Intelligence Department run by Major-General Sir Charles Mac-Gregor. A select group of multilingual army officers fanned out from there and travelled into the countries surrounding India's borders, seeking information on Russian troop movements. Only the previous year MacGregor had published a confidential handbook, *The Defence of India*, which had been so specific about Russian intentions against the sub-continent (and the need for greater military preparedness) that the Gladstone government had taken fright and suppressed it. The *Pioneer*'s Howard Hensman had drawn on MacGregor's knowledge in writing his history, *The Afghan War*, and had subsequently made a journalistic name for himself on the basis of his despatches from the summer capital, where he had been a confidant of Lord Ripon and General Roberts, the newly appointed Commander-in-Chief of the Indian Army.

The *CMG* owners no doubt had their own reasons for wanting a good correspondent in Simla. They were the equivalent to what today would be called a town Mafia (an eminently respectable Mafia, of course). James Walker had been appointed President of Simla Municipality the previous year, taking over from Horace Goad – like himself a former police officer – who was also a director of Walker's Alliance Bank. The Goad family was Simla's biggest landlord – owning some thirty-three houses (at one recent count) with a rent roll of 38,000 rupees (£2857) a month. George Allen was not so directly involved but, with his business interests dependent on continued army manoeuvres, he was particularly aware of the town's importance for intelligence (both commercial and political) and deal making. So considerable thought had gone into Rudyard's appointment. As a journalist he would inform

CMG readers of important government decisions, while taking them behind the scenes at the parties, dinners and amateur theatricals that were essential ingredients of life in the summer capital. At the same time, he would have a public relations role – part court jester and part promoter of the *CMG* syndicate's political and business interests. Perhaps James Walker was taking a gamble, but he was confident it would work.

Having just celebrated his nineteenth birthday, Rudyard took his forthcoming duties seriously. Faced with the prospect of regular balls in Simla, he felt he should at least know how to waltz properly. Although he had previously always claimed to dislike dancing, he now immersed himself in lessons. His father noted graphically how Rudyard's 'grievous blotch on his cheek, appearing and disappearing as he revolves, like the red bull's eye of a light house, worries him sorely and keeps him humble'.[14] The young writer was helped in his efforts at self-improvement by Trix who was not only a fine dancer but also a head-turning beauty. Lockwood realised that she had 'a radiant merry look about her', but he did not understand the sexual innuendo of the elderly General Murray's repeated comment to Alice, 'But she's very bonny, your daughter.'

The route to Simla would soon become familiar. Rudyard first took the train to Umballa which, with good imperial sense, was both an important railway junction and a military garrison. There, he hired a two-horse tonga for the journey up into the hills. He followed 'the wandering road, climbing, dipping, and sweeping about the growing spurs' until, about five miles beyond Kalka, the atmosphere began to change and he could feel the cool, bracing air from the snow-peaked mountains above. As in the story 'Garm – A Hostage', 'Now and then we would meet a man we knew going down to his work again, and he would say, "What's it like below?" and I would shout "Hotter than cinders. What's it like up above?" and he would shout back: "Just perfect!" '

Approaching Simla from below, the town fitted Lord Dufferin's description as 'an absurd place ... hanging by its eyelids to the side of the hill'. It looked like the corner of a bizarre university city, set in a Surbiton transported to Switzerland. Mock-Tudor public buildings straddled a narrow street (inevitably known as The Mall), leading up to a Bombay-Gothic Anglican church and then, through the deodars (a Himalayan variety of cedar tree), to the heights of Mount Jackko above. Dotted around the hillside were pockets of Swiss chalet-style villas, including the Viceroy's Peterhof and the Commander-in-Chief's Snowdon. And then there was the other Simla: the 'crowded rabbit warren', perched higgledy-piggledy beneath The Mall, where the native population lived and loved, and where, as Rudyard was bound to notice, courtesans discussed 'the things which are supposed to be the profoundest secrets of the Indian Council'.

First used as his summer headquarters by the Governor-General Lord William Bentinck in 1829, Simla had once been the home of the beautiful Irish-born Marie Gilbert, who was celebrated as the exotic dancer Lola Montez on the London stage in the 1840s. It came into its own as India's most fashionable resort two decades later, after the Viceroy, Sir John Lawrence, chose it as his summer capital. He needed somewhere large enough to accommodate the various offices of state. But in the wake of the Mutiny his camp followers were happy simply to find a town which offered some peace and quiet. For every visitor who liked Simla, such as the civil servant Walter Lawrence (no relation to the Viceroy),[15] who called it the 'brightest, wittiest, most refined community I ever knew', there were detractors like the artist Val Prinsep who, after passing through in 1877, commented disapprovingly, 'Simla is like an English watering place gone mad ... Real sociability does not exist. People pair off immediately they arrive at a party ...'[16] Rudyard's own attitude was summed up in his later comment to a friend: 'Simla's a queer place – isn't it?'[17]

Having reached Simla in late April, before the general influx of holiday-makers, Rudyard found little to do. So, after suffering a mild attack of dysentery, he decided to convalesce on a trek in the Himalayas. For his travelling partners on the Tibet road he latched on to a low-level railway engineer, Stanley De Brath, and his wife. With Rudyard riding a temperamental pony, general progress was slow; on the first day, having taken five hours to cover eight and a half miles, he felt as if 'hot irons were stuck down my marrow bones'.[18] As they traversed breath-taking 10,000-feet-high passes, he began to find the engineer's undemanding company strangely relaxing. On Day Six, dropping down to 3000 feet and a sunny poppy-filled valley, they rented a house in the village of Kotgarh where Rudyard was fascinated with the beauty of the women. He was not particularly surprised to learn that the local clergyman – 'one of the queerest little devils ever cast away forty miles from anywhere'[19] – had been accused of sexually molesting his female flock. But rather than protest against this abuse of native women, Rudyard confided naïvely to his diary, 'Should like to be Padre in these parts.'[20] (In the novel *Kim*, the exotic Woman of Shamlegh reveals that a sahib had once looked on her with favour, and that she had lived inside a mission house. It emerges that she had lived in Kotgarh and had been abandoned by her lover. 'Then I saw that the Gods of the Kerlistians lied, and I went back to my own people.' Rudyard was always careful with his source material: he also used this story as the basis for his Plain Tale 'Lispeth'.)

The curmudgeonly, exploitative side of Rudyard's nature surfaced again two days later when, on the way back to Simla, with everybody's spirits at a low ebb after more torrential rain, his ubiquitous bearer Noor Ali picked a fight with some locals who had been employed as coolies. Since one of the coolies had his eye cut, Rudyard, fearful of litigation within the jurisdiction of an unknown raja, decided to pay blood money. He later took it out on the unfortunate Noor Ali: seven hard lashes to his servant's back, which were borne 'quietly'.[21] Journeying on through the middle of a thunderstorm, he was further disquieted when he chanced upon a family of bears and decided to run. He could only 'thank heaven' when he 'got back to civilization'.[22]

Back in Simla, there was still not much happening. So Rudyard 'loafed' about, exploring the town and waiting 'like Micawber for something to turn up.'[23] In a clearing between the pine trees and deodars to the south of the town he would have discovered the Annandale sports complex, which served the community as race-course, cricket pitch, polo ground, croquet lawn or venue for any other pursuit that the more energetic Simla residents wished. (It was here that Rudyard staged his archery contest in the story 'Cupid's Arrow'.) On the High Street there was the 'Abbeyville', where the Simla Amateur Dramatic Club currently performed, and Peliti's, the continental-style café owned by Lord Lytton's former chef.

Behind its official and sociable façade, the town had a repu-tation as a place for serious spiritual enquiry. Students of the occult flocked there in search of the mysteries of the ancient East. As Rudyard wrote in the epigraph to his story, 'Consequences': 'Rosicrucian subtleties / In the Orient had rise; / Ye may find their teachers still / Under Jacâtâla's Hill.' These seekers after enlightenment ranged from the sadhus and fakirs of the hills, the prototypes of the lama in *Kim*, to Westerners like the enigmatic A. M. Jacob, who owned a jewellery and curio shop on The Mall (nobody is sure quite where) and who featured later as Lurgan Sahib in that same book. Theosophy was particularly fashionable in Simla at that moment, having enjoyed the patronage of two local inhabitants, Alfred Sinnett, editor of the *Pioneer* (until he was dismissed in 1883) and Allan Octavian (A. O.) Hume, an influential former civil servant. It had received a fillip in 1880 with the visit of its colourful leader Madame Blavatsky, who claimed to have travelled to Tibet and been initiated into the Hidden Brotherhood of Himalayan Masters. After attending one of her seances, Lockwood Kipling pronounced her 'one of the most interesting and unscrupulous impostors'[24] he had ever met. Rudyard observed and took note.

Slowly, as the town came to life, Rudyard began to produce for the *CMG*. In his desultory Simla Notes of 12 May, he applauded the fall of Gladstone's Liberal government and welcomed its replacement by Lord Salisbury's Conservatives. Gladstone's vacillation was widely believed to have encouraged the Russians to march into Pandjeh; now Salisbury was expected to take a tougher line – even to the point of declaring war on the Russians. In the circumstances some instruction in civil defence was appropriate. But Rudyard's report of a Home Guard-style lecture on weaponry at Simla's United Service Institute disappointingly lacked the satirical bite of his later recollection (in *Stalky & Co.*) of the tub-thumping MP's visit to Westward Ho!. It was memorable only for the lecturer's reference to a revolver as a 'type of armed civilization with a life in each chamber'.

While the state of Anglo-Russian relations remained uncertain, the Simla season officially started with a ball at Government House on Queen's Day, 25 May. Feeling like 'an abject worm', Rudyard was forced to attend with the mark on his cheek still so inflamed that he had to paint it over. When his mother and Trix travelled up from Lahore to join him, they all stayed at North Bank, a house owned by Sir Edward Buck, a languorous, old-fashioned civil servant (a 'vague clever creature' Trix called him) who had befriended Lockwood Kipling when he was Secretary of the government's Revenue and Agriculture Department (which nominally dealt with the promotion of 'art manufactures') and who had now carved out a useful niche for himself in Simla as Secretary to the Viceroy's Council.

When Lockwood arrived in August, he was occupied with the job of overseeing the refurbishment of the official residence of Sir Charles Aitchison, Governor of the Punjab. Unfortunately, his coming posed a problem over accommodation; North Bank was too small for the whole family, especially since Rudyard insisted on having his own office. So the younger Kipling went to stay at Kelvin Grove again with his influential friends the Walkers. Their house was full of people and Rudyard had 'a madcap sort of a time'.[25] Horace Goad was in and out with his 'blear-eyed, evil-visaged pendulous lipped bulldogs', who met their match in the fearless shape of the Walkers' nine-month-old nephew, Erik Hogan, who was staying with his parents and who captivated

Rudyard – to the extent of becoming the subject of one of the earliest of his sentimental pieces about children, 'His Excellency (by One of his Sincerest Admirers)'. A local doctor, 'Banjoe' Hayes, and his wife were also guests: 'Wish they wouldn't put married couple next door to me with one ½ plank between,' complained Rudyard about these rooming arrangements. 'Saps one's morality.'[26]

Despite his dancing lessons, Rudyard soon bored of the daily round of concerts, parties and balls. As he told his Aunt Edith, 'The best way to sicken a youth of frivolity is to pitch him neck and crop into the thick of it on the understanding that he is to write descriptive matter about each dance, frivol etc. . . . As it is, it is the dullest of dull things to be *chroniqueur* of a Gay Season in the hills.'[27]

He kept himself amused by observing the different ways in which his mother and sister coped with sexual attention. Witty, attractive and still flirtatious given the chance, Alice conformed to the Simla norm by surrounding herself with men young enough to be her sons. No less pretty, Trix was more shy and exuded a *froideur* that frightened off suitors of her own age (who called her The Ice Maiden) but brought a host of admirers aged fifty or more. Rudyard turned this into an entertaining poem, 'My Rival', which had Trix, a gauche seventeen, speculating about her forty-nine-year-old mother's sex appeal.

Away from these distractions, Rudyard turned his mind again to his non-journalistic writing. *Echoes*, the book he had written with Trix the previous year, had been well received: it had even been reviewed in *The World*, the London newspaper edited by Alice Kipling's old friend Edmund Yates that had published his schoolboy poem in 1882. *The World* had particularly welcomed his 'Nursery Rhymes for Little Anglo-Indians', with their cynical *bons mots* about the sort of people Rudyard was now meeting in Simla – such as the woman who left her husband on the plains and made for the hills:

> I dragged my little husband's name
> Through heaps of social mire,
> And joined him in October,
> As good as you'd desire.

As a result of the book's success in India, Thacker Spink and Company, a leading book publisher in Calcutta, offered to produce a second edition. But relations soured after Rudyard thought their estimates too high and, uncharacteristically, appended some abusive caricatures to a letter to the publisher. One reason for his high-handedness was that the *CMG* had just invested £5000 in new printing machinery and Chalmers, the Scottish foreman at the works, assured him that his own employers could do the job as expertly as a firm of specialist publishers in Calcutta. However Plan B seems to have been over-ambitious, for no second edition of *Echoes* appeared.

Rudyard had specifically been granted permission to write for other papers while in Simla. Many of his new verses were cast in the world-weary style of the 'Nursery Rhymes' that *The World* had commended. In a series of so-called 'Bungalow Ballads', produced intermittently for the *Pioneer* (rather than the *CMG*), Rudyard mocked gently at the hapless civil servants and army officers who surrounded him in Simla – men like the 'pretty and pink' Rattleton Traplegh who was addicted to flirting with a Mrs Saphira Wallabie Smith. Unfortunately for him, Mrs Smith's servants wore the same blue uniforms as those of an older Simla matron called Mrs Canterby. When, one night, young Traplegh came across a closed rickshaw being carried by men in blue, he immediately thought it was Mrs Smith's, jumped in and 'whispered stuff ... he "hadn't orter" '. Since the two women loathed each other, a scandal was only averted by Traplegh leaving town.[28]

Two of the six 'Bungalow Ballads' were to appear the following year in Rudyard's collection *Departmental Ditties*, which also included 'Possibilities',[29] his wry observation on the fleetingness of life, even in the most privileged circles, in India:

Ay, lay him 'neath the Simla pine –
A fortnight fully to be missed,
Behold, we lose our fourth at whist,
A chair is vacant where we dine.

If Rudyard's poems had a lilting musical beat, this was because he often conceived them as melodies and sang as he wrote. He himself noted how this tendency was enhanced in India, where Europeans had a tradition of verse-making which stretched back to the young factors and writers in the early days of the East India Company and which was perpetuated in the assortment of tuneful stanzas published in Indian papers under pseudonyms like 'Latakia' and 'Cigarettes'. Often, at the office, Rudyard would knock off a poem, in response to some piece of news on the wires. One of his editors, Kay Robinson, recalled how he would think for a moment and then say, ' "I have it. How would this do? Rum tiddy um ti tum ti tum, Tra la la ti tum ti tum" or words to that effect, hummed in notes that suggested a solo on a bugle.' Robinson never had to worry about delivery. He simply held open the requisite space in the paper and within twenty minutes Rudyard returned with his completed verse. He would hand it to Rukn-Din, the daytime foreman, who said, 'Your potery very good, sir; just coming proper length today. You giving more soon?'[30]

By exploring the foibles of Anglo-Indians in their summer retreat, Rudyard had struck a rich seam of material. In this respect the 'Bungalow Ballads' also anticipated his *Plain Tales from the Hills*: for example, the theme of his 'Rattleton Traplegh' poem was later echoed in 'False Dawn', his *Plain Tale* about mistaken identity in a sandstorm.[31]

As he settled into his third season in the hills, Rudyard was finding his stride as a writer, rather than a mere journalist. From time to time he toyed with his novel, *Mother Maturin*. He also worked on two stories that are illuminating about his state of mind. He later described both 'The Phantom 'Rickshaw' and 'The Strange Ride of Morrowbie Jukes', slightly cagily, as ghost stories.

But they were considerably more than that: following from the precocious 'The Dream of Duncan Parrenness', they were brilliant meditations on the dilemma of someone such as himself, who is struggling to balance being both a colonialist and an artist eager for the truth of India.

Indeed, his epigraph to 'The Phantom 'Rickshaw' referred directly back to this earlier story: 'May no ill dreams disturb my rest, / Nor Powers of Darkness me molest,' it quoted, from the hymn 'Glory to Thee, my God, this night'. Rudyard often used a few lines of verse in this way to provide enigmatic clues to the provenance and meaning of his stories. In 'The Phantom 'Rickshaw', a semi-delirious civil servant called Pansay (Rudyard seemed to be anticipating the sense of weakness and effeminacy) tells of his holiday romance with a Mrs Wessington on a liner returning to India. He soon abandons her for his fiancée, Kitty Mannering, in Simla. But the older woman does not forget him – even after, it eerily transpires, she has died. For, soon after her demise (the result of a broken heart, the reader is led to believe), Pansay sees her rickshaw, pulled by four servants in her livery and, from it, she hails him. When several similar incidents occur he begins to doubt his sanity. A Simla doctor tries to cure him, saying, 'You've too much conceited Brain, too little Stomach, and thoroughly unhealthy Eyes. Get your Stomach straight and the rest follows.' But Pansay does not improve, the ghostly rickshaw reappears and eventually he makes such a fool of himself that his prospective bride cancels their wedding.

Before being framed with a trademark Kipling introduction, this story started with the bald statement, 'My doctor tells me that I need rest and a change of air.' This clearly referred to Rudyard's physical and mental condition when he went to Simla – and helps explain why he was there for so long. The doctor in the tale might have been talking specifically of Rudyard in his diagnosis of Pansay as suffering from a combination of over-agitated brain, poor eyesight and knotted stomach. Rudyard's digestive system was to be constant irritation throughout his life.

But what was causing this psychosomatic condition? The story points to two areas of particular anxiety. Pansay's hallucinations parallel Rudyard's continuing thoughts about Flo Garrard. A few months later, in November, he was still asking his cousin Margaret to check up on Flo's progress at the Slade School. 'I only want to know if the girl looks well and – so far as your eyes can judge – happy.'[32] At the same time, Rudyard functioned like Pansay who, reacting to his ghosts, overcompensated and worked too hard – a lifestyle that, according to the narrator, 'started his illness, kept it alight, and killed him off, poor devil'. In other words, he cracked, which is exactly the image Rudyard uses: 'There was a crack in Pansay's head and a little bit of the Dark World came through and pressed him to death.'

The notion that Rudyard was revealing something about himself gains credence when 'The Phantom 'Rickshaw' is considered in tandem with 'The Strange Ride of Morrowbie Jukes'. He had actually written much of the latter story at the start of the year in Lahore. The eponymous hero is an engineer working in a desolate part of the Punjab – a hundred miles south-west of Lahore on the Sutlej river. While out riding, his horse slips and he falls down a slope into a horseshoe-shaped crater with walls of shifting sands, from which there is no escape. He finds himself in a curious netherworld of aggressive Indians who, for one reason or another, did not die on their ghats as intended. He even knows one of them, Gunga Dass, who used to be obsequious and helpful, but now is demanding and rude. Showing the influence of Edgar Allan Poe, another of Rudyard's favourite American authors, the story tells of Jukes's terrors as he contemplates this nightmare. Being an engineer, 'with a head for plans and distances and things of that kind', he tries to use his expertise to calculate the angle of the slope, in the same way that some previous incumbent had used his gun barrel to help him measure his way across a quicksand. But Western scientific knowledge proves useless; the lunatics have taken over the asylum. When the Indians eat his horse, they claim this is reasonable because they are now a Republic and, aping the utilitarianism of their colonial masters, they are providing 'greatest good of greatest number'. Jukes sees he is in 'a Republic of wild beasts penned at the bottom of a pit, to eat and fight and sleep till we died'. He is saved by his faithful servant (a familiar figure in Rudyard's work) who has tracked his master's horse to this desolate point.

Introducing this *deus ex machina* is an unsatisfactory device because it detracts from the point of 'The Strange Ride', which is a parable of Rudyard's (and the Anglo-Indian's) creeping paranoia in the face of an Indian population beginning to mouth home-grown British political slogans and aspire to democracy. While such feelings were common among expatriates, his articulation of them suggests his own devils were playing up. The effects of heat, lovesickness and niggling concerns about his health were combining with occasional opiates to exacerbate Rudyard's insecurities about India's political future.

Simla was an appropriate place for these fantasies, since the Walkers' neighbour, Madame Blavatsky's lieutenant Allan Octavian Hume, was, even then, finalising plans for the inaugural meeting of the Indian National Congress in December 1885. Something of Simla's ersatz spirituality has worked its way into the fabric of these 'ghost stories'. This was a town which, along with its lamas and theosophists, specialised in manifestations of the occult. In August, Rudyard's poem 'A Tale of Yesterday's Ten Thousand Years' told of

> One Hakim Khan, astrologer, nati-
> vity, and fortune-teller, came to my
> Hotel with leaden dice; and broke my peace
> With prophecies of Marriage and Decease
> And Wealth and Wisdom – all for five rupees ...

Even the most genteel Anglo-Indian ladies dabbled in fashionable 'psychic research' – among them Alice Kipling, with her Celtic gifts of second sight. It was no coincidence that Alice's influence on Rudyard was at its height this summer. He told his cousin Margaret in September that playing polo was the only vice he hid from his mother and 'the only thing outside office work that she hasn't the fullest authority in and uses it, bless her'[33] – a half-truth, in fact, in the light of his dabbling with opium. Unfortunately, Trix was too suggestible for the Simla spoon-benders: as Rudyard was to admit, Trix's later mental instability resulted from her meddling with the occult – 'on the road to Endor' – around this time.

The more sceptical Rudyard himself took this esoteric piffle in his stride. Although his writings tell of his other anxieties, one would not have known it from his demeanour when he returned to Lahore at the end of August. Affecting an air of general ennui in his 'Carmen Simlaensa', he complained:

> I've danced till my shoes are outworn
> From ten till the hours called small;
> I've cantered with Beauty at morn –
> And even made love at the ball …
> Lord! What was the good of it all?[34]

Luckily, as he had struggled to understand his position in India, his art had advanced significantly. And his four months in the hills cleared up his skin complaint.

Back 'on station' in Lahore, Rudyard soon reverted to 'bad' old habits. On 1 October his friend Y. L. French had just come down from the hills and wanted some action. 'Dug up a couple of opium dens in the city,' Rudyard's diary recorded. 'Queer night altogether. Suddhu is his name.' The links between Rudyard's personal life and his writing were unusually clear when 'Section 420, I.P.C.' was published in the *CMG*. This title, a reference to that part of the Indian Penal Code which forbids the obtaining of money by false pretences, was changed when the story was later republished in book form as 'In the House of Suddhoo'. It tells of an old man, Suddhoo, who owns a seedy lodging house near the west gate of the Old City. His tenants comprise a couple of Kashmiri-born prostitutes and an astute seal-cutter who devises an elaborate but bogus magical ceremony to keep his credulous landlord informed about the fate of his son who is badly ill from pleurisy in Peshawar. The seal-cutter takes money from Suddhoo for providing the latest medical reports and more again for summoning the right spirits to ensure that the boy's parlous state of health improves. Since these bulletins from the astral plane are invariably correct, Suddhoo only becomes more impressed and more gullible. What he does not know is that, before their mumbo-jumbo ceremonies, the seal-cutter has gone to the trouble of getting up-to-date information on the young man's condition by telegram. While Rudyard's experiences in the opium dens with French were probably different, he was able to turn them into a neat tale – with the ironic twist that the Indian seal-cutter called on the latest Western technology to perpetrate his fraud. In his fiction, at least, Rudyard could envisage the old and the new happily coexisting.

Along with opium, Rudyard was exploring the use of another common Indian drug, hashish. This is the evidence of his poem 'The Vision of Hamid Ali', published by the *Calcutta Review* that same month of October 1885. Set in a brothel within earshot of the muezzins of the Mosque of Wazir Khan, it tells of Hamid Ali who, after 'Drinking the ganja, drowsy with its fumes / Above the dying chillam', breaks into an airy Coleridge-style fantasy about the overthrow of all the world's religions, including Christianity and his own Islam. Although he is much troubled by this reverie, his friends tell him it is only 'an idle dream'. The Pearl, the courtesan, reassures him sensuously, 'I dreamt no dream but ye. My breasts are real; / My lips, my love, O Hamid! Nothing else ...' Rudyard, as the story-teller, is enthralled not only by the powerful effect of this drug-induced dream but also by its origins. Was it the ganja that caused Hamid Ali to blaspheme in this way? Rudyard leaves the question open, but the manner in which he poses it suggests he was not simply a disinterested observer of hashish users, but wanted an answer to an epistemological problem that concerned him personally.

More conventionally, he was putting the finishing touches to his two stories, 'The Phantom 'Rickshaw' and 'The Strange Ride of Morrowbie Jukes', so that they would be ready, along with material from his father, mother and sister, for inclusion in *Quartette*, a 125-page supplement to be published by the *CMG* at Christmas. Rudyard needed all his skills at handling Indian workers to ensure that the publication came out on time. When Ram Dass, the Hindu head printer, told him that the 19 December deadline could not be met, Rudyard encouraged a spirit of religious rivalry, telling him how his Moslem colleagues would have risen to the occasion. On the night of production, Ram Dass needed a tot of brandy before being fired into action, while the men running the presses would only put in the requisite overtime after Rudyard promised to supply tobacco for their hookahs and allow them to smoke in the press hall in half-hour shifts. (An English shilling bought twelve pounds weight of their favourite tobacco mixture.) They made an eerie sight in the candle-light – 'full of bobbing shadows and reflections; the mob of white and red and green turbans tossing round the raised platform in the centre of the room'.[35]

Since the type was worn out, Rudyard employed a trick he had learnt when producing the *Chronicle* at Westward Ho!: he would 'pack the lay' with gum and bits of paper so as to ensure as even a surface as possible. After further cajolery, bribery and a lot of hard work, the edition was completed around five o'clock in the morning. Chalmers, the foreman, told Rudyard as he left, 'Seein' the stupeedity o' these men an' conseederin' the material at our deesposal, I may say, Mister Kipling, that we have done vara weel.' Rudyard's proprietors agreed and increased his 'screw' or salary to £500 per year. As a mark of their approval, the Walkers invited him to join them in Agra, home of the Taj Mahal, over Christmas, but the wretched Stephen Wheeler said the young man could not be spared.

Amid whoops of joy that the *Bombay Gazette* had compared his 'Morrowbie Jukes' to the work of Wilkie Collins, Rudyard later recounted this workroom tale to his cousin Margaret as the latest detail in a fascinating debate they had been conducting by letter during the autumn on the fraught subject of British rule in India.[36] When she expressed pious sentiments about the advancement of the natives, he told her that it was not a matter – as Crom Price fondly believed – of taking liberal enabling measures, such as allowing Indians to work abroad. India's problems were much more basic: 'What I mean is that the population out here die from purely preventible causes, are starved from purely preventible causes, are in native states hideously misgoverned from their rulers' own folly and so on.'[37]

Indian culture suffered from a basic inertia that prevented it from tackling these issues, Rudyard argued. So it was left to his real heroes – British men working in the field as doctors, engineers and administrators – to show what could be done through practical, replicable measures, such as constructing small dams to stave off drought. As a journalist, he himself even had a small part to play. 'People won't stir quickly for abstracts of reports. Go down and look at the place yourself and write all you know on the running pen. Serve hot and something is sure to come of it.'

When Margaret was sceptical about the motives of these colonialists and enquired if they really had Indians' welfare at heart, Rudyard was offended. 'Oh Wop! If you had met some of the men I know, you would cross out that sentence and weep. What else are we working in the country for? For what else do the best men of the Commission die from overwork, and disease, if not to keep the people alive in the first place and healthy in the second?'

And when, as an aside, she told him about the effete men now to be found about London, who hid their 'nobler selves' behind the 'neat ease of mockery and disrespect', Rudyard, showing the first signs of a lifelong revulsion to this type, became vituperative. He blathered that this sort of 'moral prevarication' came from idleness and was not to be found in India where, presumably picking up on the *double entendre* exploited by Oscar Wilde, he said, ' "Earnestness" ... means an infinite capacity for boring the other man with details of your own work or driving the government wild with appeals for more money for your district.' And he urged her to tell her friends that God does exist. 'You see him work out here which in your fenced in, railway ticket, kind of life at home you can't well do. Better still send some of the boys out here to catch murderers, or run canals, or make railways. It would tan 'em and clean their rotten little brains a little. My faith! How angry have I grown over naught.'[38]

Calming down slightly, Rudyard claimed that the way to deal with Indians was to understand their culture and idioms: they were 'men with a language of their own which it is your business to understand; and proverbs, which it is your business to quote (this is a land of proverbs) and bywords and allusions which it is your business to master; and feelings which it is your business to enter into and sympathize with. Then they'll believe in you and do things for you, and let you do things for them.' At the same time, though, Indians were incapable of acting autonomously, they always needed a sahib figure to direct them, and if the English ever left the country it would dissolve within six months into 'one big cock pit of conflicting princelets'. Indians were 'a queer people indeed. Touchy as children; obstinate as men; patient as the High Gods themselves; vicious as Devils but always lovable if you know how to take 'em.'

At the end of the day, he admitted the British in India had very little in common with their subjects.

And faith if you knew in what inconceivable filth of mind the peoples of India were brought up from their cradle; if you realized the views – or one tenth of the views – they hold about women and their absolute incapacity for speaking the truth as we understand it – the immeasurable gulf that lies between the two races in all things you would see how it comes to pass that the Englishman is prone to despise the natives – (I must use that misleading term for brevity's sake) – and how, except in the matter of trade, they have little or nothing in common with him.

Outside the civil lines lay 'the dark and crooked and fantastic, and wicked, and awe inspiring life of the "native" ' which British rule could only put a fence round and prevent from being disturbed. He hoped to penetrate this mysterious world in his novel *Mother Maturin*, but admitted, 'My experiences of course are only a queer jumble of opium-dens, night houses, night strolls with natives; evenings spent in their company in their own homes (in the men's quarter of course) and the long yarns that my native friends spin me.'[39]

For all their odd inconsistencies, Rudyard's politics were not very different from the 'gas and sewerage' Benthamism he had expounded to Mrs Tavernor Perry three years earlier. As he had quickly discovered, this basic utilitarianism, underpinned with a moral imperative, lay behind many British initiatives in India. It provided a justification for much of his own journalism, such as his attacks on the Lahore Municipality for the filthy state of its drains. (As he told his old schoolmaster, W. C. Crofts: 'Drains are a great and glorious thing and I study 'em and write about 'em when I can.'[40]) And it allowed him to campaign strongly against the Hindu custom of child marriage – his 'pet subject', he told Crofts – since it led to early widowhood and then (in seventy-five per cent of cases, he claimed) to prostitution. When in January his groom asked him for a five-pound loan because his twelve-year-old son was getting married to a girl of nine, Rudyard angrily refused.[41] But, as he told his Aunt Louisa, he knew full well that nothing he said would prevent the wedding from going ahead anyway.

In admitting this, Rudyard was expressing a fundamental anxiety of the Anglo-Indian who realised that, for all his drains and bridges, certain aspects of Indian life would never change. Having thought about the reasons for this, Rudyard tended to blame the dead weight of the Hindu religion, with its rag-bag of warring and copulating gods. He was happy to show off his command of local languages by sprinkling his articles with Urdu or Hindustani phrases. He might well trade proverbs with his workers. But he had no respect for the philosophical under-pinnings of Hindu life, as was clear in his review of a translation of the Hindu epic, the *Mahabharata*. After quoting a verbose passage, Rudyard commented, 'Page upon page might be filled with extracts equally profitless ... The fantastic creations of the Hindu Mythology have as much reality in their composition and coherence in their action, as the wind-driven clouds of sunset.' Lumping the *Mahabharata* with the other national epics, the *Ramayana* and the *Rig Veda*, he concluded that 'the working world of today has no place for these ponderous records of noth-ingness'.[42] (Learning that William Morris had chosen the *Maha-bharata* as one of the world's hundred best books, Rudyard was incensed and ventured to suggest to Crom Price that his 'Uncle Topsy' simply had not read the book.)

Predictably, given the paper he worked for, Rudyard was articu-lating the opinions and prejudices of a minority community of roughly 70,000 expatriates who, for all their colonialists' author-ity, often felt ill at ease in a country of two hundred million indigenous people. Their sense of powerlessness reflected authen-tic political grievances. A series of three poems by Rudyard in December 1885 and January 1886 showed that, along with worries about Russia and the Indian National Congress, the average Anglo-Indian was concerned about his standard of living. 'Exchange' attacked the official policy of bimetallism, which linked the pound to the gold standard and the rupee to silver – to the detriment of the latter currency, which was regularly falling in value. 'The Rupaiyat of Omar Kal'vin' and 'The Quid Pro Quo' took the government to task for introducing an income tax of two per cent. The 'Rupaiyat', with its references to Edward Fitzgerald, played on the word 'rupee' and on the name of Sir Auckland Colvin, the Financial Secretary. Colvin, something of a literary man, took it in good heart, penning a reply in the *Pioneer* and telling Rudyard it was 'a joy to find that the days of wit and delicate humour are not yet dead in the land'. Rudyard may not have been aware of the close identity of interests between the *Pioneer*'s proprietor George Allen and Colvin, whose brother Walter was the leading lawyer in Allahabad. In 1884, during a lull in frontier wars, Allen's Cawnpore boot factory had sought further capitalisation and Sir Auckland had authorised a government loan of 500,000 rupees.[43]

In the circumstances, Anglo-Indians were loath to give up any powers to indigenous politicians, and devised all sorts of ways of denigrating Hindu culture and aspirations to justify their position. On cue, in November another of Rudyard's poems, 'The Indian Delegates', had mocked the behaviour of three Indian national politicians who had gone to London to explain their country's aspirations in advance of a general election in Britain. In Gilbert and Sullivan style, Rudyard showed the Indians initially making a favourable impression with their fluency and knowledge of British philosophy. But their mission failed after the Great British Public began to learn more about Indian customs and showed its disgust. The 'GBP' articulated the thoughts of Rudyard, George Allen, Lockwood Kipling and any number of Anglo-Indians when it concluded:

Urgent reforms you need – See that you get 'em.
Make *women* of your wives; don't cuff and pet 'em.
Doctor them when they're ill – they die like flies.
Reform corrupt Municipalities.
We worked our freedom out through thirty reigns –
Show your own power to manage your own drains.
Don't howl for Government when things look black.
Grow moral backbone in your moral back.
Try to speak the truth – you've years before you plenty –
And marry on the other side of twenty.[44]

Six

Wit and Sex Appeal

1886–1887

Regrouped within the family square that winter of 1885–6, the severe head prefect of two years earlier had fleshed out into a more relaxed-looking young man, with a heavy moustache and markedly cleft chin. At the age of twenty, Rudyard was never going to be taller than 5 foot 6 inches, and his weight – 8 stone 4 pounds[1] – hardly fluctuated during his adult life. 'A kind of scrubbed boy – a lawyer's clerk,' he scribbled from *The Merchant of Venice* on the back of a photograph showing him with his hair centre-parted.

Now that the Kiplings had been in Lahore for over a decade, Bikanir House was the town's nearest equivalent to an intellectual salon. As an acknowledged expert in Indian art (with his reputation only enhanced by his editorship of the *Journal of Indian Art* from 1884), Lockwood's professional advice was sought by rich collectors, two of whom were to play significant roles in Rudyard's life. From a wealthy New York background, Lockwood de Forest had teamed up with the painter Samuel Colman, the interior designer Candace Wheeler, and the glass designer Louis Comfort Tiffany in 1879 to form the Associated Artists group, whose blend of aestheticism and good craftsmanship had a similar influence on American design to William Morris in England. Encouraged by Tiffany, who had praised the Indian artefacts in the British Museum, de Forest and his wife Meta paid a prolonged visit to India in 1881–2 to investigate the sources of Indian craftsmanship. He set up the Ahmedabad Wood Carving Company to make well-designed, traditional products for the American market. His filigree friezes and teakwood furniture became sought after features in houses designed for the wealthy clients of Associated Artists (and later, when the group folded, of de Forest himself). While in India, he discovered a fellow spirit and passionate admirer of Indian design in Lockwood Kipling. He visited Bikanir House, where he observed with amusement how his host's two pet black crows would steal silver objects and hide them behind the stairs leading to the roof. He searched out material for the Lahore Museum, and, in 1883, encouraged Lockwood Kipling to write a long, authoritative article on 'Indian Art in Metal and Wood' for the New York-based *Harpers Magazine* – an initiative that acted as a useful advertisement for his own business.[2]

The Duke of Connaught was a very different creature – Queen Victoria's third son who, after leading the Guards Brigade at the Battle of Tel el Kebir in Egypt (the aftermath of which Rudyard had witnessed on his voyage out to India), had taken command of the Indian Army garrison at Meerut, north of Delhi. Lockwood Kipling was one of the first people the Duke met on his arrival in India in late 1883: the curator of the Lahore Museum was supervising the Punjab stand at a grand international exhibition in Calcutta. Lockwood was subsequently invited to Meerut to submit designs for an Indian billiard room the Duke and his wife were building at their house at Bagshot in Surrey. When the Connaughts visited Lahore in December 1884, their admiration for Lockwood was manifest in the Duchess's diary comments on the Mayo School of Industrial Art. 'Mr Kipling, a most charming, clever man, most interesting and original and most obliging, is the Principal and has done *much* for it.'[3]

Rudyard became used to the 'incessant come and go of travellers, savants, specialists etc. on their way through India who sooner or later would stay for a time in my father's house'. When the French imperialist Gustave Le Bon passed through in 1885, he jabbered 'like a Maxim articulate' about the merits of French colonialism, frequently referring to his country's '*emprise morale*'.[4]

The Kiplings introduced such visitors to their local friends, who included Flora Annie Steel, a civil servant's wife who had just published the first of her many books, a collection of Punjabi folk-tales called *Wide-Awake Stories* ('She is not pretty and a cold world might consider her plain,' Lockwood informed a friend, 'but as bright as an Afghan knife and every bit as sharp'[5]), and Dr Elizabeth Bielby, the Punjab's first woman doctor, who had recently taken up a post as Professor of Midwifery at Lahore Medical School. 'A dear, round, tubby darling,'[6] she soon became a friend of the family, as well as doctor to its female members. As a role model, she inspired Trix in a short-lived ambition to do what her brother had balked at and obtain a medical quali-fication – in her case as a nurse. For a period in early 1886 Trix attended Dr Bielby's lectures, but received little support from the brother who publicly advocated direct action by doctors and engineers. After she had made careful notes about the causes of childhood convulsions ('due to ricketts, worms or small glottis'), Rudyard jotted down his own cure, 'Regulate bowels', and added that he was 'much shocked at the contents of this Infamous Book'.[7]

Rudyard's journalistic year started with a visit to Lahore's railway workshops, whence he reported in fascinated detail (with precise Morrowbie Jukes-type measurements) about the tests on various guns deployed on an armoured train, including a five-barrelled Nordenfeldt machine-gun. Although the experts were blasé about this piece of weaponry (which used obsolete tech-nology, they said), Rudyard was amazed at its potential. 'Most impressive of all to see the weapon feeling its way foot by foot to the required range, and marking each step with a little cloud of dust a hundred yards distant; finally settling upon the target with a volley of venomous precision.'[8]

Once again he was telling his readers that India needed such exactness – the attention to detail he had witnessed in different circumstances in the regiments filing past the Amir at Rawalpindi. In his eagerness for more of that breast-swelling experience, he volunteered to report on the military expedition that had been sent to quell a rebellion in Upper Burma a couple of months earlier. But Stephen Wheeler again decided he was indispensable at the office. Rudyard was left with a romantic affection for Burma, a country he was later to visit and remember nostalgically. Hearing that a USC contemporary, Lieutenant Robert Dury, had been killed in this campaign, he wrote 'Arithmetic on the Frontier', one of the *Departmental Ditties* he published in June 1886:

> A scrimmage in a Border Station –
> A canter down some dark defile –
> Two thousand pounds of education
> Drops to a ten-rupee jezail –[9]

Prevented from following the army in Burma, he made a point of finding out about military life from other sources. In February he reviewed *From Recruit to Staff Sergeant*, an account by N.W. Bancroft, an uneducated soldier, of the Bengal Horse Artillery's role in the First Sikh War of the 1840s. He enjoyed its 'stories of camp fire jest, rough banter and practical jokes'[10] and, in his poem, 'Snarleyow', four years later, he recalled directly Bancroft's description of the wounded horse at the battle of Ferozeshah.

He also took the opportunity to get to know the soldiers on his own doorstep. He would ride over to the military cantonment at Mian Mir, where mess dinners were served on sparkling plate, with the regimental band playing between courses. There he met careless young subalterns who could 'stand up and sing "Auld Lang Syne" without a quaver'. One week this type was a callow recruit being 'broken in' (a favourite Kipling metaphor), the next he was leading punitive expeditions against dacoits in the Deccan. Rudyard encountered him at theatrical evenings in the barracks, at dances in Montgomery Hall and at the Lahore racecourse, with its adjacent polo ground. They also met at Fort Lahore, where officers from Mian Mir commanded the Infantry Detachment. Often, on his nocturnal prowls in the Old City, Rudyard dropped in to see them. As he recalled in 'Haunted Subalterns', the more sensitive young men felt the ghosts of the former Sikh ruler Ranjit Singh's wives, and found the place eerily oppressive.

He also came to know and admire the foot soldiers of the British Empire, the rank and file of his 'Mulvaney' stories. Commentators have wasted much ink discussing the origins of the 'Ould' Regiment to which his Soldiers Three – the Irishman Terence Mulvaney, the Cockney Stanley Ortheris and the Yorkshire-born Jock Learoyd – belonged. Rudyard's own testimony – in his uncollected story 'Quo Fata Vocant' – states incontrovertibly that the 'Ould' or Old Regiment was the 2nd Battalion The (Royal) Northumberland Fusiliers, 5th Foot, for whose paper, the *St George's Gazette*, this sketch was originally written.

With its complement of 1080 men, the 5th followed the East Lancashires at Mian Mir from 1885 to 1887 and was undoubtedly the regiment Rudyard knew best. He first became aware of it when he bundled a drunken squaddie into an ekka[11] near Lawrence Hall, and so helped him avoid an officer who passed a moment later on his way to play polo. (Rudyard recalled this incident precisely at the start of 'Garm – A Hostage', his story about Ortheris and his love of his dog.)

He later ventured into the sergeants' mess and the regimental canteen at Mian Mir. In his book *Sixty Years in Uniform*, John Fraser, a former colour sergeant with the 5th (the Tyneside Tail Twisters, Rudyard called them), remembered being asked by a young officer to take Rudyard to the canteen and introduce him to some of the men. His visitor was a writer who, for professional reasons, wanted to get 'into direct touch with Tommy Atkins', he was told. The sergeant took Rudyard to meet the musketry fatigue party headed by Corporal MacNamara who, he claimed, was the spitting image of Mulvaney in Rudyard's later stories.

As always, Rudyard drew on many aspects of his experience for his stories. Later, after he had moved to Allahabad in late 1887, he met another regiment, the 1st Battalion The East Surrey, 31st Foot, which added some colour to his portrayal of the Ould Regiment.

'A London recruited confederacy of skilful dog-stealers, some of them my good and loyal friends,' he called it in his autobiography. And sometimes he was simply confused, as when he suggested in *Soldiers Three* that the 'Ould' had served in Afghanistan, Burma and the North-West Frontier – something that no British regiment ever actually did.

Rudyard appreciated the humour and resolution with which the ordinary soldier endured the hardships of India, on behalf of Missis Victorier, the Widow at Windsor. They put up with appalling conditions at Mian Mir – a 'dreary, dismal cantonment', recalled one senior officer, which 'with its baking hot weather and oven-like barracks, its boiling rainy season and marrow-chilling winter, its sorry bungalows and brackish water, is still the dread of every regiment in the Bengal Presidency – with what good reason its teeming graveyards and overflowing hospitals too sadly show'.[12] But the rank and file took these adversities philosophically, only occasionally grumbling, like Mulvaney, 'Mary, Mother av Mercy, fwhat the divil possist us to take an' kape this melancholious counthry? Answer me that, sorr.'[13]

Since his profession as a journalist gave him privileged access (as he put it, the ability to 'move at will in the fourth dimension'), Rudyard took up these soldiers' complaints directly. He was incensed at the cant over the men's sexual activities. Although licensed regimental brothels existed in both Mian Mir and Lahore, where one of the first 'lock' hospitals specialising in venereal disease had been introduced in the 1860s, the official attitude to sex remained ostrich-like. Because of the influence of missionaries and pressure in England to reform the Contagious Diseases Act (one of the new moralists, W. T. Stead, the editor of the *Pall Mall Gazette*, had proved in a series of sensational articles that it was possible to purchase young girls for 'white slavery'), bazaar prostitutes were not medically inspected and the rank and file were not taught even the most basic precautions. Rudyard claimed that this failure of common sense ensured that there were 9000 'expensive white men a year always laid up from venereal disease'.

He wished that he had 600 priests, preferably bishops, to put through the arduous and disease-ridden regime of his soldier friends.

Rudyard had an additional motive for visiting Mian Mir in early 1886. He had developed a crush on Amy, the slender, dark-eyed daughter of the Reverend William Duke, the military chaplain attached to the barracks. To his family, Rudyard enthusiastically compared her looks to Emma, Lady Hamilton. To his former classics master Crofts he went further, describing her as having 'the face of an angel, the voice of a dove and the step of a fawn'.[14] Although Padre Duke was a graduate of Trinity College, Dublin, and had worked as an Anglican clergyman in several military outposts including Multan and Quetta, he and his family were not on the Lahore social circuit. So if Rudyard wanted to see Amy, he had to ride out to the cantonment and sit through her father's crashingly boring sermons. (At least, the church had the reputation of being the prettiest in the Punjab.)

The previous autumn, after a bout of fever at a time when his mother was still in Simla, Rudyard had joked to his cousin Margaret about his need to find a wife: 'I began to understand faintly why so many good men perpetrate matrimony. It's temporary insanity superinduced by intermittent fever.'[15] Rudyard had expressed a preference for an older, caring woman – 'a lady well versed in domestic knowledge, not less than twelve years my senior, and by preference, some other man's wife'. But Lockwood Kipling had not been convinced of his son's sincerity and had offered him a hundred pounds a year if he should marry. Now Lockwood had an interest in seeing if he might have to pay up: '[Rudyard] is vastly funny about it,' he told Margaret, 'and I cannot make out whether there is anything in it.' The romance did not prosper, however, even after Trix introduced Miss Duke to her brother at a *thé dansant*. After three dances, Amy was sitting on her own and Rudyard later complained to Trix about his inamorata's appalling bad breath. This was hardly the 'knowing' lover Beresford had noted. Not for the last time, Rudyard had admired a girl from afar and then rejected her as soon as he ventured close.

The need to strike a better balance between his outer and inner selves – between his professional advancement and emotional development – contributed to his decision in April to join the local Freemasons' Lodge Hope and Perseverance No.782. With its ideals of brotherhood, goodwill and charity, Masonry had played an important part in bridging social divisions, both within the British community, and between Anglo-Indians and the local people. Over the previous thirty years it had made substantial progress in the Punjab, where there were now twenty-two lodges, with nearly 600 members. Lodge Hope and Perseverance No.782, the largest of four in Lahore, was formed in 1858, the year after the Mutiny. Its spacious hall, known locally as the Jadughar or 'witchcraft' house, was built in the Anarkali area, where many Indians lived, and became the headquarters of the District Grand Lodge in 1872. Significantly, Rudyard was proposed by Colonel Oswald Menzies, Lahore's most influential police officer, with a dual role as Inspector General of Police and Under-Secretary in the Punjab government's Home Police Department.

Rudyard welcomed Masonry's ecumenicism. In his auto-biography he noted approvingly how it introduced him to 'Muslims, Hindus, Sikhs, members of the Arya and Brahmo Samaj, and a Jew Tyler, who was priest and butcher to his little community in the city. So yet another world opened to me which I needed.' The movement also provided a social network, which Rudyard particularly valued when he was travelling. Once, when visiting Jamalpur, a railway manufacturing town in Bengal, he consoled himself with the thought that, at the local Lodge, St George in the East, there were 'men who will talk to me as though they had known me all their lives on subjects which both I and they will be able to discourse about with freedom and cama-raderie'.[16] There he probably met the model for Olaf Swanson, the mail train driver who was 'Past Master of the big railway Masonic Lodge, "St Duncan's in the East"' in his didactic story 'The Bold

'Prentice'. Olaf provided another reason for being a Mason: within the Craft, Rudyard would come to know a hitherto unfamiliar body of men, the mechanics and foremen who ensured that British India ran efficiently. Through these blue-collar labourers, and the middle-class engineers and public works officials at the Club, he honed his ideas about the importance of work and duty for both the individual and the community. A specialised version of these qualities was to be found at Mian Mir. Accordingly, Rudyard used to visit the soldiers' Lodge St John the Evangelist No.1483 in the cantonment, where fellow Masons included a Surgeon Terence Mulvaney of the Army Medical Department and a Lieutenant Learoyd of the Royal Artillery. Like many authors, he appropriated these names for his work.[17]

The Craft was not just a companionable society. It served a personal need, which explains why Rudyard took his Masonic membership – unlike that of the 1st Punjab Volunteer Rifles, for example – so seriously. He never mocked the movement's rituals as he did governments or civil servants. Instead, he participated fully, helping decorate the bare walls of the Masonic Hall in Lahore, and lecturing on the 'Origin of the Craft First Degree' and 'Popular Views on Freemasonry'.[18] Within a year he had been elected Secretary of his Lodge.

The reason was that Masonry, with its ethical and metaphysical elements, provided the nearest equivalent to a coherent belief system for a young man who, for all his knowingness, was still floundering to make sense of India's mass of conflicting creeds. He himself was not religious in a formal sense (the church at Mian Mir was the first Christian place of worship he had entered since his return to India). But he was fascinated by the way religions sought to explain the more complicated issues of human existence. Until now, India had seemed a spiritual bazaar, with salesmen, from the Sufis of Lahore to the Theosophists of Simla, pushing their wares. To ground himself he needed a philosophy with an intellectually satisfying explanation of the world and its mysteries. Freemasonry provided a structure which allowed him to dart among different faiths and to address such esoteric issues as the Talmudic theory of Creation, as seen from the point of view of a Moslem potter (the subject matter of 'The Seven Nights of Creation' published in the *Calcutta Review* that April). Rudyard loved the give and take of ideas, writing happily in 'The Mother-Lodge' about how, after an evening's chatting at the Lodge,

> An' we'd all ride 'ome to bed
> With Mo'ammed, God, an' Shiva
> Changin' pickets in our 'ead.

The Craft also provided something more: since its basic tenets harked back to Solomon's construction of the Temple in Jerusalem, referring frequently to precise units of measurement, they provided not just a useful metaphor but also an ideological frame for those movers and shakers working to develop India on the lines of Rudyard's dreams. Little wonder he spoke of another world being opened to him, which he 'needed'. (Later he added that Freemasonry was the nearest thing to a religion that he knew.[19])

When the heat of summer hit the plains in early May, Alice and Trix headed for Simla. Lockwood was scheduled to join them in August, but Rudyard did not expect to get away until September. Sweltering in Lahore, his journalistic nerve was exposed at the end of May when Wheeler sent him at short notice to report on the collapse of a roof at the local high school. Three pupils had been killed in the wreckage and the sight of the carnage caused Rudyard literally to be sick. He was perhaps lucky not to go to Burma as he would have been unable to cope with the casualties. Having retched violently, Rudyard's eyes started playing up and he had nightmares about the dead children he had just seen on stretchers waiting to be buried. His hallucinations continued for the best part of a week: morphia administered by the doctor seems to have brought some relief, but possibly intensified his delusions.

He put his solitariness to good use by collecting his more

recent poems (including some of the 'Bungalow Ballads' from the previous year) in a volume called *Departmental Ditties*. This was published on the *CMG*'s presses in mid-June[20] in an attractive new format – with the cover made to look like one of the light-brown envelopes used in government departments, tied with red tape and officially 'sealed'. The envelope was addressed to 'All Heads of Departments and all Anglo-Indians' from 'Rudyard Kipling, Assistant, Department of Public Journalism, Lahore District'. This light-hearted tone also applied to the contents – a literary *amuse-gueule* for sweaty civil servants to take on their holidays. Rudyard turned his penetrative eye on the petty nepotism and sharp practice of daily Anglo-Indian life in poems like 'Study of an Elevation, In Indian Ink', which speculated about how much the narrator's ex-lover Mehitabel Lee had contributed to the successful career of a rival, Potiphar Gubbins, CE, or 'A Code of Morals', about an uxorious young officer who flashes his wife a Morse Code message (read by his colleagues) warning her to reject the advances of the snowy-haired Lothario, Lieutenant-General Bangs. 'Giffen's Debt' tells of a character (similar to McIntosh Jellaludin in the later *Plain Tale*, 'To be Filed for Reference') who 'went Fantee', living like a native, perpetually drunk, until a flood engulfs his village and, by some irrational process, he is elevated into 'the Tutelary Deity / Of all the Gauri valley villages, / And may in time become a Solar Myth'. In 'Pagett M.P.', Rudyard explored a widespread Anglo-Indian prejudice (which had rapidly become his own) about a politician who came out from England to 'study the East' and was inveigled into staying over the summer, by the end of which time his pious nostrums about the 'bloated Brahmins' serving the Raj had rather dissolved in the heat.

The overall theme of the poems was encapsulated in the aptly named 'A General Summary', an up-beat statement of Rudyard's view that there was nothing new under the sun – from the artist who filched another's painting and 'Won a simple Viceroy's praise / Through the toil of other men' to the delightfully cynical verse:

> Who shall doubt the 'secret hid'
> Under Cheops' pyramid
> Was that the contractor did
> Cheops out of several millions?
> Or that Joseph's sudden rise
> To Comptroller of Supplies
> Was a fraud of monstrous size
> On King Pharaoh's swart Civilians?[21]

Readers enjoyed speculating about the real-life models for the poems: it was generally believed, for example, that General Bangs was based on Sir George Greaves, the sleek, white-haired Commander-in-Chief of the Bombay army. Because they gave voice to the frustrations and aspirations of the Anglo-Indians (telling them, as Rudyard put it, 'what they knew'), the poems were immediately popular, the first 500 copies selling out within a month. By the end of the year, a second edition had been printed by the once reviled Thacker Spink in Calcutta, and *Departmental Ditties* was receiving respectful reviews in Britain – including one that Rudyard cherished, from Andrew Lang, the eminent poet and critic, who told readers of *Longman's Magazine*[22] that 'Giffen's Debt' was comparable to the work of Bret Harte.

Rudyard himself would gladly have traded any reputation for a good night's rest. Towards the end of June, when the monsoon rains came, he described himself as 'a raw red lump of prickly heat'.[23] Since he was clearly suffering from insomnia and over-work, his proprietors took pity and allowed him up to the hills on 3 July. Unlike the Blastoderm, the superficially similar protagonist of his story 'The Conversion of Aurelian McGoggin', he did not take long to recover in Simla. Three days later, on his father's birthday, Rudyard dashed off a whimsical cele-bratory sonnet which posed a question every curious child considers at some stage: how can a parent ever have been young? Lockwood, who was merely middle-aged, was put out, telling his son this was hardly a compliment. Why shouldn't he have been young once like other people? he enquired.

Once again Rudyard was billeted with the Walkers at Kelvin Grove, where he was 'a sort of spoilt child of the house', according to his father, who added, 'It would be surprising if, when made so much of, he was not at times inclined to be bumptious – but his sense of humour saves him.'[24] Rudyard enjoyed the 1886 season much more than the previous year, when the courtiers at Simla had been on edge, waiting to see how Lord and Lady Dufferin would perform in their first summer in town, and he himself had been feeling his way in a hierarchical society. Now the Dufferins were more relaxed, even if, high-handedly, the Vicereine insisted that her official house, the Peterhof, was too small and plans had to be drawn up for a larger Viceregal Lodge.

The Kiplings benefited socially from the Dufferins' increased participation in the activities of the town. Like the Duke of Connaught, the Viceroy sought Lockwood's advice on collecting Indian art, while his daughter, Lady Hermione Blackwood, later attended his art classes. Dufferin himself frequently wandered into Lockwood's sketching room, where he made complimentary remarks about Rudyard's *Departmental Ditties*, professing himself 'greatly struck by the uncommon combination of satire with grace and delicacy'.[25] He was also attracted to Alice in her Simla prime. 'Dullness and Mrs Kipling cannot exist in the same room,' his Lordship once said admiringly.

At one stage it looked as though the two families might enjoy an even closer liaison. For Lord Clandeboye, Dufferin's feckless heir, conceived such a passion for Trix (who at last had a suitor of her own age) that, on several occasions, he asked her to marry him. Despite the attractions of becoming a peer's daughter-in-law, Trix held back: 'I've always liked Irishmen, but I drew the line against marrying them somehow,' she later said.[26] The upshot – according to the Kiplings' side of the story, at least – was that Dufferin became embarrassed at the attention his son was paying the daughter of an art teacher and asked Alice to take Trix to another hill station. Mrs Kipling drew herself up to her fullest height and replied that perhaps it was Clandeboye who should move.

Rudyard had been intending to make a mark on the local theatre that summer. In February he had told Crofts he was under contract – apparently from a Mrs Le Mesurier – to write a comic operetta 'on an Anglo-Indian subject' for Simla that season. He claimed to have it 'all out in the rough and it only needs pulling together'. But there is no record of his producing anything. Perhaps his breakdown from overwork and insomnia held him back.

Instead, a combination of theatrical, military and family connections drew him to one of the leading lights on the Simla amateur dramatic scene. Forty-year-old Isabella Burton was the fiery Irish-born wife of an intelligence officer attached to the 1st Bengal Lancers, better known as Skinner's Horse. Her husband, Major Francis Burton, was the nephew of the artist Frederic Burton (now Director of the National Gallery in London), Uncle Ned's friend whom Rudyard had met at The Grange while on holiday from Southsea. As with several officers Rudyard knew, Major Burton had first come to prominence during the 1878–9 Afghan War when, with his talent for languages, he proved a successful Political Officer. Riding to the north of Kabul in May 1880, he mysteriously acquired a gold armlet, which is today displayed in the British Museum as the Oxus Treasure. According to his account, he surprised a gang of brigands after they had stolen a valuable hoard of gold and silver from some travelling merchants who, in their gratitude, allowed him to purchase the armlet, which in 1884 he sold to the South Kensington Museum for the then substantial sum of £1000. The discovery of this personal booty had not harmed his career. With his moustache and steely military bearing, he was in Rawalpindi at the time of the 1885 durbar for the Afghani Amir, though there is no record of his meeting Rudyard there. That same year he was appointed Assistant Adjutant-General, under Major-General Sir George Greaves, who moved to Meerut.

His wife, Isabella, was a petite woman with a darting, original intelligence. A warm Irish smile lit up her rounded face, with its full lips, largish nose and flashing violet eyes. In Simla, she was considered eccentric, partly for her unconventional views and partly for the way she dressed: she usually wore a combination of yellow and black which, on top of exceptionally small feet, made her look like a busy wasp. (In fact, she was simply displaying the colours of her husband's regiment.)

She had first met Rudyard the previous year. A subsequent letter from him refers to their knowing each other in 1885 and, although there are no further details, this strongly suggests that she had helped him with the composition of his *Departmental Ditties*. (Indeed, given her husband's appointment in 1885, it rather confirms that General Greaves was indeed the original for General Bangs in 'A Code of Morals'.) Rudyard, who was precisely half her age, was immediately captivated by her *savoir vivre*. Ostensibly a typical Simla 'lady who lunches', she became the inspiration for one of his most enduring characters, the wily Lucy Hauksbee, who uses her wit and sex appeal to penetrate the heart of the Simla government machine and get what she wants. While many of Isabella's personal traits went into this fictional character, who 'had the wisdom of the Serpent, the logical coherence of the Man, the fearlessness of the Child, and the triple intuition of the Woman', in real life she was more cultured and better read than the often crudely manipulative Mrs Hauksbee. Unusually among Simla women, Isabella liked to discuss philosophy and ideas. She had dabbled in religions, including the local brand of Theosophy, and found them wanting. (She was thrown out of the Theosophists for being too cynical and she had ruled out a move to Rome because – on the evidence of 'The Education of Otis Yeere' – that would only mean 'exchanging half-a-dozen attachés in red for one in black, and if I fasted, the wrinkles would come, and never, never go'.) So she was a Stoic, a follower of the Roman Emperor Marcus Aurelius, whom she urged Rudyard to read, along with her beloved French novelists. (Rudyard balked at 'the licensed prig, Marcus Unrealius' whose concern with his soul was too impersonal, he felt.[27] But he was happy to continue his exploration of French literature.)

Though Isabella's bookish Stoicism was little more than a euphemism for her sharp cynicism, she taught Rudyard – who, as the *Departmental Ditties* indicated, could be as sardonic as the next man – to take a step further back, to adopt more 'edge' and to explore the complex motives of Simla camp followers, with their obsessions with power, office and sex. She pointed out interesting story-lines and devices (she was the source for his adoption of the globe-trotter as a device for obtaining a fleeting image of a place) and she suggested ways of improving his craft. As an additional aid in these tasks, she presented him with a Bible and advised him to read it. He described the 'good book' as 'a singular eloquent oracle to me. By virtue of it, I have turned out a lot of quaint work and it is good for the chastening of riotous and over-luxuriant English.'[28] (Biblical references now began to appear more regularly in his stories.) However, he remained sceptical of its spiritual worth: 'Oh! to think that that collection of Durbar lists, taxes, Deputy Commissioners' reports and Municipal Sanitary arrangements should be given to an innocent and long-suffering world as the work of the Most High! Great Heavens!'

Isabella Burton is best described not in the *Plain Tales from the Hills*, as is often suggested, but in the slightly later story, 'The Education of Otis Yeere', where Rudyard adopts a Wildean tone to describe a woman's world where her *alter ego*, Lucy Hauksbee, and her friend Mrs Mallowe 'talked chiffons, which is French for Mysteries', or, in other words, female matters.[29] These two women are dissatisfied with life: Mrs Hauksbee suffers from a spiritual lethargy that not even the lead role in the latest play can requite, while Mrs Mallowe echoes a general complaint of the Simla wife that the government has 'eaten' her husband, a civil servant. 'All his ideas and powers of conversation – he really used to be a good talker, even to his wife, in the old days – are taken from him by this – this kitchen-sink of a Government.' When Mrs Hauksbee wonders if she should start a salon (after all, she is acknowledged for her skills in 'managing a team' of male admirers), her friend points out that the transitoriness of Simla existence would not allow for this: 'In two seasons your roomful would be scattered all over Asia. We are only little bits of dirt on the hillsides – here one day and blown down the *khud* the next.' (A *khud* is a steep hillside or cliff.)

Mrs Hauksbee remains determined to 'act, dance, ride, frivol, talk scandal, dine out, and appropriate the legitimate captives of any woman I choose, until I d-r-r-rop'. (There is a modern ring to that: she will 'bop till she drops'.) But the more discerning Mrs Mallowe ('her one bosom friend, for she was in no sense "a woman's woman"') suggests a different approach: 'Take a man, not a boy, mind, but an almost mature, unattached man, and be his guide, philosopher and friend. You'll find it the most interesting occupation that you ever embarked on.' Since this was exactly how Isabella approached the education of Rudyard, there is much of him in Otis Yeere, who even 'wears a dress-shirt like a crumpled sheet of the *Pioneer*'. Mrs Hauksbee takes him in hand, encourages him to wear better clothes, inspires more fire and self-assurance in his manner, even rewrites his memoirs of his period in some remote station in Bengal. Her Pygmalion exercise comes to an abrupt end, however, when he misinterprets her actions and tries to kiss her. (This does not seem to have been in the original script between Isabella and Rudyard.) A more mature Otis makes his exit with some apposite verses from Elizabeth Barrett Browning, drawing the wry observation from Mrs Mallowe, 'My experience of men is that when they begin to quote poetry they are going to flit. Like swans singing before they die, you know.' (Since Mrs Mallowe had no obvious model, she possibly represented another, more controlled side of Isabella.)

A fusion of Mrs Burton's playful, cultured Stoicism and Lockwood Kipling's second-generation utilitarianism was apparent in the harder attitude of Rudyard's lesser-known pieces around this time. In 'Naboth', with its tell-tale Biblical name pointing to

Isabella's influence,[30] Rudyard related 'an allegory of Empire' – about an Indian who took up residence at the bottom of the narrator's garden, and proceeded to colonise the place with his family and business – or, simply, the latest in Rudyard's paranoid visions of the consequences of allowing the natives too much licence. A week later (3 September) his tongue-in-cheek article, 'A Nightmare of Rule', told of a frenzied search for the 'Government' and of attempts to destroy IT. (The capital letters were adopted to give added significance to a numinous presence.) The narrator consults a Mahatma who reveals enigmatically that the IT is a woman. He remains incredulous until 'there fell from the Clouds a Powder-puff and a Fan, and a left-hand shoe in white satin, whereof the number was Two, and the heel two and a half inches ... Thus was it that we found the Government of India – the IT that we set forth to destroy. But we let IT go.' In other words, Mrs Burton not only had 'it'; she was IT.

Returning to the plains towards the end of August, Rudyard had no time to explore the insights gathered at Isabella's feet. His obligations to his proprietors required him to stop off at Dhariwal, near Amritsar, to write a 'puff piece' about the local Egerton Woollen Mills. He neglected to explain in his article 'A District at Play' in the *CMG* on 27 August that the Mills, after a period of financial instability, had been acquired by George Allen and some fellow Allahabad-based businessmen, who had installed W. S. Halsey, one of the well-known family which had spawned Lockwood Kipling's friend, Sibyl Colefax's father, as manager. A country fair was taking place in Dhariwal at the time, with competitive sports such as swimming and wrestling. Rudyard was agreeably surprised at the orderliness and efficiency of the place: electric lights at night and not a policeman in sight. He came away with renewed admiration for the type of unassuming Briton who lives in remote corners of India and gets things done. In contrast to the tergiversations of Simla, the direct talk of a group of canal officers and engineers was refreshing:

After long residence in places where folk discuss such intangible things as Lines, Policies, Schemes, Measures and the like, in an abstract and bloodless sort of way, it was a revelation to listen to men who talk of Things and the People – crops and ploughs and water-supplies and the best means of using all three for the benefit of a district. They spoke masterfully, these Englishmen, as owners of a country might speak, and it was not at first that one realised how every one of the concerns they touched upon with the air of proprietorship were matters which had not the faintest bearing on their pay or prospects, but concerned the better tillage or husbandry of the fields around.[31]

Here was a living model of the paternalism Rudyard was convinced India needed.

Back in Lahore, a new editor was temporarily in charge of the *CMG* while Wheeler was on leave. Kay Robinson had actually arrived in June, before Rudyard went on holiday. He was on secondment from the *Pioneer* where he was highly regarded as the latest member of a journalistic dynasty that the tough-minded George Allen was attempting to nurture. His father, Julian Robinson, a former clergyman, had been the *Pioneer*'s first editor, and his elder brother Phil an assistant editor. In 1878 Phil had written *In My Indian Garden*, a book of pen portraits that Rudyard admired and may have used as a source for stories: his 'Rikki-Tikki-Tavi' looks back to Phil's 'The Mungoose', for example. But the daily grind of journalism did not detain Phil Robinson for long. He became a foreign correspondent, reporting the 1878–80 Afghan and the 1884 Egyptian wars for the *Daily Telegraph* and the Cuban civil war of 1895 for the *Pall Mall Gazette*. Then, in mysterious circumstances, he had a British newspaper, the *Sunday Times*, bought for his amusement by a girl-friend, Alice 'Princess Midas' Cornwall, who had made a fortune in mining in Australia.

Refreshed by his stay in the hills, Rudyard immediately struck up a good working relationship with his new boss, who was seven years his senior. For the first time, he enjoyed himself in a newspaper office. Unlike Wheeler, Robinson did not take himself too seriously: having been ordered to 'put sparkle' into the paper, he ordered a bottle of champagne from Mr Nedou's, otherwise the Sind and Punjab Hotel,[32] over the road. He observed Rudyard's working practices with some amusement: never had he seen anyone throw so much ink about the place. At the end of the day Rudyard looked like a Dalmatian dog, he recalled. 'He had a habit of dipping his pen frequently and deep into the ink-pot, and as all his movements were abrupt, almost jerky, the ink used to fly. When he darted into my room, as he used to do about one thing or another in connection with the contents of the paper a dozen times in the morning, I had to shout to him to "stand off"; otherwise, as I knew by experience, the abrupt halt he would make, and the flourish with which he placed the proof in his hand before me, would send the penful of ink ... flying over me.'[33]

Soon, with these two in charge, the Rag, as they called the *CMG*, was 'humming'. After redesigning the paper on the model of *The Globe*, the London evening paper he once worked for, Robinson asked Rudyard to write some short stories, along the lines of his *Departmental Ditties*, for publication as 'turnovers' – the first section appearing on the front page, with the rest tucked away inside the paper. Rudyard saw this as an opportunity to commit to paper some of the ideas he had recently mulled over with Mrs Burton in Simla. While his *Departmental Ditties* had been trifles, these stories would offer a sophisticated synthesis of his attitude to India.

The so-called *Plain Tales from the Hills* are remembered primarily for their pithy portrayal of Mrs Hauksbee and the personal politics of fringe members of the Imperial 'court' at Simla. One of the first stories, 'Three and – an Extra', published on 17 November, tells of a woman, Mrs Bremmil, who loses her looks and zest for life, following the death of a child. While at Simla, her weak husband is ensnared by Mrs Hauksbee, a skinny, witty woman – no great beauty, but possessed of large blue eyes and 'many devils of malice and mischievousness'. Although she knows that her husband and Mrs Hauksbee ride together and eat at Peliti's, Mrs Bremmil does nothing until the day of the Viceroy's ball. First, she declines to attend, but then, wearing a fine new dress, she makes a late entrance. After filling her card, she leaves three dances vacant, forcing her husband to abandon his commitments to a now furious Mrs Hauksbee, who tells the narrator, 'Take my word for it, the silliest woman in the world can manage a clever man; but it needs a very clever woman to manage a fool.'

In 'The Rescue of Pluffles', which appeared in the *CMG* only two days later, Mrs Hauksbee gets her own back by extracting a raw young subaltern out of the clutches of a deadly rival, Mrs Reiver, who was not 'honestly mischievous' like herself, but 'bad from her hair – which started life on a Brittany girl's head – to her boot-heels, which were two and three-eighths inches high'. (In another story, 'The Broken-Link Handicap', a horse named in Mrs Reiver's honour is called The Lady Regula Baddun.) In writing about the 'Seven Weeks' War' between these two *grandes dames*, Rudyard explores a favourite theme – how, on arrival in India, young officers need to be 'broken' like a horse. After Mrs Reiver's harsh treatment, Pluffles prefers Mrs Hauksbee's gentler style of holding him on the snaffle. He responds to her talking to him like a mother – just one of the twenty-three sides of her character, according to the narrator.

This light social farce provides a façade for Rudyard's more serious critique of the British in India. The entire collection of thirty-nine (later forty-two – the total varied with editions) is more than the sum of its parts. It provides an absorbing picture of an India uncomfortable with itself and its place in the world. The country suffers from the debilitating drawback that people at home know so little about it. When Phil Garron (in 'Yoked with an Unbeliever') quits England for a job in 'tea', he has no idea what this involves and his mother thinks his intended destination, Darjeeling, is a 'port on the Bengal Ocean'. Yet this introverted society has to put up with interference from do-gooding Westminster politicians, such as Lord Benira Trig, the Radical peer (an ennobled version of Pagett M.P.), who is seen off by the common sense of Rudyard's soldiers, 'The Three Musketeers'.

Such globe-trotters have no conception of the fears and aspirations of Anglo-Indians who, having survived the Mutiny, are beset by disease, by threats on their borders and by internal communal tensions.[34] As a reaction, Indian society turns its back on these interlopers (and the succour they give to Indian nationalism) and locks itself in political paralysis. Apprehensive of change, it is merely careful not to upset the delicate balance of interests that allows the country to function (so in 'Pig', for example, the sensibilities of the Moslems of Upper India have to be considered).

In the circumstances, the country's Little Tin Gods (Rudyard appropriates this general term of abuse for the government in his epigraph to 'A Germ-Destroyer') are loath to do much. The Viceroy, a man with 'no name – nothing but a string of counties and two-thirds of the alphabet after them', retreats to the hills where he makes a virtue out of non-intervention. 'No wise man has a Policy,' he says. 'A policy is blackmail levied on the Fool by the Unforeseen.' Rudyard seems to agree, but one of his skills as an author is to remain ambivalent enough to be interesting.

That does not hold him back from satirising the pomposity and dullness of Simla. He attacks the town for being cut off from the real world. Thus, in 'Tods' Amendment', the Supreme Legislative Council is informed about native Indians' reactions to a bill on land rights in the Sub-Montane Tracts by a six-year-old child, one of a succession of Rudyard's grating child heroes, whose function is to subvert and show up the established order. This government is malleable enough to be susceptible to pressure from mad inventors such as Mellish in 'A Germ-Destroyer' and to intrigues by women like Mrs Hauksbee. The result is a condition of 'inherent rottenness',[35] 'where nothing changes in spite of the shiny, top-scum stuff that people call "civilization" '.[36]

This was hard-hitting stuff. But Rudyard had not finished with his satire. If the daily round in the hills was boring, so much more so the lot of the average Anglo-Indian official in his distant station. *Plain Tales* is notable for its depiction of the loneliness of civil servants such as the engineer Moriarty in 'In Error', who embodies the adage 'a man who has been alone in the jungle for more than a year is never quite sane all his life after'. On their own in the 'Mofussil', these foot soldiers of the imperialist ideal are often overwhelmed by the stark reality of India, a country where, as Rudyard put it in 'Wressley of the Foreign Office', there are no half-tints worth noticing. As he says in another story, 'By Word of Mouth', 'Few people can afford to play Robinson Crusoe any-where – least of all in India, where we are few in the land and very much dependent on each other's kind offices.'

All too frequently, they succumb to mental breakdown: like Moriarty, they go mad, beginning with 'suicidal depression, going on to fits and starts and hysteria, and ending with downright raving'. Or else they commit suicide. As B. J. Moore-Gilbert has chronicled, India experienced an epidemic of suicides in the 1880s. The papers were full of the details, accompanied by anguished enquiries into the causes. When Colonel F. D. Harrington, Deputy Commissioner of Gujarat, took his own life in 1883, the *Pioneer* noted he had worked alone for eight years – 'one of the severest forms of punishment'. Changes were introduced to guard people against isolation – a phenomenon, the *Pioneer* reported, that, paradoxically, increased after 'the extension of railways and tele-graphs' encouraged one man to do what three might previously have done.

The subject of solitariness – and the resulting breakdowns and suicides – was close to Rudyard's heart, as is clear from the plight of the all too sensitive 'Boy' who fails to be 'broken in' in 'Thrown Away'. The narrator and the Major have to concoct their great lie about The Boy's death. As they bury him, the Major indulges in 'awful stories of suicide or nearly-carried-out suicide – tales that made one's hair crisp. He recalled that he himself had once gone into the same Valley of the Shadow as The Boy, when he was young and new to the country; so he understood how things fought together in The Boy's poor jumbled head.' Rudyard had been there too.

Later Rudyard was to explore this issue rather more deeply. During his period in India, there was considerable interest in the research into suicide conducted by the Italian Enrico Morselli, whose 1881 study *Suicide: An Essay in Comparative Moral Statistics* received the unusual accolade of two separate reviews in the *Pioneer*.[37] The French sociologist Emile Durkheim was to take this debate much further in his book *Suicide*, published in 1897, partly as a rebuttal of Morselli. In a well-known essay, 'Kipling's Place in the World of Ideas', Professor Noel Annan has suggested that Rudyard was influenced by Durkheim in evolving his own theory of society.[38] While there is no evidence of Rudyard having read Durkheim, his magpie intelligence would have absorbed comment about the Frenchman's concepts of 'anomie' and suicide, and used them to develop his own reflections on the need for community and purpose.

For the time being, Rudyard advised his readers to avoid The Boy's mistake and not to take India too seriously, 'the mid-day sun always excepted'.[39] In 'Thrown Away', he offers a cynical list (*à la* Isabella Burton) of things that simply do not matter on the sub-continent, such as flirting (because everyone is on the move) and good work (because another person usually takes the credit). Later he developed these reflections on keeping a wry distance from life's problems into more mature ideas on the restorative effects of mirth.

The *Plain Tales* are notable for their occasional poignant evocations of native Indian life, such as 'The Story of Muhammad Din', about his servant's infant son who creates a pleasing series of designs with the narrator's polo ball as its centre-piece, before withering and dying. (There was nothing inconsistent in this:

Rudyard had no gripe with the Indian people; it was their would-be political leaders he abhorred.) However, the stories are unhelpful as portraits of Indian (as opposed to Anglo-Indian) society. And they are unrelenting in their projection of the message that there can be no bridging the gap between European and Indian cultures. Trejago's love for Bisesa in 'Beyond the Pale' leads inexorably to the sawn-off stumps of his lover's arms. Equally, it is no use trying to become one of them, like Strickland, the policeman who – following the footsteps of a better-known Burton: the explorer Sir Richard – is the only man in Upper India able to 'pass for Hindu or Mohammedan, hide-dresser or priest, as he pleases', or McIntosh Jellaludin, the former Oxford scholar who goes native. (This stricture also applied – mutatis mutandis – to the babus who followed English ways, a type Rudyard had satirised in 'What Happened' in *Departmental Ditties*.)

The best that an Anglo-Indian can hope in the circumstances is to keep to the straight and narrow. As Rudyard says in the epigraph to 'In the House of Suddhoo':

> A stone's throw out on either hand
> From that well-ordered road we tread,
> And all the world is wild and strange.

This is not a formula for dynamic change. Indeed, in the *Plain Tales* Rudyard shows a political passivity at variance from his letters to his radically minded relatives in London. To Aunt Georgie and to Cousin Margaret he had expressed his aversion to child marriage. But in these stories Rudyard shows respect for customs such as arranged marriages. 'We are a high-caste and enlightened race,' he writes in 'Kidnapped', 'and infant-marriage is very shocking, and the consequences are sometimes peculiar; but, nevertheless, the Hindu notion ... of arranging marriages irrespective of the personal inclinations of the married is sound.' This point of view feeds his prejudice against missionaries who try to change such customs, as in 'Lispeth'. It also ensures that his own politics differ little from his father's paternalism – the sort that he had recently witnessed at the Egerton Woollen Mills. While his earlier article on the Mills had been a public-relations puff, the *Plain Tales* suggest that such a community can play a positive role in guarding against loneliness and potential madness. He was able to convey more effectively in fiction than in journalism that this kind of paternalism works best when underpinned by power. As he noted in 'His Chance in Life': 'Never forget that unless the outward and visible signs of Our Authority are always before a native he is as incapable as a child of understanding what authority means, or where is the danger of disobeying it.'

Although Rudyard raises these issues, he offers no real solution. While he sees a future for Indian ways muddling along in tandem with technological advance (like the hocus-pocus in 'In the House of Suddhoo' which functions – under portraits of the Queen and the Prince of Wales – because of access to the telegraph), he is content also to fall back on ideas of inevitability. The Turkish word kismet, or fate, crops up more than once in these stories. In 'A Germ-Destroyer' he simply admits, 'Fate looks after the Indian Empire because it is so big and so helpless.' The title and the unravelling of the story 'Consequences' points to a Western variation on this determinism.

Rudyard's uncertainty emerges in various stylistic devices. He mixes the 'knowingness' that annoys some commentators with a diffidence that enables his narrator to say, 'No man will ever know the exact truth of this story' (in 'False Dawn'). From time to time, he deliberately turns away from the action with the catch-phrase – 'but that's another story . . .' In his virtuosity, he nods appreciation at influences such as the French writer Guy de Maupassant and plays with new techniques of writing. And while his plotting can be rudimentary, Rudyard often manages to achieve a sparse and moving lyricism. In 'False Dawn', for example, after the confusion of the sandstorm, the picnickers are waiting by the tomb in the 'deep, dead stillness that followed the storm' when, like a scene from a Fellini film, the errant Edith Copleigh returns. She kisses Saumarez, the man who mistakenly proposed to her sister instead of to her. Using an appropriately histrionic image, Rudyard observes, 'It was like a scene in a theatre, and the likeness was heightened by all the dust-white, ghostly-looking men and women under the orange-trees clapping their hands – as if they were watching a play – at Saumarez's choice. I never saw anything so un-English in my life.'

The coming of the new year in 1887 witnessed a period of double celebration at Bikanir House. On 30 December Rudyard had attained his majority, and on 1 January Lockwood was appointed a Commander of the Indian Empire. Despite this official recognition, there was no escaping that the son was now more famous than the father – largely because of the success of *Departmental Ditties*. As he had told his Aunt Edith in December, everyone he knew had read that particular book. 'I have made a mark – I say it with all the modesty that a youngster who has had a fill of butter can say so.' As a result, 'strangers in trains, and hotels and all manner of out of the way places come up to me and say nice things. Also – last proof of notoriety – people turn their heads and look and ask to be introduced to me when I dance or dine in strange places beyond my district.'[40]

Rudyard was happy to be widely known, since he knew this would help him in his efforts to publish a new book, a collection of his *Plain Tales*, and so raise further his literary profile. For this important job he returned to Thacker Spink, the Calcutta publishers he had fallen out with over a second edition of *Echoes* in 1885. His dealings with this company show Rudyard's skill as a businessman – and his powerful sense of his own worth.

Surprisingly, he had approached Thacker Spink again the previous July (1886) to see if, as specialist book printers, they would handle a second edition of between 300 and 500 copies of *Departmental Ditties*. He was down to the last fifty of his original run of 500 from the *CMG* presses in Lahore. However, this first edition had been 'abominably printed. The margins are cut down to the quick; the inking is unequal and the type not of the newest or set up in the straightest way. These defects a firm of your standing will of course remedy; supplying better paper, broader margins and a superior style of binding.' To make the second edition more saleable, he offered to 'throw in' a few extra ditties.

When Thacker Spink expressed an interest, but wanted the copyright also, Rudyard was annoyed, arguing that he only required a regular print job. He was also adamant that they should keep as nearly as possible to his earlier 'departmental envelope' design. When they said that this would be difficult, he demanded that they should at least refrain from stamping the bindings with any gold or silver, or raising the price beyond one and half rupees per copy. He wanted the book 'as sober and as official looking' as possible.

To people already enquiring about a second edition, he issued a printed postcard to enable them to subscribe. Within a month, he had eighty-nine reservations, from as far afield as Quetta, Ceylon, Karachi and Mandalay. (Eventually he had 420 such replies.) Growing into his role as a salesman, he suggested to Thacker Spink from Lahore in mid-August 1886 that if they hurried with the job (terms had been agreed), they could easily sell forty copies in the six final weeks of the Simla season. But he warned that, although Williams & Co., the hill station's book-sellers, only demanded a ten per cent commission, 'they want the book shoved under their noses and brought to their very doors before they will take the trouble to buy it'.[41]

He had recently trailed another book which he hoped Thacker Spink might like to publish. 'By the time we have squabbled over the division of the profits and finished our correspondence over the publishers' bill, you may perhaps be willing to launch my Anglo-Indian Novel 'Mother Maturin' – a story of Eurasian and native life in Lahore city.'[42] But six months later, in February 1887, this idea was shelved and instead Rudyard started to think seriously for the first time about publishing the *Plain Tales*, which had been so well received by *CMG* readers the previous autumn. Although only a couple of months earlier, in December, he had denied to his Aunt Edith[43] wanting to collect these stories in a book, he now asked Thacker Spink to quote for their publication in a similar form and type to *Departmental Ditties* – to be 'made up of 12 stories of native and twelve of English life in India; the whole to be called "Punjab People Brown and White" and to take up not more than 120–30 pp.'[44] Although the title was hardly catchy, it showed that at this stage the *Plain Tales* were intended as a different sort of book, giving as much weight to 'Indian' stories such as 'In the House of Sudhoo' as to the more obvious Simla sagas involving Mrs Hauksbee and her cohorts.

In replying with the good news that their new edition of *Departmental Ditties* had practically sold out, Thacker Spink proposed a different deal for 'Punjab People'. They themselves were prepared to take the risk of any loss, but, in return, they wanted to share in all the profits. In other words, they sought to be publishers, rather than mere printers. By May the title had altered, and he was calling the stories *Plain Tales from the Hills*, but he was wary of these new terms. He claimed – justifiably enough, given the reaction to the original stories when they were printed in the *CMG* – that the book 'could be very popular'. The *Pioneer* had already made an attractive offer, but, he said, 'I should naturally prefer the book to come out under the auspices of a book-publishing firm'. The following month he changed his mind: he was happy to go fifty:fifty, with Thacker Spink taking the risk, because he felt this would spur them to advertise this book more extensively than the previous one. By the end of June, having completed some additional *Plain Tales*, he asked Thacker Spink to hurry the lot through the production process because, once again, he wanted the new book on sale in Simla before the end of the season. Eleven days later he was forced to apologise because he had failed to send them one of the stories, 'The Madness of Private Ortheris'.

In mid-August Rudyard returned to the hills, where inevitably there was speculation about the characters in the *Plain Tales*. Rudyard was skilled at fusing and disguising his models so, even now, it is hard to be specific. Mrs Bremmil appears to have been based on Mrs Douglas Straight, wife of a prominent judge in Allahabad; the adorable Venus Annodomini was a Mrs Parry-Lambert, wife of a colonel in the Public Works Department; 'Wressley of the Foreign Office' drew on attributes of Sir Lepel Griffin, the lascivious Agent to the Governor-General of Central India who had written on Punjab (as opposed to Rajput in the story) chiefs, and Strickland owes much to James Walker's friend, Horace Goad, whose 'extraordinary knowledge of the native language and customs, combined with a genius for disguising himself, rendered him a terror to all evil-doers within his jurisdiction'.[45]

Since Rudyard was still in thrall to Mrs Burton, he naturally gravitated to her passion, the local theatre, which was enjoying an *annus mirabilis*. After several seasons of a peripatetic existence, the Simla Amateur Dramatic Club had finally secured its own premises – in the New Gaiety Theatre which opened in the Town Hall on The Mall in time for Queen Victoria's Jubilee at the end of May. For many years the Club had teetered on the verge of bankruptcy, and had been saved through the energy and financial generosity of Lord William Beresford, the turf-loving military secretary to three Viceroys, who had been responsible for developing the Annandale recreation complex. Beresford had run the Dramatic Club with two other officers, Colonel 'Joey' Deane of the King's Dragoon Guards and Colonel Philip Henderson, the Superintendent for the Suppression of Thuggee and Dacoity. For the new theatre's opening, Deane wrote a prologue, to which Rudyard penned a tongue-in-cheek reply, asking why Deane had felt it necessary to stress the chasteness of the Simla stage.

The diversity of the theatre (and its links with the military) were underlined when Sir Frederick Roberts, the Commander-in-Chief, allowed a small stage to be built in the ballroom of his official residence, Snowdon, for a variety performance in aid of

Homes in the Hills, the charity his wife had started to provide holiday accommodation for nurses. This time Rudyard wrote a more subdued prologue, which was spoken by his sister Trix who had clearly pursued her paramedical studies as she was dressed in a nurse's uniform. At the end of August Rudyard was reunited with Isabella in a production at the new theatre of *A Scrap of Paper*, a farce by the popular French playwright Victorien Sardou. Rudyard played Brisemouche and Isabella his lover, Susanne de Ruseville, though this time there was the added interest of Major Francis Burton in the lead role of Prosper Couramont. Burton had just completed his period of service at Meerut and was shortly to be transferred to Peshawar as second-in-command of his regiment. Though the relationship between Rudyard and Isabella was not consummated sexually, the Major's presence must have added a piquancy to proceedings, as is suggested in 'The Education of Otis Yeere', 'We have to remember that six consecutive days of rehearsing the leading part of *The Fallen Angel* at the New Gaiety Theatre where the plaster is not yet properly dry, might have brought about an unhingement of spirits which, again, might have led to eccentricities.' *A Scrap of Paper* itself met with mixed reviews: Lord Dufferin found Rudyard's performance 'too horrid and vulgar' and rather relished the possibility that 'the actors whom he has been cutting up in his paper will now be able to have a shy at him.'[46]

Outside the theatre, Rudyard had befriended one of Trix's former dancing partners, Captain Ian Hamilton, a high-flying army officer who was ADC to General Roberts. He and Rudyard used to lunch every Sunday at the house of the Viceroy's ADC, Lord Herbrand Russell (later the Duke of Bedford). Like another ADC, Colonel Neville Chamberlain (the inventor of snooker who had written a burlesque version of *Lucia di Lammermoor* for the charity gala at Snowdon), Hamilton liked to dabble as a writer, having once been military correspondent of the *Madras Mail*. Since he liked Rudyard's work, he offered to send one of his friend's stories to his brother Vereker, a writer and artist in

London, with a request that it should be passed to Andrew Lang for his comments. According to Hamilton, Lang dismissed the piece (said to be an early draft of 'The Mark of the Beast') as 'extremely disagreeable', which was odd, given that only the previous year he had gone out of his way to compliment *Departmental Ditties* in *Longman's Magazine*.

Generally, the pushy young journalist from Lahore was not popular, particularly among men who were tired of seeing their wives entranced by Rudyard's wit and then exposed to ridicule in his stories. Even in 1887 the majority of the summer population in Simla were women, who came up from the plains, leaving their husbands working 'on station'. Writing in June to Mrs Maunsell, a strong candidate as model for the woman in 'On the Strength of a Likeness', Rudyard could hardly disguise his relish at the forthcoming Simla season: 'Seven women per head of male population. Amen.'[47] The explorer Colonel Francis Younghusband, an irregular member of Colonel MacGregor's Intelligence Department from 1885, spoke for many fellow officers when he recalled that they looked on Rudyard 'with great disfavour', regarding him as 'bumptious and above his station'.[48] Louis Dane, a Punjabi civil servant, provided more of a Lahore perspective when he described Rudyard as a 'pretty impossible' companion, adding that the young journalist had a 'caddishly dirty tongue', spent his whole time in the Lahore Bazaar and 'everyone thought he was going for a mucker with the harlotries therein'.[49]

Although Dane's later recollections should be treated sceptically, Rudyard had again been talking of using his time in Simla to make some progress on *Mother Maturin*, his on-off novel about Lahore's low life. Instead, he was locked in correspondence with Thacker Spink, as the *Plain Tales* project continued to be delayed. At one point he played the racial card, complaining about the printing: 'There is a haziness – more Punjabi than Bengali – in locking up the formes and dropping out letters.'[50] In September, unhappy with the literals still to be found in the second proofs, he demanded a revision. And he wanted to know: 'When do you begin advertising?' Even then, as he was leaving Simla, he still hoped the edition would be ready the following month to catch the stragglers in the hills.

He was also considering a third edition of *Departmental Ditties*, which led him to hit upon another seemingly bright idea. He told Thacker Spink he had changed his mind and would be happy to divest himself entirely of the copyright in that book for the modest sum of 500 rupees (£37.50).[51] They could then print any cover they wanted and he would have no further say in the matter. If they wanted to publish additional poems in future editions, he would provide them at their market price. His calculation of his royalties for the first two editions showed that, so far, each of his poems had been worth 43.2 rupees (£3.24). He would willingly sell future poems for 30 rupees (£2.25) – until, that is, his prose began appearing in English magazines and he was confident his name would increase in value.

Thacker Spink interpreted this gesture as a sign of weakness that he might allow them to acquire the copyright of the still unpublished *Plain Tales*. There is no record of the price they offered, but on 3 November Rudyard told them emphatically that wild horses would not induce him to part with his stories at four times their offer. He believed that his *Plain Tales* were worth at least 5000 rupees (£375).

A week earlier he had been disappointed to hear that Isabella Burton had passed through Lahore 'like a thief in the night', accompanying her husband on their way up to his new posting in Peshawar. Writing to her on 26 October, he recalled his dire experiences in that town before the 1885 durbar – in a manner that confirmed he had not met Major Burton there at the time. Instead he filled her in with the latest gossip from Lahore, before plucking up his courage to ask if she would mind the *Plain Tales* being dedicated to her.

If I put on the title page, sans initials or anything, just this much – 'To the wittiest woman in India I dedicate this book' –

will you, as they say in the offices 'initial and pass correct'? ...
I have put a fair amount of trouble and time and prying about
in queer places into the three hundred pages that will carry my
name ... However if you have the faintest doubt about mixing
yourself up even indirectly with a 'new man's' bid for public
favour, you can always with that convincing candour which is
one of your most startling attributes promptly deny the dedication and turn up your nose at it – *c'est à dire* if you are ever
so left to yourself as to turn up your nose.'[52]

He need not have worried. Within a week, she had given her
approval of this dedication. By now his own future was clearer.
His bosses had decided it was at last time for him to move to their
senior paper in Allahabad where, on an increased salary of 600
rupees a month or £540 a year, he would be both the *Pioneer*'s
'special correspondent', with a licence to roam (initially, he was
excited to learn, in Rajasthan), and editor of the *Week's News*, a
new literary supplement they intended to publish. But before
boarding the train for the capital of the North-West Provinces,
Rudyard still had columns to fill and he called once again on
Isabella. He claimed that he had not had an original idea since
last seeing her in Simla. Lahore bred nothing but mosquitoes and
he had become a 'discursive loon' through having to write leaders.
Consequently he pleaded, 'As the Scripture says, "Write over and
help us." Suggest a new Anglo-Indian horror for a Christmas
story. I've got to make one and the printer's devil is my witness
that I have no material to make it from.'[53]

Seven

Allahabad and Home

1887–1889

Sitting in the peaceful garden of the Allens' large house in Allahabad on a balmy late-November afternoon in 1887 was pleasant enough. Rudyard had not realised before how unclean the air of Lahore had been. But, having made the switch to the heart of his proprietor's business empire, he felt lonely – 'like a rabbit in a strange warren'.[1] He had forgotten to bring Mrs Burton's inspirational pocket Bible. His train journey down the Punjab had been uncomfortable: somewhere after Meerut he had been hit in the eye by what he described as a 'piston crank' (probably only some soot from the engine) and was ministered to by a kind lady from Calcutta who gabbled about her family. He arrived in Allahabad in the wake of the horse-whipping of someone (unnamed) at the Club whom he clearly disliked. He enjoyed telling Isabella the details: the whip 'was of a rhinoceros hide and it curled, Madam, it curled all round and about him and he squealed after the manner of hares when you capture them squatting in the snow. It was good – even the account of the flogging from the man who had administered it cheered me immensely.' Then he had to attend a party for the outgoing Governor Sir Alfred Lyall and his replacement Sir Auckland Colvin, with whom Rudyard had traded jovial insults in the *Pioneer*. The braying voices of the official guests only made him feel more alienated.

He was happy to make a quick turnaround and set off again on his way to Rajasthan, 'the home of a hundred thousand legends and the great fighting pen of India'.² Professionally, he had *carte blanche* to write anything he wanted and, on a personal level, he welcomed the opportunity to wander freely 'under no more exacting master than personal inclination, and with no more definite plan of travel than has the horse, escaped from the pasture, free upon the countryside'.³

Rudyard's journey started, in easy touristic style, at the place he had been prevented from visiting the previous Christmas – the Taj Mahal in Agra. Like most visitors to this Persian-inspired marble memorial to the wife of the Mughal Emperor Shah Jehan, he was profoundly moved, finding it 'full of sorrow – the sorrow of the man who built it for the woman he loved, and the sorrow of the workmen who died in the building – used up like cattle. And in the face of this sorrow the Taj flushed in the sunlight and was beautiful, after the beauty of a woman who has done no wrong.' There was no archness in Rudyard's tone now; any mocking was reserved for one of his (and Isabella's) regular *bêtes noires*, the globe-trotter – in this case, a young man from Manchester who was ticking off the sights and hoping to be back home by Christmas.

Rudyard remained in an unusually cheerful mood: even when his tonga broke down on the way to Udaipur and he had to hitch a lift in another vehicle, where he was subjected to prodding and poking by the other travellers, he refused to be ruffled, simply inferring that he might have been happier if a railway, that symbol of colonial efficiency and integration, had already been laid on that stretch of his journey.

Only when he reached the ancient mountain-top city of Chitor was his good humour rudely interrupted by an unexpected encounter with the other side of India that still fascinated and repelled him. He had just climbed Chitor's nine-storey Tower of Victory looking out over the desert, when he decided to visit the Gau-Mukh (literally, cow's mouth), a shrine which was billed as a set of springs built into the side of a cliff. Descending some slippery steps, he arrived at a dull blue stretch of water or 'tank', where, suddenly, he was confronted with an alarming image. 'In a slabbed-in recess, water was pouring through a shapeless stone gargoyle, into a trough; which trough again dripped into the tank. Almost under the little trickle of water, was the loathsome Emblem of Creation, and there were flowers and rice around it.'⁴

In this hillside grotto, Rudyard had come face to face with a statue of the elemental Hindu creative force, the phallus. In one of those momentary experiences that stick in one's mind and shape one's attitudes, Rudyard was overwhelmed by the potency of this sacred Lingam. Amid blatantly sexual oozings, sproutings and pourings, he felt he had been led 'first, two thousand years away from his own century, and secondly, into a trap, and that he would fall off the polished stones into the stinking tank, or that the Gau-Mukh would continue to pour water until the tank rose up and swamped him, or that some of the stone slabs would fall forward and crush him flat'. He had an overpowering urge to get out: 'he desired no archaeological information, he wished to take no notes, and, above all, he did not care to look behind him, where stood the reminder that he was no better than the beasts that would perish. But he had to cross the smooth, worn rocks, and he felt their sliminess through his bootsoles. It was as though he were treading on the soft, oiled skin of a Hindu.' Coming up out of this nightmarish dungeon (which he was to recreate in his novel *The Naulahka*), he was sweating profusely. 'There was something uncanny about it all. It was not exactly a feeling of danger or pain, but an apprehension of great evil.'⁵ Later that evening, determined not to give in to this irrational panic, Rudyard felt compelled to venture into Chitor again. This time the sight of the moonlit city and the sound of braying jackals helped compose him – providing an arresting image for his later *Jungle Books.* Nevertheless, he much preferred visiting the Anglicised princely states of Jaipur, with its gas lamps, Museum and wide boulevards, and Jodhpur, whose ruler, dressed like a pukka English gentleman, insisted on taking his visitor on a tour of his spotlessly clean stables where, he was proud to say, no horse was ever shot. Rudyard's access to this and other princely courts again came in useful when he wrote *The Naulahka*.

On his way, Rudyard contemplated an issue that, he said, puzzled every foreigner in India. A friendly meeting with Moslem soldiers at Boondi caused him to reflect that, like his father, he preferred Moslems to Hindus. The former were easier to deal with: 'A Hindu is an excellent person, but ... but ... there is no knowing what is in his heart, and he is hedged about with so many strange observances.'[6] He admitted that in Rajasthan, the political residents preferred Hindus, finding them more trustworthy. But he had given way to prejudice and was obsessed with the idea that the Hindu pantheon was both monstrous, as in Chitor, and inane, as he had argued in his *CMG* review of the *Mahabharata*.[7]

Returning to the holy Hindu city of Allahabad, Rudyard was pleased to find the railway stations in the nearby 'Cow Belt' plastered with posters announcing his series of 'Anglo-Indian Studies' for the *Week's News*, the *Pioneer*'s new supplement. Once again, he stayed at the Allens' palatial residence, where the guests included Sir Lepel Griffin, another admirer of Mrs Burton, and a couple of sprightly young girls up from the sticks of Bhopal to be 'brought out' by Mrs Allen. Rudyard 'could have fallen on their necks bared to the light of gas for the first time and kissed them', he told Isabella. But this was not Simla and he was roundly rebuffed: 'They were full of their exceeding importance as young ladies and before we have been thirty-six hours together gave me to understand that I was "quite a boy".'[8]

After accompanying the girls to a 'singularly mournful' performance of *Cinderella* at the Mayo Hall, he concluded that Allahabad was not very different from Lahore. Institutional social life revolved round a large, well-appointed Club where, apart from a preference for the game of poker rather than whist, the main features, including the conversation, were familiar enough. There was even a resident Regiment, the 21st East Surrey, in the local Fort. Rudyard noted how a bastion of the Mughal-built Fort stuck out into the River Ganges. This had the effect of stopping the flow of partially burnt corpses down the river. The corpses would pile up outside the subalterns' window and someone had to be employed to keep the bodies moving. 'In Fort Lahore we dealt with nothing worse than ghosts,' noted Rudyard sourly.[9]

His month in Rajasthan had whetted his appetite for the road. As when indulging in opium, he liked to cast off his official persona from time to time and travelling seemed an agreeable way of doing this. Writing about his recent experiences, he said, 'There is no life so good as the life of a loafer who travels by rail and road; for all things and all people are kind to him.'[10] This wanderlust was reflected at his place of work, where he found George Allen's presence intimidating. While day-dreaming about new places to visit, he was, by his own admission, often casual in rehashing the week's news for the paper of that name.

However, he liked the creative side of his job. Having argued to his proprietor that it was unnecessary to buy in stories from authors such as Bret Harte because he could fill the space himself, Rudyard was delighted when Allen took him up on his offer. As he wrote in his autobiography, 'My head was full of, to me, infinitely more important material [than the regular news]. Henceforth no mere twelve-hundred *Plain Tales* jammed into rigid frames, but three- or five-thousand word cartoons once a week. So did young Lippo Lippi, whose child I was, look on the blank walls of his monastery when he was bidden decorate them!'[11]

In this positive mood, he started in early 1888 on a new round of 'soldier tales, Indian tales, and tales of the opposite sex',[12] most of which were to appear, first, in the *Pioneer* or the *Week's News* and then collected in distinctively packaged volumes of the Indian Railway Library a year or so later. Examples of these different genres that made their way into the newspaper during his first month in Allahabad included 'The Gods from the Machine', a slight story (with some annoying attempts at dialect) in which Mulvaney and his colleagues foil the elopement of the Colonel's daughter; 'Gemini', about confusion in the identities of two Indian landlords who were brothers; and, a nod and a wink to Mrs Burton, 'A Wayside Comedy', about sexual shenanigans in a small, remote British community. Rudyard was particularly happy about the conciseness ('economy of implication', he called it) he achieved in this last story, which again stressed the psychological pressures of being cut off in a 'prison', 143 miles from the nearest station.

Before long, Allen was having second thoughts about his use of Rudyard's talent. He could see that his protégé was no longer committed to the daily grind of journalism. Rudyard's flippant tone attracted frequent complaints from departments of a government that was much closer, both physically and politically, to the *Pioneer* in Allahabad than to the *CMG*. So the paper's owners decided that Rudyard might, as he himself put it, be 'safer on the road than in my chair'.[13]

Towards the end of January he was despatched, in his role as 'special correspondent', to a number of politically interesting places in the east of the country. Even at this stage the book of the *Plain Tales* was not ready and Rudyard had to restrain himself in a letter to Thacker Spink: 'I am a man of peace and will *not* be angry because you have taken about nine months to publish the booklet.'[14] He had to beg them to send him six copies within a week, because, after that, 'I go out again into the wilderness for an indefinite time'.

By the time he received a copy, he was seventy-five miles down the Ganges at the holy but 'very dirty' city of Varanasi, or Benares, where he was disconcerted to see a girl who was the spitting image of Flo Garrard. 'Did I ever, in the gabblings of my egoistical youth, tell you about a woman who first taught me to believe in my soul and took me in hand and formed me when I was an objectionable little boy of fourteen and three quarters?' he asked Isabella Burton revealingly. 'Providence has sent to this Hotel for my sins the very double of this Woman – her likeness in face, figure, gait, gesture and speech. I am clearing out tomorrow. I don't approve of magic in private life.'[15] He enclosed a copy of the newly published *Plain Tales* with his letter, confessing he was not satisfied and willing Isabella to tell him it was a fine piece of work. 'I can picture you waving your hands above the pages in a manner of which I firmly believe no other woman in the world has the secret,' he gushed, 'and saying with the sniff of lofty disdain, "And this thing was a tribute to ME!". Candidly, haven't you done something of the sort already? Forgive me, it is crude and imperfect as you have said.' His continuing debt to Isabella was clear in his story 'The Bride's Progress', which appeared in the *Pioneer Mail* on 8 February. As he later confirmed, he used her perspective to tell of a young English bride passing through Benares, being assailed by smells, bells and images of lewd gods, and passing quickly on – oblivious of the cultural context and happy that India was simply 'an incident' on her trip.

Following the railway forty miles downstream to Ghazipur, he visited Harry Rivett-Carnac, his old family friend, who had secured himself one of the cushiest sinecures in the Indian Civil Service – as Opium Agent, earning 3000 rupees a month or £2700 a year, at the Ghazipur Factory, the country's leading centre for processing opium, largely for the Chinese market. In his autobiography Rivett-Carnac admitted candidly that the job afforded him 'the greatest comfort', allowing considerable leisure to pursue his own interests. Rudyard did not reveal this personal connection in his piece for the *Pioneer*, but was open about his interest in being there shortly before the start of the spring opium production season. He watched the drug arriving in 'challans, regiments of one hundred jars, each holding one maund,[16] and each packed in a basket and sealed atop'. Every challan was accompanied by a number of forms attesting to its quality and signed by the district officer where the opium was picked. The factory had its own quality control: an expert Indian taster, called a purkhea, took a sample of the drug in his fingers, rubbed and smelled it, and called out the class, which was written down by another official. When the jars were empty they were smashed up and put to serve as part of the revetment that guarded the factory against encroachment by the River Ganges.

From Ghazipur Rudyard crossed the River Ganges to visit a memorial of the Mutiny, the 'Little House at Arrah', where a heroic magistrate and his small defensive force had held out for eight days against a besieging army of thousands of sepoys. He was amused to find that the house was now occupied by a judge, whose servants had no idea of its historical interest and were more concerned to show the inquisitive sahib visitor their master's boots and saddles.

Moving down to Jamalpur, in the north-west corner of Bengal (now Bihar), he found a model railway town, basking in an area 'fat and greasy with good living'. He appreciated the fact that there was only one employer here, the East India Railway. When a loud buzzer sounded at 11 o'clock every morning, the whole place ground to a halt, as all the workers downed tools and ate their tiffin. In vast sheds, housing up to twenty-four locomotives, he watched engines being stripped and reconditioned, and concluded, oddly, that they were 'as distinctly feminine as a ship or a mine'. In this smooth-functioning community, where no expatriate had to fear 'anomie', his own welcome by the local Masonic lodge, St George in the East, confirmed his faith in the Craft as a universal brotherhood of action.

By now accustomed to living out of a suitcase, he penned a wry poem 'A Ballade of Bad Entertainment', also known as 'A Ballade of Dak Bungalows', about the primitive food available in government-run lodging houses. To the south of Jamalpur, the poorly maintained Giridih coalfields kept his interest for only a short time and he struggled to convey something of the monotony of the mine engineers' existence in his journalistic report to the *Pioneer*. Probably for this reason, this account was not published until after his related but fictional piece of 'social realism', 'At Twenty-Two'.[17] As was often the case, Rudyard was sympathetic to the plight of the Indian masses (it was the babus he did not like). This time he made a powerful case for the miners, presenting the colliery company as cold and greedy (changing their employees' allotments every six years so that they would not acquire proprietary rights), and idolising the coal-face hero whose long experience of the positioning of the shafts helped extricate himself and his colleagues from a flooded mine. Rudyard ended his story with reference to Zola's *Germinal*, suggesting that his enthusiasm for miners' rights was as much a literary homage as an expression of new-found political activities.

One of his more strongly held opinions – his hostility to educated Indians – could not have been more blatantly expressed when he reached Calcutta. After sizing up the unaccustomed bustle of the Raj's capital, an administrative and commercial centre that was as close to a European city as anything in India, he reverted to type, ascribing 'the Big Calcutta Stink' which assailed his nostrils to the city's limited measure of self-government, which ensured that 'the municipal Board list is choked with the names of natives – men of the breed born in and raised off this surfeited muck heap'.[18] A visit to the debating chamber of the Bengal Legislative Council only confirmed his prejudices, as he heard a babu spouting John Stuart Mill in a live version of his nightmare in 'The Strange Ride of Morrowbie Jukes'. 'We made that florid sentence,' Rudyard railed. 'That torrent of verbiage is Ours. We taught him what was constitutional and what was unconstitutional in the days when Calcutta smelt. Calcutta smells still, but We must listen to all that he has to say about the plurality of votes and the threshing of wind and the weaving of ropes of sand. It is Our own fault.'

Some calm was restored when an expatriate officer of the Calcutta police ('as fine a five-score of Englishmen as you will find east of Suez') was on hand to accompany Rudyard on a tour of the red-light district or 'City of Dreadful Night' (a title, lifted from James Thomson's poem, that he must have liked, since he had already used it for his story in Lahore). Rudyard was bowled over by the beauty of a jewelled tart called Dainty Iniquity. She was clearly well known because Rudyard had informed Isabella of his intention to visit her a few weeks earlier. 'Take one of the fairest miniatures that the Delhi painters draw,' he wrote, 'and multiply it by ten; throw in any of Angelica Kauffmann's best portraits, and add anything that you can think of from Beckford to Lalla Rookh, and you will still fall short of the merits of that perfect face!'[19] However, he was appalled to find a white, albeit Eurasian, woman plying her trade, commenting, in another reference to his current literary interests, that it would have taken a novelist, probably a French one, to do justice to her story.

He himself had to be satisfied with penning 'The Ballad of Fisher's Boarding House'. In a dockside bordello frequented by sailors, a fight breaks out over the favours of a hooker, known as Anne of Austria. When Hans, a blue-eyed Danish seaman, is killed, she steals his lucky charm, with its picture of his girl-friend. While lusty and colourful, this poem is interesting because its subject matter was close to Rudyard's side-lined novel *Mother Maturin*. Unusually, a diary fragment survives[20] of 'notions to be worked out': it shows the ballad was finished on 22 February and published in the *Week's News* a fortnight later.

The late spring heat of Calcutta was becoming uncomfortably sticky in early March, when he received a letter from Isabella (possibly at Fisher's boarding-house) informing him, along with some constructive criticism of his *Letters of Marque*, that she was leaving India by the end of the month. The suddenness of her decision surprised him: reading between the lines, she found life in Peshawar unbearable and her marriage was suffering. Rudyard begged her to stay in touch, telling her that he now expected to return to Britain himself the following April and running over the many stories he had recently written with her in mind – not just 'The Education of Otis Yeere' and 'A Wayside Comedy', but also 'The Sending of Dana Da' and even 'Wee Willie Winkie' (suggesting the possibility – though the ages are different – that the precocious child in that tale was her twelve-year-old son Francis).

Back in Allahabad at the end of the month, Rudyard did not

wait long before finding a replacement muse. He had first met Edmonia (known as 'Ted') Hill when passing through the town over Christmas. She was tall, dark-haired and dainty, with a broad face, thin lips and an inscrutable smile. Well educated and amusing, she had an American candour not unsimilar to Isabella's Irish bluffness. Seven years older than Rudyard, she was the Methodist daughter of the President of Beaver College for Women, near Pittsburgh, Pennsylvania, and the wife of an Ulsterman, Alexander Hill, an amiable bearded meteorologist, who for eleven years had been a science professor at Allahabad's Muir Central College. At their first meeting, over dinner at the Allens', Rudyard had made a beeline for Ted, as she stood by the fireplace, and had quizzed her about her country. Unfazed, she told her younger sister Caroline in Beaver about her new acquaintance who 'looks about forty, as he is beginning to be bald, but he is in reality just twenty-two. He was animation itself, telling his stories admirably, so that those about him were kept in gales of laughter ... He is certainly worth knowing.'[21] When she invited him to her house to play badminton, he declined any exercise, but was keen to continue his so far literary-inspired study of the American tongue, which he claimed was 'the one language I have long and ardently desired to learn'. Having decided he was returning home the following year, he probably already contemplated journeying eastwards and home across the United States.

Rudyard also had to tell someone about Ted and his confidante was Isabella. '[I] have fallen in love with an American woman – the wife of a man in the Educational. She isn't much more than 12 inches taller than I but she is original and says surprising things in a soft cooing drawl and keeps a team of youngsters – four of 'em – in beautiful control. I want her for a character in a story of mine, and have told her that. She is everything that is beautiful and fascinating. She thinks that I'm a "very nice little man" and asks me to Badminton – jumpy, jerky, shrieky, squeaky Badminton!'[22]

Ted Hill quickly assumed Isabella's (and, before her, Alice

Kipling's) position as Rudyard's main critic and confidante. But where Isabella was inspirational and Alice pushy, Ted was more supportive and objective. As a childless woman, she easily adopted a maternal role though, still only in her late twenties, she was hardly matronly. Several factors made for mutual understanding: for example, they both came from Methodist backgrounds and they both suffered from painful and debilitating headaches. More important, she provided emotional security at an unsettled time in both his personal and professional life. For, at the age of twenty-two, he had cast loose from his family for the first time in India. His roving Viking gene had surfaced on his recent travels and was making him restless. But for the time being he needed to apply himself to serious creative writing.

The Hills' quiet house, Belvedere – which, unusually for Allahabad, was set back from the main road down a long tree-lined drive – provided a welcoming environment where Rudyard could withdraw from the clatter of the printing works and the tedium of the Club. The garden, with its bougainvillaea and its fruit trees, was a delight – as he affectionately recalled in his *Jungle Book* story 'Rikki-Tikki-Tavi'. He even liked the unassuming Alex Hill, whose hobby of photography intrigued him. From now on Rudyard's writings were peppered with references to this newish phenomenon. In February, 'The Sending of Dana Da', his spoof on Madame Blavatsky and the Theosophists, contained an elaborate metaphor about the developing fluid needed to interpret the mumbo-jumbo of spirits on the astral plane. Before long he helped Alex publish articles on 'Amateur Photography in India' in the *CMG*. Later in the summer he memorably compared a moonlit trip through a Himalayan pass to 'hurrying through miles and miles of platinotype photoes – all as soft as velvet mixed with cream'.[23]

In late April, with stories flowing from his pen in a notably prolific period of his working life, Rudyard called on the 'brilliantly clever'[24] Mrs Hill for assistance on 'Poor Dear Mamma', the first part of *The Story of the Gadsbys*, his latest attempt to convey the cynical, sexual politics of Anglo-Indian relationships – in this case, the engagement and marriage of a young officer. Providing an insight into his research methodology for 'The Education of Otis Yeere', Rudyard claimed he needed to get into the 'innermost recesses of a young ladies' [sic] boudoir', but was finding it difficult 'with the limited amount of knowledge at my disposal to get the hang of conversation between girls'. So he asked Ted, who had recently left for her summer holiday in the hill station of Mussoorie, if he could 'trespass' on her kindness 'so far as to ask you on some idle afternoon to look over and check the thing in proof? You shall have the widest of margins as befits the wisest of Censors and your commands will be obeyed.'[25]

In May, requiring Rudyard out of the office again, the *Pioneer* was thinking of sending him to report on the continuing war in Burma. Instead, he was asked to return to Lahore to edit the *CMG* while Robinson was temporarily absent. Having 'stuffed the weekly with tales for the next seven weeks', Rudyard proceeded north with mixed feelings. On the one hand he claimed to prefer the rough Pathans and Baluchis, whom he understood, to the 'frog-like' inhabitants of Allahabad.[26] On the other he now realised one Club was like any other and, returning to the Lahore version, he found the 'same men, same talk, same billiards – all connu and triply connu, except for what I carry in my heart, I could almost swear that I had never been away'.[27]

For four months – while he was in Lahore and then, briefly, with his family in Simla – Rudyard amused Ted with long gossipy letters about his literary efforts, his family and the people he met. After he had published a poem, 'The Song of the Women', in the *Pioneer*,[28] praising Lady Dufferin's endowment of a fund to provide medical care for native women, the Viceroy wrote a letter of thanks, asking him to 'accept the accompanying volume of mine which will be followed by a very good photograph of Lady Dufferin as soon as the supply which we are expecting arrives'. Unlike his parents, Rudyard had remained lukewarm towards the Dufferins – partly out of youthful arrogance, partly now from an atavistic, puritanical aversion to aristocratic pomp that had been rekindled by Mrs Hill's American lack of pretension. (Around the same time the *Pioneer* had printed a leader, ostensibly on Matthew Arnold's *Civilisation in the United States,* which maintained that no Englishman of taste would consider living in North America. Rudyard was incensed at this 'impertinence', but admitted to Ted that 'I have been in my readings and training an American for so long that I am perhaps prejudiced'.[29])

One tedious evening at the Lahore Club, Rudyard was collared by a love-sick subaltern, Lieutenant David Beames, of the 19th Bengal Infantry, who poured out his heart about his passion for a seventeen-year-old beauty he had met in Simla. Rudyard was fascinated by the reactions of a youth whose attitude to women was even more impulsive than his own. Superficially, he feigned annoyance that 'whenever a man is in a row or in love or sick or something'[30] he unburdened his secrets on him. In fact, realising he gleaned useful insights into human behaviour this way, he plied Beames with best Burgundy and noted what he said – for possible inclusion in his *Gadsby* stories. In the end, Beames served less as a model for literature than as a sounding board for Rudyard's views about the role of females in Anglo-Indian life. As with many of his opinions, his attitude to women was both complicated and inconsistent. While the young maidens in his stories tend to be whimperers, the middle-aged matrons are manipulators above all else. Sexual passion is generally restricted to lower-class army camp followers such as Mulvaney's Dinah Shadd or native girls like Bisesa in 'Beyond the Pale'. Yet Mrs Hauksbee is intelligent and not unattractive: a credible prototype of a modern woman managing her own life.

Rudyard could not make up his mind whether women were a positive or negative influence in India. In the *Plain Tale* 'His Chance in Life', Rudyard admits that a woman's presence can be useful: 'When a man does good work out of all proportion to his pay, in seven cases out of nine there is a woman at the back of his virtue.' But by the time of *The Story of the Gadsbys*, his views had altered abruptly: women are now an encumbrance to men trying to fulfil their duty. 'A good man married is a good man marred,' as Gadsby's friend, Captain Mafflin, put it, or, 'He travels the fastest who travels alone' – from the much quoted explanatory 'L'Envoi' at the end of the book. This was odd because Rudyard had just been in Allahabad, where the Hills' marriage, which he had witnessed at close quarters, was enduring and mutually supportive.

The reasons for this change of view are unclear. Perhaps it is wrong to read too much into Rudyard's fiction. Perhaps he was simply thinking about leaving India and wanted no ties. There was a laddish swagger in another of his well-known lines (from 'The Betrothed', published in the *Pioneer* in November), 'A woman is only a woman, but a good cigar is a smoke.' The feeling of 'loaferdom' that he frequently noted in the *Letters of Marque* about his Rajasthani travels had made rather more impression on him than he imagined.

Rudyard also had other females on his mind at the time. Shortly after returning to Lahore he started telling Ted Hill about a mysterious woman he referred to vaguely as 'My Lady'. The extravagant terms in which he spoke of this person have led some commentators to suggest that she was either a figment of his imagination or else a vehicle for stating his affections for Ted Hill herself. The latter idea is unlikely since he switches distinctly in his letters from discussing his 'Lady' to addressing questions directly to Ted. The only satisfying solution to this mystery is the most obvious. There really was a woman, whose name is unknown, with whom Rudyard was besotted. Mrs Hill herself stated as much in a note she later appended to one of his letters, 'About RK's love affair which he got bravely over. The girl was not worthy – she wouldn't marry such an "ineligible".'[31] As she wrote to her family in Beaver, when Rudyard visited Mussoorie briefly *en route* to Simla in mid-June, 'He is the most susceptible person I ever knew. As he came up the winding road he glimpsed a girl's head in a window, "a golden-haired beauty", and he has been talking about her ever since. I think I know her, so I hope they can meet at a dance.'[32]

Clearly, while at ease with older women, Rudyard had problems relating to girls of his own age – and there was a history of such distant and unobtainable women, from Flo Garrard to Amy Duke. No name has survived for this latest fancy, suggesting again a lack of physical contact. Nevertheless, his colleagues sensed something afoot because, even while he was at Lahore a rumour surfaced that he was engaged to Amy Parry-Lambert, daughter of the sub-Hauksbee Simla schemer who featured in 'Venus Annodomini'. But, from Rudyard's uncharitable comments, Amy was not his 'Lady': finding her ugly and talentless, he forecast that she would be a burden on her mother's hands for the rest of her life. Six weeks later, in Simla, Gussie Tweddell, a prettier girl with literary aspirations, pressed herself upon him. After forcing him to sit through a recitation at dinner, she sent Rudyard a copy of her execrable verses, which were read out, to general amusement, in the family square. Teased by his mother that Gussie might be a suitable woman to marry, Rudyard had to admit that the girl, who was half German, had a 'beautiful name for a comic opera'.[33]

Rudyard's attitude towards marriage in the *Story of the Gadsbys* also reflected his complicated emotional reaction to Isabella Burton's leaving India. Her final departure was delayed until the end of April, allowing her enough time to tell Rudyard that his latest story – unnamed, but possibly a reworking of 'The Hill of Illusion', about a married woman who decides at the last minute not to elope from Simla with her lover[34] – was 'not bad – very bad – but it lacks depth'. Typically, she left a couple of time bombs to remind people of her. One was her article, 'Play-acting', about 'the vanities and stupidities of a provincial group of amateur actors'[35] which appeared in the *Pioneer* on 27 April, the day she sailed from Bombay, and which, three days later, Rudyard informed Ted Hill, had already made some of the targets of her satire furious. ('Poor dears!' he added.) The other was the unsatisfactory conclusion of her latest liaison with Sir Lepel Griffin, Agent to the Governor-

General for Central India. He had been scheduled to accompany her home, but for some reason cried off. Speculating to Ted Hill that Isabella had hoped to act as a political confidante to Griffin – 'she is one of the few women in the world who have a man's ambition beating in a 23-inch figure'[36] – Rudyard noted that, with her temper, he would not have liked to have been her companion at table during her voyage home. And he recalled the line in his story 'Consequences': 'If Mrs Hauksbee were twenty years younger, and I her husband, I should be Viceroy of India in fifteen years.'

By then, Rudyard seemed almost relieved at this outcome. He told Ted that Isabella had been kind 'in her curiously cynical way and I owe her thanks for half a hundred ideas and some stories'.[37] His own mother was certainly delighted to see the back of a woman she felt had been a bad influence. Referring to 'The Hill of Illusion', with its cool dissection of the fickleness of Simla's social mores, she said, only half admiringly, 'It's clever and subtle and all that and I see the morality in it, but, O my boy, how do *you* do it? Don't tell me about "guessing in the dark". It's an insult to your old Mother's intelligence. If Mrs Hauksbee enlightened you I'm not sorry she's gone home.'

After his short stay in Mussoorie, Rudyard arrived in Simla towards the end of June, for what was to be his final visit. Lockwood had left for England, so the Kiplings were renting Craigsville, a smaller house than usual, next door to Hardinge's Hotel in The Mall, where Rudyard nominally stayed, though he only used his room as a retreat in which to smoke. The atmosphere of the town was subdued because Rivett-Carnac's friend, the German Kaiser Frederick III, had just died, only three months after succeeding his father, and the Viceroy and his 'court' were observing what Rudyard felt was an unnecessarily long period of mourning. No sooner had Rudyard arrived than his mother realised that their relationship had changed. Rudyard had grown up living away from home in Allahabad. Was there a note of jealousy in her voice, a sense that her role in his life had been usurped, when she observed, matter-of-factly, 'You belong to yourself,' and Trix picked up the thread: 'You don't belong to us at any rate'?[38]

One member of the party disagreed – Vixen, the finely bred fox terrier which had become his faithful companion the previous year. When his 'fat, white waddler' forsook Alice and Trix, who had been looking after him, and transferred her affections back to Rudyard, he preened, 'I shall think better of myself henceforward,' whereupon his proto-feminist mother noted caustically, 'Hear him! Anyone but a man would have said that he would think better of the dog.'[39] As Rudyard had already suggested to his cousin Margaret, and as he later underlined in his story 'Garm – A Hostage', Vixen was the first of many dogs that took on the role of the woman in his life. (In 'Garm', he told how Vixen would sleep in his bed, 'her head on the pillow like a Christian; and when morning came I would always find that the little thing had braced her feet against the wall and pushed me to the very edge of the cot'.)

Before the end of the month the Kiplings had decamped to the relative luxury of The Retreat, an English-style 'country house' that Sir Edward Buck kept at Mashobra, six miles outside town. (The Allens had a similar cottage nearby.) In his precious manner, Sir Edward prided himself on his garden to which he had imported Simla's first rhubarb plants, as well as mushroom beds, English pears, strawberries and, as Rudyard put it, 'all the hundred fads and whimsies with which a wealthy bachelor is at liberty to surround himself'.[40] At one stage he had owned a pet tiger cub, which was kept on a long steel chain, until it clawed the flesh off a hillsman's leg and had to be sent to the zoo.

At The Retreat he ran a hospitable open house, though he was never quite sure who was visiting or staying. On this occasion the Kiplings found themselves in the company of Lady Roberts, who kept herself to herself, and Mrs Napier, the capricious, bossy wife of Colonel George Napier, commander of the 1st Dragoon Guards in Rawalpindi, who saw herself – now more than ever – as a pretender to Mrs Hauksbee's crown. Having attracted Lord Dufferin's eye, she kept his indolent son Lord Clandeboye as a hanger-on. But when she imperiously asked Rudyard to write her a story he refused. As far as he was concerned, her role model Mrs Burton had 'more wit in her little finger than Mrs N. ever heard or knew of in her life'.

Since Lockwood Kipling was in England, Rudyard found himself in the unfamiliar role of *pater familias*, having to deal with an army officer who was badgering Trix to marry him. Normally Captain John Fleming would have fascinated Rudyard. The son of a distinguished army doctor, he too had served in Afghanistan (with the King's Own Scottish Borderers) in the wake of General Roberts in 1879–80. Later he had taken part in punitive expeditions against the Mohmands, north of the Khyber Pass and, further east, across the border, into the Laghman Valley, before being seconded to the Survey of India in July 1885. In different circumstances Rudyard would have wanted to know more about Fleming's experiences across the North-West Frontier and would have enquired about the Survey of India, the mapping unit, based in Dehra Dun, which provided essential topographical information about the frontiers of the Raj and beyond. As well as map-making, the 'pundits' employed by the Survey often gathered military and political intelligence as they travelled in the hills and beyond to the steppes of Central Asia. Indeed the Survey of India complemented Colonel MacGregor's military Intelligence Department in Simla as the Raj's espionage service. If Fleming had met Trix a year earlier, Rudyard might have used him as a model for his policeman, Colonel Strickland. Later, after he came to know him better, Rudyard may have drawn on Fleming when he created Colonel Creighton, the head of the Ethnographical Department to which Kim reported. Was it simply a coincidence that one of Fleming's best friends in the Survey of India was a Colonel Crichton who married Rudyard's old flame, Gussie Tweddell?

But at this stage Rudyard considered Fleming an interloper into the family square and had no time for him. He was not impressed that his sister's suitor came from a distinguished Scottish family and was a fine water-colourist (a useful attribute in a map-maker). For Rudyard felt he had a family duty to perform. The two lovers had begun seeing each other in Simla the previous summer. As a result of parental pressure, Trix had subsequently halted their romance. Lockwood Kipling thought that, though 'a model young man', Fleming did not have the right tastes for his daughter, 'not caring for books, nor for many things for which our Trix cares intensely'.[41] Now Fleming was pressing his suit again. Initially Rudyard's reaction was to forbid his sister to see 'that objectionable cuss'. But Trix had wept so much that Alice begged her son to be merciful, arguing in a Machiavellian way that if the two lovers saw each other, their ardour might abate. So Rudyard told Fleming 'that while I hated him just as much as ever (poor brute, he was *so* humble) I liked my sister's peace of mind more and consequently he wasn't to stay at the Club making a gibbering baboon of himself but to come down to see the maiden now and again with the assurance that I would not regard him as a burglar or an assassin'.[42]

Rudyard's sixth season in the hills (his fifth in Simla) confirmed that he had had enough. He pushed himself through the usual social hoops, visiting the Viceregal Lodge ('to call and tell lies'[43]) and dining with the Lieutenant-Governor of the Punjab, Sir James Lyall ('a portentous dull affair'[44]). More observant now about the way the government operated in its summer retreat, he was amused at the role of Donald Mackenzie Wallace, the Viceroy's private secretary, who acted as a modern spin doctor 'executing a sort of official war dance between him and the outer world to keep off the profane crowd. A good watch dog is the faithful Donald, and when he is on duty he refuses to bend.'[45] Oddly, this buttoned-up figure was soon to play a significant role in Rudyard's life. For he had previously been the correspondent of *The Times* in both Moscow and Constantinople. While in the latter post, he spent six months in Cairo assisting Lord Dufferin on his special diplomatic mission following the Egyptian defeat at the battle of Tel el Kebir. Dufferin subsequently invited him to join his staff in India, and when the Viceroy's term of office finished, Mackenzie Wallace returned to *The Times* as its Foreign Editor in London.

As light relief, Captain Edmund Hobday, one of the Viceroy's ADCs, had written a revue called *Bluebeard* that ran at the small theatre in the Commander-in-Chief's residence, Snowdon. At Trix's insistence, Rudyard went to see it twice, wrote it up for the *CMG* and even included one of Hobday's songs at the end of his story 'The Man Who Was', published a couple of years later. More men were now coming to Simla, bringing a more masculine, even misogynistic culture, if a joke told Rudyard by Andrew Scoble, the Legal Member of the Council, is anything to go by: 'What medicine does a man take when he is blessed with an obstreperous wife?' And the punch-line ran, 'He takes an elixir' (he takes and he licks her). With hindsight, the high point of Rudyard's visit was riding up The Mall with General Sir Frederick Roberts who earnestly quizzed him, as the author of the Mulvaney stories, about army conditions. After asking Rudyard what the average Tommy really thought about his housing and leisure facilities, the General thanked him as 'gravely' as if the young writer himself had been a full colonel. Or, at least, these were Rudyard's recollections in his autobiography nearly half a century later, when his vision may have been coloured by his subsequent adulation of Roberts.

Rudyard's sense of *déjà vu* made him more determined than ever to leave India. He had been reading Walter Besant's novel *All in a Garden Fair* about a young man making his way in bookish circles in London. Well-informed about developments in British publishing, he probably knew that Besant had started the Society of Authors four years earlier and he realised it was now possible to make a living as an independent writer. Although his letters to Ted Hill show he was under no illusion about the fickleness of London's literary salons, he was 'hungry for the theatres because

I have yet to write my play – and long summer days at Richmond, Datchet, Virginia Water, and rests on the borders of Epping Forest, perhaps the most beautiful in all the world'.[46] He was encouraged by his family who said, 'You must go home next year, and go home round the world. You're blue-moulded with India – fagged, dull and self centred.' George Allen proved sympathetic and offered him a freelance contract, worth £200 a year, to write from London for the *Pioneer*. But for the time being he still needed Rudyard's services in Allahabad. The rigours of another Indian summer had laid his staff low: George Chesney, the editor, was ill, Maitland Park, his young assistant, was still raw, and Howard Hensman, the experienced Simla correspondent, was set to accompany a punitive army expedition into the Black Mountains in October.

When Rudyard returned to Allahabad in the sweltering monsoon heat of July, the Hills took pity and invited him to stay at Belvedere, rather than sweat it out in his usual lodgings at the Club. Motivated by a touch of jealousy that her son should be living with a rival muse, Alice Kipling wondered whether the Hills would be able to tolerate his 'moods and devils and falling into clouds'.[47] But Alex and Ted knew what they were letting themselves in for. Since their guest bungalow was under repair, they accommodated him in a spare room inside the main house, allowing him access to their so-called Blue Room as a study. Rudyard quickly adapted to the easy pace of Belvedere, one of the few houses in town to have survived the Indian Mutiny. (It had cloth ceilings to create an air pocket under the thatched roof. Once, when a powerfully unpleasant smell pervaded the house, it was traced to a small dead squirrel trapped under the roof – an incident that Rudyard used in his story 'The Return of Imray'.) The highlight of the day at Belvedere was breakfast on the back veranda. Indian cooks were notably uncreative, particularly in serving Western dishes. But the Hills' kitchen was run by a culinary genius called Booj, a dab hand at everything from mutton chops to exotic American dishes such as chicken and corn dodgers, and the house speciality – pancakes, dripping with butter and honey. After his morning meal, Rudyard went to his office in his trap – his 'Pig and Whistle', as he called it – leaving behind his dependable servant Kadir Baksh to look after his domestic arrangements. When in October Alex Hill needed to go up into the Satpura Hills of the Central Provinces to report on the weather stations, Ted accompanied him, leaving Rudyard in charge of the house.

Living in Belvedere allowed Rudyard to complete his year's work. During the summer more of his soldier tales had been running in the *Pioneer* and the *Week's News*, along with episodes of his marital saga *The Story of the Gadsbys*. In September he signalled an end to this series by publishing 'The Last of the Stories', an amusing conceit about a visit to a limbo-land inhabited by his fictional characters. On one level it allowed him to run a roll-call of everyone from Mrs Hauksbee to Mulvaney, and them to get their own back. On another it provided an insight into his own working methods: later he liked to talk of the daemon who guided him as he wrote; in this story, he wrote of this daemon's cousin, the Devil of Discontent, who lives at the bottom of his ink pot and 'emerges half a day after each story has been printed with a host of useless suggestions for its betterment'.

Rudyard also worked to ensure that the stories he had written over the past year or so were gathered in book form. Hoping for the widest possible dissemination, he entrusted the job not to the stuffy Calcutta publisher Thacker Spink, but to A. H. Wheeler & Co., a local Allahabad firm, which had the monopoly on bookstall sales on Indian railway stations. Rudyard licensed Wheeler's enterprising senior partner, Emile Moreau, to publish his stories in cheap booklet form, with covers in grey-green card, illustrated by his own father. Starting in the autumn, the six volumes of the Indian Railway Library began to appear, priced at just one rupee, and soon they were being read not only on trains but in drawing-rooms throughout the world.

Even as he was mentally winding down from India, Rudyard

was not afraid to tackle new material. The fifth of his booklets, *The Phantom 'Rickshaw and Other Tales*, contained the intriguing tale 'The Man Who Would Be King' – about a couple of ne'er-do-wells who travel beyond the furthest reaches of Empire to Kafiristan, a remote mountain tract to the north of Afghanistan, where they are determined to establish their own 'kingdom'. Their task is made easier when they are greeted as long-lost white Gods of tribal legend. They find they can maintain their authority by offering the natives a mish-mash of Masonic ideology. Significantly, their thrall is broken by a woman. Having promised each other not to be diverted by sex, Dan Dravot unilaterally decides to relax this rule. But when his native wife bites him in a dispute and he bleeds, he is seen to be only human, and the game is up. Dan is killed, and his colleague Peachey Carnehan crawls back to the narrator (clearly Rudyard in his newspaper office) with his tale of an improbable escapade gone badly wrong.

The story works on several levels – as a madcap adventure; as a scholarly examination of the nature of kingship, and the myths that are required to sustain it; and, anticipating a theme Rudyard would later develop, as a cautionary tale of an imperialistic venture which goes wrong because it fails to live up to its original moral principles.

Various models for Dravot and Carnehan have been suggested, but no-one quite fits the bill. Rudyard would have known the stories of, perhaps even met, like-minded Englishmen such as the army deserter 'Jungli' Wilson, who established a semi-independent fiefdom with its own coinage at Harsil, north of Musoorie, in the middle years of the century. As usual, he was able to draw on many sources, including W. W. MacNair's appendix on Kafiristan in General MacGregor's 1884 volume *The Defence of India*. (Another contributor had been Major G. C. Napier, husband of Mrs Hauksbee's putative successor.) The names of the two adventurers were suggested by the Hills, and additional information on Kafiristan was culled from the *Encyclopaedia Britannica*.

In keeping with its title, *Wee Willie Winkie and Other Child Stories*, the final volume of the Indian Railway Library also addressed new subject matter – the psychology of children. It included a recent tale, 'The Drums of Fore and Aft', about two delinquent young drummer boys who, with their rousing rendition of 'The British Grenadiers', spur a dispirited regiment to victory in an Afghan border skirmish. Rudyard's interest may have been inspired by Mrs Hill's three-year-old god-daughter, Edna Irwin. He was so charmed by her frequent visits to Belvedere (with her father, the local doctor) that he wrote 'Imperious Wool-Booted Sage', a gushy poem in baby-talk, for her birthday in October. As he noted in his preface to these stories, 'Only women understand children thoroughly; but if a mere man keeps very quiet, and humbles himself properly, and refrains from talking down to his superiors, the children will sometimes be good to him and let him see what they think about the world.' An impressed Ted Hill told her family in America, 'I never saw anyone more devoted to children, and there are so few in this station.'

Rudyard was also stimulated to dredge up painful memories of his time at Southsea. 'Baa Baa Black Sheep' is a gut-wrenching tale of a young boy sent from India to live in the care of a cruel guardian in England. Although presented as fiction, it is uncompromisingly autobiographical. Ted Hill later noted, 'It was pitiful to see Kipling living over the experience, pouring out his soul in the story, as the drab life was worse than he could possibly describe it ... When he was writing this he was a sorry guest, as he was in a towering rage at the recollection of those days.' The curious thing was that Rudyard should have chosen to write this story now. Over the previous six years in India, he had never bothered to rail against a system of education that required young Anglo-Indian children to go back to the 'mother country'. (Indeed he had attacked a scheme to set up a USC type college in India, because he believed it would produce children of Empire with a provincial rather than the necessary metropolitan frame of mind.) However, the presence of a lively American woman may have encouraged Rudyard to speak of his own childhood experiences for the first time. In the process, some of his suppressed hostility towards his parents surfaced.

As well as arranging for these stories to be published as books, Rudyard worked feverishly at self-promotion, particularly in England where, until then, sales of *Plain Tales* had been poor: only sixteen subscriptions to the second edition which Thacker Spink had shipped in sheet form. The tide began to change after a notice of the book in the London-based *Saturday Review*,[48] which praised Rudyard as 'a born story-teller and a man of humour into the bargain. He is singularly versatile, and equally at home in humour and pathos.' Three months later the grand old man of Indian letters, Sir William Hunter, compiler of the Statistical Survey of India, who had recently retired from the Supreme Council, penned a sympathetic review of the third edition of *Departmental Ditties* in the *Academy*. Lockwood Kipling's home leave in the autumn also helped advance his son's name: a review of *Soldiers Three* in the *Spectator*,[49] was probably written by his friend George Hooper, who worked there. Hooper had received the early Indian Railway Library edition that Rudyard had mailed to anyone he vaguely knew, including even his old colleague Stephen Wheeler, now in harness at the *St James's Gazette*.

Meanwhile, Rudyard was still arguing with Thacker Spink. Their initial accounts for *Plain Tales* showed that, after paying his royalty, they had made a profit of 2235 rupees on sales of 2500 copies at four rupees each and Rudyard was not satisfied. On 9 August 1888 he wrote, 'We will now talk business. I am a little bit too well known to continue this extravagant rate of buying publicity. Therefore as soon as the first edition runs out I will resume my property and publish elsewhere, using and altering the book as I please. If you are anxious to secure any lien on the *Plain Tales* you are welcome to the copyright for the sum of Rs 10,000, or, in other words, the price of three editions. I feel sure that when you look over your books and see what the

Departmental Ditties and *Plain Tales* have done for your profit you will admit that it has been a pleasant and profitable connection between us.'[50]

Two months later, in October 1888, after *Departmental Ditties* had received renewed coverage in Britain, Rudyard could not resist asking Thacker Spink, 'How much by the way did you make on your Rs 500 purchase [of that book]?' Although Rudyard had told Ted Hill that he did not like the company's production of the latest, third edition,[51] he cannot have been too unhappy because he now offered the Calcutta publisher 'for outright sale a volume of verse – mostly ballads of incident and action, entirely or almost entirely Anglo-Indian, and certain to take with the public if they haven't changed their minds. Also it is a likely volume for home consumption as it would introduce the Englishman to a life that he knows very little about.'[52] What he was soon calling 'my Barrack Room Ballads and other Poems which includes 2 soldiers songs and a variety of Anglo-Indian sentimental and descriptive work'[53] were offered outright for 2000 rupees, later raised to 2500 rupees, or just £187.50. This shows that Rudyard was already working on his *Barrack-Room Ballads*, well before they began to appear in *Macmillan's Magazine* towards the end of the following year.

Although concentrating on his books, Rudyard did not neglect his daily contributions to the Allahabad papers, nor his talent for annoying the great and the good. Despite their personal friendship, he upset General Roberts in his September 1888 poem 'A Job Lot', which suggested that the Commander-in-Chief was dispensing his official patronage too liberally to his friends. As Rudyard later commented, 'I don't think Lord Roberts was pleased with it, but I know he was not half so annoyed as my chief proprietor.'[54] Rudyard also antagonised his old *bête noire*, Lord Dufferin, in his poem 'One Viceroy Resigns', which purported to reveal, in robust Browning style, what Dufferin said to his successor Lord Lansdowne when he left his job. Rudyard put his own ideas into Dufferin's mouth:

You'll never plumb the Oriental mind,
And if you did, it isn't worth the toil.
Think of a sleek French priest in Canada;
Divide by twenty half-breeds. Multiply
By twice the Sphinx's silence. There's your East . . .

But they fell out over something entirely different. The original newspaper version of the poem included lines suggesting that Dufferin intended to publish some letters written by his mother, Helen. The quondam Viceroy thought that his friend Alice Kipling had betrayed his confidence to her on this subject and she was forced to write a grovelling letter denying this. 'Since [Rudyard] left us, now more than a year ago, we have only seen his work as the general public sees it when published and have been grieved to note from time to time offences against these which no cleverness, nor even genius itself, can excuse. His youth and inexperience of the world in which he does *not* live, are I feel sure the explanation of what no one regrets more keenly than do his parents. The parody will not be republished.'⁵⁵ In fact, Rudyard had received his information not from his mother, but from another of Dufferin's favourites, Mrs Napier. But Alice's writ on this issue held good and the offending lines were not printed again.

In an end-of-term vein, Rudyard could not resist a final, unusually explicit attack on the rarefied atmosphere of Simla in 'The Masque of Plenty',⁵⁶ a pastiche for the *Pioneer* which drew on Captain Hobday's summer entertainment *Bluebeard*. A few days earlier the official Private Services Commission had concluded a lengthy report on the condition of farming labourers with the complacent view that there was no cause for 'any anxiety at present'. Rudyard had already attacked the 'side-show' of the Commission in the *CMG* and had satirised its activities in a series of stories, known as *The Smith Administration*, about a man's efforts to run his household of squabbling Indians with a suitable dose of paternalism. Now he took to verse to tell how, after being

despatched from the 'wooded heights of Simla' to enquire into
the economic well-being of the land, the Commission encounters
a peasantry reeling from the effects of drought and famine:

> The well is dry beneath the village tree –
>   The young wheat withers ere it reach a span,
>   And belts of blinding sand show cruelly
>   Where once the river ran.

But the delegation sees none of this. Returning to Simla, 'attired
after the manner of Dionysus, leading a pet tiger-cub in wreaths
of rhubarb-leaves, symbolical of India under medical treatment'
(a dig at Rudyard's recent host Sir Edward Buck), it gives a glowing
report: 'The bunnia and the ryot are as happy and as quiet / And
as plump as they can be!'

The gist of Rudyard's message was that the Indian peasantry
deserved better. But he remained adamant that this could not
come from political concessions to babus and their fellow travellers. His intransigence became clear when the Indian National
Congress held its third annual conference in Allahabad at the end
of December. The provincial Governor, Sir Auckland Colvin, had
earlier tried to initiate dialogue with A. O. Hume, only to be told
that the organisation's sole opponents were 'a tiny knot of Anglo-
Indians, mostly officials, whose organs [are] the *Englishman* [a
Calcutta paper], the *Pioneer* and the *Civil and Military Gazette*'.
So George Allen and his editor George Chesney must have gritted
their teeth when they attended the Congress gathering in their
home town. Rudyard also flitted in and out – enough to write a
piece on 1 January 1889 that dismissed the whole exercise as a
putli nautch (puppet show) and referred derogatorily to a 'brown
Captain' among the 'half-castes' in the 1200 delegates.[57] There was
no doubting whom he meant – 'Captain' Andrew Hearsey, the
maverick son of a distinguished general, who had thrown in his
lot with the Congress. On the day of publication an incensed
Hearsey marched round to the *Pioneer*'s office and horsewhipped

the editor. For this act of aggression he was arrested, fined and sentenced to one month in prison. Later, after he was released, Hearsey took the *Pioneer* to court and it seemed that Chesney might have to stand trial – until Allen intervened to say that he had written this latest article. After some judicial gerrymandering, the case was forgotten.

Rudyard reverted to the Old City of Lahore for 'On the City Wall', which provides an insight into what he really thought about India when he abandoned his tub-thumping mode. This sophisticated story, much admired by the imperialist romantic Andrew Lang, takes place in a high-class brothel, allowing Rudyard to explore his ambivalence about the relationship between European and Indian cultures. When, at the start, he notes how, in the West, Lalun's profession of prostitution is criticised on moral grounds, while, in India, it is hereditary and respected, he leaves little doubt that he favours the latter attitude. Though he continues with the dead-pan observation that this is 'distinct proof of the inability of the East to manage its own affairs', he is clearly being sarcastic, particularly when he satirises the failures of a Raj whose Civil Service can delude itself that it is preparing Indians for self-government, while burdening them with so much bureaucracy that, on Judgement Day, 'the youngest Civilian would arrest Gabriel on his own responsibility if the Archangel could not produce a Deputy-Commissioner's permission to "make music or other noises" as the licence says'.[58]

Even in such a regulated society, the natives still take their pleasures. Rudyard looked to personal experience for the loving detail of his description of the room in which Lalun plies her trade. He notes the hideous huge pink-and-blue cut-glass chandelier, the delicate latticed window of carved wood, the profusion of 'squabby pluffy cushions' and the silver hookah, with its 'special little carpet all to its shining self'. Here Lalun entertains her eclectic clientèle of Shiahs, Sufis, Pundits and Lahore notables. She plays songs on her sitar, makes their pipes and presumably, though this is not stated, goes to bed with them. When she trades verses of poetry, they are Persian, bawdy and 'with a triple pun in every other line'.

While one would be hard put to find a more Orientalist scene (in the modern cultural sense), Rudyard portrays it as indissolubly Indian. This is Lalun's kingdom, where the long arm of the English law cannot reach. She does not allow Jews to enter and she objects to the mission-educated Wali Dad even speaking English. Wali Dad is more intelligent and amusing than the usual babus Rudyard mocks. His only trouble is that he suffers 'from education of the English variety and knew it'. In his own words, he is a Product, a 'Demnition Product', of his schooling and 'cannot make an end to my sentence without quoting from your authors'.

Outside Lalun's window is Fort Amara, the fictional Fort Lahore. Imprisoned within its battlements is Khem Singh, a once-fiery Sikh leader who had fought the British and been exiled to Burma. Subsequently, he was brought home to serve out his sentence in the Fort – but only when he was old and offered no threat to the regime. The narrator of the story wonders about this caged lion and pesters Wali Dad for more information. Wali Dad initially refuses even to give the old war-horse's name, stating ambivalently, 'I belong to a nation of liars.'

One night the peace of this civilised brothel is disturbed by a riot in the streets below. Hindus and Moslems are playing out one of their ritual battles on the annual feast of Moharram. Amid the chaos, with army officers still in evening dress arriving hastily from the Club, and with the Garrison Artillery standing by, itching to bring its big guns into action, the narrator is asked by Lalun to help an old gentleman with a gold pince-nez make his way to the Kumharsen Gate on the other side of the riot-torn Old City. He duly obliges and returns to Lalun's house to find Wali Dad sobbing hysterically. This self-professed 'Agnostic and Unbeliever [was] shoeless, turbanless, and frothing at the mouth, the flesh on his chest bruised and bleeding from the vehemence with which he had smitten himself. A broken torch-handle lay by his side, and his quivering lips murmured, "Ya Hasan! Ya Hussain!"'. Only later does the narrator understand that, in the confusion, Khem Singh has escaped from the Fort and he himself has helped escort the old warrior through the crowds to freedom. In the process the sahib has unwittingly been turned into a pawn of the Indian masses. As Lalun earlier joked, he has become her Vizier, or Councillor.

At the end of this precise story several apparent truths are turned on their head: in keeping with the clubman's view of Indians' emotional development, the Western-educated young man reverts to form as a fanatic as soon as a religious-inspired mob surges nearby; the sahib is tricked into undermining the interests of the Raj; and, as a final irony, the great warrior gives himself up, returning to his lonely but generally satisfactory life under guard in Fort Amara because he finds that he cannot hack it in an outside world that has moved on since his glory days. Rudyard was a master of such subtle contradictions.

He had to wait until January 1889 before agreeing severance terms with the *Pioneer* and arranging to accompany the Hills on their voyage back to America in March. He did little writing during his final three months in India (his piece on Hearsey and the Congress may have seen to that), but his life was not without incident. He was devastated in January when Ted Hill was laid low and seemed near death, following a fever – at one stage diagnosed as meningitis – which drove her to the edge of madness. As a result he had to give up his room to a nurse and move back to the Club. From there, he plied Ted with letters which ached with his sincere concern and affection: 'There is no news to tell you. How could there be any with the light of your countenance withdrawn from the station?'[59] Rudyard even had a bout of sympathetic sickness, bringing on such an acute depression that he admitted to his cousin Margaret he had been suicidal. Yet he was not conventionally 'in love' with Mrs Hill. He saw her husband regularly at the Club. It was more that he idolised her and was distressed when not in her company – as can be observed in four rough sketches[60] he made to amuse her. The first, with the rubric 'Study (after the fashion of Whistler) in the NWP Club from 6.30 to 8 pm. It was anything but pleasant ...' shows Rudyard's black face, nocturne-style, with a pipe. The second depicts Rudyard with a worried look, and the note, 'Result of abortive attempt to drive away care with drink. Time 7.55 p.m.' Then there are studies of a 'Futile attempt at taking interest in billiards' and 'Final collapse'.

Rudyard obtained useful advice for the road from the adventurer Moreton Frewen, a friend of George Allen. After a colourful career prospecting for gold in the Rockies, the well-connected Frewen had been working as private secretary to a former Prime Minister of the wealthy princely state of Hyderabad. He had also contributed articles to the *Pioneer* on his favourite topic of bimetallism. On meeting Rudyard, Frewen was struck by his potential and offered to help him find outlets for articles about his forthcoming trip. Frewen informed his American-born wife Clara (sister of Lord Randolph Churchill's wife, the former Jenny Jerome)[61] that Rudyard was 'a sallow young man who had incredible knowledge of every facet of Indian life ... He really has a talent.' But his friend Edward Levy-Lawson, proprietor of the *Daily Telegraph*, did not agree. Having been sent a copy of *Plain Tales*, Levy-Lawson replied discouragingly that Rudyard's work had merit, 'but hardly reaches the standard required of a position on the staff of the *Daily Telegraph*'.

In late February Rudyard travelled to Lahore to bid farewell to his family and friends. At Bikanir House they declared him to be in good shape – rather spoilt by Ted Hill's waffles and short pastry, in fact. But a pen-and-ink sketch by his father, who was back from England, captured the recent thinning of Rudyard's face, the sadness at the corner of his eyes and the slight baldness beginning to appear on his head. No longer was this the confident young man who had arrived in India six years earlier. (Touchingly, Ted had given him some 'hair developer' for his pate – a practical present and a private joke since the most heavily advertised product of Peake, Allen, the general-merchants arm of George

Allen's business empire, was a brand of patent 'hair restorer'.)

Trix was in good form. Her relationship with Captain Fleming had blossomed to the stage that she was now engaged. As a result, she was weighed down with trinkets and rings from her fiancé. Rudyard reported to Ted, 'I walked round and round her till she was dizzy asking: "Where did you get this?" and the invariable answer was: "Oh, Jack gave that to me, ages ago. Didn't you know?"'

Lahore was now firmly on the globe-trotters' map (partly the result of the friendship that had developed between Lockwood Kipling and Frank Cook, of the travel firm Thomas Cook and Son, when the latter had handled the travel arrangements for the 1887 *hajj*, or Moslem pilgrimage to Mecca). As a result the town's bazaars were denuded of suitable artefacts when Rudyard tried to buy last-minute souvenirs – though he did manage to find a plaque of Ganesh, the elephant-headed Hindu God of good fortune (whose swastika symbol he later adopted as a trademark for his books), and a red copper open-work box for Ted. He also made sure he had a letter of introduction to the Freemasons of the United States from the District Grand Master of the Punjab.

After the fifty-one-hour railway journey direct from Lahore to Calcutta, carrying a huge flagon of whisky provided by his mother, he still had a couple of business matters to settle, including, on 7 March, the sale of the copyright in his Indian Railway Library books to A. H. Wheeler for £200 down, and a royalty of four per cent. As a result, he had £1000 in his pocket when, two days later, he joined the Hills at the s.s. *Madura's* berth on the Hughli for the first stage of their journey to the United States. Looking back in a final letter to his cousin Margaret, 'I've had a good time. I've tasted success and the beauty of money, I've mixed with fighters and statesmen, administrators and women who control them all, and "much have I seen, cities and men". It was vivid and lively, and gloomy and savage. I've tried to get to know folk from the barrack room and the brothel, to the Ballroom and the Viceroy's Council and I have in a little measure succeeded.'[62]

While with Moreau in Calcutta he had received finished copies of his last Railway Library book, *Wee Willie Winkie*, one of which he inscribed for Ted on board ship:

> I cannot write, I cannot think
> I only eat and sleep and drink. –
> They say I was an author once,
> I know I am a happy dunce,
> Who snores along the deck and waits
> To catch the rattle of the plates,
> Who drowns ambitions in a sea
> Of Lager and of Tivoli.[63]

He elaborated on his extraordinary sense of release in the first of his articles for the *Pioneer*: 'I understood with what emotions the freed convict regards the prison he has quitted – insight which had hitherto been denied me; and I further saw how intense is the selfishness of the irresponsible man.'[64] Within days, 'A glorious idleness had taken possession of me; journalism is an imposture; so is Literature; so is Art.' And this wave of indolence infected the other two in the party. Rudyard told the story of the venerable Professor, Alex Hill, going below deck to fetch his instruments so he could perform his regular scientist's duty of measuring the weather, being waylaid by the offer of a drink and deciding against any further work.

For the next two and a half months, until they reached San Francisco at the end of May, Rudyard and the Hills sat back and enjoyed themselves. Their favourite pastime was the latest American card game Euchre. Occasionally, Rudyard would hum what he called his 'Tommy Atkins Ballads'. But Ted was wrong to imagine that she was 'present at the inception of Ruddy's *Barrack Room Ballads*', since his communications with Thacker Spink indicated that this happened six months earlier. Alex Hill took so many photographs that he began to complain he was a slave to his camera. Rudyard later playfully reminded him of this, annotating a book of Alex's pictures 'The Professor is cursed with a large and active camera' and adding comments to various shots: against a snap of some sullen Malays smoking on deck, Rudyard subversively (as if to emphasise his bemused disagreement) wrote the words of the popular hymn, 'Onward Christian Soldiers':

> We are not divided
> All one body we,
> One in hope and doctrine
> One in charity.

At the first port of call, Rangoon, the capital of Burma, Rudyard behaved like one of his despised globe-trotters visiting India for the first time. He was overwhelmed by the dazzling colour of this Buddhist country – and, in particular, by the prettiness of Burmese girls. Anticipating the sexual longing that permeates one of his most famous poems, 'Mandalay', written the following year, he reacted immediately:

> I love the Burman with the blind favouritism born of first impression. When I die I will be a Burman ... and I will always walk about with a pretty almond-coloured girl who shall laugh and jest too, as a young maiden ought. She shall not pull a sari over her head when a man looks at her and glare suggestively from behind it, nor shall she tramp behind me when I walk: for these are the customs of India. She shall look all the world between the eyes, in honesty and good fellowship, and I will teach her not to defile her pretty mouth with chopped tobacco in a cabbage leaf, but to inhale good cigarettes of Egypt's best brand.

Further down the coast, when his ship made an unexpected stop at Moulmein, he claimed he did not even notice the pagoda – 'the old Moulmein Pagoda, looking lazy at the sea' – because he was so struck by a Burmese beauty on the steps. But, as Kipling aficionados have pointed out, Rudyard's sense of geography deserted him: Moulmein had no 'road to Mandalay' where 'the old Flotilla lay'. He must have been confusing that experience with an earlier one in Rangoon.

As he sailed down the Malay Peninsula to Singapore, and on to Hong Kong, China and Japan, three things stood out in his reports to the *Pioneer*. One was his guarded response to the orderliness of the Chinese people. In Singapore, he found that the Chinese ate their lunch in a trice, whereas Indians spread themselves out and lingered for hours. This discipline led him to speculate that Britain might have done better commercially if she had conquered China rather than India. However, when he made a side-trip from Hong Kong to Canton on the river-craft the *Ho-Nam*, he was unnerved by the steely hostility of the Chinese – a sudden realisation that brought on something of the blind panic, and symptoms of a breakdown, that he had experienced in Chitor. Having left India, he quickly became sentimental for the old place and wished that South-East Asia had been colonised by Indians rather than by Chinese coolies. The second highlight was his distaste at meeting Americans *en masse* for the first time. (He particularly took against a cocky eight-year-old 'American-German-Jew boy' on the s.s. *Nawab* between Singapore and Hong Kong.) The last was his continuing fascination with brothels – whether talking to a German madam in Singapore, or visiting a Hong Kong establishment which procured English-born girls from San Francisco. 'Corinthian Kate', a hard-drinking tart he felt should have been painted by Alma-Tadema, promised him the pick of West Coast hookers if he could give her some information about the appalling scourge of cholera which had just killed a friend of hers.

Rudyard's first landfall in Japan was Nagasaki, from where, at an extra cost of one hundred rupees paid to Thomas Cook and Sons, he and the Hills were able to sail through the Inland Sea to Kōbe. Instantly preferring the Japanese to the Chinese, he decided that they smiled a lot because they were like children – in his terms, neither natives nor sahibs. He enjoyed exploring the Japanese countryside, which offered spectacular changes of scenery within short distances. Although most of his literary output on this trip was in the form of travel articles for the *Pioneer*, he also produced the odd turnover for his 'first mistress and most true love',[65] the *CMG*. In the guise of fiction, 'Griffiths the Safe Man'[66] told of someone so security conscious that, after strapping his bag very tightly, he could not open it to find the passport he needed for an internal journey between Kyoto and Otsuki. Mrs Hill later confirmed that the ridiculous Griffiths was based on her husband:

After leaving Lake Biwa and resuming our rickshaw trip we stopped at a little Japanese Inn – up stairs we were – I can see the picture of the increasing crowd and the growing wrath of Mr Hill – while RK grinned an unearthly grin. It seemed that we must give up our passports overnight. The landlord was worried – one after another official appeared – and still Mr Hill searched – everywhere but in the right place – I can see that yellow bag with its obstreperous lock yet. The passport was one of the most ridiculous things in Japan in those days. We promised not to disfigure the temples and not to go to a fire on horseback.[67]

Rudyard's own passport was made out in the name of Radjerd Kyshrig.

Before joining the s.s. *City of Peking* for the voyage to San Francisco, Rudyard was annoyed to find pirated American copies of *Plain Tales from the Hills* on sale in a bookshop in Yokohama. His mood improved when he came across a full set of his Indian Railway Library books on board, but he was not happy that the boat was laden with American missionaries and soldiers. They confirmed his suspicions of the United States as a global power, with ambitions that might clash with Britain's in China and the Far East. His own nosing about on his travels had made him increasingly aware (and proud) of Britain's imperial role. He had become used to considering local developments in terms of their consequences for the future of the Empire. In Hong Kong, for example, he had visited the island's greatest merchant, or Taipan, whose opulent life-style left him gasping. But he wondered if it was really prudent to force on China 'all the stimulants of the West', including railways, tramlines and arms. 'There's no sentiment in business,' he was told, 'and anyhow, China will never go to war with England,' but he was not convinced.[68]

Now he began to think of possible rivalry between the United States and England. He must have known about the recent contretemps over fishing rights in Canada (which had brought the Liberal Unionist politician Joseph Chamberlain to Washington to negotiate). But he was taken aback to hear an American passenger on the *City of Peking* telling him that, because of the general lawlessness brought about by the excesses of democracy, 'a war outside our borders would make us all pull together'.[69] Consequently, his first sentiment on reaching the American West Coast on 28 May, after twenty days' pitching on the Pacific Ocean, was not excitement at reaching the homeland of literary heroes such as Emerson and Bret Harte, but relief that the blockhouse guarding the 'finest harbour in the world' could be silenced by two gunboats from Hong Kong 'with safety, comfort and despatch'.

Rudyard described, rather fancifully, how the horde of journalists at the quayside convinced him he was 'a bigger swell' in America than he had thought. Their persistence in seeking interviews annoyed him and, after the Hills had left for Ted's home in Pennsylvania, he holed up in the seven-storey Palace Hotel, where the staff, he observed, seemed so intent on proving that they were freeborn Americans that their service was abysmal. Fighting his sense of loneliness, even alienation, he buried himself in writing his travel pieces for Frewen and the *Pioneer*. He only began to feel better when he received a warm letter from his Aunt Georgie, telling him of a friend to look up in San Francisco and inviting him to stay when he reached England.

Replying to her, he claimed, 'I love not the Americans in bulk! They spit even as in the time of Dickens and their speech is not sweet to listen to – 'specially the women's.'[70] In his pieces for the *Pioneer* he confirmed his distaste for Americans' language ('they delude themselves into the belief that they talk English'), eating habits (they stuff 'for ten minutes thrice a day') and politics (their democracy had not only given power to anybody who could afford to buy up votes but also citizenship to black men about whom he was gratuitously racist).

As he started to relax, he did at least like the females he met, who confirmed the favourable impression of American women he had gained from Ted Hill.

> They are original, and look you between the brows with unabashed eyes as a sister might look at her brother ... They are self-possessed without parting with any tenderness which is their sex-right; they understand; they can take care of themselves; they are superbly independent.[71]

He also appreciated San Francisco's general air of 'recklessness'. Inspired by an evening of high spirits at the city's Bohemian Club, his curiosity (or voyeurism) got the better of him and he could not refrain from visiting the flophouses of Chinatown. As a professed Sinophobe, he was ill-advised to enter a Chinese tenement building, slipping 'past Chinamen in bunks, opium-smokers, brothels, and gambling hells', before alighting on a poker club, where a gun-fight broke out. When he picked himself up off the floor, Rudyard found that everyone else had fled the room. As when visiting the Hindu shrine in Chitor, he was beset with a sense of terror, particularly since one of the gunmen was Mexican and he thought, plausibly enough, that he himself looked Mexican. 'All the tides of intense fear, hitherto held back by intenser curiosity, swept over my soul,'[72] he recalled.

Having recovered his composure, he made his way up the West Coast on the first leg of his four-thousand-mile railway journey to New York. In the forests of Oregon he went fishing and, after a memorable tussle on the river bank, landed a twelve-pound salmon. In Vancouver he succumbed to the blandishments of a smooth-talking English salesman and bought what he called 'Ruddy's folly', two vacant property lots in the Mount Pleasant district. In Montana he met cowboys for the first time – each day 'some new character madder than the last'[73] – and appreciated the mildness of Milwaukee beer. Despite the aggressive nationalism of Yankee tourists in Yellowstone National Park on the Fourth of July, he found himself warming to Americans. Not that he could quite put his finger on the reason for his attraction: 'They are bleeding-raw at the edges, almost more conceited than the English, vulgar with a massive vulgarity which is as though the Pyramids were coated with Christmas-cake sugar-works.'[74] He simply had a gut feeling, based on a racial vision of the future where the 'Anglo-American-German-Jew' would carry all before him, producing the finest artists, writers and administrators the world had ever seen. 'Sixty million people, chiefly of English instincts, who are trained from youth to believe that nothing is impossible, don't slink through the centuries like Russian peasantry.'

This optimism was tempered when he reached Chicago and discovered the ugly face of American capitalism. Everyone was obsessed with 'progress' and making money: 'All that Sunday I listened to people who said that the mere fact of spiking down strips of iron to wood and getting a steam and iron thing to run along them was progress. That the telephone was progress, and the network of wires overhead was progress.'[75] In a fit of nostalgia, India seemed almost desirable: at least it enjoyed a certain quality of life, he noted, congratulating himself for having understood the importance of Indians maintaining their traditions.

Luckily there was someone in America who sympathised with his mixed feelings. After pining for Ted's company most of the way across America, he was delighted to arrive in Beaver, the home town of her parents, the Reverend R. T. and Mrs Taylor, in Northern Pennsylvania.

In Rudyard's pieces for the *Pioneer*, Beaver became Musquash,

Pa., a haven of peacefulness and abundance on the Monongahela river. Since the students of Beaver College were on vacation, he was accommodated on campus in a spacious suite of rooms, complete with a bath. The town being strictly Methodist and officially 'dry', he had to obtain a doctor's prescription if he wanted beer, and have it made up by the local pharmacist. To welcome their daughter Ted, and their distinguished guest Rudyard Kipling, the Taylors held a reception, with special caterers hired from Pittsburgh. True to their principles, however, they allowed no drinking or dancing.

During the long hot afternoons Rudyard lounged in a hammock in an apple orchard behind the Taylors' house. Before long he was attracted to Caroline, one of Ted's two sisters (the other was called Julia). Carrie, as she was known, was an earnest, plumpish girl who, after her BA degree at Beaver College, had recently completed a year-long 'graduate' course at the all-women Wellesley College in Massachusetts. Rudyard liked her company since she was interested in ideas. Hoping to amuse her, he decorated some plates with verses relating to the fruit in the Taylors' orchard and, as a bonus, added motifs which played on Carrie's initials, CAT – including a cat's tail, the monogram CAT, a cat's head and a picture of a cat on a wall.

In this idyllic but sterile atmosphere, with no possibility of sexual malarkey and no old Simla hands to snigger, Rudyard felt confident enough to fall in love with Carrie. This was a remarkable departure: not only was it his first reciprocated romance since leaving England in 1882, but also he was clearly wooing one sister so as to stay close to the other. Within two weeks he was unofficially engaged to Carrie, who already planned to accompany Ted back to England in September.

Before joining the transatlantic steamer at Jersey City for the voyage to Liverpool, Rudyard still needed to complete the last stages of his American safari. Diverting north on a personal quest to track down Mark Twain, he travelled to Buffalo, Toronto and Boston (where his guffaws as he read Robert Louis Stevenson's

The Wrong Box nearly had him ejected from his hotel dining room). He was preparing to go to Maine when he discovered that Twain was staying at his holiday villa in Elmira, New York. His breathless interview there showed all his sophomoric enthusiasm at meeting an American literary hero. (Twain was not expecting him and, a year later, when he first began to hear about Rudyard as an author, he claimed he had no recollection of this encounter.)

Rudyard returned again briefly to Beaver, before making his way to Washington, which impressed him with its beauty and its proximity to power (his meaning when he said it 'smelt Simlaish'),[76] Philadelphia and Wellesley, where he arrived unexpectedly, to the alarm of Carrie Taylor's formidable one-time history Professor, a Miss Coman. But on reaching New York he ignored Carrie and turned to her sister for immediate assistance. He had been to see his Uncle Harry Macdonald, who was pathetically grateful for a visit from a family member, and Lockwood de Forest, the well-heeled Indian art collector who had befriended Lockwood Kipling in Lahore. After receiving him cordially in 'one of the very luxuriousest houses' Rudyard had ever seen, de Forest offered to introduce him to the leading American publisher, Harper and Brothers. At this stage, Rudyard wailed in a letter to Ted, 'Oh how I wish you were here to help.'[77] In the event, Henry Harper waved him away, stating loftily that he ran a house 'devoted to the production of literature'. To Rudyard, this only proved that American publishers were bigger fools and charlatans than he had hitherto imagined and when, on 25 September, he finally boarded the *City of Berlin*, with Ted, Carrie and their cousin Edgar Taylor, he was more determined than ever to succeed as a writer once he reached London.

Book Three

But the Devil whoops, as he whooped of old: 'It is clever, but is it Art?'

Eight

Poet of the Music Halls

1889

With his receding hair and stiff bearing, Rudyard may have looked forty, as Ted Hill had noticed. Remarkably, he was still only twenty-three when, on 4 October 1889, he landed in Liverpool, his first port of call in England after 'seven years' hard' in India. And, behind his puckish manfulness, he remained extraordinarily callow – in a way not even the reassuring presence of a 'fiancée' could disguise. During his apprenticeship in the sub-continent he had, professionally speaking, been a big fish in a small pond. Pressured by his mother, watched over by his father, kept in line by the demands of a daily newspaper, he had cleverly expanded on his schoolboy role as the slightly boisterous, well-read swot. His curiosity and bookishness had combined with his flair to create an original concoction from the hemmed-in world of Anglo-Indians, with their petty corruptions and high-minded racialism.

But London was very different from Lahore and, from Rudyard's initial reactions, he did not realise how much. The British capital was now the centre of a vibrant, embryonic mass democracy. The introduction of compulsory primary education in 1870, together with various Reform Acts (the latest in 1884), had led not only to wider political awareness but also to greater literacy. One consequence – something that Rudyard could not have conceived in India – had been the sort of working-class agitation which resulted in the Bryant and May match girls' strike of 1888 and the month-long stoppage that had brought London's docks to a halt as recently as September. Much of this agitation was justified: 1889 saw the publication of the first volume of Charles Booth's sociological study *Life and Labour of the People in London*, which showed that at least a quarter of the city's population lived in poverty. As a result many women were forced into prostitution: despite the Victorians' reputation for prudery, the area either side of the Strand was a vast open-air brothel. The brutal murder of four prostitutes by 'Jack the Ripper' in the East End in September 1888 had only highlighted the extent of this practice, while the Cleveland Street scandal of July 1889 showed the demand for paid sex among homosexuals (including some of the highest in the land: Lord Arthur Somerset was implicated, and so, it has been suggested, was Prince Eddy, son of the Prince of Wales.)[1]

At the same time, the repercussions of a more literate population were being felt. Since the 1870s, a variety of middle-brow journals such as the *Fortnightly Review* had provided useful outlets for book serialisation. The publication in 1881 of the first penny dreadful, George Newnes's *Tit-Bits*, began to change the market, as did the early pictorial magazines, with their line engravings. Rampant commercialism encouraged writers to think of issues such as copyright protection (the Society of Authors dates from 1884) and to write slicker, more saleable single-volume books, instead of old-fashioned 'triple-deckers', which were geared to the needs of a cosy publishing world dominated by the big lending library, Mudie's. No coincidence, 1889 saw the first use of the word 'best-seller' as noted by the *Oxford English Dictionary*.

As always, writers and artists sought to reflect the spirit of a restless age. Already the words *fin de siècle* were being bandied about: in a July 1889 preview of Oscar Wilde's novel *The Picture of Dorian Gray*, to take one example. They (and, indeed, *Dorian Gray*) reflected a culture moving steadily away from mid-century philosophical certainties. Fixed concepts of reality were coming under fire from different directions – from ideas about the nature of time and perception, from psychical research (these two categories combining in the formidable figure of William James, brother of novelist Henry James), from new scientific disciplines such as anthropology and comparative religion (Rudyard was fascinated by James Frazer's *The Golden Bough*, which began to appear in 1890) and from technical innovations, such as George Eastman's first roll film in 1889. These developments were stirred into the intellectual melting-pot, helping to sustain new movements, from the impressionism of the artist James McNeill Whistler to the latest political creed, socialism. (George Bernard Shaw's *Fabian Essays* were published in 1889.) The close relationship between art and politics was spelt out two years later, in 1891, with Oscar Wilde's *The Soul of Man under Socialism*, which envisaged a Utopia where, by liberating men and women from the tedium of work, machinery would allow them to attain their true potential.

Wilde's concern for both sexes reflected a topical issue at the time Rudyard reached England: in this fast-changing society, what was to be the role of women? As with most of Rudyard's Indian output, the musings of Mrs Hauksbee had hardly moved this debate along from her eyrie in imperial Simla. But Nora, the heroine of Henrik Ibsen's *A Doll's House*, which opened in London in June 1889, had emphatically done so when she left her Norwegian home, affirming she had other duties as sacred as those to her husband and children. (Over the next year various sequels were published, ranging from Walter Besant's, which showed Nora returning to a family in a state of moral collapse, to Bernard Shaw's, which had her converting her husband to feminism.)

Sadly, no input on this matter survives from Bikanir House, Lahore, where Alice had stifled her own ambitions in favour of promoting her son's advancement and where Trix had set aside her nascent nursing career for marriage (in Simla on 11 June 1889). Otherwise Rudyard's awareness of sexual politics on reaching London might have been clearer. He certainly knew something (his portrayal of Mrs Hauksbee showed that). He also realised how removed he had become from metropolitan culture: that was one reason why he had decided to return to London now. But how much did he understand that he was about to become a pawn in a complicated social debate? His early advocates – critics like Walter Besant and Andrew Lang – were the ones who had taken the most vociferous anti-feminist stance in recent years. Besant had written the (originally anonymous) *The Revolt of Man*, a paranoid fantasy of a matriarchal twentieth-century England. Together with W. E. Henley and Edmund Gosse, Lang had hailed the works of Robert Louis Stevenson and, more recently, Rider Haggard as providing a romantic, masculine response to George Eliot's more feminine novels of manners. Now, on the basis of Rudyard's soldier stories, these same writers saw him as their latest standard bearer – someone 'so clever, so fresh, and so cynical' (in Lang's words) that he could challenge the cultural radicals on their own terms and provide inspiration for another offshoot of democracy, the country's growing pride in its imperial role. If he could breathe new life into English fiction, that was almost secondary.

And so the Kipling bandwagon started to pick up steam. While Rudyard was making his way across America, Sidney Low, editor of the conservative daily newspaper the *St James's Gazette*, took an afternoon off to read *Soldiers Three*, the first volume in the Indian Railway Library. Low had been recommended the book by his assistant Stephen Wheeler and was duly impressed. At dinner that evening he could not stop talking about a new talent 'who had dawned upon the eastern horizon'. His host sceptically noted that Low's enthusiasm would hardly be justified even if the author were a new Dickens. 'It may be that a greater than Dickens is here,' countered Low huffily.[2]

In August Andrew Lang (belying his reported response to 'The Mark of the Beast' two years earlier) was so complimentary in the *Saturday Review* about two further Railway Library volumes that he urged Wheeler's London agents, Sampson Low, to issue all six books in Britain. Rudyard had copied out a selection of such notices and forwarded them to Ted Hill when he was in Boston, commenting that she had done well to advise him to persevere with *Mother Maturin*, because that seemed more in keeping with 'the uncultured British taste' than his tales of Simla infidelities – or as he put it, quoting Shakespeare's *Henry V*, 'anything of the "chartered Libertine" brand'. Certainly, Rudyard's 'native' and soldier stories struck most chords with reviewers, who saw them as natural extensions of the exotic escapism of Rider Haggard.

But, having arrived in London on the crest of a wave, Rudyard was quickly disillusioned. Within a month, after Ted and Carrie had left, the English were 'fools', London 'vile' and his spirits 'most awful low'. He was lonely, homesick and suffering profound culture shock.

Rudyard was determined to live in the thick of it. No high-stepped Kensington mansion nor airy Bloomsbury flat would suffice for the new Dickens. With Ted and Carrie's help he found two unfurnished rooms on an upper floor of Embankment Chambers in Villiers Street off the Strand. The flat cost £55 a year and he gave his Uncle Ned's name as a reference. One window looked east across Embankment Gardens, towards the grey, misty River Thames, and out over the distant docklands to the enigmatic Orient that had recently been his home. And the other window faced south-west into the smoke and hubbub of Charing Cross railway station – a symbol of the modern industrial world that was his new constituency.

The area around his house 'was primitive and passionate in its habits and population',[3] and that was how he wanted it. The clubs of St James's and the publishers' offices in Covent Garden were a short walk away if he needed them. But, as if he were living in the Old City of Lahore rather than the civil lines, he claimed that his immediate aim was to 'get in touch with the common folk here, to find out what they desire, hope or fear, and then after the proper time to speak whatever may be given to me'.[4]

First he needed to furnish his rooms. Ted and Caroline helped him find some essentials – a bed, couch and wardrobe. Before sailing from the Royal Albert Docks on 25 October, they gave him a list of additional items he needed from the Oxford Street drapers D. H. Evans. The very evening they left he wrote them a letter (which, though nominally to both, was clearly intended for Ted). 'You had made my life happy and delightful for two years,' he announced, 'given me help, sympathy, encouragement and council and a host of things which it is easy to think but not so easy to write down in black and white.'[5]

Then he set about the job of fixing up his new home. After meeting a fat old man with a dew drop on the end of his nose who claimed to be a painter, Rudyard paid him fifteen shillings to varnish his floor. He went shopping for additional creature comforts, including a white sheepskin rug (an ordinary carpet would not fit his asymmetrical main room), three yards of matting for the bedroom (so his feet would not freeze when he walked to his washstand every morning) and a hollowed chair which allowed him plenty of movement when he sat down to writing. Slowly a working environment evolved – part clubman's study, part bazaar merchant's ante-room. The effect was dark and smoky: the walls were papered in a dull green, interwoven with a gold that had lost its sheen. In an effort to make this more inviting, Rudyard added touches of colour – soft-tinted Persian rugs and a sofa spread with a large posteen rug, bordered with astrakhan and embroidered in rich yellow silks. As a more personal touch, he hung military pictures on the walls. His one admitted luxury was a tall Japanese screen, with a lurid design of dancing skeletons that stimulated his imagination late at night.

Any illusion of comfort or good taste was destroyed by the impedimenta of a travelling writer – battered luggage, scrapbooks, old magazines, prized fishing rods. And there was no disguising the function of two solid desks – one a roll-top bureau in darkened oak with twisted brass handles, the other a larger, more business-like table, also with drawers, where Rudyard did most of his writing and where he later carved the words: 'Oft was I wearied as I toiled at thee.'

Before this could happen, Rudyard needed a daily routine.

He would rise at eight o'clock and take a bath. For a generally undemonstrative man, he liked to dress sham-exotically, as if trying to communicate with the various peoples and places he wrote about. His main garment was usually a loose blue serge suit, buttoned high to his throat, Indian style. Over that, in the early mornings at least, he wore a recently acquired Japanese dressing-gown. On his feet were monkey skin slippers and often his head was topped with a jaunty Egyptian fez.

His breakfast usually came from William Harris, known as 'the Sausage King', who had a restaurant at the foot of his stairs. (For tuppence, he could buy enough bangers and mash to last through the day.) If he was feeling slightly more opulent, he feasted on a meal of bloaters and bacon. Never in a rush to get to work, he then enjoyed a pipe and sifted through his mail. Around ten o'clock he sat down at his desk by the window overlooking Charing Cross. If there were no further distractions, such as lunch with an editor, he worked till four, with a short break at two for any food he might have set aside.

In mid-afternoon, he shaved and went out for fresh air. Then his day would develop in one of two ways. Sometimes his constitutional turned into an extended walk that took him as far as Knightsbridge (and his Aunt Aggie) or even Kensington, where Aunt Georgie could be relied on for a cup of tea. He might then stay for an evening meal with 'nice people who did not eat sausage for a living'[6] – his way of describing his solidly middle-class family and their friends.

Otherwise he skipped the tea and socialising, and carried on working. At some stage he would step out to eat at one of the restaurants down the street, calling in on his way home at Gatti's Music-Hall, where fourpence bought admission and a pewter jar of beer. Rudyard loved the 'compelling songs' from the Lion and Mammoth Comiques, interspersed with riveting repartee and improvisations from the audience. In 'the smoke, the roar, and the good-fellowship of relaxed humanity'[7] at Gatti's – and round the corner at the Tivoli in the Strand – Rudyard met the working people who he romantically hoped would put him in touch with contemporary Britain. Mixing with office clerks, railway commuters and off-duty Guardsmen, he was interested to find signs of a vibrant working-class culture, unaffected by the hallowed tones of mid-Victorians such as Tennyson.

Recognising the critical enthusiasm for his soldier stories, he hoped the music-halls would provide the same raw material for his writings as the barrack rooms of Mian Mir had done. After visiting Gatti's one night in November, Rudyard told Ted Hill he was wondering if London needed 'a poet of the Music Halls'. Next morning, he lay in bed composing 'My Great and Only',[8] an evocative story for the *CMG* about the rapport between a music-hall star and his audience as, to their raucous accompaniment, he sings an earthy ditty about a Life Guard's inexpert romancing of an under-cook. Typically, Rudyard composed his own song, which ran through the piece, with the refrain:

> And that's what the Girl told the Soldier,
> Soldier! Soldier!
> An' that's what the Girl told the Soldier.

Hearing the drawn-out howl that accompanied the word 'Soldier', Rudyard felt the gallery would never let go. (Later, he so liked this song that he wrote another stanza for Ortheris in his 1893 story 'Love-o'-Women'.) He used to listen to this frenzied baying in the company of an elderly barmaid who liked to illustrate the 'basic and basaltic truths' in the songs with her own real-life stories. Her recollections of 'a friend o' mine 'oo was mistook in 'er man' provided the background for his verses 'Mary, Pity Women!' – a poignant rejoinder to critics who accuse him of persistent misogyny.

The music-halls encouraged Rudyard to develop his bluff Mulvaney soldier of the Indian Railway Library into the engaging Tommy Atkins of his *Barrack-Room Ballads* – one important difference being that the latter was more aware of his role as a tool of Empire. As Rudyard made his way in London society, understanding more of the changing intellectual climate, he came to regard this character, with his robust opinions, as the only repository of common sense.

After finishing late at Gatti's, Rudyard would stagger home, running the gauntlet of the prostitutes who thronged outside his Embankment Chambers, speaking a language that was 'epic but unprintable'. As he wryly observed in 'In Partibus', one of his first poems in England,

> And when I take my nightly prowl,
>   'Tis passing good to meet
> The pious Briton lugging home
>   His wife and daughter sweet,
> Through four packed miles of seething vice
>   Thrust out upon the street.[9]

For Rudyard this 'shifting, shouting brotheldom'[10] provided the same voyeuristic window on the world as his nocturnal prowls in Lahore. Once he looked out of his Villiers Street window and saw a man with a shirt-front 'dull red like a robin's' falling crumpled to the pavement, having cut his own throat. Within a short while, the hand ambulance from the other end of the Strand had arrived to pick up the body. Seconds later, a young boy with a pot of hot water washed the blood off the gutter and the small crowd of spectators dispersed.

Sometimes Rudyard's walks took him further afield. Over the following year, Soho and its restaurants became familiar territory. North of Covent Garden, around Seven Dials, he found a Dickensian barber or, as he remembered it, 'half bird shop and half barber's' where all the customers had nicknames and a small boy rubbed in the lather while his fat father gashed my chin'. From childhood he knew the vast hinterland of Kensington, including the area around Brook Green, Hammersmith, that he appropriated for his story 'Brugglesmith'.

But the other side of London – the City, the East End and the docks – was *terra incognita*. So often, as if wanting to be closer to the land he had left behind, he set out in that direction. His itineraries are not known, but he may well have walked the streets of Whitechapel where Jack the Ripper had operated only the previous year. Around Mile End, he discovered for himself the social hardship which some authors were beginning to think was the stuff of English literature. Not to be outdone, he joined the trend for 'realistic' stories about the English underclass in his 'Record of Badalia Herodsfoot'. And, as 'The New Dispensation', a despatch to the *CMG*, shows, Rudyard also made his way to the Royal Albert Docks where, in the wake of the recent devastating strike, he met missionaries and sailors newly arrived from abroad. Trix later noted he 'liked going to the docks – Limehouse and so on', though she gave no reason for his interest, apart from his love of observing the world and talking to people. Perhaps, in the process, some seaman might have directed him to a Limehouse opium den where he could rediscover narcotic pleasures he had enjoyed in India.

Life at this stage was a dream – one, Rudyard later acknowledged, that seemed to allow him to 'push down walls, walk through ramparts and stride across rivers'. Villiers Street at least provided a base to launch upon 'that queer experience known as a literary career'.[11] The reason for Rudyard's headiness was that he was being treated like a star. At the invitation of his mentor Andrew Lang, he was soon dining at the Savile Club in Piccadilly, where London's top journalists, writers and publishers met to gossip. The Club had arrived on the scene fifteen years earlier, when Robert Louis Stevenson wrote, 'Here gather daily those young eaglets of glory, the swordsmen of the pen ... They are all young ... And they are all Rising.'[12]

Now Rudyard was following in their suit. 'Besant goes there and everyone seems to know me,'[13] he bragged to Ted and Carrie within a week of their leaving London. In the Savile's smoke-filled atmosphere, he rubbed shoulders with like-minded writers, such as Rider Haggard and Edmund Gosse, and with editors seeking to publish his work – among them, Henley of the *Scots Observer*.

All the same, Rudyard was wary of identifying too closely with any literary faction. Besant had advised him of a basic rule of literary politics: if you are in with one lot, you are out with another; it is best 'to keep out of the dog-fight'.

So, for the time being, Rudyard preferred to pace his entry into London. He wanted to spend some time with his family and, in particular, with his cousins who had grown up while he was abroad. During the short period when he was waiting for his own rooms, he stayed with the Burne-Joneses at The Grange, which had lost its once isolated semi-rural character and was becoming increasingly suburban, following the extension of the underground railway in the 1870s. He was disappointed that his favourite cousin Margaret was seldom around, since she had married Jack Mackail, a clever, if dour Scottish classicist with socialist leanings. At Balliol, where he had taken a first and won the Newdigate Prize, Mackail was credited (with Cecil Spring-Rice) with composing the well-known lines about their contemporary:

> My name is George Nathaniel Curzon
> I am a most superior person.[14]

Visiting the newly-weds in their 'funny little-old house' in Young Street, Kensington, Rudyard was impressed by their 'quiet little menage'.[15] But she now had her own domestic life and opportunities for seeing her were limited. Her lackadaisical brother was a poor alternative. Although sociable and not untalented as an artist, twenty-five-year-old Philip had emerged from his traditional education at Marlborough and Oxford entirely deficient in common sense. He had befriended Oscar Wilde at university, wooed various high-society ladies and even painted the odd picture. But his career was going nowhere: his days were spent pathetically hanging around his father's studio. Now, in an effort to make some money, 'phool Phil', as Rudyard called him, had written a racy autobiography and sold it to a down-market newspaper. So, within a month of arriving in Villiers Street, Rudyard had to obtain power of attorney from his cousin and negotiate the story back from the editor.

His two Poynter cousins, who lived at Albert Gate, Knightsbridge, were not much better company. Hugh was only seven and liked playing trains, while – initially, at least – twenty-two-year-old Ambrose was painfully lacking in confidence. (At school at Harrow, another cousin, Stanley Baldwin, had run into trouble – and was lucky to avoid being expelled – when he sent Ambrose at Eton some mildly provocative pornographic literature.) As Rudyard was leaving Albert Gate one night in November, Ambrose thrust a couple of manuscripts into his hands and demanded his opinion. One was a volume of poems and the other 'A Five Act Tragedy in Blank Verse'. Rudyard found them both as dire as this daunting title suggested – self-conscious meditations where sexual urges gnawed at religious doubts. 'He wants my verdict not so much for his poems as his psychological condition,'[16] Rudyard informed Ted. After deciding it might be unwise to commit his thoughts to paper, he invited his cousin round to discuss the matter over a pipe. As Ambrose relaxed and opened up, Rudyard revised his opinion and, by early December, was describing his cousin as 'a keen tongued cynical young dog'.[17]

Within weeks, nevertheless, Rudyard had experienced an odd role reversal, with himself, the colonial 'new boy', taking the initiative on behalf of his sophisticated London relations. The tables were turned slightly when, as a gesture of thanks, Phil invited Rudyard to Barnum and Bailey's show at Olympia, not far from The Grange. Surprisingly, Rudyard, who had seen freak exhibitions in India, was not amused, much as he appreciated the technical excellence. 'The monsters made me almost sick. I do not like people without legs or hands and I hate a two-headed boy.' Similarly, when he was invited to the burlesque *Ruy Blas, or the Blasé Roué* at the Gaiety, he opted out. 'Theatres ain't my shape.

I can't stand 'em,' he told Ted.[18] This attitude was uncharacteristic, given his recent enthusiasm for amateur dramatics. It suggests Rudyard was consciously holding back from involvement in the theatre, unable to understand why Ibsen was now preferred to his own favourite Sardou. A year later he tried to write a play, but it never materialised. For the time being, he reserved his applause for the lively proletarian music-halls.

His uncles and aunts did at least provide social opportunities for Rudyard to feel his way into London society. As always, the Burne-Jones family had an eclectic circle of friends, through whom Rudyard, in a roundabout way, found himself a publisher. The Stephens were one of those distinguished late-Victorian families who combined professional service at the highest level (mainly in the law and in India) with real intellectual achievement. Ned Burne-Jones had known the family since his bachelor days when he was accepted into the 'Little Holland House' set by Julia Stephen's aunt Sarah Prinsep. 'Aunt Sarah' introduced Ned to Julia, whose square, doleful features were the model for his *Annunciation* in 1879, after she had married Leslie Stephen, the stern editor of the *Dictionary of National Biography*.

Through the Stephens Rudyard met an extraordinary woman who, as well as introducing him to her publisher, Macmillan, took on the important role – only recently vacated by Ted Hill – of his older female muse. At her house at 26 Colvin Road (and later in Chilworth Street, Paddington), Lucy Clifford, a blousy forty-three-year-old novelist, hosted a regular salon whose members spanned fifty years of literary history from George Eliot through Henry James to Noël Coward. Virginia Woolf, the Stephens' daughter, penned an unflattering portrait of her in January 1920 – 'large codfish eyes & the whole figure of the nineties – black velvet – morbid – intense, jolly, vulgar – a hack to her tips, with a dash of the stage'[19] – trying unsuccessfully to reproduce her successes of thirty years earlier, talking of nothing but money, royalties, editions and reviews, and pathetically palming off her books because she needed the money. Others were more charitable: Trix described her as 'a warm-hearted impulsive widow with thick lips', while Henry James said she was 'a soul of generosity and devotion'. If nothing else, Woolf conveyed a sense of Mrs Clifford as a professional wordsmith, deeply versed in the business of writing, which were qualities Rudyard needed just now.

She had taken to her career around 1880 following the death the previous year of her husband, William Kingdon Clifford, a brilliant scholar whose official post as Professor of Applied Mathematics at University College, London, only hinted at the range of his academic interests. After two modestly received early works, she became a household name with her 1885 novel *Mrs Keith's Crime*, and later caused a mild sensation with *Love Letters of a Worldly Woman*, published in 1891, shortly after meeting Rudyard.

With her vitality and lack of sophistication, Mrs Clifford was the kind of woman Rudyard liked. According to her friend Marie Belloc Lowndes, Rudyard gave Lucy 'a portrait his father had etched of him; showed her all his work in manuscript and was constantly in her house'. At this stage, she had read his *Plain Tales* and recognised their 'high quality'.[20] He was delighted when, within two months of his arriving in London, she provided an entrée to her ebullient publisher, Frederick Macmillan, whose family firm had been responsible for such best-selling authors as Charles Kingsley (including his *Westward Ho!*) and Alfred Lord Tennyson.[21] Following her own successes, Macmillan valued her judgement: according to Charles Morgan's history of the firm, 'She had an intuition for literature, and an incapacity to lie about it whether in flattery or in spite.'

By early November Rudyard was dining at Frederick Macmillan's mansion in St John's Wood and fighting back uncivil thoughts about the authors' profits that had paid for the surrounding luxury. There he met another kind of woman, of a type he found less congenial. Pretty and articulate, Mrs Ashton Dilke, sister-in-law of the politician Sir Charles Dilke, was a member of the London County Council. Rudyard took offence at her advocacy of female education – in a tone that made him want to 'kick her round the room forty times'.

Six weeks later, he was invited to 'an awful dinner'[22] in Kensington with George Macmillan, Frederick's cousin, who also worked for the family firm. Over the meal, his host's wife told him that India was ready to govern itself and how 'we in England' (a catch-all phrase, he felt, for 'ultra liberal idiots') were 'in earnest' about putting things to rights there. Perhaps aware that her husband had once travelled round Greece with Oscar Wilde, Rudyard looked her in the eye and told her steelily that she was suffering not from earnestness but from hysteria because she had too little to divert her mind. His hostess could only look at the ceiling in exasperation 'as one who said: – "Just Heavens! what barbarian am I entertaining?" '

At the Poynters, Rudyard was introduced to a more conventional crowd, whom he found equally infuriating in their attitudes. As a leading academic genre painter, Edward Poynter was now part of the cultural establishment, taking a particular interest in art education, as former Slade Professor at University College, London and (from 1875) director of art at South Kensington, where he was also Principal of the National Art Training School, with input into Lockwood Kipling's work in Lahore. He had recently become secretary of a society dedicated to the preservation of Egyptian antiquities – not that Rudyard was impressed, describing his uncle's current work, the much touted *The Queen of Sheba's Visit to King Solomon*, as a jumble of Orientalist clichés.

Rudyard liked some of his Uncle Edward's friends, such as the sculptor Hamo Thornycroft, who shared his studio complex, and Thomas Anstey Guthrie, a lover of the music-hall, who penned funny stories for *Punch* under the name F. Anstey. Guthrie, who had never fulfilled the promise of his humorous 1882 novel *Vice Versa*, recalled Rudyard as a 'vivacious and amusing talker', regaling the Poynters' dinner guests with tales of the problems of producing a newspaper in India.

But Rudyard learned to avoid the company of the Poynters' more formal acquaintances, telling Ted – apropos Mrs Norman Grosvenor, the wife of a former liberal MP and businessman – that he did not care to tame his conversation 'to suit the needs of the grain fed matrons of Belgravia'.[23] Rudyard fared less well when his Aunt Aggie dragged him off to tea in Stanhope Gate with the 'hoight av society'. Rudyard found himself backed into a corner by three titled dignitaries. As they 'poured melted compliments' down his throat, Rudyard felt he was being treated like 'a purple monkey on a yellow stick'. In a sense he was no different from his soldier hero Tommy, with his ' "Special train for Atkins" when the trooper's on the tide' – or, in his case, as he told Carrie Taylor, 'O it's "dear Mr Kipling, *please* come as often as you can and we'll talk".'[24]

He gave vent to his self-conscious frustration at such events in a satirical piece, 'On Exhibition'. In this story the narrator looks back fondly to India where tea is a 'function at which any one who is passing down the Mall may present himself'. At a formal English tea party, he is assailed by preening reviewers and by vast women parading their social consciences. He overhears a 'weedy young gentleman with tow hair' and a tiny woman with beady black eyes discussing his work as though he were dead, 'and they talked of "tones" and "notes" and "lights" and "shades" and "tendencies" ' – modish words which might have come from any aesthete talking about the paintings of Whistler. As they are leaving the house, a fellow author, who has written a book of social realism, *Down in the Doldrums*, informs him that he is only there 'as a small deputy lion to roar in place of a much bigger man' and that he should 'wait till they've made you jump through hoops and your turn's over, and you can sit on a sofa and watch the new men being brought up and put through their paces'. At that stage, he 'gulped a great gulp of sorrow and homesickness'.[25]

At least, Rudyard saw people with Indian connections from

time to time. He met Moreton Frewen, who still wanted to publish the letters Rudyard had written on his travels, Mrs Griffiths, the wife of his godfather in Bombay, and James Walker, one of the proprietors of the *CMG*. He also visited Sir George Birdwood, the eccentric India Office civil servant who had become the arbiter of Indian art in Britain, to ask him about finding an assistant for his father, who was due some extended leave. Birdwood advised Rudyard that, if he wanted to progress as a writer, he should study English Literature at Oxford University. The young man balked at this suggestion, but there was a satisfactory outcome to his enquiries about an assistant for his father. The following February, Fred Andrews took up his job as Vice Principal of the Mayo School, from where he kept Rudyard informed of local developments, such as the exploits of Aurel Stein, an archaeologist at Lahore University who had embarked on a career of excavation.

Lockwood Kipling needed to return home because he was not very well. Rudyard was worried enough about his father's blood pressure to seek an interview with Lord Cross, Secretary of State for India. This led to an invitation to dine with Clinton Dawkins who, having recently stepped down as Cross's private secretary, was happy to introduce him to his successor, Arthur Williams Wynn. The dinner stuck in Rudyard's mind because Dawkins's wife asked him naïvely, 'And how do you think of your characters, Mr Kipling?' Once again, after only two months in London, Rudyard was moved to tell Ted Hill, 'I am sick of this.'[26] The only benefit was that Rudyard and his host stayed up till one o'clock chewing over India Office gossip. This provided the young author with material for a choice Liberal-bashing story about William Gladstone's overweening self-importance, which he sent to the *CMG* under the title 'Adoration of the Mage'. Earlier,[27] Rudyard had politely declined Birdwood's invitation to lunch with Dadhabai Naoroji, the Parsee former Westminster MP who had served as President of the Indian National Congress. This too had sparked a story, 'One View of the Question', an Indian Moslem's wry observation of England and the English, which included what Rudyard described as a 'whack' at the Congress.

In early November his sub-continental connections led him to Dorking to stay with Colonel Thomas Lewin, a former Indian Army officer and administrator, who was a friend of Ned Burne-Jones. Lewin had written books about India and was knowledgeable about Indian languages. His step-daughter had married the son of the novelist George Meredith, the sort of person Rudyard might have enjoyed meeting. But this was not the case. When he went over to Meredith's house in nearby Box Hill, Rudyard found the author of *The Egoist* a garrulous gasbag who 'fizzed' epigrams that gave him an instant headache and were completely forgotten five minutes later.[28] At the Lewins', Rudyard met a 'whole tableful of minor stars' whom he claimed he was quite happy to forget.

Everywhere he went, he felt affronted by what he considered to be the level of mediocrity. Through Wynnard Hooper, Financial Editor of *The Times*, he was introduced to the lively Irish journalist and MP Justin McCarthy. (Hooper was the son of George Hooper whose sister-in-law was one of the 'dear old ladies' of Warwick Gardens.) However, Wynnard Hooper's sister Margaret was dismissed as a 'Socialistic-artist', McCarthy himself, who had translated *Omar Khayyám*, was derided for talking 'cheap Orientalism to amuse me' and pretending to speak Persian, and his sister described as a virgin of 'emancipated lustre' who discussed divorce cases in a way that made Rudyard want to punish her for being a 'brazen little hussy'.[29] He made his excuses and left, commenting priggishly to Ted Hill, 'As long as Providence gives me the instinct to know when I am among second-rate people I am not wholly lost.'

Rudyard was not comfortable with these educated middle-class women. In India he had been quietly respectful of similar ladies. Here, away from his family and without the good sense of Ted Hill and Carrie Taylor, he felt threatened by their unfamiliar political views. When Aunt Aggie dragged him along to a small dance and tried to introduce him to three girls, Rudyard took fright – 'their eyes scared me', he told Ted – and walked home alone in the dark.

Only one sort of female – apart from earthy bar-girls and working-class do-gooders – was certain to interest him. His evening at the George Macmillans had been saved for him by the presence of a Miss Corbin, whose father, an American financier, was President of a Pennsylvanian railroad. Her giggles reminded Rudyard of Ted Hill, her accent soothed him and, oddly for someone obsessed with his career, 'she didn't talk about my bl**** blessed books'. Another favourite was Edward Poynter's Yankee niece by marriage whom Rudyard found 'fresh and girlish'. What he implied was that American women were more relaxing to meet because they had not been brought up in the shadow of the Doll's House.

These daughters of the revolution at least offered a respite from the inertia Rudyard saw in London. What with fellow-travelling Indian nationalists, unthinking socialites, 'new' women and aesthetes, Rudyard was appalled by the lack of 'bottom' in London society. He felt that the Empire, and the people who dedicated their lives to its prosperity, were being undermined by a disastrous *trahison des clercs* who 'dealt in varieties of safe sedition'. He still retained his sense of outrage when he came to write his autobiography nearly half a century later: 'They derided my poor little Gods of the East ... Their aim was peaceful, intellectual penetration and the formation of what today would be called "cells" in unventilated corners.' The metaphor was appropriate because it reflected the specious scientific concept (taken up in Max Nordau's best-selling book *Degeneration*) that society was being eroded by disease-like organisms. The decadence Rudyard felt he saw around him only rekindled his admiration for his music-hall heroes and encouraged him to develop his philosophy extolling the merits of action. One can imagine his astonishment when, at dinner with the Poynters on 11 December, he met a militia subaltern who claimed he was qualifying for the Scots

Guards 'because my mother doesn't want me to go on active service, y' know'.

Having decided on Macmillan as his book publisher, Rudyard naturally looked to its in-house magazine as an outlet for his stories and verse. There were other contenders for his occasional pieces and from time to time he obliged them. But for his regular material he plumped for *Macmillan's Magazine*, a reputable monthly which had demonstrated its firmly conservative credentials by turning down Thomas Hardy's *Tess of the D'Urbervilles* in 1887 for showing 'too much succulence'.

Rudyard was probably swayed by the fact that the journal was edited by Mowbray Morris, son of a former manager of *The Times*. Morris was known to Rudyard because, after becoming editor of *Macmillan's Magazine* in 1885, he had simultaneously contributed trenchant pieces of art criticism to the *Pioneer* by mail. Despite hating Rudyard's Uncle Ned, whom he described disparagingly as the 'Good Jones', Morris had taken to the work of Philip Burne-Jones, whose first publicly exhibited painting, based on Henry James's 'Madonna of the Future', he had recommended to readers of the *Pioneer* in June 1886.

As a start to their professional relationship, Morris was eager to publish more of the pithy stories of Indian society that Rudyard had developed in *Plain Tales from the Hills*. He was not worried if they dealt with the same characters. In addition, Rudyard was free to contribute verse along the lines of his *Departmental Ditties*.

For his first venture Rudyard wrote the rollicking 'Ballad of the King's Mercy' which – to confuse anyone who finds his 'imperialism' easy to interpret – is studiously respectful of the brutal workings of royal Afghan justice in the Khyber hills. Still wary of putting his head too far above the parapet, he signed his poem with the pseudonym 'Yussuf' – not that many readers were deceived, given the subject matter.

On 9 November Rudyard was to be found fighting his way

through the crowds at the Lord Mayor's show, making his way to Macmillan's offices in Covent Garden. Morris had invited him over to 'smoke a cigar over Terence Mulvaney'. It transpired that he considered a new *Plain Tale*, 'The Incarnation of Terence Mulvaney', 'too drunk' or outspoken for the sensibilities of his middle-class readers and wanted to discuss cuts of thirty lines. Unused to such courtesies from the *Pioneer*, Rudyard read him a 'border ballad' he had finished over breakfast. This was the 'Ballad of East and West', with its misunderstood lines:

> Oh, East is East and West is West, and never the twain shall
> meet,
> Till Earth and Sky stand presently at God's great Judgment
> Seat;
> But there is neither East nor West, Border, nor Breed, nor
> Birth,
> When two strong men stand face to face, though they come
> from the ends of the earth!

Morris pronounced this 'damned good' and opted to run it immediately. 'Stayed for lunch, talked Scott and discussed next month's story,' wrote Rudyard to Ted Hill, approving of his editor's civilised style.

The following day, Morris wrote to his friend Albert Baillie, Queen Victoria's godson and later Dean of Windsor, in glowing terms about his new discovery. 'He will do I hope a lot of work for me. He wants looking after, as he is apt to be unnecessarily frank, rather what the French call *brutal*. He is a most amusing companion, full of life and fun, and I think not likely to be spoiled. Unfortunately he is a nephew to Burne-Jones – not by blood, however, so there is hope for him.'[30]

Having bided his time, Rudyard could take stock of his journalistic progress in early November 1889 and express himself satisfied. His main source of income in London, *Macmillan's Magazine*, promised to bring him in £300 a year, on top of the

£100 a year he was guaranteed from the *CMG*. This was a tidy sum, even before his pieces for the *St James's Gazette*, or the *Fortnightly Review*, or the dozen other papers that competed for his material. An Australian journal had offered five guineas for anything he wanted to write, and there were several American outlets that Ted and Carrie wanted him to explore.

To deal with this incidental journalism, and to allow him to get on with the serious business of writing a book, he decided to seek an agent. On the recommendation of Walter Besant, he employed Alexander (A. P.) Watt, an indefatigable fifty-five-year-old Scot, with a solid grounding in the books business.[31] As an agent in the late 1870s, Watt had skilfully played all sides, working for publishers to secure syndication deals, printing the magazine *The Author* on behalf of the Society of Authors, and representing writers such as Arthur Conan Doyle, Rider Haggard and Thomas Hardy. Watt had read the *Plain Tales* and liked them. It is a testament to his personal and business skills that he never fell out with the demanding Rudyard, despite taking ten per cent of his earnings.

Watt's knowledge of the market helped double Rudyard's income in the three months to March 1890. The scanty evidence available suggests he did this by clearing up Rudyard's problems with Thacker Spink and by maximising his sales to American media such as *Lippincott's Magazine* and to new syndication outlets, which included Besant's own Authors' Syndicate (which Rudyard intriguingly promised an unidentified contribution on 'war – bloody war ... tho' adultery a *partie carrée* has its seductions'[32]) and the well-bankrolled *McClure's* in the United States.

With the burden of day-to-day negotiating with editors and publishers taken off his shoulders, Rudyard was free to think about longer-term projects. 'Hurry up your novel and become rich,' Watt encouraged him. This reference to *Mother Maturin* reminded Rudyard to ask his parents to send him the manuscript from Lahore. But there is no evidence that it arrived and by early

1890 the literary press reported that he was working on something called *The Book of the Forty-Five Mornings*.

Progress was slow, however, because, away from work, Rudyard was desperately unhappy. A wave of depression had overwhelmed him almost as soon as the Taylors left and it continued to afflict him throughout the long winter months of 1889–90. As early as 15 October he could tell John Addington Symonds, another of the literary figures keen to meet him, 'There is no light in this place, and the people are savages living in black houses and ignorant of everything beyond the Channel.'[33] In mid-November he woke up one 'evil-evil' morning and was unable to see through a yellow pea-souper of a fog. He could only hear the trains at Charing Cross station whistling to each other in the darkness. Feeling in the depths of despair, he sat down at this stage to write his 'doleful ditty', 'In Partibus', which he described as 'the wail of a fog-bound exile howling for Sunlight'. Recalling his early days in Lahore when he had been homesick for London and its hansom cabs, he lamented that now he was there:

> And half of it is fog and filth,
> And half is fog and row.

Truly, he felt he had come to the land of the heathen, as the unspoken part of the poem's title – In Partibus (Infidelium) [In the lands of the unfaithful] – indicated. Even at that early stage in Britain he was impatient with the country's feckless artsy crowd and he yearned for an Indian Army man

> Set up, and trimmed and taut,
> Who does not spout hashed libraries
> Or think the next man's thought,
> And walks as though he owned himself,
> And hogs his bristles short.

Before lunch the blackness had thickened and Rudyard had to

light his reading lamp. To cheer himself up he bought a print of some drunken soldiers coming out of a canteen, wearing each others' hats. Adding this to the militaria on his walls, he wallowed in nostalgia for the 'good old days gone by', sighing pathetically in a letter to Ted Hill, 'Ah me!'[34] He went downstairs, bought two big cherry-wood pipes and enfolded himself 'in the mists of fancy'. Initially his smoke-filled reverie was productive: he thought about future topics for stories and about pieces of dialogue that needed improving. But then real unhappiness took over and he found himself weeping audibly. (Only the previous year, the Irish poet W. B. Yeats had felt much the same: 'I feel like Robinson Crusoe in this dreadful London,' he complained.)

As the winter drew on, one underlying reason for Rudyard's chronic depression became clearer – the pointlessness of his engagement to Carrie Taylor. Writing to her in early December, he combined unconvincing protestations of love with mock-jovial insinuations that she was 'a casuistical little villain'. As the letter showed, she had become concerned – on what evidence is not clear – that he was drifting towards Roman Catholicism. So he needed to disabuse her of this idea and reassure her that he was a paid-up member of the Church of England – baptised into that denomination in Bombay and confirmed by the Bishop of Exeter while still at school. He took the opportunity to set out his theological stall: he believed in a personal God, he was agnostic about the Trinity and, while agreeing with the need for some sort of retribution for evil, he rejected the idea of eternal damnation or reward. In other words, as his stories suggested, his personal religion was strongly influenced by the Methodism of his forefathers. As he now told Carrie, he believed in the doctrine of justification by works rather than faith. And while admitting his fascination with the 'whole skittledom' of the Roman Catholic church, he suggested plausibly that she should ask her brother-in-law Alex Hill if he was really 'the sort of person likely to hand over will and conscience to another's keeping'.[35]

While objectively, Rudyard's basic Protestantism was never in doubt, he had never been overtly religious and it is curious that the issue surfaced now. In his perambulations in the East End, Rudyard may have seen enough of the ravages of the dock strike to have welcomed the efforts of Cardinal Manning, the Archbishop of Westminster, to mediate. Something of his respect for Roman Catholic spirituality is found in Brother Victor of the Order of Little East in 'Record of Badalia Herodsfoot' which, though not published till November 1890, appears – on the evidence of a copy in Dalhousie University watermarked 1889 – to have been written around this time. Although this proves nothing in itself, it supports the supposition that Rudyard was toying with religious thoughts within a few months of his arrival in London. Indeed, on Sunday 15 December, only six days after his letter to Carrie, he crept along to St Clement Dane's to attend church. 'Don't laugh,' he told Ted Hill sheepishly.

Shortly afterwards, on Christmas Day, his mood had deteriorated once more. He braved empty streets to dine with Ned and Phil Burne-Jones at their favourite Solferino's restaurant in Soho. But he did not enjoy himself. Indeed, he wished he were dead. 'These beasts hereabouts will be sweet and sugary to me just as long as I have any success, but you'd be just the same if I turned up without a whole shirt on my back and broken boots. That's why I hate 'em – hate everybody and chiefly myself.'[36] He wished he were back at The Belvedere where he had spent the previous Christmas. These emotions, however, were unburdened not to his fiancée but to her sister Ted, for whom he retained his puppyish affection.

Add to this the excess hours he was putting in at his desk ('overwork's only murderous idleness,' he put it, with back-to-front Methodist logic in his novel *The Light that Failed* the following year), and it came as no surprise when a month later, on 24 January 1890, Rudyard was in touch again, this time with Alex Hill, apologising that he was unable to write anything that week: 'My head is all queer and I am going to have it mended some day.' Within a few days he had elaborated slightly to Ted. He was having one of the minor breakdowns he had last experienced on the *Ho-Nam* on the Canton River. 'My head has given out and I am forbidden work and I am to go away somewhere.'[37] Although, for the first time in his life, he had begun to look seriously to religion as an emotional support, he felt that nobody else could help him: 'I must go on alone now till the end of my time. I can do nothing to save myself from breaking up now and again ... I am physically in perfect health but I can neither work nor think nor read.'

Apart from his parents and the Taylor girls, Rudyard was missing the ministrations of his faithful servant from Allahabad. This emerged from 'The New Dispensation', a curious despatch to the *CMG* in early December. In it, he claimed to be so upset at the absence of Kadir Baksh that he had gone to the Albert Docks and hired an unkempt Tamil sailor as a replacement. He had resorted to this after taking on a maid. But he had experienced difficulties with her because of his lingering Oriental sahib's confusion about the roles of service and sexuality. When his new maid refused to sew his buttons, Rudyard noted, 'I strove to ingratiate myself with her, believing that a little interest, combined with a little capital, would fix these buttons more firmly than anything else. Subsequently, and after an interval – the buttons were dropping like autumn leaves – I kissed her.'

Both strands of this story are so vivid – in the style of his other direct reportage – that there seems no doubt that they are factual, particularly when Rudyard chose to write another, clearly more fictional, interpretation of the events in his story 'The Limitations of the Pambé Serang', which was published in the *St James's Gazette* three days before the *CMG* version.

His recollection of the maid was similar to a story he had told Ted Hill the previous month. Aunt Georgie's servant girl Annie had made a special journey across London to deliver his letters when she could more easily have posted them. Rudyard concluded that she wanted to chat, even to flirt, and offered her a cup of tea. But she only took this as an excuse to remark on his frayed collars and to suggest that it was time he settled down and married a nice steady woman. 'I *do* hope she doesn't mean herself,' Rudyard commented archly.[38]

But Rudyard made no mention in his letters of any incident which related to 'the Camel' (as his fellow servants were supposed to call the Tamil seaman in the story). This may simply have been a fancy that crossed Rudyard's mind on one of his East End strolls. The juxtaposition of these two events suggests, however, that Rudyard found 'class' in Britain as much of a problem as sex. He told his *CMG* readers how local wives got locked in a cat and mouse game with their servants, because their husbands were out at the office and they themselves had nothing to do. This echoed one of his more general thoughts about women in society – that they can be a nuisance when they have time on their hands. His Aunt Georgie may have contributed to his confusion. Despite her socialist principles and despite the loyalty of her maid Annie, she described the relationship between servants and employers as 'either a bloody feud or a hellish compact'.[39]

Rudyard found companionship with various journalists during the early part of 1890. At least newspapermen did not have the pretensions of the braying literary scribes of the Savile Club. They kept him informed of the latest political developments and they reminded him of happier days at the *CMG* and *Pioneer*. The closest local equivalent to those journals, the 'paper of record', was *The Times* where he knew several journalists. Some were merely acquaintances, such as William Stillman, the paper's correspondent in Rome. Stillman's Greek-born wife, the palely beautiful Marie Spartali, had been one of the three Greek-born Graces painted by Uncle Ned. Others he knew better, including Humphry Ward, whose wife was a celebrated novelist. Wynnard Hooper, the paper's Money Editor, was also a regular companion.

At this stage another *Times* journalist, who was an important influence on Rudyard's career, appeared on the scene. Moberly Bell was an intriguing character with an interesting 'Orientalist' pedigree. His mother was the daughter of a sister of Miss Williams who had accompanied Lady Hester Stanhope on her travels to the Levant in 1810. (Lady Hester was also this Mrs Bell's godmother.) Bell had been destined for the Indian Civil Service, but opted for health reasons to follow his father into Peel and Company, a firm of merchants in Alexandria. His attention was more attracted to politics and journalism than to business, however, and for a while he had acted as an unofficial correspondent of *The Times* in Egypt. In 1880 he and two friends started a local English-language paper, the *Egyptian Gazette*, which is still published more than a century later. During the subsequent decade, as Britain assumed full administrative control of Egypt in the wake of the Khedive's political and economic disarray, Bell became the official and highly influential correspondent of *The Times* in Cairo. A confidant of Britain's agent and consul-general, Sir Evelyn Baring, later Lord Cromer, Bell also reported on the background to events further south in Sudan, during the Mahdist revolt and General Gordon's ill-fated attempts to relieve Khartoum in 1885.

In the process Bell had become a convinced imperialist, an attitude reinforced in 1888 when he was visited in Egypt by Flora Shaw, a forceful, pretty Anglo-Irish writer in her mid-thirties whose experience of the poverty of the East End of London had convinced her that colonies were required to absorb the energies and numbers of the working classes. (This was a view she shared with the politician Joseph Chamberlain, a radical Liberal Unionist and imperialist.) Bell's own skills and energy came to the attention of the Walter family, which owned *The Times*. In February 1890, in an attempt to boost dwindling circulation, Arthur Walter, the latest family member to take the helm at the paper, decided to recall Bell to London as Assistant Manager (soon to be Manager), in which capacity he was quickly in contact with Rudyard.

One of Bell's responsibilities as Manager was the foreign department. For the position of Foreign Editor he secured Donald Mackenzie Wallace, whom he knew from Egypt and whom Rudyard had met as Dufferin's private secretary in India. And, because he was convinced of the growing importance of colonial news, Bell set up a parallel Colonial department, with Flora Shaw as *de facto* Colonial Editor – an incredible feat, given the prejudice against women in such positions at the time.

One reason for Bell's recall was that *The Times* was going through a difficult period. Its dry academic editor, George Buckle, had been struggling to halt a marked decline in its circulation. In early 1887, in an effort to boost its profile, it published a series of letters of dubious origin which purported to show that Charles Parnell, the Irish Nationalist leader in the House of Commons, had direct links with the Fenian terrorists who had murdered the Chief Secretary for Ireland Lord Frederick Cavendish and his Under-Secretary Thomas Burke in Phoenix Park five years earlier. After an inconclusive court case, Parnell demanded a special committee of Parliament to clear his name. The Conservative government offered instead to appoint a three-man judicial inquiry which it hoped to be able to control. But, after shilly-shallying, the inquiry refused to do the government's bidding. Instead, it ruled in February 1890 that the letters were forgeries and Parnell was therefore exonerated.

In his upstairs room overlooking Charing Cross, Rudyard was so incensed at the verdict that he dusted off some lines ('At the Bar') he had written four years earlier for the *Civil and Military Gazette* attacking judicial chicanery in the Madras presidency. He worked them into 'Cleared', his first poem to deal with an overtly British political theme, which railed against the hypocrisy of the judges in the inquiry who had managed to overlook the involvement of the Irish Nationalists in Parliament in the original Phoenix Park murders. 'We are not ruled by murderers, but only – by their friends,' he intoned.

Ironically, 'Cleared' was rejected by *The Times*, which was acutely embarrassed at its involvement in the affair. Rudyard then took it to 'a Mr Frank Harris', as he later disdainfully described the journalist and sexual athlete. Harris was editing the *Fortnightly Review*, which had recently published Rudyard's 'One View of the

Question'. Unusually, Rudyard had failed to take notice of the journal's politics, which were traditionally radical. Nor had he got the measure of Harris, whom he later described as 'the one human being that I could on no terms get on with'.[40] Harris, predictably, read the powerful verses with 'shrinking and dislike', fearing that their publication would exacerbate racial tensions between English and Irish.[41] So, after he too had rejected the poem, Rudyard deposited it in the waste-paper basket.

His luck changed following the success of his poem 'Danny Deever', whose appearance in the *Scots Observer* on 22 February led David Masson, the usually undemonstrative Professor of Rhetoric and English Literature at Edinburgh University, to dance before his astonished students, waving the paper and exclaiming, 'Here's Literature! Here's Literature at last!' Telling the story of a soldier hanged by his regiment for shooting a colleague, 'Danny Deever' was rhythmic, insistent, melodramatic and brilliant. With its traditional question-and-answer style, the ballad has been praised not only by Masson, but by fellow poets, ranging from W. B. Yeats, who was coming to prominence at the same time, to T. S. Eliot, who called it 'technically (as well as in content) remarkable', and noted, 'The regular recurrence of the same end-words, which gain immensely by imperfect rhyme (*parade* and *said*), gives the feeling of marching feet and the movement of men in disciplined formation.'

Will Henley, the editor of the *Scots Observer*, was a big, bluff bear of a man, whose romantic Johnsonian Toryism made him a natural leader of the Conservative reaction to contemporary cultural trends. A cripple from birth, his wooden leg had provided the model for Long John Silver in his friend R. L. Stevenson's *Treasure Island* published in 1883. Over the years, as a literary journalist, he was more important for his influence (through what Max Beerbohm described as his 'Henley Regatta' of fellow thinkers) than for the wide dissemination of his words. Even at its height, the *Scots Observer* boasted a circulation of no more than 2000. His imperialism dated from the end of 1888 when he

went north to edit the paper, which was owned by a group of Edinburgh-based Tories.

According to a family story, Henley had first been alerted to a new talent by Captain Edward Boyle, his seafaring brother-in-law, who had read a poem by Rudyard in an Indian newspaper during one of his distant voyages. The two writers met at the Savile shortly after Rudyard arrived in England and soon were corresponding. Rudyard warmed to a man he described as 'more different varieties of man than most'.[42] His first contribution to the *Scots Observer* in February was his enigmatic poem 'The Explanation', a wry, Jacobean-style meditation (first written in India) which tells how, after Love and Death have drunkenly mixed up their darts, old men are fated to love and young men to die.

However, it was 'Danny Deever' that made Henley – and the rest of the literary world – sit up. Shortly after its publication Rudyard was visited at Embankment Chambers by Fitzroy Bell, the *Scots Observer*'s proprietor, accompanied by the lawyer Herbert Stephen, another of the Stephen clan (Sir James Fitz-james's son and Leslie's nephew), who had also encountered the young author at the Savile. Pacing across his rug, toying with his spectacles, Rudyard could not resist reading his distinguished visitors a new ballad called 'Fuzzy-Wuzzy'.[43] When Bell asked if he had anything else to offer, Rudyard fished in his waste-paper basket and came up with 'Cleared', which was published to acclaim in the *Scots Observer* of 8 March.

Before long *The Times* was itself quoting the verses and (on 25 March) published an unsigned article which tried to assess the literary merits of their author. Now known to have been written by Humphry Ward (the *Times* network was working in Rudyard's interests), the piece complimented Rudyard's efforts to 'lift the veil' on Anglo-Indian society. Basing its observations largely on his Calcutta editions, it even compared him with the great French writer Guy de Maupassant. True to form as the voice of the establishment, *The Times* had its reservations, however, taking

Rudyard to task for 'wanting in style' and warning – as if he did not already know – of the dangers of writing himself out. 'Modern magazines and their eager editors,' it thundered, 'are a dangerous snare in the way of a bright, clever, and versatile writer, who knows that he has caught the public taste.'

Frank Harris remained a dissenting voice: writing thirty years later, he could still summon some of the frustration he felt at the rigidity of Rudyard's opinions. The young Kipling was open to textual changes in his copy, he recalled, but quite unwilling to accept that there might be another side to his arguments. His problem, Harris felt, was that he had no idea of the dialectical process and that it might be possible to arrive at some synthesis of the truth. 'Rudyard Kipling was proud of being a partisan, proud of holding and asserting the English view of every question. Nine times out of ten he even preferred the Tory English view to the Liberal. One day I spoke bitterly of the exploitation of the poor by the powerful in Great Britain. It did not seem to interest him.' When, another time, Harris attacked an English judge for defending class interests, Rudyard was adamant that this could not be the case. English judges were the fairest in the world, he said, not least because they were the best paid. But this only confirmed to Harris that Rudyard 'had the prejudices and opinions of a fourth-form English schoolboy on almost every subject coupled with an extraordinary verbal talent: the mind of a boy of sixteen with a genius for expression'.[44]

This deficiency was most obvious, Harris felt, on the subject of India. He found that Rudyard often repeated himself, regurgitating clubhouse stories and the 'rinsings' of his experiences. 'He always assumed that the English rule was the best thing that had happened to India: the Pax Britannica held to peace a score of warring races and conflicting religions.' Rudyard did not see how this had led to the 'enslavement and impoverishment' of millions, argued Harris, wearing his post-1918 anti-imperialist hat. 'He had never considered that side of the matter. The English had given railways to India: was the sufficient answer.'

With the success of 'Danny Deever', followed by 'Tommy' and 'Cleared', Rudyard no longer needed Harris or the *Fortnightly Review*. His contributions to the *Scots Observer* now came fast and furious. Over the next few weeks he produced a series of thirteen poems, now known as the *Barrack-Room Ballads*. (Confusingly, different collections were made under this title, though the definitive volume is *Barrack-Room Ballads and Other Verses* published by Methuen in 1892.) Instead of such romantic paeans to Pathan nobility as the 'Ballad of the King's Mercy' and the 'Ballad of East and West', the so-called 'border ballads', Rudyard now spoke more directly of the British soldier's day-to-day experience – from the baggage trains of 'Oonts', through the perks of battle in 'Loot' (which is deemed to be tongue-in-cheek, or not, according to one's political point of view) and the devotion of an Indian water-bearer in 'Gunga Din', to the stresses and strains (told in resounding vernacular) of policing the world for 'The Widow at Windsor'. The subject matter incorporated Rudyard's understanding of broad imperialist themes, as refracted through conversations with Moberly Bell and Henley. But in the observations of his soldier heroes he also showed the humour, pride and emotion that comes from their role in holding ''alf o' Creation' for the Widow. Nowhere is this more touching than in the splendid 'Mandalay' – a returned squaddie's lament for his lost 'Burma girl' who, in contrast to 'fifty 'ousemaids outer Chelsea', knew all about the art of loving. He recalled 'them spicy garlic smells / An' the sunshine an' the palm-trees an' the tinkly temple-bells', and claimed that 'If you've 'eard the East a-callin', you won't never 'eed naught else.' So, he beseeched,

> Ship me somewhere east of Suez, where the best is like the
> worst
> Where there aren't no Ten Commandments an' a man can
> raise a thirst.

After being acclaimed by the critics these verses, in Charles

Carrington's words,[45] soon 'escaped from the literary salons and spread like a bushfire into the wide world, into the public houses and "the Halls"; they were set to music and sung at "smoking concerts"; were recited, quoted, copied, anthologized, translated'. Already in April, James Whitcomb Riley, the popular dialect poet from the American state of Indiana, was asking a friend, 'Have you struck anything of Yussuf's verse or prose? England has just punched him out from under the woodpile. His real name is Rudyard Kipling, and he's only 24 years of age. His work is great – with the East in it – the Indias – the frontier British soldiers – barracks – camps – courage – fire and tar!' Riley could not have quoted more forthright, masculine lines to make his point:

> Four things greater than all things are –
> Women, and horses, and power, and war,
> And since we know not how war may prove
> Heart of my heart, let us talk of love.

In the context of Rudyard's recent unsatisfactory relations with women, these sentiments had a certain wishfulness, if not irony.

Nine

Artistic Rejection

1890

Trying to be positive, Rudyard had regaled Carrie Taylor on 2 January 1890 with a vision of the exciting life they would enjoy as man and wife in the United States. They would share a flat, with its own janitor and electric light, in a city such as Pittsburgh, from where they would be able to get away to the seaside during summer.

But by this stage Rudyard was fighting a lost cause and was only trying to convince himself, rather than his fiancée, that they had a future together. A week later he wrote to Carrie's brother-in-law Alex Hill in Allahabad expressing his doubts about the whole affair, and comparing it, misquoting rather wildly, with Romeo and Juliet's romance –

> Too sudden, too ill-advised, too rash
> Too like the lightning that doth cease to be. [*sic*]

Rudyard must have said rather more for on receipt the letter was torn up. Only four thin strips of paper survive, with Ted Hill's pithy annotation, 'It's drugs, I believe. Anyway it's impossible.'[1]

Rudyard's cries of anguish to the Hills about his head feeling 'queer' and needing mending were followed by his total breakdown later in January. Reading between the lines of his more guarded letters to her, his mother Alice in Lahore became concerned and diffidently asked Ted Hill if she had any other news.

The two most important women in Rudyard's life had been in touch the previous month after Ted, on her return to Allahabad, found that Rudyard had forgotten the phaeton, or four-wheeled carriage, in which he had used to travel around town. After thanking Ted for being her son's 'Guardian Angel', Alice asked her to auction the phaeton and send her the proceeds so she could pay off some bills (amounting to 300 rupees) that Rudyard had left behind. Ted also helped when Trix passed through Allahabad *en route* to Calcutta, where her new husband had been unexpectedly evacuated, after falling sick on a brief tour of duty with the Indian Survey in Burma.

During February Alice became more anxious about her son. By then Trix had returned to England with her invalid husband and she had sent indications that not all was well with Rudyard. After being reassured by Ted that this was only a passing phase, Alice wrote, 'I too have seen the boy through many moods and tenses, and gladly accept the encouragement of your assurance as to his coming out all right.'[2]

That did not make the reality any less alarming. When Trix called on her brother at Embankment Chambers on 11 February, she was shocked at his mental and physical state. He admitted now that his engagement to Carrie Taylor was over. But, to add to his own mental confusion, he also told Trix that he had recently met his former girl-friend Flo Garrard in a London street and this chance (he claimed) encounter had confirmed to him that he still loved her.

Flo may have been visiting her Aunt Esther Ruck (her father's sister) in Courtfield Gardens, South Kensington, where she had stayed during her final year at the Slade School in 1887. Since then, she had moved to Paris and enrolled in another art school, the fashionable Académie Julian, where, unlike British establishments, the course included working from life models. Started in 1873, Julian's studio had attracted many British, American and Irish students, including the poet George Moore, who recalled how its eponymous founder – 'a typical meridional: dark eyes, crafty and watchful, a seductively mendacious manner, and a sensual mind' – had '[thrown] open a door of Parisian life' for him. The main studio was in Montmartre, but by 1890 it had spawned several other branches, including one for women in the rue Vivienne. One of Julian's selling points was that his students' work was viewed and criticised by the influential artists of the day. But Moore grew disillusioned with Julian's factory approach: 'All the poor folk that go there for artistic education are devoured ... After two years they all paint and draw alike, every one had that vile execution – they call it execution – *la pâté, la peinture au premier coup ...'*

Slowly, during March, Rudyard began to emerge from the psychological doldrums. After meeting Flo and regaining his enthusiasm for work, he wired his parents in Lahore and begged them to hurry home. His message was hardly conventional, reading simply 'Genesis 45:9'. On consulting their Bibles, Lockwood and Alice read: 'Haste ye, and go up to my father, and say unto him, Thus saith thy son Joseph, God hath made me lord of all Egypt: come down unto me; tarry not.' This apt quotation (with its use of Rudyard's 'real' name) managed to convey the hugeness of his success and his urgent need for the support of his family square. Even so, his father was still concerned: 'I won't pretend, dear boy, that we have not felt very anxious about you,' he wrote on 2 March, 'and though your last letter is somewhat reassuring, I shall want much better news of you before I am quite content. I do hope you have knocked off work altogether and gone out for a complete change and rest. You've been on full stretch for so long – you must be brain weary – it couldn't be otherwise. Your work takes a great deal out of you – more than you know.'[3] Lockwood begged his son not to worry about finding him and Alice a place to stay in London. He said they would be quite happy to spend time with the Walkers. Failing that, they would seek lodgings in the north or north-west of London rather than the West End, which could be fearfully expensive in summer.

As soon as his parents reached London in early May, Rudyard

felt free to pay a flying visit to Flo in Paris. Her original sketch-book,[4] bought in the Faubourg St Honoré, records the emotional intensity of the four days he spent there. Her own drawings are predictable sub-Academician stuff. But Rudyard in holiday mood unburdens himself in a series of cartoons executed in his familiar spindly black hand. *A Tale of Absinthe* shows a man in increasing stages of intoxication as he imbibes first 'just one liqueur', then another, then another. In each succeeding frame the wild beasts on the wall become bigger and more threatening, though in essence they are the same fantastic creatures that Rudyard had drawn from his school-days.

Flo's sketch-book contains several more elaborate 'story-boards' by Rudyard. There is a detailed tale, with captions, of Flo setting off into the woods for a day's sketching. After lighting a cigarette (evidence of her unconventional Bohemian habits, no doubt), she tosses the match away and Rudyard neatly captures her surprise as people rush out, shouting 'Fire! Fire!'. 'Of course she thought it was a joke,' runs the last subtitle. Another such series of cartoons, *The Bull That Meant no Harm, or How the best handmade split bamboo rod was lost*, shows Flo fishing, oblivious of the presence of a bull in the same field.

There are also caricatures of four people on an outing in the French countryside – Flo and Ruddy, and two companions called Charles and Jack. The party seems to be having a good time, as is confirmed in a separate sketch of *The strong man Charles* playing tennis. The identities of Charles and Jack are not spelt out, but it is reasonable to guess that the former was Charles Furse, the protégé and friend of John Sargent, who had studied with Alphonse Legros at the Slade and was enrolled at Julian's around this time. Furse also had links with Rudyard's India. A close friend of Vereker Hamilton, who had tried to interest Andrew Lang in Rudyard's early story 'The Mark of the Beast', he became semi-official artist to General Sir Frederick Roberts, whom he painted astride his favourite horse Vonolel.

The only factor missing as far as Rudyard was concerned was

any reciprocal demonstration of affection from Flo. For she had come under the influence of a fellow student, Mabel Price, the daughter of an Oxford mathematics don, later to become Master of Pembroke College, and the two women were living in a lesbian relationship. Herself three years older than Flo, Mabel had studied at the Slade School in Oxford and at Calderon's studio in London, before going to Julian's where, like the vivacious Maria Bash-kirtseva before her, she had impressed the most distinguished visiting teacher, the Academician Tony Robert-Fleury. This had led to some professional success, with one of her paintings being exhibited at the Paris Salon in 1889. Flo and Mabel shared an annexe or 'pavillon' in the garden of a pension in the avenue d'Iéna, where they occasionally staged amateur theatricals with Nigel Playfair, a fellow student who married into the Price family and became a notable impresario. A family memoir tells of these three thespians putting on a version of *La Tosca* (by the French playwright Victorien Sardou, who had been so popular in Simla). Flo took the leading role, originally created for the actress Sarah Bernhardt.

Back in London on 28 May, Rudyard wrote to Gosse that he had been in Paris, where he had suffered a 'surfeit of pictures and consequent indigestion'.[5] If this sounded vaguely upbeat, Rudyard was hamming it. Although he now was clear that his relationship with Flo was finished, his overall mood was as confused as ever. So, under the watchful eye of his father, who often spent the night on his couch at Embankment Chambers, he worked to transmute his recent experiences into the novel that Watt felt would make his name, drawing together his impressions of early-1890s London, his second-hand knowledge of the Sudan campaign, his halting forays into the art world and his meditations on an unsuccessful love affair.

Over the next eleven weeks, Rudyard's only distractions were one short trip with his father for fishing and 'loafing' in Devon (where they stayed with Crom Price) and the occasional composition of a *Barrack-Room Ballad*. (Price's diary recorded that

Rudyard wrote a ballad while staying at the United Services College: possibly 'The Gift of the Sea', which was published in the *English Illustrated Magazine* in August.) Otherwise Rudyard's time was occupied with rejigging his book, *The Light that Failed*. Critics have seldom been kind about the outcome, portraying it as a damp squib after the pyrotechnics of his Indian stories. But it should be read as a quirky piece of Kipling's art – a quietly experimental novel, which moved his literary output beyond the predictable confines of Anglo-India and tackled more serious issues of sex, art and destiny in contemporary society. Though it is full of brilliant cameos and provides a fascinating metaphor for Rudyard's life at the time, its main drawback is that it is a 'grown-up' novel by an emotionally immature man.

Ostensibly, it tells of Dick Heldar, a war artist, and his unrequited passion for Maisie, with whom he had been brought up in an environment similar to Rudyard's in Southsea. After covering campaigns in Egypt, he returns to London where he unexpectedly meets her again. He tries to resurrect their relationship but, encouraged by her friend, a red-haired girl whom he instantly dislikes, Maisie plays the New Woman and rejects him in favour of her own artistic vocation. When Dick/Rudyard fails to develop his own career as an artist, he is drawn back to his old life as a war correspondent – reporting the latest in a long line of campaigns against the Mahdi in Sudan, where he is killed.

This historical setting was interesting since, although *The Light that Failed* was set in the contemporary art world, it drew its military background from General Wolseley's 1884–5 expedition to relieve General Gordon in Khartoum. Even six years later, Sudan remained unconquered and Rudyard would have read accounts of the latest act in the unfolding drama in North Africa – H. M. Stanley's much publicised trip to rescue Emin Pasha in Equatoria. This scenario established a classic antithesis between art and action, and allowed Rudyard to explore the role of the imaginative artist in an age when mechanisation was leading to increasing exactitude of reproduction. The Ruskin-Whistler libel

trial that had interested Rudyard as a boy seemed to establish that
the painter should be true to line and form. But the advance of
photography at the time of the colonial wars of the 1880s and 1890s
helped to undermine this received opinion, which was already
crumbling under attack from different directions. These were the
last conflicts in which the war artist proved an essential intermediary in conveying the details of fighting. By the Boer War,
photo-reproduction had come into its own. During these last two
decades of the nineteenth century, as engravings gave way to
lithograph and mezzotints, popular magazines such as the *Illustrated London News* and the *Graphic* demanded quicker and more
exact representations of war, which were disseminated not only
through the press but also through popular galleries devoted to
stereoscopic and panoramic images.[6]

Leading exponent of the genre was Richard Caton Woodville,
whom Rudyard had almost certainly heard of through his father's
connection with the Duke of Connaught. At Queen Victoria's
behest, Caton Woodville had painted the Duke leading the Guards
at the Battle of Tel el Kebir. He also did a picture of Indian troops
in Egypt that was acquired by the Duke after being published as
a fashionable chromolithograph by Ackermann's in January 1883.
Lockwood would have discussed this type of official military
portraiture with the artistic Duke in Meerut. Returning from
India in 1889, his son must have noticed Caton Woodville's illustrations for Rider Haggard's recent book *Cleopatra*.

For additional material on the Sudanese conflict, Rudyard only
had to look at back numbers of the *Illustrated London News*. The
magazine was represented on Wolseley's expedition by Melton
Prior, who sketched the 'Death of Mr Cameron, special correspondent of the *Standard*, in the battle of January 19'. Cameron
was depicted leaning against a camel, like Dick at his death in *The
Light that Failed*. Among the others present was Bennet Burleigh,
the arrogant correspondent of the *Daily Telegraph*, who was a
likely model for Torpenhow – down to the agency he represented. (In the book Torpenhow works for the Central Southern

Syndicate, a similar name to the Central News for which Burleigh was working a couple of years earlier during the battle of Tel el Kebir.)

Rudyard could also call on a recent memoir, *With the Camel Corps up the Nile*, by Lord Edward Gleichen, as well as eye-witness accounts from Moberly Bell, his school friend Dunsterville, Lord Charles Beresford, Captain Ian Hamilton from India, and perhaps even George Wyndham, spirited son of his Uncle Ned's friends, Percy and Madeline Wyndham, who, to the disgust of his radical cousin Wilfrid Blunt, went to Suakin on the Red Sea to fight the Mahdi's allies, the Hadendowas (or Fuzzy-wuzzies, of Kipling's poem). Not only did Wyndham send back colourful reports to his family, but he had literary, as well as political, ambitions, and had started writing for Henley's *Scots Observer* in 1890.

Having accumulated this detail, Rudyard peppered *The Light that Failed* with insights into his own way of life. On a mundane level, there are details about contemporary journalism, with organisations such as the Central Southern Syndicate reflecting the new professionalism of McClure's and similar agencies. When Dick returns to London at the start of the book, he is infuriated to find that the Central Southern wants to keep his prints, arguing that it has invested time and money in bringing him to the public's attention – the sort of acquisitiveness over copyright that Rudyard was beginning to learn was widespread.

More significantly, the novel's debate on the meaning of Art reflects Rudyard's own contradictions. As a modern war artist, Dick advocates a super-realism that can be faithfully reproduced in the pages of a modern journal. His real-life author's voice can be detected in his complaints about having to attend tea parties (at the unearthly hour of five o'clock) and to listen to 'half a dozen epicene young pagans' twittering about Art and the state of their souls – 'as if their souls mattered'. Dick claims to have heard more about Art and seen less of it in a few months in London than in the rest of his life.

In discussions with Maisie, who paints 'fancy heads' with a

'queer grim Dutch touch' (a fair description of Flo's style in her sketch-book), Dick advises her to ignore her Paris teacher's Whistler-like emphasis on colour, and to concentrate on line which 'doesn't allow of shirking'. In other words, she must draw what exists, rather than her particular style of heads 'with a bunch of flowers at the base of the neck to hide bad modelling' – or, as Rudyard was to put it in a poem a couple of years later, she must draw what she sees 'for the God of Things as They are'. (Rudyard never really resolved this debate: in his own field he was clear that fiction offered a better stab at truth than fact.)

Despite Rudyard's understanding of the issues – a legacy of conversation with his father and his uncles – this artistic debate is never fully engaged, let alone resolved. Dick only comes alive when he urges Maisie to share his wanderlust, or 'go-fever', and journey with him to distant lands. He tells her of some of the attractions of India, and pleads: 'Maisie, darling, come with me and see what the world is really like. It is very lovely, and it's very horrible ... and it doesn't care your life or mine for pictures or anything else except doing its own work and making love.' Dick could not have expressed Rudyard's frustrations with London better – nor his sense that he needed to get away to find his vocation as a writer and lover.

Rudyard also fails to spark an intelligent discussion about women's role in the world. Looking like a little mouse in her mantle of grey, Maisie lacks sufficient sex appeal. Rudyard's own confusion is painfully evident as Dick veers between addressing Maisie as an honorary 'chap' to fantasising about making love to a Negroid-Jewish-Cuban woman – 'with morals to match' – on a ship to Australia.

On the one hand, Dick tells her she is 'a work-woman, darling, to your boot-heels and I respect you for that'; on the other, harking back to Rudyard's (and before him, his father's) view of Indians, he is unable to countenance the possibility that women are capable of art. Consequently he rejects women (and art and society) and returns to his familiar male stamping grounds. It is no accident that Maisie's wild revolver shot, back in their youth, had anticipated his blindness. Women are like that, Rudyard implies. They take away your powers. Or as Dick's journalist friend Torpenhow comments, in arguing that a woman cannot be part of a man's life, 'She says she wants to sympathize with you and help you in your work, and everything else that clearly a man must do for himself. Then she sends round five notes a day to ask why the dickens you haven't been wasting your time with her.'

The Light that Failed is full of clues about Flo Garrard and her friend Mabel Price. Flo/Maisie comes across as the lively ingenue of Rudyard's sketches in her notebook. The red-haired girl, on the other hand, is a scheming sexual predator, who is jealous of Dick's attentions to her lover. As an expression of her distaste for Dick, she draws him in the impressionistic Whistler style he has advised Maisie against: 'it was the merest monochrome roughing in of a head, but it presented the dumb waiting, the longing, and, above all, the hopeless enslavement of the man, in a spirit of bitter mockery.' And then to emphasise her loathing, she destroys the drawing.

Rudyard's own attitude to Flo and their doomed relationship was reflected in the poignant poem which prefaced one of the chapters:

> Roses red and roses white
> Plucked I for my love's delight.
> She would none of all my posies –
> Bade me gather her blue roses.

When Flo Garrard later made her only known comment on Rudyard, she implied that it was he, rather than she, who had made impossible demands. This, at least, was the burden of her inscription in her personal copy of *The Light that Failed* that she left to the companion of her later years, Miss Frances Egerton:

If you happen to read this singular & somewhat murky little

story you are very likely to wonder if *real* people could be quite so stupid and objectionable as this crowd … It looks to me rather like its image reflected in a Distorting Mirror appearing all distorted and grotesque. For instance, in the case of the Blue Roses (I didn't refuse any other colour) but as a matter of fact, Dick, with his usual obliquity of vision failed to observe that I wasn't exacting them of him, but *he* of me.

Flo's reference to her one-time friend's 'obliquity of vision' reflects the novel's dominant visual metaphor. As various comments to the Hills suggest, Rudyard was fascinated with the developing science of photography – both as a technique which supersedes art by providing absolute verisimilitude in reproduction and, as a branch of optics, an interest linked to his problems with his own eyes. As Dick's sight began to fail, he showed classical signs of astigmatism: 'It was true that the corners of the studio draped themselves in grey film and retired into the darkness, that the spots in his eyes and the pains across his head were very troublesome, and that Maisie's letters were hard to read and harder still to answer.'

On the evidence of *The Light that Failed*, Rudyard took his study of phenomenology rather further. From time to time Dick's story is told in a series of brilliant images as if seen from a fast-moving train or, alternatively, as if projected in an early movie. Thinking of his earlier involvement with Maisie, 'the pictures passed before him one by one'. Then, turning to his own life, 'From the beginning he told the tale, the I-I-I's flashing through the records as telegraph-poles fly past the traveller.' Elsewhere, particularly when dealing with events outside England, Rudyard's style is sharp, vivid and kinetic.

Rudyard's autobiography throws light on this background. In seeking to dress up *The Light that Failed* with a suitable literary–historical pedigree, he tells how, as a thirteen-year-old accompanying his father to the 1878 Paris Exhibition, he saw Pascal Dagnan-Bouvert's painting of the tragic death of the

demi-mondaine Manon Lescaut, and this later led him to read
the Abbé Prévost's original proto-romantic story of that name, in
tandem with Scarron's picaresque *Roman Comique*. He says this
encounter with French literature took place when he was 'about
eighteen', which would place it in 1884, or shortly after he had
arrived in India and was experiencing the pangs of his broken
romance with Flo. Rudyard suggested that these seeds lay dormant
until he moved to London and that *The Light that Failed* was a
'sort of inverted, metagrobolized phantasmagoria based on
Manon'. The unusual adjective 'metagrobolized' is an Angli-
cisation of a French word used by Rabelais meaning 'to puzzle
out'. Beside giving the novel another French literary antecedent,
its use in conjunction with 'phantasmagoria' – a reference to the
magic lantern shows which had flourished since the start of the
century – helps explain Rudyard's cartoon-like doodles on Flo's
notebook, as well as his narrative technique, both in this novel and
afterwards. Only three years earlier Thomas Edison, an unsung
Kipling hero, had patented the first motion picture camera, which
by 1891 was working successfully.

Rudyard completed *The Light that Failed* (he called it a *conte*,
or short story) within three months, in time for its deadline of 15
August, when it was delivered to Macmillan (in the middle of a
heatwave) – together with his promised *Book of the Forty-Five
Mornings*. The effort had been immense: as he wrote that very
day to Margaret Clifford, Lucy's younger daughter, with whom
he had developed a playful relationship, 'I am nearly broked in
two. I have done my two books an' I'm dead tired frabjous an'
muzzy about the head.'[7] Almost at once, he was having second
thoughts about the latter compilation, asking Macmillan for
changes on 17 August, 'Please be good enough to place "The
Sacrifice of St Helen" (enclosed) immediately before the tale called
"Where" and "The Seven Nights of Creation" after the story called
"New Brooms".' Curiously, this volume was never published,
suggesting it was assembled from old material with little relevance
to Rudyard's current output. Two of these four named pieces are

unknown, while 'The Seven Nights of Creation' was originally published in the *Calcutta Review* in April 1886, and 'New Brooms' in the *CMG* in August 1888. The package may also have included some of the travel articles Rudyard had written in America and had discussed republishing with Moreton Frewen. Wiser counsels prevailed and this collection was cancelled in the autumn.

Having, at least temporarily, absolved himself of these commitments, Rudyard found himself drawn into a literary dispute he would rather have avoided. On 20 June *Lippincott's Magazine* had published Oscar Wilde's novella *The Picture of Dorian Gray* which, in a curious way, covered the same ground as *The Light that Failed* – the role of the artist, the aesthetic movement, sexual roles, homosexuality; one of the characters was even based on Whistler. The perspective was clearly different: while Rudyard had taken a conservative, anti-feminist approach to this material, Wilde adopted a radical, nihilistic view. Since Rudyard never referred to it directly, the consternation with which he greeted Wilde's literary efforts can only be imagined.

The reaction of the *Scots Observer* (which had recently added the words 'an Imperial Review' to its masthead) offers a clue. Henley's assistant, Charles Whibley, weighed in: 'Mr Wilde has brains, and art, and style; but if he can write for none but outlawed noblemen and perverted telegraph-boys, the sooner he takes to tailoring (or some other decent trade) the better for his own reputation and the public morals.'[8] Wilde returned fire in a series of letters to the paper and, having clearly decided that the Henley Regatta was united against him, weighed into Rudyard in the September issue of *Nineteenth Century*, where he described the author of the *Plain Tales* as 'a reporter who knows vulgarity better than anyone has ever known it'. Rudyard rose to the bait: he resurrected an old India poem[9] as 'The Conundrum of the Workshops', which pointed out that Wilde's criticisms of art (in *Dorian Gray*) were not new; some devil was always asking of people's efforts: 'It's clever (or pretty), but is it Art?' With the years, Rudyard's views on this matter firmed: by mid-1891 when he wrote

'Tomlinson', the aesthetic view on art was roundly attacked and later, in his memoirs, he referred to the 'suburban Toilet-Club school favoured by the late Mr Oscar Wilde'.

Rudyard would have preferred to keep clear of any literary mud-slinging, and to continue writing. But a classic metropolitan literary tiff was unfolding. As if to display Rudyard's colours more clearly on the Regatta's mast, Henley asked Whibley to review the latest English editions of *In Black and White* and *The Story of the Gadsbys*. In his piece, published on 20 September, Whibley fêted Rudyard as 'a man of genius', while clearly attacking Wilde with his jibe, 'It would be an easy matter, by an unscrupulous choice of examples, to prove that Mr Kipling was little better than a smart journalist.'

In thanking Henley (with certain reservations) for this puff, Rudyard admitted he was 'wondrous miserable just now'.[10] As so often in such circumstances, his father tried to help him out. Since returning from Lahore, Lockwood had been putting the finishing touches to his Indian-inspired Billiard Room for the Duke of Connaught's house at Bagshot Park. This had gone so well that the Duke's mother, Queen Victoria, asked him to work on a similar Moghul-style Durbar Room for her house at Osborne in the Isle of Wight. Because Lockwood was occupied with this, Rudyard often stayed overnight at the Kiplings' rented accommodation at 101 Earls Court Road. This allowed Lockwood time to collaborate with his son on a story, 'On Greenhow Hill',[11] which drew on his own recollections of Yorkshire customs and dialect to re-create the stark, primitive world of rural Methodism. Rudyard liked the outcome, telling William Canton, a literary-minded journalist on the *Glasgow Herald*, 'I want to make these people understand that it has been given to me to describe, when God chuses, country village rusticity in the North whence I come; "for my birth and kin Ise Yorkshire and Stingo". '[12]

A second joint effort, 'The Enlightenments of Pagett M.P.', satirised the posturings of a parliamentarian who backed the Indian National Congress without knowing the first thing about

India. With this story,[13] Rudyard's perspective on the land of his birth took a new turn. His earlier poem 'Pagett M.P.' had taken an Anglo-Indian viewpoint to attack the 'travelled idiot' who visits India briefly to 'study the East'. In 'Cleared' he focused more directly on British domestic issues as he railed against the Liberal party's role in the Parnell Commission. Now again (with his father's help) he adopted an Anglocentric viewpoint as he vented his anger against radical politicians wanting to dismantle the Empire. Rudyard was beginning to regard himself as an Englishman rather than an Anglo-Indian.

As a proud father, Lockwood chose to see his son's development in a positive light. 'In one year this youngster will have had more said about his work, over a wider extent of the world's surface, than some of the greatest of England's writers in their whole lives,' he told Edith Plowden. 'He has kept his head wonderfully, steadfastly refused to go into society and seems to care for naught but his work, his Mother and a very few friends.' After almost a year in London, Rudyard had certainly made his mark. But Lockwood did not give the full story, glossing over his son's unhappiness and wranglings with the literary world, and ignoring the brooding, unexpected presence of the Balestier family.

Ten

The Family from Vermont
1890–1892

'Rudyard Kipling?' Wolcott Balestier had asked contemptuously when first told about the author of *Soldiers Three* in 1889. 'Is it a man or a woman? What's its real name?' Yet by the end of the following year this fragile, charismatic literary entrepreneur from Vermont had taken Rudyard's career in hand, begun to collaborate on an oddly unsuitable book and made him part of his dysfunctional family. Rudyard needed Balestier's American drive to complement his own hard-won Eastern wisdom and help him deal more positively with contemporary society.

Balestier's no less exotic name reflected his origins as a member of a Franco-Hispanic (possibly once Huguenot) family, a branch of which had prospered in the sugar business in Martinique. With the abolition of slavery after the Napoleonic Wars, Wolcott's grandfather, Joseph Balestier, surfaced in the American frontier town of Chicago where, working with John Harris Kinzie, the leading trader with the local Indians, he amassed a fortune in real estate. He, it has been claimed, was the 'young lawyer' whom Harriet Martineau met when she visited Chicago in July 1836 and who 'had realized five hundred dollars per day the five preceding days, by merely making out titles to land'. A Unitarian (like Martineau), Joseph became an ardent Whig (as Republicans were then called), writing for the party's daily newspaper, the *Chicago-American*, and serving in the delegation which nominated Abraham Lincoln for President in 1860. In his upward mobility, he attracted the hand of Caroline Starr Wolcott, daughter of a doctor (related by marriage to the Kinzies) who had come to Chicago in the boom of the late 1830s. Hers was a prominent East Coast family (originally from Somerset in England) that had spawned three governors of Connecticut, including Oliver Wolcott, a US treasury secretary, whose father, also Oliver, signed the Declaration of Independence in 1776. To underline her impeccable WASP background, her great Aunt Maria was the daughter of Paul Revere, whose 'minutemen' or riders harried the British at Lexington, while among her other English antecedents was John Drake, brother of Sir Francis, the Elizabethan privateer.

From Chicago, the Balestiers moved to New York where Joseph added to his considerable wealth, enabling him to retire in 1868, aged only fifty-four. Since he suffered from gout, he decided to join the fashionable exodus to the leafy town of Brattleboro, on the confluence of the West and Connecticut rivers, 195 miles north in Vermont. Brattleboro's waters were believed to have restorative qualities and many New Yorkers took summer houses there – at least until its natural advantages attracted a sanatorium for people with nervous diseases in the 1870s. The town enjoyed an agreeable New England mixture of well-ordered conservatism and energetic grass-roots capitalism. Its established families, such as the Brookses, Holbrooks and Cabots, had rendered the community sterling service over the years. The summer visitors from New York were treated warily and had to prove their worth.

The Balestiers avoided any ostracism, demonstrating their desire for permanent roots by buying an old white farmhouse, which they called Beechwood – though its position, set in 380 acres of land, some four miles from the centre of Brattleboro, reflected their distance from the mainstream of town affairs. In 1860 one of their four sons, Henry, married Anna Smith, daughter of Erasmus Peshine Smith, a lawyer and writer from Rochester, New York. Smith's efficiency in the Department of Claims in Washington during the Civil War led to his appointment as legal adviser to the Japanese Foreign Ministry from 1871 to 1876, shortly after the restoration of the Meiji. Smith antagonised his mentor, the United States minister Charles de Long, with his familiarity with the Japanese. De Long accused him of leaking official American secrets and disgracing his country by living with a local concubine and indulging in 'perfect orgies' of drinking.[1]

During ten years of marriage, Henry and Anna Balestier had four children, Wolcott, Caroline, Beatty and Josephine. For a while, Henry worked as a lawyer in the same New York office as his father, but he disliked the profession and drifted out into the insurance business. However, his health was poor and in 1870, a year after Josephine's birth, he died in Boston.

Anna's early widowhood was unsettled as she and her children shuttled uneasily between Rochester and Balestier family houses in Brattleboro and New York. (In Brattleboro, she usually avoided Beechwood and stayed in a local lodging house.) Wolcott, her eldest son, who was born in 1861, was a sickly child, who retained his pallor as he grew into a tall, intense young man, with swept-back hair. For one year (1800–1) he attended Cornell University, but his formal education was, as a friend put it, 'desultory'. The spirited Balestiers were not great stickers and Wolcott found the prospect of a career as a writer more exciting.

His sister Caroline, who was one year younger, was no more conventional. She was a plain, dark-haired, eccentric teenager, with 'the air of habitually living in a world apart from those around her ... her mind ... being filled with a desire to visit far countries and live a life of activity which was far from being the "ladylike" ideal for the feminine sex in those days'. During the short period Wolcott was at Cornell, she managed to spend several weeks in Ithaca, the local town, where she amused herself in poetry and painting. Brother and sister cut colourful and unconventional figures. The Rochester Historical Society reported that they were both 'fond of extremes in dress, wearing the largest and loudest checks, when checks were in fashion, and outraging convention in the matter of color and size of hats and ties'.[2]

Having left Cornell without a degree, Wolcott dabbled in journalism. His brief career on the *Rochester Post-Express* was notable only for his coining in an article on 5 August 1882 of the word 'telepheme' as a synonym for 'telephonic despatch' – one of only two such uses admitted in the *Oxford English Dictionary*. He submitted at least one piece to the distinguished man of letters William Dean Howells, who had married a Brattleboro woman and was now writing for the influential *Century Magazine*. But family connections encouraged him to seek his fortune in the state of Colorado, which was enjoying a mining boom. On this occasion his chest was not healthy enough to cope with the bracing mountain air. So, returning to New York, he wrote his first story, 'A Potent Philter', for the local *Tribune*. He also found a job at the Astor Library where he was able to immerse himself in newspaper files and so churn out a pot-boiler biography of James G. Blaine, the Republican presidential candidate in 1884.

He hoped to be rewarded, if Blaine were successful, with a foreign consulship which would allow him to write. In this way he would follow in the steps of his Peshine Smith grandfather, though a more immediate model was his mentor W. D. Howells who, nearly a quarter of a century earlier, had been given the sinecure of United States Consul in Venice after writing a campaign biography of Abraham Lincoln. When Blaine failed to win office, Wolcott decided to try his luck again in Colorado where his enterprising sister Caroline (known as Carrie) had gone in April to stay with Amy Graves, an old school friend.

Once again Wolcott did not take to the outdoor life-style and soon continued on his travels through the South-West and Mexico, where he wanted to collect material for future stories. Returning to New York, he assumed the editorship of *Tid-Bits*, a lowish-brow magazine that the John W. Lovell publishing company had started the previous August. Even at this stage Wolcott was a martinet, calling on the artist Charles Dana Gibson to attend him at the theatre (where he himself was invariably late) and demanding drawings at noon, which had to be ready for the presses within three hours.

After three years at *Tid-Bits*, Wolcott was given a more challenging job. The international book trade was changing. American publishers were beginning to realise they could no longer pirate books by foreign authors and unscrupulously refuse to pay royalties. Following a raft of complaints, stretching back to Charles Dickens, a law of copyright was about to be introduced. John Lovell had the novel idea of pre-empting the courts and sending an agent – in this case, Balestier – to London, where he could court British authors and encourage them to sign up with a 'reputable' American firm such as his own. They would ensure simultaneous publication of their British 'sheets', or printed proofs, in the United States, while Lovell, who had once been as exploitative as the rest of them, would steal a march on both the pirates and his more legitimate competitors.

Balestier arrived in London in December 1888. (His decision to make the move may have been facilitated by the knowledge that he would inherit some money, under the will of his grandfather, who had died three months earlier, leaving an estate worth $600,000.) Not knowing anyone, he paid an early call on W. D. Howells's friend Edmund Gosse, who frequented the local literary scene. As agent for *Century Magazine*, Gosse was familiar with all the city's authors, whom he generously introduced to Wolcott. Gosse later remembered the 'thrill of attraction' at his first meeting this stylish newcomer – 'a mixture of suave Colonial French, and the strained nervous New England blood'; simultaneously a fop, with cravats to compete with the most hardened aesthete, and a driven man, possessed of almost demoniac energy, very different from the lassitude of the 'decadents'.

Through force of personality, Balestier soon made his own friendships among English authors. As well as dangling potentially lucrative contracts before them, he spoke an enticing and unknown language of copyright protection and promotional budgets. As Gosse subtly noted, 'He possessed a singularly winning mode of address with strangers whose attention he wished to gain.' And not only was Wolcott a dynamic businessman, but he also seemed genuinely interested in the finished literary product.

Before long, Balestier wrote home to a family friend Molly Cabot, 'I have met all the novelists, of course.'[3] Gosse, in particular, had been a useful contact. Not only did he know the literary world, but he was also a friend of artists and actors. His wife Nellie was one of five daughters of a prominent homeopathic physician, George Napoleon Epps, whose family was well known for manufacturing cocoa. Her sister Laura was married to the Dutch-born painter Lawrence Alma-Tadema. Wolcott, who had his own artistic ties through a family relationship with Whistler, reminded Molly of the Epps cocoa advertisement and its punchline, 'Grateful and Comforting'.

Since business was initially slow, he continued his own writing, in particular a new book, *Benefits Forgot*, based on his Colorado experiences. A casual comment to Molly suggests the extent of his ambition. For he confirmed that he had not enjoyed his time in the Rockies and had only been there to gather material for a debunking novel. Now, having embarked on a 'vicious and thoroughgoing "doing up" of the Great, Big, Boundless', he hoped to 'make a volume which shall be the vade mecum of all who hate the West; or rather, those who understand the West. To understand it *is* to hate it ... There are ten chapters, now in proof.'[4]

After finding lodgings in Belsize Road, Swiss Cottage, he needed somewhere permanent for his business premises. On a visit to the Gosses in May, Alma-Tadema had been making sketches in the background. Wolcott offered to accompany a fellow American home. She was Mrs Joseph Pennell, who later wrote a life of Whistler with her artist husband. On the way, she insisted on stopping to look at what she described as a 'picturesque' house on the Embankment which she felt would be an ideal office. Her sense of geography was wayward, for it turned out she was referring to a set of rooms that overlooked not the River Thames but Dean's Yard, in the shadow of Westminster Abbey, close to the Houses of Parliament. Balestier was intrigued: having decided against the usual publishers' stamping grounds, such as Covent Garden, he agreed that this quiet spot would provide appropriate headquarters for his mission to feel 'the pulse of English literature'. 'People are beginning to think I am an Englishman,' he told Molly, delightedly.

During the summer of 1889 his family started to visit him from America. First to arrive, on 1 June, was Carrie who, after landing in Glasgow, stayed in Scotland with some friends, the Kelseys. Later that month Wolcott wrote to Molly Cabot suggesting she might like to join them 'when Carrie and I are established in our house'. At the same time he could not help being curious about developments in Brattleboro – his younger brother Beatty had become engaged to an attractive local girl, Mai Mendon. Beatty was the black sheep of the family – a charming, hard-drinking spendthrift, with a quick temper. However, his decision to stay in Brattleboro, rather than seek his fortune elsewhere, had endeared him to old 'Madame' (as she liked to be called) Balestier. Now that he was getting married, Beatty, her favourite, was allowed to buy Maplewood, a farm on the family's Beechwood property, plus the surrounding 170 acres, for a knockdown price. Wolcott was not amused, commenting wryly that the newly engaged couple would 'both need a guardian appointed'. Carrie quickly adapted to London life, becoming friendly with Gosse's artistic wife Nellie.

During the summer of 1890, after nearly two years in London, Wolcott finally found his feet. His writing was still bogged down, but his various business interests began to flourish. With his contacts in the New York book world he knew that, after setting up a syndication arm for the *Century* magazine, the entrepreneurial S. S. (Samuel) McClure had recently branched out on his own. So, as well as his regular work for John W. Lovell, Wolcott now sought contributions for McClure's syndication service. (McClure's brother Bobby came to London to work with Balestier on this: Conan Doyle and Stevenson were among their first clients.) At the same time Wolcott set up a new company with William Heinemann, who had recently started his eponymous publishing firm in London. Having been educated in Europe, Heinemann was convinced he could attack the German Baron Tauchnitz's monopoly in publishing limp-bound editions of English fiction on the Continent. With this aim, the company Heinemann and Balestier was launched, with its imprint the English Library. The two other directors showed the epicurean Heinemann's range of contacts – Bram Stoker, soon to be famous as the author of *Dracula*, but at the time Henry Irving's manager at the Lyceum Theatre, and W. L. Courtney, a former academic making his mark on the *Daily Telegraph*. As secretary for the new business, Balestier chose Arthur Waugh, just down from Oxford and recommended by his cousin Edmund Gosse.

By then, Wolcott had met Rudyard, though the precise moment is not clear. Gosse claimed he introduced the two writers, but his biographer Ann Thwaite suggests they had already encountered one another at Humphry Ward's house. Initially the relationship was friendly rather than commercial, with Rudyard showing more attention to Caroline Balestier, one of his favourite breed of American women, which must have added to his general con-fusion. Writing to her sister Josephine in New York as early as 18 March 1890, Carrie told how she had introduced Rudyard to typing and how he intended to name the machine he had used 'Jemima Anne'. Some of his verses were to be engraved on it in silver plate. 'It's so nice to have him in the typewriter fold,' gushed Carrie. When he learnt that she wanted to send Josephine a buckle, he insisted on helping her choose and dispatch it. 'He is a crank over old silver and insists it is most of it vilely bad.'[5]

27-year-old Carrie was living with Wolcott in Neville Street, Kensington, in a house owned by Thackeray's 'Aunt Job', Jane Brookfield. As well as acting as his house-keeper, she had helped decorate her brother's office at Dean's Yard, taking special pleasure in the acquisition of a custom-made William Morris carpet. She enjoyed meeting her brother's bookish acquaintances, even asking for autographs from favourites, including Ouida, Olive Schreiner and Bret Harte.

But this one friend particularly interested her and, anticipating a life-time's activity, she began to help Rudyard collate his written output. She was looking forward to receiving an early version of *The Light that Failed* which she would arrange and bind for Wolcott. At this stage, Wolcott appeared more as a book collector than as a professional adviser. And this was how Carrie saw herself, telling Josephine proudly that she had acquired at least one manuscript autographed: 'CSB from Rudyard Kipling'. But she added, 'The last chapters [of *The Light that Failed*] are not done yet and there is no telling when they will be.'

Carrie enjoyed telling her sister about the gossip surrounding her new writer friend. When she had seen Rudyard the previous day, he had been 'rejoicing over what a cheque he had just had from India' – for the sale of 7000 copies of his books. 'Fancy what a reading public he has, for he has "His Own People" [i.e. the Anglo-Indians] in addition to England and America.' She referred to Rudyard's aversion to Edmund Gosse who made 'a great fuss over him always' but whom 'he does not trust'. And Rudyard had had a request from Italy to translate his books. He had accepted and said that 'soon there will be no race free from the curse'.

His friendship with both Balestiers had quickly flourished, for Carrie also noted, 'He keeps his clothes partly here and insists that a place be placed for him always so it is at dinner and supper, and he was much disgusted because it was not looking as if he was expected the other day when he popped in on his way to lunch at the Savile Club, so that I should have to have it done for lunch now.' She and Wolcott were preparing to visit Europe, and there was a possibility that Rudyard might accompany them part of the way. 'He is always game to go anywhere. It is staying that bothers him. He has Go fever every three minutes.' (This was exactly Dick Heldar's complaint in *The Light that Failed*.)

But for the time being Rudyard preferred not to look to Wolcott for professional advice. As young Arthur Waugh remarked, Kipling 'was a more dilatory conquest than usual' for Balestier. At the very start of his employment in June, Waugh was sent to

Embankment Chambers to ask permission to publish an American edition of Rudyard's *The Book of the Forty-Five Mornings*, then being widely touted in the press. 'Extraordinarily importunate person, this Mr Balestier,' retorted Rudyard in his darkened rooms. 'Tell him that *The Book of a Hundred* [*sic*] *Mornings* is all over my bed and may never get finished. Tell him to enquire again in six months.'[6]

At the time Rudyard was still struggling to meet his August deadlines for both this book and *The Light that Failed*. This did not stop him visiting Wolcott for tea in Westminster in July. Josephine had taken over from Carrie, and she reported back to her sister in New York, 'You can fancy about my amazement – or rather you can't – when, as Wolcott was standing with Mrs. Gosse and me on the balcony, he said quite casually, "Ah, there's Kipling; I asked him to come over this afternoon to meet you." He is not at all a "woman's man" and young girls are always afraid of him, so of course I was on the defensive and declared to myself that, if I hadn't been afraid of Henry James, I certainly was not going to be of Rudyard Kipling. So I chatted away with him and then he came and "sat down beside me", but little Miss J. was not frightened away, and we had a very jolly time. He is very clever and it was exciting and great fun keeping the ball rolling; Wolcott was amused at the glorious way we got on . . .'[7]

During the autumn the situation changed, as Rudyard experienced further professional and personal setbacks. In September, he was furious when Harper and Brothers, the company which had snubbed him in New York less than a year earlier, informed him casually that, without his prior permission, it intended publishing a cheap edition of six of his stories. It had bought serial rights for five of these (which made its action questionable, but strictly legitimate), but for the sixth, 'The Incarnation of Krishna Mulvaney', it did not even have this basic cover. To make matters worse, it offered a £10 'honorarium' which Rudyard described to Henley as 'the wages of one New York road scavenger for one month'.

Rudyard learnt of this at a time when he had been drawn inadvertently into the squabble between the Henley Regatta and Oscar Wilde; he was being pestered by Gosse, an advocate of Ibsen, to write a play which never materialised; and he was not happy with *The Book of the Forty-Five Mornings* – a view shared by a literary friend, Robert Barr, who told him that it was only as good as – and certainly no better than – *Plain Tales from the Hills*.

Then once again he was plunged into a personal crisis. On 23 September Alex Hill had unexpectedly died of typhoid fever in Allahabad. Although he felt grief at the loss of a friend, Rudyard was presented with an extraordinary possibility: one day, he might be able to marry Alex's widow, Ted, for whose company he had endured his ill-advised engagement to her sister Caroline Taylor. Ted was a free woman again, and Rudyard was not sure what to do.

His solution was to follow the example of Dick Heldar and flee. The *Athenaeum* of 4 October carried his protest about Harper and Brothers' theft of his copyright. It also printed a short paragraph: 'We regret to hear that Rudyard Kipling has broken down from overwork. He had been ordered to take a sea voyage and sailed on the P & O steamer *Shannon* for Naples. His illness will probably delay the publication of *The Book of the Forty-Five Mornings*.' Rudyard covered his tracks well and the only place he is known to have been to, apart from Naples, is the nearby town of Sorrento where Lord Dufferin, the British Ambassador to Italy, had a summer villa. Quite why Rudyard wanted to spend time with an aristocrat he had never liked is a mystery. He may have felt Dufferin was familiar enough with both East and West to be able to advise him where his true interests lay. Possibly he was worried about his father's future and hoped that the former Viceroy might use his influence to obtain Lockwood a suitable pension when he retired in 1893. His wily mother was perhaps concerned about her financial future and encouraged Rudyard to seek this mediation. Certainly she was uncommonly grateful for Dufferin's support, writing later, 'The kindness and sympathy which [Rudyard] received from you and from Lady Dufferin is the brightest recollection he retains of a time when he was neither well nor happy.'[8]

After returning to London in a more relaxed frame of mind, Rudyard found his dispute with Harpers taking a new turn in late November, when three leading British writers, Sir Walter Besant, Thomas Hardy and William Black, wrote to the *Athenaeum* defending the American publisher as generally honest.[9] In retrospect, their appeasing line might have been designed to assist negotiations on an international copyright agreement. But Rudyard's wrath could not now be contained. He burst into print on 6 December in a furious ballad 'The Rhyme of the Three Captains' which told how, after his ship had been raided by a piratical Yankee brig, a skipper battled to regain his cargo and crew, despite the equivocation of 'three captains' intent on convincing him that this sort of activity was time-honoured fair trading. The target of Rudyard's satire was clear as he shamelessly punned, 'the bezant is hard – aye – and black'. Harper and Brothers had compounded its offence in his eyes by printing a snide attack on him by W. D. Howells in its magazine – 'criticizing stolen work with adjectives stolen from England', wrote Rudyard to Henley.[10] Now it backed down, removing the offending story from its forthcoming edition of Rudyard's work, substituting 'The Record of Badalia Herodsfoot', for which it had legitimate serial rights. But, in apologising, it claimed it had treated him much better than any real pirate would. Later, in 1898, a more reflective Rudyard thought he had acted hastily: 'I should have taken their money and held my tongue but in those days I thought I did well to be angry.'[11] Part of Rudyard's fascination at this stage of his career was that he could be impulsive and raw. But this was not the last time he would tangle with American publishers over copyright.

This row at last gave Balestier the opportunity he needed to make himself useful. How much he advised Rudyard on strategy towards Harper and Brothers is not known, but the dates suggest he played a role. More important, he arranged for Lovell to publish an 'authorised' edition of Rudyard's works in the United States, starting in November 1890 with the first collection of the *Barrack-Room Ballads*. The word 'authorised' was what counted, for this would cut the ground from under the pirates, though Rudyard's lingering resentment can be discerned in his letter to Lovell: 'Gentlemen, Your country takes the books of all of the other countries without paying for them. Your firm has taken some books of mine and has paid a certain price for them though it might have taken them for nothing. I object to the system altogether but since I am helpless, authorize you to state that all editions of my property now in your hands have been overlooked by me.'[12]

Balestier convinced Rudyard to scrap *The Book of the Forty-Five Mornings*, as was confirmed in a letter from Carrie in London to Josephine in New York (the two sisters changed places again in the autumn). This referred to 'a long book he was going to give the world called The Something of the Forty Nights. I read them in proofs and agreed with Wolcott who made him stop them, that for the most part they were not the stuff that he ought to give the world now, they were the youngest thing he had by him and it was a shame to let them see daylight here.'[13] Nevertheless Carrie urged her sister to read 'the beanie story and the Elephant yarn' ('Bimi' and 'Moti Guj – Mutineer'), the only tales he had been allowed to bring from this aborted book. They would now be incorporated into twelve predominantly Indian stories for publication under the title *Mine Own People* in the United States in the spring of 1891, with a 'critical introduction' by Henry James, who had met Rudyard through Wolcott in November. Before the expanded British edition of this work appeared in August 1891, Rudyard found another new book with the same title, so he changed his own to *Life's Handicap* – a name he had once given to the verse epigraph to his May 1887 *Plain Tale*, 'In the Pride of his Youth':

Stopped in the straight when the race was his own! ...
Maybe they used him too much at the start;
Maybe Fate's weight-cloths are breaking his heart.

Its use now showed that, even in the midst of success, Rudyard feared that some unexpected reverse might prevent him attaining his goals. The new volume had a wry introduction, originally intended for *The Book of the Forty-Five Mornings*, which meditated on the difference between Eastern and Western narrative approaches. In India, a traditional weaver of tales had one object – to tell an old story well – while in England Rudyard was always under pressure to come up with something new. The dialectic between repetition and innovation was a constant theme in his work, even in his style, which often gained its effect from the subtle reiteration of words and sounds.

Balestier also suggested Rudyard should put out two versions of *The Light that Failed* – his original 'sad' story, which would be published in volume form by the United States Book Company (the latest incarnation of the financially troubled John Lovell) in the United States and Macmillan in London, and a shorter alternative, bringing Dick and Maisie happily together, which would be easier for him to syndicate. (This was duly published in *Lippincott's Magazine* in January 1891.)

As Rudyard came to know Wolcott through this business arrangement, their friendship flourished and they agreed to collaborate on a novel, *The Naulahka*. Sadly, no material survives to confirm the division of labour, or even to say who initiated the idea. But, as a former journalist, Rudyard was always quick to capitalise on his raw material and he must have been chafing that he had not already turned some of his American experiences into fiction. What better way than to contrast that country's dynamism, however ambiguous his feelings about it, with a very different culture, the elusive, fatalistic East, he knew so well? At the same time, he could make another attempt at exploring the question of women in the modern world.

The Naulahka tells of a politically ambitious young American, Nicholas Tarvin, who believes that the development of his small High Plains town of Topaz depends on having the railroad call there. His girl-friend Kate Sheriff does not share his parochial vision, preferring to help the wider world as a medical missionary in Rhatore, a princely state in Rajasthan. As an excuse to be near her, Tarvin conceives a plan to steal a magnificent jewelled necklace (the Naulahka) from Rhatore and deliver it as a gift to the wife of the railroad chairman, who has promised in return to influence her husband to build a station at Topaz. However, the political faction fighting and cultural impenetrability of the East hinders them both. Although Tarvin acquires the necklace, it brings too many problems and he casts it aside, opting instead for the hand of Kate. In this respect *The Naulahka* is a happy version of *The Light that Failed*, with action-man Tarvin winning the love of 'new woman' Kate who agrees to marriage, after first rejecting it. What makes the book more than just a familiar anti-feminist tract is its examination of the experiences Kate, in particular, needs to go through in order to reach this understanding. She finds Indian women spurn her medical care because she does not share their 'life experience'. As the verse preface to one chapter puts it, she 'stands beside the Gates of Birth, / Herself a child – a child unborn!'. It finishes with the haunting refrain:

> Our sister sayeth such and such
> And we must bow to her behests.
> Our sister toileth overmuch,
> Our little maid that hath no breasts.

It was as though Rudyard was saying that young women such as Kate had no role in the development of an established culture such as India. More matronly figures, the Isabella Burtons of the sub-continent, might get involved, but not the Gussie Tweddells. With Wolcott ill and Rudyard still hammering out his different versions of *The Light that Failed*, little progress was made until

January 1891 when, according to Carrie, 'Wolcott booms on with the Little Jewellery and I hope they will have made great strides by this time next week. It will be sport to hear the no-end gabble that will be babbled about the combination.' Although Henry James did not believe the collaboration would work, Rudyard was 'ripe for the doings'.[14] A month later Wolcott was telling his friend Howells of progress on a book that was 'as American as a roller skating rink and as Indian as a juggernaut'.[15]

Something of Carrie's character emerges in her letters home to Josephine. She was bossy and opinionated, advising her sister to study more English history ('Edward the Confessor may not seem of any earthly use in America . . . but he will fill a deeply felt want here, if you only turn around once')[16] and to tread carefully in her new career as a writer ('Please don't forget that being a plain woman who does a woman's work is not a career to easily turn away from . . . For myself I do not care for literary women, not those that I know').[17] But Carrie could also relax and be frivolous. When Josephine enquired about the latest fashions, Carrie informed her that Scotch plaids were *de rigueur* in London and Paris. If Josephine wanted a new dress she should supply a 'waist' – 'the one that fitted you best (they use the Southern body)' – and Wolcott might pay for it out of some money he owed their mother.

Carrie now had some acquaintances to discuss with Rudyard – the de Forest family, whom she had recently met in New York. She confessed to Josephine, 'I find the young man the pleasantest article in London, he is so refreshingly unEnglish. And for some unknown reason I have never had any shyness with him and can be myself when he is about which is a great relief because it is a nagging bother to be overwhelmed and unable to be oneself all the time.'[18] But Rudyard was not an easy socialiser: when she introduced him to a retiring New England friend, Gertrude Hall, conversation ground to a halt. Three times Carrie attempted to start the two talking, but without success. When he sensed her once again girding herself to break the ice, Rudyard begged, 'Please, don't try again. We can have a nice talk, and she can't or won't.' Mr Kipling was 'much too clever about things', Carrie commented with admiration.[19]

In later years, Carrie used to remember 28 November as a special anniversary in the history of her relationship with Rudyard. Possibly this marked the occasion she told Josephine about – when he skipped an engagement with a male friend and, with Wolcott away, 'stayed to dinner with plain me'. He told her in confidence about his alternative endings to *The Light that Failed*. 'Next time we meet we shall have something not to talk about,' she trilled. But she could also have been referring to Rudyard's first avowal of affection to her. Ted Hill was due in London a couple of days later, but he had clearly decided against pursuing any further relationship and pointedly only saw her and his ex-fiancée Caroline Taylor once during their time in the capital.

The reason was quite clear. Before the end of the year he was more part of the Balestier family than ever and Carrie (Balestier) was telling her sister Josephine of the fun they had had at his twenty-fifth birthday dinner, 'the nicest thing which has happened since we returned to London'. She and Wolcott had given Rudyard small presents – she, a typical American corn popper, with corn from Fuller's which annoyed her because it did not pop properly, and Wolcott a pipe: Rudyard had been a 'great dear' about it all.

At the time, Carrie was also experiencing problems with Edmund Gosse, whom she had never liked and who she felt had snubbed her unsophisticated brother Beatty on a visit to London with his new bride Mai. Putting a strain on her friendship with Nellie, she speculated, 'They [the Gosses] are wildly jealous of our intimacy with Kipling, though, of course, I never mention his comings and goings to them. But he does not mind as I do, and they hear as everyone else does and to see him here is enough, for he acts as if he were familiar with it all and, of course, they have not the sense to know that he would do that any way.'[20]

Others also became jealous of this closeness. Lucy Clifford told Rudyard frankly that she did not consider Carrie the right woman for him – with damaging consequences for their own friendship. As her friend Marie Belloc Lowndes coyly put it, 'A foolishly frank answer on Lucy Clifford's part caused him to leave her house, never to return.' Lucy was devastated and whenever she subsequently saw Rudyard at various functions, 'a sensation of such pain filled her heart that she had at once to leave the room where he happened to be'[21] – a reaction that supports Trix's view that Lucy was infatuated with her brother and wanted to marry him. Trix, who discerned signs of Rudyard in Jim Alford, the character from Lahore in Mrs Clifford's 1895 novel *A Flash of Summer*, used to recall his arriving at the Kiplings' in Earls Court one night, in a state of shock because Lucy had raised the subject of matrimony.

More significantly, Alice Kipling had watched this young American woman warming to her son and did not like it. 'That woman is going to marry our Ruddy,' she said, as soon as she met Carrie. Lockwood Kipling took a different perspective, referring to Carrie's organisational talents, and perhaps rather more, in his comment that she was 'a good man spoiled'. Alice feared that her son, in his naïveté, was repeating his mistake with the Taylor sister and was attaching himself to this new Carrie because of his friendship with her brother Wolcott. Carrie Balestier sensed Alice's wrath because, in telling Josephine of Rudyard's support for her efforts to bring her mother Anna to London, she claimed that this was because he was in a rather similar position. Only in his case his mother was refusing to visit him. Carrie put this down to Alice being 'selfish' but, more likely, Rudyard's mother was making some kind of protest against this new liaison.

With Rudyard still suffering occasional relapses in his health, Lockwood and Alice turned up on cue to accompany their son to Brighton for a short New Year holiday. In a letter to George Allen, thanking him for a paper knife that must have been a birthday present, Rudyard showed a touching faith in the south coast's ability to deliver the sunshine he craved. 'I'd sell all my success just now for ten hours of hot sunshine . . . England is the vilest land alive. Mercifully I ought to be back in Lahore next September.'[22]

Mention of Lahore suggests that his parents and, in particular, his mother were putting pressure on him to take a break. Alice wanted him to recharge his batteries by seeing more of the world (and, the unspoken message went, getting away from Miss Balestier). Needing to appease his demanding mother (and reassure her of his love), Rudyard wrote the stark emotional poem 'Mother o' Mine' as the dedication to the English version of *The Light that Failed* when it was published in March 1891. Still determined to prise Rudyard away from London, Alice fed her son the line: 'And what should they know of England who only England know?' Rudyard responded with 'The English Flag', a verse distillation of his expansive nationalism, with its vision of an England covering all corners of the earth and its call to his countrymen to 'go forth, for it is there!'. The poem sat well in Henley's fiercely patriotic *National* (formerly *Scots*) *Observer*, which was taking up the fashionable cry of 'imperial federation', or a formal treaty to bind English-speaking nations.

In the circumstances it became increasingly difficult for Rudyard to ignore his own propaganda, particularly when in May, Gosse added his voice: 'Go east, Mr Kipling, go back to the Far East. Disappear! ... Come back in ten years' time with another precious and admirable budget of loot out of wonderland.' (Could he, with his dislike of Carrie, have colluded with the older Kiplings?) There was no doubting Gosse's belief in the young man. 'Kipling is one of the most extraordinary beings ever created, out of Naples or Malacca,' he wrote the following month.

> He is like an infant might be that smoked manilla cigars all day and was none the worse; or a tarn among mountains with a volcano concealed underneath ... What he really and soberly is most like, I suppose, is the child of god-fearing dissenting parents, who has run away and enlisted in a thoroughly black-guard cavalry regiment. Only that does not account for the Malay element and a suspicion of knives whipped into your vitals. Not a commonplace young gentleman, Mr R. K.[23]

An opportunity for travel unexpectedly presented itself at the end of May when Rudyard's Uncle Harry in New York sent word that he had a fatal cancer and did not have long to live. Harry's brother Fred Macdonald decided to visit as representative of the family and Rudyard went with him. For the sake of peace and quiet, they both agreed to travel under the name Macdonald. But, when they reached New York, word had seeped out that one of the Macdonalds was actually Mr Kipling – a story that Uncle Fred was not skilled enough in media relations to be able to rebuff. The visit came to an abrupt halt when the two men discovered that Harry had died two days after they set sail. Unhappy at the subsequent intrusion on his privacy, Rudyard turned round and booked a passage on the next ship home, s.s. *Aller* of the North German Lloyd line, whose staple menu of boiled pigs feet and sauerkraut he came to loathe.

No sooner was he back in England than he claimed 'the brutes of doctors are trying to chase me out of England again on another sea voyage'.[24] Although he told a correspondent (in July) that all work was forbidden, he made some attempts at the sort of fiction that would occupy him later in life – incorporating themes of spiritual enquiry, disease, healing and madness into his essentially rationalist synthesis of metaphysical experience. Three stories from 1891 stand out in this context. 'The Finest Story in the World' was his first study of reincarnation in a Western context. Inspired, so Ted Hill later noted, by his cousin Ambrose Poynter's diary, it showed all Rudyard's ambivalence about women: the love of a girl can make Charlie happy, but it 'kills remembrance', or that special ability to be able to remember his past lives. 'The Children of the Zodiac' demonstrated a growing and imaginative interest in the symbolism of astrology. On a personal level, it reflected his concern that Uncle Henry's cancer might run in the family and strike him before he had completed his life's work. 'The Disturber of Traffic' drew directly on his own experience of mental breakdowns. Inspired by Rudyard's visits to Balestier's holiday cottage on the Isle of Wight, this told of a lighthouse keeper in the Dutch

East Indies who goes mad watching the streaks created by the water's ebb and flow – to the extent that when he suspects that passing ships are disturbing the patterns, he seeks to divert them. As was Rudyard's habit, this was a tale within a tale, related by another lighthouse keeper on the English Channel. When this narrator completes his intense and detailed story, Rudyard's relief at the passing of his real-life psychotic episodes is only too obvious as he describes the calm after the storm – the dawn breaking, the fog disappearing, the birds starting to sing and the freshness of the country smells. The last line of the story – 'Then we were both at liberty to thank the Lord for another day of clean and wholesome life' – has led to the idea that Rudyard's own instability resulted from sexual guilt (linked to a homosexual attachment to Wolcott). This emphasis on a 'clean and wholesome life' is intriguing, but since this type of hallucination dated back to his boyhood, this seems far-fetched.

When, two years later, Rudyard collected this story in his book *Many Inventions*, he prefaced it with his mysterious 'The Prayer of Miriam Cohen', indicating that his problems came from a hyperactive mind occasionally overreaching itself and trying to delve too deeply into the secrets of the universe. For this poem, later expanded from three to five stanzas, states that man needs the shroud (or, given his other obsessions, the lie or even the solid assurance) of revealed religion in his quest for meaning in life: staring into the void is too blinding. Rudyard's plea

> A veil 'twixt us and Thee, dread Lord,
> A veil 'twixt us and Thee:
> Lest we should hear too clear, too clear,
> And unto madness see!

should be read as a milestone on his journey of spiritual enlightenment.

Since Henry James later wrote of an idyllic afternoon ramble over the downs to Freshwater, Wolcott's cottage has been assumed to be near that town, within easy walking distance of one of the Isle of Wight's two lighthouses, at The Needles in the south-west. However, Rudyard's preamble to this story more accurately describes the other lighthouse at St Catherine's Point, close to the village of Chale, where Wolcott indeed had a house by the sea called The Five Rocks. Heinemann did not like Balestier's habit of absenting himself from Dean's Yard, apparently on grounds of illness: 'Your idea of running a London office from the Isle of Wight is about as sensible as steering a ship in a storm from the top of a lighthouse.'

Wolcott was happy to leave Dean's Yard in the hands of Will Cabot, the brother of his Brattleboro friend Molly. Although trained as an engineer (in which capacity he had worked on railroads in the mid-West) Will had literary ambitions and was being groomed for a partnership. In June he had (at Wolcott's behest) been looking forward to assisting Rudyard on an unnamed project – possibly the proofs of *The Naulahka*. But nothing materialised for, as Will noted, Rudyard was 'very retired as to the world in general just now. He is working hard.' Within a month Will had to admit he did not see a future for himself in Heinemann and Balestier. As a mutual American acquaintance, the artist Charles Bacon, had told him, 'Wolcott Balestier is a good friend but allows *no one* to stand in the way of his success. He is a Czar in his family. No one apparently expects that anyone can suit him or get on with him in business because of his electrical ways and dictatorship.'[25]

Since Wolcott was more or less ensconced at Chale, Rudyard frequently visited him there, bringing him increasingly into contact with Carrie. From his later moves, the prospect of marriage had clearly been raised. But influenced, no doubt, by his mother, Rudyard was determined not to repeat the mistake he had made with Carrie Taylor – of getting engaged and then regretting it. So he decided to bow to pressures and 'get clean away and re-sort myself'.[26] His idea was to travel to Australia and New Zealand, where he hoped to find a ship to take him to Samoa to meet a literary hero, Robert Louis Stevenson. The two men had enjoyed a sporadic correspondence for nearly two years, addressing each other in the styles of their own fictional creations, Terence Mulvaney and Alan Breck Stewart. Henry James had kept Stevenson informed of 'the infant monster of a Kipling'. Normally Stevenson would also have been told of this new writer by his old friend Henley. But these two Scotsmen had fallen out in 1888, after Henley rumbled that Stevenson's American wife Fanny Osborne had plagiarised a story he knew to have been written by a cousin, Katherine De Mattos. Possibly, Rudyard had hopes of effecting a reconciliation.

With the help of his father's friend Frank Cook, Rudyard booked a passage for the first leg of his journey to the Cape on the s.s. *Moor* on 8 August. However, putting his business in order detained him longer than he expected and it was not until 22 August that he finally left on the Union Line's s.s. *Mexican*. Always happy to communicate with young children, he told Ethel Clifford, Lucy's elder daughter, that, though he was 'off on a small excursion to the other end of the world', she should not expect 'a white kangaroo' on his return.[27]

From his infancy in Bombay, through his chats with Captain Holloway, to his schooldays at Westward Ho!, Rudyard had liked the sea. Now, among his fellow passengers he met a naval officer, Captain E. H. Bayly, travelling to take up a new command at the main Southern African base of Simonstown and they became good friends. Rudyard began to explore the romance of the ocean and, by the time he reached Cape Town, he had completed a new poem, 'The Long Trail', recounting how when 'your English summer's done', 'it's time to turn on the old trail, our own trail, the out trail, / Pull out, pull out, on the Long Trail – the trail that is always new!'. The first five stanzas, depicting the crash on a ship's bows, 'and the drum of the racing screw', as she made her way south from Cadiz, were published in the *Cape Illustrated Magazine* in November.

Cape Town reminded him of India, with cows ambling through

the streets, colourfully dressed native women and a Muslim quarter for the Malays who had crossed the Indian Ocean to work. Rudyard's health was soon restored by 'the dry, spiced smell of the land and the smack of the clean sunshine'. Invited by Bayly to the officers' mess at Simonstown, he enjoyed the warmth of naval hospitality and the rowdiness of their high jinks. There was a running joke about Lieutenant S. de Horsey who, on taking command of his gunboat the *Gryper*, had barked out an order that the 'top mast wants staying forward'. These words only had to be mentioned in the mess and the place went berserk, the 'rag' continuing until the entire room had been rearranged. Rudyard liked de Horsey, however, and made him the model for 'Bai-Jove-Judson', hero of the first of his sea tales, his divertissement about imperial pretensions in Southern waters, 'Judson and the Empire'.

In the warm sunshine of the Cape he developed an unlikely friendship with Olive Schreiner, a writer who today would be called a radical feminist. He admitted that they both shared the 'same creed' (as writers), but potential differences of opinion were clear in his advice that she should ensure 'that the very vehemence of your own desire to help others does not lead you into sorrow'. In other words, he was saying she should not get too emotionally involved in her subject matter – a line that, as a fighter for racial justice, she rejected. Nevertheless, Rudyard offered to put her in touch with his agent Watt, and left her with the intriguing thought, 'If all the girls in all the world sat quiet and still at the right moments by all the men in the world when these were in trouble we should all be perfectly happy instead of being hurt and worried. I'll show you about this time next year why Maisie was made as she was.'[28]

Rudyard had hoped to travel to Kimberley to see the diamond mines on which South Africa's wealth was being built. (He claimed to have sighted the magnate Cecil Rhodes briefly in a restaurant in Adderley Street, Cape Town, but not to have spoken to him.) However, the mail boat for the next stage of his journey could not wait, though he had seen enough of southern Africa to realise that he would like to return. He continued on his way, rolling across the southern Indian Ocean for twenty-four days[29] in the Shaw Savill Line's s.s. *Doric*, to Hobart, Tasmania and on to Wellington, New Zealand – a voyage 'Fra' Cape Town east to Wellington' celebrated in the din of the engine room in his poem 'McAndrew's Hymn'.

Establishing himself in Wellington's Oriental Hotel, he announced himself to the 'station' through the Anglo-Indian habit of leaving his card at the Club. Before long, he found he was enjoying himself. The visit to Stevenson disappeared from his itinerary: he said this was because the captain of the fruit boat that might have transported him to Samoa was habitually drunk and would not give him a proper schedule. He may also have received notice that Stevenson's wife Fanny was suffering from depression and would not have welcomed the intrusion. In New Zealand, his favourite spot was Auckland – 'last, loneliest, loveliest, exquisite, apart', as he wrote in 'The Song of the Cities'. Having learnt from his American experience, he had become skilled at fobbing off the media with throw-away lines, such as he had only 'come for a loaf' and wanted to see 'natives and wonders'. But sometimes, perhaps inadvertently, he was revealing, as in an interview with the *Weekly Press* in Christchurch, when he loosed off at a species of 'white man at home', who read all the same books and had become 'divorced from the knowledge or fear of death'. He recalled a particular type of smile to be found in London that 'expresses tempered grief, sorrow at your complete inability to march with the march of progress at the universities, and a chastened contempt'. Because those pampered types 'have everything done for them, they know how everything ought to be done, and they are perfectly certain that new pavements, policemen, shops, and gas-light come in the regular course of nature. You can see with these convictions how thoroughly and cocksuredly they handle little trifles like colonial administration, the wants of the army, municipal sewage, the housing of the poor and so forth.'[30]

All in all, as his New Zealand story 'One Lady at Wairakei' shows,[31] he was impressed with the country's potential. He could feel a nation building up a useful bank of experience, which would make for interesting tales, though he was typically sceptical of talk 'about a Distinctively Colonial Literature, a Freer Air, Larger Horizons, and so on'.

Crossing with him to Australia on the s.s. *Talune* from Bluff, in the extreme south of New Zealand, was 'General' William Booth, leader of the Salvation Army, whom Rudyard had first seen coming on board 'his cloak blown upwards, tulip-fashion over his grey head, while he beat a tambourine in the face of the singing, weeping, praying crowd who had come to see him off'. Arriving in Melbourne in the teeth of a mid-November gale, Rudyard was struck by the country's similarity to the United States. Unfortunately he felt it was 'second-hand American', which created specific problems. Adopting what was to be a familiar Cassandra pose, he sounded a grim warning about the potential threat from the Chinese he had encountered a couple of years earlier: 'There is a big score to be wiped out, and if you Australians could see them as I have in their native towns, where you meet the eyes in every crevice until you think the very stones are made of flesh and blood, then you might get an idea of the force you will have to reckon with.'

At Melbourne's Austral Salon, Rudyard was content to play the benevolent author on a promotional tour, only balking when someone, clearly muddled, asked him about his 'beautiful, beautiful book, *Caesar's Column*'. However, he discovered the disadvantages of celebrity status when the *Melbourne Argus* published rumours about his personal life. The paper delighted in noting that Rudyard had 'expressed his view on the marriage question so clearly in all his writings that it comes upon one with rather a shock to find that our distinguished visitor contemplates the great leap in the dark himself'.[32] It claimed to have seen a personal letter from someone in England who, in relating idle gossip about her friends, had stated, 'Florrie Garrard is engaged to a Mr Rudyard Kipling, a fashionable author.' Marriage might have been in the air, but not between this couple. The paper had probably obtained sight of a garbled letter to a member of the extended Garrard family living in Australia.

After two weeks in Australia, which included a trip to Sydney, Rudyard was back on board ship – this time, the s.s. *Valetta* – for the next stage of his trip to Colombo. Once again, 'General' Booth was a passenger, though Rudyard threatened their developing friendship by asking him about the problem of female missionaries 'living native-fashion' in India. This was an issue Rudyard was wrestling with in *The Naulahka*. His attitude reflected his ambivalence not only to women but also to the whole question of Indian advancement: on the one hand, he claimed to despise certain Indian cultural habits; on the other, when Westerners went into the villages and tried to change matters, he became defensive and felt they were encouraging political subversion. Booth washed his hands of the matter: 'But what *am* I to do? The girls *will* go, and one *can't* stop 'em.'

At Colombo Rudyard left the ship, crossed to Tuticorin in Tamil Nadu, whence a series of trains took him slowly up from the wet red soils of the south, through parts of India unknown to him, and deposited him four and a half days later in the cold, bright sunshine of Lahore. Scholars have speculated how much this 2400-mile journey contributed to his knowledge of Central India in his story 'William the Conqueror' and the *Jungle Books*, and have concluded: not a lot. Stepping on to Indian soil again was as emotional an experience as nine years earlier: 'the beautiful smell was there, the brown, slow-moving crowds were there (white is rather a leprous tint when you come to think of it, and it doesn't match backgrounds).'[33] But this was as nothing when he reached Lahore on 18 December. Rudyard was overwhelmed by the vivid colours, even down to the splashes of vermilion provided by soldiers of the King's Own Scottish Borderers (now on Fort duty). 'It is awful to think that in England they have never seen any of the primary colours,' he speculated, 'and that they know nothing of drapery, the folds of well worn unsewn clothing that falls in great laps and curves, gathered round the neck and under the armpit in robes of richest deep shadowed wrinkles.' The Old City brought back happy memories of his night-time prowls ('there, arrogant and unashamed was Lalun's naughty little house'). In the bazaar, Rudyard was fascinated by the capacity of an impoverished people to find money for fripperies, including embroidered hats, cheap jewellery and cricket bats and stumps (a significant development of the past couple of years). When looking around, he saw the four minarets of the mosque of Wazir Khan pointing to heaven and was moved to applaud, 'What need to cry five times a day that God is great?'

Several friends were on hand to greet Rudyard, including his much-missed former servant Kadir Baksh ('pearl among khitmatgars'), 'Stalky' Dunsterville (who, after being bitten by a dog, had recently been to Paris for inoculation against rabies by the pioneer microbiologist Dr Louis Pasteur) and his Aunt Edie, who had accompanied his mother to India in September and was thriving in the pre-Christmas festival atmosphere. As expected, he had business details to attend to. His main concern was that, in November, the London publisher Sampson Low had advertised plans to publish two new books by him, to be called *City of Dreadful Night* and *Letters of Marque*. His agent Watt had been furious and, with Rudyard himself incommunicado in Australia, had despatched a series of letters to Lockwood Kipling in Lahore, asking for details. Perhaps, he suggested, Rudyard had negotiated a separate contract, as with *The Naulahka*. (That episode clearly rankled: 'I may here mention that, if the price which I hear he got for the serial use of "Naulahka" is correct, he lost a very large sum of money by not putting this in my hands, as, in fact, he promised to do with all his work.'[34]) It emerged that the two books were collections of Rudyard's old journalism from the *Pioneer*. The entrepreneurial Emile Moreau had bought the publishing rights to this material from the Allahabad newspaper, and repackaged it for the Indian and (through Sampson Low) British markets.

For a while Sampson Low took a high-handed approach, informing Watt that, far from being 'accused of raking up old material (as you implied) for the purpose of trading on Mr Kipling's present popularity',[35] they had in fact laid the ground-work for the author's high reputation by publishing his original Railway Library volumes. The matter revolved around whether the *Pioneer* retained the copyright on Rudyard's articles from a couple of years earlier. Luckily George Allen was in London at the time and offered to waive his rights. He promised to use his influence to stop publication of these two books and any further editions of Rudyard's Indian journalism that might arise.

In Lahore Rudyard had to sign affidavits finalising this agree-ment, which also covered *The Smith Administration*, another book of his Indian stories that Moreau proposed to publish under the A. H. Wheeler imprint in Allahabad. The *Pioneer*'s editor, G. M. Chesney, wrote explaining the paper's role in the affair, adding a request that Rudyard might consider delaying his return to a dreary English winter and embark instead on another tour for the paper, this time to Central India, where he could write 'some more *Letters of Marque* – about which there shall be no quarrel'.[36]

Rudyard is unlikely to have been tempted. The matter was dramatically removed from his hands on Christmas Eve, when he received the shattering news that Wolcott Balestier had died from typhoid fever in Dresden, Germany, on 6 December. Rudyard immediately dropped everything and hurried home by sea from Bombay, reaching London in record time on 10 January 1892.

There he was told the full horror of what had happened. Wolcott had set out for Leipzig a fortnight before his death, intending to visit Albert Brockhaus, the English Library's German agent. On reaching Berlin he felt ill and decided to divert to Dresden where he had friends (the von Funckes, relations of the Cabots). His mother and sister Josephine had come to Europe to see Carrie and were in Paris. All three at once travelled to the Carola Haus, Dresden, where Carrie realised her brother was badly ill when he did not scold the maid for failing to open the door at once. On 30 November Wolcott still had strength to ask her to check some *Naulahka* proofs and send them to America. But despite regular infusions of port, beef tea and milk, and a bath three times a day, his temperature fluctuated wildly. Badly emaciated, he became delirious and finally 'slipped away'.[37]

Wolcott's friends in London were stunned at his death, and both Henry James and William Heinemann saw fit to set off for Dresden immediately – Heinemann's grief painfully apparent in his postscript to a letter from Hall Caine to Bram Stoker on 7 December, 'Pardon my not writing myself, dear fellow, I am simply off my head. *He* of all! Is it not horrible! What am I to do?' James and Heinemann arrived in Dresden two days later, just in time for the funeral the following morning. James travelled back from the suburban cemetery in a coach with 'poor little concentrated passionate Carrie' who, he told Gosse, was 'remarkable in her force, acuteness, capacity, and courage – and in the intense – almost manly nature of her emotion. She is a worthy sister of poor dear big-spirited, only-by-death-quenchable Wolcott.'[38]

That very day, she took control of her brother's affairs and wrote to Arthur Waugh that she wanted all his books (except his Bible) wrapped – each volume in a different piece of paper – and put where her mother and sister Josephine, who had taken Wolcott's death badly, could not see them. A day later, after Waugh had sent some money, drawn on a Brown Shipley draft, she asked to see Wolcott's obituary notices (including Gosse's in *The Times* and Conan Doyle's in the *Pall Mall Gazette*). But again for her mother's and Josephine's sakes, she wanted Waugh to cut out any photographs. She also requested her brother's American newspaper subscriptions to be redirected to her as Mrs Wolcott Balestier.

By 6 January 1892, when Rudyard was still on the high seas, strange news had begun to filter back to Brattleboro. Molly Cabot had heard that Carrie was engaged to be married to Rudyard. She discussed this with Mai Balestier who told her that Rudyard had 'paid devoted attentions' to both sisters and was 'something of a flirt'. Mai did 'not understand how it happened to be so positively cabled unless true' and felt that Carrie would 'suffer more for Wolcott than anyone and such a marriage would be the only adequate consolations'.[39]

Four days later Rudyard arrived back in London and the very next morning, on 11 January, he confirmed the truth of the rumour by taking out a special licence to marry Carrie. According to Edmund Gosse, Carrie's telegram to Rudyard in Lahore had read simply, 'WOLCOTT DEAD STOP COME BACK TO ME STOP.' On hearing the news of his friend's death, Rudyard had the same overwhelming emotional urge as James and Heinemann to do something to help. His reaction was to cable Carrie and, putting an end to months of indecisiveness, to ask her to marry him.

Now there was to be no hitch. The wedding was set for a week later, on 18 January, at All Souls, Langham Place. On the eve, staying in the Langham Hotel across the road, Rudyard wrote to Crom Price with the news, confirming that his affair with Carrie had endured 'months of delay and tribulation' and that he felt he ought to feel bad but instead was in 'a state of sinful joy'.[40] To W. E. Henley he pointedly did not even bother mentioning his marriage, enclosing his latest poem 'Tomlinson' and noting, 'I've been walking with Almighty God under the world where the British Empire is OK. If I could meet you and tell you what I saw!'[41]

On the day, most of Carrie's and Rudyard's relatives – Mrs Balestier, Josephine, Aunts Aggie and Georgie, Phil Burne-Jones – were struck down with flu. So the service was a sombre affair, attended by only Ambrose Poynter (Rudyard's best man), Henry James (who gave Carrie away), William Heinemann (who arrived late, clutching a bunch of flowers) and Edmund Gosse, his wife, daughter and son. Gosse told Gilder in America that Rudyard had been 'hurried into matrimony, like a rabbit into its hole ... At 2.8 the cortège entered the church and at 2.20 left it, the sharpest thing of modern times. . . . Both bridegroom and bride are possessed by a very devil of secrecy and mystery, and hope that no one will know of the event.' And, as if to ensure no misunderstanding, he added, 'It is Caroline, of course, not pretty Josephine who is now "Mrs R. K." '[42]

Rudyard and Carrie spent their wedding night at Brown's Hotel in Mayfair, which was to become a home from home. They stayed there for a week's quasi-honeymoon, at the end of which Henry Ford, the manager, told them that, as a gift, their bill for £22 had already been paid. They moved to 101 Earls Court Road for one more week. But already they were rushing frantically to finalise their plans to sail to America on the s.s. *Teutonic*, leaving Liverpool on 3 February.

One immediate problem was to tie up Wolcott's estate and this raised the question of what was to happen to jointly held literary properties such as *The Naulahka*. This proved no difficulty as Wolcott's share in the copyright passed to his mother, who gave Rudyard complete control. He then had to sort out the matter with Watt, encouraging him to sell the book to the Century Company (and, failing that, Macmillan) in the United States, but not for a month since there was 'a rather doubtful American firm which owes me royalties and will pay up piously as long as it believes there is a chance of my giving it *The Naulahka*'.[43] At no stage did Rudyard realise this was an incorrect spelling. In Hindustani, the word Naulakha means nine lakhs (of rupees) or, since a lakh is 100,000, 900,000 rupees. It must have been written wrongly at the start and nobody thought to change it.

On his own behalf Rudyard had to finalise the selection of poems for the British edition of the *Barrack-Room Ballads*. The previous May he had opted to take this book to Methuen whose reputation was slightly more 'literary' than Heinemann (Balestier's publisher, which was handling *The Naulahka* in Britain) or Macmillan, Rudyard's main imprint. He had been encouraged not just by the £250 advance but by the fact that Leonard Whibley (brother of Charles, from the *National Observer*) was a partner there. When he had gone away to the

Antipodes, this project was put in abeyance and now had to be quickly resuscitated.

His poem 'Tomlinson', which was published in the *National Observer* on 23 January, was both a repayment of a debt to Henley, who had written an embarrassing homage to Rudyard called 'The Song of the Sword', full of bombast about the destiny and nobility of war, and an advance indication of Rudyard's impending departure from fashionable literary London. Once again, it expressed Rudyard's distaste for young London aesthetes who so burden themselves with received, bookish opinions that they manage to lose their souls (the theme of his interview to the *Weekly News* in Christchurch a few weeks earlier). The poem provided a sequel to his earlier 'The Conundrum of the Workshops', attacking more unequivocally the shallowness of metropolitan life in contrast to the manly and human values of his favourite soldiers. In rushing 'Tomlinson' to Henley at this particular moment (according to Carrie, it had been written the previous April),[44] Rudyard was saying that he had finished with this life and was looking forward to a future with Carrie in the United States.

There was now only one more (unimportant) poem to be written – 'The Ballad of the Bolivar', published in the *St James's Gazette* on 29 January after Rudyard had completed the final touches in the editor Sidney Low's office the previous day – and Rudyard was able to send his complete selection of *Barrack-Room Ballads* to Watt for publication by Methuen in March. But, first, he drew on his poem 'The Blind Bug' to compose an emotional dedication to Wolcott, beginning 'Beyond the path of the outmost sun through utter darkness hurled'. Then he rewrote 'The Long Trail' to make it a poem for his new wife. He added verses about his return from southern climes, changed one word in the line 'Ha' done with the Tents of Shem, dear lad' to 'dear lass' (a source of confusion to commentators such as Martin Seymour-Smith, determined to imply that Rudyard was fudging his homosexual desires for Wolcott) and concluded romantically,

The Lord knows what we may find, dear lass,
And The Deuce knows what we may do –
But we're back once more on the old trail, our own trail,
  the out trail,
We're down, hull-down, on the Long Trail – the trail that
  is always new!

This then became L'Envoi to the *Barrack-Room Ballads*, the
ending that complements the dedication to Wolcott. (Rudyard
was starting a habit of framing his volumes of poetry and stories
very precisely.)

On 2 February the newly married couple, travelling with Mrs
Balestier and Josephine, were seen off at Euston Station, *en route*
for Liverpool, by a heavyweight literary guard of Henry James,
Edmund Gosse, William Heinemann and Bram Stoker. Henley
was rather visibly absent. Having seen one favourite, Stevenson,
disappear into the hands of an American woman, he was concerned that Rudyard would follow suit. As he told Charles
Whibley, 'Rudyard's marriage is a blow; but we must e'en make
the best on't.'[45]

Book Four

But the Glory of the Garden lies in more than meets the eye

Eleven

En Puissance de Femme

1892–1896

With the wedding following so closely on the funeral, an uneasy pall of mock cheerfulness and numbing grief hung over Rudyard's party as the *Teutonic* ploughed its way through the bleak mid-winter Atlantic Ocean. Getting to know his new wife in the presence of her bereaved mother and sister cannot have been easy. As a diversion, Rudyard occupied himself with thoughts of India, composing the verse chapter headings for *The Naulahka*. In keeping with the novel, in which the sub-continent repels all boarders, he took a detached view of the life he had once led:

Now it is not good for the Christian's health to hustle the
    Aryan brown,
For the Christian riles, and the Aryan smiles and he
    weareth the Christian down;
And the end of the fight is a tombstone white with the name
    of the late deceased,
And the epitaph drear: 'A Fool lies here who tried to hustle
    the East.'

More immediately, these epigrams for *The Naulahka* provided a stark commentary on the early progress of his marriage. There was a sweaty erotic charge to the lines:

> I was the Lord of the Inca Race, and she was the
>   Queen of the Sea.
> Under the stars beyond our stars where the reinless
>   meteors glow,
> Hotly we stormed Valhalla, a million years ago.

He had intimations of Carrie's fiery, implacable nature, which could lead to his instant rejection:

> Now we are come to our Kingdom,
> But my love's eyelids fall,
> All that I wrought for, all that I fought for,
> Delight her nothing at all.

He showed he was learning to cope with the situation. There was love and respect in the way he admitted he was yielding the emotional upper ground to his wife, as he tried to adapt to her ways ('The Law whereby my lady moves / Was never Law to me, / But 'tis enough that she approves / Whatever Law it be') even though he did not fully understand them ('The Law that sways my lady's ways / Is mystery to me').[1]

Rudyard seemed content mixing family and literary commitments. A fellow passenger, the author Henry Adams, found him an 'exuberant fountain of gaiety and wit', though, perhaps picking up an idea of his friend Henry James who had introduced them, he felt, rightly, that 'somehow, somewhere, Kipling and the American were not one, but two, and could not be glued together'.

Rudyard could not help feeling uncertain about his future. His initial enthusiasm for the United States had been inspired by its literature and reinforced by Ted Hill's intelligence. When he was there three years earlier, he had liked the people, but was alarmed at their lack of tradition, which, he felt, masked a potential for lawlessness that could erupt unexpectedly and, on the international stage, could even threaten the British Empire he loved. As so often, he was influenced by his father who once said, 'If I possessed any rupees I could spare, I would prefer to send them to Sitting Bull, Crazy Horse and Old Crow and other warriors of the Sioux, away on the Yellowstone River, who have been half exterminated by the possibly beneficent but certainly rowdy and murderous civilisation of America.'[2] By collaborating with Rudyard on *The Naulahka*, Wolcott Balestier had helped his friend confront his mixed feelings about America. But a sense of ambivalence remained.

The immediate plan was that, after escorting Mrs Balestier home, the newly-weds would take a honeymoon in the Far East, where Rudyard still wanted to visit Robert Louis Stevenson in Samoa – the destination he had failed to reach a few months earlier. As usual, he would pay his way by writing about his travels, an important consideration now he was married and no longer enjoyed an income from the *Pioneer*. A. P. Watt had undertaken to contact newspapers offering his latest series of articles. Rudyard himself had approached Moberly Bell at *The Times* who promised to publish anything he produced.

In New York, Rudyard and his new American relations were met by his father's friend Lockwood de Forest, who had arranged for them to stay at the Brunswick Hotel in Madison Square. Carrie's husband was introduced to the family matriarch, old Madame Balestier, who still travelled between New York in winter and Brattleboro in summer. Her opinion of the bustling little Englishman is unknown, but her maid Kate Monks, a feisty Irishwoman who had been with her for forty-five years, probably reflected her views when she told a friend of her distaste for Carrie's affected English ways. This, however, may simply have reflected the Balestiers' capacity for bickering. The death of grandfather Joe in 1888 had added disputes about money to the resentments that festered between the families of his four sons, who never visited Beechwood at the same time. One of them, John Balestier, particularly disliked the hold that Kate Monks had over his mother and avoided all contact as long as the maid was in residence.

If Rudyard had known more about this infighting he might never have agreed to live in the Balestier heartland of Vermont. But having said he would do so, he and Carrie needed to make some arrangements before departing on the second stage of their honeymoon. Leaving the 'roar and rattle' of New York, they travelled to Brattleboro, where Rudyard was boyishly thrilled to find himself, for the first time in his life, in a picture postcard New England winter. The temperature was minus thirty degrees Fahrenheit when Beatty Balestier, on his best behaviour, met them off the train. Looking like walruses in hairy goatskin coats, with caps over their ears, and draped in buffalo robes and blankets, they made their way by sleigh to Maplewood, Beatty's farm in the neighbouring parish of Dummerston. During the half-hour drive, Rudyard gaped around in amazement. 'But for the jingle of the sleigh-bells the ride might have taken place in a dream, for there was no sound of hoofs upon the snow, the runners sighed a little now and again as they glided over an inequality, and all the sheeted hills round about were as dumb as death.'[3] Crossing the then covered bridge over the West river, they travelled north for a couple of miles until reaching the Waite Farm, where they branched off to the left up a winding hill through snow-draped trees. Passing Madame Balestier's grand family house, Beechwood, they crested down, a mile further, to Maplewood, where the boisterous Beatty (pronounced 'Batey' in these parts) lived with his wife Mai and bubbly baby daughter Marjorie.

Wolcott's old friend Will Cabot was on hand to inform Rudyard about local lore. Even in London his ability to tell where he was going by the stars had been impressive. Now this 'quiet, slow-spoken man of the West' (Rudyard's reference to Will's time in the mid-West as an engineer) showed how to distinguish a fox's spoor from a dog's track, and recounted stories of the deer which wandered down from the Canadian border along deep-trodden tracks called 'yards', only to be captured and photographed by a certain type of modern hunter wielding a 'Kodak'. Wearing snow shoes (which, to Rudyard, looked like two giant tennis racquets strung with hide), Will gestured to the furthest range of hills and to the tallest mountain, which stuck up 'like a gigantic thumbnail pointing heavenward', and told Rudyard this was Monadnock, an Indian name (like many surrounding places) and one well known to him from Emerson's poem and the whale in Melville's *Moby Dick* with its 'Monadnock hump'.

Initially, the Kiplings hoped that big, bluff Beatty might be willing to sell them Maplewood outright, thus easing his financial, if not his drinking, problems. On reflection, this smacked too much of out-of-town relations flaunting their wealth. So, after some wrangling, they agreed to purchase eleven and a half acres (mostly meadowland, useful for hay, but also two acres of pasture) in a plot across the lane from Beatty's house. Since her brother had a reputation for blustering, irrational behaviour, Carrie insisted on sealing the deal (the purchase price of $750 was considered on the high side) through the offices of a New York lawyer. Then she arranged for a family friend, Herbert Rutgers Marshall, a fashionable if second-rate New York architect, to build a house, estimated to cost $7200, rising eventually to $11,175.[4]

Before crossing North America to Vancouver, where he and Carrie would join the s.s. *Empress of India* for Japan, Rudyard penned the first of his latest letters of travel, 'In Sight of Monadnock', about his initial impressions of Brattleboro. Unknown to him, in London Watt was having difficulty syndicating this output. He had contacted a select group of papers in Britain, the United States, Australia, India, Singapore and Europe. But the *New York Sun* refused to pay forty pounds for American serial rights to up to thirty proposed pieces.[5] The *Bombay Gazette* could only manage four guineas, while, embarrassingly, at *The Times*, Arthur Walter, son of the proprietor, overruled Moberly Bell, who had offered twenty-five pounds, saying that twenty-one pounds was the paper's limit. In the event, when the articles began to appear, *The Times* protected its copyright forcefully, taking out an injunction against the *St James's Gazette*, an evening paper, for daring to print part of 'In Sight of Monadnock'.

On board ship the Kiplings befriended a middle-aged English couple, the Hunts. The representative of a London firm of importers, Alt and Company, H. J. Hunt liked to pen light verses as a sideline. He and his wife offered to put up the Kiplings when they reached Yokohama. As usual, Rudyard was struck by the smells of the Orient as soon as the *Empress of India* docked on 20 April. (This manner of signalling his arrival in a different land was becoming a cliché.) With the Hunts as hosts, the honeymooners enjoyed a sociable few days in Yokohama and Tokyo, where Carrie was fêted as the granddaughter of Erasmus Peshine Smith, the Mikado's former legal adviser. Also visiting Japan was George Hooper's friend Edwin Arnold, whose influential poem 'The Light of Asia', about the Gautama Buddha, Rudyard had read as a schoolboy. Arnold probably encouraged the Kiplings to visit Kamakura, twenty miles outside Yokohama, the site of a great bronze and gilt statue of the Buddha, gazing out to the sea. Seeing it, Rudyard wrote his dignified poem 'Buddha at Kamakura' which, in contrast to his work in India, advocated tolerance towards other religions. (It was indicative of his relaxed state – and of his generally open, optimistic approach to his marriage – that, having left India, Rudyard was reviewing his strident anti-Hinduism and adopting a more balanced approach to religion.)

The general euphoria came to an abrupt halt, however, when the New Oriental Bank Corporation, where Rudyard had £2000 in savings, folded. This collapse was not totally unexpected: the bank's predecessor, the Oriental Bank, had failed in 1884, a victim of the falling price of silver, to which most of the Asian currencies it traded were tied. Both Rudyard and Carrie had links to the institution: he because it had started life as the Bank of Western India in Bombay and she because, after it had grown into Britain's largest multinational bank, with a branch in Yokohama, it had acted as financial adviser to the Japanese government, floating the country's first two foreign loans in 1870 and 1873, when her grandfather was there. As a result, Rudyard had deposited the bulk of his savings with the bank. While he lived, Wolcott also kept a small account, but had advised Rudyard to pull out. Rudyard had ignored this suggestion and now found himself virtually penniless. To make matters worse, after an earthquake the previous day, Rudyard had been to the local branch that very morning to draw ten pounds and the manager had asked if he wanted more.[6]

This financial setback at the start of his marriage was a severe blow. Although Rudyard was eventually repaid around £1000, he and Carrie decided they could not continue to the South Seas. So, after a few more days in Japan, they reluctantly returned to Vancouver, where William van Horne, chairman of the Canadian Pacific Railway, sensing an advertisement opportunity,[7] provided a free passage across Canada. As he made his way sedately eastwards across North America, Rudyard discovered the romance not just of the railway but also of the machine. He was still in honeymoon mood as he observed how this train ambled across the countryside 'with its hands in its pockets and a straw in its mouth' – a different experience from England where 'the railway came late into a settled country fenced round with the terrors of the law, and it had remained ever since just a little outside daily life – a thing to be respected'.[8] He began to play with the idea (developed in 'The Derelict', for example) of machines as quasi-animate beings enjoying a special relationship with humans. 'A week on wheels turns a man into a part of the machine ... The snort, snap and whine of the air brakes have a meaning for him, and he learns to distinguish between noises – between the rattle of a loose lamp and the ugly rattle of small stones on a scarped embankment – between the "Hoot! toot!" that scares wandering cows from the line, and the dry roar of the engine at the distance-signal.'

Arriving in Montreal on 22 July, the Kiplings had more pressing matters to attend to. Carrie was now three months pregnant (another factor which influenced their decision to return), and they needed somewhere to live until their house was built. Her mother found them a small place in Brattleboro, not far from their own site, that could be rented for ten dollars a month. Bliss Cottage was a modest workman's dwelling on a neighbouring farm owned by the Bliss family. They installed a second-hand stove to keep warm in winter and moved in on 10 August.

Initially, Rudyard was happy to enjoy the spectacle, as the maple and beech trees in the hills around him turned russet-coloured, then flame-red, in the glorious New England autumn. He did little writing, preferring to spend time out of doors, attending to necessary domestic chores, such as piling spruce boughs around the white clapboard house to prevent draughts. On his frequent trips into town he began to meet local people, including Wolcott's friends the Cabot family. But when Molly Cabot was invited to Bliss Cottage for lunch, she found Rudyard remarkably naïve about the most elementary matters. He had not even learnt to turn his buggy: rather than cramp the wheels, he was happy to hand her the reins.

The general population remained wary. The arrival of a world-famous author in a small Vermont town had stimulated considerable interest. But, friendly and easygoing though he seemed, Rudyard often unknowingly antagonised Brattleboro residents with his unkempt appearance (which they felt to be disrespectful) and with his blunt manner. He was accused of looking like a farm-hand, as he drove into town with trousers tucked into his boots, coarse coat flying open and a wide-brimmed hat on his head. And there was resentment at his attitude in 'In Sight of Monadnock', which seemed to sneer at Brattleboro's 'hatreds, troubles and jealousies', leading to a snide comment in the summer burlesque at the town hall.

Not that Rudyard worried about his image. Forgetting how he had surprised Mark Twain only three years earlier and showing supreme disregard for the modern art of public relations, he gave two reporters from Boston short shrift when they came to seek an interview in mid-October. Retreating behind barbed wire, he told them – revealingly for a former journalist – that American newspapers were immoral and it was an 'outrage to be assaulted on the public highway and asked to give the details of one's private life'. When told he was considered famous enough to have something 'valuable and interesting' to say, he thundered, 'That's another reason why I can't afford to be interviewed. I can get more by writing it myself and selling it to some English magazine, and then I suppose your American publishers would steal it, as they have most of my books.'

Rudyard was more concerned with making his mark in literary circles in the United States. His initial contacts revolved around the *Century* magazine, edited by Wolcott's old friend Richard Watson Gilder. While passing through New York in February, he had lunched at the *Century,* which had begun to serialise *The Naulahka.* Also owned by the same company was the *St Nicholas Magazine* for children, but its editor, Mary Mapes Dodge, had fallen out with Gilder and was not present at this meeting. Perhaps out of spite, when she heard from a colleague of Rudyard's presence in town, she contacted him directly to ask if he would contribute to her journal which, she did not seem to recall, had turned down his schoolboy poem in 1879. At the time Rudyard had nothing to hand. But, on his return from Japan, elated that Carrie was pregnant, he felt more inclined to write children's stories and contacted Mrs Dodge about a 'notion' he had – a story about a princess in a pickle bottle.[9]

He also offered 'a thing that I picked up in far Japan', a finished tale about a cockatoo. What he did not spell out was that this story, called 'Polly Cla', was written by his Yokohama friend, H. J. Hunt. Thinking she had an original Kipling piece, Mrs Dodge seized on it, offering £250 if she could run it in her December issue. To embarrassment all round, Rudyard had to insist that the signature H.J.H. was not his nom de plume. As a result, he felt obliged to send her something of his own. Along with his jaunty Hindustani rendering of 'Humpty-Dumpty', he submitted his completed 'notion', 'The Potted Princess', which turned out to be a sunny recollection of his childhood in India, almost a corrective to 'Baa Baa Black Sheep', his dour story about Southsea which

had upset his parents – a point he tacitly acknowledged by requesting the return of the manuscript so he could send it to his mother.
In addition he provided Mrs Dodge with rough outlines of some
stories about children in India. One of these – 'the tale of the
Thibetan lama and Kim o' the Rishti' – needed to gestate before
becoming his novel *Kim* nearly a decade later. But his other ideas
soon developed into the *Jungle Book* stories, the first of which,
'Toomai of the Elephants', was published in the *St Nicholas* the
following December. Significantly, this whole process covered the
period of the birth of his first child. The prospect of parenthood
was having a mellowing effect on Rudyard. He always enjoyed
young people's company and he meant it when he said, 'I would
sooner make a fair book of stories for children than a new religion
or a completely revised framework for our social and political
life.'[10]

In London, Rudyard's main correspondents were Henley (for
literary gossip) and Heinemann and Watt (for business). His next
collection of stories (*Many Inventions* published in May 1893) was
taking shape – a mixture of material from the previous year
(including 'The Disturber of Traffic'), plus two (later four) new
stories, one of which, he told Heinemann in November, was
'strange and quaint being in the nature of . . . well, anyhow, if you
say anything to anyone about the new tales I myself will presently
take ship and murder you'.[11] The piece he was coy about was
almost certainly 'In the Rukh', a trial run for the *Jungle Book*
stories he was discussing with the *St Nicholas*.[12] Till now Rudyard
had ignored India's fauna and flora, preferring to describe
people, towns and social dynamics. But a combination of the
Vermont hills and his father's book *Beast and Man in India*
(originally published in 1891, and now in a second edition)
had encouraged him to think again about the physical world
in the land of his birth. Mowgli in 'In the Rukh' was an en-
vironmental (as opposed to spiritual) version of the lama
Rudyard was developing for *Kim* – a rootless figure from somewhere 'towards the north', with such an innate understanding

of the jungle that he was happy to bring up his own child with wolves.

At this stage, Mowgli was a man – soon to metamorphose into the boy of the *Jungle Book* stories. Recalling how this idea had arisen, Rudyard said that, as a child, he had read a fanciful story (in the *Boy's Own Magazine*) about a hunter who fell among a pride of lions who, being all Freemasons, were able to join him in an alliance against wicked baboons. More recently his imagination had been stimulated by Rider Haggard's *Nada the Lily*, based on a Zulu tale of a boy who ran with the wolves. 'After blocking out the main idea in my head,' Rudyard noted, 'the pen took charge, and I watched it begin to write stories about Mowgli and animals, which later grew into the *Jungle Books*. Once launched there seemed no particular reason to stop, but I had learned to distinguish between the peremptory motions of my Daemon, and the "carry-over" or induced electricity, which comes of what you might call mere "frictional" writing.'[13]

This daemon was the force to which Rudyard attributed his creativity. With understated English mysticism, Rudyard considered himself a medium for an unconscious process. It was more than mere inspiration: 'When your Daemon is in charge, do not try to think consciously. Drift, wait and obey.'[14] Rudyard had alluded to this form of compulsion in a different context in 'My New-Cut Ashlar', the poem he used as L'Envoi to *Life's Handicap* where, referring to a piece of stone masonry, he wrote,

> If there be good in that I wrought
> Thy Hand compelled it, Master, Thine...

As Rudyard contemplated his wolf boy, his daemon encouraged him to evoke a magical jungle that, on one level, was an entertainment for children and, on another, a backdrop to explore ideas about society and the rule of law. From his first encounters with the United States in 1889 he had been agitated about the country's unpredictability and potential for chaos. As he became more familiar with his adopted homeland these impressions persisted. As he told Henley in November 1893, 'The moral dry rot of it all is having no law that need be obeyed: no line to toe: no trace to kick over and no compulsion to do anything.' Turning the premise of *The Naulahka* on its head, he compared America with India – with defects in all its workmanship. 'So far the immense natural wealth of the land holds this ineptitude up ... Au fond it's barbarism – barbarism plus telephone, electric light, rail and suffrage but all the more terrible for that very reason.'[15]

Already, in India, Rudyard had pondered the nature of society and concluded the need for some shared sense of purpose. In the *Jungle Books* he sought to extend these ideas into universal truths about the rule of law, as examined in the fictional laboratory of a tropical jungle. In the face of caterwauling from the Bandar-Log – those monkeys outside the Law who represent the unthinking democracy Rudyard viewed so warily in the United States – the young Mowgli is advised to stick to the rational, well-founded precepts of his elders. Without their make-believe furniture of trees, rocks and anthropomorphic animals, Rudyard's theories appear naïve: their most important insight being that the law acts as a social and moral glue, a sixth sense that individuals carry on their backs like a giant creeper, constricting their ability to act in an antisocial manner. He later mixes banal observation, 'For the strength of the pack is the wolf, and the strength of the wolf is in the pack', with stern authoritarianism:

> Now these are the Laws of the Jungle, and many and
>   mighty are they;
> But the head and the hoof of the Law and the haunch and
>   the hump is – Obey![16]

This was didactic stuff for unruly American children who, initially, were unimpressed. No-one bothered to write to the popular 'Letter Box' feature of the *St Nicholas* magazine to express an opinion about the stories. But the *Jungle Books* were the sort of reading a responsible adult could recommend to any young person and they soon became extremely popular. Within a year there was a Braille edition and Rudyard was telling Charles Eliot Norton that if he had known that, he would have written 'specially touch-and-smell' tales.[17]

Feeling his way as a political philosopher, Rudyard focused his attention on other matters during his first autumn in the United States. He watched as the foundations of his new house were dug and filled with rocks blasted from the hillside. He stood helplessly by – a foretaste of servant problems that were to afflict the Kiplings throughout their life – as a Swedish maid called Anna Anderson came and went, unable to stand living in the cramped quarters of Bliss Cottage. With the completion of her pregnancy fast approaching, Carrie prevailed on an old friend, Susan Bishop, to act as a perinatal nurse. Then, four days after Christmas, she gave birth to a daughter. Rudyard claimed mock annoyance that the infant (called Josephine after her aunt) had arrived on Gladstone's birthday, 29 December, telling Henley that if she had been a boy he would have disposed of her 'lest she also should disgrace the Empire'.[18] But his delight in this tiny creature with blue eyes, chubby features and a chin unmistakably his own was only too obvious: as he noted in a postscript to the year in the diary Carrie had started around the time of her marriage, 'All well – and the Good God be thanked for the ending of the happiest year in my life.'[19]

The main business of 1893 was the construction of his house. As a diplomatic gesture he hired his brother-in-law Beatty, who always needed money, as overall foreman of the works. As soon as the weather allowed in the spring, a burly Quebecois builder called Jean Pigeon appeared with a team of navvies, who put up a dormitory for themselves alongside the site and set to work. Before long, a vast, ark-like structure, clad in olive-green shingles, took shape on top of the solid foundations. At the back, powering the unit from the stern, was a giant furnace, next to the kitchen (though its heating did not extend to the servants' rooms above).

A long corridor ran the full ninety-foot length of the hillward (west) side of the house, with eleven rooms giving off it, looking out east across the Connecticut River valley through generous picture windows. At the prow (south) of the 'ship' was Rudyard's study, leading on to a loggia. Anyone wanting to talk to Rudyard had to pass through an ante-room – 'the dragon's chamber', as it was known locally – where Carrie would sit and sew, establishing a precedent that lasted through their married life that she controlled access to her husband. For a while, the nursery was above the study, with a veranda where the baby slept in warm weather. But this proved too noisy for Rudyard, and Josephine's quarters were moved back on the first floor. At the top of the house, the attic was given over to a vast play-room, which provided a useful space when Rudyard later wanted a billiard table to match one he had seen at Mark Twain's house in Elmira. In memory of Wolcott, the Kiplings decided to call their matrimonial home Naulakha, though this time Rudyard made sure the spelling was correct.

Outside, a split-level stable was built, incorporating accommodation for the horses on the ground and storage for hay above, with cramped living quarters for a servant at the back. Dynamite was used to blast a driveway through the uneven rocky hillside. Since there was no other water source, a 325-foot-deep well had to be bored. With the ground so hard, progress was slow – roughly three feet per day – and at least one drill-head was ruined. To lift the water, a windmill was constructed, but it proved noisy and inefficient. So, at a cost of $2000, Rudyard later bought a low-power atmospheric pump, which was capable of giving the house 1200 gallons of water a day.

With its fortress-like exterior, unrelieved by decorative detail, Naulakha's uncompromising command of the hillside caused Brattleboro tongues to wag again. The local *Windham County Reformer* reported the griping partially:

> What makes them build at all ... when there are plenty of large farms with good enough buildings for anybody to be bought

for half the price? ... It is rumored that when finally installed in this much-disapproved of dwelling, Mrs Kipling will keep three servants! It is 'presumed' that she cannot get them. We all know how it must be – breakfast late, luncheon at all hours, and dinner at night – absurd custom anywhere, but worse in the country. And Mr Kipling actually puts on a dress-suit when, ten to one, there isn't a soul there but his wife![20]

However, a woman who lived the other side of the valley was happy to see the house nearing completion. 'Be you the new lights 'crost the valley yonder?' she asked Rudyard when she met him on one of his long walks. 'Ye don't know what a comfort they've been to me this winter. Ye aren't ever goin' to shroud 'em up – or be ye?'[21]

In mid-June, with Naulakha at last taking shape, Rudyard was visited by his father. Rudyard's pleas to Lord Dufferin in 1890 had had the desired effect of obtaining Lockwood an adequate pension. 'The Pater' had finally left India in April. But while Alice remained in England to look for a house in Wiltshire, close to Ned Burne-Jones's friends the Wyndhams, Lockwood had continued his journey to America – this time in the company of the Society of Authors stalwart Walter Besant, who was travelling to New York to deliver his latest broadside against rapacious publishers. Rudyard met them both in New York, where his conversation with Besant must have been interesting since, for all his wariness towards publishers, he had been guilty of 'crossing the picket lines' after being drawn – inadvertently, it seems – into a rancorous feud between publishers and agents in London.

As with Rudyard's dispute with Harpers two and a half years earlier, this debate was conducted rather too publicly and angrily in the pages of the *Athenaeum*. After William Heinemann had railed in the magazine against the Society of Authors being 'a trades union more complete, more dangerous ... more determined in its demands than any of the other unions', Rudyard had written to him expressing some sympathy – a point of view that

Heinemann proceeded to quote in a further letter to the *Athenaeum*. Rudyard was not amused, telling the magazine[22] that his had been a private communication with Heinemann. Otherwise he might have expanded on his conclusion: 'My practice (for I have bought my experience in the market) is to deal with publishers entirely through an agent.' Inevitably, this led to a *froideur* between Rudyard and the clubbable Heinemann who was now more of a friend than publisher. He wrote some angry verses, but this time thought better of sending them. In a letter of 12 March, he was clearly biting his tongue when he promised to let the matter rest, and the polite postscript from Carrie, who valued her friendship with Heinemann, indicated why: she was keen that her mother should be paid for Wolcott's share of *The Naulahka*.[23]

With Lockwood away, Alice stayed with her sister at The Grange, whence Georgie wrote to her old friend Mary Wyndham (now Lady Elcho), expressing *sotto voce* her sense of the injustices of domestic life: 'Alice has to find a little house and get it ready for her husband's return, as he has been ill and is not to be fussed with anything.'[24] That did not prevent Lockwood, who suddenly seemed in rude health, accompanying his son on a tour of Canada and New England, where Rudyard enjoyed getting to know the old family friend Charles Eliot Norton, who initiated him into the high-minded but disappearing world of the 'Boston Brahmins'. Like father, like son: not for the last time, Rudyard upset Carrie by going off on his own, leaving her to cope with moving into Naulakha on 12 August. To make matters worse, two servants had just resigned – the maid because she refused to wear a cap with lace frills and the cook who walked out in sympathy. Carrie did at least have some support from her mother and sister Josephine, who were both up from New York. But Anna Balestier kept her accustomed distance from the main Balestier property, preferring to stay in a local boarding-house.

As often in the past, Lockwood was on hand to help his son with an important story. In his poetry Rudyard had been developing a new line about the romance of the sea. But in his fiction he was still happy to draw on Indian subject matter. On one level, 'The Bridge-Builders' recalled Rudyard's old themes of the selflessness of the Anglo-Indian official and, more generally, the redeeming value of work. But this time his tale showed a much greater awareness of the overall cultural background. When the engineer Findlayson's great bridge across the Ganges is threatened by a severe storm, his headman, a Rajput former sailor called Peroo, offers some opium to calm him down. As a result Findlayson has a drugged vision of a panchayet of Hindu gods discussing what to do: Mother Ganga is angry at the taming of her powers and wants the bridge destroyed. But wiser counsels prevail and Find-layson's solid construction, with its girders and piers, withstands all buffeting. After the storm passes, the spendthrift local maha-raja sails up in his steam launch to see if everything is all right, before departing to a puja in his local temple with the words, 'They are dam-bore, these religious ceremonies, Finlinson, eh?' The ascendancy of engineering over mumbo-jumbo is preserved, though Rudyard shows more understanding than before of the compromises needed between modernity and Hindu culture. Almost despite himself, he cannot refrain from advancing the cause of a new cult of machinery, one so powerful that Peroo (a symbol of the new local forces of change) prays to the low-pressure cylinder when he first enters the engine room of a steamer.

This more sympathetic attitude to India was also apparent in the *Jungle Book* story 'The Miracle of Purun Bhagat', which tells of an Indian who, after becoming Prime Minister of a native state and gaining a knighthood, decides, in the manner of traditional Brahmins, to turn his back on the world and live spiritually as a sannyasi or holy man. Rudyard writes approvingly of the enlight-ened Sir Purun Dass's priorities: he has worked and tried to improve the world, before seeing to his religious duties. Rudyard's observation of American society helped bring about this change of perspective: his revulsion against the excesses of raw capitalism encouraged a new-found respect for India's ways – but only if mitigated with a British sense of values. (As so often Rudyard's point of view could change radically: in 'The Bridge-Builders', the Western-educated maharaja was a figure of fun, but a year later Sir Purun Dass, with his endowments for his countrymen to study English medicine, was a hero.)

While Lockwood Kipling could usually stimulate his son with ideas for stories about India, he was not much help in writing about women. With his professional sense of the market, William Heinemann had been pressing Rudyard to focus again on the topical issue that had eluded him in *The Light that Failed* – the position of women in modern society. Rudyard claimed to be giving some thought to the subject, but his comments were usually accompanied by a caveat – ' 'Tisn't a thing that could be done unless it came and I make no doubt that some day it will come' – and not even his father could inspire progress on a story on these lines.[25]

Rudyard was more occupied with a real woman for the first time in his life than with any theoretical consideration of the 'female question'. Carrie's influence, as well as his baby daughter's, had clearly contributed to his greater open-mindedness, even mellowness. Never one to indulge in intimate revelations, he did once get as far as telling his cousin Margaret of his enjoyment at giving Carrie regular massages, though the circumstances hardly indicated great passion – 'it's a beautiful thing for making tired folk untired'.[26]

Carrie herself was blossoming in marriage and motherhood. Within three weeks of her daughter's birth, she astonished neighbours by driving into Brattleboro in her 'Maryland' wicker basket sleigh, decorated with yellow mountings and a cock's feather between the horse's ears. Until common sense prevailed, she was talking about travelling to India in the spring. Rudyard spoke with some relief of the infant Josephine tying and taming his wife's 'adventurous soul'.[27]

Instead Carrie had to learn to channel her energies, and one outlet was as her husband's financial manager. Now that Rudyard was earning significant sums, she adroitly took on the role of Rudyard's intermediary in his business dealings with his agent and publishers. Every week, the post brought some new payment: $582 from Moreau for the Indian Railway Library sales in January, a cheque from Heinemann for £296. 3s. 11d as his half-share in *The Naulahka* in March, $1460 in Macmillan royalties in May. At a time when Rudyard was receiving one hundred dollars (twenty pounds) per thousand words from the *Youth's Companion*, the *Barrack-Room Ballads* had sold 7000 copies in its first year of publication and Macmillan was happy to offer a royalty of up to thirty per cent, Carrie was almost insulted when the *National Observer* sent fifteen guineas for her husband's poem 'The Dove of Dacca': 'better nothing at all,' she wrote in her diary.[28] Only a year earlier, financial ruin seemed to stare the Kiplings in the face. But, after April 1893, when the New Oriental Bank Corporation made its first repayment, they began to feel more comfortably off. Initially, most sums were quickly turned around, as the outgoings on materials and construction for the new house were substantial. Since Beatty was nominally works supervisor, Carrie made regular transfers to her brother, all meticulously noted in her diary – five dollars in cash here, a $257 cheque there.

At least as part of the 'Committee of Ways and Means' the methodical Carrie could flourish. Inside the house she had less of a sure touch – not so much a natural housekeeper as a shrew, insisting that everything was done exactly as she said. As Molly Cabot noted, she 'provided only bare necessities and slender allowances for her life, made much of the difficulty of conducting a household far from the source of supplies, and kept the machinery of life always in evidence. An unexpected guest at luncheon would have been an impossibility. Nor did she know how to make a house attractive.'[29]

So the internal decoration of Naulakha had no particular style: none of the sub-Old Master paintings that hung at Beechwood or even the French-style furniture, a legacy of the Balestiers' ancestry, at Maplewood. The Kiplings' new home offered only, and perhaps inevitably, a variation on the Orientalist theme Rudyard had pioneered at Embankment Chambers: hand-blocked muslin curtains, a gift of his parents, covered the windows; a wrought-iron gate manufactured to Lockwood's design in Lahore helped prevent baby Josephine tumbling down the stairs; a kaleidoscopic range of Eastern rugs covered the floors. A few pieces of furniture, such as an oak sideboard, were commissioned from a local carpenter. Otherwise the effect was simple, almost stark. One of the house's few original features was the sentence from St John's Gospel that Lockwood moulded in plaster above the fireplace in his son's study: 'The night cometh when no man can work.'

In July word filtered back to Henry James in London that the Kiplings were living in blissful domesticity, which he viewed with a sceptical but benevolent eye. He told a friend that he had heard that Rudyard was 'supremely content ... *en puissance de femme*'. But then, as he admitted, the Englishman had few needs that Vermont could not satisfy, and 'almost none of the civilized order – London, English life, "culture", etc. were for instance a superfluity for him. He charged himself with all he could take out of India when he was very young, and gave it out with great effect; but I doubt if he had anything to give ... But what he *did* – in two or three years – remains wonderful.'[30]

Henry James would not have known it but, even in this idyll, there were tiny, tell-tale signs of tension. When, before the end of the year, Carrie complained to Nellie Gosse that her husband took no interest in either the house or its grounds, and that he liked to berate her for 'mis-managing' them,[31] she thought she was being light-hearted. She had little idea of the basic truth behind her words: that Rudyard was beginning to feel uneasy about living in the United States.

He did his best, however, and there was something harsh about the way she belittled his efforts to brighten his property. His vast correspondence is enlivened by his brisk, inconsequential letters to tradesmen, such as the Boston seed firm he thanked for their roses, hollyhocks, peonies, zinnias, asters and marigolds, and asked for 150 strawberry plants capable of surviving the Vermont winters. 'I should also be obliged if you would send me your catalogue *as soon as possible*, as I wish to order some Tea roses &c for indoor blooming this winter.' (He published his wry observations on seed catalogues in his light, flowery poem 'Pan in Vermont'.) Already he received up to 200 letters a week, many requesting autographs. In return, he asked for payment of $2.50 to the *New York Tribune*'s Fresh Air Fund for disadvantaged children. Since the paper listed all contributions, he would monitor its columns and only perform his part of the transaction when he saw the required sum had been paid. However, he was often disappointed: one batch of petitioners brought no money, only a flood of abuse from people asking how much Rudyard pocketed for himself.[32]

Rudyard's interest in flowers extended to the countryside around him. He took every opportunity to engage correspondents (such as Ripley Hitchcock, chief editor at the publishers Appleton's) about local fauna and flora. His observation of horses frolicking in the Back Pasture, on Beatty's property, prompted his story 'A Walking Delegate', which is both an affectionate memoir of lazy days in the Vermont sunshine and a political allegory about a new kicker from Kansas who tries to stir his fellow nags into revolt against their masters – until the old bay Rod brings him up short: 'America's paved with the kind er horse you are – jist plain yaller-dog – waiting to be licked inter shape,' an echo of Rudyard's thoughts about the country's inhabitants. (In domestic political terms, the new horse referred to the People's Party, which was stirring up populist protest following a marked economic downturn.)

Before this story was published, Rudyard wrote a more factual account of Vermont, 'Leaves from a Winter Notebook', which he read to Molly Cabot when she visited in early January 1894. This was a sensual description of the changing seasons, as the autumn's 'insurrection of the tree-people against the waning year' becomes the punishing, glorious winter when 'snow turns into chalk, squeaking under the heel, and their breath cloaks the oxen in rime'. Although this appeared objective, certain passages struck a more personal note, such as Rudyard's reference to the New England summer having Creole blood: 'She went away, red-faced and angry to the last, slamming all the doors of the hills behind her, and Autumn, who is a lady, took charge.' In a cryptic manner, Rudyard was describing the behaviour of his wife, with her part-West-Indian (Creole) origins.

A few days earlier, on New Year's Day 1894, the Kiplings invited a dozen friends to dinner, followed by dancing in the barn. To the accompaniment of a local fiddler, Rudyard and the pretty, lively Molly Cabot led the guests in reels. She was amused at the way he had fastened pieces of paper to the walls of his barn, with inscriptions such as 'Here are the marble pillars!' and 'This is the gilded divan'. As Rudyard's main literary confidante in Brattleboro (with her knowledge of New England novelists, she understood at once when he referred to a local resident as 'the best story Mary Wilkins never wrote') Molly loved his habit of rattling off verses whenever they met, drumming an accompaniment on the table to give him a rhythm. She noted that he was writing a play that he practised in a child's theatre he had bought from F. A. O. Schwartz. (This was probably just an entertainment for the baby since there are no other references.)

The following month she invited the Kiplings back to her house in Brattleboro for a gourmet's feast – lobster *à la* Newburg with beer, followed by beef olives *farcis* with crackers, then marrons glacés, and a glass of Maraschino liqueur provided by her sister Grace, whom she told triumphantly, 'As I brought out one course after another, Kipling's eyes swelled with amazement, and he told me that it was "a perfect supper". I never have seen him so brilliant. I am sure he had a good time.'[33] Small-town New England society being what it was, there was no question of romance. But there was clearly a difference between impulsive, efficient Carrie, who could not help looking matronly, and soft, sensual Molly, who knew how to make her guests comfortable and happy.

It was, perhaps, fortuitous when, in late February, the Kiplings took a break, not in India, but in Bermuda. One result of their trip was a lifelong friendship with the wealthy Catlin family from Morristown, New Jersey. Julius Catlin, a leading dry goods merchant in New York, had died the previous year, and his widow and three daughters, Julia, May and Edith, were taking a short holiday to recuperate. During the *Trinidad*'s voyage between New York and Bermuda a storm blew up and the cabin doors began to bang. The first time twenty-one-year-old May Catlin saw Rudyard he was standing in blue pyjamas, 'keen eyes behind gig-lamps and bristling eye-brows', asking politely, 'Do you mind if I fasten your door? The banging is disturbing my wife.' On reaching Bermuda, no porter was available, so Rudyard offered to carry her bag.[34]

Apart from bright spring sunshine, the attractions of Bermuda were limited. With its dockyard and naval station, the island was a cultural backwater, paying its way in the world through exports of agricultural produce to the East Coast of the United States. Rudyard may well have been encouraged to go by Mark Twain, a regular visitor, whom he had seen in New York the previous year. The Kiplings parked themselves in the Princess Hotel,[35] where they saw much of the Catlin girls – Julia, soon to marry Trenor Park, a millionaire industrialist with one of the largest yachts in the world, the *Trenora*; musical May who, under the name Raymond Hunt, published, in 1896, a setting of the lullaby 'Shiv and the Grasshopper' from the *Jungle Book*; and Edith, who had ambitions to write. With the Catlins at the same stage of grieving about Julius as the Kiplings had been about Wolcott a couple of years earlier, the two families joined up for picnics on the rocks, and for parties with the Governor and the Admiral where Rudyard befriended his host's six-year-old daughter and fed her six slices of ham at lunch – to Carrie's evident disgust, Edith Catlin recalled.[36]

Early in his stay Rudyard met a sergeant from the resident

regiment, the Royal Berkshires, who invited him and Carrie to tea in his married quarters. The soldier recounted his experiences at the Battle of Maiwand in Afghanistan in July 1880, when many of his colleagues had perished beside the colours along with their colonel, while the others retreated ignominiously to Kandahar. Rudyard used this material for a poem, 'That Day', which, as vividly as anything he wrote, tells of a soldier's conflicting emotions in the heat of battle.

Returning briefly to Brattleboro to pick up Josephine, before setting off for an extended summer holiday in England, the Kiplings were dismayed to find that their coachman Bogle had decided to quit (though Carrie quickly rationalised the advantages: they would not have to pay the man during their four months' absence). In London they stayed for a fortnight in lodgings arranged by Nellie Gosse in Ebury Street. Rudyard dutifully made the rounds of relations and Savile Club friends, but felt little involved. He made a half-hearted attempt to see Henley, who had left the *National Observer* and was about to take on the editorship of the *New Review*, William Heinemann's attempt to publish a tied journal along the lines of *Macmillan's Magazine*. But when Rudyard breezed in to see him Henley was occupied, later telling Charles Whibley: 'He [i.e. Rudyard] promised to come back – or rather he asked permission to come back – in the afternoon. But didn't.'[37] Rudyard felt his time in London was like entering a theatre in the middle of the second act: 'You see all sorts of situations and hear a deal of vastly fine dialogue but not being privy to events that led up to all the row, you are only a little amazed and more than a little bored.'[38]

He was happy to move to Tisbury, near Salisbury in Wiltshire, where he paid forty-five pounds for a three-months' rental on Arundell House, a rambling six-bedroomed house with a fine view over the downs, half a mile closer to the centre of the village than The Gables, his parents' modest new home. The main object of the exercise was to show off young Josephine to Lockwood and Alice, and the bouncy baby, now sixteen months old, did not disappoint: Flat Curls (or Bo or Bips), as her adoring father called her, was 'in enormous form; learning a new word every ten minutes; playing with the coal scuttle, eating pencils, smearing herself, bumping her head; singing, shouting and babbling from dawn till dark'.[39] Less predictable was Alice Kipling, who was still wary of Carrie and needed careful treatment: why else had Rudyard made such a fuss a couple of months earlier when Trix had written to him about their mother and he had been so upset that he could not work?[40] During almost three months in Tisbury, Rudyard wrote many letters, including several chatty notes to family members like Louisa Baldwin and to his new friends the Catlins. He discussed his father, Josephine and the appalling weather, but never once Alice. His mother was such a sensitive subject that she could not be mentioned. During his visit, when he was thinking of building a holiday cottage by the sea (possibly near Lulworth in Dorset, which he liked), Carrie noted that such an undertaking was unlikely, for 'at present family reasons make England of course undesirable'.[41] Her diary entries were often short and, if touching on personal matters, ambiguous, but this one suggested a family impasse rooted in Tisbury rather than Brattleboro.

Living in close proximity, Carrie and Alice found what they had always suspected: that they were almost too similar – both powerful, intelligent, emotional women who liked to take charge. One specific reason for their coolness was suggested in a letter from Rudyard to his cousin Stanley Baldwin the following April: 'Don't believe a grandmother is infallible. It's generally so long a time since a grandmother has had a baby that they forget things or get 'em mixed up and the results are apt to be disastrous for the Kid.'[42] And if mother- and daughter-in-law quarrelled, ostensibly over the baby Josephine, Carrie was not in the best of spirits, showing distinct signs of post-natal depression. As Rudyard told his cousin, 'A woman isn't well before her child comes bodily but it's her spirits and mind that are all on edge afterwards.'[43] Trix, who might have acted as a useful go-between, had returned to India with her husband, who was now fully recovered.

In Tisbury, the benevolent, white-bearded Lockwood Kipling had already been adopted as *ex officio* cultural guru (a role which might have been tailor-made) to three local landowners – Percy Wyndham, known to him through his friendship with Ned Burne-Jones; the hugely wealthy Alfred Morrison, who collected coins and other artefacts at Fonthill Splendens; and Lord Arundell, owner of Wardour Castle, on whose estate Rudyard now lived (and enjoyed fishing rights).

Through his father Rudyard came to know all three families, particularly the Wyndhams, who lived at Clouds, a lavish modern house, built for them by William Morris's associate Philip Webb, on a 4200-acre estate at East Knoyle, ten miles from Tisbury, and hung with paintings by Burne-Jones, Poynter and others. The Wyndhams gave him (and his father) an entrée to a cosy late-Victorian world of enlightened privilege. Along with his artistic interests Percy Wyndham, son of the first Lord Leconfield, who owned Petworth in Sussex, had married Madeline Campbell, granddaughter of the radical Irish peer Lord Edward Fitzgerald. He himself had been an independent-minded MP who opposed British intervention in Egypt before resigning from parliament in 1885 in protest against the extension of the franchise. Two of the Wyndhams' five children had peripheral roles in Rudyard's life. At Stanway in Gloucestershire their daughter Mary Elcho played host to the Souls, a small group of cultured aristocrats who prided themselves on their ability to mix fun with intellectual rigour. Their dashing son George, the writer and MP who may have advised Rudyard on the Sudanese background to *The Light that Failed*, had acted as private secretary to his sister Mary's admirer, probably lover, Arthur Balfour, while the latter was Chief Secretary for Ireland from 1887 to 1891. Rudyard himself was never received into the Souls (nor would he have wanted to be). But it is significant that when in early 1897 he needed to name an influential friend, he mentioned the Balfour brothers, Arthur and

Eustace, and his old sparring partner Lord Dufferin.[44]

During June the weather was appalling (cold, wet and 'only fit for marine monsters').[45] Unable to fish, Rudyard spent rather more time indoors than he wanted, looking out over 'fat and fleecy and green'[46] Wiltshire downs, and dreaming up stories he described as 'full of the purely male horse-play and schoolboy rot that womenfolk bless 'em find it so hard to understand'.[47] He told correspondents he was itching to return to Naulakha (he wanted to be 'back in Main Street Brattleboro Vt. U.S.A. and hear the sody water fizzing in the drug-store ... and then go home, an easy gait, through the deep white dust with the locust trees stinking to heaven and the fire flies playing up'.[48] But this was typical Rudyard camouflage: his fiction ideas show he was grappling with two very different themes – the insidious attraction of the English countryside and the phenomenon of the American at large in the wider world. Both topics were touched on in 'My Sunday at Home', completed at Tisbury, and more clearly delineated in 'An Error in the Fourth Dimension', written on his return to Brattleboro in October. This latter story tells of an American plutocrat, Wilton Sargent (after Wilton House, the nearby house of the Earl of Pembroke, and John Sargent, the American artist patronised by the Wyndhams) who, having decamped to England, thinks his wealth allows him to flag down an express train running through his estate. Such New World chutzpah was not acceptable in Rudyard's newly romanticised view of Britain, with its 'fourth dimension' of customs and traditions, impenetrable to the outsider, but so essential to the ordering of society.

The evidence of these stories is that, at the age of twenty-eight, Rudyard was thinking deeply about his roots. In more modern parlance, he was having a minor crisis of national identity. Inspired by his love for Carrie, he had moved happily, but without great foresight, to the United States. Now the first flush of his enthusiasm for matrimony had worn off, he sensed a lack of purpose in his life. Much as he loved Naulakha and its countryside (his homesickness when in England was genuine), he had no real bond with the American people or culture. In Vermont he never experienced the panic – the desperate sensation of peering over the edge of an abyss – that he had in India. But he had felt threatened by the teeming mass of people and, as he told Henley the previous year, he had been aware of the similarities between the United States and the land of his birth. He worried about the influx of immigrants into North America: one result, he observed, was the politics of a democracy had become a matter of biddable ethnic lobby groups. Perhaps he feared, like Wilton Sargent in reverse, that he might some day make a fool of himself and some dreadful faux pas would show him up as an alien. But where could this rootless creature really feel at home? In metropolitan London, a few weeks earlier, he had been no more at home than on his return to England in 1889. Now, in Wiltshire with his dependable father to guide him, he tested his reactions to English rural life, and the evidence of 'My Sunday at Home' suggests he was beginning to feel comfortable.

The essence of 'Englishness' intrigued him: although not published for a dozen years, 'The Puzzler', one of his Tisbury ideas, explored the peculiar genius of a people who could produce three dignitaries, a senior lawyer, artist and engineer, whose idea of fun was seeing if an organ grinder's monkey could climb a monkey puzzle tree. As if to confirm his sense of wanting to belong, he even joined the local Tisbury cricket club. And, to show what he was rejecting, he wrote the execrable poem 'An American' for the *Pall Mall Gazette* (ironically, owned by a rich American, William Waldorf Astor). In this he contrasted the indomitable Yankee spirit with the new unthinking breed of American with an energy

> ... That bids him flout the Law he makes
> That bids him make the Law he flouts ...

With the help of his father, Rudyard also started some new animal stories, the forerunners of the *Just So Stories*, which he illustrated himself in what his wife described as Aubrey Beardsley style.

Ever since his father had designed covers for the Indian Railway Library, illustrations had been features of Rudyard's work, often requiring separate negotiations with potential publishers and editors. (In the United States, he had to plead for his characters not to look too American – or his Indians like redskins – though he was delighted with the drawings of the New England artist Mary Hallock Foote for *The Naulahka*). His own style had evolved into a unique mixture of Beardsley's art nouveau, Japanese engravings, Oriental prints, old county maps and surrealism *avant la lettre*. Typically, Rudyard devised his own monogram – often a rebus of an ark, set in a capital letter 'A', reading phonetically 'Ark A' or his initials RK.

When Henry James came to stay in Tisbury, Rudyard spared him his observations on Americans abroad (a theme which his guest had already made his own) and read him his paean to a Scottish ship's engineer, 'McAndrew's Hymn', which would appear in *Scribner's Magazine* in December. No doubt Rudyard, in expansive mood, adopted the broad accent of his Macdonald forebears. For this was a poem he had been working towards. He knew he could always write some ditty based on the aspirations of the soldiers' mess, but he needed new subject matter. Over the previous two years he had been exploring the nature of romance: was it really achievable in an age of season tickets? he asked in 'The King'. As he looked back over British history, he felt this elusive quality could still be found at sea and suggested as much in several poems in the early 1890s, ranging in style from 'A Song of the English' to 'The Ballad of the "Clampherdown" '. His personal contribution to the established genre of nautical verse was to invoke the role of machinery on the ocean wave. He achieved this in 'McAndrew's Hymn', which chronicles the heroics of a ship's engineer in command of his 'purrin' dynamoes' as they gave out their message (reminiscent of Rudyard's own politics): 'Law, Orrder, Duty an' Restraint, Obedience, Discipline!'

Twice he travelled up from Tisbury to London for formal dinners, including one at the Grand Hotel on 3 May, given by

W. W. Astor for contributors to his *Pall Mall Gazette*.[49] Rudyard made a well-received speech, sitting next to Field Marshal Lord Roberts, about whom he had penned the affectionate poem 'Bobs' in June 1893. On these occasions he stayed, as on his honeymoon, in Brown's Hotel, slipping out once to tea with his 'dear ladies' in Warwick Gardens where he met the explorer Mary Kingsley, just back from her first West African expedition. She fascinated everyone with tales of cannibals: in the *Journal of the African Society*, Rudyard recalled, 'Her even, disinterested tones were in precise key with the Victorian atmosphere and surroundings; but the manner of her discourse was heathen and adventurous.'[50] In his autobiography, Rudyard told how, after walking home, he had asked her up to his rooms to finish their conversation. She agreed, then quickly changed her mind, saying she had forgotten she was a woman.[51] While the story showed up the irony that this new woman could travel in distant lands but not accompany a man to his room, it was not true. The local geography indicates that he simply accompanied Miss Kingsley a few hundred yards from Warwick Gardens to her flat in Addison Road where, with his diffidence, he probably declined to go to her rooms because he was a married man. Rudyard was on more familiar ground when he went with his father to Westward Ho! to pay his respects on Uncle Crom's retirement as headmaster of the USC.

Back in Vermont, needing to replace Bogle, Rudyard put an advertisement in the *New York Tribune*: 'Coachman, married, English preferred, to take charge of three horses in the country: must be thoroughly good driver and understand furnace; permanent home for a steady man; wife could do family washing if competent. Write to Rudyard Kipling, Brattleboro, Vt.' He received a reply from a seedy Bowery hotel, where Matthew Howard claimed to have worked in the Leicestershire stables of Lord Grey de Wilton. (If this was indeed what he said, Rudyard should have been wary, as the last nobleman of that title had died at the beginning of the seventeenth century.) Somehow, nevertheless, Howard knew the servants' protocol the Kiplings expected (to the amusement of the locals) and he did not mind wearing his redcoat uniform. On his salary of thirty-five dollars a month, plus the furnished room in the stable, he arranged for his wife to join him from England. Although he neglected to inform Rudyard of his eight children this proved no problem: only two came to Brattleboro while the Kiplings were there and Carrie happily took them on as maids.

Within two months, Howard had proved his worth. On 27 October he was driving Carrie, Josephine and Armstrong, the baby's English nurse, into town, when Rick, one of the two horses, inadvertently caught his leg over the pole connecting his harness to the carriage. After the other horse, Rod, bolted for the best part of a mile, a wheel broke on a corner, the carriage overturned and the passengers were thrown out. During this nightmare couple of minutes Carrie had the presence of mind to wrap the baby up tightly and place her at the bottom of the carriage. Luckily no-one was hurt, though Carrie was badly shaken. Rudyard showed his appreciation of Howard's coolness by writing him into 'An Error in the Fourth Dimension' as a butler.

Carrie was again in the wars in January 1895 when, upon opening the door of Naulakha's furnace, the flame burst out and singed her face. Her friends rallied round, notably Meta (wife of Lockwood) de Forest, who sent her cook from New York. The previous month Rudyard had given his wife a Persian cat because she had been feeling low after her carriage accident. Now, hearing from Dr James Conland, the local doctor who had delivered Josephine and who had become a good friend, that Carrie needed a 'tonic', Rudyard entered negotiations to buy Nip and Tuck, a couple of young brown Morgans (a local breed of horse) from Beatty for $650. Despite her injuries, Carrie, in adventurous mode, insisted on trying her tonic – though with her face covered in bandages she looked like an Egyptian mummy as she drove her new horses round the local lanes in failing light and three feet of snow. Rudyard was happy enough to keep his brother-in-law solvent because he himself was feeling rich. As Carrie's diary recorded, he had earned $20,000 (£4000) in 1894. As the daughter of a one-time insurance salesman, she encouraged him to lock some of this cash away in two large life insurance policies – a $25,000 endowment policy with the Equitable Life and a further $10,000 option policy with the National Life Insurance Company. The total annual premiums were in excess of $1000.

As in the previous year, the Kiplings were determined to avoid being marooned in Naulakha during the severest part of the winter. On 25 February they journeyed south for a few weeks' holiday in Washington, the capital city Rudyard had noted for its 'Simlaish' smell six years earlier. Curiously, for all his frequently voiced antipathy to American democracy, he knew little about the mundane realities of national politics. In the United States he had cheerfully traded on his reputation as the soldiers' poet, but generally, like any self-respecting writer, he had kept clear of party political issues, only occasionally offering an opinion on local topics such as the tram. His letters to England, where his Uncle Alfred Baldwin sat on the Conservative benches in Parliament, showed no special interest in Congressional matters in Washington. He gave little indication of awareness that American politicians faced the same underlying pressures as in Europe. Confronted by an agricultural depression which had dragged on since the 1860s (one of the reasons for the founding of the People's Party) and by the growing struggle between monopoly capitalists and organised labour, Republican activists had been calling more vocally for new markets overseas and for a more powerful American navy. Only two years earlier President Grover Cleveland, a Democrat, had stamped on a move to annex the Pacific islands of Hawaii. Now expansionist-minded Americans were again eyeing opportunities in China and Latin America. Certain newspapers were whipping up anti-British feeling over a boundary dispute between British Guiana and Venezuela.

In Washington the Kiplings paid fifteen dollars a day for some unsatisfactory rooms, but since Carrie's eyes were still hurting from her accident and baby Josephine fell ill, they moved to the Grafton Hotel in Connecticut Avenue, where they paid forty-five dollars a week. Having installed themselves, their first callers were John Hay, the Anglophile Assistant Secretary of State, and Cecil Spring-Rice, from the British embassy, both accompanied by their wives.

As a result, Rudyard was assured not only of an interesting social life but also of an excellent grounding in the new politics of expansionism, as seen from a Washington perspective. Hay had once been Lincoln's secretary and Rudyard had wanted to meet him, since being recommended by their mutual friend Henry Adams in 1892. Part of a bookish élite, Hay had spent several years in London, where he had befriended writers and politicians, including Joseph Chamberlain, who had left the Liberal party and was now a leading Conservative advocate of imperialism. His observations of the British social order had led him, like Rudyard, to reject democracy in favour of the stratified society outlined in his book *The Bread-winners*. At the same time, he was both an American hegemonist, having backed the annexation of Hawaii in 1893, and a passionate believer in Anglo-American co-operation, which he favoured on grounds of similarities of race and culture. Hay introduced Rudyard to like-minded people, among them the senator Henry Cabot Lodge and the influential lawyer William Hallett Phillips.

Spring-Rice had been one of Hay's London friends, though Rudyard had initially met him in Tokyo. The up-and-coming British diplomat, whose grandfather had been Chancellor of the Exchequer in Lord Melbourne's government in the 1830s, took Rudyard to the zoo, where the author expressed an interest in a colony of beavers, and to a session of Congress, which was intent on displaying its own brand of bestiality. Spring-Rice recalled the hubbub as members screamed abuse at each other: 'A great many were smoking. Some were chewing and each was provided with the necessary spittoon.' Viewing the scene, Rudyard said he would never bring Carrie there, 'as she was an American and wished to respect her country'.[52]

Before long, Rudyard met another member of the Hay–Adams circle, Theodore Roosevelt, a charismatic rough diamond who was a Civil Service Commissioner and rising star in the Republican party. Unlike Hay, he was not a natural Anglophile. As a man of letters, he had taken issue with English critics of American culture (coincidentally echoing Rudyard in damning Matthew Arnold's *Civilisation in America* in 1888). Priding himself more on physical toughness than intellect, he had spent time as a young man among the cowboys in the badlands of Dakota – an experience he developed into his best-selling 1888 history *The Winning of the West*.

Sensing a fellow restless spirit, he had initially viewed Rudyard's progress with suspicion, congratulating his friend Brander Matthews, the writer and Columbia University professor, three years earlier for blackballing the British author from the Players Club in New York, because 'he is at bottom a cad'. When the two men first met over dinner on 7 March, they regarded each other warily. Roosevelt described Rudyard as 'bright, nervous, voluble and underbred', displaying an occasional truculence towards America which required 'very rough handling'.[53] But appreciating the genius behind those brittle defences, Roosevelt persisted. Although he found Carrie 'fearful',[54] he introduced Rudyard to friends, such as his Harvard contemporary Owen Wister (who later wrote *The Virginian*) and took him to the Smithsonian Institution where, looking at Indian relics in the ethnographic department, the two men argued heatedly about the fate of native Americans – with Rudyard recalling his father's strictures and mocking the smugness of the white settlers who had successfully exterminated the country's aboriginals and Roosevelt causing the glass cases to shake with his rebuttals,[55] as he thanked God that he, a man of Dutch origins, had not a drop of British blood.

Roosevelt was determined that his new English friend should understand the reality of America's power. Appropriately for a future Assistant Secretary of the Navy (whose first book had been *The Naval War of 1812*, a study of an earlier flare-up between Britain and the United States), he pointed Rudyard towards the Navy Yard to see for himself the vast strides the United States had taken to build 'a navy second to none'. This was a development that Rudyard had followed closely. Five years earlier US Admiral Alfred Thayer Mahan had published his highly regarded book *The Influence of Sea Power upon History*. His masterly record of how Britain's control of the seas had led to the growth of its empire had been seized upon by American expansionists calling for a more powerful navy. Mahan's arguments had been noted in London, where he was fêted the previous year, and even the German Kaiser William II praised the American admiral's book. It is inconceivable that Rudyard, with his wide reading, did not also know of Mahan. Indeed, his fascination with the sea – as a theme in his poetry and, increasingly, in his stories – was closely paralleled in Mahan's admiration for 'that English nation which more than any other owed its greatness to the sea'.

Roosevelt[56] also wheeled Rudyard in to see the scientist Professor Samuel P. Langley, Secretary of the Smithsonian, who the following year was to pioneer the first heavier-than-air flight – the sort of technical development that fascinated Rudyard, not least for its military potential.[57] Langley plied him with Smithsonian publications, including one about Eskimos, which Rudyard used for the background to 'Quiquern', a new departure as a *Jungle Book* story.

More conventionally, Spring-Rice was responsible for Rudyard meeting British Minister (as ambassadors to the United States were then called) Sir Julian Pauncefote, a veteran diplomat whose legal training proved useful in various potentially dangerous disputes with the United States, and Miss Mary Leiter, the wealthy department store heiress who, having spurned Spring-Rice's advances, was shortly to marry his old friend George Curzon, the ambitious British politician just back from a gruelling trip to India and Afghanistan.

Outside this close circle of conservative politicians and diplomats, Rudyard lunched with the theatrical impresario Beerbohm Tree, who was touring the United States, and received A. P. Watt, who came down from New York. Rudyard also met Max Beerbohm, Tree's half-brother (who was travelling as his secretary) and together they discussed the latest developments in the Oscar Wilde affair. Following the opening of *The Importance of Being Earnest* in February, Wilde had been described as a 'somdomite' (*sic*) by the Marquess of Queensberry, the father of his lover Lord Alfred Douglas. He had responded by issuing a writ for libel, which was due to be heard in London on 3 April, two days after this meeting of expatriates in Washington. Passing through New York the following week, Rudyard learnt that Wilde had lost his case and had subsequently been arrested, carrying, it was wrongly reported, a copy of the *Yellow Book*, with its lascivious illustrations of Wilde's *Salome* by Aubrey Beardsley, a young friend of Burne-Jones. When John Lane, the *Yellow Book*'s publisher who was in New York at the time, panicked and irrationally sacked Beardsley, Rudyard, an unlikely supporter of the aesthetes' canon, intervened on the artist's behalf.[58]

To Rudyard's satisfaction, Watt had managed to buy back the copyrights (outside India) of his Indian Railway Library books from Emile Moreau for £1200. Surprisingly, 16,000 copies of the Sampson Low one shilling edition of these books remained unsold in England: under the terms of the agreement they had to be either destroyed or taken to India for sale at the original agreed royalty of four pounds per 1000, or eight per cent. As Rudyard explained to Ripley Hitchcock, this transaction had been possible because Macmillan had offered a good deal to repackage the material.[59] He was hoping to add more stories, including one about Mulvaney's death. He never achieved this and Macmillan published a lacklustre edition of *Soldier Tales* (*Soldier Stories* in America) in 1896. Nevertheless, there was no doubting Rudyard's assertion, 'It means a good deal to me – even at long prices – to control my early books.'

Towards the end of his Washington visit, on 5 April, he also met Roosevelt's political opponents. Invited to visit Daniel Lamont at the War Office, he was led in to see the full US Cabinet and President Grover Cleveland. Rudyard was singularly unimpressed, describing these men as a 'colossal agglomeration of reeking bounders – awful; inexpressible; incredible'.[60] That evening he saw Roosevelt, Hay, Wister and a few others for a final dinner before leaving for New York the next day. By now, Roosevelt was converted, telling Brander Matthews, 'When one knows him, it seems preposterous to mind anything he says about the United States. He is both parochial and sensitive himself, and as there is plenty that is parochial and sensitive about us he of course hits at it; but his small peculiarities do not interfere with his being a very pleasant companion as well as a writer of genius. It has been a great pleasure meeting him.' The proverbial fly on the wall would have enjoyed this last gathering, described in Carrie's diary as 'a man's dinner, amusing'. Well might Henry Adams exude quiet satisfaction when he told a British correspondent later in the year that Rudyard had 'grown rather thick with our little Washington gang'.[61]

After the excitement of the capital and New York, Rudyard returned to New England where the issues of the day were no more pressing than the water level (happily replenished by ample rains while he was away), the fencing of his property (a problem he had discussed with the head of the zoo in Washington), the siting of a sunken garden and his petition for a new post office at Waite's Farm. This had grown out of his unsuccessful campaign against Brattleboro's tram. Since he had claimed that travelling into town would be dangerous, it was logical he should attempt to cut out such journeys and establish an independent community, with its own post office, at the intersection of the road from his house with the main Brattleboro highway. With the help of his new friend, the Washington lawyer William Hallett Phillips, his request was granted by the Fourth Assistant Postmaster-

General in June. Surprised to find that a bureaucracy could act quickly and sensibly, he told Phillips it was the first time in his life that he had ever felt benevolent to members of a government department ('as a journalist in India of course I fought 'em on principle,' he said, with an element of wishful thinking).[62] Thereafter, he proudly headed his letters: Naulakha, Waite, Windham County, Vermont.

Since the interior of his house remained unfinished, Rudyard called on Lockwood de Forest who, although no longer in formal partnership, was still associated with the glass designer Louis Tiffany. Along with rugs and other knick-knacks, de Forest had already supplied two Tiffany stained-glass windows for the writer's study. Now Rudyard asked if Tiffany could mould a globe to case an old candle-hanging light that had long been in the Balestier family.[63] (As a present he sent de Forest some maple syrup from Beatty's farm.) While he had been away his Uncle Ned had sent four paintings, which he had to collect from Molly Cabot who had been looking after them.

To mark the annual visit of the Episcopalian Bishop Hill at the end of April, Molly was invited to lunch. She was amused to hear the Bishop of Vermont refusing Rudyard's request to baptise Josephine on the grounds that this should be done by the local vicar. Bishop Hill referred disapprovingly (to Molly) about his host's 'presumption', while Rudyard later spoke unfavourably of the British-born prelate's ecumenicism, attributing it to his Cowley Father training, which he equated with the Jesuits, and telling a correspondent, 'Let us "discourage enthusiasm and preach the Church of England", as the old order ran.'[64] Josephine seemed to agree, screaming, 'Take him away! I don't like Bishunts!' A sense of Rudyard's swagger drifted across the Atlantic when the newly knighted Sir Walter Besant made a tongue-in-cheek call for him to be given a peerage: 'Lord Brattleboro of Vermont would, methinks, sound well.'

Washington had given Rudyard the impetus to complete one important piece of work. He had been wanting to write a definitive story about India and had toyed with an idea (which he admitted was improper) about a fat civil servant who, after being shot in the backside by a poisoned arrow, had the wound sucked by his devoted assistant. He did not proceed with this saga, which was open to misinterpretation, opting instead for the tale of William Martyn, an English girl keeping house for her brother in India. Having stated she likes men 'who do things', William accompanies her brother to the scene of a famine, where she falls in love with the tireless Scott of the Irrigation Department, and takes on his work when he falls ill with a fever. As far as Rudyard was able, the story is a grudging generic tribute to the 'new woman' but, not surprisingly, it is hardly a feminist tract: as with Maisie, William looks and acts like a boy and, like Ted Hill, who has been suggested as a model, carries a boy's name. Yet Carrie was delighted: '[Rudyard] has got the hang of quite a new sort of woman,' she confided to her diary, 'and she is turning out stunningly.'[65] Her unusually ebullient reaction suggests that she had convinced him, at the end of long-running domestic discussions, that this kind of female could, unlike Kate Sheriff in *The Naulahka*, play a useful role in the running of a country such as India. Within five days of starting the story (titled 'William the Conqueror') on 20 March, Rudyard was offering it to Edward Bok for use in the December issue (a full nine months thence) of *Ladies' Home Journal* at a price of $140 per thousand words. Having thoughtfully added a Christmas scene, complete with carol, at the end, he told Bok, 'I think the story ought to give your women readers a little notion of a woman's life where life is rather trying.'[66] In this sense it was not only about India, but also a contribution to the political debate in the United States – albeit he exposed his usual difficulties in writing about women as independent, let alone sexual, beings. To him, they could only be helpmeets in the common glorious enterprise of work.

Nearly four years after his last visit to India, Rudyard was feeling nostalgic for the sub-continent. He had been trying to write his story about a boy, Kim o' the Rishti, who 'went to the River of

Healing'[67] (he had promised it to the *St Nicholas* again the previous September), but the subject matter continued to elude him. Now – prodded perhaps by Carrie – he may have felt the need to refresh his sense of its place. He had mentioned bringing his Mulvaney stories to a conclusion in a letter to Ripley Hitchcock in January, and he referred to a series of Jungle Tales (perhaps a third *Jungle Book*) – the first of which, 'The Manx Cat', he sent to Watt for publication in the *Pall Mall Gazette* in June, though with the slight change of title to 'The Maltese Cat'). He informed people of his plans to go to India in the autumn: a report to that effect made its way into the *Vermont Phoenix* and he even proposed to *Cosmopolitan* magazine that he should write a dozen letters describing the land from the point of view of one for whom it was 'home'. Mark Twain promised to repay Rudyard's visit to him in Elmira in 1889, adding in cod Anglo-Indian: 'I shall arrive next January and you must be ready. I shall come riding my ayah with his tusks adorned with silver bells and ribbons and escorted by a troop of native howdahs richly clad and mounted upon a herd of wild bungalows. And you must be on hand with a few bottles of ghee, for I shall be thirsty.'[68] But then suddenly in June Rudyard's journey was called off. Instead, he and Carrie made a short (one-month) trip to England, leaving their two-year-old Josephine with her grandmother Anna Balestier, and aunt, also Josephine, at the Fairview Inn in East Gloucester, Massachusetts.

The main reason for the change of plan was that Carrie was pregnant again. It also coincided with a deterioration in Rudyard's relationship with his brother-in-law. Beatty objected to the Kiplings' attempts to cut back the grass in front of Naulakha and to build a sunken garden, believing he had an agreement that this land should be left unmown for his animals to graze. The crunch came at the end of June when Beatty, as foreman of the works, sought to settle his regular accounts. He was $145 overdrawn, having used house funds to support his own life-style.

Rudyard's mood was not improved when, passing through Boston on the Fourth of July, he was subjected to unnerving

American triumphalism. (He should have known this was unlikely to be an Anglophile environment, particularly with the crowds agitated by the Venezuelan border dispute and, as Carrie noted in her diary, with the fireworks only adding to the 'horror'.) As a gesture of friendship, Henry Adams offered to share his deck-suite on the luxury transatlantic liner *New York*, since Rudyard initially appeared to have been travelling on his own. But the offer was declined: Rudyard said he had work to finish. The Washington gossip factory was not convinced. William Hallett Phillips, the Washington lawyer who had secured Rudyard his post office, told John Hay, 'He blamed it on his proof, but I think he was not proof against the reproofs or blandishments of the wife, as he ended by taking another steamer and the wife too.'[69] In the event, Rudyard and Carrie sailed from Hoboken on the less salubrious German ship *Saale* on 9 July.

Arriving in Southampton five days later, Rudyard found himself pitched into the last few days of a fierce general election campaign. With his political antennae sensitised by his time in Washington, he took more interest than usual in the issues. He did not need explanations that important changes were taking place. The polls confirmed Lord Salisbury's imperially orientated Conservatives in power with a large majority. Following the break-up of Gladstone's coalition over Home Rule for Ireland the previous year, an era of Liberal ascendancy had passed. Now, with the single-minded former Liberal Unionist Joseph Chamberlain at the Colonial Office, London could be expected to pursue a more robust policy towards its colonial possessions – in particular in South Africa, where support for the beleaguered British minority in the Boer republic of Transvaal would lead to the bungled Jameson Raid at the end of the year. As Chamberlain stated unequivocally in his first speech to the House of Commons, 'I believe in the British Empire and I believe in the British race.'

London was full of Americans which, for some reason, Rudyard found amusing.[70] At the beginning and end of his trip, he and Carrie stayed in their original honeymoon suite at Brown's Hotel,

which enabled him to see all his Poynter and Burne-Jones relations. As if he were not already aware, the new government's
aggressive nationalism was not favoured by his Uncle Ned and
Aunt Georgie. At his son Phil's insistence, Uncle Ned had sheepishly accepted a baronetcy from the departing Liberals. But he told
his studio assistant T. M. Rooke that he disliked the materialism of
the new jingoists. 'I love the immaterial in English achievements,'
he said, adding, 'Let's have no more dominant races, we don't
want them.' On the day after the election, Rudyard found time to
meet Aubrey Beardsley, still smarting from his *Yellow Book* row.
He doubtless took up the story six days later when, visiting his
parents in Wiltshire and staying at the Bennett Arms in Tisbury,
he and Carrie dined with the Percy Wyndhams and the Marchioness of Queensberry, whose son and now divorced husband
had been the cause of Oscar Wilde's downfall. Doubtless, there
was political gossip: George Wyndham, still an MP, was married
to Sibell Grosvenor, a former lover of George Curzon, who had
just been appointed Under-Secretary at the Foreign Office. And
Rudyard might have let slip that he had been sounded out as Poet
Laureate – a notable honour for someone still in his early thirties.
But he had declined to take on the mantle last worn by Lord
Tennyson, and the post passed to the lacklustre Alfred Austin.
Lockwood Kipling was working flat out to complete his drawings
for the *Second Jungle Book* (published in England in November
with an advance order of 35,000) and Rudyard was so delighted
with his efforts that he could only stand behind his father 'and
ask for more'.[71]

   Returning to Vermont on 23 August, Rudyard was pleased to
find that Howard had kept Naulakha in excellent condition and
even more so that his naturalist friend Ripley Hitchcock, from
Appleton's, had sent a book to help him identify birds on his
property. Over the next three weeks he played the amateur orni-
thologist, as he explored the woods around him. 'What bird is it
that nips off aster buds for fun and then laughs at you?'[72] he asked
his mentor.

He was helped in his research by William Hallett Phillips, who passed through Brattleboro *en route* between staying with John Hay in New Hampshire and his own home in Washington. Phillips was the sort of well-rounded polymath who always fascinated Rudyard; as well as a lawyer, he was a writer, outdoorsman and specialist in American-Indian culture. Rudyard liked him best of all the people he had met in the capital, as he conveyed in his letter of invitation,

> Come and we will sit still, enjoying Kif together, – considering the ways of man and the land which Allah has made. When there is a need to speak we will speak together. When there is need to be silent we will cease speaking and lie upon our bellies upon the warm rocks.[73]

For his help over the post office, Rudyard dubbed Phillips 'Sitting Fox', one of the 'Trues', the North American Indian gods, and warned him he would have to help Josephine build a wigwam because he himself could not 'put two boughs together without their falling down'.[74]

The early September evenings at Naulakha were cold enough to require a fire. By its warmth, Rudyard read Phillips what he described as the last of his Jungle Tales, as well as another story, 'How Tabitka Killed the Seals', which he had written as a tribute but which seems to have been lost. During the day Phillips would 'hear Kipling's voice challenging me to go forth' and the two men would make their way to the 'jungle' near his house. 'Into it we crawl,' Phillips noted, 'and I listen to what the Master of the Jungle tells; and what talk! . . . What a wonder that fellow is! What felicity and what fecundity!'[75] Rudyard, for his part, made the most of Phillips's knowledge of the countryside. When his guest told him that the frogs in a stream were good to eat, they 'went out after them with a pistol and a small Marlin repeater. Result 22 pairs of legs.' For Hay, Rudyard sketched a picture of an intrepid Phillips 'raking in the water for a body. You'd think it was bears at least'.[76]

To Ripley Hitchcock he reported, 'I've been out getting frogs legs in a marsh stream and very nearly dropped my hand twice on an adder!'[77] Here was a man who was thoroughly enjoying himself.

Back in his study, puffing on his briar pipe, Rudyard had already started work on a 'story of dream life'[78] (as Carrie put it), rather at variance from his recent output, almost as if he were defying readers' efforts to typecast him. 'The Brushwood Boy' tells of the conventional upbringing of a young army officer, George Cottar, who throughout his early life enjoys the distraction, pleasure and sometimes terror of a recurring dream sequence. This usually had two main features: he would enter and leave his dream along a beach road that ran past a pile of brushwood to a lamp-post and there was a beautiful girl in the background to whom he gave the name Annie*an*louise. Returning from India, Cottar meets a girl whom he instantly recognises. When he talks with her he learns that she has had similar dreams and is indeed the girl in his own visions. The autobiographical elements of the story are striking: banished to a nursery in the far west wing of an English country house, Cottar starts weaving his own worlds at the age of six. In his later 'Brazilian Sketches', Rudyard recalled how, as a child, he had once wandered into a Fifth Quarter of the World where everything was 'different from all previous knowledge'; in 'The Brushwood Boy', Cottar finds himself in 'a sixth quarter of the world, beyond the most remote imaginings of man'. But his flights of fancy are repressed during the course of a regular English public-school education that does 'not encourage dreaming'.

In India Cottar spurns contact with older, usually married, women, preferring to keep himself for the girl, literally, of his dreams. During his fantasy voyages he has to run the gauntlet of spirits he describes as 'They', 'Them' or 'It', which can prove either comforting, frightening, or, in the case of a laughing duck, merely bizarre. Having completed these journeys of discovery, he returns to England to find his other half (in Jungian terms, his anima). In a reprise of Rudyard's 'The Dream of Duncan Parrenness' eleven years earlier, Cottar is then ready for the business of manhood, the propagation of the race with a young woman who, in an intriguing twist, is called, outside of the reverie, not Annie or Louise but by the unambiguous Jewish name Miriam.

The autograph manuscript of this story in the J. P. Morgan Library in New York shows that Rudyard cut a section in which Cottar asks the regimental doctor in India about his dreams and is told,

> Oh that's easy enough. You've got two sides to your brain, you see, and they ought to work together but they don't always. One side gets a fraction of a second in front with a thought specially when you're half asleep and your reason, you see, isn't at work.

Perhaps he thought this was too didactic: in October he admonished Sarah Orne Jewett, a New England writer he admired, for spelling things out in a story, 'and I loathe an explanation'.[79] He certainly did not offer much help in relation to 'The Brushwood Boy'. However, his clear description of the Tisbury landscape and his use of Wiltshire names such as Morrison and Bassett suggest that, as in the previous year, his time in England helped him work out pressing issues. Watching his contented father and his wife carrying his baby (was it to be the son everyone said he longed for?), he reflected deeply about his upbringing (and particularly his school years) and concluded that a complete man needs to strike a balance between his masculine achieving and feminine imaginative sides. As he later would boast, he himself had two sides to his head – something for which he thanked the Lord or, as he put it with a typical flourish, Allah.

Having completed the story on 8 September, Rudyard sent it to *Century Magazine*, asking $170 per thousand words. (His fees had been leaping up.) Since it was accepted for the *Century*'s Christmas issue, he even allowed the editor, Gilder, in deference to squeamish readers, to alter the boil on Cottar's thumb to a cut. (Usually, he refused such petty censorship, as when Bok at *Ladies'*

Home Journal wanted to remove scenes referring to alcohol in 'William the Conqueror'.)

According to Carrie's diaries,[80] the original title for 'The Brushwood Boy' was 'The Infants of Bohemia', which provides a clue to the story's provenance, helping explain why, when Rudyard seemed involved with other more weighty issues, he turned his attention to a story of psychic communication. For the previous autumn, over Thanksgiving, he had been visited by the pugnacious Anglo-Irish author Arthur Conan Doyle, who was accompanied by his brother Innes, a second-lieutenant in the Royal Artillery. Doyle was in the middle of an American lecture tour (a means of promotion the commercially minded but more retiring Rudyard had always scorned). As autodidacts, the two authors had a remarkably similar range of interests. They had moved in the same circles in London at the start of the decade, but they had never been close – despite the fact that they shared the same agent, A. P. Watt, and Doyle had been an early client of the syndication services of both Wolcott Balestier and Sam McClure. (Doyle's appreciation of Wolcott in the *Pall Mall Gazette* was particularly warm, praising the American's 'power and delicacy in conversation ... felicity of expression and ... quickness of sympathy'.[81]) Perhaps they saw themselves as rivals and an element of this tetchiness survives in Rudyard's comments to Robert Barr about Doyle's eagerness 'to explain his burning love for the [United States] and its Institutions at $1 a love – reserved loves $2' and in Doyle's initial unwillingness to visit Naulakha because he said he felt 'raw' at Rudyard's failure to answer a couple of his letters. 'We're a rummy lot, we children of the ink-pot,' Rudyard commented sagely to Barr, a recent guest.[82]

When they did meet at Naulakha, they argued about America. Doyle was an unreconstructed Americanophile, having dedicated his 1891 novel *The White Company* 'To the Hope of the Future, the Reunion of the English Speaking Races This little Chronicle of our common Ancestry is inscribed'. Rudyard liked this idea, but remained sceptical; Doyle had to beg him, 'For God's sake, let's stop talking about spittoons.' But other subject matter would have drawn the two men together – Southsea (where Doyle had practised as a doctor), photography, drugs and, in particular, the paranormal. A member of the Society for Psychical Research, Doyle was fascinated with experiments in telepathy. It would have been just like Rudyard to nod recognition towards Doyle in his title 'The Infants of Bohemia' (Doyle's 'A Scandal in Bohemia' had been the first of his stories agented by A. P. Watt) and then to change his mind. By the end of Doyle's short stay the two men were getting on famously. They relaxed by playing the newly fashionable game of golf. Doyle had clearly benefited financially from his American lecture tour. As a gesture of thanks, he later sent Rudyard a gift of some skis, so he could try another form of exercise.

When the New England leaves began to turn, all sorts of people discovered a liking for Naulakha hospitality, however limited it might be. During the autumn of 1895 the Kiplings played host to Owen Wister, Mrs Pen Browning ('wife of the bad son of a good father', Rudyard noted, referring to his idol Robert Browning), Kay Robinson, his old *CMG* colleague, and Frank N. Doubleday, a large, genial young man, who came from Scribner's, the publisher, to discuss a collected edition of his works. Charles Eliot Norton and his family were now great friends, so there was regular two-way traffic between Naulakha and both Shady Hill, his delightful fifty-acre estate in Cambridge, and Ashfield, his summer retreat in north-west Massachusetts.

In his avuncular way, Charles Norton was concerned that Rudyard, with his new-found interest in politics, should remain in touch with developments in England. Lockwood Kipling told his friend not to worry: Rudyard preferred to keep his distance from metropolitan life. 'There is undoubtedly a freer outlook from America for a man who prefers to think for himself than from London.'[83] Nevertheless, Norton insisted on sending his second-hand copies of *The Times* to Naulakha, where Rudyard kept himself informed, at a time of rising international tension, on the debate about the ties Britain should develop with her colonies. The idea of imperial federation, the sort of thing that had appealed to W. E. Henley, was giving way to the principles of the British Empire League, founded in 1894, which 'put more stress on voluntary co-operation, better communications and the augmentation of inter-imperial trade than upon the federal ideal'.[84]

Rudyard had reflected this debate in his poems about his country's relationship with the sea, notably in 'A Song of the English'. Now, in late September 1895, with the debate moving on to the issue of whether Britain's colonies should help defray the costs of the Royal Navy, he pitched in with some rousing propagandist verses, 'The Native-Born', which hailed the common heritage and purpose of the English-speaking peoples. He might have published them in the *Pall Mall Gazette* (a regular outlet for his poetry), or kept them for his forthcoming book *The Seven Seas*, but Norton insisted he aim higher and send them to *The Times*. Moberly Bell replied enthusiastically, despite admitting some editorial hesitation because the paper had never 'published a poem not written in relation to any one definite event before'. Rudyard replied that this was ridiculous: he had followed the colonial navy question closely and though he might be a 'verse-writer by accident', he was 'a journalist by education'. At least Bell agreed to Rudyard's request that, since 'The Native-Born' was written with 'A Moral Object', he should be rewarded with a free subscription, rather than the usual cash fee.[85] Not only would Rudyard remain well-informed, but his habit of sending poems to *The Times* on national issues had begun.

However, there were more pressing matters at home. As the year drew to a close, it was clear that the problem of Beatty remained. Unfairly, Carrie the 'dragon' was seen locally as the villain of the piece. Embarrassed by her hard-drinking hick of a brother and eager always to protect her husband's peace of mind, she upbraided Beatty at every opportunity and refused to bail him out financially. Since this was not how close-knit Vermont families were expected to behave, it only exacerbated the general criticism of her stuffy 'English' ways. Grace Holbrook, Molly Cabot's sister, who was close to Beatty's wife Mai, went further. 'Perhaps Carrie K. is partly (or wholly) insane,' she told Molly on 24 October. 'It is the most charitable conclusion to arrive at concerning her.'

Rudyard's feeling that he was among hostile natives was not alleviated when, towards the end of December, the transatlantic row over the border between British Guiana and Venezuela suddenly escalated. He had seen this coming since July, when Washington had sent an official note warning that any attempt to alter this boundary would be considered a violation of the Monroe Doctrine, its codified prescription to prevent foreign powers meddling in its 'backyard'. With Lord Salisbury rejecting all offers of arbitration, an ugly tiff threatened between the two main Anglo-Saxon powers. Partly to diffuse this tension Rudyard had written 'The Native-Born', with its emphasis on the common destiny of English-speaking peoples. But, inspired by President Cleveland, who sought to take a leaf out of his Republican opponents' book and to play the nationalistic card in the run-up to his own elections, the United States bandar-log was unmoved by the poet's fine words. Instead, it turned up its anti-British rhetoric. Rudyard was appalled at the number of Americans who endorsed the German Kaiser William's letter of support to President Kruger of the Transvaal, following Dr Starr Jameson's abortive raid which started on 29 December, the eve of Rudyard's thirtieth birthday. Genuinely fearing he might have to leave Vermont quickly and flee across the border into Canada (he told Charles Norton he had at least provided for the pregnant Carrie with the house and his copyrights), he penned two more poems, which struck a pained patriotic note.

One was the angry, dirge-like 'Hymn Before Action', which anticipated the better-known 'Recessional', written the following year, in appealing to an old-fashioned God, three parts Old Testament wrath to one part New Testament compassion, who is the special deity of the British Empire. This poem was based on the Church of England hymn 'The Church's One Foundation', which had originally been composed by S. J. Stone thirty years earlier as a statement of Anglican unity in the face of Bishop Colenso of Natal's controversial doubts about the historical truth of the Bible. As Peter Keating has pointed out, 'Kipling's use of religious language seems to have little theological or doctrinal meaning: rather, it serves to establish an appropriately solemn tone and a set of values that is crucial to the maintenance of "the Law". When Kipling addresses the British people in this way, he is not calling on them to be more religious, but to be true civilising imperialists. That involves, centrally, the application of Christian principles and the exercise of religious tolerance.' It was another of Rudyard's contradictions that, as an agnostic, he could so easily stir British sentiment with an appeal to an outdated mid-Victorian religiosity.[86]

The second poem, 'Et Dona Ferentes', written in easier, more colloquial style, also referred to the Englishman's inherent qualities, but these were rather different – his capacity, for all his lack of emotion, to strike when riled by any of the 'pentecostal crew' of foreigners:

> Oh, my country, bless the training that from cot to castle
> runs –
> The pitfall of the stranger but the bulwark of thy sons –
> Measured speech and ordered action, sluggish soul and
> unperturbed,
> Till we wake our Island-Devil – nowise cool for being curbed!

In one of his more famous lines, Rudyard counselled people to beware when his country grew polite. He sent both poems to English newspapers, but while the *Pall Mall Gazette* was happy to print 'Et Dona Ferentes', *The Times* sat on 'Hymn Before Action', considering it too provocative in circumstances that had not reached a state of war.

Perhaps Rudyard should have taken note of his comment to Henry Norman, a well-connected English journalist who had reviewed his own writings favourably in the *Daily Chronicle*. Norman was that creature of the moment, a Liberal Unionist turned eager imperialist. At the beginning of the year, he had been thinking of starting an imperialist magazine, to be called, tentatively, *The Seven Seas* (later, actually, *The World's Work*) – both meaningful names to Kipling enthusiasts. Rudyard declined an offer to edit this periodical, but did counsel Norman, 'You don't want to preach Imperialism. It has to be sweated into the system or injected hypodermically same as I have occasionally managed to do.'[87]

That very month, early on 2 February 1896, at the height of Rudyard's anguish over events which threatened to destroy his ideas of English-speaking co-operation, the Kiplings' second daughter, Elsie, was born at Naulakha. Weighing a healthy nine and a half pounds, she was (in accordance with Kipling family tradition) given a name sometimes used by her grandmother Alice. In telling Molly Cabot that mother and baby were well, Rudyard added, in the plaintive way his father used to address Edith Plowden, 'Wish you'd come up some afternoon and play with *me*. You see I can't go far away and we could snowshoe or something.'[88]

As an escape from his responsibilities, Rudyard took to cycling and playing golf (one memorable game in the snow required the use of red balls). Having rejected a further plea from Heinemann in connection with his 'woman book' with the words, 'In regard to the work on the Other Sex my advice to you is: go swiftly and get married and if after four years you feel able to explain even the fringe of its many mysteries, I will buy all the edition before publication',[89] and having decided to abandon *Kim* until he could call on his father's help, he turned his attention in mid-February to *Captains Courageous*, an extended story about fishermen operating out of Gloucester, Massachusetts. Luckily, his main source, forty-four-year-old Dr James Conland, was often in the house attending to Carrie and the baby. As a young man, Conland had worked on fishing boats on the Grand Banks, a shallow area of the North Atlantic, 300 miles south-east of Newfoundland. He had come to Brattleboro in 1875, working initially in a drug store, before taking a medical degree at the University of Vermont and becoming an old-fashioned country doctor. He told Rudyard of his experiences (which led to criticism that the ensuing book was at least twenty years out of date). The two men travelled to Gloucester, once taking a boat from Boston – a voyage which hardly registered on Rudyard's mind as he was violently seasick. Before long he had enough material for a 50,000-word story about Harvey Cheyne, the spoilt son of a shipping and railroad millionaire who, after falling off an ocean liner near the Grand Banks, is picked up by a fishing vessel out of Gloucester. Because the *We're Here*, a seventy-ton two-masted schooner, is at sea for several months, Harvey has no option but to change his brattish ways and learn (reluctantly at first) to play his part as a responsible crew member. While paying tribute to the professional skills of the sailors who operate an old-fashioned, soon to be superseded vessel, Rudyard shows how involvement in the shared ritual of work makes a man of young Harvey.

Rudyard was thrilled with his achievement when he wrote to his friend Robert Barr on 11 March:

> I'm most [*sic*] through with my first genuine out and out American story – a long one – ... and oh Rrrobert it is a beauty. You'll hear the continent sit up as one man over it and the band will begin to play ... It raises no questions, it doesn't criticise. There's no one in it. It's plain narrative done from the inside and I'll give a year's growth to publish anonymous. It's a corker – ... I'm sinfully proud of it. This in confidence because I always told you I would write a tale.

Rudyard's excited comments showed the importance he attached to writing a 'tale' that went beyond his usual length: after the disappointment of *The Light that Failed* and the curiosity of *The Naulahka*, *Mother Maturin* had been forgotten and *Kim* shelved until he could work on it with his father. But here was something he was proud to offer in their place. Although it would never have the literary impact he hoped, it skilfully conveyed his own ambivalence about America – no more so than in the contrast between the efficiency of the railroads that bring the ruthless Harvey Cheyne Senior across the United States from San Diego and the old-fashioned camaraderie of the fishermen.

As a treat, in mid-March Rudyard took his growing family for a month's stay at the Laurel House, a small luxury hotel in the fashionable resort of Lakewood, New Jersey, close to their friends the Catlins, in Morristown. While there, he met Joseph Pulitzer, the flamboyant proprietor of the *New York World*, who offered him his best wordage rate yet – $1000 for 1000 words on the subject 'Why America could not conquer England'. But, taking his cue from *The Times*, Rudyard decided that tub-thumping nationalism was inappropriate at this stage and declined prissily, saying that acceptance of the commission would involve discussing the armed strength of the Empire, 'a question on which no British subject has any information for sale'. Instead, he offered a light-hearted poem, 'How Breitman Became President on the Bicycle Ticket', which, while enthusing about his latest pursuit of bicycling, landed some punches about the populist nature of American politics.

Rudyard and Carrie had only been back from their short spring holiday for eight days when their dispute with Beatty came to a head. A couple of months earlier, Beatty had been threatened with financial ruin when two local firms, Crosby and Company, and Pratt, Wright and Company, petitioned him for insolvency. Carrie, at her most schoolmarmish, pressed her mother to join her in refusing to make further payments on Beatty's Maplewood mortgage, which they had both guaranteed. News of this gambit got back to Beatty through his sister Josephine who had tried to remain neutral. To Beatty and his wife Mai, this seemed to confirm that the acquisitive Carrie was determined to get them out of their farm. Only recently, she and Rudyard had offered to buy Maplewood and look after Mai and young Marjorie if Beatty would leave town for a year to dry out and find a job. But to the young Balestiers this had smacked of typical Kipling arrogance and insensitivity.

Now, in early May, Beatty was convinced that Rudyard had been discussing his financial affairs with people in Brattleboro. The brothers-in-law next met in woods to the south of Bliss Farm. Rudyard had just fallen off his bicycle and was picking himself up, when Beatty drove up in his buggy and shouted that he wanted to talk to his brother-in-law. 'If you have anything to say, say it to my lawyer,' replied the crumpled Rudyard. Beatty, who was drunk and flustered, did not consider this the Vermont way of doing things and exploded (for effect, it is best to keep the censored text of the contemporary report in the *Vermont Phoenix*), 'By *****, this is no case for lawyers. If you don't retract those ***** lies, I will punch the ***** soul out of you. I will give you a week in which to retract, and if you don't, I will blow your ***** brains out.' When Rudyard answered, 'You will only have yourself to blame for the consequences,' Beatty saw this as another attack and bawled out, 'Do you mean to threaten me, you *****.'

Rudyard, who claimed he feared for his life, immediately contacted his lawyer, State Attorney C. C. Fitts, who filed a complaint, which led to Beatty's arrest three days later by Sheriff Starkey for 'assault with indecent and opprobrious names and epithets and threatening to kill'. The case attracted considerable media interest, and journalists came to Brattleboro from New York and Boston for the hearing the following week. They met Beatty, who turned on his formidable charm and befriended eager reporters over drinks. Up at Naulakha it was a different story: when one newspaperman arrived at the Kiplings' unannounced, he was unceremoniously ejected by a servant. By 12 May, the day of the hearing, Beatty, sensing he was winning a public-relations battle, had rediscovered his composure and swagger. Had he threatened the distinguished author, Mr Rudyard Kipling? Justice William S. Newton asked. Indeed he had; with a licking. Beatty's bluster was matched by Rudyard at his most elusive. As a result, the proceedings deteriorated into farce. The reporter of the *Boston Daily Globe* noted, after hearing Rudyard repeat Beatty's threats, 'This sounds serious and dangerous, but when the manner of the speaker is jovial and even humorous, when he winks to by-standers and laughs at the jests of counsel, one gathers the impression of a consummate actor rehearsing his part in a farce comedy.' And he added, as a member of the Beatty fan club, 'There is a feeling here ... and notwithstanding the numerous debts which Beatty owes to local tradesmen, he is the more manly man of the two.'

When, towards the end of the day, the judge asked for a bond, pending a further hearing, Beatty said he was not prepared to pay it. The judge then said he might have to send him to jail and Beatty, understanding the embarrassment this would cause Rudyard, asked for an hour's freedom to take his wife and young child home. At this stage Rudyard jumped up and offered to pay his brother-in-law's bail. But Beatty refused to accept this offer: eventually his lawyer posted his surety for $800 and a new hearing was set for September. Rudyard retired to Naulakha dejected: although he had won the legal skirmish, he had lost the battle. The following day Carrie's diary recorded, 'Rud a total wreck. Sleeps all the time. Dull, listless and weary. These are dark days for us.'[90] Over the next three months he completed some poems (including 'The "Mary Gloster"' about a tough, self-made shipping magnate preparing to hand over to his cultured son, educated at 'Harrer an' Trinity College', like Rudyard's cousin Stanley Baldwin, in similar circumstances at his family iron manufacturing firm); after receiving identical offers for *Captains Courageous* of $10,000 from both the *Century Magazine* and *McClure's Magazine*, he opted for the latter, which contracted to pay in gold dollars.[91] He then went on a fishing holiday with Lockwood de Forest in Newfoundland.

But, despite the support of people who mattered to him, such as Dr Conland, Rudyard could not throw off his feeling of list-lessness. Still believing his life was in danger, he chose to spend his *Captains Courageous* windfall on a new $10,000 life insurance policy on 1 July. After his exposure in a Brattleboro court room, he felt he could never raise his head in the town again. Having already taken measures to leave America, if only temporarily, it was not difficult to speed up arrangements and make them more permanent. In late August he finished packing Naulakha and left Howard in charge. Then, proceeding via the Catlins' in Morris-town, he and his family boarded the s.s. *Lahn* at Hoboken on 1 September, bound for Southampton. It was a week before the hearing was to have resumed and the papers again had a field day.

Shortly before the Kiplings left Brattleboro, Molly Cabot had visited them to say goodbye. Carrie was in tears and Rudyard 'seemed frozen with misery. He said it was the hardest thing he had ever had to do, that he loved Naulakha. I spoke of the touch of Autumn already on the distant hills – as he put me in the carriage – which brought the tears to his eyes. His last words, in a tone of piercing sadness, were, "Yes! 'tis the Fall. Goodbye, Miss Cabot!" '[92] Rudyard, for all his intelligence, had made a fatal error in the fourth dimension.

Twelve

Sobering Down

1896–1899

Returning to England in September 1896, Rudyard might have been expected to settle close to his parents and to spend his growing fortune on a substantial country property, with access to the caste-based life-style he had admired on visits to Tisbury during the previous two summers. But he was not in good mental shape. Although relieved to be home, he also felt defeated and dejected: his efforts to forge a new life for himself in the United States had come to nothing.

As a result, he was in no condition for decision making and left it to Carrie to arrange where they should live. She opted for the village of St Marychurch, near Torquay in Devon, the family home of Edmund Gosse's stepmother Eliza. If Rudyard had considered this, he might have objected. (He never liked Gosse, describing him as 'a dish I love not' later in the year.) But Carrie, in her role as domestic 'fixer', had carte blanche to contact her best friend in England, Gosse's wife Nellie. Plucked reluctantly from the bosom of her family, Carrie had no desire to live too near her prickly mother-in-law Alice, but she needed a place that would engage Rudyard's interest. The sea won out over the land.

The Rock House was an imposing mid-Victorian grey stone building, at the top of reddish sandstone cliffs, which dropped to the waters of the English Channel two hundred feet below. In the other direction the house looked over the rolling green expanses of Dartmoor. But the view that mattered was the one from Rudyard's study which, he explained,[1] gave the illusion of hovering on the decks of fishing craft as they came in to shore to tend their lobster pots. He and Carrie could 'sit like swallows on a telegraph wire', gazing over Tor Bay to the promontory of Portland Bill, sixty miles away. A steep, narrow lane ran down, a mile away, to a small, enclosed bay, which gave Rudyard that powerful sense of English nautical history he had felt when visiting Lulworth Cove a couple of years before. It was the sort of landing spot pirates would have used earlier in the century. Yet, strangely, enclosed by cliffs, with its rich red soil and vivid green vegetation down to the sea, it had a tropical atmosphere. The locals called this part of the world the 'English Riviera' and when it rained, as it frequently did, Rudyard laughed at their pretension. But at other times he understood, particularly when, in early October, little Josephine complained, 'This England is stuffy.'

Taking up from where he left off in Gloucester, Massachusetts, Rudyard set to learning about the nitty-gritty details of British seafaring. He was rewarded with tales of derring-do on the high seas when he visited the Royal Navy's training school, HMS *Britannia*, twelve miles down the coast at Dartmouth. He had an opportunity in late September to go out to sea in a destroyer, but a heavy storm blew up, damaging several boats, and he was thankful, with his history of seasickness, that he had declined. A visit to Plymouth to observe the steam trials of a new warship was similarly postponed because of the weather. But he was able to wander round the harbour at Torquay, where the captain of a ten-ton rigged cutter offered to take him (and his father who was visiting) out to his usual fishing grounds – a mere three weeks' sailing away (shades of the *We're Here*). Rudyard was so concerned at the way the sailors' hands had been gashed by ropes that he wrote to Dr Conland asking him to send a pair of 'nippers', the protective mittens used by fishermen in New England. Hearing someone speak French, he tried out the language and found he was talking to a sailor delivering potatoes from Jersey in a neat black ketch that he felt had 'smuggler' written all over it. (Torquay itself Rudyard did not like. In keeping with his new-found country-house view of the world, he thought that the town's seaside gentility was 'smugly British' – so much so that he wanted to dance naked in its streets, with only pink feathers to preserve his modesty.)[2]

As for work, Rudyard was determined not to burn himself out – the cause of his undoing in 1889–90. Apart from familiarising himself with the English nautical tradition, he had no all-engrossing literary project. He signed off the proofs of *Captains Courageous* and advised Frank Doubleday at Scribner's on the packaging of his collected Outward Bound edition (a gold elephant head medallion, photographed from an original drawing by Lockwood Kipling, was used as frontispiece to each of eleven volumes). Having finalised poems for *The Seven Seas*, he was delighted at the response when the book was published in November (by Methuen in London and Appleton in New York). In Britain, 22,000 copies were sold prior to publication and the reviews were almost universally favourable, including one in *Atlantic Monthly* by sixty-nine-year-old Charles Norton who wrote, 'This splendid continuous fertility of English genius, this unbroken expression of English character and life from Chaucer to Rudyard Kipling, is unparalleled in the moral and intellectual history of any other race.'[3] Rudyard replied that Norton was the only man, apart from his father or Uncle Ned, whose opinion made any difference to him.

Equally intent on not repeating his Vermont mistake of living in a fortress, cut off from the community, Rudyard spent time in the pub, the Thatched Tavern, knocking back the local tipple, sloe gin, with a motley crew including a Roman Catholic priest and the sergeant instructor of the local company of volunteers (a breed of men lauded in his poem 'Pharaoh and the Sergeant', which appeared in August 1897, marking the first phase of Kitchener's campaign to wrest back control of the Sudan from the Mahdi). He accepted an invitation from the volunteers' captain to shoot rabbits on a nearby fifty-acre farm (using a ferret to flush out the warrens), but his preferred sport was fishing. While the English weather might not be ideal, it was at least good for reeling in pike and trout. 'Dry fly fishing is the kind of thing we may do when we go to Heaven if God gives us wisdom,'[4] he said enthusiastically. With Rudyard in this mood, everything seemed right: 'The land is more full of beauty than ever I had imagined. England after all *is* literature. One can't believe that the whole landscape hasn't come out of a novel.'

Carrie's new passion was cycling. No longer able to drive into Brattleboro, sitting sedately behind her horses in her red phaeton, she bought special suits from the Cyclists Touring Club. Between bouts of sickness that were possibly the first signs of her latest pregnancy, she prevailed on Rudyard to join her in forays along Devon's hilly, banked lanes, occasionally visiting Torquay's cinder-tracked velodrome, an early leisure facility for the masses. 'I spend my time doing nothing very hard – chiefly on a wheel,'[5] he claimed, not unhappily, to Dr Conland. A local tradesman recalled Rudyard careering down the long steep hill into Torquay, 'singing at the top of his voice', and on another occasion, hitting a bad rut about which he had 'spoken very strongly "and not in French"'.[6]

Otherwise the Kiplings devoted themselves to entertaining a succession of visitors – Rudyard's parents; his Aunt Edie (last heard of staying with Lockwood and Alice in Lahore and now living in spinsterish style with her sister Louisa Baldwin in Worcestershire); his cousin Florence Macdonald, who had ambitions to write; more cousins, Ambo and young Hugh Poynter; Crom Price; and, between 23 and 27 January 1897, the newly knighted Sir George Robertson, the former political agent in Gilgit, who the previous year had raised faint British hearts by stoutly resisting overwhelming native attacks in the hilly state of Chitral, at the furthest north-western reaches of British influence in the Hindu Kush.

Carrie wrote of the two men in her diary, 'They talk and talk,' and well they might. Four years earlier Robertson had visited the border state of Kafiristan, the scene of Rudyard's 'The Man Who Would Be King'. In Chitral he had clashed with the bullish Captain Francis Younghusband, who had recently published *The Relief of Chitral*, with his brother George. Rudyard was interested to hear about not just the expedition itself, but also George Curzon, who had passed through the remote kingdom during his 1895 Asian tour, and the Younghusband brothers, towards whom he had previously been cool. Francis Younghusband was now a correspondent of *The Times* in South Africa, under the wing of Rudyard's friend Moberly Bell, and a reconciliation was in the offing.

A doctor who had transferred to the sharp end of soldier-diplomacy, Robertson was hardly scintillating company. But Rudyard was reminded of the world of politics and intrigue that he had – a tribute to Carrie's management – been missing in Devon. Back in Vermont, in the summer, she had been afraid that if her husband returned to England he would become obsessed with politics. She had told Molly Cabot, 'Once there, he will become so much absorbed in the Imperial Federation and other questions of National importance that he will sacrifice his literary career to them.'[7] For a few months she had kept him from the political fleshpots. But now it became more difficult. Even on the day of Robertson's arrival, Rudyard dashed off a letter to Moberly Bell, sending what must have been a poem which, he modestly affirmed, 'though I say it, is a Beauty'. (The evidence is not clear, since it did not survive.)

Realising he was bored in Devon, Rudyard needed little encouragement to pick up his metropolitan ties. Twice in February he was in London for the best part of the week. Although there is no record of his movements, it is easy enough to work out what he was doing. The day before his first visit Crete had rebelled against its Turkish rulers. In an effort to stop Turkey being drawn into an eastern-Mediterranean war, the great powers acted smartly to prevent Crete gaining its objective of unification with Greece. Within a short time three papers had contacted Rudyard with offers to go to the area as a journalist.[8] But, with Younghusband in mind, he only wanted to work for *The Times*. As he reminded Moberly Bell, 'You promised me my choice three years ago, and there's heaps more fun in it than writing a fistful of odes.'[9]

However, the paper had specialist correspondents dealing with the conflict and Bell's attention was focused on another matter. A few days earlier Cecil Rhodes, the English-born businessman turned statesman who had masterminded the Jameson Raid at the end of 1895, had arrived in London to appear before a House of Commons select committee looking into whether Rhodes's British South Africa Company had violated the terms of its charter.

The bulky, walrus-faced Rhodes had originally made his fortune through the De Beers diamond mine in Kimberley. A clergyman's son from Bishops Stortford in Hertfordshire, his experiences in South Africa had led him, as early as 1877, to dream of 'a secret society with but one object, the furtherance of the British Empire and the bringing of the whole uncivilised world under British rule, for the recovery of the United States, for making the Anglo-Saxon race but one Empire'. However, when a decade later the economic action shifted to the gold-bearing reefs of the Witwatersrand, near Johannesburg, Rhodes's scope was limited by the awkward reality that this part of southern Africa came within the Boer republic of Transvaal. In his eagerness for new resources and new peoples to civilise, he had prevailed on the British government to grant an old-fashioned charter giving his British South Africa Company (BSAC) a free hand to the north in what are now known as Zimbabwe and Zambia. At the same time, as Prime Minister of the Cape Province since 1890, he had enjoyed a political power base from which to juggle his economic interests. But the Transvaal remained outside his influence – until he championed the cause of the 7000 (largely British) Uitlanders who had fuelled the gold boom and made Johannesburg a thriving capitalist centre at the core of an obscurantist Boer republic.

There was no doubting Rhodes's support for Dr Starr Jameson's ill-fated raid in support of a supposed Uitlander uprising. But how closely had 'e connived with the new Colonial Secretary Joseph Chamberlain? In the light of subsequent revelations in South Africa, the British government had been forced to act. Despite Ned Burne-Jones fulminating that 'Dr Jameson is a fool who should be whipped at the cart's tail and not dignified by a trial',[10] the Doctor and several of his party were brought to court and given short prison sentences, while Parliament set up a select committee to look, in particular, into whether Rhodes had violated the terms of his charter by allowing BSAC personnel to participate in the invasion of a foreign country. Rhodes had a trump card in various telegrams *The Times*'s Colonial Editor Flora Shaw and others had sent him before the raid, clearly indicating Chamberlain's support. When he threatened to reveal these, the British government backtracked. After all, what had the raid been but the furtherance of Chamberlainite imperialism by other means? Rudyard's friend, the MP George Wyndham, who had so frequently backed Rhodes in the House of Commons that he was disparagingly referred to as the 'Member for South Africa', was despatched to the Cape to make a deal. Since Rhodes had been forced to resign his Cape premiership after the raid, Wyndham had to go to 'Rhodesia' (with its capital called after the Prime Minister Lord Salisbury), where Rhodes was in what he called 'my north', suppressing a rebellion of the Ndbele people. If Rhodes could promise that his lawyer would not reveal incriminating telegrams at the inquiry, Wyndham would ensure that the BSAC's charter was safe.[11]

Not that Rhodes had much to fear in London. With its own complicity in the affair, *The Times* fêted him from the moment he arrived. As for the select committee itself, its five Conservative members included both Chamberlain and Wyndham, while its Liberals were compromised by earlier support for Rhodes. Even before 5 March, when Rhodes finished two weeks of cross-examination, Rudyard had written another poem, this time noted in Carrie's diary for 27 February: 'Rud writing verses on Mr Rhodes. Never published.'

It is hard to escape the conclusion that Rudyard had met Rhodes during his visits to London in February (perhaps also attending the select committee hearings) and had been inspired by his vision. From now on, Rudyard would never be quite the same. He had found a man who was striving on a huge scale to implement his own ideas of work and Empire. The following year, when asked what was his dream, Rudyard told Rhodes, 'You are part of it.'[12]

Until this point Rudyard had been trying to assure himself he enjoyed his desultory existence in Devon. After all, he had no pressing schedule and he was spending more time than ever with his wife. However, things were not as relaxed as they seemed. Although he still told American correspondents he missed New England, Carrie indicated his real feelings when she divulged that, in reality, she could not even inform him of her sister Josephine's engagement to Dr Theodore Dunham of New York in November 1896. As she told Molly Cabot, 'As Mr Kipling never talks of Brattleboro, or reads a letter from America, or does anything which remotely reminds him of that last year of calamity and sorrow, I have not told him this piece of family news.'[13]

Now the excitements in London, and further afield, convinced Rudyard that he was bored in Devon. Looking around for reasons, he decided the Rock House was to blame. When a cistern broke, he discovered that Carrie felt, like him, 'a gathering blackness of mind and sorrow of the heart'[14] when in the house. As a measure of their lack of communication they had been unable to admit this to one another. Rudyard looked to his Far-Eastern travels for an explanation: 'It was the Feng-shui – the Spirit of the house itself – that darkened the sunshine and fell upon us every time we entered, checking the very words on our lips.' Having been informed of an earlier suicide at the Rock House, he expanded on this feeling of psychic unease in his 1909 story 'The House Surgeon'.

But while his Macdonald sixth sense made him sensitive to his environment, he was happy to find an excuse to get away. Somehow, the English countryside had not proved quite as he expected. Reality had a nasty habit of intruding on to the unsullied pages of English literature. Carrie was not likely to stand in her husband's way: in Vermont, her two children had been born at home, with her family around, but in Devon she too felt cut off and now wanted to complete her pregnancy with people she knew, such as Rudyard's aunts.

In April 1897 the Kiplings decided to cut their losses and pay off the remainder of their one-year lease on the Rock House. The following month they moved *en famille* to London, where they took a suite in the Royal Palace Hotel overlooking Hyde Park, until they found somewhere more suitable to live.

In the intervening period Rudyard flitted between Devon and the capital. On 2 April he met Rhodes again at dinner at the Moberly Bells', where his fellow guests were Sir Alfred Milner and George Buckle, editor of *The Times*. The stiff, half-German Milner had made his name as a financial administrator in Egypt. Having established his imperialist credentials with his book *England in Egypt*, he was waiting to go to the Cape as High Commissioner but had delayed his departure to ensure that the select committee did not demand evidence from the incumbent Sir Hercules Robinson.[15] This dinner, which was recorded in Carrie's diary,[16] indicated that Rudyard was now accepted as one of the promoters of Rhodes's imperial dream.

That same day Rudyard was elected to the Athenaeum Club – then, as now, a meeting place for high-minded civil servants and establishment intellectuals. His original proposer had been his uncle, Ned Burne-Jones, and his seconder Henry James. However Sidney Colvin, keeper of prints and drawings at the British Museum, had suggested that Rudyard should be spared the normal membership procedures and invited to join under the

Club's Rule 2, which admitted distinguished people without the usual balloting, and this had been accepted.

In keeping with this new status, he took the opportunity, between house hunting, to meet the great and the good. Before the end of May he attended dinners and receptions at – *inter alia* – the Royal Academy, the Royal Society and Balliol College, Oxford, where the old India hand Sir William Wilson Hunter was a fellow. (Repaying an old debt, Rudyard introduced Hunter to A. P. Watt and helped him publish his *History of British India*.) So determined were the Balliol undergraduates to give Rudyard a standing ovation that they prevented the Master from saying grace. The meal was followed by a Bach concert, specially performed in Rudyard's honour and notable for the fact that he himself failed to mention it in his account of the evening to Conland. Classical music was not an important art in his scheme of things.

Because of his family background, he knew more about painting, but was hardly an art enthusiast. His uncle, Edward Poynter, had recently been appointed President of the Royal Academy. In recognition of the office he had been awarded a knighthood but clearly considered this not good enough. Rudyard was amused at his uncle's transparent campaign to follow Ned Burne-Jones into the baronetcy by becoming 'ex officio member of about every utterly uninteresting society in England' and spending his evenings 'eating with bores'. He himself was quite happy to attend the Academy's dinner on 30 April, when he sat next to the leading actor-impresario Sir Henry Irving and the Poet Laureate Alfred Austin, and met his old acquaintance, the sculptor Hamo Thornycroft – 'brother to *the* Thornycroft who builds torpedo-boats,' he explained to Conland, establishing his order of priorities. As a result he was invited to attend the steam trials of a new thirty-knot destroyer that the family firm of Thornycroft had built at Chatham Dock. As soon as the captain of the vessel, HMS *Foam*, pulled out of the Medway into open sea and shouted 'full steam ahead', Rudyard was astounded at the change of pace. 'I nearly fell down on the deck. The little bitch jumped from 22 to 30 like

a whipped horse – and the three hours trial had begun! It was like
a nightmare. The vibration shook not only your body but your
intestines and finally seemed to settle on your heart. I staggered
aft above the twin-screws and there saw a blue-jacket, vomiting
like a girl; and in the ward-room which is right in the stern of her,
I felt my false teeth shaking in my head!'[17] After returning to shore,
Rudyard took two days to get the 'jumps' out of his legs. (The
teeth were a result of long hours he had recently spent at the local
dentist, who cannot have improved his general health by using
arsenic dressings as pain-killers.[18])

Compared with this excitement, London was remarkably tame.
Almost as compensation, Rudyard decided to explore an interest
from his earlier days. He had liked the theatre as a boy, but had
kept a surprising, perhaps safe, distance from it when in London
prior to his marriage. Now, as evidence of his new-found sociability (he joked he was seldom without frock-coat and top hat[19]),
he accepted an invitation to the Lyceum on 28 May from the
owner, Henry Irving, who was angling for him to write a play.
From their box, the Kiplings watched Irving and his protégé Ellen
Terry in *Madame Sans-Gêne*, a drama about Napoleon written by
the thespian knight himself in an effort to upstage his rival George
Bernard Shaw's *The Man of Destiny*.

Rudyard must have noticed that, only ten days earlier, the same
theatre had witnessed a reading (to protect the dramatic rights)
of *Dracula*, a new novel about a Transylvanian vampire by Irving's
general manager Bram Stoker. Oddly, Rudyard had just composed
a poem which dealt with the same basic subject matter. He had
written 'The Vampire' to help his feckless cousin Phil Burne-
Jones, whose career had been proceeding in its usual fitful manner.
Phil had long nurtured a passion for Beatrice Tanner, the beautiful
Anglo-Italian actress who, as Mrs Patrick Campbell, had been
taken up by the Souls after her successes in the London theatre.
Phil plied her with jewellery, but she rejected him and took up
with a fellow actor, Johnston Forbes-Robertson. In response, the
jealous Phil painted a frenzied Gothic fantasy of a wasted youth,

lying on a bed, straddled in suggestively sexual manner by a wild-eyed woman with sharp teeth and dark long hair, and entered it for the tenth summer show at the New Gallery, which had usurped the Grosvenor Gallery as the fashionable place to exhibit. Rudyard seems to have agreed to write his poem as a promotional gimmick, to ensure that his cousin's painting was noticed. He himself shed no light on his motivation, the most telling, rather oblique, contemporary reference being Uncle Ned's pathetic assurance to Rooke, his studio assistant, that Rudyard had written a long poem for the New Gallery catalogue. When Rooke queried whether 'The Vampire' was really that long, Ned insisted, 'Yes, it's so long that the catalogue will consist for the most part of Ruddy's poem about Phil's picture, with a few figures and other unimportant details about the rest of the pictures. Isn't that magnificent?'[20] In fact, Rudyard's poem was short and devastating, the first three lines (out of eleven) running:

> A fool there was and he made his prayer
> (Even as you and I!)
> To a rag and a bone and hank of hair ...

To ensure the widest dissemination, it was published in the new *Daily Mail*, as well as in the Gallery catalogue. The painting itself disappeared from public view after the exhibition: it had served its purpose and Phil was not prepared to sell it. Stoker subsequently sent Phil a copy of his book when it was published on 26 May and, to add to the general incestuousness, when 'Mrs Pat' became ill later in the year she went to Tisbury to stay with Sybil, Marchioness of Queensberry. The whole affair smacked of some bizarre theatrical in-joke.

The 'Vampire' episode was all the more odd, since Rudyard was concerned with weightier matters. His meeting with Rhodes had inspired him to think expansively and in greater detail about colonial affairs. At the end of April he had penned 'Our Lady of the Snows', a propagandist poem which praised Canada for unilaterally adopting a central feature of British Colonial Secretary Joseph Chamberlain's economic protectionism, a preferential tariff for British Empire goods. The verses were slipped into *The Times* in advance of the Colonial Prime Ministers' conference in London in June. Once again, Rudyard made no charge, telling Bell, 'She comes under the head of Promiscuous and Patriotic.'[21]

Despite this modest political success, other issues still exercised Rudyard – the conflict over Crete (where Britain's navy had again proved its worth, he felt),[22] the growing threat from Germany (particularly after the bullish Alfred von Tirpitz had been appointed Naval Secretary at the beginning of June), the situation in South Africa and the continuing impasse between Britain and the United States. In March – indicative of a strategy discussed if not with Rhodes, certainly in Rhodes circles – Rudyard was already looking forward to Germany, with its pro-Boer sympathies, damaging itself by being sucked into a war in South Africa.[23] (He later called the Jameson Raid 'the first battle in the war of 14–18 – a little before its time but necessary to clear the ground'.[24]) As for America, official relations remained poor, but Rudyard hoped for an improvement, following the appointment of his friend John Hay as US Ambassador to London by the new Republican President William McKinley.

For a while his gaze was averted, as he and his fellow Britons prepared for Queen Victoria's Diamond Jubilee on 22 June. Rudyard had been asked by Moberly Bell to write a commemorative poem for *The Times*. But he had proved curiously reluctant, claiming he had used his best notions in 'A Song of the English'[25] and suggesting that this was the sort of thing the Poet Laureate, Alfred Austin – whom he disliked – was supposed to do. Rudyard also turned down a similar request from Sir Douglas Straight, now back as editor of the *Pall Mall Gazette*. As he told William Hallett Phillips, he was 'the sole, solitary, single and only "poet" who isn't writing a Jubilee Ode this year'.[26] (This was his last communication with Phillips, who drowned a couple of months later. Rudyard's poem 'The Feet of the Young Men', published in *Scribner's*, was a tribute.)

In reality, Rudyard was struggling for the right tone to sum up his feelings about the country in the latter years of the reign of 'The Widow at Windsor'. Intriguingly, he started 'some verses on the "White Man's Burden" '[27] around the time of the Colonial premiers' conference in June, but set them aside for another occasion. Clearly, not only the Jubilee, but also the prevailing imperialism, was populist in mood. Yet this was the side of the forthcoming Jubilee that disturbed him. He was sickened to find on 1 June that London was 'simply packed and double packed. There are stands and seats everywhere: and like the Embassies the Police are praying for the day to be over without accidents.'

More personally, he was worried that, at the time of this invasion of London, he himself was still 'a houseless gypsy'.[28] Ever since settling into the Royal Palace Hotel, the Kiplings had been looking for somewhere more permanent to live. After drawing a blank in Kent, they had been invited by Ned Burne-Jones to continue their search in Sussex, basing themselves at North End House, his holiday home in Rottingdean, a hamlet nestling in a small valley, where the downs rolled down to the sea, only four miles east of the fashionable Regency resort of Brighton. When the Burne-Joneses first went there in 1882 they wanted some of the peace and quiet that The Grange had lost since being swallowed up by West London's suburbs. At the time, there was only one horse-drawn bus to Brighton every day and the journey took forty minutes. Rottingdean had chickens running in the streets and, up on the wind-swept downs, one could smell 'a thousand grasses', as Ned nicely put it. Fifteen years later the village was becoming more accessible, particularly since the 1896 opening of the Brighton and Rottingdean Seashore Electric Railway, otherwise known as the 'Daddy-Longlegs' Railway, which rumbled along the shore – much too noisily for the Burne-Joneses – on spindly steel girders rising twenty-four feet above rails set in concrete piers on the seabed.

In the meantime Rottingdean had developed into a colony for the extended Kipling family. The Burne-Joneses had initially acquired Prospect House, on the west side of the village green. (It was here that Rudyard had spent his last few days before departing for India.) Needing somewhere bigger, they bought the next-door Aubrey Cottage in 1889 and knocked the two properties together to form North End House (with a special gap in the wall as a point of access for Ned's canvases). Across the green at the Dene lived Edward Ridsdale, who was the village's nearest equivalent to a squire. Ridsdale, a former Master of the Mint of impeccably Liberal Unionist pedigree, had spawned a large and eccentric family. Visiting the Burne-Joneses, Rudyard's cousin Stanley Baldwin had fallen in love with Ridsdale's sporty daughter Lucy, known as Cissie, whom he married the following year. The newly-weds suffered the tragedy of having their first son stillborn in January 1894. But, as Stanley had settled down to life as a director of his father's iron manufacturing firm, they had had three more children and lived contentedly at Astley Hall in Worcestershire, occasionally showing up in Rottingdean, where Cissie's sister Lily and her three brothers – Aurelian, the austere stockbroker MP for Brighton, Julian, an invalid, and Arthur, the local doctor – were effortlessly assimilated into the Macdonald cousinhood.

The day of the Jubilee, 22 June, was dull and foggy. After looking at the necklace of bonfires glowing along the downs that evening, Rudyard sat down and summarised his thoughts. Since these were written on a sheet of paper headed 'After' and later called 'Recessional' (a word defined by *Chambers Twentieth Century Dictionary* as: 'hymn sung during recession or retirement of clergy and choir after service'), his intention was clearly to lift his countrymen's sights, now that the festivities were over. But once again he was not happy with the results and cast them aside.

At the same time he had been working on a poem about Britain's modern warships (published the following May in *McClure's Magazine*, as 'The Destroyers'). So he welcomed the opportunity, a couple of days later, to accompany his father to the

Jubilee naval review at Spithead. In Berlin von Tirpitz had begun
to articulate a naval policy that identified Britain as Germany's
natural enemy and advocated the construction of a fleet of battleships. But for the time being, Britain retained clear numerical
superiority, and had been making important advances in technical developments such as turbines and wireless. Rudyard caught
the general mood of pride and even complacency as he observed
the Royal Navy's spectacular display of 165 warships drawn up in
five lines over thirty miles of the English Channel. 'Never dreamed
there was anything like it under Heaven. It was beyond words –
beyond any description!'[29]

During the Review, Rudyard again made contact with Captain
Edward Bayly, his fellow passenger on the *Mexican* travelling to
South Africa in 1891. Now in command of his own cruiser, HMS
Pelorus, Bayly invited Rudyard to join him on board for the regular
naval manoeuvres, which were to follow the one-off Review.
During the course of these nautical war-games, which took him
along England's western approaches as far as the north coast of
Ireland, Rudyard rubbed shoulders with several senior officers,
including Admiral Sir Henry Stephenson, commander of the
Channel Squadron, who did not impress him, and dined with
Captain Prince Louis of Battenberg, Assistant Director of Naval
Intelligence. Despite 'throwing up a meal or two', he noted appreciatively the ordinary midshipman's command of language, using
a slang borrowed 'from the engine-room, the working parts of
guns, the drill-book and the last music-hall song' and 'delivered
in a tight-lipped undertone; the more excruciatingly funny parts
without a shade of expression'.[30] Talking to the crew, the cooks
and the brisk young officers, he picked up 'tons of new notions'
and returned to shore 'chock full of new tales'.

Back in Rottingdean in July, Rudyard found Charles Norton's
daughter Sally was also staying. With the triumphal Review fresh
in his mind, he decided to take another look at his sheet headed
'After'. According to the official version of the story, Sally recovered
this from the waste-paper basket and urged him to publish it. But

this seems unlikely, particularly as she was not there when he wrote it and Carrie's own diary recorded that he read the poem to Sally, possibly to get an independent reaction. When he remained unsure, he agreed to allow his Aunt Georgie to arbitrate on the matter. She was hardly a political ally: over the years she had become increasingly radical, encouraging the parish council, to which she had been elected, to adopt William Morris-inspired measures of social reform.[31] It was a mark of Rudyard's respect that, when she suggested that the verses should indeed be published, he sent them to Bell at *The Times*, noting, 'We've been blowing up the Trumpets of the New Moon a little too much for White Men, and it's about time we sobered down.'[32]

This time there was no delay. The poem was published in the paper the very next day, 17 July, along with Queen Victoria's letter of thanks to her people and a leader praising the note of 'moral responsibility ... in Mr Kipling's stirring verses'.[33] Having been refined over the course of a month of jingoistic show, 'Recessional' had emerged, much as it started, as a warning against overriding ambition in national affairs.

> If, drunk with sight of power, we loose
>   Wild tongues that have not Thee in awe,
> Such boasting as the Gentiles use,
>   Or lesser breeds without the Law –
> Lord God of Hosts, be with us yet,
> Lest we forget – lest we forget!

Commentators have queried why Rudyard could take this elevated tone at a time when he was rooting for war in South Africa and had started his *Stalky* stories, which sought to turn his school-days, with their snook-cocking and petty violence, into a light-hearted improving tract for modern youth. Seizing on 'Recessional's' dismissal of 'lesser breeds', such observers have interpreted the poem as nothing more nor less than a hypocritical apology for imperialistic greed. 'Posing as a warning against complacency,' argued Martin Seymour-Smith, 'it was exactly what complacent people wanted to hear: that their sense of supremacy would be justified only if they were vigilant of it.'[34]

While there is truth in this, it fails to admit the power of Rudyard's contrary imaginative genius – the two sides to his head – which allowed him, in bardic, prophetic mood, to feel and say things apparently at variance from his other views. His clearest statement on the poem came in *Something of Myself*, where he claimed simply that the Jubilee celebrations had exuded 'a certain optimism that scared' him. The country needed vaccinating against over-confidence, or, as he put it, it required a *nuzzur-wattu*, or averter of the Evil Eye.

In retrospect, he was conducting an internal debate – working out his own complicated view of the nature of democracy. On the one hand he had been apprehensive about the popular patriotism associated with the Jubilee; on the other he could sense, as he began to tell correspondents around this time, that the future belonged to the common man. As he informed Jack Mackail, who had written him a note of congratulation on the day of 'Recessional's' publication, 'The big smash is coming one of these days, sure enough, but I think we shall pull through not without credit. It will be the common people – the 3rd class carriages – that'll save us.'[35]

In other words, he realised that his form of imperialism relied on the man in the street, but could not stop himself from warning against manifestations of the popular will. In communication with Rider Haggard he admitted that his fears on this score had been rather overstated. Claiming that he did not like the way his poem was quoted as an excuse for not doing anything, he added, 'What I wanted to say was: "Don't gas but be ready to give people snuff" – and I only covered the first part of the notion.'[36] Of course, he readily agreed when, towards the end of July, Captain Caius Crutchley, Secretary of the Navy League, a recently formed lobby group, asked permission to use the verses in a pamphlet to be distributed on Trafalgar Day in October. 'The general tenor of your writing is so patriotic', wrote Crutchley, 'that I cannot resist the impression that you would be willing to assist the Navy League in the work it has undertaken in endeavouring to arouse the apparently dormant spirit of patriotism in the rank and file of the British people.'[37]

Was Rudyard also admitting to apprehension in advance of a new arrival in the family? On 17 August, exactly one month after publication of 'Recessional', Carrie gave birth to her third child, a son called John, who would grow up to the increasingly strident sound of his father's calls for military preparedness. Three weeks later Rudyard was crowing happily about 'a jolly little kid ... said to be very like me with big black eyebrows'[38] and talking seriously about sending him to the naval college HMS *Britannia*. With North End House now too crowded, Rudyard was forced to redouble his efforts to find a home. Accompanied by Thomas Hardy, he explored likely sites in Dorset. At one stage he thought he had found the right place on the other side of Sussex near Hastings, but the owner took too long to make up his mind. So Rudyard signed a three-year lease on The Elms at the northern edge of the Rottingdean village green. (He used to say one could throw a cricket ball between it, North End House and the Ridsdales at The Dene.) Although slightly dilapidated, the red-tiled, stucco-fronted house had the advantage of being cheap – three guineas a week – and warm. It had a pleasant walled garden with elms and vast ilex trees, and Rudyard was convinced that its deep cellars meant that it had once been a smugglers' haunt.

A couple of months later the Kipling clan was visited by Crom Price, who was struggling as a teacher in an army crammer. Price came with Sydney Cockerell, former secretary to the late William Morris. One of their objectives was to see the stained-glass windows that Burne-Jones had designed (and Morris's firm executed) for St Margaret's church in the village. Both men stayed at the Mermaid pub where, Price remembered, Rudyard called in during the evening and 'after much bantering chat ... read a school-tale, the "Escape", in which happily I am a respectable figure'.[39] Now well immersed in his *Stalky* stories, Rudyard had been asking Price for the addresses of old boys such as G. C. 'M'Turk' Beresford. (In fact, since there was no story called 'Escape', Price probably meant 'In Ambush', the latest completed by Rudyard.)

After 'Recessional' and *Stalky*, Rudyard was getting a habit for declaiming his work. Taking after Uncle Ned at The Grange a quarter of a century earlier, he always found time for any children around. Baby Elsie still spent most of her time in the big south-west-facing day nursery, where she had learnt to address her sturdy-looking brother as ' "Dear John" in wilting tones'.[40] Jose-phine, now an enchanting four-year-old with fair hair and blue eyes, preferred the company of her second cousin, the Mackails' daughter Angela, whose visits from London were eagerly awaited. Together these two girls perfected a routine where they acted as Cavaliers in mock battles with the Roundhead Rudyard. In the evening they converged on his study, where he began reciting the *Just So Stories* he had toyed with in Brattleboro. According to Angela who, as Angela Thirkell, later wrote best-selling novels about upper-middle-class life, the printed version of these tales could not compare 'with the fun of hearing them told in Cousin Ruddy's deep unhesitating voice. There was a ritual about them, each phrase having its special intonation which had to be exactly the same each time and without which the stories are dried husks.'[41]

One of Rudyard's few friends in the vicinity was Leslie Cope Cornford, a lively if undistinguished journalist who had written on naval topics for Henley's *National Observer*. Coming from an old Sussex family, he lived in Brighton, where Carrie used to call on his wife for advice on local schools and servants. When, towards the end of the year, Cornford revealed that Henley was in dire financial straits, Rudyard gladly agreed to serve on a com-mittee to lobby for a pension for his old editor. In the event, Rudyard resorted to personal contacts, writing to George Wyndham, who prevailed on his sister's beau, Arthur Balfour the Home Secretary, to grant Henley £225 a year from the Civil List.

The general thesis of 'The House Surgeon' – that the Rock House in St Marychurch had been responsible for Rudyard's depression – was undermined when, even after the birth of a son and moving to a new house in a supportive family environment, his black moods persisted. The *Stalky* stories had acted as a form of personal therapy (which explains their sometimes laboured humour). But, as he reached his thirty-second birthday at the end of December, he wrote to Dr James Conland about the 'darkness and gloom' that had enveloped him – since April, he said. At the start of the previous year Conland had sent him to a Boston specialist with similar symptoms. Now Rudyard consulted a London doctor, who told him his problem was not 'liver', as he had been led to believe, but a colon distended with wind, exacerbated by too much smoking.

Having been recommended to work less and to spend time in a better climate, Rudyard made plans to take Carrie and the children to South Africa in the new year. He was hoping for three things: one was simply the winter sun (he found the English coast cold and blustery out of season); the second, that feeling of expansiveness that is often sorely missed by people brought up in the tropics when they return to the grey skies and limited horizons of England (Rudyard was feeling this when he told Rider Haggard in July, 'I want to see South Africa again – badly'[42]); and third, more elusive, an infusion of the dedicated idealism he had seen in district administrators in India and was convinced that his hero Cecil Rhodes was now bringing to Africa.

His party, augmented by Lockwood Kipling, a nurse and a governess, left Southampton on the Union Castle line's s.s. *Dunvegan Castle* on 8 January 1898. On board was John Hays Hammond, the energetic American mining engineer who had been given his head by Cecil Rhodes. Two years earlier, Hammond's report that there was no gold in either Mashonaland or

Matabeleland had played a role in encouraging the Jameson Raid because Rhodes needed to ramp up the depressed price of shares in his British South Africa Company. Hammond no doubt informed Rudyard about the latest developments in the colony. After being cleared by the British select committee, Rhodes was planning to wrest back control of Cape politics as leader of the new Progressive party.

While Rudyard enjoyed talking to the Yale-educated Hammond, he also found time for the children on board and, in particular, a well-read young girl called Morton, who left an acutely observed account of him unwinding.[43] On 14 January, a couple of days after docking briefly at Madeira, he suddenly appeared on deck, 'got into a chair between Mrs Nathan and myself and began to talk. He says he is half a Macdonald – but not a Highland Macdonald – and he talked a good deal of nonsense and some verse and was very amusing.' He recounted tales about Tennyson, advised her to read Scott ('everyone should read Scott once a year, just by way of medicine') and showed considerable enthusiasm for Dickens. 'He sprawled on the deck and taught a small boy how to play with soldiers arranging them in squares and in marching order and in double file and so on.' Carrie was not in the same class. 'She may have been pretty before she got fat, but she gobbles her food and is dowdy – does not even dress the children nicely, and they are dear little things.' Miss Morton noticed that Rudyard spoke to his wife 'as in duty bound'.

Nine days later, nearing Cape Town, he gave his young friend his autograph, adding a verse from Emerson. When she claimed she hated illustrations in books because they detracted from the text, he countered that he disliked plays based on novels 'because they spoiled the characterisation'. In an effort to wean her away from this aversion, he showed her the illustrations for the first twelve volumes of Scribner's De Luxe edition of his works. These had been photographed in black and white from bas-reliefs by his father. She encouraged Rudyard to publish them in England and he said he would ask Scribner's. 'We talked lots – he is really nicer than his books, has nice feelings about things and is absolutely outspoken,' Miss Morton told her mother.

Rudyard's arrival in South Africa was marked by the publication in the *Cape Times* of some verses, 'Welcome to Mr Kipling', purporting to come from an ordinary soldier. The author of this tribute had been making a name for himself in the local press, writing occasional 'Tommy verses', a popular form which had developed in the wake of the *Barrack-Room Ballads*. His name was Edgar Wallace and at the time he was a young private in the Medical Staff Corps working at Simonstown Hospital.

> O, good mornin' Mister Kiplin'! You are welcome to our shores:
> To the land of millionaires and potted meat:
> To the country of the 'fonteins' (we 'ave no 'bads' or 'pores')
> To the place where di'monds lay about the street
>   At your feet;
> To the 'unting ground of raiders indiscreet...

Rudyard had checked with Haggard about accommodation in the Cape Town suburbs of Wynberg or Constantia. While almost as young as Rudyard in India, the author of *King Solomon's Mines* had been Master of the High Court in the Transvaal. On his advice the Kiplings based themselves at the Vineyard, a boarding-house in Newlands, a leafy seaside suburb eight miles to the east of Cape Town. The landlady, an Irishwoman, was fierce, but the children enjoyed discarding their winter clothes and gambolling barefoot in the sun.

Soon that easy tropical feeling returned and the Kiplings could forget the troubles of the last couple of years:

> We shall go back to the boltless doors,
>   To the life unaltered our childhood knew –
> To the naked feet on the cool, dark floors,
>   And the high-ceiled rooms that the Trade blows through...[44]

Rudyard and Carrie had taken the trouble to pack two bicycles in their vast baggage train (but not, it seems, the tandem, nicknamed 'Two Tails', that Sam McClure had given them as a present in the summer). Out on their 'wheels' on the lower slopes of Table Mountain, they met Cecil Rhodes who invited them to lunch. Still smarting from the failure of the Raid (and its aftermath), Rhodes was in subdued mood, 'as inarticulate as a schoolboy of fifteen'.[45] The latest stage of his great Cape-to-Cairo railway project had only been opened in November, but for the time being his mind was focused on local issues such as combating rinderpest and developing a viable fruit export industry. Treated to a tour of the Cape, Rudyard was impressed by the dignified old Dutch farmhouses, 'stalled in deep peace' – one of which, Groote Schuur, set among pine trees and hydrangeas on 1500 acres of the lower slopes of Table Mountain, had been transformed by Herbert Baker, a local architect, into a spacious modern palace for Rhodes himself.

Having met the local dignitaries, including Sir Alfred Milner the new High Commissioner, and John Merriman, a former colleague of Rhodes who had thrown in his lot with the opposition South Africa party, Rudyard accepted Rhodes's offer of a special De Beers train to visit the diamond centre of Kimberley. Observing the native labourers in their guarded enclosures, Rudyard had no trouble accepting either the explanation, 'Kaffirs steal diamonds', or the gift of a $3\frac{1}{2}$-carat gem. Rhodes was determined that Rudyard should see 'his' new country in Matabeleland. So Rudyard pressed on, like the 'satiable Elephant's Child in the *Just So Story*, 'to the banks of the great grey-green greasy Limpopo River', and then to Bulawayo, 1000 miles north on the new railway.

Passing through Kimberley on his return, Rudyard visited the writer Olive Schreiner whom he had met on his 1891 trip. Despite her opposition to Rhodes's white supremacy (her brother was a leader of the liberal South Africa party), she still warmed to Rudyard, whom she described as 'a real man, a most lovable little human creature'.[46] From there he doubled back to Johannesburg where his father had arranged for him to stay with an old India hand. (Lockwood Kipling had been in Durban where he showed his own political colours with his fears that the Indians were likely to cause trouble – 'for they are many, and the Natalians are few'.) In Johannesburg, Rudyard was fêted at a dinner at the Rand Club, the heart of the Uitlander establishment. In a speech to the sixty-four guests, he hedged his bets about their future ('I didn't want to get my hosts into trouble by talking sedition and the place was full of spies'). But an American mine manager's reply, full of 'red-hot Revolution', left him in no doubt of his audience's wish for the Transvaal to be brought under British control. His growing sense of German uncouthness was reinforced when he was forced off a Johannesburg pavement by a detachment of the Kaiser's officers who were supervising the mounting of some heavy Krupps artillery. 'Say then in '98 I had a closer notion of the Hun peril and you won't be far wrong,' he later told a correspondent.[47]

By the time Rudyard and his family set off for home on the *Norham Castle* in mid-April the Cape rainy season had started, reminding him of Indian monsoons. Back in London on 30 April, after a stormy voyage, they booked into the Royal Palace Hotel for a few days as he familiarised himself with the latest news – five days earlier the United States had declared war on Spain, following the destruction of the USS *Maine* in Havana harbour two months earlier. That very night he dined with the US Ambassador John Hay, who was increasingly expressing himself in terms of the common interests of Britain and the United States. Three nights later these two dined again, only this time there was a third guest, Cecil Rhodes, who had travelled to England in early April to lobby for his interests. No record of these meetings exists, but the co-ordination of an Anglo-Saxon world view must have been high on the agenda. Rudyard indicated as much in 'The Houses', described by Carrie as his 'verses on "Anglo-Saxon alliance"', published in the *Navy League Journal* later in June.

Returning to Rottingdean, Rudyard rediscovered a taste for riding, as if South Africa had reminded him that an activity he had neglected since India was acceptable for a decent, patriotic Englishman. Carrie noted that he 'seems to like it', though when, during the next week, he was thrown twice and badly shaken, he changed his mind and took up cycling again. Anyway, as he told a Johannesburg correspondent, he was busy catching up on work, or, as he cheaply put it, he was 'back in the collar again, working *not* like a nigger because S. Africa rather shook my faith in the black man's industry'.[48]

An early commitment was his talk at a dinner of the Anglo-African Writers Club, a propagandist organisation founded by Rider Haggard. With many of the guests crammed into an over-flow dining-room, Haggard, as chairman, set the tone, hailing their speaker as a true 'watchman of our Empire'. Rudyard did not disappoint, drawing loud cheers as he told how, after his 'little visit down South', he had learnt 'that there were no men among the strong men who were working for our Empire throughout the world who needed and deserved our sympathy more than our countrymen in South Africa'. As for the situation in the Transvaal, he again hedged his bets, counselling hard work in the field and diplomatic patience, though adding, 'If there should be con-tinental interference and a shindy in that part of the world, it might be our opportunity and our duty to clean the whole thing out.'

Rudyard did little writing at this stage as his schedule was interrupted by the sudden death of Uncle Ned at The Grange in London early on the morning of 17 June. Rudyard was devastated: since moving to Rottingdean, he had grown closer than ever to his uncle, who combined an engaging innocence with formidable scholarship. If anything, the Oxford-educated Ned was better read than Lockwood Kipling, who was more practical and worldly. Over the previous autumn, Rudyard had found it both 'joyous and refreshing' to discuss English history with his uncle. 'The things that that big man does not know, and cannot help in, might be written on a postage-stamp,' he told Charles Norton.[49] 'Just now we are deep in the Roman occupation of Britain (this with an eye to stories) and he sends me volumes on volumes; but one talk is worth libraries.' The seeds of his book *Puck of Pook's Hill* had been sown. In return, Ned enjoyed the stimulus that his son Phil could not provide. One of his last acts, after playing dominoes with Georgie the night before he died, was to write to Rudyard – 'one of his wild, nonsensical "lark" letters . . . a beautiful tissue of absurdities', the object of which was to say when he was coming to Sussex.[50]

After cremation, Uncle Ned's ashes were brought to Rottingdean and laid, in their box, on his drawing table before the altar in St Margaret's church. The family kept a watch throughout the night before the funeral. Rudyard's hours were from four to six in the morning, during which time he had cause to meditate, 'For the life of me I could not connect the man who was three parts a God with the little oak box before me. The drawing table and the windows were much more *him*.' Rudyard was amazed at the show of love and respect for his uncle: Ruskin and Swinburne sent flowers, Uncle Crom was clearly shattered, and Martin, the gardener, insisted on watering the grass on the parched lawn for the sake of a 'humane man'. Yet even after the funeral and the memorial service in Westminster Abbey, Rudyard could not bring himself to cry. He felt 'broke – broke – broke', but could not weep. 'At least I don't seem able to have found out the way yet and I don't think it will come either. It's all a sort of a clot in my head because one has to realize that the man won't come back.'[51]

Rudyard's writing schedule that summer showed his usual range of interests. The lively nationalism of the *Barrack-Room Ballads* and even the 'Song of the English' had given way to more insistent propagandising, in poems such as 'The Truce of the Bear', which went into *The Times*'s new supplement, 'Literature' (somewhat to Rudyard's displeasure because he thought its anti-Russian political message would be 'smothered' there rather than in the main paper),[52] and 'Kitchener's School', a fund-raiser for a new secondary school in Khartoum, which informed the Sudanese defeated at Omdurman in September of their mad victors' plans to bring them schooling (and the mysterious game of cricket): 'For he who did not slay you in sport, he will not teach you in jest.'

The role of education in an individual's and a country's formation was explored in further *Stalky* stories, which were published at regular intervals in *McClure's* and other magazines until the middle of the following year, when they were collected between hard covers. Schoolmasters predictably objected to the depiction of their careless brutality and literary critics tended broadly to agree. Rudyard himself later admitted that *Stalky & Co.* was an 'atrocious book', though he defended King, the character most teachers loathed, but his younger readers rather liked. Finding this strange, he could only suggest they felt they were 'getting their money's worth from the long words and laboured sarcasm'.[53]

Formative communal experience of a different kind lay at the core of *A Fleet in Being*, which drew on a second trip on HMS *Pelorus* in September, as well as on his experiences at sea the previous year, to provide a lively manifesto for the Navy. Although Rudyard's account included interesting historical detail (on the crew's concern about the dangers of its two fourteen-inch above-water torpedo tubes, for example), it provided only a superficial account of the dynamics of the ship's community. (Rudyard kept these observations for his Pyecroft stories in the new decade.) *A Fleet in Being* was little more than a public relations exercise – so blatant that the *Spectator*, now owned and edited by his friend St Loe Strachey, congratulated him for ignoring service grievances, particularly among engineers.

Less bombastically, in October Rudyard published *The Day's Work*, his first collection of short stories for five years. Although all the material had been issued before, he gave it a focus and artistic integrity by starting the book with 'The Bridge-Builders', dating back to 1893, one of his most successful explorations of the duty and commitment required by the empire maker, and progressing to the final piece, 'The Brushwood Boy', which launches into uncharted territory, where the secret world of dreams needs to be squared with objective reality. Rudyard's precise positioning of these stories indicates that he saw the collection as his own bridge between a youthful naturalism and a later sparser, more allusive style. Further evidence that he was thinking along these lines came in his efforts in August to make another start on his Indian tale *Kim*.

In America, both *The Day's Work* and *A Fleet in Being* were published by a new firm, Doubleday and McClure. Frank N. Doubleday (whose initials Rudyard immediately seized on, dubbing him Effendi, a Turkish honorific for men of distinction) had jumped ship from Scribner's and set up his own company with the ubiquitous Sam McClure. Rudyard initially tried to deter Doubleday, fearing his friend did not have the necessary capital resources, but was happy to take his wares to the new firm as soon as it was functioning.

In Britain, he consigned his fiction to Macmillan and poetry to Methuen. But he was still friendly with the resourceful William Heinemann, who had not given up trying to interest him in one-off publishing projects. The old idea of a 'woman book' had been quietly forgotten and nothing came of a proposal Rudyard rather liked to write a verse version of *Cinderella*.[54] However, he provided copy for *An Almanac of Twelve Sports*, an upmarket calendar Heinemann had put out for the 1897 Christmas gift market. Rudyard's involvement had come about through his sitting for a portrait for the *New Review*. Henley had sent the ambitious young William Nicholson to make a woodcut *in situ* in Rottingdean. At the same time, the artist was working on the *Almanac*, a separate book commission for Heinemann, who owned the *New Review*. Seeing Nicholson at work, Rudyard offered to write accompanying verses, adopting a pithy, knowing style that looked back to *Departmental Ditties*. Where Nicholson illustrated the month of August with a woodcut on Coaching, Rudyard suggested the lines:

> Youth on the box and Liquor in the boot,
> My Lord drives out with My Lord's prostitute.[55]

When Heinemann deemed this not suitable for the family audience he had in mind, Rudyard reassembled his thoughts:

> The Pious Horse to church may trot.
> A maid may work a man's salvation....
> Four horses and a girl are not,
> However, aids to reformation.

When Rudyard billed Heinemann (fairly modestly) for his time, the publisher could not restrain himself from making a dig at Watt:

> Has the impeccable 'What's his name' taught you so inadequately what every little precious word you write is worth? Seriously I cannot accept the thing at such a figure. It is worth much more to *me* at least and therefore I've thought (unable still to trace the Byron-Murray figures) of 'a Pound a Line' & here's my cheque. You must be very considerate & generous please with me in my delirium and just say it's alright. I am now and always your debtor & now for once at least (how I wish it were for ever), Your publisher, William Heinemann.[56]

The following year, hoping to repeat the *Almanac*'s success, the wily Heinemann bombarded Rudyard with further ideas. When he suggested some verses on 'London types', Rudyard said this was in Henley's line of work. However, the publisher did obtain one lasting memento from Nicholson's visit to Rottingdean: the artist sketched the windmill at the back of Burne-Jones's house, which became the trade-mark (or colophon) for the William Heinemann company. And Nicholson himself so liked the village (and Rudyard) that he returned at regular intervals, eventually coming to live there in 1909.

In Rottingdean, Rudyard had just gone on the electoral register and was able to vote for the first time in his life. With a neophyte's enthusiasm, he felt this brought responsibilities: although he eschewed joining the parish council, claiming it was intrinsically corrupt, he was happy to spend time organising the Village Boys Club – so much time, in fact, that Carrie noted plaintively that he was occupied there every evening for weeks. With a Victorian's paternalistic instincts, he wanted to build a reading room, but the boys did not like this idea and 'rebelled'. They were happier when he decided to sponsor a rifle club. As a diversion, his wife characteristically found a role for herself 'superintend[ing] the execution of some dozen or two small jobs in the plumbing, carpentry and gardening line'.[57] But at least they were both beginning to feel at home: he even went to the trouble of asking his solicitor cousin, young George Macdonald, to enquire, unsuccessfully, about buying The Elms. Instead he paid £920 for a plot of land on the cliff top facing the sea to the east of the village, where he cannily envisaged that villas would one day be built.[58] He also bought two more properties – a one-acre field beneath the windmill, where he later erected a drill hall for the rifle club, and a smaller plot called North Bank Meadow.

Rudyard was now beginning to plan for his regular winter holiday abroad. As he told Robert Barr, he had had enough of 'grey skies and boiled potatoes' and was 'going over to where the sun shines and oysters is cheap' – in other words, the United States. Given his continuing discomfiture from his experiences in a Brattleboro court room only two and a half years earlier, the destination was probably decided by Carrie: Rudyard told his school friend Dunsterville that he made the trip 'so as to enable the wife ... to see her mother'.[59] (Carrie overruled Alice Kipling's objections to a transatlantic crossing in mid-winter, reported Charles Carrington.[60]) Bright little Josephine probably had her say, recalling her early days in the Vermont countryside. But he himself had his own reasons for making the journey. Apart from visiting his new publisher Doubleday and McClure, he wanted to see for himself how America was coping with its new colonial role. One of its heroes during its invasion of Cuba had been Theodore Roosevelt, who had insisted on participating with his voluntary cavalry force known as the Rough Riders. Since the fighting was reflected in a domestic newspaper circulation battle – 'You furnish the pictures and I'll furnish the war,' William Randolph Hearst, publisher of the *New York Herald Tribune* told his correspondent Frederic Remington in Cuba – Roosevelt's exploits were well-publicised. As a result, he was adopted as the Republican candidate for the governorship of New York state and elected to office in November. After what John Hay cynically described as 'a splendid little war', Rudyard was keen for the United States to exact as much as possible from its peace with Spain. He was not disappointed that the Treaty of Paris in December gave the United States control over the old Spanish colony of the Philippines – even though this would require further suppression of an indigenous nationalist movement.

To show his solidarity, he dusted down his poem on 'The White Man's Burden' from the previous year and sent copies to Roosevelt and to *McClure's Magazine* for publication in February. This time there was none of the ambiguity about the meaning of 'lesser breeds without the Law' (his phrase from 'Recessional', which was deemed to refer to the Germans). Rudyard called on Americans

> To wait in heavy harness
>   On fluttered folk and wild –
> Your new-caught, sullen peoples,
>   Half devil and half child.

As Roosevelt rightly commented, it made 'rather poor poetry, but good sense from the expansionist point of view'.[61]

By the time the poem was published Rudyard himself was in New York, accompanied by his family and a nanny, Lucy Blandford. The *Boston Globe* reported his arrival from Liverpool on the s.s. *Majestic* on 2 February: he was wearing a dark suit, a heavy overcoat with a fur collar and a derby hat, while Carrie was in a short sealskin coat. The paper speculated that because Howard, the English coachman who had stayed to look after Naulakha, had recently bought a new horse, the Kiplings would go on to Brattleboro and then to the south-west and Mexico. Characteristically, Rudyard gave no clues, telling newsmen, 'I have absolutely nothing to say.' During the crossing, which had been particularly rough and unpleasant, the two girls, Josephine and Elsie, had picked up bad colds and were bundled off to bed with suspected bronchitis as soon as they arrived at the Hotel Grenoble on West 56th Street on 2 February. With press interest focusing on his return to the United States and on the controversy round his poem 'The White Man's Burden', Rudyard's own equanimity was not improved by two further developments. First, because Scribner's edition of his collected works had lost momentum in the wake of Doubleday's decision to branch out on his own, a rival publisher, Putnam, had stepped in with an unauthorised Brushwood Edition, an act of piracy that was to lead to protracted legal action. Second, hearing that Rudyard was back in the country, Beatty wasted no time in telling eager reporters that he intended to sue his brother-in-law for malicious prosecution and false arrest. Beatty seems to have seized an opportunity for a few further minutes of fame, for there is no evidence of any sequel to this threat.

Nevertheless, the prospect of endless dealings with lawyers cannot have lifted the Kiplings' spirits. Soon Carrie joined the children on the sick list, but while she quickly recovered, on 20 February Rudyard also became feverish and was confined to his room. Luckily Carrie's sister Josephine had married a Harvard trained doctor, Theodore Dunham, who took charge of the situation. He called in a leading specialist, Dr Edward G. Janeway, who diagnosed an inflammation of the right lung. But while Rudyard seemed to rally (three days later he was sitting up in bed working on a story), Josephine's condition did not improve.

Bizarrely, given her state and the medical help to hand, a decision was taken to transfer her twenty-one blocks south to East 35th Street where Lockwood de Forest's sister, Julia, lived. Whatever the reason, the move was unsuccessful, for poor Josephine never rallied and died on 6 March. (Was Carrie worried that her daughter's illness would get in the way of her husband's recovery? She said her hands were 'more than full' and she felt she 'could not properly attend her'.[62]) Curiously, in this way, she repeated her mother-in-law's behaviour. A quarter of a century earlier, Alice had preferred to stay beside her husband in India rather than be with her children in England. That was the way women behaved in the Kipling family.

By then Rudyard's own condition had deteriorated again, with the infection (now described as pneumonia) spreading to his left as well as his right lung. In his fever, he kept up a non-stop monologue. So fascinated was he with these ramblings of his unconscious mind that in a calmer moment he hired a local stenographer to take down what he said. This record of his delirium, which unwittingly found its way into his papers at Sussex University, provides a fascinating insight into his fears and prejudices.

It starts with a New York girl called Bailey or Brady – he cannot remember which – producing letters and other papers which accuse him of having 'larked around with a great many girls both before and after my marriage'. When New York society (with his brother-in-law Dr Theodore Dunham to the fore) takes up the claims of this 'unclean-minded person', he allows himself to be talked into a submarine journey (shades of the 'thirty-mile ride' in 'The Brushwood Boy') to visit Robert Louis Stevenson in Samoa. However, this provides no escape: the stewardesses on this underwater trip are his two real-life nurses, Miss Warner and Miss Ryerson, who both turn out to be not only reporters but also sexual teases, with the latter, in particular, 'dressed throughout in soubrette style, with short skirts, clock stockings and high heels'. Rudyard finds himself back in a nightmare, which alternates between being threatened with lynching in America and escaping from Ireland in a ship owned by the Rothschilds, with himself 'dressed in the clothes of an abbé without any undergarments'. (With the Irish appearing as regular villains, the racial origins of his original accuser are no surprise.) Rudyard makes his way to a sleepy town, but 'cannot tell for sure whether I am in England or America'. Another 'thirty-mile ride' takes him across the Central Asian steppes, where he remembers precisely the names of the camps that the Russian General Alikhanoff stopped at during his alarming advance to the borders of British India in 1884 (reports of which Rudyard used to translate for the *CMG*). Returning to New York, he convinces himself he is held against his wishes in an asylum. But nothing happens when he demands the intervention of his embassy. Dunham and the other doctors, all in league with New York society, continue to stick things into Rudyard (with the nurses dancing attendance in their tarts' uniforms). He himself is reduced to sending the English government a cable, saying this provocation has amounted to *casus belli*.

Suffice it to say that these ravings included sexual fantasies, racial stereotyping and paranoid feelings of personal inadequacy (on another occasion he finds himself in New York town hall wearing nothing but a night-gown). And what should be made of the Rothschilds' role? Rudyard appeared to believe that Jews had some special ability to rescue him.[63]

Given the circumstances, interpretation is invidious. For in early March 1899 Rudyard was struggling for his life. As the seriousness of his illness became known, telegrams and letters of support flooded in from all parts of the world – from Mark Twain and Henry James (writing to 'my dear, demonic, indestructible youth') to the 'working people of Rottingdean' and even the reviled German Kaiser William who cabled Carrie, 'God grant that he may be spared to you and to all who are thankful to him for the soul stirring way in which he has sung about the deeds of our great common race.' (Ironically, at roughly the same time,

Lord Curzon, newly arrived as Viceroy in India, was telling Queen Victoria that Calcutta society was not nearly as bad as it had been painted in the 'too cynical stories of Rudyard Kipling'.[64])

Around 9 March, Rudyard slowly began to improve. By then his beloved Josephine had been cremated, but because of his condition he could not be told for a week. Among the various friends who rallied round was Frank Doubleday who proved, in Sally Norton's words to her father, a 'tower of strength', taking over Carrie's duty of answering the mass of mail, sitting beside Rudyard when no-one else was around and even cooking the patient's light meals, which improved from milk and ox blood on 9 March to sweetbreads in white sauce and yellow jelly a week later. On 16 March, Rudyard was moved to a lighter, airier room on the third floor of the hotel and began to receive visitors. Sally recalled how, sitting 'by his bed with his hand in mine, it was wonderfully pathetic to see the look of extreme sensitiveness in his face, about the mouth and eyes, and the look of sadness there, even his smile did not dispel'.[65] As they indulged in small talk, she 'kept carefully away from anything that might touch the springs of feeling and emotion' and he spoke wearily of the long period of convalescence that stretched out before him.

Carrie herself maintained a brave face, corresponding with Augustus Gurlitz, a New York copyright lawyer, about the Putnam case and even sending ten pounds to Aunt Georgie in Rottingdean with requests to pay five pounds to Martin (who cut the grass and looked after The Elms), ten shillings on account to Martin's wife who cleaned, and two pounds to Shergold, a groom, plus two pounds for forage for Gill, the pony that had been acquired for Josephine only the previous October.[66] At least the arrival of Lockwood Kipling from England on 29 March provided a tonic, causing Sally Norton to comment, 'Oh that blessed English temperament, so steady, so matter of fact even,' which she unfairly contrasted with Carrie who was 'so splendidly restrained and self controlled, but vibrating with sensitiveness, and bodily worn by it'.[67]

When the time came for Rudyard to move, four railroad companies fought for the honour of providing private cars to transport him to Lakewood, New Jersey, for recuperation at the Laurel House where the Kiplings were given the same rooms as three years earlier, at the west side of the hotel. Rudyard managed to put on fifteen pounds in three weeks but, despite regular drives in the pine woods, he was still very run down. He perked up when he and his family moved to Fairholme, the Catlins' house at Morristown, where extra security staff were hired to keep the curious public at bay. His biggest laugh for weeks came when the Catlins' valet Mike managed to send Lockwood Kipling to a dinner in New York with Frank Doubleday's trousers, and vice versa. Over the course of his month's stay at Fairholme, Rudyard spent time talking to Edith Catlin, who was having difficulty making up her mind whether to be a writer or an artist. He advised her, 'Copy the great for craftsmanship, write as much as you can like Dickens, imitate Henry James, study Thackeray. Out of all this you will evolve a style of your own. Only, write! write! write! and – WORK!'[68] He impressed on her the need to avoid clichés: when she showed him a story, he crossed out the word 'partake', marking it 'vile oh vile', and 'scorned such expressions as "blue ether", "rugged features", "pointing with disdain" and other journalese'. He told her his own two favourite books – the ones he would take if he had to go to prison – were the Bible and the Dictionary.

By early June, Rudyard was sufficiently well to be able to spend a few days at Frank Doubleday's house at Cold Spring Harbour on Long Island, while Carrie accompanied her mother to Brattleboro, where she found Howard had kept Naulakha in 'excellent order'. A few days later the Kiplings were ready to board the s.s. *Teutonic* for their sorrowful journey home. Doubleday insisted on going too, in case there were any problems. He had agreed to produce a special Swastika Edition of Rudyard's work, to kill the sale of unauthorised sets such as Putnam's Brushwood edition. Rudyard explained to Edward Bok, the editor of *Ladies' Home*

Journal, who also was on board, that the swastika ('pronounced Swas-ti-ka to rhyme with Car's ticker')[69] was an auspicious Indian sign. Subsequently Rudyard persuaded Bok to name his new house, in Merion, Pennsylvania, 'Swastika', adding, 'The sign on the door or the hearth should protect you against fire and water and thieves.' Having cheated death, Rudyard was more famous than ever – as he discovered when his fellow passengers on the *Teutonic* insisted on poking cameras at him at every opportunity. 'Folk with no manners,' observed the formidable Carrie. Eventually, on 24 June, six months exactly since leaving for America, they returned to The Elms and began the painful process of 'taking up the threads'.

To ease their workload the Kiplings took on a secretary, whom they initially shared with Aunt Georgie. Sara Anderson, an efficient, self-contained woman in her mid-thirties, lived in rooms opposite the Black Horse above Dr Ridsdale's surgery. Having already worked for John Ruskin, George Meredith and George Moore, she was ideally suited: Rudyard was to call her 'a woman apart; all the others were just secretaries. She knew by the way I pronounced "damn" just how to answer any letter. And she was utterly discreet.'[70]

But this organisational luxury did nothing to mitigate the family's personal pain. Wherever they went at home, Josephine's presence could be felt. Lockwood Kipling described to Sally Norton how Rudyard and Carrie had 'found going back to The Elms much harder and more painful than they had imagined. The house and garden are full of the lost child and poor Rud told his mother how he saw her when a door opened, when a space was vacant at table – coming out of every green dark corner of the garden – radiant and – heartbreaking. They can talk of her, however, which is much, for Carrie has hitherto been stone-dumb.'[71] One slight bonus, if it can be so called, was a thaw in relations between Carrie and Alice Kipling, with the American finally able to break down and weep in the presence of her mother-in-law. Did Rudyard cry? There were reports of tears in his eyes, but nothing more. The general consensus was that a great sadness had descended on him. Angela Thirkell wrote of a barrier that came down, as 'much of the beloved Cousin Ruddy of our child-hood died with Josephine'.[72] And he, more than anyone, continued to see his daughter at every turn. She was there when he visited St Loe Strachey in Surrey, where memories of her frolicking on the River Wey were affectionately recorded in his poem 'Merrow Down', and she was there in his story 'They', about the spirit children brushing the narrator as he visits a house in the Sussex woods.

The Kiplings' troubles did not come as single spies. With malevolent timing, Rudyard's sense of Josephine's ghostly pres-ence coincided with psychic manifestations of a different kind in his sister Trix's troubled mind. She had returned from India with her husband, now Colonel Fleming, the previous autumn. But she had immediately plunged into a catatonic state that would today be diagnosed as schizophrenia. Her healing process was not helped by either the antipathy between the Kiplings and Fleming (whom they thought – unfairly, given his ability to paint sensitive water-colours – too dour for their daughter) or Alice Kipling's determination not to admit that her daughter suffered from mental illness. So Trix had been sent to a quack called Dr Robert Colenso who lectured on 'artistic anatomy' at the Camberwell School of Arts and Crafts and was a strong believer in the benefits of diet and massage. She then stayed with her parents in Tisbury where, during Rudyard's illness in New York, she babbled con-stantly. As Alice told Georgie, 'The emotion which was at first so trying has changed to almost constant talk – & Oh – my dear – nearly all nonsense.' At times Trix was normal but then drifted 'into a world of her own, always a sad one – into which I cannot follow her'. Trix wept when she heard about Josephine's death, which Alice rightly realised was a good thing. But as she wailed to her sister, 'Oh, my Georgie, my heart is bursting full – both my dear children so smitten.'[73]

The Kiplings' attentions were diverted from their problems when they received a welcome offer from an unlikely source. Andrew Carnegie, the Scottish-born American steel magnate, was the sort of person to whom Rudyard would normally have given a wide berth: not only was he an enthusiast for union between the United States and Canada, but also he wanted to plough his fortune back into international peace-keeping efforts (among them the Permanent Court of Arbitration at The Hague and the Carnegie Endowment for International Peace). But Rudyard had met the millionaire through Doubleday and was happy to accept an invitation to use The Manse, an old Presbyterian minister's house at Creich, six miles from Carnegie's Skibo Castle on the Dornoch Firth in Sutherlandshire and seventy miles from John o'Groats at the northern tip of Scotland. Optimistically he had told the industrialist that he hoped to convert him to imperialism.[74]

Living at The Manse was basic: there were kerosene lamps and a single bathtub. But the Kiplings and their two children were determined to relax and enjoy themselves. They were joined by Edith Catlin, over from New Jersey, Phil Burne-Jones, Lockwood Kipling and, for a short while, Stanley Baldwin. Sir Phil (as he now was, having succeeded to his father's baronetcy) was working on a commission to paint both Rudyard and Carrie. He had made a start on his cousin: in the competent likeness now in the National Portrait Gallery Rudyard is depicted sitting thoughtfully at his writing table at The Elms, with a picture of HMS *Pelorus* in the background. He had found that maintaining one position, trying to look natural, for longer than fifteen minutes, gave him appalling cramp, but trained himself to do so for up to three-quarters of an hour. Now Phil wanted to use his time in Scotland to work on Carrie. With startling lack of regard for others in the house he appropriated the front drawing-room, with its clean, starched antimacassars, as his studio. His picture of Carrie is more successful, showing a formidable, slightly overweight, handsomely composed woman in green, with what appears to be a key dangling from her midriff – Carrie, the eternal chatelaine.

With a gillie from Skibo as a guide, members of the party fished (but seldom caught anything), rambled over moors of purple heather and pedalled bicycles along country lanes. Carnegie was a generous host, inviting them over for leisurely trips on his steam yacht *Sea Breeze*. Once they sailed down the Firth to Dunrobin Castle, home of the Duke and Duchess of Sutherland. The beautiful Duchess, known as Meddlesome Millie for her social and educational reforms, was another figure to whom Rudyard would not usually have been attracted. He almost alienated her by bounding up the lawn and asking the first person he met – a woman in a long silk dress, carrying an ivory-coloured parasol – where he could find the Duchess and, of course, he was speaking to her. But she did not mind and later returned the call at The Manse. Rudyard's flirtation with the British landed classes – hitherto a localised Wiltshire affair – was gaining momentum.

The Kiplings' best moments came in the evenings when, after an early supper – usually grouse and cold potatoes, washed down with Dewars whisky provided by Carnegie – they pulled out their pencils and paper, and settled down to an evening of word games and charades. (Carrie did not participate. She preferred to sew, chiding the others for wanting to go back to school.) A favourite amusement involved writing letters down one side of the page and up the other, and trying to make words. Faced with A–O, Rudyard unsuccessfully tried to claim that the Aino were a species of small carnivorous birds which lay hairy eggs and live in northern Japan. In the 'alphabet game', Edith remembered, G stood for an author the Kiplings particularly disliked. (She appears to have been referring to the unfortunate Edmund Gosse. Of the other possible candidates, Rudyard had no known opinion about George Gissing and he later suggested John Galsworthy to Buckingham Palace as a worthy recipient of the Order of Merit.[75]) Rudyard amused himself observing the sexual chemistry between foppish Phil and down-to-earth Edith. '*She* was a type that Phil had never seen before and *he* was a type she had never, never seen before and their manoeuvrings around and about each other were very fine.'[76]

Although Rudyard appreciated Carnegie's hospitality, he assimilated none of his pacifism. Returning strengthened to The Elms on 15 September, he found the burning issue in British politics was, more than ever, South Africa. Over the course of the year the ambitious Milner had become increasingly insistent that the Uitlanders needed British support in their struggle for political rights in the Transvaal. During August, when most ministers were on holiday, the British High Commissioner had lobbied strongly for a show of strength to force Paul Kruger's hand. As a gesture of solidarity, as war preparations began, Rudyard penned a poem called 'The King' which, in elliptical style, lauded the British people's ancient struggle against tyrannical monarchs. They soon would need to fight once more for their liberties, he implied, since they were confronted by a false 'King' in the shape of Kruger. On 28 September these verses were published in *The Times* as 'The Old Issue', with an editorial note, explaining that the Boers had 'sought safety in the discredited services of despotism, resisted and overthrown by our fathers at home centuries ago, as Mr Rudyard Kipling bids the world mark, in the spirited poem we publish this morning'.

Milner's campaign to draw the Transvaal into a confrontation was now reaching its climax. On 9 October Kruger issued an ultimatum, threatening war within forty-eight hours unless Britain stopped interfering in his country's affairs. This foolhardy gesture was greeted with great enthusiasm by the pro-imperialists. (Moberly Bell set the tone: 'The ultimatum was excellent in every way. An official document is seldom both eminently amusing and useful but this was both.'[77]) Rudyard rushed to London to dine with Chamberlain on 11 October, the day the Boer War officially started. At such a moment the Colonial Secretary might have had other priorities, but he found time to see Rudyard. There is no record of their discussion, but it is a safe bet that Rudyard was encouraged to use his pen to rally the nation behind the Army

Corps, now preparing to sail from Southampton under the command of Sir Redvers Buller.

This was a moment Rudyard had been waiting for. Britain was finally taking on the Boer and this would lead to a united self-governing South Africa, confirming it as part of the British Empire and a magnet for British settlers. One of his notions was to start a local corps of volunteers, though he doubtless had to withstand much criticism from his anti-war Aunt Georgie during their 'long talk on family and village matters'[78] on 14 October. However, as Carrie's diary makes clear, Rudyard was also concerned about the condition and fate of the troops sailing to South Africa. Friends like George Wyndham, now Under-Secretary of State in the War Office, may have alerted him to the potential dangers of the expedition: fighting the Boers in their own terrain was not likely to be easy.

On 16 October, Rudyard started writing 'The Absent-Minded Beggar', the latest of his music-hall style 'Tommy songs'. While stirring members of his audience to think of the 'gentleman in khaki ordered South', Rudyard had an additional message: he wanted them to contribute to a fund for these soldiers' dependants, even the

> ... girls he walked with casual. They'll be sorry
>   now he's gone,
>   For an absent-minded beggar they will find him,
> But it ain't the time for sermons with the winter
>   coming on.
>   We must help the girl that Tommy's left behind him!

Looking for an outlet, Rudyard turned to Alfred Harmsworth, proprietor of the mass-market *Daily Mail*, which, in its three years' existence, had helped fuel the popular mood of imperialism. When Rudyard offered to forgo his copyright, Harmsworth agreed to make the poem the centre-piece of a huge campaign to raise money for his paper's Soldiers' Families Fund. After publication in the *Daily Mail* on 31 October, the verses were reprinted and sold in pamphlet form. A fortnight later they were set to music by Sir Arthur Sullivan, the composing half of Gilbert and Sullivan. 'The song was sung and played in music halls, at smoking concerts and drawing room recitals, and cranked out on barrel-organs all over the country ... The words were printed on every kind of paper and on silk, satin and linen, and the famous Caton Woodville illustration of a wounded Tommy appeared on tobacco jars, ashtrays, cigarette packs, pillow cases, plates, card holders, knives, mugs, jugs and every other conceivable china, brass, or metal object.'[79] Maud Tree, wife of the actor-manager, raised a reported £70,000 by reciting the verses at the Palace Theatre every day for fourteen weeks. The fund eventually topped £300,000, providing wounded soldiers with everything from clothing and cocoa to wine and deck-chairs, as well as giving a welcome circulation boost to the *Daily Mail*. Within a short time many people were heartily fed up with the insistent poem: the Irish playwright and patriot Lady Gregory, W. B. Yeats's friend, refused to allow it, or 'God Save the Queen', to be recited in her house in Ireland ('in our country the Queen's name and Mr Kipling's name have come to mean the same thing as the Union and the extinction of our distinctive nationality'[80]), and even Rudyard admitted he would have killed the author if he had not been committing suicide.

Opinion was by no means unanimously in favour of the war, which made Rudyard's determination to raise public awareness all the more significant – as the Prime Minister, Lord Salisbury, recognised when he sent his private secretary, 'Pom' McDonnell, to offer him a knighthood. But, as with the Poet Laureateship, Rudyard refused, saying he could work better without the honour. The shattering news of the sieges of Kimberley, Mafeking and Ladysmith, and of British reverses at Stormberg, Magersfontein and Colenso were coming in and, as he entered his thirty-fifth year, he wanted to be in South Africa to support his 'cook's son – Duke's son ... each of 'em doing his country's work'. As he told

William Fraser in Canada, he was 'offended with no one except the "simple and pastoral" Boer who seems to be having us on toast'.[81]

Thirteen

Flannelled Fools

1900–1902

Rudyard had a history of taking the 'long trail' when he was in low spirits. This time he had every excuse: following Josephine's death, he had come through the most traumatic year of his life. Unexpectedly, however, towards the end of 1899, he began to feel better. Visiting Rottingdean in October, Henry James had found him 'as solid as if his hideous ordeal of last winter had been a mere bad dream; Carrie was as fresh as a rose, and the youngsters as blooming as peonies'.[1]

The onset of the Boer War had given Rudyard a new focus. As he prophesied to his friends the de Forests, the conflict was set 'to do untold good to our army and it has the merit of being the one war that has been directly fought over the plain issue of elementary freedom for all white men ... England is slowly waking up to her possibilities and when the war is ended will be a different land.'[2] Once he had decided to go to South Africa, he moved so quickly that he forgot to tell a disgruntled Moberly Bell, who had to be placated: 'If I find that it will be useful to say anything, you'll probably know all about it. But why be hurt?'[3] Henry James was equally uninformed: as late as 30 January 1900 he told Carrie's mother he had read in one London paper that the Kiplings 'have "just sailed" for S. Africa, babies & all, and in another that they have done nothing of the sort but are sitting close about their hearthstone'.[4]

By then the Kiplings had been on the high seas for ten days in

Alice Kipling, née Macdonald:
'dullness and Mrs Kipling cannot
exist in the same room'

John Lockwood Kipling, with his
'sage Yorkshire outlook and wisdom'

The baby Rudyard

Top left Rudyard, young horseman
Top right Rudyard and dog (probably his 'fat white waddler' Vixen) in India
Above The mature schoolboy, together with fellow pupils at the United Service College, Westward Ho!, Devon

So Flo set off to sketch the pine trees

Having ignited a cigarette

Accused of - Browsing in the Streets of causing obstruction to Earl, wishing to enter the House of Lords, of battering same with a hammer, thus causing him to sit suddenly on the Artist's palette, with dire results. The Artist here took umbrage at the unseemly behaviour of the Earl and made some rather unpleasant remarks.

And alas about the Police. There being it was considered enough seem to have Graced what had become of the Work of Art. The Lion (who by the way was a Period Lion and consequently a gentleman, for there were gentlemen in those days) felt most uncomfortable about this Work of Art affair. and he too, was quite of opinion, that the Police (so far, at any rate) had not moved in the matter, one way or the other.

Three views of 'Flo' Garrard (*clockwise from top left*): Kipling's cartoon of her (from her sketchbook, 1890); her comic strip image of herself in jail (from her illustrated book *Phantasmagoria* in the British Library); what is believed to be a late self-portrait (from her sketchbook)

Rudyard in his 'Pig and Whistle' outside the Hills' house in Allahabad

Isabella Burton, the original for Mrs Hauksbee

Above 'Trix' Kipling: the 'Ice Maiden'

Above right Rudyard and his mother, December 1890, shortly after his first meeting with Carrie Balestier

Right Wolcott Balestier

A youthful Carrie Kipling with
her first-born child Josephine

Rudyard Kipling,
man about town

Husband and wife,
Paris, 1902

Rudyard in his element on
board ship

Rudyard – the only
known photograph of
him as an adult with-
out glasses

Father and his roses. Summer at Naulakha.

Father on his skis. Winter at Naulakha. sliding down the mead

By the brook behind the hill.

After Father had learned to ride a bicy

Rudyard at play at Naulakha

...od — with mummie

'September' 1896

Bo and Ettie at Rock House
Torquay (England) spring '97

in charge of the condensed
... Mother's study. Spring. 96.

Opposite the greenhouse
door. 'Rock House'. 97. We
came away from Rock House
March 1. 1897.

The Kipling children at The Rock
House, Torquay in early 1897 (Bo
is Josephine and Ettie Elsie)

The Kipling family

Kipling and son

John, the boy soldier, 1901

Right Max Beerbohm's jaundiced cartoon of Kipling carrying off the Nobel Prize for Literature in 1907. The English quotation 'Lord God, they ha' paid in full!' is from Kipling's poem 'The Song of the Dead', which celebrates those who have died in the service – and as the price – of empire. The other figures are Algernon Charles Swinburne and George Meredith (disinterested, in the clouds) and Hall Caine

Below Rudyard (back right) in formal pose with the Bishop of Perpignan and Field Marshal Lord Roberts and Lady Roberts, Perpignan 1911

Below right Colleagues on *The Friend*, Bloemfontein, March 1900: (standing) H.A. Gwynne (seated, from left) Perceval Landon, Kipling, Julian Ralph

John Kipling (centre) with fellow members of the Irish Guards, Warley, 1915

Rudyard at a recruiting rally in Southport, 1915

Facing page War correspondent in Rheims, August 191

Rudyard (centre) with his friend Perceval Landon (right) and with French army liaison officer Captain F. Monroe (left), near Thann, France, August 1915

Cousins – (left to right) Sir Philip Burne-Jones, Rudyard, unidentified figure, Carrie, Stanley Baldwin, Margot Baldwin, Diana Baldwin, Elsie Kipling

Rudyard and Carrie in the garden at Bateman's with dog (probably Mike), 1930s

Rudyard's installation as Rector of St Andrews University, 1923, with 'cousin Stan', Stanley Baldwin (far left)

Below and below right
George and Elsie Bambridge, marriage at St Margaret's, Westminster, 1924, and, later, with dogs, Paris, early 1930s

Rudyard Kipling: reflective, troubled, mature bard, 1924

the *Kinfauns Castle*. Arriving in Cape Town on 5 February, they went straight to the Mount Nelson Hotel in the pine trees beneath Table Mountain. Rivalling Shepheards in Cairo or Raffles in Singapore as one of the most gracious hostelries on the imperial grand tour circuit, the 'helot's rest' had been commandeered by newspapermen and other camp followers. To get his bearings, Rudyard latched on to a group of journalists, including Leo Amery, the young chief correspondent of *The Times*, Julian Ralph, an American representing the *Daily Mail*, the donnish Perceval Landon, who also worked for *The Times*, and Howell Gwynne, a reporter for Reuter's news agency, who had recently arrived from China. Amery left a familiar picture of a man whose 'talk was jerky, and full of swift exchanges' and who 'was supremely interested in people who did things and inquisitive to learn how and why they did them'.[5]

The next day Rudyard spent an hour with the Commander-in-Chief, who was no longer General Sir Redvers Buller but 'Bobs', his old friend from India, now Field Marshal Lord Roberts. Following the British defeat at Colenso in mid-December, Sir 'Reverse' Buller had been replaced by the ageing but still sprightly Roberts, who had suffered the personal tragedy of losing his only son Freddy in the same battle. Although due to depart for the front that evening, at the onset of the campaign that would lead to the fall of Bloemfontein in March and the turning of the tide in the war, Roberts briefed Rudyard on the fighting in the Orange Free State. Two days later, over a leisurely dinner, Rudyard was updated on local political developments by the High Commissioner Sir Alfred Milner, whose main concern was the loyalty of the Cape Boers.

Rudyard knew many of the leading players in this 'first-class dress-parade for Armageddon'. With the promotion of the diminutive Roberts, the Army's Indian 'ring' had superseded the African, which was associated with campaigns in Egypt and Sudan. Old friends such as Colonel Ian Hamilton and Colonel Robert Baden-Powell were in the thick of hostilities. In addition, several divisions had sailed directly from India as reinforcements. As a result, Rudyard's old mentor George Allen was thriving. In 1900–1, his North-West Tannery Company in Cawnpore produced 944,713 pairs of footwear for the army in South Africa. When, three years later, Rudyard wrote his famous Boer War anthem, 'Boots', 'We're foot – slog – slog – slog – sloggin' over Africa', he had a direct personal interest.[6]

Rudyard's social contacts also proved diverting and useful. George Wyndham's brother Guy was a brigade major, though at the time out of communication, under siege in Ladysmith. Similarly incapacitated, within the walls of Mafeking, was Major Lord Edward Cecil, the engaging fourth son of the Prime Minister Lord Salisbury. According to the historian Thomas Pakenham, Cecil had volunteered as Baden-Powell's second-in-command so as to get away from his attractive, bossy wife Violet, who had found a role for herself, stiffening the resolve of the High Commissioner in Cape Town.[7] She was a woman Rudyard had known slightly for many years. Her father, Admiral Maxse, was a Crimean war veteran, who provided the model for his friend George Meredith's novel *Beauchamp's Career*. Apparently she had met Rudyard when he had visited Meredith in late 1889. She and her sister Olive had been drawn (and, indeed, taught to draw) by Ned Burne-Jones, who was always susceptible to pretty young girls. For a while she studied at Julian's in Paris, where she befriended the rising politician Georges Clemenceau. Her brother Leo (like Milner, one of Benjamin Jowett's boys from Balliol) owned the *National Review*, a Chamberlainite magazine to which Rudyard occasionally contributed. Offered the chance by Milner to edit the *Cape Times*, Leo Maxse refused because, according to his sister, he had to 'stay in England to warn the people of the German danger'.[8] By the time Rudyard arrived in Cape Town, Lady Edward had completed her initial conquest of Milner and moved out to Groote Schuur, Cecil Rhodes's home close to the Mount Nelson. Rhodes was away until March, under siege in Kimberley, but Rudyard was to see much of him (and his house guest) when he returned.

One of George Wyndham's proudest feats as Under-Secretary for War had been to establish an Imperial Yeomanry, as support for regular Mounted Infantry units. To an extent, this was a complicated piece of social engineering, reflecting Wyndham's ties to South Africa. For the Yeomanry was financed by Wernher-Beit, the largest pro-British gold mining firm in the Transvaal, whose agent Percy Fitzpatrick hoped that a body of footloose English farmers and country gentlemen might stay and provide good settler stock for the future. As a further example of the interlinking of various strands in Rudyard's life, Wyndham arranged for Patrick Campbell, the ne'er-do-well husband of his sister's friend 'Mrs Pat', to join the 10th Imperial Bucks Yeomanry. But Campbell, who had unsuccessfully sought his fortune working for De Beers, was killed soon after arriving at the front in April.

The war had brought a large number of wives to Cape Town – so many that Queen Victoria herself was moved to express her disapproval of the 'hysterical spirit which seems to have influenced some of them to go where they are not wanted'. Inevitably, the city was a hotbed of gossip: Rudyard told his new friend the Duchess of Sutherland he found 'stories and three-volume novels walking about those streets by the hundred'.[9] Fifteen years earlier he would have made Lady Edward Cecil into a new Mrs Hauksbee figure. Now, probably encouraged by Roberts, he accompanied her on visits to wounded soldiers in the Cape hospitals in Wynberg and Rondebosch. He later rather exaggerated his role: 'In the Boer War I controlled many many pounds of cake tobacco and millions of cigarettes to distribute; and the entire British army ran after me wagging its tail.'[10] But there is no doubt that his presence in South Africa provided a significant morale booster. On 22 February he joined a Red Cross ambulance train travelling 600 miles north to the railhead at Modder River to pick up casualties from the Battle of Paardeberg. Captain Llewellyn Phillips, who was in the same carriage, recalled that when Rudyard got out he 'was immediately surrounded by about fifty "Tommies" and seemed in his glory conversing with them. I never saw such hero worship as at Beaufort West. It had leaked out that he was travelling by that train, and the whole of the town ... crowded into the station to get a glimpse of him. This morning I received a packet containing two bottles of laudanum from him ... I administered the first dose of it this morning and when I told the man from whom the medicine had come, his eyes gleamed with appreciation.'[11] Returning on the same train to Cape Town, he arranged bandages and took every opportunity to put his talents to good use, writing letters home on behalf of the wounded.

The following month the tide of the war began to turn. Following the relief of Kimberley, Rhodes came back to Groote Schuur and told Rudyard and Carrie about the vision he had had during the siege of building a house, next door to his own, for writers and artists. He wanted the Kiplings to have first refusal and use it whenever in South Africa. Less than a week later, after recapturing Bloemfontein, one of Roberts's first moves was to revive the local paper, the *Friend of the Free State*, as a propaganda sheet to win the backing of the local population and boost his own soldiers' spirits. He asked four war correspondents – Ralph, Landon, Gwynne and F. W. Buxton of the *Johannesburg Star* – to act as editors for the four weeks or so that the troops would be in the vicinity. When Landon tentatively telegraphed Rudyard, asking for a contribution for St Patrick's Day, he received by return a few short lines which were published in the second issue. That same day Roberts decided to invite Rudyard to join the staff. The man with the universally recognised bushy eyebrows did not have to be asked twice. Having been heralded in advance in the paper, he arrived at the Free State Hotel in Bloemfontein on 25 March.

Although he had not sat behind a desk in a newspaper office for over a decade, Rudyard immediately felt at home at the *Friend*. Sucking on his pipe, he turned his hand to anything that was required. He dashed out short inconsequential fables, which found their place in the paper alongside official 'Proclamations to the Burghers of the Orange Free State'. He contributed to a series of 'Kopje-Book Maxims' (a Boer War version of 'Hafiz', with disrespectful lines such as 'The nearer to the Press Censor, the further from the Truth'). He edited scraps of verses sent in by the private soldiers (usually in imitation of his own style). He railed against the mistakes of the Dutch compositor. And, occasionally, he penned a worthwhile poem, notably his solemn tribute to the fallen Boer Commandant-General Piet Joubert, which accorded with a strategy he had discussed with Milner – to take every opportunity to wean the Boers to the idea of a united country after the war. As the poem 'General Joubert' put it,

> Later shall rise a People, sane and great,
> Forged in strong fires, by equal war made one.

Rudyard's appeal to the people of the Free State (written with Julian Ralph) came as close to a statement of his political creed as anything he ever produced. British principles, he said, included 'The absolute independence of the individual, so long as he does not interfere with his neighbour's rights. Prompt and equal justice, before the Lord, to all men. A natural and rooted antipathy to anything savouring of military despotism, in any shape or form. Absolute religious toleration and freedom of belief for all people ... The right of every man to make his home his castle.' Soon the circulation of this sleepy provincial paper had jumped from 400 to over 5000 and whenever anyone came to the office for a copy Rudyard would say, with a hint of pride, 'Haven't any; go to Barlow's shop around the corner.'[12]

When Sir Alfred Milner visited newly liberated Bloemfontein, the staff of the *Friend* held a dinner for him and Lord Roberts in the dining-room of the railway station. Introduced by Julian Ralph, with a throw-away comparison with Shakespeare, Rudyard, in similar high spirits, recalled the words of Whistler who, when an acolyte said, 'Master, you and Velasquez are the greatest exponents of the art of painting,' replied, 'True, true, but why drag in Velasquez?'[13] Rudyard proposed a toast to

> the man who had taught the British Empire its responsibilities, and the rest of the world its power, who has filled the seas with transports, ... who has turned the loafer of the London streets into a man, ... who has made the Uitlander of South Africa stand shoulder to shoulder with the boundary rider of New Zealand, and taught the men of New South Wales to pick up the wounded men who wear the maple leaf – and all in support of the mother-country. Gentlemen, I give you the name of the Empire-builder – Stephanus Johannes Paulus Kruger.

One of the other correspondents with Roberts's army in Bloemfontein (not working for the *Friend*) was the poet A. B. 'Banjo' Paterson. Since he had often been described as the Australian Kipling (his 'Waltzing Matilda' dates from five years earlier), he took a special interest in the new arrival, whom he described as having a 'quick, nervous energy ... His talk is a gabble, a chatter, a constant jumping from one point to another. In manner, he is more like a businessman than a literary celebrity. There is nothing of the dreamer about him.'[14] Sitting next to Rudyard at a dinner, Paterson got the impression of 'a sort of Dr Jekyll and Mr Hyde' who was able to 'put off the toga of the politician and put on the mantle of the author. It was most fascinating. He yarned away about shoes and ships and sealing-wax and cabbages and kings; interested in everything; jumping from one subject to another, from his residence in New York to border battles on the Indian frontier; from the necessity of getting your local colour right, to the difficulty of getting a good illustrator. As he spoke, his face lit up and you began to notice the breadth of his head and the development of the bump of perception over his eyes.' Paterson felt that 'you could have dumped Kipling down in a splitter's camp in the back-blocks of Australia and he would have been quite at home; and would have gone away, leaving the impression that he was a decent sort of bloke that asked a lot of questions'. Rudyard told his new friend he was off to London on the eleventh of the following month: 'I'm not going to wait for the fighting here. I can trust the army to do all the fighting.'

Rudyard had a rude shock when, on 28 March, he took what was intended to be a leisurely day trip to watch a British force trying to secure an advance position at Karee Siding, twenty miles north of Bloemfontein. With him went Bennet Burleigh, the veteran correspondent of the *Daily Telegraph*, who had accompanied Lord Wolseley's 1884–5 expedition to relieve General Gordon in Khartoum. The two journalists were driven in a cart full of provisions to a ridge, beside a Boer farmhouse where, drinks in hand, they might have hoped to discuss the Sudan and observe the fighting in some comfort. Instead, a detachment of Light Horse passed close by and suddenly, as the Mausers, pompoms (or rapid-firing light artillery) and Krupp cannon loosed off around him, Rudyard was in the thick of the battle. His first experience of being under attack left sharp impressions: 'Then to the left, almost under us, a small piece of hanging woodland filled and fumed with our shrapnel much as a man's moustache fills with cigarette smoke.'[15] He would recall the setting, with the trees 'withered by fire', in his story 'A Sahibs' War', later in the year. There he would suggest that the Boers in the farmhouse had been acting treacherously, a theme he stressed in a non-fiction piece, 'The Sin of Witchcraft', sent to *The Times* the day after he returned south to his family on 3 April. Now he no longer laughed when he saw people with shell-shock taking cover when they heard the clattering of an approaching Cape Town trolley car. The encounter at Karee Siding had another sequel when a Geneva newspaper alleged that Rudyard had participated in atrocities at the farmhouse. He marked this down to the efficiency of the German propaganda machine and was confirmed in his anti-German sentiments.

Without Rudyard to comfort her, Carrie felt the loss of

Josephine badly and was 'ill and depressed'.[16] She was cheered by Mary Kingsley calling in for 'a Christian tea'. Kingsley, a niece of the author whose novel had provided the name for Rudyard's school, was another of the hordes who had arrived to offer their services to the war effort. As a qualified nurse, she had signed up to work among Boer prisoners in the hospital at the Palace barracks in Simonstown where, as she told the Kiplings over dinner, the conditions were appalling. Two months later she succumbed to typhoid and died. Although she had vehemently opposed his ideas of the white man's burden, Rudyard was distressed, later describing her as 'the bravest woman of all my knowledge'.[17]

Returning to England in late April, his first task was to visit Kingsley's friends, his three 'dear ladies' from Kensington, and inform them of her progress. He felt buoyed by his experiences in South Africa: as Carrie noted in her diary, he 'has had the greatest of times and feels he has joined up all his ideas with the others of many years ago'. This was partly true: Rudyard's belief in the nobility of the British Empire had been enhanced, while his penchant for the 'go-fever' world of *The Light that Failed* had been confirmed. But he had made little progress in exploring the sort of dream worlds he had begun to map out in 'The Brushwood Boy'. Nevertheless, South Africa had had its intended effect of revitalising him. Now, as he told his uncle, Alfred Baldwin, he was convinced the 'real crux of the war' was in Britain, where he hoped to be 'of some little service'.[18]

Essentially his role was still propagandist. But, now he was home, he could afford to be more critical of the war's prosecution than he had been in South Africa. As he explained to Conland,

War is a rummy job – it's a cross between poker and Sunday School. Sometimes poker comes out on top and sometimes Sunday School – but more often poker. The Boers hit us just as hard and as often as they knew how; and we advanced against 'em as if they were street-rioters that we didn't want to hurt. They spied on us at their leisure, and when they wanted a rest they handed up any old gun and said they'd be loyal subjects. Then they went to their homes and rested for a week or two; and then they went on the war path again with a new coat and a full stomach. They are an elegant people: and we are the biggest fools, in the way that we wage war, that this country has produced.[19]

As well as Boer fifth columnists, he was obsessed with more strategic matters. One was the need to introduce the right kind of settler into South Africa after the war. They did not necessarily have to be English: 'For a big country we want a man who had been born in a big country and not sent to school between fences.'[20] Another was that the fighting there was still only a prelude to a conflict brewing in Europe. Despite Chamberlain's espousal of a London–Berlin axis, German (and European) opinion had been predominantly pro-Boer. The Prince of Wales, the future King Edward VII, was not amused when his nephew the German Kaiser William urged him to accept defeat in South Africa in the noble spirit that the England cricket team had bowed to Australia in the Ashes series the previous summer. Queen Victoria's spring visit to the French Riviera was cancelled because of anti-British sentiment – a sensible move, given the failed assassination attempt by a Belgian anarchist on the Prince and Princess of Wales in Brussels in April 1900.

Rudyard addressed these themes in various writings, notably in 'Four Stories of the War' published in serial form in the *Daily Express* in June and early July. When he showed one of these, 'A Burgher of the Free State', about the duplicity of the citizens of Bloemfontein, to his Aunt Georgie, she, a pacifist opponent of the war, was not amused. Nor did she take kindly to his insistence that Rottingdean should celebrate the relief of Mafeking by firing a cannon from the cliff. But Rudyard was determined that his home village should back him in supporting the war effort. He had already had a run-in with Edward Blaber, the publican of the Plough, at the opposite end of the village green from The Elms, who took his cue from Georgie and was a determined anti-imperialist.

Now was the time to set up a local rifle club, with two sites – a 1000-yard range at the top of East Hill on the downs for fine-weather shooting and later, during the winter, a seventy-five-foot miniature range in the tin Drill Hall on his own recently acquired land in the centre of the village. Up to fifty villagers received regular training from Sergeant Johnson, the physical education master at the local St Aubyn's prep school – with input also from the local coastguards. As well as basic (Lee Enfield) rifle practice, they learnt Morse Code and semaphore, and performed gymnastic exercises. Before long, the club was challenging other villages to shooting matches, in which Rudyard enthusiastically competed whenever he was in Rottingdean.

In taking this initiative (and in his commitment to the Navy League), Rudyard was hoping to influence the course not just of the Boer but of some future European war. As his story, 'The Army of a Dream', begun in November, indicated, he was thinking of a scheme of volunteer-based national service. 'What I saw during the war of our arrangements and notions of work scared me, and I thought it might be good to train people before a real war came.'[21]

With this in mind, Rudyard made frequent trips to London to see Amery, Moberly Bell and Chamberlain (to whom, he pointedly informed a South African contact, he related things 'he had not heard before'[22]). He was delighted (and steeled to his task) when visited by two colleagues from the *Friend*, Perceval Landon and Julian Ralph. In Bloemfontein they had discussed setting up a club, called The Friends, with a mock ritual, based on their shared knowledge of Freemasonry. Getting into the spirit of their quasi-secret society, Rudyard wrote an elaborate constitution and commissioned Tiffany, the jeweller, to produce a gold enamelled badge, with the motto 'Inter proelia prelum' – which he told Ralph to inform enquirers meant 'Drinks between engagements' rather than 'In the midst of war, the (printing) press' – and the letters R.L.K.G. – not for 'Roberts let Kruger go', as Rudyard joked to Ralph, but the initials of the four founder members (though they also 'initiated' their colleague F. W. Buxton, Lord Roberts and Lord Stanley, the wartime censor).

The Kiplings were more sociable than usual because they had quickly taken up the latest advance in the transport revolution – the motor car. It was inevitable that cars would appeal to a man of Rudyard's questing, childlike sensibilities. The arrival of the noisy, steaming automobile had been greeted with dismay by traditionalists who feared its effects on the peace of the countryside. But this only encouraged a man who enjoyed loafing (whether on bicycles or ocean liners) as much as new technology. Rudyard's introduction to automobiles had come in October 1899 when Alfred Harmsworth, the newspaper magnate, had driven to Rottingdean to show off his new Mercedes. Harmsworth, who had started his career as owner of *Bicycling News*, was an eager advocate of motoring, which he declared was 'like being massaged at speed'.[23] He was a friend of Claude Johnson, the Secretary of the Automobile Club, the main lobby group for motorists, with about 540 members. Johnson's father had worked throughout his life at the old Department of Science and Art in South Kensington, where he is likely to have known Lockwood Kipling. As later became clear, Harmsworth was keen to encourage Rudyard, the apostle of steam and mechanical engineering, to write about motor cars. On this initial outing he took the Kiplings for a twenty-minute trip, which left them 'white with dust and dizzy with noise'. But, as Rudyard admitted, 'the poison worked from that hour'.[24]

Later that year, before going to South Africa, Rudyard hired a 'Victoria-hooded, carriage-sprung, carriage-braked, single-cylinder, belt-drive, fixed-ignition Embryo which, at times, could cover eight miles an hour'. The cost, driver included, was three and a half guineas a week and, now in the summer of 1900, the car provided useful service as the Kiplings set about house hunting. (The lease of The Elms needed to be renewed in the spring and the owner was keen to develop some land adjacent to the property.) At least this gave them an excuse for indulging in an activity they both enjoyed. Apologising to James Conland for not having written, Rudyard enthused about motoring:

> It's just the kind of play that would delight you – a cross between steering a boat and driving an engine. But England being crowned with small and fascinating villages one never knows from one minute to the next what one will find. We go out together, the wife and I, after breakfast, get out twenty or thirty miles, lunch at some sort of hotel and come home in the cool of the evening. Our pretence is that we are hunting for a new house, but as a matter of fact we simply lounge around and get the skin peeled off our noses by the sun.[25]

(Harmsworth seems to have been still pressing for some copy about cars. An entry in Carrie's diary on 15 May stated baldly, 'Rud declines a further publicity scheme for the *Daily Mail*.' The previous month the *Daily Mail* had sponsored a Thousand Mile Trial for vehicles throughout the United Kingdom and Harmsworth may have wanted Rudyard to build on this success. Though he declined to write promotional copy, Rudyard took the hint. By the end of the year he had begun writing the verses *The Muse among the Motors*, which were later published in the *Daily Mail*.)

Rudyard's longest foray by car was roughly fifty miles to Guildford to see St Loe Strachey, another early motoring enthusiast. For more distant journeys he still used the railway, as, for example, when he travelled to Tisbury and found his usually ebullient father in poor spirits, worn down by the exertions of living on a small pension and looking after Trix, who had been going through a new phase of wildly swinging moods.[26] (Alice was still unwilling to admit the possibility of mental illness – a position that annoyed no-nonsense Carrie and put an end to the rapprochement between Alice and her daughter-in-law.)

Further afield, Carrie had located some distant relations of her own in Warwickshire. She had lived in the United States without having much to do with her extended family. But now she discovered a cousin who was a direct descendant of the Kinzies who had founded Chicago. Juliette (known as 'Daisy') Low was a grand-daughter of John Harris Kinzie, Chicago's first 'President'. Her father, William Washington Gordon II, was an old fashioned Southern gentleman from Savannah, Georgia. In 1886, she had married a Scotsman, Willie Low, whose father had made a vast fortune as a factor (or financier cum middle-man) in the Savannah cotton trade. She had settled in a grand house at Wellesbourne Hall, near Stratford upon Avon, where she entertained in grand style. From Savannah she brought a black cook, Mossiana Milledge, whose father Tom, the Lows' butler in Savannah, had so impressed William Thackeray when he visited Georgia in 1856 that he made him the model for Gumbo in his novel *The Virginians*. Mossiana's Southern cuisine greatly impressed a neighbour, the Earl of Warwick, who, never remembering her name, used to call her 'Mozambique'. It also made a wider mark since a fellow cook at Wellesbourne was Rosa Lewis who successfully introduced Mossiana's recipes to the fashionable Cavendish Hotel she later ran in London.

In 1898 Daisy's younger sister, Mabel, had followed her across the Atlantic and married an Englishman, the Honourable Rowland Leigh, a barrister who was the younger son of the landed Lord Leigh. But by then Daisy's own marriage was in difficulties. She had not properly understood that her husband was a playboy – one of the libertine Marlborough House set centred on Edward, Prince of Wales. Gradually Willie Low drifted away from her and, in keeping with his friends, he took up with a beautiful widow, a Mrs Bateman.

The Lows were living uneasily together at Wellesbourne when the Kiplings came to stay in November 1900. Carrie had learnt of her cousins after being contacted by Daisy's mother Nellie. She and Rudyard had called on Nellie and her husband who were visiting England. Carrie had asked about her English ancestors, Nellie noted, 'especially the Drake line, which she wants on account of her children'. Nellie promised to send her details when she returned home, along with some lily bulbs from her Savannah garden.

Despite the domestic tensions at Wellesbourne, Rudyard enjoyed the luxury of being served by butlers and valets. Although unmusical, he was fascinated by his host's mechanical organ, which played tunes from perforated rolls.[27] Touchingly, he understood that the visit was important because it gave the often painfully homesick Carrie some genuine status in England. He told Conland, 'I had a gay time and it did me good because Carrie was the guest of honour and I was only the man who had married her.'[28] Rudyard was reminded of American generosity, as he and his wife were sent on their way with three hams (Maryland, he said, but probably Virginia), several pots of begonias and a prize Persian cat that Carrie had coveted as a replacement for the one Rudyard gave her after her carriage accident in Vermont in December 1894.

In the midst of politics and family, Rudyard still had professional matters to attend to. As he was well aware, one result of his high-profile support for the war had been a critical backlash. He had always had his detractors, who tried to pin various versions of Oscar Wilde's accusation of vulgarity on him. But the coarse laddishness of the *Stalky* stories had turned even admirers such as Henry James against him. After reading the first of these schoolboy farces, James told Grace Norton of his disappointment: Rudyard wrote 'almost nothing civilized save steam and patriotism ... almost nothing of the complicated soul or of the female form or of any question of shades'. He had once looked on Rudyard as a potential 'English Balzac', but had given up 'in proportion as he has come down steadily from the simple in subject to more simple – from the Anglo-Indians to the natives, from the natives to the Tommies, from the Tommies to the quadrupeds, from the quadrupeds to the fish, and from the fish to the engines and screws'.[29] James reiterated this opinion a couple of years later, after the publication of *Stalky* in book form: 'I can't swallow [Rudyard's] loud, brazen, patriotic verse – an exploitation of the patriotic idea, for that matter, which seems to me not really much other than the exploitation of the name of one's mother or one's wife.'[30] The Scottish critic Robert Buchanan picked up on this in his excoriating attack on Rudyard as the antithesis of the humanitarian tradition of English letters, and the epitome of 'all that is most deplorable, all that is most retrograde and savage, in the restless and uninstructed Hooliganism of the time' – a view echoed in the first full-length critical study cum biography by Richard le Gallienne in 1900.

In answer to these criticisms Rudyard made a determined effort to finish *Kim*, the Indian story that had occupied him, in one form or another, for so long. As his autobiography makes clear, he had broken the back of this project a couple of years earlier. But there was still work to be done. At least it would provide some stimulus for his despondent father whose background knowledge and ideas had been so essential so far. As an additional *aide-mémoire*, he sent for his copy of *Mother Maturin*, which was in safe keeping with A. P. Watt.

Rapidly, over the course of the summer, Rudyard's most delightful and enduring novel took final shape – an extraordinary feat for, as far as anyone could discern from his recent behaviour, Rudyard had degenerated into a political propagandiser, with little subtlety to his art. Yet in 1900 he produced a book that transcended the imperialist rhetoric that had blighted his writing on India over the previous decade, showed none of the Anglo-Saxon supremacy he adopted in South Africa and had enough 'complicated soul' and 'shades' to please the most demanding critic.

Writing at book length allowed Rudyard to deal with the pace and the space of the sub-continent. More than any other of his works, *Kim* demonstrates his love and understanding of India. He makes no attempt to portray the colonialist's existence as superior to the native's. Indeed his manuscript shows that he took special care to tone down any possible racialist traits in his European characters and to build up his Asians – in particular, the lama, who had earlier been rather too ingratiating and child-like. For the first time he deals sympathetically with Indian reli-gion. Everyone, in his or her way, is a 'seeker', searching for fulfilment or merit. For the first time, too, Rudyard acknowledges something he had known but, for various reasons (including cowardice), had rejected while in India: the similarity between Indian philosophy and his own metaphysical interests – between the Buddhist concept of dharma (the law) and his own developing ideas of a corpus of received wisdom, also known as 'the law', that is necessary for the health of a community; between the East's familiarity with the powers of the mind (inherent in its traditions of reincarnation and time travel) and his fascination with dreams and psychic phenomena, as seen in 'The Finest Story in the World' and 'The Brushwood Boy'; and between the play-like quality of life in the East and his own heavy-handed Western equivalent in his *Stalky* stories.

Both cultures are involved in the Great Game of being. (It was coincidental that this was also the name given to the more ephemeral struggle between Russia and Britain for political power in Central Asia.) Ultimately, in *Kim*, Western action wins out over Eastern contemplation: the eponymous boy hero does not follow his lama, but prepares to take up his historical position as a young 'great gamer' with Colonel Creighton. Thus Edward Said, scourge of the Orientalist tendency in Western culture, can call *Kim* a 'master work of imperialism' and rightly suggest that Rudyard failed to reflect the developing independence struggle in India. But Said acknowledges that somehow Rudyard transcended his political agenda and thereby achieved a novel of 'aesthetic integrity'.

But then Rudyard did not write *Kim* to accord with the criteria of an academic nearly a century later. *Kim* shows Rudyard at his most subversive, turning his usual opinions on their head, affirming the benefits of cultural and intellectual pluralism, asserting the right to see things from different angles, crying out for the freedom of the artist to follow his daemon and, if necessary, to take contrary views. And he ascribes such insight firmly to his Indian experience:

> Something I owe to the soil that grew –
> More to the life that fed –
> But most to Allah Who gave me two
> Separate sides to my head. . . .
>
> I would go without shirts or shoes,
> Friends, tobacco or bread
> Sooner than for an instant lose
> Either side of my head.[31]

Although *Kim* was finished in August, and Rudyard would have liked to have published it before the end of the year, *McClure's Magazine* offered £5000 for the serial rights and its schedule had to be accommodated. This meant that, though the serialisation began in December 1900, the book did not appear until the following October. As soon as he read it, Henry James was thrilled that Rudyard had again tackled something commensurate with his talents. Writing from Lamb House, his newly acquired home in Rye, along the Sussex coast towards Kent, James called *Kim* a

> magnificent book . . . The way you make the general picture live and sound and shine, all by a myriad touches that are like the thing itself pricking through with a little snap – that makes me want to say to you: 'Come, all else is folly – sell all you have and give to the poor!' By which I mean chuck public affairs, which are an ignoble scene, and stick to your canvas and your paint-box. There are as good colours in the tubes as ever were laid on, and *there* is the only truth. The rest is base humbug. Ask the Lama.[32]

Delighted as Rudyard was to receive such praise, there was never any question of his abandoning his new-found political interests. As a diversion he worked on a play based on his *Jungle Books*. But his guru, Cecil Rhodes, was much more demanding than any Tibetan lama. With his thirty-fifth birthday approaching, Rudyard decided to leave for his winter holiday in South Africa earlier than usual. Under the terms of his lease, The Elms needed painting and he (or, rather, Carrie) wanted this, and some additional repairs, completed while they were away. By 30 December 1900 (in retrospect, almost exactly half-way through his life), he and his family were ensconced in The Woolsack, the new house Rhodes had built specially for them in Cape Town.

Ten years earlier, during the summer of 1890, Rudyard had been painted by John Collier, a fellow member of the Savile Club. Most artists (including his brother-in-law) tended to make him look worthy, cerebral and intense. But Collier had a knack of suggesting additional features in his subjects. His 1890 portrait had subtly indicated the Oriental dimension to Rudyard's personality. Rudyard must have appreciated this, for a decade later he agreed to sit for him again. (A further incentive was that Collier had offered to give the finished product to Carrie, in return for various rights of reproduction.) This time he captured Rudyard's Kim-like quality – his playful, innocent intelligence. The hair might be receding, the moustache droopy and walrus-like, but the painting showed Rudyard's emotional fragility and approachability in such a direct way that it almost justified Carrie's efforts to guard his space.

Arriving in Cape Town on Christmas Day 1900, the Kiplings were met by Rhodes's carriage. They were taken to their new house, set among huge oak and pine trees, with the Table Mountain rising from the back and a long view down the narrow front garden to the Drakenstein mountains in the distance in front. Rhodes's Groote Schuur was literally next door – a short walk through a hydrangea-covered ravine. As for the house itself,

Herbert Baker had skilfully adapted a traditional Cape Dutch design to produce a modern serviceable bungalow, comprising two whitewashed wings, with shutters and heavy doors of oiled teak, built round a smallish colonnaded open court. The beds were made, milk had been ordered, ice was in the chest: the family simply had to unpack.

Within ten days Carrie decided the place was 'enchanting' and told Sally Norton that its 'beauty and peace' were helping her 'rather troublesome nerves to a normal state'.[33] While Rudyard relaxed in 'God's sunshine' (she preferred this to his working), Carrie set to making her mark. This, typically, did not mean changing the décor, which remained stark and utilitarian, but ensuring the efficient running of the household with its multi-national staff – the young black houseboy supplied by Rhodes, the Malay gardener, her trusted Scottish cook Georgina Grant, as well as a governess and a nurse she had brought from England. (Miss Thompson, the governess, had originally come during the autumn as a substitute nurse. Popular with the children, she had the enviable knack of inspiring them to enjoy their lessons. As she had an eye problem, which doctors said would benefit from sunshine and good air, Carrie, belying her reputation as a dragon with servants, had suggested that she come along as a governess. The previous incumbent, Gertrude Blogg, had just become engaged to be married to the writer and publisher Rex Brimley Johnson – not that Carrie was impressed; as she told a friend revealingly, 'I would not marry a literary man for worlds, they are always doing too much and one can only give them help by being hopelessly dull, so they may relax their minds and rest themselves in the security of one's stupidity. They really need to do nothing more exciting than catch flies when they are not on the stretch.'[34] Sadly, Gertrude never made it to the altar, as she was struck by a bus and killed while out bicycling. Her sister Frances was more fortunate, marrying G. K. Chesterton in 1901.)

The Woolsack was paradise for Elsie, who had her fifth birthday in February, and for John, who was three. Life had not been easy for them since their sister Josephine's death. Inevitably, their parents had been protective and, according to several observers, the children were timid and slow-witted. (Rudyard himself noted his daughter's 'difficulties with human speech':[35] when he taught her Beggar-my-neighbour, she said she was playing a new game, Govern my Negro. Georgie talked about John's speech being 'a foreign language to outsiders'.[36]) At The Woolsack they no longer had to be on their best behaviour, as Mr Kipling's well-brought-up children. Barefoot in the garden, they could rootle among the myrtle and plumbago hedges, and enjoy the profusion of exotic fruit and flowers. They had access to the menagerie of kangaroos, zebra and emus which roamed on the neighbouring Groote Schuur estate. Rhodes even kept a private zoo, with a couple of lions from the Matabele bush. When a new-born lion cub was having difficulty surviving, he sent it over to The Woolsack to see if the Kipling children could raise it by hand. After discovering that the Ndbele for lion was *umslibaan*, Elsie and John christened the cub Sullivan. They weaned him with a bottle until the moment, recorded by Rudyard, when the baby's eyes, hitherto dull and stupid, suddenly became a 'grown-up lion's eyes, soft and blazing at the same time, without a wink in them, eyes that seemed to look right through you and out over all Africa'. Then they had to return the growing and now healthy Sullivan to his parents. And when they tired of their immediate environment, the children went with their nanny, Lucy, to the sandy white beaches at Muizenberg. Because of an outbreak of plague in February, however, Carrie was careful not to let them travel by public transport, though she admitted that trains might be safer than trams 'because only white people go first class'.[37]

The Boer War had now entered a protracted and nasty guerrilla phase. With the main fighting over, Lord Roberts had been replaced as Commander-in-Chief in December by General Lord Kitchener. But over the course of the following year Boer resistance refused to knuckle under. Blaming civilian support for the enemy for his own failure to reach a conclusive peace, Kitchener began to herd Boer women and children into 'concentration camps'. When liberal do-gooders such as 'the unspeakable' (in Rudyard's phrase) Emily Hobhouse revealed the inhumanity of some of the Boers' treatment, popular support for the war dwindled at home, making an overall settlement more vital.

Although this final resolution would not happen for a year, Rudyard was happy to spend time discussing post-war prospects for both South Africa and Empire. With his health beginning to fail, Rhodes had come up with a plan to establish a scholarship fund to allow sixty students from the British colonies, a hundred Americans and fifteen Germans to study at his alma mater, Oxford University. He used to discuss this with the Kiplings over dinner at either Groote Schuur or The Woolsack and was impressed by Carrie's practical suggestions. When she said that his scholars might have difficulty surviving a full year away from home on £250, he raised the stipend to £300. Rudyard acted as his interpreter on these occasions: 'What am I trying to express?' Rhodes would blurt. 'Say it, *say* it.' And Rudyard would tailor an appropriate phrase.

Many of Rudyard's friends from the previous year were no longer in Cape Town. He saw little of Milner, who in February moved his headquarters to Johannesburg and was shortly to return to England to recruit his 'kindergarten' of Balliol graduates who would rule the new South Africa after the peace. Instead, Rudyard befriended Colonel Robert Baden-Powell, hero of the defence of Mafeking, who was beginning to develop his ideas on scouting, a mixture of personal initiative and cult of Empire that partly justifies his description as 'the true Stalky'.[38] During the siege of Mafeking, Baden-Powell had written *Aids to Scouting for NCOs and Men*. Although no records survive, he probably discussed with Rudyard how this military text could be adapted to civilian use. In *Mowgli's Sons*, an entertaining account of the relationship between Kipling and the Boy Scouts, Professor Hugh Brogan points to early scouting references in Rudyard's 'The Way that He Took' (which had been published the previous June) and in his *Just So Story*, 'The Tabu Tale'.

Rudyard also met Baden-Powell's sister Agnes, and his brother Baden, a Scots Guards officer who had pioneered the use of military kites in signalling. Agnes had recently been courted by the Italian-born scientist Guglielmo Marconi who, following his invention of wireless telegraphy in 1895, was interested in the possibility of using Baden's kites in his ship-to-shore wireless experiments. A couple of years earlier, Marconi had accompanied Sam McClure to lunch at The Elms. Having kept his ears to the ground, Rudyard was able, back home in September 1901, to write 'Wireless', a story that, with references to Marconi, explored the relationship between psychic communications and the new science of telegraphy.

With no pressing literary endeavour to concern him, Rudyard also enjoyed the company of another great advocate of Empire, his old colleague Howell Gwynne, the Reuters' correspondent, to whom he presented his 'Friend' medal. Gwynne's rumbunctious manner amused him: he noted that when Gwynne said he had not stayed in a hotel for a month, he meant he had not visited a brothel. This was probably true: Gwynne told his friend G. E. Morrison, the Australian-born correspondent of *The Times* in Peking, 'Pretoria and Bloemfontein are the two most immoral towns in the world. The dear Dutch girls and the Hollanders have no scruples and very little virtue.' Any idea that Rudyard accompanied him to the brothels of Bloemfontein must be discounted: Gwynne simply did not communicate with him on the same level as with Morrison: 'Give my love to all the little Chinese girls', or 'This is a splendid country for f*****g. The Australians have shown the way...'[39] He and Rudyard dealt with loftier matters of Empire.

Sex was not the reason for Rudyard (as he told Rhodes) 'seeing a good deal of the Australians lately'[40] – even if Gwynne did accompany him to tea with Colonel James Mackay, the Australian chief staff officer of Overseas Colonial forces, and remembered the occasion for his introduction to Mrs Willie Mitchell, a beautiful Australian widow who, he noted, was worth £13,000 a year. Rudyard was simply impressed by the way these white-skinned colonials had rallied to the imperial cause: 'a cleaner, simpler, saner, more adequate gang of men I've never met up with.'[41] (His poem 'The Young Queen', published the previous October, had already expressed his appreciation of the decision of the six Australian colonies to join in a new Commonwealth.)

Invited to stay at The Woolsack in early April, Gwynne found Rudyard as 'delightful and as full of energy as ever'.[42] The Kipling children loved him and Carrie prevailed on him to ask Morrison in Peking for some jade. 'Mrs Kipling has fallen in love with jade,' Gwynne told his Australian friend, who knew Rudyard slightly through his boss, Moberly Bell. 'Could you get for her some jade rings, combs or such like? She would be awfully grateful.'[43] After a leisurely lunch one afternoon, he listened with rapt attention as his host recited his latest work, including 'one beautiful poem' Gwynne remembered as 'The Body Guard' (probably 'Bridge-Guard in the Karroo') and a 'perfectly lovely' story, 'A Sahibs' War'. Later, after a 'glorious dinner', 'we talked like blazes till ten when went to bed finding I had talked too much. Kipling has splendid ideas for the "Friends" Society – to be an organisation for the empire.'[44]

Rudyard returned to England in early May 1901 in more sombre and reflective mood than Gwynne's upbeat account suggested. The weather at home was poor and he had continuing problems with rogue American publishers. (After more than two years, the Putnam case had still not been concluded.) Reacting in much the same way as when he came back from India in 1889, he found the British way of life lazy and effete. Recalling his words in 'Recessional', he told Charles Norton on 19 May, 'We were bung-full of beastly unjustified spiritual pride as we were with material luxury and over much ease.' The country had become 'soft-rubber-tyred', but 'now we are slowly coming back to the

Primitives and realizing that a lot of what we called civilization was another name for shirking'.[45] Rudyard promised that 'presently I'm going to sing verses about it'.

Like a good intelligence officer *manqué* (his Indian background had its uses), Rudyard played a long game, with both foreign and domestic dimensions. Narrowly, he had identified Britain's Liberal party as the villain of the piece (and the peace). He had already given an indication of his thinking in 'The Science of Rebellion', a pamphlet written for the Imperial South African Association in February, shortly after Queen Victoria's death. There he attacked those elements in the Liberal party who, contrary to the wishes of the generals, were prepared for the stalemated guerrilla war to continue, because this would lead to an increase in domestic income tax, turning the British public more decisively against the war, and so giving succour and political voice to the Bond (the Cape Boers), who would impede the sort of Anglo-Saxon-dominated peace that Rudyard, Rhodes and their friends had in mind.

More broadly, Rudyard was convinced of his country's need to learn from its South African failures. In his poem 'The Lesson', published in *The Times* on 29 July, he proclaimed a twin message: on the one hand railing against Britain's lack of preparation for war; on another calling for it to raise its sights and adopt an expansive, global outlook rather than a narrow insular one. Again recalling the introspection, if not the mood or metre, of 'Recessional', he intoned,

> We made an Army in our own image, on an island
>   nine by seven,
> Which faithfully mirrored its makers' ideals, equipment,
>   and mental attitude –
> And so we got our lesson: and we ought to accept it
>   with gratitude . . .

and ended,

We have had an Imperial lesson. It may make us an Empire
yet!

Strangely, Rudyard's own life showed no corresponding change
of 'attitude'. His main pastime during the summer was pottering
about the countryside in a new American-built Locomobile steam
car. Not that he covered much ground: with a boiler heated by
petrol burners, which regularly blew out in a cross wind, the car
spent most of its time in the garage. As Rudyard told John Phillips,
general manager of *McClure's Magazine,* who had helped him
purchase the vehicle, 'Her lines are lovely; her form is elegant; the
curves of her buggy-top are alone worth the price of admission.
But, as a means of propulsion she is a nickel-plated fraud.'[46]

He continued, it is true, to promote his village rifle club. (He
was thrilled when 'Earle Hodgson, the military expert man and
one Simpson [an inventor and therefore a maniac]'[47] came to
Rottingdean to test the latter's patent rifle rest.) But while this
might guard against future military unpreparedness, it hardly
broke the mould. Nor did his decision to join the Channel fleet
on naval manoeuvres in July.

The events surrounding Rudyard's short period at sea suggest
that his mind may have been preoccupied with personal problems. For Carrie continued to be plagued by her 'nerves'. As
was professional practice at the time, her doctor ascribed this to
'female troubles'. In her fortieth year, she was thought to be
suffering from an inflammation of the womb. A visit to a specialist
in June suggested she might need an operation. Although this
diagnosis was soon altered – she would not, after all, have 'to be
scraped about and messed about by doctors',[48] – she did require
time for rest and a course of massage. Since Rudyard was scheduled to go out with the fleet in July, Carrie arranged through her
friend Mrs Cornford to rent a cottage for two and a half guineas
a week in the village of Crowborough, some twenty miles away
and at 700 feet one of the highest and reputedly healthiest spots
in the generally flat county of Sussex. Her idea was that her two

children would spend a couple of weeks there, in the company of their nanny Lucy and her new young assistant Miss Parker. She would then recuperate with her own nurse and masseuse while Rudyard was away.

Her plans did not work out that way. Before joining his ship, the *Nile*, Rudyard went to stay with his parents. This immediately raised Carrie's hackles. Her diary recorded,

> July 16 Four wires from Rud. He returns to Tisbury which appals me. A night of agony.
> 17 Rud goes to see Willoughby Manor. I sink down leagues in my declining stride to reach my actual physical state when not braced by necessity. An awful ghost to live with.
> 18 Down and down I go.

Carrie was expressing her reaction to Rudyard making further enquiries about a house, near Salisbury, that he had seen the previous winter before going to South Africa. In January she had been unconcerned, telling Sally Norton that the place was 'rather far from the railway station but, with motors, that is no bar'.[49] The new wing was Elizabethan, the main house from the reign of William II and there was a grave of one of Arthur's Knights of the Round Table who was 'supposed to ride round the mound in full armour in summer evenings'. Six months later – abandoned by her husband and in a state of nervous fatigue – she saw things differently. Not only would Rudyard be close to his mother, which she still found difficult to take, but also the ghost resurrected the spectre of the Rock House and memories of her depression there.

Carrie continued to record her feelings in this hysterical manner for the next three weeks until

> August 6 A night of mental agony leaves me down in the bottom of the pit and well nigh hopeless for the black future.
> 7 Rud arrives at 6 p.m. Great rejoicings.

Her pleasure in her husband's company was endearing. But the corollary was that it put inordinate pressure on him to be with her. Doubtless, as when he disappeared on a tour of North America with his father shortly before Carrie moved into Naulakha in 1893, Rudyard could be selfish. But now, as she grew increasingly neurotic and demanding, his wife threatened to become less a helpmeet attending to the necessities of his daily and business life but rather a jailer, who kept him from friends and intellectual nourishment. Carrie's possessiveness was to be a constant and unwelcome feature for the rest of Rudyard's life.

When Rudyard returned to the political arena his eye was off the ball, for his poem 'The Reformers', published in *The Times* in October, was wilfully obscure. He explained to Gwynne he wanted 'to make people see how the 200,000 or 300,000 men trained to deal with the inevitabilities [of war] must on their return carry over their training into our soft slack civil life'.[50] But even this was not enlightening. The note, said to be an 'extract from a private letter', which accompanied the poem in the paper was marginally more helpful: 'The men who have been through this South African mill will no longer accept the old outworn explanations. They know too much, and it is to them we must look, when they come back, for the real reform in every direction.' But Rudyard's frame of mind was all too plain in his comment (echoing Josephine in the Rock House four years earlier) to Rhodes on 24 October, 'England is a stuffy little place, mentally, morally and physically.'[51] When 'Banjo' Paterson visited the following week, a local butcher seemed to confirm this depressing view. Rudyard took his Australian friend for a long drive and somewhere they stopped to buy some lamb. Playing up to his guest, Rudyard told the butcher he should buy all the Australian lamb he could and keep the money in the Empire. He received the frosty reply: 'The Empire. Ha! My customers don't bother about the Empire, sir. It's their guts they think about!'

Rudyard was more successful when he was invited by Lord Roberts, who was closely associated with the newly formed National Service League, to 'write some stirring lines to bring home to the public the danger of allowing ourselves to be a second time in the same risky position without any properly trained troops in the country'.[52] 'The Islanders', his main poetic blast of the year, was completed in December, just as he was departing once more for South Africa. Startlingly, it showed the extent to which Rudyard's faith in British society had been shattered by the Boer War. Five years earlier, in Tisbury, the colonially reared boy had fallen in love with well-ordered English country life. But in the Cape he had witnessed the complacency of the ruling classes, while his regard for the sterling qualities of the ordinary man had been strengthened. His poem attacked the establishment – mainly the landed gentry who, with their 'witless learning' and 'beasts of warren and chase ... grudged' their sons to military service and refused to allow their estates to be used for army training, but also, more generally, the chattering classes who were more interested in professional sport than matters of national destiny. It was in this context that Rudyard wrote his famous lines,

> Then ye returned to your trinkets; then ye contented your
> souls
> With the flannelled fools at the wicket or the muddied oafs
> at the goals.

Rudyard confirmed to Moberly Bell that the verses were a call for conscription and asked him to back him with an editorial. *The Times* obliged, but rather half-heartedly: it opposed compulsory national service and suggested that Britain's continuing naval power undermined some of Rudyard's arguments.

England happened to be in the middle of a cricket series with Australia when the poem appeared on 4 January 1902. (Rudyard cannot have foreseen this when he wrote it a month earlier.) Over the next three weeks the paper published twenty-seven letters about 'The Islanders', only six of which seemed to take issue with it. Rudyard was delighted at the furore he had created. When one correspondent noted the number of cricketers who had laid down their lives, Rudyard told Rider Haggard, 'It was delicious to see *The Times* backing and filling – and those d****d hired pros, taking cover behind the names of good men, who happened to be cricketers, dead at the front as some excuse for their three day £1000-gate performances. I ought to have written *hired* fools instead of flannelled. That might have made my meaning clearer.'[53]

The poem emphasised the extraordinary turnaround that the Boer War had produced in some of Rudyard's basic ideas, so that even he seemed uncertain where he stood. Was he attacking the sort of society that could produce professional cricketers, or was he calling for national service? Little over two years earlier, in October 1899, when his *Stalky* stories were published in book form, he was convinced of the benefits of the English education system: 'India's full of Stalkies – Cheltenham and Haileybury and Marlborough chaps – that we don't know anything about, and the surprises will begin when there is really a big row on.' But the big row had come and he had been disappointed. His altered view of this Stalky type is apparent as early as 'The Outsider', one of the stories published serially in the *Daily Express* in June 1900, where the stuffy Lieutenant Walter Setton gets his come-uppance from Private Jerry Thrupp who is clearly much cleverer than he. This officer shows no Stalky-like resourcefulness. 'When he could by any means escape from the limited amount of toil expected by the Government, he did so; employing the same shameless excuses that he had used at school or Sandhurst . . . For the rest, he devoted himself with no thought of wrong to getting as much as possible out of the richest and easiest life the world has yet made; and to despising the "outsider" – the man beyond his circle.'

At least Rudyard had started a debate, as he discovered, with a sense of *déjà vu*, when hordes of journalists thronged the docks to meet him off the *Kinfauns Castle* in Cape Town on 7 January 1902. South Africa was in the middle of a heatwave and Rudyard had little energy for anything much more creative than compiling his *Just So Stories* for a book. These dated back nearly a decade to just before Josephine's birth, when Rudyard first mentioned writing a 'camel tale' to Mary Mapes Dodge at the *St Nicholas Magazine*. At the time, he probably had not differentiated them in his mind from the *Jungle Books*. But he had always been interested in simple tales of natural phenomena, whether native fables from India or North-American-Indian legends, as related by his folklorist friend William Hallett Phillips. When Josephine started asking probing questions about the world, he told her these stories, partly as afternoon entertainments in the woods and partly as evening soporifics in bed, where they had to be told 'just so', or else she would 'wake up and put back the missing sentence'. Their particular style recalled Rudyard's childhood at The Grange, where the family would read Lane's *Arabian Nights* and parody that author's modes of address in the manner taken up in the *Just So Stories* – 'Best Beloved' or 'O Enemy and wife of my Enemy'. Over the previous autumn Rudyard had worked on his drawings, with their mixture of runic detail, map-like precision and deft Japanese-inspired line. Lockwood had been so impressed that he encouraged his son to include them in his book of the fables. All Rudyard had to do now was finish a couple more stories, 'The Cat that Walked by Himself' and 'The Butterfly that Stamped', and the completed manuscript would be ready for the publisher. (The former was a tribute to his wife's love of cats – and, in particular, of her new Persian.) The completed text was another Kipling paradox – a children's book with an enduring, magical tone that was the opposite of the raucous antics of Stalky only three years earlier. Critics did not know what to make of them, G. K. Chesterton eventually deciding to describe them as 'like fairy tales told to men in the morning of the world'.[54]

With the war virtually over (the Boers would surrender in May), Rudyard had been hoping to go 'up country',[55] probably to Johannesburg. But a sharp deterioration in Cecil Rhodes's health detained him. Rhodes had been in England until early February, but after he returned he was clearly not well and retired to his seaside cottage at Muizenberg, where he hung on to life for over a month, until he died on 26 March, mouthing the words, 'So little done. So much to do.' He was forty-eight. Within two days, Rudyard composed some obituary verses, which were recited at a short private service at Groote Schuur on 2 April. Rhodes's body lay in state in the Houses of Parliament, before being taken in procession to the Cathedral. Rudyard thought it the most marvellous thing he had ever seen – 'a whole city of 60,000 moved as one man with a common grief and reverence!' – even if he did complain vociferously that marching up Adderley Street in slow time was no joke, leaving his lumbar muscles almost as 'sore' as his heart.[56] For this reason Rudyard opted not to accompany his friend's body on its final railway journey through the African bush to Rhodes's chosen burial place in his eponymous new country of Rhodesia. Rudyard felt that 'half the horizon of my life had dropped away'.[57]

The death of a friend always had a powerful emotional effect on Rudyard and Rhodes's was no different. Although he had just written a poem about his love of 'Sussex by the sea', Rudyard now began to regard Africa as his own country – the place where his love of Rhodes obliged him to be. He had to return to England to see to various business matters. But, as he told Ted Hill, he did not intend waiting until winter before visiting South Africa again. He hoped to be back soon after the coronation of Edward VII in June, for 'this land is the nearest approach to Anglo-Indian in many of its ideas that I know and it has been pulling at me more and more the past four years'.[58]

Rudyard convinced himself of his duty to promote his dead friend's agenda for southern Africa. Even before the peace treaty, he could see that the Progressive party in the Cape was floundering without its mentor Rhodes's inspiration and was giving up ground to the pro-Boer Bond. As a result he lobbied for 'the old fetish' of Constitutional government to be delayed 'till the loyalist who has borne the burden of the day, has overtaken his neglected or ruined business and is in a position to meet the unharmed and astute rebel in the legislature'.[59] (In this, he had a powerful ally in the High Commissioner, the now ennobled Lord

Milner.) Conscious of the power of the media in such situations, he arranged for Maitland Park, assistant editor of his old paper the *Pioneer*, to take over the editorship of the *Cape Times*. Rudyard told Park to look to Jameson for direction: 'He represents Rhodes and Rhodes was Africa.'[60] And to Jameson he admitted how much he was putting his own reputation on the line with this recommendation: 'If he (P) doesn't dig out like a nigger and unreservedly embrace Cape Colony, my face will be blackened and I want P. to understand this.'[61]

Rudyard's pattern of political behaviour – in South Africa, at least – had been established for the next few years. His objective would be to delay the Boers gaining a voice in the Cape, while assisting Milner in settling the newly annexed Transvaal and Orange River Colony with British (or Anglo-Saxon) emigrants. One of his ideas, as he told Lady Edward Cecil, was for every English county to finance some of its best men to go to allotted farms in South Africa.[62] The nearest he got was arranging for some Sussex mechanics to join the diamond firm De Beers. For support, he looked to a new generation of rand millionaires – in particular, Sir Abe Bailey, who had acquired a vast house in the Sussex town of East Grinstead.

Two days after the Boers' surrender in Pretoria on 31 May, Rudyard needed all his diplomatic skills to quell a more domestic row, for his Aunt Georgie had responded to the armistice by hanging a banner across the front of North End House, stating uncompromisingly 'We have killed and taken possession'. Although her point of view had some support in Rottingdean, it did not go down well with villagers who had lost sons in the conflict. On the night of 2 June, Rudyard had to defuse a noisy demonstration outside her home.

His plans for a quick return to South Africa were delayed because, a few days earlier on a trip to Crowborough on 23 May, Rudyard had read in the local paper that a grey stone house that he and Carrie had seen and loved two years earlier had come back on the market. Bateman's was a run-down Jacobean mansion, with no bathroom and no electricity, on the edge of the Wealden village of Burwash. Remembering that the owner, a stickler-like stockbroker called Alexander Scrimgeour, had wanted in excess of £10,000, Rudyard prevailed on Leslie Cope Cornford to contact a Bond Street firm of estate agents, to find out the price and to arrange a viewing in the name of Smith.[63] (The Cope Cornfords were proving the sort of practical no-nonsense friends that every family needs. Earlier in the year Leslie had acted as intermediary when Trix Fleming, now recovered from her illness, published some Coronation verses in the *Pall Mall Gazette*. He had even negotiated a modest fee when a woman wrote in and wanted to set them to music.)

As so often, the Locomobile was out of order on 26 May, so Rudyard and Carrie had to take a train to Etchingham and travel on to Burwash by fly. Bateman's was one mile outside the village, along 'an enlarged rabbit-hole of a lane' that dropped steeply down a one-in-ten gradient to a hollow by the River Dudwell. Thinking – so Rudyard liked to say – that the place was inaccessible, and apparently unaware of the identity of his new purchaser, Scrimgeour was now happy to sell Bateman's, plus the old mill on the river and some surrounding farmland (thirty-three acres in all) for £9300. Rudyard felt he had struck a bargain, but the wily city man had not sold cheaply, since the value of the land was minimal and he had bought the house, without the mill, from a local farmer, Albert Jarvis, for £6500 less than five years earlier. (Scrimgeour later emerged as the main financier of the fiercely anti-semite William 'Lord Haw-Haw' Joyce's National Socialist League, a markedly pro-Hitler break-away from Oswald Moseley's British Union of Fascists.)

Rudyard hired his architect cousin Ambo Poynter to supervise a programme of minor improvements. Having acquired a more reliable Lanchester car, he himself spent much of July toing and froing between Rottingdean and his new property. (His story 'Steam Tactics' suggests his pleasure in this temperamental two-cylinder, ten-horsepower, air-cooled car.[64]) However, in late

August, a few days before they were supposed to move in, he and Carrie drove to Bateman's to make one final check and found the alterations woefully behind schedule. 'Dear Ambo,' implored Rudyard that evening, 'TAKE NOTICE! We have just returned from Bateman's – a long day: and we find there is only one carpenter at work.'[65] He reeled off a list of failings, such as the pantry partition that had not been fitted and the dining-room hatch that was missing. Rudyard begged his cousin to get more carpenters on the job.

Just over a week later, on 3 September, his (and, more so, Carrie's) worst fears were confirmed. Having shut up The Elms, the Kiplings arrived to find Bateman's in chaos. The builders had not done their job and the removers' foreman was drunk. 'Labour and struggle to put things right,' Rudyard noted.[66] Initially he and Carrie were forced to stay at the local Bear Inn. But when the children and servants arrived on the 6th, they had to spend their first night at the house. 'We came in over the bodies of two and twenty "leaders of revolts in Faenza",' Rudyard told Cope Cornford philosophically, referring to a favourite passage from Robert Browning's verse drama *A Soul's Tragedy*. 'They called 'emselves, variously, plumbers, white-washers and so on, but the main point is that we are in.'[67]

Fourteen

Most Wonderful Foreign Land

1902–1907

Rudyard had a line he trotted out to friends towards the end of 1902: England is 'the most wonderful foreign land I have ever been in'. More to the point was the throw-away comment he added to Charles Norton: 'It is made up of trees and green fields and mud and the Gentry: and at last I'm one of the Gentry!'[1] Just as he began to rail against the established order, this foreigner was coming home to rediscover a potent combination of land, status and history.

His new house was set in the cradle of what once was the Sussex iron industry. The gurgling River Dudwell at the bottom of the garden had provided power for an upstream forge that had flourished, initially in Roman times, and later in the sixteenth and seventeenth centuries. The wood to the south bristled with the sweet chestnut and hornbeam that had provided charcoal to fuel the furnaces, and stray pigs of iron could still be found speckling the Wealden clay.

Bateman's itself was built in 1634 – the date proclaimed under the curlicues above the rounded arch of the front porch which, like the walls and mullioned windows, were fashioned from local sandstone, 'hint[ing] at the first tentative intrusions of the Renaissance into this obscure part of Sussex'.[2] Having announced his arrival in the gentry, Rudyard, with typical inconsistency, noted appreciatively that this was not a vast manor, with a lodge 'or any nonsense of that kind', but 'just the kind of house that a successful

Sussex iron master builded himself two hundred and fifty years ago'.[3] In fact, the original owner, Northampton-born William Langham, was probably a London merchant. At least the house escaped mutilation in the mid-Victorians' enthusiasm for renovation, as it had been owned by the local vicar and housed his bailiff who, for forty years, 'lived in peaceable filth and left everything as he found it'.[4]

The inside was dominated by dark panelling and woodwork (including the staircase) in oak, or the 'Sussex weed', as it was locally known. One entered through a black-and-white-tiled hall which, Rudyard told Charles Norton, had 'a deep window seat and high leaded windows with lots of the old greeny-glass panes left and a flap-table of Queen Elizabeth's time (the worst of the place is that it simply will not endure modern furniture) and benches and a stone arched fire place backed by old Sussex iron work'. This set the tone for the rest of the house which, even after fine eighteenth-century English 'Cordoba' leather hangings had been acquired from the Isle of Wight (probably at the suggestion of Lockwood Kipling who had been trawling the dealers of Southern England), and after furniture and other artefacts had been recovered from Naulakha, remained uncompromisingly heavy, as if the Kiplings were settling in for another long siege.

The heart of this armadillo of a house was upstairs in Rudyard's study. His desk was a ten-foot-long early seventeenth-century French walnut draw-leaf table, set on a large Indian woven rug, and littered with pens, papers and writer's paraphernalia. Two thousand books lined the walls ahead and to the left of him (a quarter were about India, with further significant holdings on the Navy and the Empire). One of Rudyard's first commissions, from Leslie Cope Cornford – an excellent carpenter, as well as everything else – was an oak couch where he would stretch out, contemplating his work in progress. As he told a visitor, 'I lie there . . . and wait for my daemon to tell me what to do.' If his daemon ('Intuition. Subconscious. Whatever you want to call it') was silent, he would keep still, smoking a Turkish cigarette. (At this stage he was still a forty-a-day man). When inspiration came he would jump up, his daughter Elsie recalled, 'go to the desk, write a line or two, make a note or a correction, then resume his place on the sofa.'[5]

The grounds provided a light, airy contrast, with a pond and terraced lawns tumbling down in ever rougher grass to the now disused water-mill. Beyond were the woods, bridleways and streams – a panorama evocative of the complex relationship between a landscape and its inhabitants through the ages. Rudyard gained pleasure and stimulation from the traces of a rich history around him – whether the remnants of the forge or the outline of a road across a field, known as The Gunway, supposed to have been used during the Armada. The whole place was 'alive with ghosts and shadows,'[6] Rudyard liked to say.

Before long, he would enjoy the age-old rituals of seeding, nurturing and harvesting his land. At first, however, he only had access to part of his demesne. The majority of his recent purchase had been cut off from Dudwell Farm, an adjoining property owned by Scrimgeour. But since the farm was tenanted until the following spring, he could only gaze fondly and dream of rooting out the hops that grew there (he believed they were too risky a crop) and planting over with grass. He looked forward to washing his apple trees (all 335 of them) with oil, limewash, salt and soap, as recommended in the agricultural textbooks he began to accumulate.

For the time being he focused his attention (and imagination) on the mill. Half wood, half brick, the present building dated from around 1750, but Rudyard insisted its origins were to be found in 1196 and later, ambitiously, liked to suggest it had featured in the 'Domesday Book'. As he wrote in 'Puck's Song', at the start of *Puck of Pook's Hill* in 1906,

> See you our little mill that clacks,
> So busy by the brook?

> She had ground her corn and paid her tax
> Ever since Domesday Book.

Even before moving in, he had decided with Ambo Poynter that the house needed electricity. Initially he put a Hornsby-Ackroyd oil engine to work, but the longer-term plan was to draw energy from the mill dam. After declutching the eighteenth-century water wheel, once used for grinding corn, he ordered a turbine from Gilbert Gilkes of Kendal and a generator from Christy Bros and Middleton, Electrical Engineers, of Chelmsford. He then laid 250 yards of deep-sea cable under the ground leading from the generator to storage batteries in a shed behind the house. As a result, the following August, he created enough power to light ten sixty-watt bulbs.

Rudyard channelled his excitement at this innovation into his story 'Below the Mill Dam', started in June 1902, three days after discussing electricity with Ambo. This witty fable showed that, journalistically, his antennae were as sharp as ever. Picking up from his disillusion with the established order, it told of two one-time enemies, a grey cat and a black rat, who have taken to living companionably in the shadowy recesses of an old mill, while a water wheel turns resolutely away. In their complacent chit-chat, the two animals reflect the old guard, while the water wheel is the symbol of plodding, old-fashioned industrialism. Their equilibrium is upset by the introduction of new technology in the form of turbines. In the ensuing *bouleversement*, the black rat, an old English breed, does not survive, though the cat and the wheel manage the necessary changes to keep the 'Spirit of the Mill' intact.

Angus Wilson interpreted the story as an attack on the Balfourite Souls tendency in the Conservative party. It was also an appeal for innovative ideas in the wake of the Boer War – a response to Joseph Chamberlain's call, 'Now a new chapter begins.'[7] A few days after Rudyard started 'Below the Mill Dam', Chamberlain was set to host a conference of colonial prime ministers. One item on the agenda was Canada's request for imperial trade preferences and, in particular, for the British corn tax, introduced to pay for the war, to be reduced, but only for colonially grown produce. This sort of imperial co-operation was exactly how Rudyard envisaged the future of Empire. It is not known if he discussed the matter with Chamberlain when he attended a reception for the colonial premiers on 16 June, two days before meeting Ambo Poynter to decide on electricity at Bateman's. But it was typical of Rudyard to reflect the mood of the moment. His sister Trix once said, 'If a thing was in the air he knew all about it.'[8] One of the issues of the day was corn tax. Therefore, by a process of literary alchemy, Rudyard's love for his own corn-grinding mill was metamorphosed into a political tract.

His attitude was percipient because in July, the following month, the Prime Minister Lord Salisbury resigned and was succeeded not by Joseph Chamberlain, as Rudyard would have preferred, but by his nephew Arthur Balfour, whose fence-sitting on tariff reform (imperial preference under another name) led to the split and subsequent defeat of the Conservative party in the election of 1906. Although in the middle of moving, Rudyard was encouraged by the added topicality of Salisbury's resignation to speed up his writing of 'Below the Mill Dam' and publish it in September, an unusually quick turnaround time.

Ironically, he placed it in the *Monthly Review*, John Murray's belated entry into the publishers' magazine stakes and in many ways the epitome of all Rudyard was satirising. Conventionally Liberal Unionist in outlook, the journal was edited by Henry Newbolt, whose famous poem 'Vitaï Lampada', from 1897, out-Kiplinged Kipling in its evocation of a desperate battle at the edges of Empire:

> But the voice of a schoolboy rallies the ranks:
> 'Play up! play up! and play the game!'

When Rudyard had published 'The Islanders' earlier in 1902, Newbolt took a dislike to its anti-public school tone and replied

in a poem 'An Essay in Criticism' which advised Rudyard to stick
to subjects he knew about:

> O Rudyard, Rudyard in our hours of ease
> (Before the war) you were not hard to please
> You loved a regiment, whether fore or aft,
> You loved a subaltern, however daft.

Newbolt's attitude was predictable since, a bit earlier, he had
complained to his publisher John Lane about critics comparing
his verses with Rudyard's: 'These donkeys who think that Tennyson invented the Arthurian legends and Keats made the Greek
mythology, of course can't believe that Kipling didn't create
England and English patriotism and the Navy and the Native and
all the rest. I understand that no one else since the "Recessional"
may write a hymn or mention God. It seems that Kipling made
Him too and took out a patent.'[9] Now the peeved Newbolt had
changed his tune and granted 'Below the Mill Dam' was 'original,
witty and up to date', though he told A. P. Watt's son, Struan, 'in
strictest confidence' that he found it 'inartistic both in design and
execution: "a clever skit by an amateur who has read Kipling", I
could imagine anyone saying, until he came to the signature'.
Nevertheless, since he had requested a contribution, he agreed
to pay twenty-five pounds which, although twice the *Monthly
Review*'s normal rate, was well below Rudyard's.

The supreme professional, Arnold Bennett, noted in 1898 that,
while H. G. Wells and William Le Queux wrote for twelve guineas
per thousand words and Stanley Weyman for sixteen, 'Kipling
stands solitary and terrible at £50 per thousand words, £200 being
his minimum for the shortest short story'.[10] Bennett was more or
less correct. While A. P. Watt offered 'The Comprehension of
Private Copper' to *Everybody's Magazine* in the United States for
fifty pounds per thousand in July 1902, he received only twenty-
five pounds per thousand from *Strand* on the home market.
This two-to-one differential between remuneration in the United

States and Britain obtained throughout the 1890s, when Rudyard's rate in the latter market grew steadily from ten pounds per thousand in 1892, to twelve pounds (paid by the *Pall Mall Gazette* for 'The Servants of the Queen' in November 1893) and twenty-five pounds per thousand for 6–7000 words of *Stalky & Co.* in 1898. In October 1904 'The Army of a Dream' was sold to the *Morning Post* for £500. So his acceptance of the *Monthly Review*'s pittance for 'Below the Mill Dam' only provided further evidence of his eagerness to place the article.[11]

By the date of publication Rudyard had moved into Bateman's and was starting to understand the mystique of land that lay at the heart of the Tory philosophy he sought to denigrate. His first lesson was in the power of labour. He had taken the precaution of bringing his gardener Martin with him. But for most jobs around the estate he had to rely on jobbing workmen from the neighbourhood, who operated a cartel and were unwilling to work for his wages. With the help of Stephen Lusted, a local builder who became *de facto* his foreman, 'one of the tidiest and neatest workmen I ever met',[12] Rudyard learnt that the secret of dealing with these Sussex villagers was to treat them as his father might – as rural artists and craftsmen, worthy of respect.

Rudyard himself was not totally jejune regarding the land. He had his experience of Vermont behind him. He had observed traditional country practices on the estates around Tisbury. He had followed round faithfully as Rhodes had shown off his experimental farms in the Cape, spouting 'progressive' ideas on everything from growing fruit to raising livestock. But over country matters he generally deferred to his doughty friend Rider Haggard, one of the few people he allowed into his study while he was writing.

Since the untimely death of his son in 1891, Haggard had retired to his farm in Norfolk, where he began observing the sorry state of English agriculture. The repeal of the Corn Laws in 1846 may have dramatically cut the price of the average British workman's loaf, but the ensuing surge in imports of foreign wheat had contributed directly to the agricultural depression of the last quarter of the nineteenth century, when landlords could no longer afford to maintain their farms and agricultural labourers suffered severely. In 1899, Haggard published *A Farmer's Year*, which focused on the vanishing way of life in the countryside. Kipling encouraged him, comparing Haggard's journal to one of his own favourite books, *Five Hundred Good Points of Husbandry* by the sixteenth-century agricultural writer and poet Thomas Tusser. As a result of the generally positive reaction to his work, Haggard opted to continue campaigning on English farming, rather than take up Moberly Bell's invitation to report on the Boer War for *The Times*.

However, the war, and its financial demands, did nothing to improve rural conditions. So, following the example of William Cobbett and Arthur Young, Haggard donned his breeches and travelled round the country, making a more detailed report on English agriculture. Though his book *Rural England* was not published until 1903, it began appearing serially two years earlier and once again Rudyard was appreciative. Subsequently, Haggard took a more specialised approach in *A Gardener's Year*, which looked in particular at his own experiments in orchid growing. Generally, although his agenda was journalistic rather than political, he shared many of Rudyard's broader ideas, such as the benefits of emigration – to South Africa and other colonies – for both Britain's unemployed and for Empire. Rudyard was keener on the advantages of colonially rigged protectionism and, as late as 1912, was hoping Haggard would return from a trip to Australia and New Zealand 'a Wild Tariff Reformer'.[13]

During the latter months of 1902 Rudyard did little apart from work on his property and entertain friends and family members who came to visit. He expanded on 'The Puzzler', one of his meditations on Englishness from Tisbury eight years earlier – an example of his intellectual waywardness, since it gave out a very different message from 'Below the Mill Dam', referring approvingly to the unfathomability of the English establishment, with its Ties of Common Funk. As before, he was convinced this was a story (at this stage called 'For Men Only') that was unintelligible to women.[14] He was still not satisfied, it seems, for he worked on it again the following August and did not publish it until January 1906. Otherwise his main output that autumn was 'The Rowers', a rant against co-operating with Germany over its efforts to collect debts from Venezuela.

Returning to the Cape at the start of 1903, Rudyard initially found that 'the strain of the war has been taken off and all the country is going ahead by leaps and bounds'.[15] But he was soon disillusioned by the concessions he felt were being made to the Boer-dominated Bond. He blamed Sir Walter Hely-Hutchinson, the Governor of the Cape Colony, for pulling the wool over the eyes of the Colonial Secretary Joseph Chamberlain, who happened to visit in February. Rudyard was disappointed to hear Chamberlain sounding a note of appeasement, because, as he told Lord Milner, the High Commissioner, 'personally – and I mean poetically – I am bound to his chariot wheels, because he is all that we have and we owe him gratitude for the past'.[16]

Despite himself, Rudyard contributed to the general mood of reconciliation in his poems 'The Settler', with its plea to

> repair the wrong that was done
> To the living and the dead

and 'Piet', his paean to the Boer fighting man. (In his more positive moments he hoped Boers – at least, the landless ones – could be recruited for the service of Empire, like the Afridis in India. For, as he said, 'The Boers were the nearest approach to the Jews of old that I have ever met, excepting my friend the Pathan, and for some reasons I was almost sorry to see them go under'.[17])

No longer able to let off steam with Rhodes, Rudyard channelled his frustrations into finishing *The Five Nations*, his first collection of poems for seven years.[18] Like 'Piet', his more recent material expressed his admiration for a new 'thin red line of 'eroes' who had survived their generals' stupidity – men like the soldier from New South Wales with his Proustian experience of the wattle at Lichtenberg, and the home-bound squaddies in 'The Return' and 'Chant-Pagan', with their subtly different messages:

> If England was what England seems
>   An' not the England of our dreams,
> But only putty, brass, an' paint,
>   'Ow quick we'd drop 'er! But she ain't!
>
> ('The Return')

> Me that 'ave been what I've been –
> Me that 'ave gone where I've gone –
> Me that 'ave seen what I've seen –
>   'Ow can I ever take on
> With awful old England again,
> An' 'ouses both sides of the street,
> And 'edges two sides of the lane,
> And the parson an' gentry between,
> An' touching my 'at when we meet –
>   Me that 'ave been what I've been?
>
> ('Chant-Pagan')

As often, Rudyard drew on his own bank of experiences and feelings, particularly in 'Chant-Pagan's' reference to riding through the dark 'forty mile, often, on end ... / With only the stars for my mark' – a throw-back to early days in India and his trip to Patiala. With the attractions of South Africa now beginning to pall, Rudyard was content, by the end of April, to leave 'this sordid and tawdry play – licensed, alas! by the Lord Chamberlain'[19], an unfavourable reference to the Colonial Secretary.

Travelling home on the *Kinfauns Castle* were Sir Abe Bailey and Gwynne, which made for an interesting trip, particularly for the children who loved the latter's company. Waiting at Madeira was a copy of a play, based on his story 'The Man Who Was', by Kinsey Peile, a jobbing actor cum playwright, who had been introduced to Rudyard through their mutual friend Thomas Guthrie (the writer 'F. Anstey'). Rudyard had agreed to Peile's request to dramatise his story, provided he first see the text. But his long stay in South Africa had held things up. While Rudyard was away, Peile had sent his script to the impresario Beerbohm Tree who, still keen for a Kipling text, had agreed to stage it at His Majesty's Theatre in a special summer gala performance in aid of Guy's Hospital.

With time running short, the play was sent to Rudyard in Madeira. Shortly after returning to Bateman's (which was 'looking divine', Carrie commented), Rudyard was visited by Tree and Peile. Although not happy at Peile's attempts to introduce some love interest ('my play was written to show the soul of a regiment – not the soul of a woman'), Rudyard reluctantly gave his permission. 'Remember that Pathan is pronounced Put'arn *not* Paythan,' he wrote helpfully. 'That mispronunciation will make people laugh.'[20] When the play was staged on 8 June, it was seen by the formidable actress Sarah Bernhardt, who was so impressed that she asked Peile to adapt another Kipling story as a vehicle for herself. Here Rudyard drew the line: 'I do not like to think of that imperious and absorbing personality ranging at large among my stories with intent to "create" a female part' where there was not one before.[21] He claimed there was a 'hash of the Gadsbys' coming out in the autumn, so by then the public would be fed up and would return to 'the legitimate drama'. (Cosmo Hamilton, editor of Edmund Yates's old paper *The World*, and a stalwart of the National Service League, wrote[22] about gaining Rudyard's approval for his adaptation of *The Story of the Gadsbys* for Cyril Maude at the Haymarket. But there is no record of it ever having been staged.)

At least Rudyard's aversion to the theatre, which had continued through most of the 1890s, appeared to have been cured. According to his wife's diary, he had been working on a play in 1900[23] and, two years later, this – or another work – even had a name, 'The Gods and the Machine'. But that was the last that was heard of it. In February 1903 he had sanctioned a dramatisation of *The Light that Failed* by 'George Fleming', otherwise young writer Constance Fletcher who was capitalising on the success of her best-selling book *Kismet*, written when she was eighteen. In South Africa that winter Carrie had kept a watchful eye on the newspapers and noted that the reviews were 'all favourable'. With Mrs Pat Campbell's former beau, Johnston Forbes-Robertson, in the lead as Dick Heldar, the play ran successfully at the Lyric Theatre. But Carrie had clearly not read the *Saturday Review* where Max Beerbohm, an inveterate critic of Rudyard's penchant for bullying and militarism, attacked his 'inevitable scent' for 'the ugly word, the ugly action, the ugly atmosphere' and took the opportunity, because of the playwright's change of sex, to question if Rudyard Kipling was perhaps the pseudonym of a woman, because only a woman would be so 'permanently and joyously obsessed' with 'the notion of manhood, manliness, man'.

A Beerbohm cartoon the following year got closer to truth, depicting Rudyard as a hyperactive little ball of energy, with the caption, 'Mr Rudyard Kipling takes a bloomin' day aht, on the blasted 'eath, along with Britannia, 'is gurl'.[24] For Rudyard was as irrepressible as ever. On the one hand he continued to work his land. As he told a friend, 'I've been spending my time laying down agricultural drains – all sizes from nine to four inches – and watching 'em choke up. It isn't Literature but it's Art of a strange sort.'[25] Now he had title, he could lay his additional acres down to grass. He could even joke, in typically dry fashion, 'Decidedly Allah knew what he was about when he cursed Adam with a taste for agriculture.'

At the same time he kept abreast of political developments. In March 1903 a vast new area of Africa had come under British rule with the conquest of northern Nigeria. Six months later Rudyard visited the man responsible, the High Commissioner Sir Frederick Lugard, and his new wife, the former *Times* journalist Flora Shaw, in their house in Abinger. 'Delightful folk,'[26] was the verdict in Carrie's diary. Rudyard spent time with Chamberlain, who announced his full-scale conversion to imperial preferences in May, but was concerned when the politician resigned from the government in September to give himself more opportunity to fight freely on the issue. Rudyard could foresee that the ensuing split in the Conservative party would let the Liberals into power, with dire consequences for South Africa and Empire. The new Viscount Milner was offered Chamberlain's portfolio at the Colonial Office, but believed he had another year's work still to do, ordering the post-war settlement in South Africa. Rudyard met him in Hatchards bookshop on 14 October, the day after Milner returned from a lengthy European holiday, and helped steel his friend for the task ahead. The following month he himself again refused an offer of a knighthood, this time from Balfour. And in early 1904 he declined an invitation to fight a by-election as a Liberal Unionist in South Edinburgh, whose constituency chairman wanted a candidate 'the more Imperialistic he may be, the better'.

By then Rudyard and his family were back in The Woolsack. Politically, he was relieved at the victory of Rhodes's rump, the Progressive party, now headed by Jameson, in the Cape elections in February. But with the economy in poor shape Milner was determined to bring the gold mines up to full production as soon as possible. As a result of lobbying from Fitzpatrick and the Randlords, who wanted to avoid a troublesome white proletariat, and the bizarre logic of imperialism which deemed it inappropriate for white men to work in the mines, the High Commissioner proposed to achieve this by introducing indentured labourers from China. This form of slavery caused outrage in South Africa and in Britain, where there were motions of censure in both Houses of Parliament. Such issues brought out the most childish, sycophantic and unpleasant side of Rudyard's nature. He told Milner he owed him an apology for not having done away with the Bishop of Hereford, the mover of an angry *ad hominem*

motion in the House of Lords.[27] He had had a chance to push the
prelate into the path of an oncoming train at Kidderminster
station the previous autumn. He added, 'I congratulate you on
the plague,' a loathsome reference to an outbreak of bubonic
plague in Johannesburg's Indian community in March. (Like his
father before him, Rudyard thought that the Indians in South
Africa signalled trouble.)

It is extraordinary that he could say such things, only three
years after publishing *Kim*. Even his sympathetic portrait of the
Sikh servant in 'A Sahibs' War' was inspired only because he
appreciated the man's backing for an imperialist war in 'the
country of the "Hubshis" [niggers]'. He himself now saw foreign
lands as little more than tourist destinations. He showed no
enthusiasm in 1902 when Lord Curzon, the Indian Viceroy, invited
him to Delhi for the Coronation Durbar. And if his regard for
Indian culture was ambivalent, his interest in the African way of
life was non-existent. No black African featured in his stories.
There was no Mowgli, Muhammad Din or even Peroo (from
'The Bridge-Builders'). Native culture held none of the romantic
appeal that it had even for his friend Rider Haggard. The most
that can be said is that his poetry showed a fine appreciation of
the veld and he himself had some understanding of Boer traditions. But generally, in Africa, Rudyard's "satiable curtiosity'
deserted him. He liked 'the sunlight and the space of it and the
great breadth of wine-dark sea',[28] but otherwise gave no indication
of seeing the continent as anything except a part in a giant jigsaw
puzzle that needed assembling for the furtherance of Empire.
Renée Durbach has commented, 'What is missing is any sense of
continuity with the past, that magical dimension that underlies
Kipling's writing about England and India ... He failed to see
South Africa as a country with a history.'[29] The trouble was,
Rudyard was too busy exploring the 'foreign land' that was
England.

Rudyard's verses *The Muse among the Motors*, which appeared in

the *Daily Mail* in February 1904, were modest fare, by his standards, as his parody of Wordsworth's *Lyrical Ballads* showed,

> He wandered down the mountain grade
>> Beyond the speed assigned –
> A youth whom Justice often stayed
>> And generally fined.
>
> He went alone, that none might know
>> If he could drive or steer.
> Now he is in the ditch, and Oh!
>> The differential gear!

The ditties provided an amusing commentary on the controversy
that the new pastime of motoring was generating. The letters
columns of *The Times* were still full of complaints from people
who considered the car both dangerous and unsociable. (To a
keen cyclist who reproved him for glorifying speed, Rudyard
replied that Ruskin had once decried cyclists as 'cads on castors'.[30])
When Filson Young, a former war reporter on the *Manchester
Guardian*, solicited his views for a book, Rudyard wrote unequivocally that 'the chief end of my car ... is the discovery of England.
To me it is a land full of stupefying marvels and mysteries; and a
day in the car in an English county is a day in some fairy museum
where all the exhibits are alive and real and yet none the less
delightfully mixed up with books.'[31]

Anyone less enthusiastic might already have abandoned motoring, for the Lanchester he had acquired in 1902 had proved hardly
more reliable than the Locomobile. It needed so many repairs
that Rudyard called it Jane Cakebread, after a notorious London
prostitute with ninety-three convictions to her name. After a six-
month overhaul in the firm's Birmingham works in early 1903
(while Rudyard was away), the car immediately broke down again.
When Lanchester provided a full-time engineer (as well as a
driver), the man had the temerity to ask for a wage increase

from thirty to forty-five shillings a week – the rate received by a colleague in similar employ in Haslemere. It was not until June 1904, when Lanchester supplied a new twelve-horse-power model (nicknamed Amelia), that Rudyard began to enjoy trouble-free motoring. After inevitable teething troubles he was happy enough in December to write a testimonial affirming that his new car had run for 4000 miles 'without flaw or failure'.

Describing a circuitous journey that seemed to go from Wiltshire to Hampshire, via Sussex, Rudyard told Filson Young that in six hours he could travel 'from the land of the *Ingoldsby Legends* by way of the Norman Conquest and the Barons' War into Richard Jefferies' country, and so through the Regency, one of Arthur Young's less known tours, and Celia's Arbour, into Gilbert White's territory'.[32] He also claimed that cars helped the causes of both temperance and education: drivers needed to remain sober and to read road signs. But his main point was that the car was a 'time machine on which one can slide from one century to another'.

Back in Sussex, he only needed to step outside his front door to feel in a time machine. He was enveloped in layers of history; he imagined them even where they did not exist. 'The Old Things of our Valley glided into every aspect of outdoor works. Earth, Air, Water and People had been ... in full conspiracy to give me ten times as much as I could compass, even if I wrote a complete history of England, as that might have touched or reached our Valley.'[33]

Rudyard was encouraged to develop some stories about English history that he had been contemplating for some time. After discussions with Uncle Ned seven years earlier, he had read widely in such books as Mommsen's *History of Rome* and Geoffrey of Monmouth's more fanciful *History of the Kings of Britain*. In August 1902 he asked his childhood acquaintance Gilbert Murray for details of the Numidian Legion in Southern England.[34] At some stage his cousin Ambrose suggested the name 'Parnesius' for a tale about the Romans in Britain.

Rudyard's historical imagination was stimulated by Aurel Stein, a friend of his father from Lahore, whom he enthusiastically invited to Bateman's in September 1903 after reading about his romantic quest for treasure in his book *The Buried Cities of Khotan*: 'We have no buried cities but Sussex was once as you know the seat of an iron industry and the buried slag heaps on my place have already yielded me an old Henry VIIIth spoon, a piece of bronze which I am told may be the cheek of a Roman bit, and a few coins. And I am hunting for pre-Roman relics as I believe our piece of country lay in the track of the Phoenician tin traders.'[35]

Rudyard's writing was held back by several false starts. He abandoned a story about a Viking arriving on Britain's south coast just as the Romans were leaving. Two further tales about Daniel Defoe and Doctor Johnson proved too complicated. It was only when, with some assistance from his father, he attempted a broader sweep that his daemon began to feel in tune with his Sussex environment.

By September 1904 Carrie noted, 'Rud at work on a fresh idea, a set of stories, the History of England, told by Puck to children.' Since John and Elsie, his attentive in-house audience, needed to know about Puck before proceeding to the history, Rudyard asked his friend Gwynne, who had returned to England to edit the right-wing *Standard* newspaper, to call at a toy shop before coming to Bateman's in early October and to buy a mask of a donkey's head, 'either in paper or cloth sufficiently large to go over a man's head and also a pair of gauze fairy wings'.[36] Rudyard pleaded that he had not gone mad, but was preparing for a production of *A Midsummer Night's Dream* in the quarry at the front of the house, with John as Puck, Elsie as Titania and himself (inside the donkey's head) as Bottom. (In the event, 'Weland's Sword', the first story in *Puck of Pook's Hill*, suggests that Gwynne failed in his commission and Rudyard bowed out, leaving John to play both Puck and Bottom – the latter in a fragile paper donkey's head out of a Christmas cracker.)

As the idea of *Puck of Pook's Hill* took root, Rudyard could claim that winter,

I have been blocking out a set of stories which concern Dan and Una, and one Puck – alias Robin Goodfellow, the oldest and only existing fairy in England. He tells the children some rather out of the way histories concerning the Gods of the early Saxons who gradually had to become fairies as their worshippers fell off; and at various times and seasons calls up for their amusement a Roman legionary, last of the Roman soldiers left in Britain; a young Norman baron who came over with William the Conqueror; a mediaeval adventurer who had an interest in a gold mine on the West Africa coast . . . an old Sussex iron master who cast guns for the Armada and persons of that sort. The first yarn is done but deuce knows when the next will be. It's awfully slow work; the audience being a really educated one. The whole thing ought to be rather an interesting study of early English history.[37]

More immediately, Rudyard had been putting the finishing touches to his collection of stories *Traffics and Discoveries*, which was published in September 1904. The title referred directly to the Elizabethan explorer Richard Hakluyt's *The Principal Navigations, Voyages, Traffiques and Discoveries of the English Nation*, which was Rudyard's theme of the moment. This book was not concerned to show England objectively with a historian's perspective, but to give a flickering cinematic impression of a nation adapting to post-Boer War realities, as it makes its psychic adjustments to political, social and technological progress. Even in the more prosaic stories such as 'The Captive', the influence of Rudyard's nagging daemon can be sensed, pushing him to create a work that is not so much conventional but metaphysical history.

The strands of his recent interests range through the book in roughly chronological order. As well as Boer War tales, there is a selection of naval stories, which draw on Rudyard's observations of sailors ashore in Devon and at sea with the Channel fleet, and tell of Emanuel Pyecroft, a Stalkyish petty officer who follows an independent line within 'the bonds of discipline'. Boundaries of space and time are broken down with motor cars and telegraphy in 'Steam Tactics' and Wireless'. The latter story also explores the more subtle overcoming of limits through the power of the mind. This theme, which had intrigued Rudyard since India, is followed up in 'They', where a magical car journey through Sussex recalls the 'thirty-mile ride' of 'The Brushwood Boy', bringing the narrator from 'the other side of the county' – from one consciousness to another, where he can see and talk to the spirits of dead children playing in a country garden. Evoking his own painful efforts to communicate with Josephine, Rudyard does not tarry long among the auras and spiritually charged colours of 'the Road to En'dor'. As the narrator tells the psychic woman at the centre of the story, 'For you it is right . . . For me it would be wrong.'

Rudyard could not restrain himself from delivering a blast of political invective in 'The Army of a Dream'. First envisaged back in 1900, this was his over-long scenario of the army of the future, where people would perform their national service with the same enthusiasm that they played team sports such as cricket and football. Taking his cue from the cricketer C. B. Fry, he foresaw mock military exercises conducted in the spirit of county cricket matches. (He hoped that giving them a folksy spirit would help rebut charges of militarism.) In real life, as he confirmed elsewhere, he himself had a more direct way of ensuring the performance of national service: anyone not volunteering should be denied the vote.[38] In his story, however, his dream is shown to be a mirage and those capable of fulfilling it have been killed in South Africa. As a tease, Rudyard liked to describe this tale as the most important in the collection – the one, he told his occasional correspondent Ted Hill, that was the purpose of the whole book.[39]

As additional political fodder he included 'Below the Mill Dam'. But the most successful and still most pored-over story in *Traffics and Discoveries* was the enigmatic 'Mrs Bathurst', written in South Africa in February. Ostensibly a rambling memoir about the unfortunate demise of a naval warrant officer called Vickery, it contrasted two forms of modern communication – mechanised transport (symbolised by the railways at the beginning and end) which resulted in loneliness and isolation for those required to travel great distances in service of Empire (an old theme from Indian days), and the cinema which provided powerful, immediate images of 'Home and Friends', as the newsreel feature in the Cape Town biograph was called.

Overlaid on this was a subject Rudyard had scarcely addressed since India: the destructive power of sexual love. Twenty-odd years before Elinor Glyn invented the It-girls, Rudyard wrote of the sex appeal of Mrs Bathurst, the barmaid whom his anti-hero Vickery had met in Auckland, ''Tisn't beauty, so to speak, nor good talk necessarily. It's just It. Some women'll stay in a man's memory if they once walk down a street . . .' (Possibly he gleaned this idea from Lord Milner, who had courted Glyn the previous summer.)

Rudyard explained in *Something of Myself* how Mrs Bathurst was based on his own recollection of a barmaid who had sold him a beer during his visit to Auckland in 1891. A decade or so later he heard a petty officer from Simonstown telling a friend about a good-natured woman from New Zealand. 'Then – precisely as the removal of the key-log in a timber-jam starts the whole pile – these words gave me the key to the face and voice at Auckland, and a tale called "Mrs Bathurst" slid into my mind, smoothly and orderly as floating timber on a bank-high river.'[40] He might have written that it came to him like a succession of cinematic images. For Rudyard had been exploring the tricks and subtleties of memory. It was possible to 'recall' events through sensory experiences (such as the wattle which acted as the 'madeleine' for the New South Wales soldier at Lichtenberg), through a relationship with the environment (thus creating 'history', the subject matter of *Puck of Pook's Hill*), or through dreams and psychic awareness (as in 'They'). Writers such as himself acted as licensed memory joggers. Now there was a new form of memory that threatened the paramountcy of words as a form of communication – the mechanical and often uneven reproduction of pictures at the cinema.

Craig Raine has argued plausibly that Vickery's guilty secret is bigamy.[41] Since no reliable model for Mrs Bathurst has been found, Rudyard's imagination may have been stimulated by a surprise meeting with his old flame Isabella Burton in London the previous October, at a time when Carrie was away with the children, staying with the Baldwins in Worcestershire. Isabella had left her husband and returned to England with her only son Francis. Rudyard subsequently wrote formally to thank her for an old Gaiety programme, which reminded him of his theatrical performances in Simla. He added that he too had enjoyed reading *The Call of the Wild* by the American author Jack London, whose tales of the wild west and frozen north were reminiscent of his old favourite Bret Harte. Although his cool tone gave nothing away, he elsewhere indicated there were strains in his marriage. 'Men and women may sometimes, after great effort, achieve a creditable lie,' he noted in 'They', as if drawing on hard-won experience. 'Mrs Bathurst' hints that, at the age of thirty-eight, he might have contemplated some indiscretion with Isabella and then banished the thought.

Reaction to Rudyard's output was mixed. When Alan Lascelles, the well-connected future private secretary to both King George VI and Queen Elizabeth II, went up to Trinity College, Oxford, in October 1905, the Rev. H. E. D. Blakiston, the President, told him that Kipling (along with G. K. Chesterton and Bernard Shaw) should be transported for life. Phil Burne-Jones informed Charles Norton that he had not actually read his cousin's latest work, but 'from all accounts' it did not 'seem to be up to the mark. The growing tendency to obscurity ... and this perpetual preaching of blood and thunder and blowing of "imperial" trumpets, must militate against the enjoyment of his writings; and I think people are beginning to feel this and not to take as much pleasure in them as they did.'[42]

Phil's world-weariness was not always shared on the other side of the Atlantic. Despite general American opposition to the Boer War, Jack London, a socialist, saw Rudyard as sui generis, a unique interpreter of bourgeois triumphalism: 'when they, the future centuries, quest back to the nineteenth century to find what manner of century it was – to find, not what the people of the nineteenth century thought they thought, but what they really thought, not what they thought they ought to do, but what they really did do, then a certain man, Kipling, will be read – and read with understanding.' In Baltimore, the iconoclastic young journalist H. L. Mencken described himself as 'a Kipling fanatic of the first chop'. He decorated his bedroom with four or five portraits of his hero and adopted Kipling models for his youthful verse.

Even at home Rudyard had unlikely enthusiasts. In September 1904 George Bernard Shaw sent his lover the actress Ellen Terry a copy of 'They' and asked if she would like to play the blind woman: 'One forgives all the creature's [i.e. Rudyard's] schoolboy ruffianisms and vulgarities for his good tidings, of which this is one of the goodest. What a pity the thrilling turning point of it – when he feels the child's kiss in his palm, and then, seeing that there is no child there, realizes – is impossible on stage!' Terry was overwhelmed. 'Thanks and thanks,' she replied. 'I never loved him before for I admired him too much, but that story was the meltingest loveliest thing. The stage would be too rough for it I fear and I should fear to touch it if I were him.'[43] She may have understood instinctively why Rudyard tended to steer clear of the theatre.

As Rudyard's use of the phrase in this particular story suggested, the Kiplings' 'creditable lie' was about coping with life without Josephine. Five years after their daughter's death they still felt her loss hugely and made a conscious effort to present a composed face to the world. Rudyard had his work and his fantasy life as country gentleman cum historian to fall back on. Carrie, the American expatriate with few friends, was rather braver. He might be uncommunicative and, at times, exasperating. But she loved him enough to overlook that side, to keep her own volatility in check and to devote herself to being the wife of a genius.

Managing her property was still her forte, though she did her best to overcome her perceived deficiencies as a home-maker. In June 1904, while Rudyard was resting after completing *Traffics and Discoveries*, she described her routine to her mother. At 10 o'clock one morning she had finished her daily load of dictating letters and was about to devote some 'quality time' to Elsie and John, who had been listening intently to their new governess, Miss Mary Blaikie, reading them Bible stories. The children were looking forward to a visit from their friends the Cope Cornford twins (one of whom, Lawrence, was Rudyard's godson). While Carrie noted poignantly, 'I like entertaining children better than grown-ups,'[44] she acted the impeccable hostess for what were invariably her husband's visitors. On another occasion, when the Kiplings were expecting a crusty house party comprising 'Stalky' Dunsterville and his wife, Gwynne and Cope Cornford, Carrie spent the morning arranging flowers, supervising the kitchen and making sure that the three guest rooms were spick and span. Outside, a gardener had just sliced off the top of his finger while sawing firewood and Carrie explained to her mother, 'Over here, an employer is liable for such misadventures to either man or woman servants, and one covers the responsibility by insuring them against accidents. We wrote the insurance people this a.m. and they and the doctor fry it up between them.'[45] She particularly enjoyed it when Rudyard took time to join her on her rounds of the property. One morning they both spent an hour 'overseeing the workmen and making out plans to make the garden more beautiful. Some bees swarmed suddenly in the mill and we watched with excitement how they were hived in a new hive to set up housekeeping fresh.' A few days later, she wrote, 'This is a perfect June day, and I have wanted everyone I love to see the outer garden. The roses in the sweet briar hedge, which encloses the little rose garden where the lead figures are, are in full bloom, and this perfume is wonderful, and the mass of pale pink blooms perfect, and the border of white pinks is in full glory and even sweeter.'[46]

But there was another, sterner side to Carrie. When in 1902 her efficient secretary Sara Anderson was forced to resign so as to look after her elderly parents, Carrie hired Elsie Parker who had worked for her as a children's nurse the previous summer. Under Miss Anderson's supervision, Elsie performed various exercises and was deemed proficient for the post.

Young Elsie was soon squabbling with her mistress. Having agreed a salary, she could not understand why Carrie refused to pay it, insisting instead on a hitherto unmentioned trial period. Elsie complained this was absurd: either she was 'competent, well recommended and fit'[47] for the work, or not. Even when the agreed money was released, Elsie was convinced that Carrie tried to bamboozle, even swindle, her by paying her by the month – with the result, she claimed, that she lost four weeks' wages during the year. There were regular disputes about petty issues such as whether Elsie should be charged not just for the wood that heated her cottage but for the electricity used to saw that same wood.

While the Kiplings were away in the early part of 1904 Elsie, like most of the staff at Bateman's, was laid off. She went to work for an American playwright, Seymour Obermer, who appreciated her services enough to want her to stay full time. (Not that it appears to have benefited him: his only known play, *The House of Bondage*, had just three matinée performances at His Majesty's Theatre in 1909.) Carrie begged her to return, offering to raise her salary to £120 (later £130) a year and arguing that it could not possibly inconvenience Obermer if she left after only two months. When Elsie wrote to inform Obermer about this she said of Carrie, 'Her health is obviously indifferent and she said to me yesterday that if I realised the struggle she is now obliged to make to get through her heavy and trying share of the work each day, I should not add to her troubles by insisting on going at such a time.'[48] Of course, Elsie could have been just a scheming girl, playing each of her employers against the other. But Carrie's emotional blackmail of her secretary was familiar to anyone who was aware of her treatment of her husband.

Elsie agreed to stay with the Kiplings but, before long, another trivial dispute arose. Carrie had given her twelve shillings to pass on to Baldwin, the chauffeur. When she did not see any note of this on Elsie's regular monthly accounts, she accused her secretary of taking the money. Elsie pointed out that all the moneys had been accounted for. In the ensuing argument Elsie resigned and then was reinstated. Finally opting to leave in October, Elsie told Sara Anderson that she was not sure what sort of reference Carrie would give her. Rudyard's would be favourable, she felt, 'for on the day I gave her notice I accidentally overheard him remonstrating with her about me. But he has no voice in anything now.'[49]

Josephine's death had the effect of bringing out the mean, acquisitive streak in her naturally efficient mother. Carrie had always kept a close eye on Rudyard's business affairs. Now her background as the daughter of an insurance salesman encouraged her to adopt more of a laager mentality. She devoted her energies to building up the family fortunes. Anyone not with her was agin her. (One can see why Rhodes found it useful to talk to her about his scholarships.)

Rudyard's income had built up steadily through the 1890s. He quickly overcame his financial set-back when he lost £2000 in the crash of the Oriental Banking Corporation. His earnings at the start of the twentieth century are estimated at £15,000 per annum. Every year up to the First World War, Macmillan sold an average of between 4000 and 8000 copies of each book in its popular pocket edition alone. Since these cost five shillings in red leather and four shillings and sixpence in blue cloth, Rudyard made around £5000 a year on his thirty per cent royalty. Methuen sold an average 9000 copies a year of *Barrack-Room Ballads*. Income from newspapers, magazines and American sales brought the total up.

Certainly Rudyard had no difficulty in finding £967 to fund his lawsuit against Putnam's in 1901 nor £450 to install electricity at Bateman's the following year. On 17 October 1905 he added to his insurance cover, taking out a further £4000 life insurance policy, costing £175. 16s. 8d per annum 'to cover death duties'.[50]

He had reached a new level of wealth around 1900. Subsequently, he regularly quizzed his more financially astute friends and relations about how to invest the odd few thousand pounds. In May 1901, for example, he turned to his old Indian employer Sir James Walker (in his capacity as owner of the Alliance Bank in Simla), asking what the bank would pay on £3000 or £4000 he wanted to salt away. 'One doesn't seem to get more than 3% on anything this side of the water,' he complained.[51] A fortnight later his nest-egg had risen to £5000, which was converted into 75,000 rupees (at a rate of fifteen rupees to the pound) and credited to Carrie's name.

Carrie was not without her own means. Under the terms of her grandfather's will she was a beneficiary, following the death of old Madame Balestier in June 1901. Independent wealth encouraged her to step up her requests for baubles from Rudyard's friends in distant places. She asked for amber when Perceval Landon accompanied Colonel Francis Younghusband to Tibet in 1904 and Gwynne had to send a shopping list to Morrison in Peking in June of that year: 'She wants £50 of the following. Jade ornaments of all kinds but not that big, some Buddhas, a few embroideries and any curious little things you may see – a little good China if it is available.'[52]

Carrie's bank balance was also boosted when Naulakha was finally sold in 1903. For seven years Rudyard's trusted English coachman Matthew Howard had held the fort – fending off visitors and despatching books and pieces of furniture, as requested, to England. It hardly mattered that his whole family (eight children in all) had moved into various parts of the property. After Rudyard's failure to visit in 1899 it was clear that, with the memory of Josephine now superimposed on that of his court case, he would never return. Two years later, in 1901, he offered the house for sale at $30,000, but there were no takers. The following year the price fell to $10,000 and still he could not find a buyer. In January 1903 he admitted to Conland, 'I feel now that I shall never cross the Atlantic again. All I desire now is to get rid of Naulakha which I am perfectly willing to part with for $5000 (five thousand dollars!). That means carriages, sleighs, etc., and everything that may be in the house at the present time! All for $5000. That's what I call a bargain ...'[53] Almost in desperation, Rudyard suggested that the Brattleboro lunatic asylum might like to use it as an annexe. In November 1903 the Cabot family – Molly, Grace (and her husband Frederick Holbrook) and Will – put Rudyard out of his misery and bought Naulakha for the asking price. The proceeds – £1000 sterling – went to Carrie, the nominal owner.

Property now became the Kiplings' most important asset, as well as most engaging joint interest. Once the Naulakha sale was finalised in November, Carrie ploughed the proceeds back into land in England, paying £923.2s. for Rye Green Farm and a large fifty-one-and-a-half-acre expanse to the west of Bateman's. Rudyard still owned three pieces of land in Rottingdean where, in August 1902, he entertained an offer of £450 from a local JP, who wanted to build a chapel on his fifty- by seventy-foot plot, North Bank Meadow. However, he made clear he had no intention of selling his rifle club site or his sea frontage 'because I should have no means of controlling the use to which the land might be put in the hands of speculative builders'. (He later sold the frontage to Arthur Ridsdale.) For a while he thought of dismantling the drill hall and bringing it, lock, stock and barrel, to Burwash. But he decided against this and contributed instead to a gymnasium in his new village (pronounced Burrush by the locals).

The Kiplings' sights were focused on accumulating land and property around Bateman's. When, in September 1904, Rudyard paid £774 for a farm called Little Bateman's, and a further nine acres, stretching northwards towards the village, Carrie explained to her mother that he had viewed it as an investment, paying two and three-quarters per cent, 'which is as good as consols and has the advantage of adding to the value of Bateman's directly by giving it more land and indirectly by preventing someone else buying it and turning the pretty old farmhouse into a villa'.[54] The same month, adjacent to Little Bateman's, he acquired a barn, lodge and two pieces of land known as Upper and Lower Oxfield (six acres in all) for £420.

On Rider Haggard's advice he sought to buy the remaining fifty-three acres of Dudwell Farm and Mill. In letters to Haggard he referred to this property, in shorthand form, as Naboth's Vineyard – not because it contained vines, but because, referring back to his story in *Life's Handicap* and, before that, to the Book of Kings, this land surrounded his own and he, picking up on Carrie's comment to her mother, wanted a ring of his own property around Bateman's. Negotiations with Scrimgeour, the owner, became tense, with Carrie referring to 'haggling' and Rudyard telling Haggard, when the deal was nearly complete, 'I believe I've got it now – but the chap is so wonky he may swivel round at the last minute.'[55] In January 1905 he had his agent A. P. Watt write to Macmillan requesting payment of everything they owed him.[56] With the £2878 thus received, the Kiplings were able, the following month, to acquire the property they wanted for £5000.

This splashing around of money was not universally popular in the neighbourhood. As a result of his improvements to Bateman's the local Ticehurst District Council wanted to double the estimated rateable value of his property. Rudyard called in his solicitor cousin George Macdonald to contest the claim. Carrie told Macdonald (in between wanting him to injunct some photographs of her husband taken several years earlier in Torquay) that, since the Council's aim was clearly to avoid having to inflict a rate rise on the poorer members of the community, Rudyard 'thinks it will be wholesome for the neighbourhood to know that he does not intend to be put upon after this flagrant fashion'.[57] A drawn-out and expensive bureaucratic battle ensued. The Kiplings had to detail their various changes to Bateman's. When the Council offered to reduce its new estimate to £125, Rudyard held out for £100, eventually agreeing to £110 – but only so as to prevent having to repeat his Brattleboro experience and appear as a witness before the Quarter Sessions in Lewes.

In the circumstances Rudyard soon learnt to appreciate his local allies. Top of the list was Colonel Henry Feilden who had moved into Rampyndene, an attractive William and Mary house in the centre of Burwash, at the same time as Rudyard acquired Bateman's. According to family legend, Feilden described Rudyard as 'an awful little bounder' after first meeting him at the Bear Hotel. But the two men shared a reactionary attitude to the world and soon were great friends. From a Lancastrian political family, Feilden had enjoyed a varied career, nicely illustrative of the opportunities for adventure and personal advancement in the service of Empire. As a result of serving with the British army in India and China, he made enough money (one source refers to his looting during the siege of Lucknow) to purchase a cargo of blankets, which he transported to the Southern states, beating the Northern blockade in the American Civil War. Attaching himself to the Confederate army, he became an ADC to General 'Stone-wall' Jackson. After marrying a Charleston belle, he travelled as official naturalist with the 1875–6 Arctic expedition – the one from which Rudyard claimed, as a small boy, to have seen HMS *Alert* and HMS *Discovery* return to Portsmouth. Feilden subsequently went back to the British army and served in South Africa. Forth-right in manner, though diffident about personal achievements, Feilden was the ideal 'Colonel Sahib' (as dubbed by Rudyard), suited, in the absence of any other candidate, to act the squire in Burwash, where he regularly read the lesson in church on Sundays.

As a symbol of his occupancy of Bateman's, Rudyard was delighted when, in June 1904, he acquired the iron bell-pull which, as a child, he had found so intriguing at The Grange. The combination of his company, Carrie's spartan but impeccable housekeeping and the surroundings of Bateman's ensured a steady flow of visitors that summer, including Joseph Conrad ('a large seaman full of amusing stories'[58]), Henry James, a relatively close neighbour at Rye, and Frank Doubleday and his wife (Doubleday had split from McClure and now ran his own firm, which still published Rudyard in the United States).

Rudyard's two most welcome guests were his Friends from Bloemfontein, Perceval Landon and 'Taffy' Gwynne, both of whom became mainstays for much of the rest of his life. Landon was an elusive character, with interests in recherché areas. Of Huguenot origin on his father's side, he was related on his mother's to the early nineteenth century Prime Minister Spencer Perceval (hence his first name). After qualifying as a barrister, he had enough of a private income to be able to travel widely and drift into a job as a foreign correspondent. When he returned from lengthy trips abroad he slipped easily into an alternative role as an aesthetic bachelor clubman, writing plays, novels and poetry, dining at the Beefsteak and befriending a wide range of mainly aristocratic women.

In 1904 he was recently back from reporting for *The Times* on Colonel Francis Younghusband's botched expedition to Tibet. The object had been to sign a commercial treaty with the country's ruler, the Dalai Lama. But this had turned into an excuse for a military exercise – 'the last great adventure of the Victorian age',[59] as Younghusband's biographer Patrick French described it. Curiously, Landon left Younghusband's party before the conclusion of the treaty and hurried back to Calcutta. This has led to speculation: did he simply want to get home to write up his account before anyone else? Or did he have some role in the intelligence services?

Arriving in England in late September, Landon went to Bateman's to work on his book *Lhasa*. On 3 October Rudyard was writing to Mary Mapes Dodge in America that 'the first man back from Lhassa [*sic*] [was] now labouring at a map of the place in the next room'.[60] Landon managed to rekindle his friend's romantic enthusiasm for far-off places. 'What a place is Lhassa!' Rudyard told Mrs Dodge. 'I've been feasting on the story of its marvels all last night.'

From then on, Landon regularly visited Bateman's at the conclusion of his foreign travels. His own immediate family was dispersed: his father had been an itinerant clergyman whose only regular work was as chaplain on the island of Madeira during the winter months; otherwise there were brothers in Sudan and India, and a lesbian sister. He acted as Rudyard's surrogate brother, giving him access to ideas and people the Sussex countryman might otherwise have ignored. In 1904, for example, Landon published *Helio-tropes or New Posies for Sundials*, an unusual collection (which he must have finished before going to Tibet the previous year) of a seventeenth-century antiquary's Latin inscriptions for sundials. Rudyard contributed his own translation of one tag:

> I have known Shadow
> I have known Sun
> And now I know
> These two are one.

This neatly encapsulated his dualistic philosophy – the idea that he had two sides to his head. It also suggested the interest in esoteric religion he shared with Landon.

In July 1905 Landon brought the Australian composer Percy Grainger to Bateman's. Grainger was collecting material for Cecil Sharp's English Folk Song Society – a pursuit that complemented Haggard's 'back to the land' concerns and encouraged Rudyard in finding out about the history and culture of his new homeland. (Grainger later worked on sophisticated choral settings of Rudyard's verses.)

Normally, Carrie did not allow anyone as close to her husband as Landon. But, perhaps because they both had Huguenot ancestors, he managed to charm her into accepting him. Before long, he was accompanying the Kiplings on their holidays and later moved into a cottage on the Bateman's estate. One possible explanation is that Landon, who was described by Peter Fleming in his book *Bayonets to Lhasa* as a 'spruce, gifted, self-important man', reminded them both of Wolcott Balestier.

Gwynne was a very different type. An ideologue and imperialist, he reflected the aggressive, imperialist side of Rudyard's personality. He had recently returned from South Africa to edit the *Standard*, the daily newspaper now owned by Arthur Pearson, the mogul who, with Harmsworth and Newnes, had been responsible for the growth of a mass-market press over the previous decade. (Carrie had astutely noted this trend and invested in Newnes in August 1897, a few days before the birth of her son.) Pearson had one over-riding political obsession – tariff reform. At the start of the decade he had promoted this idea in his newspaper the *Daily Express*, edited by the expatriate American R. D. Blumenfeld, one of the first journalists in Britain to understand the impact of the mass media. Despite Blumenfeld's sloganising – 'Tariff Reform Means Work for All' was one of his creations – the attack on free trade had still to fire the public imagination. In July 1903 Pearson had helped set up the Tariff Reform League and in November 1904 he beat off competition from John Montagu, the motor-loving heir to Lord Montagu of Beaulieu, to acquire the *Standard* as a platform for Joseph Chamberlain, who continued to fly the imperialist flag, arguing his case for tariff reform from the back benches. On Chamberlain's recommendation, Gwynne was summoned back from South Africa to edit the paper. It was not long before Pearson was being hailed as 'the "champion hustler" of the Tariff Reform League'.[61] (Rudyard, however, still turned to *The Times* to publish his verse appreciation of Chamberlain, 'Things and the Man', in August 1904.)[62]

Away from Bateman's, indicative of his influence, Rudyard was invited to spend an evening with Admiral Sir 'Jacky' Fisher, Commander-in-Chief at Portsmouth. Soon to become First Sea

Lord, Fisher might have thought – reasonably enough on the basis of Rudyard's army campaign – that the prickly author would support him in his crusade for modernising the British fleet. But Rudyard refused to take up the cause of the Dreadnoughts and, instead, backed Fisher's implacable opponent, the more conservative Admiral Lord Charles Beresford, who argued that the construction of these modern capital ships would leave the Royal Navy too thinly stretched to be able to meet any real threat. Rudyard was influenced by Cope Cornford who, as a naval correspondent, regularly attacked Fisher's pretensions. Possibly, the two men were too similar: like Rudyard, Fisher was small, bristling with ideas and had been brought up in the Indian sub-continent. But the main reason for their failure to see eye to eye became clear when Rudyard returned to South Africa in the winter. One of Fisher's first initiatives as First Sea Lord was to reduce the size of – *inter alia* – the naval squadron based at Simonstown in order to pay for his new battleships. Rudyard considered this an abrogation of responsibility to both South Africa and the Empire, and so started the campaign that lasted into the 1980s of promoting Simonstown as a key to the defences of first Britain and then Western democracy.

The Cape continued to exert a powerful attraction (or ju-ju, as Rudyard with his penchant for the exotic, often anthropological phrase, might have put it). An important link was Lord Grey who, as a trustee of Rhodes's will, was a quietly dedicated promoter of the imperialist ideal. As a young man, Grey had been a high minded Liberal Unionist MP, a friend of the then editor of the *Northern Echo*, W. T. Stead, and much influenced by the federalism of the Italian politician Giuseppe Mazzini. In the late 1880s his life changed when Stead introduced him to Rhodes. Like Rudyard, he saw an opportunity to put his ideas into practice. As director of the British South Africa Company and, later, administrator of Rhodesia, he used his British contacts, particularly with Chamberlain, to orchestrate support for Rhodes.

One of Grey's current concerns was the construction of a

monument to his hero in Cape Town. He wanted to build a massive statue that would be visible to incoming ships. Rudyard was not convinced about the site, and liaised with Rhodes's architect Herbert Baker about a more appropriate memorial on Table Mountain, incorporating G. F. Watts's equestrian statue *Physical Energy* and a verse inscription by himself.

An elderly survivor from the pre-Raphaelite heyday, Watts was approached by Grey personally for this statue. When he protested that it was unfinished, Grey replied, 'So is Rhodes's work.'[63] Certainly the prognosis for Rhodes's political legacy was not good. Jameson's Progressive party government in the Cape had given rise to an 'English' opposition, the South African party, headed by that old liberal bugbear John X. Merriman, who made cause with the Boer Bond. Milner's scheduled departure in April 1905 was marred by a row a few days earlier over the flogging of Chinese indentured labourers. Rudyard hurried through 'The Pro-Consuls', his tribute to the retiring High Commissioner, which was draped with powerful Masonic imagery.[64] But the controversy over 'Chinese slavery' refused to go away, becoming an issue in British domestic politics in the run-up to the general election in January 1906, when the Liberal party trounced the Conservatives and Unionists, condemning them to opposition for the next decade.

By then, Rudyard was back in South Africa and ruefully but accurately predicting the course of events. The new Liberal government in Britain did as promised, overturning Milner's nominated executives and introducing 'responsible government' to the Transvaal and Orange River Colony. Democracy led inevitably to the election of Boer governments in these two states in 1907, to Jameson's defeat in the Cape the following year and to the establishment of a Boer-dominated Union of South Africa in 1910. There was an irony in the way that Rudyard, who so recently had railed against the army as a symbol of a decaying social order, could travel to South Africa on the *Armadale* in December 1905 in the company of the Duke of Connaught, the Inspector-General of the Forces, who remembered him and his family from India, and that he and Carrie, an Anglo-Indian and an American, could draw up a list of the 'First Fifteen' most influential people in the Cape for the benefit of the Duchess.

The amiable Connaughts now got to know a second generation of Kiplings, with whom they enjoyed another link through Rudyard's Sussex neighbour Moreton Frewen. While serving in Ireland, the Duke had fallen passionately in love with Frewen's American sister-in-law, Leonie Leslie. His daughters Princesses Margaret and Patricia were great friends of Frewen's lively daughter Clare, who sported plants from both the Connaughts and the Kiplings in her 'friendship garden' at her father's house at Brede Place in Sussex. Rudyard thrived on the royal patronage. He presented the Duke with a poem, 'The Silent Army', about British soldiers buried in South Africa. Carrie dutifully sat for the artistic Princess 'Patsy' who was accompanying her parents on the voyage.

Rudyard tried to summon interest if not enthusiasm for the new political realities because, as he disarmingly told Ted Hill, 'My half-year at the Cape is always my "political" time: and I enjoy it.'[65] He visited the Chinese miners and, predictably, could not understand the fuss about their conditions. 'It looks rather better grub than in barracks and I couldn't see any bars and padlocks.'[66] He railed at the way the Liberals had come to power on the back of a 'lie'[67] about 'Chinese slavery' and could not hide his bitterness at the way 'the work of years [had been] chucked away for the whim of the English electorate'.[68] The situation reminded him of India, where he had always felt that Westminster had undermined the work of years. '*You* know,' he told Mrs Hill, 'how civilians in India have to grin and bear the wreck of their administrative hopes now and then. Imagine a whole sub-continent going in fear and distrust of its own people at home; and you get some notion of it.'

He returned to South Africa the following two winters. The place was like drink: 'One curses it but one comes back to it,'[69] he told a friend in April 1907. But by then he was going through the motions. Before his last visit in January 1908 to 'see the corpse buried' (a regular phrase around this time), he told Robert Duck-worth Ford, a macho bear-shooting Englishman serving with the American army in the Philippines and one of several like-minded correspondents he collected in different parts of the world, that he would now have to 'hunt for another country to love'.[70] Once ensconced at The Woolsack, he told Milner dejectedly, 'We do nothing: we see nobody (there is no one left to see) and the few people who had English leanings have gone bad on our hands. We sit on the stoep and listen to hours going by.' Looking back, he felt the crucial mistake had been the failure to suspend the Cape Constitution after the Boer War.[71] He recapitulated to Lord Selborne, the new High Commissioner, that Lord Milner had been 'sent out to do certain work, on certain lines, in furtherance of certain principles. Later on, the English abandoned those principles, obliterated the main lines of Lord Milner's work, and handed over absolute control of the details to another race'.[72] He kept his spirits up playing golf with Jameson, whom he trusted to implement Rhodes's ideas as far as possible. His main goal now was to keep Rhodesia out of the inevitable federation of South Africa: 'It's the last loyal white colony in the sub-continent.' If he took heart from anything, it was his observation that the Boers needed the 'ring fence' of the Royal Navy and understood the long-term benefits of maintaining their ties with Britain.

When the Duke of Connaught returned to South Africa to preside over the opening of the new Union parliament in late 1910, Rudyard drew up for him a dossier on the country's politics and personalities, such as Abe Bailey ('multi-millionaire: unscrupulous financier, a bad enemy') and Bender, the chief Rabbi ('alert, quick and intensely modern Jew, but proud of his race and takes a great interest in Jewish emigrants and poor ... Knows his Bible').[73] The document attested to Rudyard's enduring interest in the practical realities of modern Freemasonry. The Duke was Britain's leading Mason, having taken over as Grand Master of England when his brother Edward became King in 1901. Rudyard informed him of the various lodges in South Africa – 'St George's 2537 is reckoned the first of the English lodges in Cape Town and Israel, the Jewish one, is rather interesting.'

South Africa had been Rudyard's surrogate India – a warm-water winter destination where he had hoped that the mistakes of the Raj would not be repeated, and that his version of the contented colony, ruled altruistically by the equivalent of the Indian Civil Service, would be realised. But Milner's kindergarten failed to deliver and, as the vision faded, he looked around despairingly for that 'other country to love'.

He was unlikely to find it in contemporary Britain. The Liberal landslide of January 1906 brought 'canker and blight', as 'every form of unfitness, general or specialised, born or created, during the last generation ... combined in one big trust – a majority of all the minorities – to play the game of Government'.[74] Sticking close to Milner, Rudyard continued to harry on domestic issues, such as tariff reform and national service, and now felt he also had to alert people to the threat of socialism (the subject of his 1908 story 'The Mother Hive'). But with Joseph Chamberlain laid low after a stroke, Rudyard could see no Conservatives capable of taking the fight to the Liberals. Joe's son Austen did not have the stature and the party's nominal leader, Arthur Balfour, was 'strange, evasive, undulating' and regarded 'with sorrowful boredom'.[75]

Obsessed with Indian parallels, Rudyard looked for the first time at Ireland. He imagined the country was in safe hands while George Wyndham was Chief Secretary from 1900 to 1904 – the period when Rudyard's own attention was focused on South Africa. Wyndham took strides towards solving intractable problems of land tenure, but was suffering from nervous collapse, related to a drink problem, when he was forced to resign. Still socially active, Lockwood Kipling liked to think he had played a supporting role in this saga, following the political uproar that arose when, in the Chief Secretary's absence, his senior civil servant presented a paper which, Unionists argued, opened the door to Home Rule. Lockwood claimed that Wyndham decided to quit the Cabinet after a 'long chat' with him at Clouds the previous day.[76] Subsequently, Rudyard kept a closer watch on Ireland, but there was no love: the country only confirmed his worst political nightmares.

By June 1907 he was urging Gwynne to check his files on Ireland and India during Gladstone's second term of office in the 1880s, when he 'would find almost verbatim the identical questions which are asked today as to lawlessness in Ireland: the identical flippant replies, and the same growth of lawlessness'.[77] The more Rudyard was aware of Ireland, the more vitriolic he became about 'the Celt' – a position which was understandable, given his political point of view, but odd, since his mother and sister both valued their Celtic heritage so highly.

With his romantic regard for the French, Rudyard cast across the English Channel for support. During the Boer War, Paris opinion had been anti-British and Rudyard had retaliated by making the villain of his story 'The Bonds of Discipline' a French spy whose imaginative approach to his job proved no match for the Stalkyisms of the Royal Navy's best. He himself was then the butt of a stinging personal attack in Jean and Jérôme Tharaud's novel *Dingley*, which examined the personal life of an imperialist British author who was forced to tone down his bellicosity after his son (with spooky prescience) was killed by the Boers. Although the book was a best-seller and won the Prix Goncourt, Rudyard's anger soon abated: Paris was Carrie's favourite foreign city and, while Edith Catlin (a student at Julian's) and later her married sister Julia lived there, Rudyard enjoyed visiting. His first move was always to ask his American friends to take his wife out and buy her some clothes. Edith noted Rudyard's need (shades of Lahore) for local colour: 'For heaven's sake', he would say, 'let's get out and see the people. Come along for a ride on the bus or a walk in the gardens.'[78]

Following the Entente Cordiale in 1904, the mood of the French boulevardier changed and Britain was fashionable again. When the French cruiser *Dupleix* visited Simonstown at the start of the year, Rudyard was invited on board ship where he was fêted by officers who knew his work in both French and English.[79] Later that year Vicomte Robert d'Humières published an interview with Rudyard in his imperialist tract *Through Isle and Empire*. The following August, when Joseph Coudurier de Chassaigne, London correspondent of *Le Figaro*, wanted to produce a French version of 'The Man Who Was', he arranged for a colleague, the much-travelled writer Jules Huret, to interview Rudyard at Bateman's. The two men enjoyed a wide-ranging conversation, touching on Rudyard's old concerns about America's lack of tradition, the 'yellow peril' and the German threat. Rudyard later felt he had been too outspoken in denouncing 'our mutual friend' for, when sent proofs, he deleted comments about Germany's lack of achievement in science, industry, literature and soldiering, and even admitted to Huret that he owed much to the poet Heine.[80]

While this exchange was trivial, it showed Rudyard trying to strike a balance between his gut aversion to Germany and his equally emotional Francophilia. The United States remained a curious no-go area: although he included two stories about the early United States among his later *Puck* tales,[81] and although he had friends and family connections there (indeed, Theodore Roosevelt was President until the end of 1908), Rudyard seemed to associate the nation with his daughter's death, while keeping up his distrust of American mass democracy. At the same time he sought to impose his own fuzzy logic on the changing pattern of early-twentieth-century alliances. He had been happy about the 1902 Anglo-Japanese treaty, encouraging Stanley Baldwin's brother-in-law Arthur Ridsdale to visit the 'Britain of the Far East' and start a collection of Japanese prints. He was less enthusiastic five years later when, in order to bolster the Entente, Britain concluded a pact with France's ally Russia, which he suspected of hostile intentions. The Winged Hats of *Puck of Pook's Hill* have often been identified as his warning about the bellicosity of pre-revolutionary Russia, whose navy had fired at British trawlers in the North Sea in October 1904. China – or rather, the Chinaman – still scared him: 'he has more guts than the Jap, and is honest'.

Rudyard's view of the wider world was often influenced by mercantile interests. Like Joseph Chamberlain, who had had family investments in the Bahamas, he recognised the potential of the West Indies as an outlet for labour and capital. As a result of his stories and poems about sailors, he had excellent ties with the shipping industry. He wrote to a friend at the start of the decade: 'Curiously enough, I've been a great deal interested of late in Jamaica and I've kept my eye out on that new banana line (but it's tourists really that should make it pay, and a hotel syndicate). The W.I. are like Newfoundland in that they are in the making – only in their case it is for the second time and we want large and adequate men to do it.'[82]

More traditionally, Rudyard maintained contacts in both Australia and New Zealand. But his most enduring efforts to find another country to love were in Canada, which he visited in September 1907. He made the journey for a mixture of personal and political reasons. At one level, Carrie had not seen her mother for eight years and, since Rudyard now adamantly refused to return to the United States, the Kiplings could at least meet Mrs Balestier somewhere north of the American border. In addition, as Charles Carrington has suggested, Rudyard wanted to pick up the honorary doctorate that McGill University in Montreal had awarded him (and he had not been able to receive) in 1899. Academic – as opposed to political – honours were acceptable to him, and in the course of a few days in June 1907 he had been awarded honorary degrees at both Durham and Oxford Universities.

But there were other Canadian influences at work that summer. While accepting his degree in Oxford, he stayed at 13 Norham Gardens, home of Sir William Osler, the Canadian-born Regius Professor of Medicine. At some stage (it is not clear when) Carrie had discovered she was distantly related to Osler's wife, born

Grace Revere, granddaughter of the early American revolutionary Paul Revere, whose daughter Maria had married one of Carrie's great-uncles, Joseph Balestier. The two cousins do not appear to have met before the Encaenia, at which the new Chancellor Lord Curzon (recently returned from India) presented an honorary Doctorate of Letters to Mark Twain as well as to Rudyard. For Osler can only have been describing two recent acquaintances when he told a friend: '[Kipling] stopped with us – such a jolly fellow, so full of fun and with an extraordinary interest in everything. Mrs K is very bright, & we fell in love with them both.'[83] Rudyard, for his part, was chastened by Osler's concern for his health. He probably treated his host to an account of his desperate need for a cigarette during the interminable degree ceremony. When someone else asked if smoking was allowed, he and Rudyard – in scarlet and grey gown, looking 'rather like an African parrot' – were directed outside the hall. 'So we went out and Mark Twain came with us and three or four other men followed and we had a smoke like naughty boys, under a big archway.'[84] After Osler suggested that this habit was bad for his health, Rudyard claimed to have taken heed and was 'cutting down my tobacco'.[85]

While Rudyard paid scant regard to Osler's professional advice (he still smoked thirty cigarettes a day), the two men enjoyed an immediate intellectual rapport. Before moving to England the professor had quoted Rudyard in a 1903 address to the University of Toronto where he called upon medical students to follow Mowgli in *The Jungle Books* and adopt a 'master word' – in their case 'work'. Once physician to Walt Whitman, he was widely read, particularly on the history of medicine. His approach to his job was based on his understanding of the power of the mind in the aetiology of disease. His epigrams, such as 'It is more important to know what sort of a person has a disease than to know what disease a person has', are still quoted. They tallied with Rudyard's thinking, and his debt to Osler was soon clear in the details of his medically inspired tales, 'Marklake Witches' and 'A Doctor of Medicine', in *Rewards and Fairies*.

Osler was also a quiet but committed imperialist. Ostensibly he steered clear of politics. The only indication in his two-volume biography[86] of any concern about matters of state was his attendance at a talk by Joseph Chamberlain on tariff reform in 1905. He was, however, closely involved with the Rhodes Trust, taking a special interest in Rhodes Scholars at Oxford. And he maintained excellent ties with the great and the good at home in Canada, where his brother Edmund was President of the Dominion Bank and Director of the Canadian Pacific Railway.

A few weeks before meeting Osler Rudyard had been visited at Bateman's by another Canadian, Stephen Leacock, later his country's foremost humorist but at the time a Conservative and imperially minded Professor of Economics and Political Science at Osler's old university McGill. With funding from the Rhodes Trust, secured by Earl Grey, who was now Canada's Governor-General, Leacock had embarked on a lecture tour of Britain and the colonies, presenting the imperialist case. Rudyard found him 'very interesting ... Goodness knows we want men of his powers in these days of fluffy irresponsibility.'[87] Leacock did his best, but when he reached South Africa he was shocked by the legacy of the war, which he described to his mother as 'one huge crime from start to finish, organized and engineered by a group of plutocrats and tyrants and carried on as ruthlessly as the wars of an Asiatic conqueror. And that is the British Empire! That imperialism!'[88]

No doubt by design, Leacock was in London prior to the third Imperial Conference of Prime Ministers in June. Concerned for the success of this meeting, Rudyard had travelled to London on 7 May, three days before Leacock came to Bateman's, for a pre-conference rendezvous with the Australian premier Alfred Deakin, in the company of a heavyweight team of like-minded imperialists – Gwynne, Milner and Dr Jameson.

With the Liberals in power in Britain, imperial preference was no longer on the conference agenda. The main topic was the setting up of a permanent secretariat to deal with common issues during the five-year gaps between formal gatherings. This was a step on the way to Rhodes's idea of an imperial parliament. However, some of the colonies (now called dominions) thought such a centralised structure would institutionalise British domination. Neither Australia nor New Zealand minded, but Canada sided with the new state of Transvaal in countering the proposal. Canada's position reflected internal divisions between the Liberal party of Prime Minister Sir Wilfrid Laurier, a Quebecois who needed the votes of the Francophone population, and the Conservatives, under Sir Robert Borden (and supported by Stephen Leacock), who were imperially 'sound'.

Jameson described Laurier as the French dancing master 'who bitched the whole show'. As a result, Rudyard was encouraged to visit Canada in order to bolster the imperialist cause. (Milner made the same journey for the same reasons the following autumn.) Having invited Crom Price to Bateman's (advising him not to bicycle in the vicinity because it was 'devilish pimply'),[89] the Kiplings joined the *Empress of Britain* in Liverpool on 20 September for a dreary six-day voyage across the Atlantic. Anna Balestier met them at the Place Viger Hotel in Montreal, where Rudyard was amused to hear his forty-four-year-old wife being addressed as 'child'. Hounded by the press, he did not like staying in big, impersonal hotels, which he found over-heated and stuffy[90] (a comment on the typically English draughts at Bateman's). As a result he was grateful to Sir William Horne, President of the Canadian Pacific Railway, for repeating his gesture of fifteen years earlier, and laying on a special green velvet and mahogany 'private car', which could be hitched to the back of any train. This allowed Rudyard and Carrie to make their way across the prairies to Vancouver and back, stopping *en route* at the major towns where he gave keynote speeches to the Canadian Clubs. While in their luxury carriage, variously described as a 'cathedral' and a 'palace', they were sumptuously looked after by William, 'a stately negro [who] received us with the airs of an archbishop, called us "Sir" and "Madam" in a deep resounding voice and whenever we dropped anything on the floor he noiselessly and swiftly picked it up. This made us feel rather like bad untidy children.'[91] William, 'our Nurse, Valet, Seneschal, and Master of Ceremonies', made sure Rudyard was ready for every appointment: 'Dere's a speech doo at ——,' he would say. 'You go ahead with what you're composin', Boss. Jest put your feets out an' I'll shine 'em meanwhile.'[92]

Rudyard's lectures mixed homespun philosophy with rousing calls for unity in the imperial 'family'. Accepting his degree at McGill University, he spoke with unusual candour, recalling his conversations with Osler, 'There is a certain darkness into which the soul of the young man sometimes descends – a horror of desolation, abandonment, and realised worthlessness, which is one of the most real of the hells in which we are compelled to walk. I know of what I speak. This is due to a variety of causes, the chief of which is the egotism of the human animal itself.' He counselled his audience to lose themselves in 'some issue not personal to yourself – in another man's trouble, or, preferably, another man's joy'.[93] More often, he simply tried to stir the sceptical Canadians into a more whole-hearted imperialism. Despite Carrie noticing 'a decided feeling of French-Canadian wet blanket',[94] he sought to allay fears about immigration and encourage acceptance of more English settlers, if only – and this argument is unlikely to have won over many waverers – because 'the Englishman is a born kicker'.

He used this last phrase in one of the 'Letters to the Family' he wrote for the *Morning Post* on his return, summarising his thoughts about Canada and its relations with its mother country. Rudyard's own ties with *The Times*, his normal outlet for political material, were disrupted. The paper had been suffering huge losses – caused, at least partially, by its expensive commitment to the Boer War. In September 1905, in an effort to boost circulation, the paper had set up a book club where, in accordance with established practice, subscribers could buy 'used' books at significant reductions. *The Times* covered its immediate losses by purchasing books at trade discounts. But when publishers eventually got round to understanding what was happening, they took a dim view and withdrew their advertising. In the ensuing 'Book War' the paper presented itself as the apostle of free trade. But Rudyard felt his own interests so threatened that he wrote saying only *The Times* could benefit from the scheme. In reply, Moberly Bell asked him to conduct an independent investigation into both sides of the argument, which he promised to publish. Rudyard did not take him up on the offer, and eventually in 1908 *The Times* had to climb down and accede to what became known as the Net Book Agreement, the price-fixing cartel, which obtained in the book trade for nearly nine decades. By then, however, ownership of what Rudyard intemperately described to Gwynne in January 1908 as 'the damned Jew-Yank sheet'[95] had changed and *The Times* was in the hands of Lord Northcliffe, the former Alfred Harmsworth, who had started the *Daily Mail* only a dozen years earlier. Rudyard had not liked Northcliffe's equivocal support for Balfour and free trade.[96] For the next few years, until the First World War, Rudyard preferred to place his work with the *Morning Post*, which recently had been revitalised as a strident nationalist paper by a new proprietor, the rich Lady Bathurst. Until 1911 it was edited by the fastidious Fabian Ware, a former director of education in the Transvaal, and thereafter by Gwynne himself.

Rudyard looked back on his trip across the Atlantic with mixed feelings. Despite the influence of the Governor-General, Lord Grey, with whom he had stayed in Ottawa, he admitted he had found Canada a 'constipating land', where he had needed to speak in what would now be called 'sound-bites' since Canadians could not 'carry anything more than three and a half lines long in their busy heads'. Their redeeming feature was 'a certain crude material faith in the Empire, of which they naturally conceive themselves to be the belly-button'.[97] And they were at least different from the Americans: showing unusual bitterness, though typical inconsistency, he claimed to be bemused that 'on one side of an imaginary line should be Safety, Law, Honour and Obedience, and on the other frank, brutal decivilization'.[98] As a result he happily cultivated his Canadian contacts, one of whom, the financier Max Aitken, became his trusted friend and adviser.

If Canada had failed as an alternative to South Africa as a country to love, it did at least affirm Rudyard's Anglo-Saxon tribalism (which today would be described as racism). His own low spirits contributed to the bleak mood of 'The Stranger', the most enduring of the poems accompanying his Canadian articles in the *Morning Post*:

> The Stranger within my gates,
>   He may be true or kind,
> But he does not talk my talk –
>   I cannot feel his mind.
> I see the face and the eyes and the mouth,
>   But not the soul behind.

At this time when Rudyard was at his most introverted, his standing in the world was at its highest. While working on his Canadian articles in November, he received notice that he had been awarded the Nobel Prize for Literature. This entailed travelling to Stockholm to receive the prize, which was valued at £7700. He was not supposed to tell anyone in advance so, typically, he complied, casually informing Arthur Conan Doyle, who had recently moved to nearby Crowborough, that he had 'to go abroad next week for a few days'.[99] The award ceremony on 11 December was muted because the Swedish capital was in mourning for King Oscar II who had died three days earlier. As in Oxford a few months before, Rudyard felt himself back at school – 'rather like a bad boy up to be caned'.[100] However, he liked Stockholm, making a point of saying how much he enjoyed the food, though Carrie would not allow him to try the things he really fancied – jellied eels, pickled herring, lobster, crab, raw ham and what he described as 'dried raw salmon' (gravadlax). While he was there, he met the new King Gustavus V, and spent an hour with Carrie in the company of young Crown Prince Gustavus Adolphus and his wife Princess

Margaret (known as Daisy), whom the Kiplings knew through her parents, the Duke and Duchess of Connaught. The return voyage from Flushing in Holland to Queenborough was stormier than Rudyard would have liked. But he had his prize proceeds to spend on improvements to the garden at Bateman's, including a sundial with the rubric (inspired by Landon) 'It's later than you think'. This served as an admonishment both to guests who tarried too long and to himself, as he viewed his life's work.

Rudyard's last despairing search for a new country to love was in the world of the past, whose detritus was strewn so abundantly around him at Bateman's. He sublimated this search into his *Puck* stories, published in two main tranches between 1906 and 1910. The link between South Africa and this history was implicit in the names he gave the two children at the centre of the tales. John and Elsie became Dan and Una, in memory of their lion cub Sullivan – Dan, after Daniel (from the Babylonian lions' den), and Una, from the virgin protected by a tame lion in Edmund Spenser's *Faerie Queen*. Some of the *Puck* stories were partly written in Cape Town, where Rudyard appreciated the university library, which allowed him to research such topics as the writings of the seventeenth-century astrologer and physician Nicholas Culpeper. He later claimed that the idea for 'A Doctor of Medicine', about Culpeper, came from observing an old, 'puffy scabby', whitish rat in Cape Town in 1901.[101]

The basic themes of the *Puck* stories were simple enough: the continuity of history, and the importance of myth, religion, legend and song in perpetuating a common sense of identity.[102] Rudyard might have wrapped them in a philosophy that was uncompromisingly imperialist – a tale of virile civilisations emerging from the succession of wars and empires that make up the matter of history. But he was more subtle than that. He did not eschew the imperialist element. A central figure was the British-born Roman centurion Parnesius, who was depicted sticking to his lonely duty as he followed his 'destiny' on Hadrian's Wall (the epitome of Rudyard's ideal Indian civil servant) rather than return to the easy life of the cities. He was able to do this, Rudyard suggested, because he remained faithful to his religion, the cult of Mithras, while his compatriots in Rome were abandoning their gods.[103]

As with *Kim*, both sides of Rudyard's head were involved in the creation of *Puck of Pook's Hill*. It is testimony to the power of his daemon that, at a time when this reactionary Conservative was railing against the betrayal of Empire, he could write stories with an alternative Whig interpretation of history, in which England progresses, with stately inevitability, from superstition and barbarism to parliamentary government, or 'The Thing', a central myth of its people. Rudyard described how military prowess led to the accumulation of wealth and this created the conditions for the first growth of British liberty, with the signing of the Magna Carta at Runnymede. 'Weland gave the Sword! The Sword gave the Treasure, and the Treasure gave the Law. It's as natural as an oak growing.'

More unexpectedly (again not unlike *Kim*), Rudyard presented a strong argument for racial tolerance. English history is shown as a process of gradual assimilation. In Parnesius's case, while anarchy reigns at the centre of the Empire (a comment on contemporary politics in Britain?), he himself adapts to his environment and has no problem being English. His approach was echoed in the anguished cry of 'The Roman Centurion's Song', which Rudyard published in 1911:

Let me work here for Britain's sake – at any task you will –
A marsh to drain, a road to make or native troops to drill ...

Legate, I come to you in tears – My cohort ordered home!
I've served in Britain forty years. What should I do in Rome?
Here is my heart, my soul, my mind – the only life I know ...

Another example of hybridisation occurs in 'The Treasure and the Law', where the early medieval Jewish money-lender Kadmiel cannot understand how Mr Meyer, a Jew living in Dan and Una's day, has become so integrated into English society that he can fire at a beater on his estate and avoid being tortured.

One race not included in this gathering of the clans was the Celt. Here Rudyard's historical research only reinforced his prejudices. In July 1908, a few months after Herbert Asquith had taken over the leadership of the Liberal party, appointing the Welshman David Lloyd George as his Chancellor of the Exchequer, Rudyard could write to Lord Milner, in the real world, 'We are paying for the historical fact that Rome did not steam-roller the Celt for four hundred years as she steam-rollered Britain.'[104]

Nevertheless, in 1963, when the firmly anti-racist Colin Mac-Innes (son of Angela Thirkell and therefore Rudyard's cousin twice removed) was writing about post-war xenophobia, he looked to *Puck* for inspiration:

> *Puck*'s message to the young is that England's essential nature, throughout its history, is to be constantly invaded by new races which the older settlers first resisted, and then accepted once the genius of each race became fused in a fresh form of the English soul. *Puck*'s lesson is that hostility to the invading race is natural, but equally so the wholehearted acceptance of its presence once it has lost its alien nature and is contributing to the mongrel glory of the English people.[105]

Several commentators, including Angus Wilson, have identified a cyclical theory of history in the *Puck* stories. However, despite Theodore Roosevelt's determinist approach in 'On Biological Analysis in History', his 1910 Romanes lecture at Oxford University, Rudyard himself stuck to proven Gibbonian empiricism. His own sense of the past was sophisticated enough to include both the Classical concept of reason and order as the prerequisites for civilisation and a Teutonic variation, which allows for the place of myth. (The critic John Coates, who has written about this balancing act, has noted the irony that Jack Mackail, Rudyard's stern socialist-minded cousin by marriage and Colin MacInnes's grandfather, was an uncompromising advocate of the Classical school – to the extent that he attributed the fall of Rome to immigration from less civilised German stock.)

George Wyndham noticed the Gibbon parallels in *Puck of Pook's Hill*. In a rambling letter of appreciation he said he had been sent back to Gibbon's *Decline and Fall of the Roman Empire* and Rudyard had emerged favourably in the comparison. While admitting that Gibbon was 'the fat heifer I ploughed with', Rudyard replied elusively, 'I swear I didn't mean to write parables – much – but when situations are so ludicrously, or terribly, parallel, what can one do?'[106]

This was a refrain Rudyard repeated several times in his second collection of *Puck* stories, *Rewards and Fairies*: that in the working out of history an individual has little choice but to stick to his or her prescribed role. (In 'Brother Square-Toes', for example, when George Washington says he must make peace with Britain on the latter's terms, he adds, 'What else can one do?') While this hinted at determinism, it was also a constant theme of Rudyard – the struggle between the individual and his environment, as he works out his destiny within the constraints of 'the law'. He was as intrigued by this dynamic tension now, as he had been when he first discovered Fra Lippo Lippi.

In grappling with these issues, Rudyard could admit, at the height of his despair in South Africa in February 1908, that he had been 'hugely enjoying' himself with his new set of *Puck* stories. Here indeed was an alternative world in which he could lose himself. His main problem was the 'very richness of the historical mine'.[107] This only inspired him to be more ambitious. 'Since the tales had to be read by children, before people realized they were meant for grown-ups', he wrote, 'and since they had to be a sort of balance to, as well as a seal upon some aspects of my "Imperialistic" output in the past, I worked the material in three or four overlaid tints and textures, which might or might not reveal themselves according to the shifting lights of sex, youth and experience.[108]

Rudyard did not elaborate on this typically ambivalent admission that he was weighing up his past imperialism. Further evidence has to be gleaned from his *Puck* stories and, in particular, their advocacy of the virtues of the practical, common man. Rudyard's heroes there are the shipwright, the apothecary, the plasterer, the centurion – the regular people (as in Hobden, the all-purpose epitome of rustic industry and good sense) going about their business. One of his least attractive characters is Queen Gloriana (Elizabeth I) examining herself in her mirror.

An underlying theme is that old saw, the nobility of work. Unable to resist tilting at the trades unions of his day, Rudyard prefers the old-fashioned community of independent craftsmen, ideally realised in the Freemasons' lodge. The prevalence of Masonic imagery in the *Puck* stories adds a dimension to Rudyard's conviction that a soundly working community – whether a cohort of Roman soldiers in Britain or an American-Indian reservation (in 'A Priest in Spite of Himself') or even the curious kingdom that Dravot and Peachey created in Kafiristan – needs its secret societies, with accepted rituals and ideals. As Rudyard made clear on his 1907 Canadian trip, he saw the British Empire in Masonic terms – 'a community of men of allied race and identical aims, united in comradeship, comprehension and sympathy'.[109]

While *Puck of Pook's Hill* suggests the need for organised religion, *Rewards and Fairies* is more explicit in presenting Christianity as the goal of spiritual endeavour. Since Rudyard was so reticent about his inner life it is difficult to say how he reached a position of Christianised Freemasonry. He seems to have arrived at a more sympathetic understanding of Christianity in the months following his depression in South Africa at the start of 1908. At the time he experienced symptoms similar to his dark days of 1890; Carrie noted in her diary, 'left eyelid dropped, left side stiff, cramp on left side of face ... the same that he had when we were engaged'. In July 1908 he admitted to Milner that he had been in 'a trough of blank, bloody pessimism'.[110] The following July he joined the Societas Rosicruciana in Anglia, an exclusively Christian society, open to Master Masons '... of high moral character ... [and] ... of sufficient ability to be capable of understanding the revelations of philosophy, theosophy and science, possessing a mind free from prejudice and anxious for instruction'. Although Rudyard was not a subscribing member of a Masonic lodge at the time (and therefore, strictly, ineligible for this inner body of Rosicrucians), he devised his own entry motto, 'Fortuna non virtute', which modestly suggested his life had been attended 'By good fortune, not by merit'. In December 1908 he could describe himself to Lady Edward Cecil as 'a God-fearing Christian atheist'.[111]

Masonic membership may be required to understand the significance Rudyard accords to the quasi-mystical status of iron, the metallic work-horse of the industrial revolution. In 'The Knife and the Naked Chalk', iron has the talismanic potency of the black pillar in Stanley Kubrick's film *2001*. It is a symbol which attracts the most forward-looking of medieval peoples, daring them to embrace new technology, even at risk to themselves. In discussing these ramifications with a friend, Rudyard indicated his enjoyment at the imaginative effort that the *Puck* stories required of him: 'My own theory is that all fairy tales of magic swords sprang from legends of stone and bone-using tribes who first came into contact – probably unpleasant – with metal.'[112]

Rudyard's sense of achievement was evident in his autobiography, where he devoted more space to the background to these tales than to any other work. Significantly, he also reported a friend's comment to the effect that the *Puck* books might prove useful tools 'towards begetting the "Higher Cannibalism" in biography'. While this showed his horror at the prospect of his life being pored over, it suggested that these two volumes were full of personal insights. The selfless mother in 'The Knife and the Naked

Chalk' is perhaps another projection of his idealised image of his own mother. There is a tribute to Carrie in the way he featured her kinsman Francis Drake in 'Simple Simon', even providing him with a dubious Sussex provenance. Generally, however, *Puck of Pook's Hill* (which came out in 1906) and *Rewards and Fairies* (in 1910) are revealing only for their overview of Rudyard's beliefs about man in society.

In the interval between these books Rudyard collected some related stories in *Actions and Reactions*, which was published in October 1909 and should be read in conjunction with the other two volumes. Although most pieces in *Actions and Reactions* had originally been printed in magazines three or four years earlier, they (and their accompanying verses, specially written for the book) provided a useful summary of Rudyard's intellectual concerns over these years. More than ever, he constructed his books as literary edifices (that Masonic influence again), attaching great importance to the order of the stories (particularly to those at the beginning and end) and to the poems which accompany each story.

Actions and Reactions (known as 'Motions and Emotions' until shortly before its publication) echoes the *Puck* stories in the importance it gives to the idea of healing. In his earlier collection *Traffics and Discoveries*, Rudyard had referred (in 'Steam Tactics') to the healing power of laughter (or mirth, as Rudyard archaically called it) – a theme taken up in 'The Puzzler' in the new collection. He now alluded more clearly to the therapeutic properties of buildings: one can have a house with good 'feng-shui' (as in the Bateman's alternative in 'An Habitation Enforced') or a bad, disorientating one (the Rock House in 'The House Surgeon'). In both cases, the dwelling has its special 'feel': as 'The Rabbi's Song', the poem which follows 'The House Surgeon', stresses:

> The arrows of our anguish
> Fly farther than we guess.

> Our lives, our tears, as water
> Are spilled upon the ground...

By including 'Garm – A Hostage' from much earlier (1889), Rudyard also pointed to the remedial role of animals and, in particular, dogs. (In 1910 he acquired two wire-hair fox terrier puppies, Jack and Betty, to which he became closely attached – his first household pets since Vixen in India.)

Actions and Reactions incorporates several other themes from *Puck*, such as the Masonic 'ties of common funk' required to shore up a community ('The Puzzler'). It departs most obviously in 'With the Night Mail', Rudyard's early effort at science fantasy. He had often written about science *qua* technology and, in particular, about machines – the engines, the ships, the railways that he brought to life in his output during the 1890s. *Puck* had dealt with the responsibilities of technology, following the discovery of 'cold iron'. 'With the Night Mail' is an eerie political fable about the use of technology in AD 2000, when science has triumphed: 'transportation is civilization'; no country is inaccessible to airships; nationalism and war have been abolished, and the planet is under the benign dictatorship of the Aerial Board of Control.

The science in the story, originally published in November 1905, is unexciting, but shows Rudyard's magpie intelligence. It incorporates elements of mineralogy Rudyard picked up in South Africa. In its vision of 'pillars of light where the cloud-breakers bore through the cloud-floor', it anticipates laser technology. Rudyard's real interest is the political consequences of global transportation. This harked back to discussions with Rhodes, whose favourite author, Wynwood Reade, had prophesied, *inter alia*, in his forgotten *The Martyrdom of Man* in 1872, the invention of 'aerial locomotion' and then, 'the earth being so small, mankind will cross the airless Saharas which separate planet from planet and sun from sun'.[113] Rhodes had seen transport as a key to the future (thus his obsession with the Cape-to-Cairo railway). Rudyard, the inveterate traveller, with his interest in railways, ships and motor cars, seemed to agree. In his address to the Canadian Club, Toronto, on 18 October 1907, he had identified the five main issues facing imperial bureaucracy as Education, Immigration, Transportation, Irrigation and Administration, which he claimed corresponded to the five points of fellowship represented in the points of bodily contact between Masons – foot to foot, knee to knee, breast to breast, cheek to cheek and hand to hand.

This bizarre statement linked Rudyard's science fiction directly to H. G. Wells, the title of whose novel *The Time Machine* he had used to describe the historical cornucopia at Bateman's. The socialist Wells was a member of the Coefficients, a dining club where Milner, Leo Maxse, Leo Amery and a handful of others met to discuss the social, political and economic development of the British Empire. In his 1910 novel *The New Machiavelli*, Wells wrote about this select group as the Pentagon. (He also paid tribute to Rudyard, saying that everyone in the late 1890s had been a Kiplingite.) In June 1907 Rudyard was invited to join this circle, but declined, pleading to Amery that it was impossible for 'a man who lives 3 hours down the South Eastern (which for practical purposes is Umtali)'.[114] This railway town in eastern Rhodesia being about as far away from Bateman's as he could imagine, he was making a clear statement of his determination that Sussex should be the remote and inaccessible centre of his universe.

Fifteen

The New Jeremiah

1907–1910

With John and Elsie established in his mind (and that of his public) as Dan and Una, Rudyard needed to make sure they did not become tangled in the undergrowth of his imagination – potentially as restrictive an environment as Lorne Lodge for him thirty years earlier. As his children grew up, he had to learn to let go, while ensuring that the sins that had been visited on him in Southsea were not repeated. For a sensitive man, known throughout the world for his hearty soldiers, it was not an easy process.

Two days before leaving for Canada in September 1907, Rudyard drove his ten-year-old son across Sussex at the start of John's first term at his new boarding-school, St Aubyn's, in Rottingdean. Amelia, the fitful Lanchester, had been replaced by Gunhilda, a more sedate parental-style Daimler. The two Kiplings stopped off at North End House, down the road from the school, where Aunt Georgie fed the small, slightly stocky John a huge tea. Rudyard left his boy reading a recent true adventure book, *The Cruise of the Cachalot*, about a voyage round the world in search of sperm whales. But although John would visit Aunt Georgie twice a week and although the headmaster of St Aubyn's, Edward Stanford, was George Wyndham's cousin and a family friend, nothing could assuage Rudyard's feeling of guilt as he drove home to Bateman's that evening. Aunt Georgie found him 'grey and pinched by the pain of parting,'[1] and he himself admitted to Crom Price, his house guest at Bateman's while he was in Canada, 'All my old miseries (with some new ones) have returned upon me. I left (John) brave enough but the misery of that first night will not be avoided.'[2]

Rudyard's sense of *déjà vu* was not helped by the fact that his son's escape route from harsh treatment at school was much the same as his own, thirty-odd years earlier – through Aunt Georgie; nor, indeed, by her insistence on calling her young great-nephew Ruddy. When she attributed her confusion to John's physical similarity to his father, Rudyard noted wearily that he hoped this was not true.

Although father and son both had poor eyesight (after consulting Arnold Lawson, a London specialist, John now wore glasses), there were essential differences, mainly in temperament. As Rudyard told Charles Norton,[3] neither of his children showed much curiosity about books. Still slow on the uptake, John was more interested in sports, particularly football (soccer, to Rudyard's dismay, rather than rugby) and cricket (making his father bowl to him in nets at Bateman's during the holidays). His preferred reading matter was the boy's magazine *The Captain*, George Newnes's lighter-hearted version of the *Boy's Own Paper* which Rudyard had read at Westward Ho!. *The Captain*, which had boasted the cricketers C. B. Fry and Pelham Warner as Athletics Editors, was known for publishing early work by P. G. Wodehouse.

In an effort to stimulate cerebral interests, Rudyard encouraged his son to take up stamp collecting. The trouble was, he proved keener than John, writing not only to say that Grandmother Balestier had sent some old American stamps, but to admit that Carrie, controlling Carrie, had forbidden him the boyish pleasure of sticking them into John's album.[4] John was much more impressed when his father obtained C. B. Fry's autograph.

Initially, possibly because of his eyesight, John could not read his father's handwriting. So Rudyard went to great trouble to print his letters, keeping his son informed about developments at home: Carrie bought a couple of miniature Iceland ponies; he himself acquired a new hive of bees and a litter of pigs; the pond in the redesigned garden was seeded with trout and other fish (though, for amusement value, this news hardly matched the account of Gwynne sinking in the birch-bark canoe in June 1908). From time to time Feilden dropped round and Rudyard went shooting with him. There were references to John's friends among the labourers, such as the carpenter Jim Lusted, killed under a horse in February that year, shortly after the death of his father Stephen, who had built the new village institute.

Rudyard's letters were friendly and amusing, though occasionally he adopted an *alter ego* ('Mr Campbell') to impart sterner advice, such as the need for John to eat or to clean his teeth. (Was this a reference to Rudyard's first housemaster, 'Belly' Campbell, who liked to wield the cane?) When John's replies were poorly spelt, Rudyard took him to task: 'Howe wood yu lick it if I rote you a leter al ful of misspeld wurds? I no yu know kwite well howe to spel onli yu wont taik the trubble to thinck.'[5] And when his son's spirits needed raising, Rudyard exhorted him with a schoolboy's version of 'If–'.

Do all that you can to win, honestly and fairly, the events for which you have entered. If you win, shut your head. Exalt not yourself nor your legs nor your wind nor anything else that is yours. To boast ... is the mark of the Savage and the Pig. If you lose remember that you have lost. It doesn't matter one little bit but it matters a great deal if you go about jawing about your handicap being too heavy or your having had a bad start or your being tripped or put off.[6]

For all Rudyard's efforts, John was never happy at school. He went through periods of depression which, like his father, were linked to problems with his sight. In May 1908, when Carrie's diary noted specifically that her son was homesick, Rudyard advised him, in alarmingly familiar terms, not to worry about his eyes. 'They will come all right and a great deal of your lack of appetite just now is because you are settling down to work again after a long holiday.'[7]

The following month, Rudyard was surprised at his emotional reaction when Elsie, now a strapping twelve-year-old, also quit the nest. He described her as 'interested in stones and rocks and trees and carries a quaintly maternal manner towards me'.[8] She looked fifteen, the spitting image of her mother. But, with her blowzy outdoor life-style, she had grown taller than she should and had a slight curvature of her spine. As a result, she was sent with her governess, Miss Blaikie, to live in lodgings in London where she received treatment every day, returning to Bateman's at weekends. Having sent her to the Army and Navy Stores to order some paintbrushes, her father complained light-heartedly that she did not praise that emporium enough. 'I prefer 'em to Harrods, I've never been to Harrods, so of course I'm right.'[9] At least the Army and Navy catalogue enabled him to inform John of something he never previously knew – that the native Indian states issued stamps.

After she had finished her course in London in October, Elsie (or Bird as she was known to her family) was no longer a child. Having tasted metropolitan life, she had lost her enthusiasm for Una's country pursuits. Now she was an experienced swimmer (part of her therapeutic regime), she attended dancing classes and, in December, she visited the theatre for the first time (a trip to the *Pirates of Penzance* with Daisy Leonard, a friend she had made in South Africa).[10] Her father boasted extravagantly that, while her interest in Gilbert and Sullivan bid fair to give her 'an abiding taste for music', her real talent was for painting and drawing.[11]

Unable to forget his own early experiences, Rudyard turned to his old school friend Colonel Lionel Dunsterville, to discuss the problems of growing children. Stalky was not the most obvious confidant: he was commanding a Sikh regiment, the 20th Punjabis, in India, from where he contributed articles to Gwynne's *Standard* about the growing problem of native unrest. Nevertheless, after a late marriage, he now had two sons, the elder of whom was five years old. 'There is much truth in what you say about parents being unfit to bring up their own offspring,' Rudyard agreed with him. 'We fought against the knowledge till we had to give way. The fact is that parents are much too interested in their own progeny to give them enough of that judicious letting alone which makes and builds up a kid's character.'[12] In the circumstances, the Kiplings were doing the best they could.

For Rudyard himself, 1908 was a crucial year as he adjusted from his bi-continental straddling of the world. Having returned in sombre mood from the political wasteland (as he saw it) of South Africa in April, he prepared to concentrate his political fire-power on Britain. Empire, national service and protectionism remained his main concerns; liberalism and democracy his bugbears. Since taking office a couple of years earlier, the Liberals had introduced a mass of legislation designed to meet the aspirations of their working-class supporters. Rudyard considered such measures as the Trades Dispute Act and Workers Compensation Act of 1906 as tantamount to socialism, and blamed them for the increase in strikes and social unrest. But the government showed no sign of relenting: it still aimed for Home Rule in Ireland, it had plans for old-age pensions, and it had already moved to limit the power of the House of Lords to veto its bills.

Initially, Rudyard kept quiet. Heavily involved in his *Puck* stories and in finalising *Actions and Reactions*, he limited his public exposure to a series of lectures in London. His comment to his son John about how much he 'detest[ed] speeches'[13] explains the lacklustre quality of his output as he addressed the Royal Literary Fund (21 May); Trinity College, Cambridge, where he received another honorary degree to mark the installation of Lord Rayleigh as Chancellor (17 June); medical students at Middlesex Hospital, where he was taken aback to see someone in the audience who was the spitting image of Ted Hill (1 October); and the Royal Naval Club (21 October).

The last talk was the most interesting – a plea for the 'spirit' of the Navy in the face of those (read Admiral Sir Jacky Fisher) who put their faith in 'ironmongery'. It was also potentially the most important, as it had some bearing on John's future. Only a month earlier Rudyard had visited Greenwich, as the guest of Admiral Sir John Durnford, President of the Royal Naval College. He told John about the paintings there of Carrie's 'ancestor', Sir Francis Drake. From the way he recounted the visit, it appears he was trying to pull strings in connection with his son's career, and the talk to the Royal Naval Club on Trafalgar Day, with Admiral Durnford presiding, was the quid pro quo.

Durnford had been Commander-in-Chief at the beleaguered Cape when Fisher introduced his naval reforms. As a result, he had thrown in his hat with Fisher's opponent, Admiral Lord Charles Beresford, whose cause Rudyard supported more strongly than ever. The expansive Lord Charles, a distant cousin of Rudyard's school friend, George 'M'Turk' Beresford, is credited with coining the name 'the Souls' for the group of high-minded aristocrats around Mary Elcho. He was a friend of Moberly Bell, who had been on board his ship, the *Condor*, when he made his name by silencing the Egyptian guns at Alexandria in 1882. But the Admiral had challenged his superior Fisher rather too often and had finally been relieved of his command of the Channel fleet in March 1909.

Rudyard's low energy level that autumn was evident when he turned down a request from Lord Kitchener, commander of the Indian Army, to write a serial for a new officially sanctioned Urdu newspaper, aimed at native soldiers, who were increasingly attracted to the vernacular, nationalist press. He was concerned about the Liberal party's concessions in the face of growing political violence on the sub-continent: the Indian Councils Act (otherwise known as the Morley-Minto reforms) of November 1908 had boosted Indian representation on the Viceroy's Council. But he refused to become directly involved, suggesting instead that four of his old Indian tales might be translated, and adding that Kitchener really needed a set of stories 'taken down at first

hand from the mouth of a retired Subedar-major in a Sikh village'.[14] (The new paper was to be published in Allahabad by the
Pioneer Press, which was still owned by the Allen family though,
following Sir George's death in 1900, the driving force was now
his financially astute son George Burney Allen.)

Rudyard kept his thoughts on British politics to himself and
his close circle of friends. When, in September, the Unionists were
successful in a by-election, he expressed disdain for the whole
process: 'We've just won a "victory" at Newcastle where 2000 tin
smiths etc. have changed their non-existent minds about our
non-effective government. What solemn pulp is Democracy.'[15] A
couple of months later, apropos the need for continuing vigilance
in national defence, he asked a correspondent, 'Do I strike you as
a "lamentable and precocious" pessimist? I swear I ain't really but,
as a people just now, we are so invincibly determined not to face
any unpleasant facts that I am sometimes scared. I have seen war
and having seen it desire it to be kept far off.'[16]

On a practical level, after three budgets had targeted the rich
to pay for social reform, Rudyard took measures to protect his
own assets. He was helped by another *ad hoc* financial adviser, a
typically gnarled and individualistic crony called Barclay Walton
who had thrown up a career as a stockbroker to sail round the
world in his yacht, the *Bantam*. Rudyard rather envied Walton his
carefree existence. From time to time the mariner would return
from lengthy voyages with gifts of red mullet and other scarce fish.
Yet he always knew exactly what was happening in the financial
markets. In May 1907, following the budget, Rudyard had asked
his advice on coping with 'a Serious Financial Crisis' (with all the
capital letters). He explained that he had 'a few thousand pounds
to invest, but thanks to C. B. [Campbell Bannerman, the Liberal
Prime Minister] and Co. I don't see my way to risking it in
anything British'. Claiming to see 'nothing but disturbance or the
promise of disturbance' at home, he asked his friend if he could
recommend 'anything outside these islands which combines
common honesty with 4% or anything reasonably permanent

within the Island at between $3\frac{1}{2}$ and 4%. I ask because I am at my wits' end.'[17]

The situation called for a wider reassessment of his business affairs. In 1907 Rudyard managed to negotiate a reduction in the commission he paid his agent A. P. Watt. Essentially, any book that had been on the market for over ten years now paid five instead of ten per cent. Not that Watt was able to sit back with a reduced workload. Carrie was immediately on to him, demanding that he should take Macmillan to task for not making Rudyard's books more widely available in South Africa.[18] A couple of years later Rudyard was complaining that he had seen only one advertisement for his new book *Actions and Reactions* and that was 'microscopical'. He told Watt, 'Hodder & Stoughton who have only one book of mine – and that a reprint of a poem in one of Methuen's books – give more space to their advertisement. As you know I hate all the press notice and puffing business of a book, but surely they [Macmillan] might print the announcement of my book so that it could be seen.'[19]

As more tangible protection against inflation and social upheaval, the Kiplings had continued during the middle years of the decade to accumulate land, as they doubled their holdings around Bateman's to just over 200 acres, including twenty-one acres west of Bell Alley Lane (purchased from Helen Egerton, widow of the former rector of Burwash), thus not only extending their property into the village but also giving them ownership of a brickworks. However, there were tell-tale signs that even land was no longer a copper-bottomed investment. In 1908, after a neighbour, Joseph Schroeter, died, his daughter tried to let the family house, Laurelhurst, the largest property in the vicinity, to the west of Bateman's. Rudyard caustically described this as a 'tribute ... to the exactions of Asquith, whereby on a person's death a house is thrown out of commission – to the improvement of England'.[20] (Schroeter was a local phenomenon – a German-born merchant who had made his money in London.)

Having opted not to travel to South Africa for the eleventh

time (including nine consecutive winters), Rudyard took a holiday with his wife and children in Switzerland in late December. He did not mind where he went; as far as he could tell, Alpine resorts were all much the same.[21] At one stage he planned to spend his three months abroad moving from one village to another. However, having consulted with Thomas Cook, he opted to stay in one place – the family-run Hotel Cattani in Engelberg, a fashionable (as it then was) resort in the sub-canton of Unterwalden. After spending Rudyard's forty-third birthday *en route* in Lucerne, the Kiplings arrived at their destination on 31 December and two days later Rudyard was writing enthusiastically to Gwynne, 'Come out! Come here! It's lovely.'[22] The skiing and luging were excellent, and his children were 'wildly happy' with their skating.

John had to leave after a fortnight to return to school. But his father, mother and sister stayed in Engelberg until the end of February 1909 (by which time Rudyard himself mastered the art of skiing and was claiming merrily that it was 'an animal life – I've left my brains at Boulogne *douane*').[23] The family then travelled by train to Rome, from where Rudyard informed his son of the historical places they were visiting, such as the bridge on the Tiber where Horatius stopped Lars Porsena. He had the good grace to admit, 'I don't know whether Rome would interest you just yet but to me the sensation of seeing the actual things one has read about – the very things that have existed, since the beginning of our civilization – gives me an extraordinary feeling.'[24] Rudyard was still satisfying his appetite for history, while drawing further inspiration for his later *Puck* stories.

The Kiplings' return to Sussex was delayed when Elsie developed measles. This allowed Rudyard to renew his acquaintance with Britain's cultured ambassador to Italy, Sir Rennell Rodd. At one stage Rodd might have become a poet: at Oxford three decades earlier he had won the Newdigate Prize and been one of Oscar Wilde's closest friends. He invited Rudyard to dinner, offered the use of a car (a suggestion tactfully declined) and even proposed an introduction to King Victor Emmanuel. (Here

Rudyard excelled with his diplomatic response: 'As to kings, this one has done me no wrong that I should bore him and you for audience.'[25]) Later, on 4 April, the ambassador invited Rudyard to the opening by the King of the Keats–Shelley Memorial House in the Piazza di Spagna in the centre of Rome. Rudyard went along, but remained undemonstrative, being the only one of several dignitaries who declined to make a speech.

Domestic realities intruded when Rudyard received news of his cousin Ambrose Poynter who, because of financial difficulties, had had to let his flat. After an ill-fated foray to Brazil, Ambo and his wife Cherry had been forced back on family charity: having stayed with his reluctant father, Sir Edward, in Addison Road, they were now with his Aunt Clara Bell and her sons, and would soon move on to Stanley and Cissie Baldwin in Queen's Gate. 'Can't help wondering what is the matter with Ambo,' wrote Lockwood Kipling. 'Must be idleness – or want of initiative. His father's dislike of him seems to me a tragic enhancement of his troubles.'[26] At a time when Philip Burne-Jones's life alternated aimlessly between the Riviera and rest cures in England (he would later admit 'the chances are I shall go to my grave with "FAILURE" branded in burning letters in my soul'[27]), Rudyard was all the more concerned about his own children when he realised that he and his cousin Stanley Baldwin were the only male progeny of the formidable Macdonald sisters who had managed to break out of a domineering family and make something of their lives.

When Rudyard returned to England in April, his worst fears about Liberal intentions to squeeze the rich had been realised. Earlier that month David Lloyd George, the Chancellor of the Exchequer, had introduced his 'People's Budget', which proposed a supertax for anyone with incomes above £5000 a year, an increase in death duties and a levy on all undeveloped land. These measures were required to balance the books if the government were to introduce a radical programme of social reform (which now included not only old-age pensions but national insurance), while maintaining its commitment to a strong defence through expenditure on 'Fisher's toys', as the Dreadnoughts emerging from the naval dockyards were known.

The Kiplings were immediately up in arms. On 14 May Carrie noted that they were 'greatly occupied with investments, the Liberal Budget having frightened us as to our hard-earned savings'. Rudyard unburdened himself to Walton, 'The budget is Desolate and I don't like to think of the amount of misery and unemployment it has already begun to cause.' He asked his friend if he could recommend any investments ('however secretive') outside England. 'We must get every penny we can out of this country before the smash.'[28]

Towards the end of the month he could hold back no longer. In his poem 'The City of Brass', begun on 31 May, he vented his spleen against a political system which built up the expectations that needed to be met through measures such as Lloyd George's budget. He attacked the 'multitude' and the leaders who pandered to its demands. In 'pull[ing] down the walls that their fathers had made them', these people neglected the country's defences:

> And because there was need of more pay for the shouters
>   and marchers
> They disbanded in face of their foemen the yeomen and
>   archers

while giving succour to the hateful, the lawless, the lazy and the indigent. Rudyard's attack on the new unemployment benefit fizzed with loathing:

> They said: 'Who is eaten by sloth? Whose unthrift
>   has destroyed him?
> He shall levy a tribute from all because none
>   have employed him.'

The sub-text was that everything worthwhile was being thrown away:

They nosed out and digged up and dragged forth
   and exposed to derision
All doctrine of purpose and worth and restraint
   and prevision...

Rudyard had laid down his mark as the leading literary scourge
of Liberalism and democracy. Although his main allies in the
press were still Gwynne at the *Standard* (soon to move to the
Morning Post), Blumenfeld at the *Daily Express* and Maxse at the
National Review, it was Hamilton Fyfe on Northcliffe's *Daily Mail*
who noted the curious dichotomy between Rudyard's uncompromisingly aggressive tone and his ambivalent standing in the
community. At Rudyard's name, he suggested, people now tended
to shrug their shoulders and comment, 'He used to be rather
good, but he's never amusing now – always telling us we're coming
to grief. Suppose he's developed a bad digestion.' According to
Fyfe, these observers failed to understand the seriousness of Rudyard's arguments, which he summarised, 'We are slipping down
the broad, easy decline which will lead to our extinction as a Great
Power with an influence to exert on the side of the angels, with a
civilizing tradition to plant all the world over.' The title of Fyfe's
piece, 'The New Jeremiah', after the Old Testament prophet who
upbraided the Judaeans in the years before the sack of Jerusalem
and their exile to Babylon, was to become ever more appropriate
as a description of Rudyard.

One issue Rudyard never tired of harping on about was national
service. Once again, the Liberals had disappointed him. After
coming to power in late 1905, R. B. Haldane, the new War Minister,
had opted for a volunteer rather than conscript army. (The War
Office had its own long-running internal debate here, mirroring
the struggle in the Admiralty between Jackie Fisher's 'Blue Water'
group and the conservative 'Blue Funk' clique around Admiral
Lord Charles Beresford.) Rudyard had never liked Haldane: when
he declined to join the Coefficients in 1907, he had provided an

additional reason to Amery, 'Besides, if I joined it would be my duty as a believer to bribe the cook to poison Haldane, and this wouldn't make for harmony in any club.'[29] Now his antipathy to the War Minister was confirmed when, to support this volunteer army, Haldane also decided to set up a Territorial Army of part-time reservists.

Such ad hoc units were hardly what Lord Roberts and his cohorts at the National Service League had in mind. (Roberts had finally retired from the army in 1905 and was now President of the League.) However, these new circumstances did create an opportunity for advocates of quasi-militaristic training for young people – among them Rudyard's friend Robert Baden-Powell, whose career had failed to advance after his heroics at Mafeking. Appointed the army's Inspector-General of Cavalry while Roberts was still Commander, Baden-Powell was more interested in his own idea of an army cadet corps, which would teach adolescents the essentials of soldiering, while addressing post-war concerns about physical deterioration and lack of discipline among working men. The Boys' Brigade had already pioneered this approach, but it suffered from an image problem. Wanting to make the Brigade more attractive, its founder William Smith asked Baden-Powell to rewrite his popular army handbook *Aids to Scouting for NCOs and Men* as a manual for younger boys. With encouragement from R. B. Haldane, who sensed useful support for his Territorials, Baden-Powell drew up a short paper 'Scouting for Boys' which, in May 1906, he sent for discussion to a small group of potential sympathisers, including the influential trio of Lord Roberts, Lord Grey and Howell Gwynne, editor of the *Standard*.

Over the next couple of years Baden-Powell developed his ideas, mixing his own army scouting experience with fashionable interest (which Rudyard had helped create) in such subjects as the outdoor lore of American Indians and the lives of frontiersmen. (In 1905 an odd group, the Imperial Legion of Frontiersmen, had popped up, drawing inspiration from Rudyard's 1893 poem

'The Lost Legion'.) Into this cultural hotchpotch Baden-Powell also drew the popular sense of a need for alertness in the face of the danger of German invasion. (1906 saw the publication of the best-selling book *The Invasion of 1910*, by William Le Queux, a journalist on Northcliffe's *Daily Mail*.)

In 1907 Baden-Powell held his first Scouts camp and the following year, with the issue of *Scouting for Boys*, initially in magazine and then in book form, the Boy Scouts Organisation (as it was then called) was formed. The publisher of both was Arthur Pearson, the tariff reformer who owned the *Standard*, whose involvement showed not only the commercial potential of such ideas but also the continuing close links between imperialists, trade protectionists and now Scouts.

While Rudyard made no secret of his support for some form of compulsory military training, his role in the origins of the Scouts is hazy. According to the historian Hugh Brogan, Rudyard and Baden-Powell 'never quite lost touch' in the five years after meeting in Cape Town in 1901. The friendliness of their next confirmed encounter in early 1906, when Baden-Powell was visiting South Africa as Inspector-General of Cavalry, suggests that the two men had been in contact and that Rudyard had played a useful advisory role in the development of Baden-Powell's thinking about the Scouts. On this occasion Baden-Powell drew a charcoal portrait of Rudyard, and also showed him a sketch of the sea and the sky that he had made on his voyage out. When Rudyard looked at this he thought it showed the veld, with a storm threatening. Having been told of his mistake, he dashed off some verses on the back of a matchbox,

> This is the ocean bright and blue
> That the *Armadale Castle* plowtered through,
> But if you turn it the other way
> It's the lonely veldt on a cloudy day,
> That is if you hold it upside down
> It's the gathering storm on the desert brown;

And very seldom since Art begun
Could you get two pictures by drawing one.[30]

By the time Baden-Powell wrote *Scouting for Boys*, a year or so later, he included not only a short bowdlerised version of *Kim*, which presented the eponymous hero as a prototype Scout, but also developed Kim's Game, in which boys were called upon to memorise a variety of objects, along the lines of the Jewel Game with which Lurgan had initially humiliated Kim in Rudyard's book. The accompanying Scout's Law, encapsulated in the words 'Be Prepared', was riddled with signs of Rudyard's influence, starting with its opening words, 'Scouts, all the world over, have unwritten laws which bind them just as much as if they had been printed in black and white.' Rudyard is said to have provided the chant for the Scouts' rallying song, 'Be prepared! Zing-a-zing! Bom! Bom!'[31] Indeed, with its proto-imperialism, Masonic sense of brotherhood and escapist fantasies of outdoor life, the early Scout movement could have been scripted by Rudyard.

The cross-fertilisation of ideas was apparent in the *Puck* stories. Dan and Una were prototype Scouts and clearly Baden-Powell saw Parnesius as a pack leader. Presiding over a wet Scout camp at Humshaugh in Northumberland in late August 1908, he waxed lyrical about the view – an ancient British fortress on one side, the great Roman Wall on the other. 'All are there to suggest what a country of fighting and romance we are in. Every rock and dingle where we are Scouting today has had its Scouts there before – Scouting for their lives, in deadly earnest, many times in the last two thousand years.'[32]

Earlier that month the Kiplings had stayed nearby with Charles Leonard, the South African lawyer whose daughter Daisy was Elsie's friend. (Leonard had other interests apart from the law. As leader of the Johannesburg Uitlanders in December 1895, he had composed the telegram calling on Jameson to intervene in the Transvaal to save 'thousands of unarmed men, women and children of our race' from the ravages of the Boers.) Rudyard met

Baden-Powell at Chollerford, close to Hadrian's Wall, where the latter's official job was commanding the Northumberland Division of the Territorial Army. Back home, he began an Arthurian *Puck* story, but was defeated by the challenge of creating a Dark Ages Kim. (He also had a wonderful idea about an Egyptian who helped build Stonehenge, but that too was dropped.[33])

Over the next half-year, at a time of increasing tension in Europe following the Austrian annexation of Bosnia and Herzegovina, the Scout movement grew substantially, numbering around 130,000 in May 1909 when Baden-Powell asked Rudyard to write a song for a giant rally in Crystal Palace. Rudyard responded with the 'Boy Scouts' Patrol Song', whose message was encapsulated in its alternative name, 'All Patrols Look Out'. As a gesture of thanks, Baden-Powell offered John Kipling a place on a select summer camp in the New Forest in August. Having been brought up a fledgling Scout, John was used to his father blurting out statements like, 'Talk of B-P's Scouts! That is the real Red Indian wood-craft.'[34] (This, in January, after Rudyard and Carrie had threaded their way round a crowd at the Hotel Cattani.) Baden-Powell now had Sea Scouts in mind: as he explained to Rudyard, 'I hope to make sailors of them this year by having them on board ship and practising cutting out expeditions, piracy, and Treasure Islands, etc.'[35] In effect, this meant that some fifty boys would spend a week at Bucklers Hard, on John Montagu's (now Lord Montagu of Beaulieu's) estate, before changing places with another group who had been on board the training ship *Mercury*, moored on the River Hamble and run on similar, if slightly more authoritarian lines by John's hero, the quintessential Corinthian sportsman C. B. Fry.

For some reason John's presence at the New Forest camp was limited to one day during a short motoring tour of the West Country. *En route*, Rudyard passed through Winchester where he was fascinated to see the graves of Jane Austen and Isaak Walton.[36] Then, leaving Carrie and Elsie to return to Bateman's, he and his son carried on to Plymouth, where John at least enjoyed a voyage round the Eddystone Lighthouse in Barclay Walton's yacht *Bantam*.

John's reluctance to join the camp may have been connected with his father's growing snobbishness. Rudyard's attitude to the Scouts had been coloured that summer by his lack of success in convening a troop in Burwash. He complained to Blumenfeld that he had provided a field for summer activities and a gym to 'fool in in winter',[37] but they had broken up – a consequence of having a poor scoutmaster, it was said, but Rudyard felt the real reason was that they were the sons of small tradesmen and did not understand discipline or effort. Once again, his views proved extraordinarily malleable when he wanted: it is hard to warrant that this was the same person who had trumpeted the heroics of Mulvaney and Tommy Atkins, or who had shown such faith in the good sense of the common man in the aftermath of the Boer War.

Because of this local experience, Rudyard now saw the Scout movement increasingly as a means of social control – a view reflected in his weary promotional piece for the *Daily Express* in November 1911, at a time of political tension, when he claimed that the Scouts 'appeal[ed] to a class of boys who go through youth unpunished and almost entirely without any notion of loyalty or discipline'[38] – in contrast to public-school boys who were 'taught the sacred gospel of jolly-well must' and needed a different bait. He still believed in the general ideology of the Scouts, however. In 1916, during the dog-days of the First World War, his influence became more explicit after Baden-Powell founded a junior branch, the Wolf Cubs, with a ritual based on the *Jungle Books*. Seven years later, to celebrate his appointment as Cubs Commissioner, Rudyard published an appropriate *Book of Land and Sea Tales for Scouts and Guides*.

Personal links between the Kiplings and Baden-Powell might have been closer, had the Scout leader developed his romantic interest in Carrie's American-born cousin 'Daisy' Low, whom he met in May 1911. Daisy's marriage had come to an end in the summer of 1901, shortly after the Kiplings visited her at Welles-bourne. When her philandering husband proved reluctant to grant her a divorce, she hired Sir George Lewis, the eminent lawyer (and friend of the Burne-Jones family) to represent her. Lewis was beginning to make some headway on the matter when, not unexpectedly, Willie Low died in June 1905. In his will, he left all his estate to his mistress, Mrs Bateman. Daisy was forced to challenge this, and eventually was granted cash and shares amounting to $550,000 (in 1906 money). As a result she remained a wealthy woman: she was able to buy two adjoining houses in London's Grosvenor Street and indulge her interests in sculpture and, as it turned out, scouting. That summer of 1911 she seemed set to marry Baden-Powell after he had holidayed with her at her Scottish fishing lodge. Although the relationship cooled, she was on the same ship when he travelled to the United States on a lecture tour in January 1912 and she subsequently set up the Girl Scouts of America, with headquarters (initially) in her home town of Savannah, Georgia.

Involvement with Scouting did not mean Rudyard severed his links with the National Service League. The closeness of the two movements was reflected in Lord Roberts's message in the first issue of *The Scout* in April 1908. The future of Britain's army was now part of the national debate: the 1909 play *An Englishman's Home* by George du Maurier's son Guy satirised the ineptness of a people without military training in the face of an invasion. Rudyard responded by opening the doors of Bateman's for local meetings of the League. He enjoyed more success than with the Scouts: 120 people attended a gathering in April 1910, shortly before publication of a series of articles in *The World* attacking War Minister R. B. Haldane's support for a voluntary army. Supposedly anonymous, the pieces were written by Lord Esher, who had helped initiate army reforms as a member of the Commission of Inquiry into the Boer War. Haldane hit back with a short book, *Compulsory Service*, for which he wrote the introduction and General Sir Ian Hamilton the main text. Rudyard considered this treachery on the part of Hamilton, who for so long had been Roberts's right-hand man, and was now the army's Inspector-General of Overseas Forces. He wrote to his cousin Stanley:

> When Haldane's Hound upon Haldane's hobbies
> Writes a book which is full of lies
> Then we find out what a first class job is
> And how Inspector-Generals rise,

adding, jokingly, 'I think Swinburne wrote this.'[39]

Jeremiah might have seen it as an omen when, after torrential rain in October 1909, the River Dudwell burst its banks, causing the worst floods in his part of Sussex for fifty years. One evening Rudyard arrived home from visiting his parents in Tisbury to find the water rising across his garden, until, around midnight, it reached the south door of his house. The next morning he went to inspect the damage – fences and footpaths had been swept away, his beloved bees flooded out and, worst of all, the dynamo by the mill made useless.

By then Lloyd George's People's Budget had set in motion a predictable chain of political events. When the House of Lords refused to pass the requisite bill in November 1909, Prime Minister Asquith asked King Edward for permission to dissolve Parliament and hold an election the following January. Rudyard forecast that, though this was 'an Election (Golly what an election!) on the strictly Roman lines of "Bread and circuses" ',[40] it would not prove decisive. However, his reasoning showed a suspect mixture of robust opinion, stirring rhetoric and racist bravado that may have made for a good prophet but would not have been suited to a political career. He believed the English had 'some grit and character yet remaining. What our alien and semi-alien politicians overlook is the fact that we are gamblers and plunderers but not cheats and thieves and we do not much applaud trickery. That is where our games save us.'

Although the British are credited with the invention of skiing as a sport, it is doubtful if Rudyard was thinking on these lines when he took his family back to Engelberg at the end of December. As soon as they reached the Grand Hotel, Carrie was confined to bed with a catalogue of complaints – a 'savage chill which gave her acute facial neuralgia, swelling of the glands of the neck, pain in tooth, eye and fore head *plus* a bad racking cough and a little more temperature'.[41] As a result, Rudyard was unable to return to England, as intended, to cast his vote in the general election in January.

Over the years Carrie's health had become a regular, disturbing feature of domestic life. Her breakdown in 1901 had been followed by increasing signs of hypochondria. In 1906, for example, she tried out a vibrator, which Rudyard explained to his mother-in-law was 'an American notion: ... if you apply it to the side of your nose when you have sniffles it seems to act as a cure'.[42] By then Carrie was under the care of John Bland-Sutton, Britain's foremost gynaecologist, with consultancies at the Middlesex Hospital and the Chelsea Hospital for Women. From modest farming stock, Bland-Sutton was a small, puckish man of wide-ranging interests and considerable showmanship. As the *Jungle Book* stories showed, Rudyard himself was already well versed in animal behaviour. But the doctor taught him to look at natural history more scientifically. Bland-Sutton himself had been granted access to perform autopsies on the animals of the London zoo. Once, when holidaying in Spain, he was allowed to dissect the carcass of a bull killed in the ring. He wrote books about his travels (with special reference to the animals) in Ethiopia and Uganda. He gave Rudyard a taste of his rigorous standards one Christmas at Bateman's (where he and his wife had become regular visitors). He had been talking about animals' gizzards when, to Rudyard's amazement, he insisted on finding a chicken to observe directly if he was right in thinking that the stones in the bird's gizzard made an audible grinding noise. Rudyard took this as an endorsement of his own view that nothing should be taken for granted. Even though checking sometimes seemed superfluous, he believed it was a necessary exercise that helped encourage and stimulate his daemon.[43]

Carrie's regular illnesses did not make for an easy matrimonial relationship. In July 1908 Rudyard showed the strain when he apologised to Elsie (during her stay in London) for appearing 'as your dear French governess says, deestray' because of 'your Mummy's pains in her inside'. Carrie had imagined the various diseases that she might have. 'She counted up 97 of them – or three. I forget which,'[44] joked Rudyard, adopting a brave face. He took her to Bland-Sutton's palatial consulting rooms at 47 Brook Street, Mayfair, where the extrovert doctor had built a remarkable hypostyle hall, based on Darius's Apadama, or Hall of Honour, at Susa on the borders of modern Iran. It was an anti-climax to learn that she was only suffering from indigestion.

After arranging for Rudyard to lecture at the Middlesex Hospital in October, Bland-Sutton advised him to give up smoking. Rudyard no longer dismissed the idea, as when Osler had made a similar suggestion, but he found it difficult to work without a cigarette or pipe in his mouth and, after a period of abstention, he soon reverted to the habit. Towards the end of the year Carrie was back at the centre of attention – laid up in bed, having had three cysts on her head removed. Cysts were a Bland-Sutton speciality: his gynaecological practice was based on his knowledge of ovarian cysts and he liked to boast that he had once removed one weighing sixty pounds from a sixty-five-year-old woman. Knowing Anna Balestier would be worried about her daughter, Rudyard tried to allay her fears by drawing a humorous picture of Carrie with her head in bandages, looking, he said, like Richard I's Spanish-born Queen Berengaria.

In Engelberg in January 1910 Carrie was again 'very far from well'.[45] Imagining once more that she had some awful affliction, she followed up the recommendation of Dr Alfred Fröhlich, an Austrian toxicologist whom the Kiplings had met at the resort the previous year, and consulted a Zurich specialist, a Dr Eichorst, who told her she had arthritis and suggested she might benefit from the curative powers of the sulphur waters at Vernet-les-Bains, a spa town in the French Pyrenees, close to the Spanish border.

Carrie perked up as a result of this diagnosis: as Rudyard noted to Fröhlich (disparagingly known as 'Golliwog' by the children), 'Her nerves are restored – and now that Eichorst had pronounced that she is not suffering from six deadly diseases she is very gay.'[46] Nevertheless it meant that the Kiplings had to change travel and all other plans, which proved disconcerting for Rudyard who wanted to finish his verses for *Rewards and Fairies*, due to be published in the autumn.

Twelve-year-old John was packed back to school. His eyesight had now put paid to his ambitions to join the Navy and Rudyard was thinking of sending him to a conventional English public school. However, John was not intelligent enough for Eton (the choice for Stanley Baldwin's son Oliver, also a pupil at St Aubyn's, and the school which, from other evidence, Rudyard might have preferred). So he had to settle for Wellington which, as its name implied, had a military background. Over the next few months Rudyard firmed up this idea. He was enthusiastic when he visited the school in the autumn, though to friends he admitted concern about the system of houses, which he felt were 'nests of all sorts of muck'.[47]

A couple of days after returning to St Aubyn's John showed his annoyance at being dumped back at school when he complained, petulantly, that he could not escape his father's influence. 'Of course we had the "Children's Song" in church this morning. I do get sick of it.' Rudyard apologised (for the third time in less than six months), adding, with a parent's white lie, 'Cheer up. I don't think there is anything in the new *Puck* tales [i.e. *Rewards and Fairies*] that can be used for scholastic purpose.'[48] (He subsequently discouraged his publisher from issuing anthologies of his work for schools.) Passing through Geneva, Rudyard indicated nagging signs of guilt when he bought his son a watch, with the boy's initials engraved. Since John had already lost or destroyed three timepieces, Rudyard adopted the persona of the manager of the shop, Golay Fils & Stahl, to counsel, 'Mais – écoutez-moi, il est défendu – verboten – prohibito, de soaker le montre en thé, ou le mettre dans les bains, ou dans la mer, ou le laisser on the cricket-field, ou le chucker at other boys' heads.'[49] (Such 'Franglais' was often adopted by the Kiplings at home as a Stalkyish mode of quasi-secret communication.)

With Elsie in tow, the Kiplings travelled by rail, via Geneva, Lyons, Avignon and then, taking four different local trains, to Vernet. In Avignon they met Lord Montagu of Beaulieu who was touring the area, testing a new 60hp six-cylinder Rolls-Royce. The stocky auburn-haired peer epitomised the excitement and political manoeuvring of early motoring enthusiasts. Schooled into the mystique of the machine by Rudyard's writings, he had, like his literary hero, worked hard to make the car respectable. Co-operating with the (Royal) Automobile Club (RAC), he had, as an MP (until succeeding his father in 1905), helped formulate even-handed laws which protected motorists from the wrath of the flat-earthers who wanted to hold back the progress of mechanical transport. (Rudyard satirised such people in his stories 'Steam Tactics' and 'The Village that Voted the Earth was Flat'.) Taking his cue from Alfred Harmsworth at the *Daily Mail*, Montagu had backed his lobbying activities with a magazine, *The Car Illustrated*. More recently, he had become a proponent of the even newer sport of flying. Always an ardent imperialist and tariff reformer (one reason why he had tried to take over the *Standard* a few years earlier), he was one of the first public figures in Britain to recognise the military potential of aircraft. In June 1909 he had been a founder, later the President, of the Aerial League of the British Empire, which aimed to ensure that Britain enjoyed the same supremacy in the air as at sea. This organisation owed something to Rudyard's story 'With the Night Mail' and something to growing fears of German invasion. Montagu had resorted to fiction to publicise the dangers of German infiltration by airship in his story 'The Mystery of Max', in *The Car Illustrated*, in 1908. In the years leading up to the First World War, Rudyard took up the baton, becoming a leading propagator of the views of an identifiable group of right-wing men like Montagu who sought to bridge the political gap between well-known issues of imperialism and protectionism, and emerging ones of German militarism and the role of new technology such as aviation.

As well as sharing an Anglocentric view of the world, Rudyard and Lord Montagu had several friends in common, including Lady Edward Cecil and the meticulous Claude Johnson, who had left the RAC and taken over as managing partner at Rolls-Royce. Johnson, who became known as the hyphen in Rolls-Royce, was accompanying Montagu on this trip to the South of France. His former secretary at the RAC, Nelly Thornton, later joined the staff of *The Car Illustrated* where she became Montagu's mistress. She had gained notoriety as the naked model used to create the Rolls-Royce mascot, Spirit of Ecstasy.

When he finally reached Vernet, Rudyard was not impressed. Julius Caesar might once have stopped there to rid his body of an English-induced rheumatism, but Rudyard loathed the sulphurous stench of the baths. He had to put up with repeated pummellings from masseurs, there were problems with the hotel and the invalids who congregated there gave it the pious atmosphere of Lourdes. The only compensations were the magnificent 'grey and black and yellow'[50] mountains, which reminded him of Africa, the spring-like weather and the fact that Carrie seemed to benefit from a purgative regime. He was relieved when, a few days later, Lord Montagu turned up and offered to take them both for lunch at Mont Louis in the hills. The Rolls climbed effortlessly through steep and winding passes until, above the snow line at 5400 feet, they were able to look over into Spain and see people were skiing. The contrast between the mountain tops and the warm town below fascinated Rudyard: he remarked to Gwynne how one moment the car was up to its ankles in six-foot drifts of snow, and an hour later was 'back among palms and oleanders'[51] in Vernet.

Since Montagu's Rolls was officially undergoing a test, it had to be driven back to Paris. When Johnson suggested that the Kiplings might like to accompany the chauffeur to the French capital in an otherwise empty vehicle, Rudyard welcomed the opportunity. On reaching Paris, Carrie seemed much improved: she 'shopped and so did the daughter and by Allah they ceased not to shop till we left that city'.[52] But Rudyard was still concerned about her health: writing to Ted Hill to commiserate over the death of her father, he confided that he hoped that his wife would soon regain her pleasure in her garden at Bateman's.[53] To Andrew Macphail he said he wanted to encourage Carrie to go a little slower. 'But', he added with a touch of sadness, 'with an executive temperament one *must* forge ahead on executive paths.'[54]

Following the election in January 1910, the political landscape was clearer, though from Rudyard's point of view more threatening. The Liberals had been returned to power with a mandate to introduce their budget, but their overall majority had been reduced to two. As a result, they were dependent on support from a rump of Irish Nationalists, who exacted their price in the promise of Home Rule. Even so, the Conservative-dominated House of Lords remained an obstacle and much parliamentary horse-trading was still required.

For a while the heat was removed from the situation with the sudden death of King Edward VII on 6 May. Rudyard reverted to his old practice of offering a poem, 'The Dead King', to several papers – the *Morning Post*, *Daily Telegraph*, *Standard* and, oddly, since he had ignored it since Northcliffe's take-over in 1908, *The Times*. But this was a special occasion, one which Rudyard hoped might have a healing effect on the nation.

Little seemed wrong with the world when the entire village of Burwash crowded into the parish church of St Bartholomew's on a hot summer's day for a service to commemorate the late King.

(Known as St Barnabas in the *Puck* tale 'The Conversion of St Wilfrid', it contained what Dan, Una and the Kipling children knew as Panama Corner – the plaque to the iron master John Collins, reading 'Orate p. annema Jhone Coline' or 'Pray for the soul of John Collins'.) Rudyard watched approvingly as five maids from Bateman's – Georgina, Ada, Ellen, Long Nellie and Elsie Martin (daughter of Martin the gardener who had come from Rottingdean) – sat together in one pew. In the countryside, at least, the peasantry was content: 'One saw just the ordinary every day people who after all make the world, just grieving for the loss of their own King and friend as they would grieve for anyone of their own blood and kin.'[55]

Throughout the summer Rudyard's friends kept him informed about developments in the wider world, either by letter or in person. After Gwynne passed through with news of machinations at Westminster, Rudyard commented that he had heard 'the not edifying history of the Government's intrigues with the Irish. A sordid tale wherein all the actors seemed to be equally bewildered – like pickpockets chased round Waterloo Station. No central plan – no definite idea. Only hate and small spites.'[56]

Several associates now lived close to Bateman's, in either Kent or Sussex. Lord Milner was established at Sturry Court, near Canterbury, where he would entertain Rudyard every Empire Day (a recent addition to the official calendar on 24 May). Lady Edward Cecil had acquired a house at Great Wigsell, near Battle, within striking distance of not only the Kiplings but her great passion Lord Milner. There she brought up her children, George and Helen, while her husband remained conveniently *hors de combat* in Egypt as Under-Secretary for Finance under Lord Cromer and his successors. Other members of Rudyard's local circle included Colonel Feilden in Burwash, Moreton Frewen, his old India friend, at Brede Place, some ten miles away, Abe Bailey who lived in style near East Grinstead, Conan Doyle at Crowborough and George Burney Allen at Free Chase, Warninglid,

West Sussex. Henry James was not far away in Rye, but seldom visited.

Despite these friends, Rudyard was delighted when, some time in 1910, the idea was floated that, between trips abroad, Perceval Landon might like to live on the Bateman's estate. When, a couple of years later, Carrie paid £650 for Keylands, an old cottage on the Fenners Farm property, it was refurbished, using new bricks from the local works the Kiplings now owned. Within months, Landon was able to move into his Wealden Woolsack, his home from home, though available for use by other friends of the Kiplings whenever he was away.

During the summer of 1910 Rudyard renewed his friendship with Theodore Roosevelt who, after two terms of office as President of the United States, was now touring the world, indulging his taste for shooting animals and occasionally giving talks such as his Romanes lecture to Oxford University on 7 June. A few weeks later Roosevelt's son, twenty-one-year-old Kermit, stayed a night at Bateman's. Rudyard liked to believe that he converted an uncouth American to British tradition: 'I took the boy to Pevensey Castle and Hurstmonceux and let them hit him between the eyes. They did.'[57] Perhaps he was correct: in the Second World War Kermit anticipated his country's entry into the war and served with British forces in Norway and Egypt. Kermit's son was given the same first name but was known as 'Kim', which was appropriate for someone who became a leading light in the early Central Intelligence Agency. (Rudyard's book of this name attained mythical status among American spies: Allen Dulles, one of the first heads of the CIA, used to keep a copy beside his bed.)

While in Oxford for the Romanes lecture, Rudyard stayed with Charles Cannan, Secretary of the Oxford University Press, the publisher of his short history of England for children, a one-off collaboration with Charles Fletcher, a Fellow of Magdalen College. Fletcher was one of the many historians Rudyard had consulted while writing his *Puck* stories. The two men shared vehemently anti-Liberal views, as well as a conviction that learning should be fun and, in particular, writing about the past should be accessible. When in May 1910 Fletcher suggested working together on a history for children, Rudyard agreed to write some verses to accompany the text. 'For babes one must give peptonized patriotism,'[58] he burbled. Fletcher took Rudyard's glib encouragement rather too literally. In their book, *A History of England*, he lamented that, although St Patrick had rid Ireland of snakes, he did not succeed 'in banishing the murderers and thieves, who were worse than many snakes'. In the West Indies, he believed the economy had declined since the abolition of slavery in 1833 and that the mainly black population was 'lazy, vicious and incapable of any serious improvement, or of work except under compulsion'.[59]

Even Rudyard was embarrassed about this output and, when Fletcher later wanted to bring the book up to date, he tried to dissuade him. As the author of the *Stalky* tales (and in particular 'The Flag of Their Country' about the Jelly-bellied Flag-flapper), Rudyard knew that such blatant tub-thumping was counter-productive. His own verse contributions to *A History of England* were more subtle, providing a useful synthesis of his ideas about his country's history. His respect for the resilience of the constitution was based on the fact that

> There are four good legs to my Father's Chair –
> Priest and People and Lands and Crown.
> I sits on all of 'em fair and square,
> And that is the reason it don't break down.

In 'The Glory of the Garden', his final poem in the book, Rudyard presented a humanitarian, almost democratic attitude to English society, peopled by 'the gardeners, the men and "prentice boys"', and emphasising that Adam was a gardener:

> and God who made him sees
> That half a proper gardener's work is done upon his knees ...

This endorsement of humble prayer suggested an emerging religiosity in Rudyard's work. Overall, there was no mistaking his patriotic vision of England as a garden 'full of stately views ... / But the Glory of the Garden lies in more than meets the eye'.

That summer of 1910, John was picked for his school's first eleven at cricket. He began to show some interest in Latin and Rudyard proudly thought of giving his son a copy of Conington's translation of Horace. He still liked to stimulate John with amusing titbits of information, such as the story of the *Dreadnought* hoax in February, when Virginia Stephen and some friends had dressed up as Ethiopian princes and persuaded Admiral William May in Portsmouth to show them round the pride of the Royal Navy – its largest and most modern warship, the *Dreadnought*. Normally Rudyard might have disapproved of such behaviour (particularly by a suffragette supporter), but he showed his lighter side in telling John he had met someone who knew the hoaxers and who had related 'some gloriously funny tales'.[60]

Again, he might have been expected to regard jury service not so much as a duty to his fellow citizens but as an important historical right. However, when he managed to avoid sitting on a jury in the county town of Lewes in July, Rudyard reacted with a Stalkyish mixture of guilt and delight, feeling 'like a boy who had shirked a licking' as he listened to twelve names being called out for service and finding his was not among them.[61]

His growing passion for gardening, rather than any desire to pay something back to the community, encouraged him to join the East Sussex natural history society, under whose auspices he held a flower show at Bateman's in early August – a piece of bravado that was not repeated. Over 1000 people attended, the lawns were badly scuffed and Carrie expressed her sense of her privacy being invaded in her terse diary summary of the day: 'Devastated.'[62]

She was on more familiar ground in October, when she wrote to A. P. Watt's son Struan, who was now working in the family business: 'Mr Kipling amused himself last night by adding up the sales of his books. The volumes sold by Macmillan have now so nearly reached a million that he wonders if they would not make a special effort next year to bring the number up to that figure.'[63] (It would be wrong to infer that the Kiplings spent their evenings poring simply over account books. There was still companionship in their marriage. One of their favourite ways of relaxing was to read to one another: 'Mother and I are buried in Queen Victoria's letters,' Rudyard told his children on one occasion. 'We read 'em to each other aloud and sit up till all hours to finish our volumes. It beats any novel I've ever read.'[64]

As the summer receded, the leaders of the two main political parties worked for a compromise that would allow the budget to pass without altering the shape of the House of Lords. They realised that failure would lead to the introduction of Home Rule which neither of them really wanted. By late autumn there was still impasse and a second election was required. But once again, Rudyard's attention was diverted, this time by the death of his mother.

Sixteen

Max, Money and Motors

1910–1914

Rudyard's concern about his parents had been one of the reasons for his low morale. For more than a dozen years Lockwood and Alice had lived modestly at The Gables, their cottage on the outskirts of Tisbury. But while Lockwood had carried on much as in Lahore – a genial, white-bearded craftsman whose range of skills was appreciated at Clouds and other local seats – Alice had found living in the English countryside more difficult. No longer the flirtatious middle-aged beauty able to turn the head of the Viceroy, she had little to occupy her in Wiltshire, except looking after Trix and exchanging occasional visits with her sisters. Racked with pains and often unable to sleep, she cut a sorry figure, remembered by her grand-daughter Elsie for her peaked and sallow face beneath a ginger toupee.

When, from time to time, Lockwood felt low, Rudyard knew what to do: he would encourage his father to lend a hand advising him on his own stories, such as *Kim*. Lockwood was still occupied with pottery and illustrations (a fund of amusement for John and Elsie Kipling as they grew up) and, as late as 1904, he declined the editorship of James Fergusson's *Indian and Eastern Architecture*, which was offered by the publisher John Murray. That year he complained that a bad attack of 'slow teasing nervous dyspepsia' had led to 'a break down in health – and what is worse – spirits'.[1] But, as when he travelled to the United States (in 1893 and again when his son was ill in 1899), or when he accompanied Rudyard's family to South Africa in 1902, he was able to slip away and recover his composure on a Mediterranean cruise – something he enjoyed so much that he went again in May 1906, this time with almost disastrous consequences, for he contracted pneumonia and wanted Rudyard to come to Gibraltar to pick him up.

For Alice there was little of this excitement. In 1902 she assisted a partially recovered Trix on a book of poems that was published by Elkin Matthews as *Hand in Hand – Verses by a Mother and Daughter* (Trix supplied sixteen and Alice ten of the leaden contents).[2] Later that year Trix returned to India, but married life in Calcutta was not easy and, over the years until her husband retired in 1910,[3] she frequently slipped home to England. Disappointed in her literary efforts and in her marriage, Trix decided to exploit her psychic gifts. During the first decade of the century she participated in a series of wide-ranging experiments into automatic writing conducted by the Society for Psychical Research and known as the 'cross-correspondences'. Adopting the pseudonym 'Mrs Holland' to avoid any embarrassment to her family, she built up a reputation in paranormal circles as a woman with remarkable powers of 'second sight'.

While she was in England, Trix tended to live with her parents in Wiltshire. At least she was able to look after them. In November 1905, Carrie could reassure herself about her husband's relations, 'His mother feeble, his father bored', but 'Trix will see them through their troubles'.[4] Rudyard's ability to influence affairs was limited by the coolness between Carrie and Alice. At one stage he was thinking of extending The Gables and putting in a nurse, but Alice opposed this and 'insisted that Trix must sleep in a cot beside her in her own room'[5] – powerful testimony to the way that her controlling influence was now being brought to bear on the sweet-natured but muddle-headed Trix. The Pater usually visited Bateman's on his own and, on the few occasions his wife accompanied him, Carrie pointedly noted her own reaction, as on 29 June 1903 when, after the Lockwood Kiplings left, she 'stop[ped] all afternoon in bed weary in soul and body'.[6]

Rudyard's worries about his parents were not calmed when in April 1907 his father suffered a forty-five-minute fainting fit and then, a couple of years later, his mother was diagnosed as having Graves disease, a variety of hyperthyroidism. These afflictions coincided with a series of deaths among his older relations and friends. In June 1906 Aunt Aggie had succumbed to cancer ('the family complaint'[7] Rudyard noted morbidly). In February 1908 Uncle Alfred Baldwin had suffered a sudden fatal heart attack. A couple of years later, in May 1910, Crom Price died, only a week after Rudyard had offered to send any books or magazines he wanted.[8]

Shortly afterwards, in November 1910, Alice Kipling was dead. Twenty-five years later Rudyard described his feelings to a friend who had just lost his mother: 'I went back for quite a while to the bewildered helplessness of a child left alone ... That's a special & eternal bond when it exists. God help the poor devils who "didn't get on with their mothers"! They've lost the other half of life.'[9] Once again, he was idealising his thoughts about a difficult relationship and was still unable to deal rationally with a woman he felt had rejected him as a young boy. Her intelligence, ambition and contacts had been essential to his success in India. But, unlike his father, who had played an equally important role, the wilful Alice had demanded recognition (the sort of pressure which had forced him to write his powerful but cringing poem 'Mother o' Mine' in 1891). Rudyard's ability to cope with his mother's demands was not helped by her disapproval of Carrie.

He had certainly not expected the way that this low-level feud would affect him after Alice's death. For this loss proved the trigger which tipped Trix back into her schizophrenia. In her grief his mentally disturbed sister worked the fault-line that existed between Bateman's and The Gables into a vast canyon. She later complained that Rudyard (as an agent of Carrie) had failed to look after her parents, condemning them to live in straitened financial circumstances in a small house without a nurse. She suggested that she had been the victim of a calculated attempt to rob her of her inheritance (this was improbable), and that Rudyard had taken the opportunity to destroy his mother's papers, including not only her will (improbable) but also his old letters to his family (much more likely).[10]

Rudyard found himself in the middle of a genetically pro-grammed showdown between Highland (Macdonald) capri-ciousness and New World (Balestier) order. He himself had driven to Tisbury on 19 November, as soon as he received a telegram telling him that his mother was seriously ill. Alice died at 7 in the morning three days later. Around 4 o'clock that afternoon, Trix claimed she was helping Miss Ensor, the local doctor's daughter, to lay out her mother's body when Rudyard 'got possession of her [i.e. Alice's] keys, opened a cupboard and destroyed many private papers of both hers and mine'. She added that Rudyard tore up what she was certain was the will her mother had discussed with her a few months earlier. 'I tried to stop him but he said, "Oh death invalidates this".'[11]

By the time of her mother's funeral on 25 November Trix's mind was wilting under the strain of conflicting emotions of grief and anger. Carrie had arrived in Tisbury the previous day. Symptomatic of her estrangement from Alice and Lockwood, she stayed at the South West Hotel in the village, which she found 'rough but not quite impossible'.[12] The next morning she went to The Gables where Trix was in 'a most excited condition' and Rudyard 'was doing everything (though J. Fleming was there)'. This suggested that Rudyard had to attend to his distraught sister rather than to matters relating to the funeral, about which Carrie had nothing to say, except that it took place at 3 p.m. and she and her husband were on the road to London at 5 o'clock.[13]

Subsequently Rudyard returned to Burwash, where he spoke twice on behalf of the local Unionist candidate George Courthope in the week leading up to the general election on 9 December. Second time round, the Liberal and the Unionist parties won exactly the same number of seats. This only strengthened the hand of the Irish Nationalists who held the balance of power, making the introduction of Home Rule inevitable.

A couple of days before Christmas Rudyard drove to Tisbury to see his widowed father. Finding him in good health, he arranged that he should stay at Bateman's during the summer. On 29 December, just before the concurrence of his and Carrie's birthdays, Rudyard escaped the growing political turmoil and again took his family to Engelberg. He had been there three weeks when he heard that his father had been taken ill with a bad cold at the Wyndhams' house, Clouds. Four days later came the dreaded news: less than three months after Alice's death, Lockwood had followed her to the grave, the victim of a fatal ten-minute-long heart attack. Rudyard and Carrie immediately hurried back to Tisbury for the funeral in the parish church of St John the Baptist on 30 January 1911. Lockwood was buried beside his wife in the churchyard, where their graves were covered unostentatiously with two plain, rectangular slabs of granite, with inscriptions of inlaid lead:

John Lockwood Kipling	Alice Macdonald
C.I.E.	Wife of
1837–1911	John Lockwood Kipling
	1910

(Mixing Scottish tradition with a touch of proto-feminism, Alice had been determined at the end to emphasise her own family line.) Before returning to Switzerland, Rudyard spent a day sorting out his father's papers at The Gables. A couple of months later, back home from his holiday, he, Carrie and the children went down to Tisbury, where they stayed for three days systematically 'break-[ing] up the little home there'. Carrie recorded the business in her diary with military precision: 'We stick at our work, Rud and John at the Library, Elsie and I at the house.'[14] When they had finished, they built a bonfire at the bottom of the garden, and burnt a quantity of letters and papers.[15] Since no will was ever found, Lockwood's estate was divided equally between his two children.

Trix felt that a will would (or, perhaps, should) have taken Rudyard's wealth into account and left her father's estate to her. When, after World War Two, she contributed fifty pounds, a significant sum, for a memorial to Lionel Dunsterville ('Stalky'), she commented acidly (and uncharacteristically, for she was normally supportive of her brother), 'If a distinguished relative had not paid (without consulting me) £40 for a houseful of carpets, curios and embroideries – half of which were mine – [in] spite of a destroyed will – I would have made it double.'[16] This referred to the settlement of the estate, a process which was not facilitated by either the lack of a will or her own fragile hold on sanity. In fact, the accounts of the estate show that the furniture and household effects at Tisbury were valued by Waters and Company at £175.8s.6d. Because he took everything in the house for himself (no doubt a high-handed thing to do), Rudyard deducted this amount from his share of the proceeds. The figure of forty pounds that Trix remembered referred to the valuation of John Kipling's library. Having also taken the books, Rudyard deducted this additional sum from his share. However, there was no record of an official valuation, suggesting that, in this instance, Rudyard did secure a bargain. He would have argued that, in order to pay for medical and residential care, Trix needed as much cash as possible from her share of her father's estate.

Back in Engelberg, John had been suffering from a prolonged attack of measles. As soon as he was better he returned to school on 13 February and Rudyard, in subdued mood, continued his holiday with Carrie to take the waters in Vernet-les-Bains. The Kiplings were joined in south-west France by Lord and Lady Roberts (the old war-horse had just completed 'Facts and Fallacies', his own book-length contribution to the National Service debate and was looking 'as fit as a flea'[17]) and by Julia, one of the three Catlin daughters, and her new husband, Chauncey Depew Jr. Having recently been widowed, she was more wealthy than ever: with an income of £30,000, she was unconcerned when her chauffeur Jules 'scarpered' with 10,000 francs, Rudyard noted, unsure whether to approve or not. He was amused at Carrie's comment when someone asked about the Depews (and Julia's sixteen-year-old daughter Frances, who played with Elsie): 'You'll know 'em well in a few years. A girl with her money simply cannot escape an English title in these days of Lloyd George.'[18]

With friends around for company, he found himself warming to Vernet – enough to write a short story for the local English-language magazine, *The Merry Thought*. His light-hearted piece, 'Why Snow Falls on Vernet', anticipated the mixture of early history, medicine and farce he brought to his later tales, recounting how two English knights, on their way home from the siege of Antioch at the end of the first crusade, called at Vernet, seeking some relief for their lumbago. Elements of future stories can be discerned in his account of a trip to the Spanish border in a long-bodied 75hp De Dietrich, stopping in Port Vendrées to watch the local fishing boats with 'tremendous timbers for their size, knees and deck beams out of all proportion' and their 'sail stuff very poor – like cotton'[19] – images that were to be recalled in his 1930 story 'The Manner of Men'. (This is not as ridiculous as it seems. At this stage in his life, perhaps because he no longer had his father to guide him, Rudyard was exploring themes he would take up much later. In October he was writing a story about the Archangel of the English, which had to wait until 1932 to be published as 'Uncovenanted Mercies' in his collection *Limits and Renewals*.)

Rudyard's reviving spirits were confirmed in his unusually red-blooded description of a lunch in Perpignan of 'a beauty and succulence which made me weep'. The meal comprised:

a locally made pâté de foie gras (fresh and lovely); oysters from Arcachon (weeping bitterly I had to pass them); omelette with tips of wild asparagus! (a dream); grilled sole (a revelation!); tripes à la mode de Caen (a delight!); fresh peas from the Spanish frontier with a tournedos sitting on a crust of bread soaked in some magic sauce!!! (indescribable!); then a soufflé unlike any soufflé that ever souffled, with strawberry jam of whole strawberries.[20]

Back at Bateman's, after a leisurely drive through France with Perceval Landon, who had also joined the Kiplings in Vernet, there were intimations of further mortality in Carrie's comment in her diary, 'Aunt Georgie has sadly aged.'[21] The more pressing problem, however, was what to do with Trix, who had not recovered her sanity. Taking after his mother, Rudyard refused to countenance his sister being certified and confined to a mental home. He admitted to Fleming that his objection was 'in large part sentimental but none the less it jars on one'.[22] As a result, Fleming's sister Moona Richardson prevailed on her brother to send Trix to a succession of homes in Scarborough, Andover and, later, Jersey. Although Trix did not mind her simple existence for much of the next thirteen years, she felt she had been banished on the orders of her Scottish sister-in-law, who did not want her presence in Edinburgh, a town where Moona's husband Ralph was a leading lawyer, or Writer to the Signet. Thirty years later Trix was complaining still she had to live on £200 a year, plus £50 a year that her father left her, Rudyard having 'snaffled the other £50 by the crude method of burning the will in my presence'. She added, 'Verily my foes have been "those of my own household" – my own brother and my husband's favourite sister.'[23]

An emotionally drained Rudyard conducted his dealings with Fleming largely through his solicitor George Macdonald. Was it conscience or good grace that, in August 1911, encouraged him to send his sister the painted fire-screen from the drawing-room at The Gables, some silver dishes and a copy of the Outward Bound edition of his works that Charles Scribner's Sons were still producing in New York? (There should now have been twenty-five out of an eventual thirty-six volumes.) Certainly there was no love lost between Rudyard and his brother-in-law. 'I think I'd have diseases with too much Jack Fleming,'[24] he told his cousin Stanley Baldwin. Carrie predictably was unsympathetic, telling her mother that the Kiplings had difficulty with Trix because 'her husband is pig headed and himself rather off his head with nerves and won't do what is best for her'.[25]

At the same time her own family had been wrestling with its problems of mental instability. For years her lively sister Josephine had behaved eccentrically. According to the disarmingly candid family history, *The Balestiers of Beechwood*, after her marriage to the distinguished doctor Theodore Dunham in 1897, 'she grew ever more precise, imperious and exacting, to such a degree that the peculiarity seemed almost psychopathic and was noticed even by a stranger after a very few minutes of conversation'.[26] In mid-1910, when she was forty and had produced four children, she suffered a nervous breakdown after losing twins at the end of a difficult pregnancy. The Kiplings' letters to Josephine and her mother at this time are full of concern about her state of health.

Henry James wrote an annual letter to Anna Balestier around the anniversary of the death of her son, his friend Wolcott. He had missed the date in December 1910 because his brother William was terminally ill. So it was not until the following May that he contacted Carrie's mother. After asking kindly after the sick Josephine, James noted, 'Rudyard's father's death added to his mother's will have swept the old scene bare for him – deeply will those losses both have ploughed into him and altered his life.'[27] Rudyard referred to his sense of loss to his old friend Ted Hill, 'Dear as my mother was, my father was more to me than most men are to their sons; and now I find that I have no one to talk or to write to I find myself desolate.'[28] This unguarded comment indicated that Rudyard was more affected by his father's death than by his mother's. However, the psychologically astute James correctly assessed that it opened up a new phase in his friend's life. For the first time, Rudyard had to face the world, and conduct his work, without Lockwood as inspiration and back-stop. Along with his inevitable grief, he was experiencing a curious sense of liberation.

*

Rudyard did at least have a new man to idolise. In November 1910, shortly before his mother's death, his approach to politics and life had been transformed by his meeting with Max Aitken, an engaging, roguish Canadian financier from Halifax in Nova Scotia. Having made a fortune in his home country, Aitken had come to Britain in July with the express aim of winning a seat in parliament. The crucial second general election of 1910 was pending and Aitken wanted to make his protectionist cum imperialist views known. With his wealth, he surrounded himself with a group of like-minded politicians and journalists (his fellow Canadian Andrew Bonar Law and the lawyer, F. E. Smith, in the first category; Rudyard's friend Howell Gwynne and R. D. Blumenfeld in the latter). After winning nomination as a Conservative candidate for the seat of Ashton-under-Lyme, outside Manchester, he used *Canadian Century*, a magazine he had founded at home, as a calling card for his first approach to Rudyard on 14 November. Probably at Gwynne's suggestion, Aitken sent Rudyard a copy of an article in the magazine on the thorny topic of reciprocity – the Canadian debate about ties with the United States, to which Rudyard had contributed various anti-American diatribes since his visit in 1907. Six days later Gwynne cabled Rudyard suggesting that, as he had offered to make an election speech, he might like to do so on behalf of Aitken in Ashton – and in the process, Gwynne felt, win several other seats in Lancashire for the temporarily waning cause of tariff reform.

By then Rudyard was incommunicado in Tisbury, seeing to his mother's funeral and related family issues. When he emerged to make contact with Aitken on 12 December, he came straight to the point: he wanted advice about investments that had been recommended by the Montreal Trust Company, a Canadian firm of stockbrokers that Aitken had once owned. Delighted to assist, Aitken cabled the Trust, telling them that any order from Mr Kipling should be 'very carefully executed'. To Rudyard he tactfully suggested that he might like to sell his Municipal and Provincial bonds and buy some of the 'many fine Tramway, Railway and other bonds which will yield you higher returns and I believe are just as safe'.[29]

A warm friendship, based on a shared interest in making money and in political sniping, had begun. Over the next year Rudyard regularly asked the newly knighted Aitken about often substantial Canadian investments. In March 1911 he took $50,000 worth of stock in Canadian Steel Foundries (which Aitken had underwritten to the tune of half a million dollars). Rudyard kept $10,000 for himself and off-loaded the rest. He asked for suggestions about selling £14,000 worth of Consols, and stumped up for $10,000 worth of Toronto and York Radial Railway Company five per cent bonds. At the end of the year he valued his US investments at $200,000 and his Canadian portfolio at $250,000.

At the same time Rudyard encouraged Aitken in his ambitions, which included a plan to acquire the *Daily Express* as a political mouthpiece. He advised his new friend on British conditions, taking him in hand as a fellow Colonial flummoxed by the odd habits of the mother country. 'As you grow better acquainted with our moist cool climate and the tricks that it plays, you will realize that you *must* eat and sleep a great deal more than would be necessary in your exhilarating Canadian air. Hence the lateness of business hours in England; the heavy lunches and the solid afternoon teas which I found difficult to understand till I had been a couple of years in the country.'[30]

As quid pro quo for investment tips, Rudyard attended dinners when Aitken's Canadian political friends came to London and needed impressing. Even with a Canadian election pending in September 1911, and the chance to remove Laurier's long-standing Liberal government, Rudyard was wary of producing political verses to order. But he happily contributed a controversial article to the *Montreal Star*, in which he argued, disingenuously, that if Canada introduced reciprocity in tariffs with the United States (i.e. free trade), she would inevitably soon be saddled with the same murder rate which, according to his calculations, stood at 150 per million people a year in her southern neighbour.

(Rudyard's interest in Canada had been further stimulated because his friend the Duke of Connaught had been appointed Governor-General in succession to Lord Grey, and Rudyard had penned another long 'situation report' for the Duchess.[31])

When news of the Conservative Sir Robert Borden's victory in the Canadian election result came through, Rudyard was staying at Aitken's new house, Cherkley Court, near Leatherhead in Surrey. Indicative of the central role that political ideas had in his life, he told Milner it had been 'some few years' since he had felt so happy. He reeled off the reasons – the Laurier–Botha liaison in 'our so-called imperial councils' was 'burst', Australia no longer had a bad example to follow and Canada would grow in stature and self-esteem, now that the idea of reciprocity with the United States had been killed. He felt imperialists and tariff reformers had been given a five-year honeymoon in which to implement their policies.[32] (Carrie may have had her faults, but lack of loyalty was not one of them. She joined her husband celebrating the 'wonderful news from Canada ... It is the first black eye that my country has ever been given, and will be very serious to them.'[33])

At the time, Rudyard's attention was focused closer to home. As expected, the Liberals had followed their election victory in December 1910 with legislation to limit the power of the House of Lords to alter Finance Bills. But the peers remained recalcitrant and, while the Unionist party dithered, with Balfour offering little in the way of leadership, Lloyd George was able to sneak in proposals for national insurance.

Rudyard's views about Balfour had not changed since 'Below the Mill Dam'. He had recently written a note to Milner, headed FROM THE STELE OF BAL-PHOUR-DUNFORUSAL CIRCA 1910 BC and containing what he purported to be the party leader's comments on the present political crisis – 'a matter of purely Historical Interest ... to be left to the Future agiz ... and sat down ... in large parts surrounded by femalz of matured views ...' – a reference to Balfour's fancy for Mary Elcho and her Souls coterie.[34]

Now the introduction of the National Insurance Bill in the

House of Commons in May 1911 allowed Rudyard to regale Aitken with his opinions. (His memo is undated, but it reads like a series of notes for a speech by Aitken at the time.) 'A general feeling in the air that people have had enough of this present Welsh Manchu dynasty,'[35] Rudyard thundered in one of his most detailed expositions of his opposition to the principle of free trade. Competition from abroad led to mobility of labour, unemployment and, eventually, Socialism or, as he put it,

> If you allow a man to be chased from trade to trade long enough he will eventually fetch up on the street corner. And that is where the Socialist is waiting for him. The Socialist has no business except on the street corner. The decent working man has no business *on* the street corner. The Socialist is like the fly that produces sleeping-sickness in South Africa. He cannot live in a decently clean and healthy district. But Free Trade is the direct parent of Socialism. Under Free Trade the workman cannot live on the wage which his European and Asiatic protected fellow workers – not the capitalist – allow him. He must therefore be treated more or less like the slave – that is to say he must be paid in kind and not in cash.[36]

As in the previous year, there was a hiatus in the proceedings to allow for royal business – this time, the new King George V's coronation in Westminster Abbey on 22 June, an important date in the Kiplings' calendar as they had been invited by the Duchess of Connaught and Stanley Baldwin had arranged additional facilities for them. Carrie went to some trouble to buy a suitable 'gown'; she and Rudyard rose at 5.45 in the morning so as to arrive at the House of Commons in time for breakfast, before proceeding to the Abbey. Noticing Rudyard's presence, George Buckle, editor of *The Times*, made another approach to see if he would write a piece for his paper. Rudyard declined, though the thrust of his argument was apparent in his comments on the ceremony, 'Of course the essential note of the thing was precisely what we are trying to throw away – the oneness of the people and the ease and intimacy that goes with it ... This must be so with a democracy of aristocrats which, at bottom is what the English are – especially the "lower classes", and that is where your alien or semi alien politician is going to trip up.' Rudyard had a couple of nice observations on his political bugbears: 'Haldane looked like a Toby dog strayed from a Punch and Judy show as he scuttled up the aisle in his unadjusted peer's robes and all the Winstonism of Churchill simply blazed up against that background of decent ritual. He looked like an obscene paper backed French novel in the Bodleian.'[37]

Rudyard's twin interests in imperial preference and shipping provided the spur when, on his return home from the Coronation, he wrote a poem about the ratification of the Declaration of London, an obscure piece of legislation – about the rights of blockade on the high seas in the event of war – which excited much interest at the time. Rudyard argued that the government's decision to allow a free vote was a sop to the pro-German lobby and ignored British nautical tradition:

> Our ears still carry the sound
> Of our once-Imperial seas ...

In August, in the middle of one of the hottest summers on record, Rudyard and Carrie took a short holiday in northern France with their new friends, Max Aitken and his wife Gladys. They returned to find that Rudyard's worst fears had come true: Britain was in the middle of a national dock strike (Gwynne, now editor of the *Morning Post*, had to wire to assure them that the cross-Channel ferries were still operating), while further afield, international tension had risen following the 'Agadir incident' when Germany despatched a gunboat in support of her interests in Morocco.

As they laid in extra stocks of food at Bateman's in case of further strikes, the Kiplings discovered that, after an expected showdown between 'Diehards' and 'Hedgers' failed to materialise, the House of Lords had finally decided to withdraw its amendments to the Parliament Bill and Lloyd George's budget could now become law. This was the end of Balfour as leader of the Unionists. However, his successor was not yet apparent: would it be the worthy Austen Chamberlain, the conventional Walter Long, or perhaps even a dark horse, the thrusting lawyer F. E. Smith? In the event, a press campaign, led by Leo Maxse at the *National Review*, supported by Gwynne at the *Morning Post* and Blumenfeld at the *Daily Express*, and backed financially by Aitken and intellectually by Rudyard, proved crucial in swinging the Unionists behind the dour Canadian-born Scot Andrew Bonar Law, who was sound not only on Home Rule but also on the basic cause of tariff reform. Asked by Gwynne for his views on a list of 'runners and riders' on 10 November, three days before the new leader was chosen, Rudyard feigned distaste, calling such speculation 'most immoral'. But since his card had already been heavily marked by Aitken, he was happy to offer his prediction. 'I say that Bonar Law will be leader. He's dead sound on Tariff reform and (NB) it's a feather in Canada's cap.'[38]

So what was Rudyard's role in all this? How effective were his behind-the-scenes probing and prodding? According to Aitken's later recollection, 'Kipling encouraged the attack upon Balfour. He did not take any active part. He did not give particular support to the selection of Bonar Law as leader. But he preferred him to either Long or Chamberlain.' More generally, Aitken observed, 'Kipling was never an active party man. He was hostile to politicians. He had a low opinion of Members of the House. He objected strongly to the failure of Conservatives to oppose many Liberal policies of social insurance etc. He was often impatient with leaders of the Tory party.'[39] In other words, Rudyard operated behind the scenes as a licensed gadfly.

Sure enough, on 15 November, two days after Bonar Law's election, Rudyard wrote to Aitken, expressing approval of the appointment (he said he would be renewing his party subscription as a result) and encouraging his energetic friend to do something about reforming the Central Conservative Organisation which, he argued, needed 'taking apart and being reassembled as soon as may be. It does not seem to know that there is such a thing as the Press even in London.' Demonstrating his interest in the mechanics of propaganda (an art he had learnt in India and would soon be advising Aitken on in a European war), Rudyard said the Unionists needed someone who could transmit confidential information to editors 'which will enable them to understand, not only what the policy of the party is, but how to lead up to, and prepare the public mind for that policy'.[40] However, when it was suggested that Cope Cornford might act as Private Secretary to Bonar Law, Rudyard, with lack of sentiment, said his friend would not be suitable.

In October, while the Unionist leadership was still being resolved, Rudyard took time off, with Carrie, to visit Ireland. He revealed little about this trip, presenting it casually as one of his tourist jaunts. While this was possible (John had just departed for his first term at Wellington), it is likely that Rudyard had been invited (or wanted) to familiarise himself with Ireland, which was certain to become the next political battlefield. The propaganda-conscious Ulster Unionists liked to entertain opinion formers and their leader at Westminster, the lawyer Edward Carson, had been Rudyard's neighbour in Rottingdean. Rudyard may also have been on a mission from Aitken, whose commitment to Unionism was sometimes tempered by his friendship with the Irishman Tim Healy. Sadly, Rudyard's few communications from Ireland during his week-long trip were extraordinarily bland. For all his interest in history, he was more concerned about the lack of penetration of the motor car into Dublin – and the consequent all-pervading smell of horse manure. He told Feilden that 'the dirt and slop and general shiftlessness of Dublin beats belief'.[41] Belfast was not much better, though he enjoyed the surrounding countryside, finding Portrush on the north coast delightful, with a 'golf course second only to St Andrews'.[42]

On his return he remained tight-lipped, though he did tell Blumenfeld that he would like to observe, preferably from a balloon, the proposed new Irish authority in Dublin attempting to collect taxes in Belfast for the first time. 'The deuce of the whole situation is that behind & over all is fear and hate of Rome – such fear and such hate as I thought had died out in the "fires of Smithfield".'[43]

Within a few days, Rudyard was working on 'an Irish story',[44] though nothing came of it. Instead, he found himself embroiled in a domestic dispute of a political nature. A year or so earlier Carrie's diary had noted how, having started some 'suffragette verses', Rudyard had 'put [them] aside'.[45] At a time when women were pressing for their political voices to be heard, Rudyard had been reading *Essays in Fallacy* by his reactionary Canadian friend Andrew Macphail. He recommended this book to Gwynne as 'ammunition for the anti-suffragette campaign', suggesting bizarrely that votes for women would lead to a weakening of Empire (presumably because the fairer sex would take an emotional view on demands for nationalist self-determination): 'You realize of course that even a limited female bill means more trouble in Egypt and India than anyone cares to think about. I don't suppose such considerations weigh with the women, but it would be difficult to underestimate the danger throughout all the East if we even enfranchise 50,000 women!'[46] To Macphail himself, Rudyard offered an even odder argument (probably honed in conversation with Bland-Sutton) – that women were ruining their reproductive systems by standing on their feet for hours and working. He probably had his own marriage in mind when he commented, 'Women knock up, knock out, go into rest-cures and under the surgeon's hand – disappear from their friends while the evasive husband says they are "not quite well" – and with them goes the promise of increase.'[47]

He did not pick up the 'suffragette verses' again until his return from holiday in France in August 1911. He then sent his completed 'The Female of the Species' to Gwynne who was now installed at the *Morning Post*. Strangely, the logic of this version ran counter to much that he had been saying over the previous year. For the woman of this poem – one deadlier and more uncompromising than the male – would surely hang on to her possessions rather than let them go in the manner Rudyard had earlier intimated to Gwynne. Now he turned this argument on its head, suggesting that men dare not include women within their councils, and

> that the Woman that God gave him
> Must command but may not govern – shall enthral
> but not enslave him.

It was not a message that went down well in certain quarters of his own household. Now fifteen, Elsie made her distaste clear and Rudyard, passing the buck, had to warn Gwynne that his daughter 'wants your editorial blood'.[48]

John, too, was showing signs of spirit. He returned from his first term at Wellington, 'looking like a beanstalk', with a cracked voice and a pronounced interest in clothes. Rudyard informed Anna Balestier, the lad's grandmother, that John was 'really a humorous chap', a bit like Wolcott in the speed and accuracy of his repartee. Once again, the boy had been quite taken aback to learn that 'his father is a sort of public man. They ask him at school if he had read any of his father's books and he says quite truthfully "no".'[49]

The Kiplings celebrated Christmas a day early that year. Rudyard gave Carrie a string of pearls and she reciprocated with a solid gold Waverley pen. He was delighted by Elsie's gift of eight costume dolls – each with a historical theme – and put them straight into a special cupboard to illustrate his *Puck* stories. John was given a gramophone and twenty-four records – reflecting his interest in the music-hall and his new-found status as a teenager. All in all, it was 'one of the nicest, happiest and quietest Christmases'[50] ever.

On Christmas Day itself, the whole family descended on the

Aitkens at Cherkley, where the Bonar Laws were also among the seventeen house guests. Rudyard had earlier composed some verses for Aitken's new visitors' book, making a spurious link between the millionaire's mansion and the household fires of primitive man. This was exactly the sort of nonsense that Aitken wanted from a scribe. On walks round his estate he liked to listen as Rudyard showed off his knowledge of British history and told stories about the Roman road running through Cherkley. Aitken was delighted when Rudyard sent a copy of *Rewards and Fairies* to his elderly father in Canada. Family links were reinforced the following March when Rudyard agreed to act as godfather to the Aitkens' third child, christened Peter Rudyard.

The personal relationship flourished because both men benefited from it. Earlier in the year Rudyard had been happy to seek Aitken's help in a dispute with Rolls-Royce. Having acquired a taste for these luxury cars through meeting Lord Montagu in France, Rudyard had ordered one for himself – a dark-green limousine landaulet, costing £1500 (with its various accoutrements) and scheduled for delivery in March 1911, following his return from his usual winter holiday in Europe. As was customary procedure, he stipulated a series 2300 chassis from the manufacturer, with a separate body from Barkers, the coach builders. Unfortunately, the order was delayed, first by a fire at Barkers, then by the King's Coronation, for which the firm had to assemble a new coach and renovate others. Rolls-Royce tried to placate Rudyard by lending him one of their cars free of charge and subsequently by sending him a limousine with a Hooper body on his chassis. Feeling he was being messed around, Rudyard rejected these alternatives and, when Barkers tried to hurry the order through in June, it made several mistakes, which only annoyed him further.

On 24 June Rudyard decided to pull strings by complaining to Aitken, who had become the major shareholder in Rolls-Royce following the death of one of the company's founders, Charles Stewart Rolls, in an air crash the previous year. Rudyard told his friend, 'It's many years since I bought quite so much trouble for $6500 – and a little more.'[51] The following day Aitken wired Claude Johnson at Rolls-Royce, 'As a private friend and not as a shareholder of your Company I warn you that Kipling is being lost to you entirely through downright neglect and ill usage.'[52] Johnson, who had just returned from a trip to the United States, responded immediately, claiming there were two sides to this story and providing a remarkably explicit account of Rudyard's pedantic, nit-picking side.

> If, as you say, Mr Kipling is being lost to us I can only say that I hope that this is true and that some other Company is to enjoy the favour of his patronage ... My feeling about Kipling is that when he gets to the kingdom of Heaven, if there should happen to be ink and paper there (which God forbid) he will plague people even then with his complaints and wailings. And the worst of it all is that he is such an expert at the job. That is to say, he has the most remarkable command of the King's English.[53]

Johnson ran through the history of the transaction, adding that, because of Rudyard's assumption that his firm was responsible for the body as well as the chassis of the car ('a view of the matter which has never been taken by any other purchaser of a complete Rolls-Royce car'), he would have to issue a specific disclaimer to future customers. However, for all Johnson's protestations, there was a note of high-handedness in his reaction – a note which was more obvious in his ridiculous comment to Rudyard the same day, 'Lord Herbert Scott, the Director who looks after our carriage building, tells me that there was only one person who could have made it possible for Barkers to do justice to your body and that is the King.'[54] In the end the matter was cleared up and Rudyard took delivery of the car he had originally ordered, but not without one final outburst to Aitken, 'What I objected to was their unwillingness to confess it was a bad body and making it a favour to me to give me another.'[55] Once he owned the car, he never looked back, maintaining his allegiance to Rolls-Royces for the rest of his life. He kept this first Rolls, which he called the Green Goblin, for two years, before exchanging it for a new model, a similar dark-green landaulet known as the Duchess, in 1914.

Later, Rudyard would look back on winters in what he described as a 'sports' hotel in Switzerland and recall that among the guests there were always German officers who, on the Kaiser's birthday, 'would dine – very well – and talk and sing of The Day with great clarity and many threats against all mankind'. This story, from his 1933 book *Souvenirs of France*, seems to have been recalled with a generous measure of hindsight. But there was no escaping the signs of looming confrontation in Europe. After their stay at the Hotel Cattani in early 1912, the Kiplings continued to Venice (an opportunity to see Thackeray's daughter Annie Ritchie, whom Rudyard had met again at a centenary dinner for her father in the Inner Temple the previous summer). Also visiting 'La Seren-issima' was the Kaiser, whose yacht the *Hohenzollern* was docked in the harbour, being washed and painted like a 'public pros-titute'.[56] A week later, staying with the Depews at their opulent Château d'Annel at Compiègne, north of Paris, Rudyard met an aristocratic young attaché at the German Embassy, who seemed 'very keen on the next war with plenty of pious wishes that it won't come'.[57]

By the time the Kiplings returned home, Britain was experi-encing further industrial unrest – this time a coal strike. Rudyard fired off a letter suggesting Gwynne should run an article on the foreign influences behind the strike.[58] He himself was more immediately concerned with the statement of intent by the Ulster Unionists in January that they would reject the authority of any Irish parliament created by the proposed Home Rule Bill. Recall-ing his few days in Ireland, Rudyard now penned verses of soli-darity with these dissenters. In his resonating hymn-like metre, he urged Ulstermen to bear in mind '... the hells declared / For such as serve not Rome'. He was happy to enlist the help of Cope Cornford to ensure that the poem had the widest possible distribution among Irish newspapers on 9 April, when Bonar Law was scheduled to make a powerful speech attacking the Home Rule Bill. 'Get the last ounce of work out of it,'[59] he urged Cope Cornford, taking care to emphasise that each reproduction must carry a copyright. Otherwise, he said, he would miss the fun of fining the pro-Irish journals in the United States, which would assuredly steal it.

A week later Rudyard might have had the poem recited in the House of Commons. When, during parliamentary question time, a Liberal MP asked the Attorney-General if Rudyard would be prosecuted for producing these seditious verses, Captain James Craig jumped up and suggested that, for everyone to know what he was talking about, he would have to read out the poem. The Attorney-General, Sir Rufus Isaacs, rejected both ideas, but not before the nationalist, William Redmond, had quipped, 'Will the right hon. gentleman bear in mind that in general opinion this doggerel ought not to be called verse at all?'[60]

Rudyard's letters to his son were now mixed with more grown-up advice. Prior to giving a talk to a literary society at Wellington on 25 May, he counselled John to keep clear of 'any chap who is even suspected of beastliness'[61] (his code word for homo-sexuality): 'Whatever their merits may be in the athletic line they are at heart only sweeps and scum and all friendship or acquaintance with them ends in sorrow and disgrace.'[62] The talk on 'The Uses of Reading' was well directed: brimming with schol-arship, but written and delivered in a style that teenagers could understand. 'Half of literature is placing fields that aren't there, and the rest of it is recording how every conceivable kind of ball that can be bowled by the Fates or life or circumstances has, at one time or another, been bowled at some wretched or happy man; and how he has played it.'

While the three issues of German militarism, industrial unrest and Ulster played around in Rudyard's mind over the summer of 1912, his attention was grabbed by another political development. For some time there had been rumblings in the Near East, as the old Ottoman Empire entered its terminal phase. Following the revolt of the Young Turks in 1908, Italy had entered the imperial game by invading the Turkish province of Tripolitania (part of modern Libya) in 1911, while the following autumn Russia had encouraged the emerging Balkan nations of Serbia, Bulgaria and Greece to take advantage of Turkish weakness and launch an attack that would bring them to Constantinople. But this only increased European tensions, as Austria, backed by Germany, was unlikely to countenance Serbian aggrandisement.

Second-guessing developments in the Ottoman Empire was an old game to Rudyard. In Lahore and Simla, thirty years earlier, it had been important to forecast how the Porte might react to Russian incursions in Central Asia or to the treatment of Moslems in India. Most recently, his attention had been re-directed to Turkey after his cousin Hugh Poynter had taken a post with the Ottoman Debt Commission. His own father's death had further stimulated a revival of his interest in the wider world. Rudyard had been desperately worried about the risks to life and limb associated with King George V's attendance at the Delhi Durbar in December, and had declined even to write a celebratory poem for *The Pioneer*. Now his spring visit to Venice had brought him closer to the action in the Balkans. Out of the blue, in May 1912, he wrote a story, 'A Reinforcement', based on the Italian experience in North Africa, for the first anniversary issue of the officially sponsored *Near East Magazine*.[63]

Over the summer his curiosity was stimulated by several visitors from abroad, including Captain Fox, a game warden from the Sudd marshes south of Khartoum, whom Bland-Sutton and 'Taffy' Gwynne had befriended on a visit to Sudan a couple of years earlier, and Sir William Willcocks, the engineer who had built the Aswan Dam in Egypt. He met Willcocks at George Allen's house, Free Chase, where the other guest was Valentine Chirol,

who had just retired as Foreign Editor of *The Times*. In his autobiography Rudyard said he had come across Willcocks ten years
earlier and that the engineer had advised on the early stages of
the construction of the Mill Dam. But from the way he described
his June 1912 meeting with Willcocks, this was their first encounter. He did not say that this was the man who helped on the dam.
He told his son, John, '[Willcocks] built the Assouan dam among
other things and has wandered through Babylon and Baghdad
making dams on the Tigris and Euphrates. One of the most
interesting chaps I have ever met. He and his wife came over here
from Mr Allen's to have lunch and he gave me good advice on
how to manage the brook.'[64]

On 16 October Rudyard asked John specifically if he was following the course of events in the Balkans, which he forecast
could be the scene of a particularly bloody war. 'The Turk is, to
put it mildly, annoyed and intends to settle the question once and
for all. Also there is the danger of Mohammedans throughout the
world taking a hand.' The following day Turkey declared war on
Serbia and Bulgaria. But, within days, Rudyard was sending his
son a report from the *Daily Telegraph* on Turkey's defeat and
was musing, 'Verily war is a queer thing.'[65] Austria's subsequent
attempts to broker a peace seemed only a threadbare cover for its
own territorial ambitions.

A couple of months later, on 8 December, Rudyard met Ellis
Ashmead-Bartlett, a Reuters correspondent who had recently
returned from the war in the Balkans. The journalist, who published a book on his experiences, *With the Turks in Thrace*, had
earlier covered the Italo-Turkish war in Tripolitania, where he
had created a furore with his account of Italian atrocities against
Arabs. It seems likely that Rudyard had used him as a source of
information for 'A Reinforcement'.

Rudyard's concern about the break-up of the Turkish Empire
was still based largely on its possible effect on India. For the time
being Egypt was effectively in the hands of the British. But what
if nationalism took root in the Middle East and the Suez Canal,

that vital stretch of water on the route to India, became part of a disputed region?

After their winter break in Engelberg in January 1913, the Kiplings decided to investigate for themselves and proceed to Egypt, where they knew several people, ranging from Lord Edward Cecil, now Financial Adviser to the British agent and consul-general, to Lionel Landon, Perceval's brother, who, a couple of years earlier, had been awarded the Egyptian decoration the Order of Osmanieh (fourth class), in recognition of his work as Inspector of Irrigation in Sudan. The connection between the Middle East and Europe was evident in Rudyard's letter to Roderick Jones, the Reuters chief in South Africa, to whom he wrote, 'We are just off to Switzerland and, if Austria will only be reasonable, for Egypt in February – maybe even Khartoum.'[66]

Carrie had her own reasons for wanting to get away. The previous autumn the lingering pain in her back had been diagnosed as another lump of fatty tissue which had been pressing on her spine, and so required the knife-happy Bland-Sutton to operate again in September.[67] She had ended the year in a run-down state, 'with no courage to start on a fresh year and very little strength'.[68] When, earlier, she had suggested to Rudyard that he might like to take up an invitation to visit his friend Duckworth Ford, now chief of police in Manila, Rudyard had declined, saying it was 'impossible for domestic reasons (13 and 15)'.[69] But now these reasons were absent (John at school, Elsie learning French with her governess in Paris) and Carrie must have been delighted as she arranged for extra funds to be transferred to Switzerland to pay for their spring holiday in Egypt.

On 7 February 1913 the Kiplings caught a train to Marseilles, where they boarded the P&O liner s.s. *Persia en route* for Port Said. In his book *Egypt of the Magicians*, Rudyard offered some limp speculation about where the East begins: was it at the St Gotthard pass, or in Venice on warm April mornings, or where one sees one's first lateen sail? It did not really matter, because Egypt showed Rudyard's remarkable facility, for all his forceful political views, to be all things to all men. To his readers, modern Cairo was merely an 'unkempt place'; to Milner the surrounding desert was likened to the Karroo in South Africa; to Feilden he said it could have been Umballa in May; and to John, at Wellington, it was 'a cross between Rome and Florence with touches of Cape Town thrown in'.[70]

Since the weather was cold and wet, the Kiplings did not stay long in Cairo, even though Lady Edward Cecil, the chatelaine of Great Wigsell, was staying at the same hotel, the Semiramis. Instead, they made their way up the River Nile to Luxor and Aswan on the s.s. *Rameses III*, owned by Thomas Cook. From Aswan they travelled twelve miles on donkey to view the dam that Willcocks built, before proceeding up stream to Wadi Halfa in Sudan, where they had arranged to meet their friends Rudyard's American publisher 'Effendi' Doubleday and his wife Nellie, who had been on a Roosevelt-type tour of Africa. While waiting at this sweltering desert outpost for the Doubledays to arrive by train from Khartoum, Rudyard asked someone the names of the intervening stations. Having learnt they were called Station Number One, Station Number Two and so on, he later liked to amuse Sudanophiles with alternative suggestions: the surnames of Kitchener's generals seemed his favourite.[71]

En route back to Cairo, Rudyard stayed at the American financier Pierpont Morgan's house in Thebes, while he visited the Metropolitan Museum's excavations in the Valley of the Kings. The Doubledays probably arranged these stopovers, though the bibliophile Morgan had been in touch with Rudyard two years earlier when he sent him a carefully restored copy of *The Golden Latin Gospels*.[72] In the Egyptian capital Rudyard at last met Lord Kitchener, the British agent and consul-general, who failed to impress:[73] there was a 'butcherly arrogance' about this 'fatted Pharaoh in spurs'[74] who had alienated the business community with his agricultural and financial reforms. He reminded Rudyard of 'a sort of nebulous Rhodes without grip or restraint'.[75] (To do Kitchener justice, Lord Edward Cecil commented of him, 'His energy is quite appalling. He starts a new scheme every morning which he wishes finished by 8 a.m. the next day.'[76] Indeed, Rudyard's antipathy to Kitchener smacks of some vendetta of Cecil's wife.)

Rudyard was more inspired by the administrators he had met further south, the Sudanese equivalents of Scott in India (in 'William the Conqueror'). These men had created a country which, 'less than sixteen years ago . . . was one crazy hell of murder, torture and lust, where every man who had a sword used it till he met a stronger and became his slave'. In *Egypt of the Magicians*, Rudyard forecast that the Sudanese would, in time, forget their precarious existence under the Mahdi:

> They will honestly believe that they themselves originally created and since then have upheld the easy life into which they were brought at so heavy a price. Then the demand will go up for 'extension of local government', 'Soudan for the Soudanese', and so on till the whole cycle has to be retrodden. It is a hard law but an old one – Rome died learning it, as our western civilisation may die – that if you give any man anything that he has not painfully earned for himself, you infallibly make him or his descendants your devoted enemies.[77]

As well as the usual travel reportage, the book provides amusing geopolitical analysis: 'Here is a country which is not a country but a longish strip of market-garden, nominally in charge of a government which is not a government but the disconnected satrapy of a half-dead empire, controlled pecksniffingly by a Power which is not a Power but an Agency.'[78] However, as its title implies, Rudyard was also interested in another side of Egypt – the one that fascinated students of esoteric religion, its history as a crucible of spiritual development. He had been alerted to this aspect by Rider Haggard, a regular visitor to the country and a friend of the great Egyptologist Wallis Budge. (On 3 March, when temporarily stuck on a sandbank between Aswan and Luxor,

Rudyard wrote to Haggard who happened to be visiting India. However, his letter ignored higher matters, complaining *inter alia* that the problem with Cook's boats was 'the fat and too-familiar-with-white-women dragoman'.[79])

The sense that Rudyard was embarked on a spiritual quest comes in the book's mock conversation with Pharaoh Akhenaton who bewails the fact that he mistook the conventions of life for the realities. When Rudyard, trying to be helpful, chips in, 'Ah, those soul-crippling conventions,' the Pharaoh corrects him, saying that he had wrongly regarded them as lies, but they were in fact invented to cover the raw facts of life – the most important being 'that mankind is just a little lower than the angels, and the conventions are based on that fact in order that men may become angels. But if you begin, as I did by the convention that men are angels they will assuredly become bigger beasts than ever.'[80]

This was a Pharaonic gloss on Rudyard's religious premise that one should not look too closely into the mind of God, for that way madness lies. It recalled 'The Prayer of Miriam Cohen', with its cry for 'A veil 'twixt us and Thee, Good Lord'. More mundanely, it can also be read as justification for Rudyard's Hobbesian political philosophy. But in this case he was pursuing a spiritual quest, as was emphasised in the poem 'A Pilgrim's Way', which accompanied the articles when they were published in *Nash's Magazine* in June 1914:

> I do not look for holy saints to guide me on my way,
> Or male and female devilkins to lead my feet astray . . .
> The people, Lord, Thy people, are good enough for me!

Not that Rudyard gave much away: as another mock interviewee, a four-thousand-year-old Egyptian nobleman, described the riddle of the Sphinx: 'All sensible men are of the same religion, but no sensible man ever tells'[81] – one more pithy echo of Rudyard's own opinion (albeit a crib from the seventeenth-century Earl of Shaftesbury, refracted through Disraeli's *Endymion*.)

Returning home on a French boat, the *Cordillère*, the Kiplings were met at Marseilles by the enigmatic Landon, who had brought their car. Together they drove through Avignon to Albi, scene of the thirteenth-century revolt by the Cathars, the heretical sect that followed the Manichean or gnostic philosophy of the dualism of the cosmic powers of Light and Darkness. The circumstances suggest that an important element in Rudyard's friendship with Landon (the man who inspired the Friends society) was their shared interest in world religion, as refracted through a filter of Freemasonry.

Getting in on the act, Carrie had bought scarabs to distribute to her relations. Angela Mackail's sister Clare received 'a little tiny Egyptian vulture of a beautiful blue ... dating from about 4000 BC (it might as well be 1 BC for all I realise!)'.[82] Once home, Rudyard had business to discuss with Doubleday, who for ten years had loyally performed a dual role as both his publisher and quasi-agent in the United States. Even after taking unsatisfactory legal action against the publishers G. P. Putnam's Sons and R. F. Fenno to protect his copyright and trade marks, Rudyard had been plagued with North American publishers who thought they could get away with pirating his work. At least, with Doubleday's help, Rudyard was learning to deal with the problem. When, in October 1909, a New York company, B. W. Dodge, put out an unauthorised edition of Rudyard's Indian journalism under the title *Abaft the Funnel*, Doubleday reacted by issuing the same collection in an edition costing just nineteen cents.

However, policing the market-place on Rudyard's behalf took up an inordinate amount of Doubleday's time. For example, the publication of 'If—' in 1910 had been followed by a rash of unauthorised editions. As Rudyard wrote of this phenomenon in his autobiography, 'Once started, the mechanism of the age made them snowball themselves in a way that startled me. Schools, and places where they teach, took them for the suffering Young ... They were printed as cards to hang up in offices and bedrooms; illuminated text-wise and anthologised to weariness. Twenty-seven of the Nations of the Earth translated them into their seven-and-twenty tongues, and printed them on every sort of fabric.'[83] Understandably, Americans concluded, from its position next to his Philadelphia story 'Brother Square-Toes' in *Rewards and Fairies*, that 'If–' referred to their revered President George Washington. Possibly Rudyard was trying to put them off the scent, and to prevent further pirating, when he later said that the poem was about his friend Dr Starr Jameson, whom he continued to revere and see regularly, long after he had stopped visiting South Africa himself.

That was no immediate help to Doubleday. In January 1912 his firm informed A. P. Watt that, after chasing up a Boston shoe manufacturer called Coleman, it proposed charging him twenty-five dollars for his unauthorised publication of 'If–'. It was pursuing three or four other offenders, but they were only the tip of the iceberg since, as Frank Doubleday noted, Americans believed that the poem was in the public domain. At the time, the pirates had just begun issuing versions of Rudyard's controversial anti-suffragette poem 'The Female of the Species'. Because of this background, Doubleday asked permission to pre-empt this latest wave of pirates by publishing the poem both as a small booklet and a ten-cents card. Rudyard appears to have sanctioned a limited edition and then reversed his decision, for on 2 April 1912 Carrie was asking, via Watt, that 'the cards, leaflets, or whatever it is [Doubleday] uses of "The Female of the Species"' be discontinued because 'they are very dreadful'.[84] Such were the demanding and often contradictory messages that Doubleday had to deal with. As a result, while in London, he had much to discuss with both Rudyard and Watt.

In addition, Doubleday had blazed the trail with his packaging of Rudyard's work. Apart from regular collections of stories and verses (and occasional one-off imprints), Doubleday Page (as Effendi's firm was now called) had produced an American edition of Rudyard's *Collected Verse* in 1907, which went through several printings before publication in Britain by Hodder & Stoughton in 1912. The American company initiated collections for children (*Kipling Stories* and *Poems Every Child Should Know* in 1909) and for some reason it published *Songs from Books*, a compilation of verses that had accompanied his stories, in 1912, a full year before the English edition, which was printed from the same proofs though not by Methuen but by Macmillan, suggesting that some dispute had delayed them.

Doubleday had started the idea of top-of-the-range 'sets' of Rudyard's work with the Outward Bound edition, which was still published by his old employers Scribner's and was mirrored in Britain by Macmillan's limited Edition de Luxe, bound in red silk. Over the years, Macmillan had produced its well-known red cloth Uniform and red-leather Pocket editions, stamped with an elephant (the Indian God Ganesha) and swastika sign. Now, in 1913, another limited edition was planned, to be known as the Bombay in Britain and the Seven Seas in the United States.[85] Both editions were limited to 1050 sets, with the first volume of each set signed by Rudyard – one of his first duties after returning from Egypt. Carrie's diaries noted on 10 April: 'Rud, with John's help, starts to sign the first volume of 1050 sets of the Bombay Edition.' (Did this mean that John handed his father the books to be signed, or did he write in them himself?)

As a result of meetings between author, American publisher and agent, it was resolved that Watt should go to the United States to sort out Rudyard's affairs. The friendship between the Kipling and Doubleday families was in no way affected. After Rudyard's strictures about Americans and publishers, Effendi was the exception who proved the rule. Rudyard called him a 'very dear personal friend', indicating to Francis Younghusband, who sought an introduction when he visited the United States in 1914, one reason for his admiration: he thought along similar imperialist lines to Doubleday, who had been 'enormously impressed with British administration'[86] in Sudan. As for Effendi's wife Nellie, she was a horticulturist who had written a best-selling book, *Nature's Garden*. While in England, she visited Bateman's and became a passionate admirer of its gardens, sending cuttings of dogwoods, trilliums (should it be trillia? Rudyard asked), dogtooth violets, asters and azaleas, for planting in May.

Thanking her, Rudyard showed an unusual degree of familiarity when he admitted that 'an epidemic of notices to leave our service has set in' and added jokingly, 'C. and I look at each other and mourn that in our relations to each other we can not just get up and say, "I'm for another situation".'[87] Even the Sussex countryside, it seems, could no longer ignore the wave of industrial unrest in Britain. Over a couple of years from mid-1911 Carrie had run through four secretaries. In June 1912 Rudyard had sacked his chauffeur George Moore after six years' service. Carrie, the probable instigator, noted that this had been necessary because of 'his hot temper which leads him to do impossible things'. Then the following month she was forced to have a 'long and tiresome talk' with Harold Martin, the gardener, who she felt had 'grown slack'. At least, when Ellen the parlour maid retired the following June after eleven years' service she received a pension and the parting was so amicable that, even twenty years later, in the early 1930s, she used to return to visit.

While the honeysuckle and wild roses bloomed extravagantly in the woods around Bateman's that summer, the whole nation seemed in turmoil. Strikers and suffragettes were still up in arms, Germany was threatening and the question of Ulster was unresolved. In the midst of all this, the press had begun a campaign of vituperative personal attacks against government ministers. (The Unionists had led the way the previous year by setting up the 'Radical Plutocrats Inquiry' to examine the sort of questions Rudyard regularly asked Gwynne to investigate, such as who were the financiers behind the Liberals.) Much innuendo was bandied around, particularly related to the racial origins of Liberal supporters. The newspapers had a field day when the Jewish Attorney-General Sir Rufus Isaacs was forced to admit that he had bought shares in the American Marconi Company shortly after its related business in Britain (which was headed by his brother) had won an Admiralty tender to build a global network of wireless stations. Isaacs had also sold some of the shares on to Rudyard's *bête noire* Lloyd George and to another minister, the Master of Elibank.

When the truth emerged, Rudyard's unruly emotions tumbled out in an ugly note to Max Aitken, 'As to the Liberals. My insular mind hasn't got any further than saying – "Thank God they ain't white". After all a Jew lawyer and a Welsh solicitor and Jack Johnson and rabbits are much of a muchness.'[88] When, three months later in July 1913, Rudyard received advance notice that Isaacs was to be appointed Lord Chief Justice, his anger knew no bounds. He produced his notorious rant, 'Gehazi', with its portrayal of Isaacs as the eponymous leper, infecting the body politic with his greed and referring to his earlier dissimulation as

> The truthful, well-weighed answer
> That tells the blacker lie –

Since the piece was potentially libellous, Rudyard did not publish it immediately. When, with a view to publication in his newspaper the *Globe*, Max Aitken asked for 'the verses in garbled form, with no particular application to the Chief Justice or the Chancellor of the Exchequer'[89] (Lloyd George), Rudyard replied, 'I can not "garble" my "Gehazi". It's meant for that Jew Boy on the Bench and one day – please the Lord – I may get it in.' In typically blistering style he castigated the *Globe* for 'the way it skirts the Marconi business. The fence is very crowded already. Isn't there a place on *this* side of it?'[90] Rudyard did later squeeze the poem into his collection *The Years Between* in 1919.

Rudyard's attention was directed towards another form of infiltration in June 1913 when he dined with Bertrand Stewart, an Old Etonian solicitor who lived not far away in Kent. The previous month Stewart had returned from a German prison where he had been held on charges of spying. A couple of years earlier, at the height of Anglo-German tension during the Agadir crisis, he had been caught red-handed with secret documents in the sensitive naval area around Bremen. Sentenced to three and a half years in the notorious Glatz fortress in Silesia, he had been given an early release as a result of a personal pardon from the Kaiser.

Carrie was impressed by her dashing guest, describing his visit as 'most amusing'.[91] Rudyard's reaction is not known, but if he imagined he was getting to the heart of British intelligence he was mistaken. For Stewart was never a serious agent. Encouraged, it seems, by the espionage mania of the time, he had presented himself to the War Office as a possible spy in 1911. He had been passed to the head of the Secret Service, Commander Mansfield Cumming, who was unimpressed, finding Stewart's ideas about espionage 'much in the manner of William Le Queux'. However, the War Office thought that Stewart should 'have a "run" and act according to his own ideas'.[92] Somehow, Rudyard's patronage of this amateur spy was telling: an indication that, under a Liberal government, a dozen years after the Boer War, he no longer had privileged access to 'insider' sources.

However, the Stalkyish schoolboy adventurer in Rudyard loved this sort of encounter, which convinced him, more than ever, of German perfidy. As always, he was invigorated when, later that month, he accompanied Gwynne to watch army manoeuvres at Elstead in Surrey. Carrie duly noted that he came home 'having had a wonderful time'[93] and he sat down the next day to write a story about his experiences. (Nothing survives, but this must have been the occasion, mentioned in his autobiography, when his Macdonald gene came to the fore and he sensed a vast horde of Boer War dead 'flickering and re-forming' in the heat haze. One can imagine him slipping out of his conscious mind into a dreamy, meditative state, as he often recorded in his stories.) Three months later, chairing a meeting of the National Service League in Burwash, he raised the spectre of invasion which 'means riot and arson and disorder and bloodshed and starvation on a scale that a man can scarcely imagine to himself'.

He also had a new hobby-horse. Popular concern about German invasion was increasingly linked to paranoia about aerial reconnaissance or infiltration by Zeppelin airships. During 1913, German dirigibles were sighted across Britain with the same regularity and lack of firm evidence as Unidentified Flying Objects eighty-five years later. This was a field in which Rudyard had become something of an expert. Since writing 'With the Night Mail', and particularly after its publication in book form in 1909, he had been widely identified with the air transport lobby. In October 1909 he told a correspondent that when he first wrote that story, 'I didn't expect that aeroplanes would be up so soon, but I will stick by it that in the long run (say 10 years) the world's passengers will be carried by the dirigible. Freight will mostly go by sea.'[94] In January 1910 he was encouraging an old India acquaintance, Major Charles Massy, to join Lord Montagu in setting up the Aerial League of the British Empire, a winged equivalent of the Navy League. 'I don't think *yet* that air ships can paralyze a country or a fleet,' commented Rudyard, 'but it won't be many years before they do.'[95] He began being visited by strange inventors, such as the Swiss Lieventhal who came to Bateman's in May 1910 to show him plans not only for a new airship but also 'a little thing like a baby typewriting machine, only not much bigger than a Kodak which could transmit messages in cypher that no one could read and then translate the cypher back into plain English. The machine itself changes the cypher all the time as it goes on.'[96]

With a link between aviation and espionage clearly established in his mind, Rudyard took the chair at a bilingual (English and French) meeting on the future of aviation in Folkestone in October 1910. A year later he revised 'As Easy as ABC', his sequel to 'With the Night Mail'. The basic tenets of the earlier story had been developed to the extent that aerial transport now really was a means of political control. Unwittingly, Rudyard's science fiction was becoming a forum for an exploration of the links between technology and power.

Not that there was much debate in Rudyard's stories. He clearly saw science as a means of control and his preoccupation with aeroplanes extended little further than their potential in the country's defences. He took a great interest in the early days of the Royal Flying Corps and, in particular, of its military wing, which was established under an acquaintance, Frederick Sykes, in May 1912.[97] After visiting the Corps in Aldershot that November, he enthused to Captain William Lewis, a young friend of the Leonards who had recently joined the Royal Artillery's No. 5 Battery in India: 'It's a rummy sensation to stand at the beginning of things – as it might be with primitive man when he first launched his canoe.' He had noticed a new smell about this service – 'not infantry (hot or cold) not artillery (which is horse sweat and leather) nor motor transport which is petrol and oil but a fourth and indescribable stink – a rather shrill stink if you understand – like chlorine gas on top of petrol fumes plus gummy calico in a shop. That's the stink of the aeroplane and (adding more gas) the dirigible.'[98]

As so often when he took up an idea, Rudyard had a good sense of its commercial possibilities. Thus, in November 1912, soon after visiting the Royal Flying Corps in Aldershot, he was recommending Max Aitken to look into E. T. Willows and Company, the inventors of an airship. He said he did not know anything about them, but he had seen their hangars, where their mechanics were working in shirt-sleeves.[99] That was enough of a 'buy' recommendation for Rudyard.

Another commercial development that interested him was oil. In 1912, the proliferation of strikes encouraged Rudyard to change from coal- to oil-fired heating in his house. Within ten years, he predicted to Blumenfeld, mining would have no role, except as a subsidiary part of the jewellery business.[100] Blumenfeld had been running a campaign in favour of oil in the *Daily Express*, probably with the encouragement of Max Aitken, his friend and financier, who had interests in oil companies. As Rudyard well knew, oil also had a strategic dimension in the modern world.

Jackie Fisher's new super-Dreadnought battleships, which began to be launched from 1911, were, for reasons of speed and energy efficiency, powered by oil. In order to ensure supplies of this precious new fuel Winston Churchill, the First Lord of the Admiralty, bought a controlling interest in the Anglo-Persian Oil Company whose discoveries in the Persian Gulf were beginning to come on stream.

Rudyard managed to introduce several of these topics into his stories. 'As Easy as ABC' was first published in a magazine in February 1912 and was the lead story in his 1917 collection *A Diversity of Creatures*. Most of the material in that book (apart from the two obvious war tales, 'Swept and Garnished' and 'Mary Postgate') was conceived and written in the short Georgian period before the First World War. As its title implies, it was a slightly unwieldy portmanteau for Rudyard's interests at that time.

'The Edge of the Evening' (initially published in December 1913) is his most obvious 'German invasion scare' story, with trademark references to the United States and its problems with immigration ('A Government of the alien, by the alien, for the alien'), an ersatz heritage estate rented from the English Lord Marshalton (né Mankeltow), aeroplanes and the Royal Flying Corps. 'The Vortex' (from August 1914) addresses issues of imperial federation, juxtaposed with more domestic concerns about bee-keeping and the role of the 'mustard-coloured scouts of the Automobile Association' engaged in their war with their 'natural enemies, the unjust police'.

'The Village that Voted the Earth was Flat' (written in May 1914 but not published before the book) is a lively satire on mass communication in the age of democracy. A variation on Rudyard's traditional revenge story, it tells how, having been dragged through a kangaroo court for speeding, four friends – two journalists, a newspaper proprietor and an MP – get their own back on the local grandee and chairman of the bench through a succession of ruses – by ridiculing his village in the press, by causing questions to be raised about it in Parliament and then, after joining forces with Bat Masquerier, a music-hall impresario with a similar grievance, by mounting an expensive charade that suggests the village is full of 'Geoplanarians' who believe the earth is flat. Rudyard has fun with 'in' jokes about modern journalism: Woodhouse (a Beaverbrook figure whose 'business was the treatment and cure of sick journals') runs two papers, referred to as 'The Bun' and 'The Cake'. However, when Masquerier, 'the Absolutely Amoral Soul', manipulates the full power of press, film and music-hall, and his song about the village that voted the earth was flat is bellowed out in Parliament (Rudyard might have recalled that his Ulster verses were threatened with this fate), the effects are both hilarious and alarming. Even Woodhouse, the brash newspaper baron, is taken aback, uncertain about the forces he has helped unleash.

Closer to home, Rudyard's two dogs helped inspire 'The Dog Hervey' (first published in the *Century Magazine* in April 1914), which elaborates on his interest in animals (and other intermediaries) as aids to physical and psychological health. The story is complicated by its exploration of the psychic ramifications of a lonely woman using her sick dog to 'project' into the reveries of a man who was once kind to her. Carrington dismisses its 'literary, Masonic, psychological, and canine clues which lead nowhere'. What is one to make of the frequent references to the goldfish that Hervey's owner, the modern 'witch' Moira Sichcliffe, sends as presents? (One commentator, Professor C. A. Bodelson, thinks they refer to her 'spiritual imprisonment'.) The tale is worth persevering with, particularly for its biographical detail: there are suggestions of Carrie in Sichcliffe, whose father had been in insurance, and of Landon in Will Attley, from whose litter of pups Hervey came. (Not only is Attley 'that rare angel, an absolutely unselfish bachelor' but also he is familiar with Madeira, where Landon's father worked.) The results were eerily effective: Elsie would run out of the room when Rudyard tried to read her extracts and complained that the squinting 'devil dog' kept her awake at night.[101]

In Rudyard's proven psychological genre, 'In the Same Boat' (first published in May 1911) tells of two 'soul-weary' individuals who are plagued by bad dreams – until they learn from the soothing Nurse Blaber that their problems can be attributed to the traumas they experienced in their mothers' womb and are not necessarily their fault. As 'The Comforters', the poem which followed 'The Dog Hervey', put it:

> Only the Lord can understand
> When those first pangs begin,
> How much is reflex action and
> How much is really sin.

Precise references (a train departs at 10.8 and a telegram is handed in at 12.46) suggest Rudyard was still toying with ideas about causation and communication beyond the boundaries of time. Curiously, for a man so fascinated with technical and commercial innovations, he took little interest in contemporary philosophical or artistic developments. Francis Younghusband was close to A. N. Whitehead and Bertrand Russell, but Rudyard knew no-one like them – only doctors (the quirkier the better), academics and the lawyers he met at the Athenaeum. As for modern culture, he ignored events such as the famous Post-Impressionist show in London in 1910–11. Occasionally he went to the theatre, but preferred the music-hall, which he liked to attend with John. ('I've taken John to divers music-halls,' Rudyard wrote to young Captain Lewis in India in December 1913, 'which always make me inclined to weep but J. thinks them "top-hole".'[102])

Both 'My Son's Wife' (written in 1913) and 'Friendly Brook' (March 1914) take up from 'An Habitation Enforced' in suggesting the therapeutic powers of the countryside. The former story tells how Midmore, a 'facile Hampstead' left-winger, comes to appreciate the 'peasantry' – assisted, to an extent, by reading the rural exploits of one of Rudyard's schoolboy favourites, the cockney grocer turned Master of Fox Hounds, John Jorrocks. The latter tale refers to the flooding of the River Dudwell which engulfed Bateman's in the autumn of 1909 and in the following three years. It focuses on the brook, with its natural, almost magical, powers to sort things out, and on the local people, epitomised in the poem 'The Land' (which accompanied the story in *A Diversity of Creatures* in 1917). The hero of these verses is Hobden, the hedger, poacher and jack-of-all-trades countryman from the *Puck* stories. He knows exactly what to do to prevent flooding (one spiles along the water-course with trunks of willow trees) and is, Rudyard implies, much more master of the land than he himself.

> I have rights of chase and warren, as my dignity requires.
> I can fish – but Hobden tickles. I can shoot – but Hobden
>   wires.
> I repair, but he reopens, certain gaps which, men allege,
> Have been used by every Hobden since a Hobden
>   swapped a hedge.

Hobden was not a figure of Rudyard's imagination. The surname was a local one and the fictional character was based on William Isted, Rudyard's main local source about country lore. In his seventies when the Kiplings first came to Bateman's, he not only was an excellent hedger (when not the worse for drink) but also knew all about poaching, from the days when it was possible to pick up a fallow deer in Lord Ashburnham's woods towards Battle. After ten years his wife began to open up and tell Rudyard her recollections of magic in Sussex in the mid-nineteenth century, when a black cock would be killed and the local 'wise woman' divined the future.

The realities of Sussex life were rather different. When Isted sat down with Rudyard, Landon and about twenty other workers for Christmas dinner at Keylands in December 1913 an embarrassed hush hung over the proceedings – at least, until Landon inadvertently upset an oil lamp. Thereafter the company's jokes were 'few and simple but highly appreciated. The menu was roast beef, potatoes, pickles and beer. Plum pudding and mince pie to follow of course. Landon's orders to Dale, his man, were not to let the pewter stand empty.'[103] At the end of the evening total consumption of beer stood at just under a gallon a head, though Rudyard claimed that he, Landon and John had only drunk one and a half pints between them. After lusty renderings of music-hall ditties, the evening ended with a communal assault on the carol 'While Shepherds Watched Their Flocks By Night'.

The Kiplings celebrated Christmas itself with the Depews in Compiègne, before moving to Engelberg for Rudyard's forty-eighth birthday. After John returned to school on 20 January they decamped to St Moritz, where the Baldwins were enjoying more fashionable surroundings. Rudyard's mind was not on winter sports this year, however. Over the previous few months he had worked himself into a lather of indignation about Ulster. Efforts to mediate there had failed, military postures had been struck both in Ulster and in the rest of Ireland and, with the Irish Home Rule Bill moving inexorably through Parliament, the 'loyalists' north of the border (and, in particular, Edward Carson's Ulster Volunteer Force) seemed ready to plunge Ireland into civil war.

For the time being Rudyard regarded Ulster as more important than Germany or any other issue. He argued that the future of the constitution was at stake: Home Rule was being pushed through without being put to the vote in an election. (Democracy could be a useful ally when he wanted.) As so often, he managed to discover links between his various concerns. Taking a historical perspective, he believed that if Ulster was pushed to the brink it would call for support in Germany. As he told Milner, 'What people can't understand is that we are on the edge of a change of dynasty – not of ministry – if Home Rule in *any* shape goes through'[104] and he added to Gwynne, whom he regularly encouraged to maintain a resolute stand in the *Morning Post*, 'An Ulster or an Ireland handed over to the Celt means an appeal for outside intervention as in 1688. That is what I fear horribly. For the moment – we cannot depend on much more than a few weeks –

the Teuton has, or pretends to have, his eye glued on Russia.'[105] There was also an imperialist perspective: 'Please hang on,' he exhorted Gwynne. 'If we die we die, but at least we can die decently. Leave it to *The Times* to tack and fill. We make a great mistake if we think we can hold the Dominions to us by a policy of compromise which they call *funk*.'[106]

Until the end of 1913 Rudyard thought it worth encouraging correspondents such as Gwynne, because he believed the government might yet back down from its Home Rule Bill.[107] From Switzerland, in January, he peppered Max Aitken with a theory that Winston Churchill, who had crossed over to the Liberals ostensibly because of agreements over free trade, might return to the Unionists in their hour of need. Rudyard did not approve: 'I believe you can cure a woman of being a personal prostitute – sometimes – but it is impossible to cure a political prostitute from whoring. Meantime the ship is alight at both ends and in the middle – S. Africa, India and Ulster – and for that reason the Conservatives will probably accept Winston when it suits him to come over. We are a Great Party!'[108]

He returned to England briefly to deliver a talk to the Royal Geographical Society (RGS) on 17 February. This was a fascinating jumble of insights into travel, confirming his delight in the immediate sensory experience of smells, touching on 'the psychology of moving bodies under strain' (nothing blurs the record of a journey so much as a few days of baths and clean clothes, he noted), and speculating about the effects of travel on mankind and his civilisation. 'Month by month the Earth shrinks actually, and, what is more important, in imagination.'

Writers and explorers were in the same business of charting the new world, Rudyard seemed to be saying. And his post-bag confirmed it. Only two months earlier, Apsley Cherry-Garrard had sent him a copy of *Kim* that had been read by members of Captain Robert Scott's recent ill-fated expedition to the South Pole. In June Sir Ernest Shackleton visited Bateman's to discuss his own proposed Antarctic voyage. In his cabin on *Endurance* he hung a copy of 'If– ' and, on his return, he sent Rudyard a copy of his book *South*. When Cherry-Garrard (who was working on his own *The Worst Journey in the World*) reviewed this in the *Nation*, his comparison of the leadership styles of Scott and Shackleton showed a familiarity with Rudyard's RGS talk.

Rudyard had time to call on Aitken in his role as investment adviser: Carrie had been selling out of 'English fluff' and wanted to buy $10,000 worth of Montana Power Company First Mortgage five-per-cent Gold Bonds, while he himself had $15,000 in Montreal that he wanted to invest.[109] He then went back to France, passing through Paris where he and Carrie had promised to buy Elsie, who was eighteen earlier in the month, a dress for her season as a débutante later in the year. At a lunch hosted there by Princess Marie of Greece, Rudyard met Dr Gustave Le Bon, whom he had not seen since Lahore, thirty years earlier. Le Bon was France's leading social psychologist, specialising in crowd behaviour. His theories of mass hysteria would have interested Rudyard and influenced 'The Village that Voted the Earth was Flat', written in May. The Princess herself was an intriguing character: she became one of Sigmund Freud's most committed followers, helping him to leave Vienna hurriedly in 1938.

Two days later the Kiplings continued to Vernet where Rudyard was startlingly bored. He now found it a 'place of Superior Dullness'. He had brought the proofs of 'The Dog Hervey' and *Egypt of the Magicians*, but all he wanted to do was to read the newspapers, which he 'devour[ed]' as soon as they arrived.[110]

The reason for this interest was that, with the return of the British Parliament in February, the long-running debate on the Home Rule Bill was reaching its conclusion. Milner had sent him the text of a declaration of support for Ulster. Rudyard was one of twenty distinguished signatories, including Milner, Lord Roberts and the composer Edward Elgar, who stated that they would do anything in their powers to stop such an unconstitutional bill being implemented, and 'more particularly to prevent the armed forces of the Crown being used to deprive the people of Ulster of their rights as citizens of the United Kingdom'. The sub-text of the message was clear: it lent support not only to the 'Loyalist' militants but also to dissidents in the British army who had expressed their unwillingness to serve in Ulster in the event of civil war. In the circumstances, Rudyard found the declaration tame. He signed it 'like a temperance man', but hoped that 'some day we shall get to something more than signing pledges'.[111] As he told Captain Lewis in India, he was in 'a League of sorts to help wage civil war. I never thought I should end as a rebel in my old age but all the best people are doing it. You never knew such a mad state of affairs!'[112]

After a new chauffeur, Eaves, brought the Rolls to Bordeaux on 18 March, the Kiplings drove home, via Paris. Each evening, Rudyard received a telegram from Landon, relating the latest news about Ulster. As Carrie explained to her mother, 'These are serious and exciting times in England ... Home Rule for all of Ireland will never be achieved and one has only to remember Kate's attitude to an Irishman or woman to understand why ... Ulster will not be governed by the Pope.'[113] (Kate Monks was old Madame Balestier's cussed Irish maid.) Following the publication of his poem 'France', putting on record his respect for Gallic civilisation at the time of the state visit of President Poincaré in June 1913, Rudyard was more than ever a celebrity. During a three-hour tour of inspection of the cavalry school at Autun[114] he faced questions on whether Britain's army, which was disobeying orders in Ireland, would show similar indiscipline if fighting Germany. In Paris he met the French Prime Minister Aristide Briand, as well as Georges Clemenceau, but was not amused at one consequence of his fame – a report in the *Gaulois* newspaper (taken up by some papers at home) that he was having treatment for some mysterious illness.

With Loyalists and Irish Nationalists stocking up their arsenals in Europe, the pro-Ulster lobby planned one last thrust before the third and final reading of the Home Rule Bill on 21 May. The previous weekend, the day after Elsie's first dance of the season at the hugely wealthy but totally insignificant Mrs Saxon Noble's, Rudyard joined his MP George Courthope at a rally in his local market town of Tunbridge Wells. In front of a Saturday afternoon crowd of 10,000, he railed against a Home Rule Bill that 'recognised sedition, privy conspiracy and rebellion ... [and] subsidised the secret forces of boycott, intimidation, outrage and murder'. He said he did not blame the Nationalists: 'They are what they are – what their particular type of their race has always been since the beginning of recorded history ... They have imposed their own ancient form of tribal administration on large tracts of Ireland – a despotism of secret societies, a government of denunciation by day and terrorism by night.'

Four days later, on 20 May, Rudyard's rousing poem 'The Covenant', with its typical call to a fearful Old Testament God, was published in a special issue of *The Covenanter* magazine in Belfast. It has been suggested that Rudyard demonstrated not only his commitment to the cause but also his considerable wealth by contributing £30,000 (the same as the millionaire Waldorf Astor) to a secret fund for the paramilitary Ulster Volunteer Force.[115] While there is no evidence to substantiate this it was clear to everyone else, if not to him, that this money was going to buy German arms.

Over the summer Carrie took part in meetings of the Women's Unionist Association with Lady Edward Cecil, while Elsie was preoccupied with her 'coming out' (though her presentation at court on 4 June was disrupted by a suffragette demonstration). Rudyard's immediate family concerns were about his son. At home, John seemed happy enough. In April 1913 he had acquired his first motorbike, a Douglas, and, the following year, after his sixteenth birthday, he was permitted to drive the Ford which Rudyard bought 'for Station work'. This allowed him to socialise with his young 'set' – his pretty red-haired cousin Lorna Baldwin and her brother Oliver; Charlie and Isabel Bonar Law; Oscar Hornung, son of the creator of Raffles; George and Helen Cecil, Lady Edward's children; and the Leonards and the Baileys from

South African days. (Sir Abe's children were called Cecil – a girl – and John after his great hero Rhodes.)

At school John had had a more troubled career. Ostensibly, he did well enough, prospering (to his father's astonishment) at mathematics and making a mark on the athletics field. But his problem was: now that he had decided against a career in the Navy, what was he to do? When, in March 1913, he indicated he might want to go to university and expressed a preference for Clare College, Cambridge, his father flattened the boy with the comment: 'Whence has come the new idea of going to the Varsity and why – oh why – Clare? Cambridge is sad enough but Clare – C-L-A-R-E – !!!'[116] (Rudyard's Uncle Ned had clearly prejudiced him towards Oxford.)

Disabused of that idea, John decided to join the Army. This was something Rudyard could enjoy: he liaised with Sir Edward Ward, the Under-Secretary for War, who had given early surreptitious support to the National Service League and who now arranged a private medical examination. On the appointed day, Rudyard drove to Wellington to pick up John and take him to Aldershot. However, the eyes that were not good enough for the Navy were not suitable for the Army either. Rudyard (and John) were left with a promise from Ward that he would 'do what he can about John'.[117]

By now the nervous strain was affecting John. The latter part of his summer term of 1913 was disturbed by a bout of glandular fever, which required a visit to the school sanatorium. (His father was quick to 'entreat and exhort and command' him to 'be careful' because he knew 'dam-well' that such places were not good for the morals.)[118] When John's symptoms persisted he was taken to Bland-Sutton, who diagnosed a thickening of the thyroid gland, banned running and demanded the right to perform an operation in October.

This episode took a lot out of John. When, six months later, he was still uncertain about his future, Rudyard asked Gwynne, who had known the boy since he was a baby, to go to Wellington to speak to him. Gwynne's advice seemed effective: John agreed to go to a crammer, Lee Evans, in Bournemouth in May. Now it was Rudyard's turn to express his confusion. 'When I was one month older than he is, I was in receipt of a salary of £10 per month, with whiskers on my face,' he moaned to Gwynne. Was there an element of competitiveness in his observation: 'Anyway he has only got a moustache' [119] ?

As the summer progressed, the Kiplings' mood turned to weariness. Their social circuit now included big country houses such as Cliveden, home of the Astors, and Taplow, where Lord and Lady Desborough, leading figures in the Souls diaspora, lived. On a visit to Taplow the previous November Eddie Marsh, the young aesthete who became Churchill's private secretary, had watched Rudyard playing a typical Souls-type game of historical charades. He noticed Rudyard's histrionic potential: indeed, he felt he was seeing 'a wasted Garrick' as Rudyard 'took the stage with Miss Montgomery, and though I don't think anyone guessed their subject which turned out to have been the High Priest giving Judas the thirty pieces of silver, that made no matter – the point was the impression they created of something on foot that was unutterably sinister and momentous'.[120] However, when they returned to Taplow at the end of May 1914, both Carrie and Rudyard had the same feeling 'that this was the end of one's sane and normal life for a bit'.[121]

The following month Rudyard turned down another request to serve as Unionist parliamentary candidate for the Midlands seat of Bordersley. He told Amery that the party should take the opportunity to get a real working man into the House of Commons.[122] He also refused Professor Osler's invitation to address an Oxford conference to commemorate the medieval scientist Roger Bacon. Rudyard claimed he did not know enough about Bacon (though he later boned up on him for his story 'The Eye of Allah'). Possibly Rudyard was aware that Osler was collaborating with his old sparring partner Mabel Price, the red-haired girl from *The Light that Failed*, in research on tuberculosis.

Though still in touch with Flo Garrard, Mabel now ran the active Oxfordshire branch of the Tuberculosis Association.

Although Ulster continued to ferment, attention was shifted back to Europe following the assassination of the Austrian Archduke Franz Ferdinand in Sarajevo on 29 June. A few days earlier Rudyard would have been happy for the ministration of either Osler or Bacon. For, after a period when he was unable to work, he was taken ill, the victim of 'overwork and over-smoking', according to Carrie's precise note. From now on Rudyard's health, rather than Carrie's, would be the centre of attention.

At least John was beginning to take control of his life. The imminence of war had concentrated his mind: from his crammer he informed his parents of his decision to be baptised into the Church of England. Rudyard made no known comment on this, but John seems to have grown tired of his father's personalised and cerebral mixture of polytheism, agnosticism and Christianity, and needed a more tangible faith which Rudyard did not have. On 19 July, a fortnight after a memorial service for Joseph Chamberlain, the Kiplings were in Bournemouth for John's baptism in St Peter's Church. Some priorities never changed: the previous day they had spent in Portsmouth, watching the Naval Review from HMS *Exmouth*, the ship of Lady Edward Cecil's cousin Henry Maxse.

Then they prepared for a family seaside holiday. The previous year they had rented Kessingland Grange, a summer house that Rider Haggard owned on the Suffolk coast, near Lowestoft. Once a coastguard station, the U-shaped Grange was situated in nine acres of land at reputedly the most easterly point in England. From its cliff-top garden one looked out over the sea as if from the prow of a ship. On 23 July the Kiplings took the train from London's Liverpool Street. Elsie had her friend Helen Cecil to stay and John joined them a few days later. However, at the end of the month Helen had to go home to see her father who, because of the deteriorating situation, had been recalled from leave to his post in Egypt.

Rudyard's mood cannot have been improved by the low state of the stock markets, though it is not clear if he was comforted by Aitken's advice on 28 July that the present financial panic would not last long and a European war would do wonders for the economies of the United States and Canada.

Carrie was suffering from a bad cold when war with Germany was declared four days later. In the circumstances, the Kiplings decided to stay where they were 'provisioned and [had] coal for a fortnight' (2 August). However, Rudyard needed money to pay for ongoing bills and wrote to Aitken requesting fifty pounds in gold (5 August). He contacted Colonel Feilden to say, 'I told you so!' and asked him to use his influence to make it clear in Burwash 'that tradesmen who take advantage of panic and ignorance to raise prices will, in the next few days, when things are wheeled into line, be made to suffer'.[123] By 7 August, as Germany pushed into Belgium, Rudyard was telling Gwynne that he thought he had heard guns from across the North Sea. He bet that when Liège fell, as it surely would, the German army would 'make such a ghastly "example" of it (with a view to striking terror)' that every adult male in Britain would rush to join up. In the meantime he looked on the future with an Oriental sense of inevitability: 'It seems that the hand of fate must have guided us here.'[124]

Book Five

But who shall return us the children?

Seventeen

What Stands If Freedom Fall?

1914–1918

The disastrous effects of the European war were already evident when the Kiplings stopped for a couple of days in London on 10 August, on their way home from Suffolk. The Germans had pushed remorselessly through neutral Belgium, and Brown's Hotel was full of 'noisy, restless and exacting' Americans who either had fled from the path of the invading *Wehrmacht* or were uncertain about the future of their Grand Tour travel plans. Three days earlier, as a British Expeditionary Force began to be mobilised, the new Secretary of State for War Lord Kitchener had called for 100,000 extra volunteers to join the modestly sized British army and John Kipling was determined to be among the first batch of recruits. When he presented himself at the War Office (the ostensible reason for his family's London stopover), he was told to make his application locally. On 17 August, his seventeenth birthday, John was taken by his enthusiastic father to recruiting stations in Hastings and Maidstone. But, once again, his eyes let him down: with his 6/36 vision, he would have had difficulty making out the second line of a standard eye chart.[1] He was dispiritedly thinking of enlisting in the ranks, when his father decided (very reluctantly, Carrie assured Lady Edward Cecil) to ask his old friend Lord Roberts, Colonel-in-Chief of the Irish Guards, if he could help arrange a commission.

Rudyard must have bristled at the prospect of his son serving with a 'race' he had denounced only a few months earlier. Not that the 'Micks' were even a regiment with much history. They had been established as recently as 1900 to commemorate the heroism of the Irish Volunteers in the Boer War. But they were drawn from both the North and South of Ireland, and from both Protestant and Catholic communities. In spirit, they were the modern incarnation of Terence Mulvaney's 'Black Tyrone'. Their motto 'Quis Separabit?' attested to both their loyalty to each other and their genuine lack of inter-Irish tribal or religious bigotry. As reassurance, they had old 'Bobs' as their titular commander. Within days John had been signed up as a Second Lieutenant. After being fitted for a uniform and inoculated for typhoid, he reported for duty on 14 September at Warley Barracks, the dingy quarters of the regiment's Reserve in Brentwood, Essex.

By then the war had progressed from bad to worse. The Germans had rolled through Belgium into France, whence came alarming reports of the British retreat from Mons at the end of August. On 9 September Julia Depew arrived from northern France, where she had been forced to abandon the château she had recently turned into a fifty-bed hospital. She confirmed stories of German atrocities that were as bad as any of Rudyard's earlier predictions. She knew an English surgeon working with the Red Cross who had had both his hands chopped off and a Belgian family whose womenfolk had been raped four times in an hour. 'It's amazing in the 20th century,' Carrie told her mother, '. . . and a bit difficult to realize it's all under a hundred miles away and it's our turn next unless we can keep them out.'[2] The battle was already pressing closer to home: from the now entrenched front came news of the first British casualties – among them friends such as George Cecil, whose mother, Lady Edward, was distraught.

As John adapted to military discipline in a barracks abandoned as unfit for the East India Company half a century earlier, his family rallied to the war effort. Rudyard was already into his stride as a recruiting sergeant for Kitchener's New Army. During August he had bided his time, as he absorbed stories of the German blitzkrieg. Then towards the end of the month he marshalled his thoughts in a poem, 'For All We Have and Are', which showed he had lost none of his Boer War gift for striking an appropriate note of swelling patriotism. Perceval Landon proved his worth as a friend, first by making 'an excellent suggestion about the verses'[3] and then by taking them by hand to *The Times*, where they were published to acclaim on 2 September. As a result of official and pirated copies, the whole world was soon aware of Rudyard's call to 'stand up ... The Hun is at the gate!' and of his resounding plea:

> What stands if Freedom fall?
> Who dies if England live?

The Times unilaterally sent fifty pounds in lieu of a fee to the Belgian Relief Fund. Rudyard, who normally received no payment for such verses, was not happy when the paper printed a note at the foot of the poem, informing its readers of his charity. Indicative of the Kiplings' old fashioned reserve, Carrie complained to Lady Milner about this 'deplorable message'.[4]

When Rudyard came to address a recruitment drive at the Dome in Brighton five days later, his poem was such a talking point that he had to repeat his short lecture to an overflow meeting.

Carrie's quiet efficiency now came into its own. Like thousands of women all over the country, she set to work with Elsie knitting winter woollens (particularly socks and gloves) for soldiers and refugees. Rudyard produced a mock business card for C. Kipling & Co, 'Highest Standard of Needlework and Finish Guaranteed ... Socks – double heel and ditto secret French pattern toe – a speciality'. (By 26 November she estimated she had used 112 pounds of wool at 4s. 6d a pound.) Meanwhile, as a faithful servant of her adopted country, she harried American friends to send her their spare linen[5] and told them the worst of the horrors perpetrated on the Belgian refugees who now 'swarm[ed] over'[6]

Sussex. As far as she was concerned, the Germans were the best recruiting agents.[7]

Before long a rumour surfaced that Rudyard was going to the United States as a goodwill ambassador. Where this idea came from is uncertain (Rudyard himself asked Gwynne to discover the source). But it had enough credibility for Sir Edward Grey, the Foreign Secretary, to threaten resignation. He informed Charles Masterman, the political appointee at the head of the War Propaganda Bureau, that, if the story had any truth, it would jeopardise all his efforts 'to keep the goodwill of the United States'. Masterman, who had already recruited a team of high-calibre literary advisers, including J. M. Barrie, Arnold Bennett, Arthur Conan Doyle and H. G. Wells, replied that he was working to prevent anti-American reactionaries like Rudyard doing just this sort of thing, adding illiberally that 'the only hope would be to get powers to lock them up as a danger to the state'.[8] (Twenty-six years later, at the start of the Second World War, this scenario was repeated, when the House of Commons decided that Noël Coward was not the right man to win over American hearts and minds.)

Grey probably obtained his information from the Post Office, which routinely intercepted overseas telegrams. For his note to Masterman was written the day after Rudyard received a truculent telegram from a German-born academic called Krebs who was living in Cambridge, Massachusetts: 'You are reported in American paper as going on platform to ask your fellow-countrymen to volunteer to risk their lives in order to support Russia in attempting to crush Germany I hereby offer you three thousand dollars and your expenses for round trip to come to New York and read (on any night you may select in October nineteen hundred fourteen) poems written by you "The Truce of the Bear" better known as "Adamzad" and "The Grave of the Hundred Head".' (The first was suitably anti-Russian and presumably Krebs considered the latter to be anti-war.) Krebs promised that any money raised, over and above expenses, would go to the Red Cross for use in England, Germany, France and Austria – 'also in Russia should you personally request'. Rudyard sent a copy of this message to Milner (thereby another possible source for the rumour) with a comment on the global reach of the German propaganda machine.[9] To Krebs himself, Rudyard sent a tart refusal: he was 'at present engaged on somewhat urgent work in connection with the late city of Louvain, Belgium' (whose ancient university had been razed to the ground by the Germans) and was doing his best to prevent a similar fate overtaking Britain's own seats of learning.[10]

Despite his official snub (not unexpected, given the divergence of his views from the Liberals in government), Rudyard understood that, at the age of forty-eight, his main contribution to the war would be propagandist – informing the world of the rightness (and righteousness) of Britain's cause. Initially, through personal contacts, he tried to stir up anti-German feeling in the United States, which was not only neutral but had a sizeable German population. By an extraordinary chance, Effendi Doubleday's business partner Walter Hines Page had been appointed American Ambassador to London the previous year by his old Princeton University friend, President Woodrow Wilson. To the annoyance of the President, Page argued resolutely for American assistance to and, later, intervention on the side of the Allies.

Realising, however, that there was no immediate prospect of America rushing to Britain's aid, Rudyard sought to prick its conscience, as he urged it to protest against German atrocities in Belgium. In letters to Frank Doubleday, Edward Bok and Theodore Roosevelt, he often repeated the same stories that Carrie was telling her mother, suggesting that the transatlantic messages emerging from Bateman's were carefully co-ordinated. Calling on Julia Depew's testimony, he stressed the indignities already suffered by American citizens. To Roosevelt, he intimated that Germany would not be satisfied in Europe and would try to attack the United States from islands in the West Indies. (These arguments were repeated in different guises to correspondents in Canada, Australia and South Africa.)

In reply, Roosevelt requested authoritative witnesses of events in Belgium. 'General or vague or dubiously authentic statements or hearsay' were not good enough. He provided pen portraits of the current crop of American politicians, including a put-down line on President Woodrow Wilson, which Rudyard later quoted appreciatively: 'He was born in Virginia, and comes from a family none of whose members fought on either side in the Civil War.' The level of understanding between the two men was clear in Roosevelt's postscript: 'I hear your son has gone to the war. I heartily congratulate you.'[11]

By mid-September the carnage in France was troubling Elsie. So many friends had already been 'killed in action', she said, that she would soon not 'know any man who's alive'.[12] As a break from the all-pervasive war, she went to stay with Carrie's distant cousin Daisy Low, the founder of the Girl Scouts in America, who had rented Castle Menzies in Perthshire. As a result, she was not at home when John returned for a weekend on 26 September. Wearing his new uniform, he swaggered and told stories about 'his' men, whose accents he mimicked well. Rudyard was impressed with the transformation: 'The Irish Guards I gather are racially and incurably mad,' he informed Elsie in Scotland. 'I am immensely pleased with our boy. The old spirit of carping and criticism has changed into a sort of calm judicial attitude.'[13]

Rudyard was also affected by the tensions of war, but typically he suffered them internally. In late September he suddenly began waking in the middle of the night with a pain in the side of his face, later diagnosed as neuralgia. For a while he had to reduce his workload to one and a half hours a day. Carrie told her mother, with quiet determination, 'I must get Rud better'[14] and, under her care, he soon recovered. The war had now entered a new phase: thousands of wounded troops were being shipped home and new recruits were arriving from all over the British Empire to take their place. Rudyard made it his business to visit the 33,000 Canadian soldiers quartered in Salisbury. The troops included members of Princess Patricia's Own Canadian Light Infantry, the regiment assembled in honour of the Duke of Connaught's popular daughter 'Princess Pat'. Carrie looked through the Bateman's library for suitable books to send them: 'When the Germans come, they will find little left,' she said, slightly grudgingly. Rudyard also went to see Indian troops stationed in the New Forest. He was so struck by their loyalty to the British cause that he included a special article about them in a five-part promotional series for the *Daily Telegraph* (later collected as *The New Army in Training*).

Although Rudyard's relations with *The Times* had improved and he once again received a free subscription, he looked to the *Daily Telegraph* in November to publish his starkly anti-German poem 'The Outlaws' in *King Albert's Book*, a volume of pieces the paper had commissioned from celebrated writers to raise funds for Belgian refugees. His poem attacked a people who

> ... set themselves to find
> Fresh terrors and undreamed-of fears
> To heap upon mankind.

The same month he wrote a solemn verse tribute to his 'clean, simple, valiant, well-beloved' friend Lord Roberts, who died of pneumonia while visiting Indian troops at the front in France, just two months after recommending John for the Irish Guards. Rudyard's ill feeling towards Germans resurfaced in his story 'Swept and Garnished' (published in January 1915) about a Berlin *hausfrau* troubled by the ghostly images of five small children, clearly killed during the German advance through Belgium.

He then turned his fire on neutral nations (in particular, the United States) in his naval story, 'Sea Constables', in February, the month when Germany introduced its policy of all-out submarine warfare. The story's theme – the refusal of four naval officers to come to the aid of the dying skipper of a neutral vessel that had been carrying oil to the enemy – anticipated (in its callousness) 'Mary Postgate', begun in early March, shortly after the first German air raids on Britain. This much-debated tale (later fatuously described by Stanley Baldwin's son Oliver as 'the wickedest story ever written') told of a prim governess who, while burning the possessions of her boisterous young charge killed in a flying accident, comes across an injured airman who has escaped from a crashed German bomber. With a frisson of perverted sexual joy, she refuses assistance to the whimpering figure in the undergrowth. When the story appeared in *A Diversity of Creatures* it was followed by the poem 'The Beginnings', which told of the time when, belatedly and reluctantly, 'the English began to hate'.

Although Rudyard had recently informed Max Aitken that he had money to invest and Russia was the country of the future,[15] the Kiplings kept celebrations to a bare minimum that first Christmas of the war. (Or was Carrie maintaining a united propaganda front when she told her mother that Rudyard's gift to her was a cheque to buy festive knick-knacks for Belgian refugees and Indian troops?) Since Cherkley came within the prescribed distance he was allowed to travel from Warley, John accompanied his family to the Aitkens' on Christmas Day. Afterwards Carrie, who had been such a rock, suffered a set-back to her own health and retired to bed. Amid the general confusion Rudyard's birthday was forgotten and for the first time in his married life this much-pampered man received no presents.

After searching for a role in the war effort, Aitken found what he wanted in the new year, when he was appointed official 'eyewitness' to the Canadian campaign in France. In the interests of efficiency, otherwise described as a blatant exercise in censorship, he became the eyes and ears of the Canadian people at the front. From time to time he called on Rudyard to help with his dispatches. (This later led to unofficial collaboration on his first book, *Canada in Flanders*,[16] which included lines from 'Our Lady of the Snows' on its title page.) In return, Aitken advised his friend on setting up a Canadian-based trust fund for John and Elsie, and on investing the tidy sum of £31,000, which had become available in mid-January.

Carrie's illness posed a problem: normally at this time of year, she travelled to Vernet (accompanied by a more or less reluctant husband). Since this was no longer possible, Bland-Sutton suggested she should try the spa town of Bath. The Kiplings went there in late March 1915, shortly after Rudyard had completed 'Mary Postgate'. As Carrie took the waters at the Bath Spa Hotel, he relaxed as he reread the works of Jane Austen, the city's best-known author. 'When she looks straight at a man or a woman,' he told a friend appreciatively, 'she is greater than those who were alive with her – by a whole head. Greater than Charles [Dickens]: greater than Walter [Scott] – with a more delicate hand and cleaner scalpel.'[17] The seeds of his 1924 story 'The Janeites', which uses Austen, Freemasonry and the war to discuss a favourite theme about the bonds of comradeship, had been sown.

With time to kill, Rudyard explored the city, where he heard what he claimed was the 'only authentic ghost-tale of the war'.[18] Someone (perhaps a member of the 10th Devons stationed there, or one of the wounded soldiers at the Mineral Waters Hospital) told him how, on three occasions during the Battle of Ypres in December, the German army turned back when it could have broken through. When a prisoner was asked the reason, he said his colleagues had seen the enormous reserves lined up behind the British lines. Recalling his experiences with Gwynne at Elstead a couple of years earlier, Rudyard was fascinated by this idea of a phantom army. 'Now whose were those Reserves?' he asked his historian friend Charles Fletcher. ' "Our Army in Flanders": Marlboro's men: old militia regiments of Wellington's time, stiffened with the bulk of the August expeditionary force? Strange notion . . . one might do verses on it.'[19]

Curiously, he does not seem to have been aware of the popular tale of the Angel of Mons, who appeared on the battle-field, riding a white horse, clutching a flaming sword, and protecting British troops during the retreat from Mons the previous August. Still less did he realise that he was partly responsible for this myth, which had gained wide currency after being published in the

Evening News as a short story called 'The Bowmen' by the jour-nalist and fantasy writer Arthur Machen. In the country's fatalistic mood of the moment, this was seized upon and embellished, both at the front and at home, by people seeking evidence of divine intervention. The Angel was invoked in Church of England pulpits and written about in the *Occult Review* by none other than Alfred Sinnett, the theosophist who had once edited the *Pioneer*. Other similar stories circulated, such as the one about the Germans being repulsed by a large spectral army of Russians who were supposed to have arrived in Flanders, via Scotland. When Arthur Machen wrote an introduction to the book version of 'The Bowmen' in 1915, he tried to play down its supernatural content and said he made the tale up after 'the Kipling story of the ghostly Indian regiment ['The Lost Legion' in *Many Inventions*] got into my head and got mixed up with the medievalism that is always there.'[20] Rudyard became fascinated by this idea of collective hallucination, and filed it away for later tales, notably 'A Madonna of the Trenches' which specifically referred to the Angel of Mons.

On his way back to Bateman's in late April Rudyard stopped in London to accompany his son to the Alhambra music-hall. Watching soldiers from all over the Empire taking a few hours' leave before returning to barracks and perhaps crossing to France the next day, Rudyard tried to understand the men who had come to fight in this war. In India, his 'soldiers three' had been noble, sympathetic creatures, but had inhabited a different universe from his. In South Africa the troops looked up to the revered poet, who visited them in hospital and handed out tobacco in an ultimately slightly high-handed manner. But these troops ambling in the spring sunshine were the same as his son and he had difficulty coming to terms with this fact. After visiting various hospitals, he tried to allay his worst fears by making insensitive remarks about the sacrifice that men from distant lands were making for the Empire. He was cheered to find Canadians showing a 'new and active hate towards the German ... And their views on the United

States ... Oh Lord!' As for the Australians, he was interested to see how their national psychology would be affected. 'I have always stuck to it that they are the most vindictive haters within the Empire on account of their heavy meat diet.'[21]

Not surprisingly, with these sentiments being voiced, the modest, shambling John was itching to show what he could do. When Gwynne heard from Lord Kerry, Commanding Officer of the Irish Guards' Reserve, that the young Kipling might not go to France for a year and a half, Rudyard urged him not to tell the boy.[22] Since even the phlegmatic John found Warley 'a living Hell on Earth', his father bought him a small Singer car so he could drive to London and occasionally visit the music-hall or join the family at Brown's. Rudyard could not resist suggesting that his music-loving son should call it Car-uso or Depèche Melba, which he admitted was 'a foul pun'.[23] He genuinely admired John's application. In his own youth, he wrote on 4 March, he himself had worked hard in an oppressive climate. But at least he was able to return to his parents' house at the end of each day. John, on the other hand, had 'to face a certain discomfort (which is inevitable) plus a certain loneliness of the spirit which is awfully hard to bear; and a certain sense of isolation which, as I remember, almost frightens a young man. And you have stood it like a white man and a man to be proud of.'[24]

John was annoyed to be incapacitated at home with flu in May when several young officers from Warley were called to the front following a spate of casualties. By early July it was clear that a big Allied push was planned and he was told to prepare to leave for France the following month, as soon as he reached the required age of eighteen. This was confirmed a couple of weeks later when, shortly after his friend Oscar Hornung was killed, the Reserve was renamed the 2nd Battalion of the Irish Guards. (The idea was that this would encourage the *esprit de corps* expected in the trenches.) When Anna Balestier wondered how one found the courage to send a boy to almost certain death, Carrie replied philosophically, but no less painfully, 'There is nothing else to do. The world must be saved from the German who will worse than kill us all if he is allowed a chance and one can't let one's friends' and neighbours' sons be killed in order to save us and our son.'[25]

Rudyard was not at Bateman's when John departed. Overcoming initial politically inspired reservations, he had been recruited to work for Masterman's War Propaganda Bureau, and the prospect of recreating the camaraderie and excitement of those few days at *The Friend* in Bloemfontein proved too seductive. Rudyard's work for the Bureau (often known by the name of its headquarters in Buckingham Gate, Wellington House) was no doubt assisted by the fact that Struan (A. S.) Watt was the organisation's literary agent, bringing his expertise to bear on thorny problems such as copyright and distribution. It was thought that writers of Rudyard's stature would help sway opinion, particularly in neutral countries subject to German propaganda, by reporting the war in an individualistic, not too obviously partisan style. One problem the Bureau wanted to address was the lack of awareness, both in Britain and abroad, of France's mood in the face of German assault. Rudyard found the subject so engrossing that, at the Athenaeum in mid-July, he ignored Henry James, who was talking to Lord Curzon, and later apologised, 'I have got hold – or rather it's got hold of me – of some work which I can't put aside. It isn't of a literary nature and will be taking all my time for some weeks to come. I should have been at your command.'[26]

Rudyard's task may not have been literary, but it did involve writing and it did require his going to France. On 12 August Rudyard departed for Paris, with Perceval Landon as travelling companion. Three days later Carrie was again on her own when John left Bateman's for the last time. In his glasses and with his round shoulders, he still looked slight in his enveloping khaki uniform. (According to his War Office record of service, John's height was five foot six and a half inches – perhaps an inch taller than his father. With a mother's eye, Carrie believed he was rather bigger, recording her son's height as five foot eight inches.[27])

Stopping at the top of the stairs, John looked back and cried to his mother, 'Send my love to Daddo.' The following morning she woke with a start at 3.30 a.m., the hour that John was scheduled to parade with his platoon. The 2nd Battalion left Brentwood at 7 a.m., travelling by train to Southampton. It crossed the Channel (under escort of a destroyer to protect against the growing menace of submarines) to Le Havre, where John wrote his first letter home from 'Somewhere in France' on 17 August. 'Today is his birthday,' Carrie told Lady Edward Cecil agitatedly, 'and I allow myself to feel it's a bit of bad luck he is neither here nor as far as I know there.'[28]

As he made his way slowly by cattle truck towards the front, south of St Omer, John had the odd sensation of reading in the local papers of his father's reception in the French lines. Rudyard was still a celebrity in France: the lowliest soldier seemed to have read the *Jungle Books* in translation and wanted to shake hands with '*le grand Rutyar*'. In Paris he met Lady Edward Cecil's friend, 'that amazing human explosive',[29] Georges Clemenceau, who shared many of his views about the war. In Alsace, after watching John's Colonel, Lord Kitchener, and the French General Joseph Joffre taking the salute at a large parade, he was escorted to within seven and a half metres (the length of a cricket pitch, he noted) of the German lines.

Proximity to the war excited him in a way he had not felt since meeting the Amir on the North-West Frontier over thirty years earlier. (Coming under fire at Kari Siding in South Africa was a more unpleasant experience.) The adrenalin of army life did something to his hormones. His letters to Carrie were full of unusual affection. Not only did he address her as 'Most dear and True' and 'My Queen', but there was a macho assertiveness: 'When I return, be prepared for a new Domestic Tyrant. I'm somebody, I've pulled the whiskers of death and don't you forget it.'[30]

At the same time he tried to give John the benefit of his experience, noting that boric acid in his socks had brought comfort when he walked for two hours through the trenches and that rabbit- or, failing that, tennis-netting was useful for guarding positions against hand-grenades.[31] No doubt he was trying to be encouraging when he said, 'It's a grand life though and does not give you a dull minute.' That was true enough: soon he was safely back in the French capital, dining with Landon in a deserted Café de Paris.

John's existence had its compensations. He was billeted with the Mayor of Acquin, a village twenty miles from the front. The amiable French official spoke no English but he had 'a very pretty daughter – Marcelle – who is awfully nice and we get on very well'.[32] Sadly, there is no evidence of John romancing, or even losing his virginity to, this French maiden. Instead, he worried about his bills at Dunhills and Slazengers, he read copies of *Tatler* and *Punch*, and he was grateful to Lady Bland-Sutton for a 'topping' sponge cake.

Then, suddenly, on 25 September, after an all-night march in the pouring rain, he learnt he would move up to front-line trenches near Loos the following day. Without further delay his battalion would then 'go over the top' as part of a massive Franco-British offensive designed to relieve pressure on Russia on the Eastern front. 'Funny to think that one will be in the thick of it tomorrow,' John wrote, as the big guns resounded deafeningly in his ears. 'This will be my last letter most likely for some time.'[33]

The 2nd Battalion was operating as part of a Guards Division originally intended as a reserve force, which would exploit any breakthrough by the rest of the British 1st Army. But the offensive went badly and it was not long before John's regiment was brought up to the front line. In a confusion made worse by a decision to use poison gas offensively for the first time, it was detailed to advance in four separate companies on Chalk Pit Wood, to the north of Loos. John's No. 2 Company sat still in their trenches while the 'accessory' was released and the artillery poured out its initial bombardment along a six and a half mile front. Emerging from behind their barbed wire, they were hit by shell fire, but moved rapidly to the far edge of the wood. Somehow, John became detached from his men and was caught up in the second wave of the attack by the Scots Guards on a salient called Puits 14 bis. In making this assault, John was shot in the head and killed. Overall, 27 September proved a disastrous day. While the French had some success further south in Champagne, the British endured heavy losses at Loos. Of 10,000 men who started the offensive, over 8000 (including 385 officers) lost their lives.

Rudyard's frothy articles from France appeared in the *Daily Telegraph*, the *New York Sun* and other outlets, shortly after he came home at the end of August. No sooner had he finished than he was off on another jaunt, visiting Royal Navy establishments on the Channel at Dover and off the east coast at Harwich. The idea was that the Navy was too much of a silent service and would benefit from newspaper publicity. Harwich was the headquarters of HMS *Maidstone*, the base for submarines patrolling the North Sea. Rudyard struck up a good rapport with the men who sailed these 'tin fish', contributing some of the poems which accompanied his subsequent articles to their in-house journal, the *Maidstone Magazine*.

Perhaps he overindulged, as he often did in navy wardrooms, because he returned on 25 September, feeling 'not at all well, depressed and chilled'.[34] Two days later, while John was engaged in the battle of Loos, Rudyard, still unwell, went to London to discuss his proposed articles with the Admiralty. Several memos give the flavour (and the seriousness) of his propaganda efforts. On 22 September George Mair, the former assistant editor of the *Daily Chronicle* who headed the Neutral Press Committee, contacted Sir Claud Schuster, director of Wellington House, explaining how he was arranging, through contacts in the Naval Intelligence Division, to have Rudyard's latest naval articles, 'The Fringes of the Fleet', published in the Greek press. On 27 September, the day Rudyard was in London, E. Y. Daniel of the Historical Section of the Committee of Imperial Defence wrote to Schuster, 'Kipling is bubbling over with enthusiasm for what he has already seen. He has been to Dover, Harwich and Grimsby and seen the submarine work, trawler work, etc., and arrangements are being made for him to visit the Grand Fleet in about a fortnight. Meanwhile he is going to work hard at his first articles which will probably be ready before he goes North.'[35]

This last stage of the operation had to be delayed. When he returned home from London that evening, Rudyard was feeling no better. Diagnosed by his local Yorkshire-born general practitioner, Dr Arthur Curteis, as having gastritis, he was put to bed on a careful diet. (When his insurance firm later needed details, Rudyard reminded Curteis of his symptoms: 'I had a great deal of wind and some pains in my stomach, with constipation, as long as I bolted my food or read papers at meals.'[36]) He was still in poor health when, on 2 October, a War Office telegram was delivered with the shattering news that John was 'missing'. Isabel Bonar Law was visiting, so Carrie had to wait until she left before informing Elsie. The following day she went round to Lady Edward Cecil, who had suffered the same heart-breaking emotions the previous year. As soon as she saw Carrie's set features Lady Edward knew the worst.

Within days, the news of John's loss began filtering out. Blumenfeld at the *Daily Express* earned Rudyard's gratitude for holding back any mention. But Gwynne 'excelled' himself (in Rudyard's caustic words) by printing a fulsome notice in the *Morning Post*. Gwynne, who lived at Dunmore, close to Warley Barracks, had contacted the regiment after his wife had heard a rumour at a party. He was told (and this was what annoyed Rudyard) that John was 'missing believed killed', rather than 'missing and wounded', as was officially the position. Realising that Gwynne's action was kindly meant, Rudyard did not hold it against his old friend, who visited Bateman's on 6 October. 'Such splendid pluck,' Gwynne reported to his proprietor Lady Bathurst. 'When I arrived he said "What did you come down for?" I said "To see what I can do." "You can do nothing," he said, but I saw a quiver in his lips which showed how the thing had gone home.'[37]

Of course, the Kiplings still hoped that John would be found.

Perhaps he had been captured, although the prospect of Rudyard's son in German hands after 'Mary Postgate' was daunting. For the next few weeks and then, less concertedly, for another two years, they followed up every lead. Aitken returned from the front with a few details. The Swedish royal family offered to help through contacts with the Kaiser. Officials of the Red Cross and American diplomats in Europe did what they could. Leaflets were dropped behind German lines asking for information whether 'the son of the world-famous author' was dead or alive.[38] Soldiers in John's company were interviewed for any slender clues they could provide. Eventually, Rudyard came to hold an image of his son dying with a smile on his face as he fired on a German machine-gun post close to Chalk Pit Wood. This was the basis of his epitaph

My son was killed while laughing at some jest, I would I knew
What it was, and it might serve me in a time when jests are few.

(Rudyard was clutching at straws. The consensus view is that John died in agony, with half his head shot away.)

Although he was devastated, Rudyard felt he had to put up a good front. Within six weeks he was telling Dunsterville manfully, 'It was a short life. I'm sorry that all the years' work ended in that one afternoon but – lots of people are in our position and it's something to have bred a man.'[39] Back at his desk, he completed the verses to go with the articles (and book) *The Fringes of the Fleet*. This was something of a labour of love. As a schoolboy aficionado of Jules Verne, he must have read *Twenty Thousand Leagues under the Sea* and first started thinking about underwater navigation. After his first sorties with the Royal Navy in the late 1890s he developed an engagingly surreal image of the submarine as 'an Egg-shell / With a little Blue Devil inside'.[40] Submariners could comfortably indulge his own Indian fantasy (arguably, at the heart of *Kim*) of being able to sail through an alien envir-onment, observing it unmolested. Now, in 'Farewell and Adieu', he came up with the warm, light-hearted lines:

We'll duck and we'll dive like little tin turtles,
We'll duck and we'll dive underneath the North Sea,
Until we strike something that doesn't expect us,
From here to Cuxhaven it's go as you please!

He sent the first three stanzas to the *Maidstone Magazine*, under the title 'An Old Song Resung' (further evidence of good times in September?) and with the instruction, 'You can finish it off for yourself, R. K.'[41] When this poem was published elsewhere, its first line: 'Farewell and adieu to you, Harwich Ladies' was altered to 'Greenwich Ladies' for security reasons.

Admiral Lord Charles Beresford, who had once dismissed submarines as 'Fisher's toys', liked the poems so much that he suggested his friend, Edward Elgar, the composer of 'Land of Hope and Glory', might set them to music. Strangely, although both men were often considered like-minded apostles of Empire (and both had signed the Ulster Covenant in 1914), relations between Rudyard and Elgar were lukewarm. In the past, Rudyard had allowed several leading composers access to his work (among others, Arthur Sullivan had written music for 'The Absent-Minded Beggar', Edward German for the *Just So Stories* and Percy Grainger for 'A Song of the English'). But he had put a stop to Elgar composing a tune for 'Recessional'. Now, according to his biographer Jerrold Northrop Moore, Elgar 'produced some hearty tunes for baritone and men's chorus, but then Kipling objected to the verses being turned to musical entertainment'. Clearly Rudyard did not think it appropriate for him yet to be associated with song making. Subsequently, he relented, and Elgar's cycle of four songs from *The Fringes of the Fleet* had a fortnight's run at the Coliseum, before going on a national tour in late 1917. But again Rudyard was unhappy and stipulated no further performances after December. 'He is perfectly stupid in his attitude,'[42] Elgar told his patron Lady Stuart of Wortley.

Rudyard's only public engagement during the remainder of 1915 was a gesture of friendship to Lady Edward Cecil – the opening of the rifle range built in memory of her son George at his old school, Winchester. On 11 December Rudyard fired the first shot and was reportedly cheered when he hit the bull[43] – testament to his Rottingdean training. In a speech, he recalled young George Cecil two years earlier looking at an atlas and saying, 'We shall be sent to prolong the French left – *here*! We shall not have enough men to do it and we shall be cut up. But with any luck I ought to be in it.'

This was the extraordinary spirit – a mixture of idealism and patriotism – in which John had approached his military service. As Rudyard urged young Wykehamists to prepare to make the same supreme sacrifice, he also focused on the future – and the post-war job of 'reconstructing, not only England and the Empire, but the whole world – on a scale which outruns imagination. Every aspect of life as we have known life hitherto will have disappeared. National boundaries and national sympathies, powers, responsibilities, and habits of thought will have shifted and been transformed.' Saying this, his stomach, the weak point in his constitution, must have tightened, partly at the prospect of a changing international political environment and much more so at the realisation that his own son would not be there to lend a hand.

Rudyard declined Max Aitken's usual invitation to Cherkley that Christmas, explaining, 'We have only a very thin skin of bravery to cover our sorrow and find it cracks at unexpected moments.'[44] A few days later Carrie wrote in her diary, 'Christmas Day but to us a name only. We give no presents and in no way consider the day John not being with us.' As she wrote to her mother, after supervising the cutting of winter firewood, 'It's rather heart rending work to go about and realize how very doubtful it is that there is a son to inherit and carry on the place. He took the keenest interest in every detail and often made excellent suggestions.'[45]

Whatever the future, the countryside was changing rapidly as a result of the start of the war. In August 1914 Rudyard had foreseen that hostilities would disrupt trade and that Britain, and Bateman's, would need to be self-sufficient in food. Initially, on Colonel Feilden's advice, he bought forty sheep. Having made clear he did not 'hanker after eternal mutton', he also built up a herd of pedigree Guernsey cows to supply the estate with milk and butter. The original breeding stock came from Max Aitken's farm at Cherkley. As each new calf was born, Rudyard carefully noted its name (usually Bateman's Blizzard, Bateman's Bunting, or some such alliterative variation) and particulars for registration by the English and Guernsey Cattle Society. After one successful mating he sent Aitken a card, 'Birth December 10th 1916: a heifer calf (Bateman's Baby) to Mrs Dene Songthrush widow of the late John Cherkley of Cherkley Court Leatherhead.'[46] Later, he was always satisfied when one of his cows carried off a prize at the Tunbridge Wells Cattle Show.

As the leases of the outlying farms ran out they were not renewed. Instead, the Kiplings used the land for growing crops and raising a herd of red Sussex Shorthorn cattle. Additional income came from poultry, fruit and pigs. However, one vital input, labour, was in woefully short supply. At the end of December 1915 only six men in Burwash had not enlisted, while 150 were already in uniform. Rudyard noted that 'all the conversation turns on the wickedness of the six black sheep'.[47] Two months later, even they could no longer hide, after Asquith's new coalition finally introduced conscription.

National service, Rudyard's goal for so long, proved a mixed blessing, because it accelerated the tendency for women to work on the land. (This was a recommendation of the committee on food production, set up by the coalition and headed by Lord Milner.) As women became familiar figures in the fields around Bateman's, they needed to be accommodated. The Kiplings had been billeting troops on the estate since the start of the war. They provided Dudwell Farmhouse as a refuge for wounded and shell-shocked soldiers, particularly Rudyard's favourite Canadians. In

June 1915 they even offered to turn Bateman's over to the War Office as a hospital. Now, in May 1916, they decided to make Rye Green Farmhouse available as a hostel for their female labourers.

The following month Rudyard summarised the situation to André Chevrillon, the French academic who had promoted his work in France and for whose forthcoming book, *Britain and the War*, he had agreed to write an introduction. Everyone at Bateman's had been called up, he said. Otherwise, there was only 'one man over age to look after 160 acres of land and 27 cattle. My sole gardener under orders and my sole help a youth and a boy and a scattering of female labour.'[48] Rudyard used Chevrillon as a sounding board for many ideas, ranging from the political and emotional awakening of a new class of clerks through the experience of war (the subject of his poem 'The Changelings'), to the need to be wary of pacifist opinion once the Germans began talking about a settlement. However, he kept quiet (strangely quiet, for the author of 'The Female of the Species') about the most radical change the war would bring: the transformation in the role of women. His female labourers did not wait long before making their presence felt. Despite the shortage of men, they introduced an element of sexual competitiveness to the workplace. In July 1916, one woman pursued another into Bateman's, where Rudyard 'found her leaning like Britannia on the pitchfork and howling "Ther dirty woman" '.[49]

Female assertiveness went together with another phenomenon of the war: the increasingly cosmopolitan nature of British life. Rudyard was not sure what he thought about this. To Ted Hill, still a regular correspondent, he noted jauntily, 'We live among troops, hospitals, refugees, French officers, Italian attachés and Russian agents, as smoothly and as unquestioningly as though we had always been what we are now, the most cosmopolitan people on earth.'[50] He referred to bilingual slang and music-hall songs as though they were part of the ideal world he had envisaged with her in the old days. However, the other side of his head revolted against the melting pot and he was truer to form when he described the United States as 'one big, uneasy refugee-camp'.[51] Perhaps, at the time, he needed to feel a sense of purpose with the people around him. For he also told Mrs Hill, uncharacteristically, 'Our common losses are drawing us together, nation by nation, as well as class by class and, for those who survive, the dawn of the new world will be worth seeing.'[52] An atavistic side of him – the one that used to prowl the streets of Lahore – still found that exciting. He recalled how on trips to London he would sit in the buffet of Charing Cross Station and listen to soldiers talking – quick oblique elliptical references to the war, to its facts and fictions, its tragedies and comedies – to all the amazing feats of prowess artlessly told by its actors.

As long as the war continued this mood of mobility and work to be done prevented the Kiplings from becoming too dispirited about their son. One of the tasks they occupied themselves with was making 'RK scrapbooks' for the wounded in hospital. Rudyard explained, 'You take a mass of magazines, weekly papers, *John Bulls, Life, Punch,* etc. – anything with fairly vulgar pictures and fairly vulgar jokes. You cut out the pictures, from ads of motor bikes to beautiful females without clothes (the hospitals like this) and you mix the vulgar jokes in the proportion of about 3 to 5.' Bateman's became a home from home for John's friends, particularly fellow Irish Guards officers such as Lieutenants Rupert Grayson, Tommy Tallents and John de Salis, who called when on leave. Stanley Baldwin's son Oliver, who was a couple of years younger than John, became a special favourite – a surrogate son, as he completed his Eton education and prepared to take up his commission in the Irish Guards in 1917. The previous December Rudyard had acted as godfather to Grayson's nephew, attending his christening in the Guards' Chapel in London.

Even in this changing society, Rudyard's popularity as an author remained undiminished. His royalty statements (or what remain of them) show that sales of his work increased dramatically during the war. In 1915, *Barrack-Room Ballads* enjoyed its best year ever, with over 29,000 copies sold, more than three times the running average. More recent works such as *The Fringes of the Fleet*, in a sixpenny 16mo. version, went through five editions (selling 34,000 copies) in the first six months following publication in December 1915. Overall royalties from the United States in 1916 (£10,392 after agency commissions) were almost double their 1910 figure. Who bought these books? Some commentators have argued that it was not the men in uniform, who were more in tune with Wilfred Owen's anti-war sentiments than Rudyard's *passé* jingoism. However, this idea is contradicted by the fact that Macmillan put out a special twenty-six volume 16mo. Service edition of his books with a clear Dolphin typeface, suitable for user-friendly reading in the trenches. Visiting a book fair in June 1916, the commercially astute Arnold Bennett found 'demand for Kipling, Chesterton, Conrad and me'[53] – a fair assessment of the market.

Rudyard was good (and popular) enough for the American writer Edith Wharton to be very disappointed when he declined to contribute to *The Book of the Homeless*, her compilation in aid of French refugees, with an introduction by Theodore Roosevelt. She somehow got the idea that Rudyard felt unable to write because of the war. Telling Max Beerbohm about this, she remarked, 'As Mr James says, "I kinder see" a portrait of Mr Kipling explaining the fact to a French refugee who happened to have read his "France"!!' But when she started to ask if Beerbohm might persuade 'dear Mr Wells' to take on the job instead of Rudyard, she thought better: 'No, I'd rather not make any other suggestion, because no other could be as good.' (In fact, Rudyard was smarting because Alma-Tadema's daughter, Laurence, had misused his name in an appeal for Poles. He certainly was not against 'charity books': indeed, in January 1917, he resigned from the Society of Authors, having donated a final £100 to its Pension Fund, because he disagreed with its policy of only allowing its members to contribute to projects that it had already officially approved.)

Rudyard also had his admirers on the other side of the trenches.

Working as a journalist, Sven Hedin, the pro-German Swedish explorer, had accompanied the Kaiser's army into France. He recalled halting in Ostend where, as a result of shell fire from the Royal Navy, he and his escorting officers dawdled over dinner, 'reciting Kipling and exchanging anecdotes'. On the French front at Bapaume, he attended a party given by Duke Adolph Friedrich of Mecklenburg, where a volunteer asked for a piano and thumped out a number of songs, including 'Mandalay', 'in a prettier and more inspirited' version than the English one. Further south, Erwin Nader, serving with the Austrian army on the Italian front, had an almost complete collection of Rudyard's works in the Tauchnitz edition and read them in the lengthy pauses between Italian offensives on the Isonzo front in 1916 and 1917.[54]

Rudyard soon rediscovered his penchant for peppering his journalist friends with oddball ideas. Since Germany had a total monopoly in the manufacture of binoculars (in August 1915 Britain had had to order 32,000 pairs through a Swiss inter-mediary[55]), he suggested to Blumenfeld that the *Daily Express* should run a campaign focusing on the number of field-glasses used at the race-track. The paper could print a photograph of a grandstand at the end of a race, showing the crowd of spectators with glasses to their eyes. It could then run an editorial advocating that these valuable optical instruments could be put to better use in the hands of troops in the field. And while Blumenfeld was at it, Rudyard said, he should adopt the word 'Boshialist' for Social-ists with Hun leanings. It was 'nasty and adhesive'.[56]

His popularity, together with his ability to think laterally, still made him a good catch for the propaganda authorities, but he did not always play their game. In March 1915 he declined to write the history of the first battle of Ypres, probably because the job would have to be done purely from the accounts of the generals involved. In September, a request from Julian Corbett, the naval historian who headed the Historical Section of the Committee of Imperial Defence, to repeat the approach of his French articles on the Russian front came at the wrong moment. (Trying to encourage him, Corbett told Rudyard, 'Our Russian experts tell us that you are the only Englishman whom the man in the street will read and you he reads with avidity.'[57]) In December Rudyard still did not feel up to the task when he turned down a proposal from Admiral Edmond Slade to report on the Grand Fleet, claiming that the Navy's failure to blockade Germany had been glossed over in everything he had thus far read.

He was more sympathetic in April 1916 when the Admiralty asked him to return to Harwich to write about submarine warfare in 'Tales of "The Trade"'. However Rudyard was not happy with his articles and asked for them to be held back. When this proved impossible, the exercise almost backfired because, in referring to submarines in the Sea of Marmara, Rudyard had remarked injudiciously that 'one cannot rejoice over dead Mahommedans unless they are Arab'. The Foreign Office demanded an explanation of Douglas Brownrigg, Chief Censor at the Admiralty: 'The serious part of the matter is that just at this moment we are especially anxious not to hurt in any way the susceptibilities of our friends in Arabia, and I think Kipling's expression may be unwelcome to the Grand Sheriff ... Possibly the wily Boche will not spot the lapse, but he probably will.' Brownrigg commented, 'One can see the Grand Sheriff, or whatever, perusing *The Times*, can't one?' but asked Rudyard to cast his eye over a prepared statement so as to 'placate the young women at the FO', just in case.[58]

Perhaps to make amends, Rudyard obliged Brownrigg four months later by producing further pieces on the Battle of Jutland, the inconclusive naval encounter between Britain and Germany in June. Reading these articles in the *Daily Telegraph* in early November (they were later collected as *Destroyers at Jutland*), Oswald Frewen, a twenty-nine-year-old officer on HMS *Comus*, was astonished to come across passages about the engagement from his letters home to his family. However, he was happy that his correspondence had been lifted in this manner. 'No honour could be higher. It transcends words. Dear old Kipling!'[59] Rudyard had been given access to the material by his neighbour Moreton Frewen, Oswald's father.

Rudyard's first piece in this series had appeared in the *Daily Telegraph* with his haunting poem 'My Boy Jack', ostensibly the lament of a mother who had lost her child at sea, but clearly a much more personal cry. Another poem with these articles was entitled 'The Neutral' (later known as 'The Question') which attacked the United States for continued fence-sitting:

> If it be proven that all my good,
> And the greater good I will make,
> Were purchased me by a multitude
> Who suffered for my sake?

Earlier in the summer Brigadier-General G. K. Cockerill, head of MO5, the 'Special Section' of the War Office (which had spawned the counter-intelligence service MI5) had been to Bateman's. According to Carrie's diary, the General was consulting Rudyard about 'handing out intelligence to neutrals' and the encounter proved so interesting that they were forty-five minutes late for lunch. One idea that emerged around this stage was for Rudyard to write some pieces about 'his' Indian soldiers in Europe. *The Eyes of Asia* was compiled largely from letters sent home from Indians at the front and obtained for Rudyard through the censorship system by the India Office's Sir James Dunlop Smith, who had been private secretary to the Lieutenant-Governor of the Punjab during Rudyard's time there. Rudyard enjoyed working with Dunlop Smith, who allowed him scope for imagination in his *ad hoc* promotional work for the India Office. In 1912 he had composed a story, 'In the Presence', about the fortitude of Gurkha guards at the funeral of Edward VII, based on an account from Dunlop Smith, who was responsible for the men. Five years later he was to write another tale, 'A Flight of Fact', drawing on Dunlop Smith's information about an airman, Flight Lieutenant Guy Duncan Smith, who had flown to the

Maldives to arrest a tribal leader suspected of sympathising with the Germans.

The year 1917 promised to be a make-or-break one in the conduct of the war. Overall prospects were improving, but the general impression left by the Dardanelles initiative, the Mesopotamian débâcle, the Easter uprising in Dublin, the battle of Jutland and reverses on the Somme was of a dithering executive. Asquith's days as coalition Prime Minister were numbered, as he found himself harried by a broad range of opponents from Aitken (now fully in control of the *Daily Express*), who simply thought him incompetent, to Gwynne, who favoured a 'nationalist' party. In December 1916, he made way for the 'Welsh wizard' David Lloyd George who, in Churchill's estimation, was the only person with 'any aptitude for war or knowledge of it'.[60] Rudyard could hardly be expected to enthuse about a man he had so reviled, but he was cheered when Lloyd George brought Lord Milner into the five-man War Cabinet that effectively ran the country. (Stanley Baldwin had breakfasted with Rudyard at Brown's in November and was relieved to find that they both agreed about the need for a change of government. 'We have common puritan blood,' Baldwin noted, 'and he said a thing I have so often said and acted on: "When you have two courses open to you and you thoroughly dislike one of them, that is the one you must choose, for it is sure to be the right one." How much happier not to be made like that.'[61]) The new Prime Minister quickly rewarded Aitken for his support by making him a peer as Lord Beaverbrook. After spending Christmas at Cherkley, Rudyard amused himself with suggestions for a coat of arms: in homage to his friend's book *Canada in Flanders*, the crest should be 'cock and bull', he joked.[62]

Rudyard himself looked forward to continuing his propaganda efforts at an interesting juncture in international diplomacy. In December, the German government had approached the United States with an offer to discuss peace terms with the Allies. President Wilson, who to Rudyard's continuing disgust had resolutely maintained his distance from the European conflict, jumped at the opportunity to act as mediator and asked both sides to for-mulate their positions. As a result, there was a period of active diplomacy, often through unorthodox channels such as the Vatican which, under Pope Benedict XV, was generally suspected by Britain of being both pro-German and pacifist.[63] Although opposition to war might be expected and even welcomed from a Christian church, Rudyard and friends like Gwynne equated pacifism – from any quarter – with support for the 'Hun' and adamantly opposed any such accommodation.

Germany's peace initiative was upset when, on 3 February, the United States was forced to abandon its fence-sitting and break diplomatic relations with Germany following the British Admiralty's success in decrypting the Zimmermann telegram, which offered Mexico her 'lost' states of Texas, New Mexico and Arizona in the event of war. Even so, the sober President Wilson remained determined to stay out of a European war if and as long as he possibly could, leaving the way clear for the Vatican to take up the standard of peace.

Rudyard must have discussed this background when he enter-tained Roderick Jones, the new head of the Reuters news agency in London, at Bateman's for a couple of nights in early January 1917.[64] An additional bond between the two men was that Jones had encouraged Dr Starr Jameson to take a financial stake in Reuters. Now Lloyd George had ordered a shake-up in the propa-ganda service and Jones, who often looked to Rudyard for advice, was about to take up an appointment as one of John Buchan's deputy directors at a beefed-up Department of Information. Unable to hide his suspicions of Catholicism, Rudyard told Jones on 8 February, 'I have never believed in any willingness on Rome's part to help civilization. If you think a minute, it must be so. England is the erring child who (for time does not exist in the Vatican) must always be schooled towards repentance and sub-mission.'[65] However, he believed that despite its President, the United States would soon enter the war on the Allied side. He therefore advised that it would be silly to jeopardise this by antagonising Roman Catholic support in the United States. He suggested the British Minister to the Vatican, Count John de Salis (whose son – also John – had recently been wounded while serving with the Irish Guards at the Somme) might 'steer' Jones about the Pope's intentions. In the meantime, he asked, could not France take a more active role in encouraging her fellow republic the United States to enter the war?

Rudyard was proved correct in his forecast for, within weeks, on 6 April, the United States declared war on Germany. Rudyard greeted the decision with his poem 'The Choice', which looked forward to the Americans recovering the road they lost 'in the drugged and doubting years'. This left the Vatican the main player in any peace negotiations. At the end of the month the young John de Salis spent a couple of nights at Bateman's and was able to help his host with a new project. A few weeks earlier, in January, Rudyard had agreed, as a labour of love, to write a history of the Irish Guards in the war. He had already begun sifting through the 1st Battalion's war diaries and maps, which were sent to him by registered post at Bateman's. His personal connection with the de Salis family, who were both diplomats and prominent Roman Catholics, is likely to have impressed on Rudyard the value of the Guards as a force for understanding if not reconciliation in Ireland. The Easter Rising of April 1916 had highlighted the still irreconcilable differences on the island. However, the regiment took in Protestants and Catholics from both the North and South of the country. It had helped ward off demands for conscription in Ireland, which even prominent Unionists such as Edward Carson realised would be disastrous. Because of his son's involvement, Rudyard had come to understand something of this and had tempered his commitment to Ulster. Nevertheless, after the Easter Rising he had refused to sign a petition of clemency for the rebel leader Sir Roger Casement. For a short period, at least, while writing the history, Rudyard's attitudes towards the Irish softened: as the book showed, he appreciated the role of the Catholic priests in battle. This did not mean any let-up in his general attitude to the war: while entertaining young John de Salis, he was doubtless willing his father, as Britain's envoy to the Vatican, not to bow to German demands at the peace table.

A week later, on 1 May, Rudyard was able to gain a more informed view when he and the faithful Landon departed on another propaganda tour – this time to Italy. Ostensibly, he was taking up a long-standing invitation from his friend, the British Ambassador Sir Rennell Rodd, who had been encouraging writers to visit an increasingly important theatre of the war – the Italian front with Austria in the Dolomites. Hilaire Belloc, Arthur Conan Doyle and H. G. Wells had all been, and had written appropriately. Hitherto, Rudyard had put Rodd off, claiming he had not been well. (Carrie's whiplash injury in a crash in a London taxi in March cannot have helped.) Now he saw an opportunity to combine amateurish diplomacy with official propaganda.

His first stop in Italy was not at the front but in Rome where, as his letters to Carrie made clear, he made a beeline for the Vatican. As soon as he reached the Italian capital on 5 May, Rudyard sought out Count de Salis and, the same evening, was put in touch with Cardinal Gasquet, the senior British official in the Vatican. Gasquet was an urbane former Abbot of Downside who had made his name in Britain as a medieval historian. Elected, like Rudyard, to the Athenaeum Club under its 'fast track' Rule 2, he was Prefect of the Vatican Archives and head of the International Commission on the Revision of the Vulgate. He invited Rudyard to attend the Pope's beatification of a Spanish-born Carmelite nun Anne of St Bartholomew in St Peter's. Two days later he lunched with Gasquet in the latter's official residence, Palazzo San Calisto. From his account to Carrie, Rudyard realised the Cardinal had his own reasons for inviting him there. 'I am a low-minded beast and I suspected from the first that we had not been asked for nothing. We hadn't: but that is a matter which I must tell you *viva voce* when we meet.'[66] Although no further record of the meeting survives, Gasquet probably briefed Rudyard about the Vatican peace offensive, which was to result in a plea to participants to desist from fighting in August 1917. (De Salis was proud of the role he had played in strengthening Pope Benedict's resolve in these negotiations and commissioned a plaque for his house in Switzerland reading 'Beati Pacifici 1917'.)

Rudyard was fascinated by Gasquet's cloistered palace, with its study full of 'priceless old prints and a genuine Holbein', and its private chapel, 'a gem of colour and design under a barrel-vaulted roof – a mixture of greys, greens and gold lovelier than aught Uncle Ned had conceived'. He recalled this occasion, with added detail from Gasquet's best-known book, *English Monastic Life* (1904), in later stories, particularly 'The Eye of Allah'. The monkish world came to represent a claustrophobic mixture of cleverness and artifice. 'This is the d**dest queerest trap-doorest world I've ever got into. Nothing resembles its external appearance in the least and when you are told to go north-east it means you ought to steer sou'east. I shall be main glad to meet real plain soldier men again.'[67]

His opportunity came three days later when he travelled northeast to the forward Italian army base on the grain-laden Venetian plains at Udine. Already impressed by the Italians' skill at road-building, he was astounded, as he climbed into the mountains, to see how they had constructed observation posts and tunnels out of sheer rock. Escorted by his liaison officer Colonel Alberto Pirelli (who later headed his family tyre-manufacturing company), he visited the deserted resort of Cortina and met the diminutive (even smaller than he) King Victor Emmanuel III, whom he described as a man of 'affairs and knowledge and guts'.[68] With shells bursting around him, he peered down from the topmost Italian positions on to Austrian troops in the valleys below. At Cormons he met a formidable pair of British women, Countess Helena Gleichen and Mrs Nina Hollings, who ran a radiographic hospital for the British Red Cross. Rudyard noted nonchalantly that they had both 'been affected by the X-Rays though I believe not to any serious extent yet'.[69] Landon knew the Countess, who had drawn several illustrations for his book on the Younghusband expedition to Tibet. Possibly a clue to Landon's activities, she was the sister of Major-General Lord Edward Gleichen, who ran the Intelligence Bureau of the new Department of Information.

In one of his five despatches for the *Daily Telegraph* and *New York Tribune* in June, Rudyard gave an amusing description of an Italian military band playing a mountain-top concert, while the Austrian army below showed its appreciation (or lack of it) by peppering the air with shell fire. A sixth article, which rashly referred to an Italian tendency to embellish the truth about their military performances, was quietly dropped.

Rudyard had been protected from the bright Alpine sun by a pair of dark glasses Carrie had thoughtfully given him before he left. She was delighted that her present had proved useful and relieved to find Rudyard 'looking browner and more fit'[70] on his return to Sussex on 17 May. A fortnight later he learnt from his cousin Stan that the government still wanted to 'give him pretty much any honour he will accept'.[71] Having restated his opposition to all politically inspired 'gongs', he was dismayed to learn soon afterwards that Prime Minister Lloyd George still intended to recommend him, first, for a knighthood in the new Order of the British Empire, then for yet another new decoration, the Companionship of Honour. Rudyard indicated his displeasure to the Chancellor, Bonar Law: 'How would *you* like to be waked on a Sunday morning by a letter from the Acting-Secretary of the Church Aid Society, informing you that your name was among the list of Bishops that had been recommended to the King?'[72] ('They stick him with a "C.H.",' wrote Carrie disdainfully.[73])

He managed to hold out against all titles, emphasising his independence in his powerful poem 'Mesopotamia', written in response to the recent report of the Commission into the military reverses which culminated in General Townshend's surrender to the Turkish army at Kut-el-Amara in early 1915. His old school friend Major-General J. C. Rimington had kept him informed of developments in this theatre of the war, and Rudyard was incensed at the incompetence of the responsible authorities in Simla, which had caused the unnecessary deaths of thousands of Indian troops. 'Mesopotamia' showed the best of Rudyard: a mixture of his willingness to take up his pen in anger (as at the start of the Boer War) when he felt injustice was being done, and his capacity to show great tenderness, as he mourned,

> They shall not return to us, the resolute, the young,
>   The eager and whole-hearted whom we gave

and he attacked the generals 'who left them thriftily to die in their own dung' and the politicians who 'promise large amends'. The *Daily Telegraph*, which was offered first refusal, found the poem too hard-hitting and it was printed by the *Morning Post* in July.

The following month Rudyard took a short holiday with his family in Scotland. In Edinburgh he had lunch with his sister and her husband John Fleming. Since Trix was still not fully recovered, the Kiplings invited her to spend some time in the wounded officers' billet at Dudwell Farmhouse. (Carrie must have had to dig deep into her fund of charity.)

On his return home, Rudyard continued to be inundated with requests for his time. He was happy to accept when Jameson asked him to become a trustee of the Rhodes Trust following the death of Lord Grey. He also agreed to join a Royal Commission to oversee the building and care of war graves. The Commission was chaired by the War Minister Lord Derby, whom he had known (as Lord Stanley) as Military Censor (and surrogate 'Friend') in the Boer War, and headed by the former *Morning Post* editor Fabian Ware. The Commission had courted controversy by deciding not to repatriate the bodies of servicemen but to bury them (making no distinction for rank, race or creed) in cemeteries as close as possible to where they died. Individual graves would have permanent but uniform headstones, with an inscription but no cross. This policy had already been fiercely attacked by the relatives of the fallen as bureaucratic and cruel – a campaign later taken up by the *Daily Mail*. Rudyard's skills as a communicator –

both as writer and skilled propagandist – were required. With his personal grief and his respect for funeral practices (dating from the sight of Hindus and their burning ghats in India), he was an excellent choice as a Commissioner.

However, having taken on this job, knowing he would soon need to turn his attention to his history of the Irish Guards, he refused a request from Carson in the War Cabinet to work on a study of the conflict in the Middle East. More personally, he declined to write the life of Jameson who had died in November, shortly after inviting Rudyard to join the Rhodes Trust. Rudyard had been one of the last people to visit Jameson at his house in London's Great Cumberland Place. Now another of his pre-war heroes, the man he claimed had inspired him to write 'If–', had departed. 'I wonder if you loved "the Doctor" as much as I did,' he later told Herbert Baker, adding a comparison with Rhodes, '. . . What's that Browning quotation – "not a fifth sound but a star". Something like that. For it's what the two fused to make. And his second name was "Starr".'[74]

Rudyard's more creative output at this stage comprised the quirky mixture of the emotional, cerebral and propagandist found in his 1919 book of poems *The Years Between*. As 'My Boy Jack' (and, to an extent, 'Mesopotamia') showed, he could call on a vast reservoir of pain at the loss of his son. With its evocative imagery, 'The Children' was as powerful and damning of war as anything Wilfred Owen produced:

> That flesh we had nursed from the first in all cleanness
> was given
> To corruption unveiled and assailed by the malice of
> Heaven –
> By the heart-shaking jests of Decay where it lolled on
> the wires –
> To be blanched or gay-painted by fumes – to be cindered
> by fires –

To be senselessly tossed and retossed in stale mutilation
From crater to crater. For this we shall take expiation.
But who shall return us our children?

Rudyard's anger was conveyed in his many 'Epitaphs of the War', including one called 'Common Form', the nearest to self-recrimination in which he indulged:

If any question why we died,
Tell them, because our fathers lied.

These short snatches of verse often adopted the religious tone of his poem 'Gethsemane' from *The Years Between*. Perhaps he was recalling John's short stay with the French girl in Acquin in the 'pretty lass' in the garden called Gethsemane. As long as the narrator talked to her, he prayed his cup might pass. 'It didn't pass – it didn't pass' and he went to his death in the gas-poisoned battlefields. As Rudyard explained to Doubleday, 'What makes war most poignant is the presence of women, with whom one can talk and make love, only an hour or so behind the line.'[75]

Religion provided some framework for understanding as Rudyard grappled to make sense of the carnage on the battlefield. He tended to temper it with the more practical insights of Free-masonry, which offered not only instant explanations but also an ethical programme for the future. As his latest stories showed, he was aware that the war had liberated the energies of a new generation of young men. As early as 1915 he recognised the plight of 'The Changelings', the head of a Walworth Bank and the grocer's clerk, who at the end of the war would look back and say,

Now there is nothing – not even our rank –
To witness what we have been;
And I am returned to my Walworth Bank,
And you to your margarine!

These young men, Rudyard realised, would not even have romantic memories of Mandalay to sustain them in civilian life. These 'sons of Martha' would recall only the hellish reality of the trenches. And their plight was all the more vivid to him because they were of his son's generation. No war poet showed as deep an awareness of this problem.

Sometimes the effort proved too much and he resorted to heavy-handed satire, as in 'On the Gate: A Tale of '16', where St Peter and his assistants grapple to cope with the demand at the gates of Heaven created by the European war. Rudyard's esoteric instruction at the hands of bodies such as the Rosicrucians bore fruit in his knowledge of the celestial hierarchies. But Carrie did not like the story (for a while also known as 'The Department of Death') and discouraged its publication.[76] When Rudyard read it to Rider Haggard (like many of his war writings at this stage, it cannot have been more than a fragment), his friend thought it 'quaint', adding, 'It would have been caviare to the General if he had [published], because the keynote of it is infinite mercy extending even to the case of Judas.'[77] (The two men were seeing more of each other as Haggard had taken a house for the winter in Sussex at St Leonard's, near Hastings.)

Rudyard's Masonic influences were more obvious in 'In the Interests of the Brethren' (dating, according to Carrie's diary, from September 1917). Showing a deep understanding of Masonic practice, this story reiterated his long-held belief in the importance of ritual for people. 'The more things are upset, the more they fly to it.' The details showed Rudyard refining his conservatism: the war had happened because rituals had been neglected and now they needed to be rediscovered. As the wise Sergeant-Major in the story put it, 'We could do much with Masonry . . . Certainly not as a substitute for a creed, but as an average plan of life.'

For spiritual values, Rudyard was still looking for accommodation with Christianity, his instinctive religion. He explained to Haggard in May 1918 that occasionally he felt the love of God but 'that the difficulty was to "hold" the mystic sense of this communion – that it passes'. True to form, Rudyard told his friend that God meant this phenomenon of the soul to be so – 'that He doesn't mean that we should get too near to Him – that a glimpse is all that is allowed'. In recording this in his diary, Haggard noted, 'I *think* R. added because otherwise we should become unfitted for our work in the world.'[78] Rudyard's reliance on Masonry as a prop, as an 'average plan of life', was clear when, that very same month he, who had taken little active part in Masonry since Lahore, joined the Correspondence Circle of the Quatuor Coronati Lodge No. 2076.

As his work, particularly his fiction, became increasingly symbolic over the next few years, Rudyard sought a balance between religion and society, with Freemasonry as the bridge. As his Masonic stories suggested, he saw lodges as refuges of enlightenment where the clerks who had discovered themselves in the war might escape the influence of more damaging doctrines, such as unbridled capitalism or even Marxism. In such centres of instruction, these people could begin to understand the burden of 'The Gods of the Copybook Headings', his paean to old-fashioned commonsense published in October 1919. As the lodge doctor in 'In the Interests of the Brethren' chirpily declares, 'Marvellous how these old copybook-headings persist.' Essentially, this was Rudyard's latest battle-tested gloss on long-held beliefs such as the nobility of repetitive work.

Alongside his sensitive attempts to resolve pain and effort, Rudyard's ranting polemical output seemed almost diabolical. During 1917 his hatred of Germans became obsessional. In retrospect, he got the worst of his attempt to convey his sense of Teutonic discipline and savagery in a verse (based on Thackeray's 'The Sorrows of Werther') that he sent his friend Fletcher in April:

> Charlotte, when she saw what Herman
> Yielded after he was dead,

> Like a well-conducted German,
> Spread him lightly on her bread.[79]

His overriding political idea was to guard against any accommodation with the enemy. Pope Benedict's peace message in August inspired 'A Song at Cock-Crow', an attack on the Roman Catholic church's unwillingness – symbolised in the image of St Peter denying the Lord – to denounce 'Hun atrocities throughout the war'.[80] The Bolshevik Revolution in early November was followed later in the month by the former British Foreign Secretary Lord Lansdowne's letter to the *Daily Telegraph* calling for a negotiated peace. (This time the *Telegraph* printed what *The Times* had turned down.) Rudyard lumped both events together in his poem 'Russia to the Pacifists', which blamed the fall of the Tsar on pacifist talk:

> God rest you, peaceful gentlemen, but give us leave to pass.
> We go to dig a nation's grave as great as England's was.
> For this Kingdom and this Glory and this Power and this
>   Pride,
> Three hundred years it flourished – in three hundred days
>   it died.

In a letter to his cousin Stanley, he attributed the *Telegraph*'s willingness to publish Lansdowne's letter to the fact that its proprietor Lord Burnham was 'a Hebrew, and was suffering from cold feet. It *is* a Semitic complaint.'[81]

Rudyard dismissed anyone who dabbled with peace proposals as an agent of either the Inquisition or international Bolshevism, as a member of a Jewish conspiracy or, simply, as weak and diseased. He marked down as traitors the growing number of British workers who either looked to Lenin for inspiration or who simply hoped for an end to the war. They had all been infected with a German cancer that needed to be excised – an idea he took to its literal, distasteful conclusion in his poem 'A Death Bed'.

Rudyard claimed that this fantasy on the last moments of the Kaiser provided a balance to his earlier 'The Dead King', about Edward VII. Insofar as it tried to contrast a war-maker with a peace-seeker, this might be true. But Rudyard's gloating insistence that only a slow death from throat cancer was good enough for the Kaiser was sadistic and nasty.

He adopted pseudo-scientific imagery in referring to Germans. 'Wherever the German man or woman gets a suitable culture to thrive in, he or she means death and loss to civilized people, precisely as germs of any disease,' he declared in May 1916.[82] 'The German is typhoid or plague – Pestis Teutonicus if you like.' Taking up the theme of his poem 'Zion', in *Destroyers at Jutland*, he seriously told Ian Colvin, Gwynne's deputy at the *Morning Post*, 'There is no question of "hate" involved now in our relations with the Hun ... One hates people whom it is conceivable that later one may care for – people, at least, of like passions with ourselves. The Hun is outside any humanity we have had any experience of. Our concern with him is precisely the same as our concern with the germs of any malignant disease.' And he stipulated how it was necessary to 'clean out, sterilize, flush down etc etc all places where they can get a foothold'.[83] Later, after the war, he suggested that an outbreak of foot and mouth disease was related to the location of prisoner-of-war camps, and asked Churchill and others to investigate. He told Blumenfeld never to capitalise the word 'hun', nor to use it with 'he' or 'whom', only 'it' and 'which'.[84]

His efforts to find a link between his various obsessions found an interesting outlet in a letter to Sir Almroth Wright, a one-time army pathologist who had developed an anti-typhoid vaccine that was invaluable in the Boer War. Of Irish extraction, Wright served as a model for his friend George Bernard Shaw's play *The Doctor's Dilemma*. Like Osler, who considered him too much of a medical innovator, Wright was well-read and precise with words, though Evelyn Waugh later described him damningly as a 'prize bore'.[85] Apart from his interest in typhoid (the disease, Rudyard may have noticed, that killed Wolcott Balestier), Wright had been a leading opponent of female suffrage. His letters to *The Times* and his book *The Unexpurgated Case against Women Suffrage*, published in 1913, played an important role in preventing women from obtaining the vote before the war. The book argued that female suffrage would imperil the state because women were not able to back their vote with physical force and that men who supported this cause were either cranks or idealistic dreamers.

During the First World War, Wright attacked the conventional wisdom about the treatment of tetanus and gangrene in war wounds. Since antiseptics did not work in the conditions of the trenches, he advocated early surgical intervention. Now, troubled by the rash of peace-making, Rudyard diffidently sought Wright's opinion as a scientist on his own bizarre theory that pacifists had an inbred masochism that responded to the German tendency to 'beastliness' and perversion (in the committing of atrocities). 'I believe that, with certain temperaments, the fact or the report of a specific type of abomination being committed, wakes, consciously or unconsciously, a certain perverted interest which may increase sympathy. It is deep calling to deep: passive responding to active.'[86] In writings of pacifists, he claimed to have noted a sense of martyrdom and 'peculiar religiosity which finds solace in the physical details of the Crucifixion, and a persistent hysteria – made worse by the riot and confusion of actual war all around – which expresses itself in terms of indiscriminate love for mankind and – unless I am very badly mistaken – merges into particular (or unparticular) love for the individual'. He linked this to 'an outbreak of intellectual lawlessness', which brought calls for 'toleration' and 'humanity' and the need to break down all contracts, 'whether with God, Nature or Man'. He claimed that the enemy exploited these weaknesses 'since he really does know something of the triple Devil he serves'. Britain's persistence in seeing its 'pacifists as sports of nature developed by the play of "politics", or as sincerely conscientious idiots' was 'a bad mistake'. These people needed to be examined calmly and scientifically, and perhaps a treatment could be found.

Rudyard's extremist attitudes found an echo in the political manifesto of the National party, which emerged at the end of August 1917 to attack the Lloyd George coalition's lack of resolution towards both Germany and Britain's increasingly restless workforce. Among its leading lights were Lord Montagu of Beaulieu, Lord Bathurst (whose wife owned the *Morning Post*) and Admiral Lord Charles Beresford, who took up the muted cries of the most reactionary of the Unionist die-hards who had opposed the Parliament Bill and supported the Ulster cause before the war.

Mindful, perhaps, of his cousin Stanley's position as Joint Financial Secretary, Rudyard had no direct links with the new party. Indeed, Baldwin made it clear that, while he approved of the party's aims, he opposed its incorporation as a separate political entity because this weakened the power of the government at Westminster.

However, Rudyard was clearly a fellow traveller. The new party's main newspaper support came from the *Morning Post*, where Rudyard made special efforts to encourage Ian Colvin, a witty and polemical Scotsman, whose journalistic career Rudyard had guided from the *Pioneer*, through the *Cape Times*, to his current position at Gwynne's right-hand side. In late September Colvin received a letter from Rudyard expressing sympathy for 'the movement',[87] and referring specifically to giving a lecture to an outfit called the British Producers. This was the newly formed British Empire Producers Organisation, one of several similar bodies at the time. At an early meeting of this group at the Savoy Hotel in May, the increasingly unpredictable Lord Beresford had created a sensation when, in the middle of an anti-German tirade, he picked up his plate and found it was manufactured in Germany by Bouscher Bros. When he smashed this offending piece of crockery the distinguished businessmen around the room followed suit with theirs.[88]

Only the previous month Rudyard had been recommending Colvin to read Bunyan's *The Holy War* as 'a weapon'. Rudyard

said the book was 'the most modern' he knew: 'Everything and
everybody is there – from the German Emperor down to the
flammenwerfer, the pacifists and the Pope – all the methods and
fighting, all the arguments, all the Labour party.'[89] At the end of
September Rudyard expressed satisfaction that Colvin was
'mining into The Holy War for propaganda'.[90] By then, he had
written his own verses based on the book. His poem 'The Holy
War' never had widespread publication in Britain: abroad it was
taken up by the *New York Times*, but at home its dissemination was
limited to the Christmas number of *Land and Water*, nominally a
recherché magazine of country pursuits, but more widely known
for its commentaries on the war by Hilaire Belloc. Rudyard told
how Bunyan had foreseen the apocalyptic battle that Britain
('Mansoul') was waging against the forces of the Devil, which he
listed with all the rhetorical power of the pulpit (capital letters
were now an essential part of his style):

> Likewise the Lords of Looseness
> That hamper faith and works,
> The Perseverance-Doubters,
> And Present-Comfort shirks,

not to mention

> ... the State-kept Stockholmites,
> The Pope, the swithering Neutrals,
> The Kaiser and his Gott...

('Stockholmite' referred to a proposed meeting of European
socialist parties, including those from enemy countries, in the
Swedish capital. Arthur Henderson, the Labour member of the
War Cabinet, was forced to resign after stopping in Paris to discuss
this gathering.)

As a footnote, the National party was not the only right-wing
group to emerge in late 1917. Noel Pemberton Billing was a

Member of Parliament who, with Lord Montagu, had championed the cause of the Royal Flying Corps and founded the Vigilante Society. A slick self-publicist, Billing might have featured in a pre-war Kipling farce, with his vampire good looks, his lemon-yellow Rolls-Royce and his background as an actor and slightly dubious inventor of flying boats. He even ran a related lobby group, the Imperial Air Convention, which promoted views not a million miles from Rudyard's Aerial Board of Control.

In June Billing had set up the Vigilante Society, whose objects were 'the promotion of purity in public life, the upholding of political honour, and the fearless exposure of corruption in the conduct of all public offices'. Its newspaper, the *Imperialist* (later the *Vigilante*), ran 'Toasts of Empire' profiles of public figures including Rudyard. In January 1918 this organ featured an article, headlined 'The Forty-Seven Thousand', which purported to reveal that the German secret service had a book that exposed the secret vices (homosexual it was implied) of large numbers of the great and the good in British society. The following month the *Vigilante* had a short piece entitled 'The Cult of the Clitoris', which suggested that the police might discover several of the 47,000 names if they raided a central London address being used to promote performances of *Salome* by the exotic dancer Maud Allen. Miss Allen decided to sue Billing for criminal libel. The trial in May was a *cause célèbre* less important – so far as Rudyard was concerned – for its content than for its apparent exposé of the links he liked to see between 'Huns' and diseased corruption.

Trix's three-month stay at Dudwell Farmhouse in the autumn of 1917 was not a success. Carrie complained to her mother, 'There is nothing in the world the matter with her except selfishness and self-centredness carried to the nth [degree].'[91] Rudyard was not so sure: he observed his bright, twittering sister, who believed she could communicate with the elephants in Edinburgh zoo, and wrote his poem 'En-Dor' which, in the context of the war, was a warning to bereaved mothers and wives not to dabble with the paranormal in their efforts to communicate with their dead loved ones. (Perhaps there was also implied criticism of his friend Conan Doyle who had announced his conversion to 'psychic religion'.)

After more than three years of war the countryside had lost its traditional independence and was beset with bureaucratic red tape. Because of the labour shortage the Kiplings had accepted prisoners of war to work in their fields. But this only encouraged a more interventionist approach from their local agricultural committee. On 10 April 1918 Carrie was 'much ruffled by a visitor from the Min. of Agriculture who tells her how to farm her land'.[92] A couple of months later Rudyard complained to Lord Northcliffe, 'I find in these days one can only just keep abreast of the daily detail of living as laid down for country people by Agricultural Departments, Barnyard Brigadiers and all the other time-wasting, work-killing Jacks and Jades in office who have been let loose upon us!'[93]

As if to confirm Rudyard's political nightmares, there had also been a revival of local labour problems. Since John's death, a succession of servants had been sacked. Already Carrie was noting the 'inadequacy' of her secretary Miss Chamberlain, who was given five weeks' notice when, later in the year, she declined to work 'regulation hours': 'a case of great ingratitude for much forbearance and great tolerance'.[94] In early 1918 there were threats of more serious disturbances when a food demonstration was planned in Burwash. Rudyard was concerned because Mrs Smith, a charwoman who had worked at Bateman's, was one of the ringleaders and he feared that she might lead a frenzied mob on the house.[95]

Rudyard must have been relieved to hear from the newly knighted Roderick Jones on 10 January that the Department of Information had decided to concentrate its resources on home propaganda – 'the working classes have to be kept in the middle of the road' – and wanted him to 'do for the Munitions and the

Army what you so finely have done for the Fleet!'[96] Rudyard replied that such work was much needed, but its success was prejudiced by 'the infernal skill with which the various censors concerned manage to knock the heart and vitality out of the stuff that they pass'.[97] As a result, not much propaganda was actually read.

Rudyard's response was his poem 'The Song of the Lathes' (a version in the British Library is dated 18 January 1918). He later explained to Doubleday about the women in the shell factories, and said their 'quiet heroism and sang-froid ... was beyond all praise'.[98] However, he added, the last verse but one contained the 'hub of the whole proposition'. This reiterated Rudyard's theme that man's hate passes but woman's endures. 'Once I was a woman,' Mrs Embsay declares in the poem, 'but that's by with me.' Despite his unwillingness to address the political consequences of female emancipation (particularly on his farm), he was very aware of the psychological strength of women and this was a sub-theme running through much of his wartime writing ('Mary Postgate' being the most obvious example).

In mid-February[99] Beaverbrook followed up Jones's approach and wanted to see Rudyard as a matter of urgency. He was about to take charge of a new Ministry of Information, with a seat in the Cabinet, and he needed Rudyard to come to Cherkley to discuss various issues with him. Even though his friend offered to send a car (the Duchess had been put on blocks, probably to avoid accusations of extravagance), Rudyard was unable to oblige, as he was putting the finishing touches to an important speech in Folkestone on 15 February when he likened Germany to a blacker version of the Thuggees of India. Turning his mind back to Beaverbrook's request a week later, he declined to take an official job with the new Ministry[100] but was happy to provide regular advice and even to make occasional speeches. He was adamant that the future of propaganda, particularly at home, was visual: 'I think Newspaper propaganda for the munition worker is dead ... The spoken word and the picture is the game' (25 February); he wanted 'not faked up dramas, but actual factory life and films from the front' (28 February).

Rudyard's interest in films and the mass media had been evident in work such as 'Mrs Bathurst' and 'The Village that Voted the Earth Was Flat'. With the growth of the cinema as mass entertainment during the war, there were several moves to film his stories. In an effort to familiarise themselves with the market, the Kiplings took the trade paper *Kinematographic and Lantern Weekly*, from which they typically peppered Watt with cuttings asking him (or the Society of Authors) to investigate if, for example, Rudyard's copyright had been violated in a new film *Maid of Mandalay*, or the Eclair company's version of *Duke's Son, Cook's Son*.[101] In the meantime Rudyard sold the screen rights to five books to Pathé Frères in the United States. The first film to be produced in 1916 was *The Light that Failed*, with Robert Edeson as Dick Heldar and Lillian Tucker as Maisie. But that was not released in Britain and the Kiplings had to wait until a couple of years later to see *The Naulahka* in London. They were not impressed as the book had been turned into a piece of exotic Orientalism, with Doraldina, a New York cabaret dancer, as the Maharani Sitabhai. Rudyard's stories do not seem the most obvious sources for sexually charged material. However, others thought differently: the most successful of these early cinematic adaptations of his stories was *A Fool There Was*, Frank Powell's racy American silent version for the Fox Film Corporation of *The Vampire* with Theda Bara, the original 'vamp', in the title role. Described in a recent history as 'Hollywood's first major sexploitation movie', it was banned by the British Board of Film Censors in June 1916 and has never been seen in Britain.[102] Otherwise Rudyard's works did not begin to translate successfully to the cinema until the mid-1920s.

As for other mass media, Rudyard had been interested when the Propaganda Bureau sent the hard-hitting Dutch cartoonist Louis Raemakers to talk with him at Bateman's in January 1916. Raemakers subsequently went to the United States where, after a slow start, his work became popular, partly because it was displayed in unusual places such as buses and trams. Knowing this, Rudyard suggested that Beaverbrook should use cartoons on the Underground. 'They are the most useful eye-stuff now available,' he said.

Rudyard's ear for music remained surprisingly unsophisticated. He liked stirring tunes, particularly the hymns which provided the beat for his early poems. As part of his recruiting effort in January 1915 he had given a talk in which he spoke of his delight in military music, recalling, in particular, the uplifting effect of the band of the 10th Lincolns playing their regimental march, that 'queer defiant tune' 'The Lincolnshire Poacher', in a demoralised cholera camp in India. He was pleased when, in January 1918, after finishing a set of verses about the Irish Guards, they were set to music by Edward German in time for a matinée at the Albert Hall in March.

Personally, his greatest delight remained the music-hall, which he celebrated in his verses 'A Recantation (To Lyde of the Music-Halls)', written in March 1918, a few days before making a major speech to munitions workers in Bristol. The poem was an appreciation of his son John's favourite singer 'Lyde', who had shown magnificent professionalism by appearing on stage on the night 'the news came in from Gaul / Thy son had – followed mine'. (The name of the singer was ambiguous: it could have suggested a Cockney variation on Lloyd – as in the star Marie Lloyd – but it is generally taken to refer to the more establishment figure Harry Lauder, who lost his son in France in 1917.)

Rudyard's reference to Lyde formed part of an intellectual game that had arisen from an innocent enquiry he had made to his friend C. R. L. Fletcher. Despite youthful misgivings, Rudyard had long been an admirer of the Roman poet Horace. Even as a schoolboy he had produced some fine pastiches (including his precociously intelligent rendering of *Odes* III. ix, 'Donec gratus eram ...' into broad Devonshire). After settling at Bateman's in 1902, Rudyard began to see Horace as a role model – the urbane man of the world who retires to his Sabine (read Sussex) farm to obtain a better perspective on the metropolitan rat race. He produced Horatian-style odes for *Stalky* and *Puck* stories, and for *The Muse among the Motors*. Addressing the boys at Wellington in May 1912 on the value of literature, he had noted, in reference to Latin authors, that there were 'bits of Odes from Horace ... that make one realise later in life, as no other words in any other tongue can, the brotherhood of mankind in time of sorrow or affliction'.[103] That same month he acquired a much-loved Medici Press edition of Horace which he kept in his safe and occasionally brought out to annotate with his translations. Later he always travelled with a copy of Horace, whom he described to Rhodes's architect Herbert Baker as 'the soundest Platitudinarian that ever was and the things he says about going slow are worth rereading'.[104]

In April 1917 he had sent a copy of *A Diversity of Creatures* to C. R. L. Fletcher, who had moved from Oxford to teach at Eton during the war. He asked his friend for a Latin 'original' for his poem 'A Translation', which appeared in the book, adding modestly that he would be grateful for information on a supposedly secret Fifth Book of Horace's Odes that someone had told him about. (He jokingly suggested he had seen reference to it in the Vatican library, but of course no such volume existed.) Fletcher confirmed this, but added that he had liked 'A Translation' and wondered if Rudyard had written any similar poems that he might discuss with his pupils as a teaching aid. Rudyard sent another Horace spoof, 'Lollius', which attacked Lloyd George's sale of honours. Fletcher thereupon suggested that, as an amusement, they might write their own Fifth Book themselves. He brought in A. D. Godley, the Oxford historian, Charles Graves, the literary journalist and, later, A. B. Ramsay, Lower Master of Eton, to help them. Rudyard provided two poems (and many more ideas) for their joint *Q. Horatii Flacci Carminum Liber Quintus*, which fooled a few people when it was published in 1920. But before then Rudyard's collaboration had come to an end: with his donnish humour Fletcher said he did not like 'A Recantation' and Ramsay claimed in the same spirit to object to the poem's identification of Lyde with Horace on the grounds that the latter did not have a son. Rudyard wrote to Fletcher on 24 March 1918, calling a halt to their wartime diversion. 'It was a very delightful game while it lasted, but one can't play under a Censorship and just now I haven't any right to play at all as I've been shoved into a heavy job that will take all my time.'[105] However, he had enjoyed his intellectual dabbling with the academics, a breed of men in whose company he increasingly took pleasure. No *amour propre* was ruffled and Rudyard continued to produce good Fifth Book glosses to accompany his later stories.

Occasionally Rudyard still asked Beaverbrook for personal favours. In March Landon had been unwell and had come over to Bateman's (from Keylands) to recover. The following month Rudyard suggested his friend's name to Beaverbrook as 'the *one* man'[106] for a Ministry assignment in Mesopotamia. In May he had a request of a more professional nature. As part of his regular work for the Ministry, he had been asked by Buchan, the Director, to write a piece for a French readership, but was prevented because his local telegraph office closed at 7 p.m. Beaverbrook took up the matter with the Postmaster General Albert Illing-worth, but discovered that keeping Burwash office open later would require the regional centre at Tunbridge Wells to stay open too and, given the delicate state of labour relations at the time, he did not want to push it. In a neat exposition of the 'An Error in the Fourth Dimension' principle, Rudyard was unable to repeat his American success in obtaining a private communications facility.

He had begun to consider collecting his recent poems for an autumn compilation – 'greatly urged to it by public and publisher', noted Carrie on 28 March.[107] (This was the forthcoming 'heavy task' he had declared to Fletcher.) As an interim measure he had decided to put out a short volume, *Twenty Poems from Rudyard Kipling*, which appeared in May and is interesting as a digest of Rudyard's favourite poems – most of them recent material, but others stretching back to 'The Long Trail' in 1892. Rudyard's work on the more substantial volume was held up, however, because of continuing pains in his stomach. On 11 May he had breakfast in bed for the first time in his married life. After going to London for X-rays, he was relieved but not hugely enlightened to be told that there was 'no tangible evidence of disease, but great irritability of the stomach'.[108] Visiting Bateman's at the end of the month, Haggard was shocked to find his friend looking 'thin and aged and worn', though the X-rays confirmed that there was 'no cancer or tumour or anything of that sort'. Rudyard's weight was down to eight stone twelve pounds and he was very depressed. He claimed that this world must be a hell for it had every attribute of it – 'doubt, fear, pain, struggle, bereavement, almost irresistible temptations springing from the nature with which we are clothed, physical and mental suffering etc. etc.' However, he said he did not want to die, but needed a 'good long rest'.[109]

There was light relief worthy of the music-hall when, on 27 May, *The Times* printed a poem that it thought had been submitted by Rudyard. The manuscript of 'The Old Volunteer' bore a passable version of his signature, but the handwriting was different and the content abysmal. When Rudyard complained that he had had nothing to do with the verses Geoffrey Dawson, the embarrassed editor, launched a full-scale inquiry. With the spectre of the Parnell letters hoax of the 1880s in his mind, he called in Basil Thomson, the suave Old Etonian Assistant Commissioner at Scotland Yard, who was responsible for the Special Branch. On at least two occasions in June Rudyard travelled to London to see Thomson, an extraordinary Kiplingesque man who had been Prime Minister of Tonga (at the age of twenty-eight), private tutor to the Crown Prince of Siam and governor of Dartmoor Prison. Of his early days in the Colonial Service Thomson recalled, 'My first native friends were cannibals, but I learned very quickly that the warrior who had eaten his man as a quasi-religious act was a far more estimable person than the town-bred, mission-educated native.' As head of Special Branch he had monitored Irish subversion and was now directing his resources to combating pro-German, pacifist and pro-Bolshevik influences. The Assistant Commissioner discussed the Casement and Pemberton Billing cases with Rudyard, but made no inroads on the forgery.

The Times also employed a private detective, H. Smale, to run a parallel investigation. At Bateman's Rudyard told Smale that the author of the offending verses was likely to be a German, a Jew, an Irishman or a Quaker, because these were types he had crossed swords with over the years. Internal evidence pointed to Ian Colvin, who had once fooled an antiquarian bookseller with a spoof Keats letter. But still no hard evidence emerged. A frustrated Rudyard was reduced to heavy-handed satire of Smale in his own autobiography: 'It was a detective out of a book, down to the very creak of Its boots ... It knew a lot about second-hand furniture ...'[110] Rudyard explained he had dwelt a lot on the incident because he did not want anyone suggesting after his death that, 'in the deepest trough of the War', he had 'step[ped] aside to play with *The Times*, Printing House Square, London, EC'.

Perhaps Rudyard protested too much for, as his Horace correspondence showed, he was fascinated with questions of authenticity. Shortly before the start of the war in 1914, he had presented Henry Tedder, the Librarian at the Athenaeum, with a faded early-seventeenth-century manuscript that he claimed to have purchased as an autograph of Thomas Coryate, the traveller, versifier and author of *Coryat's Crudities*. The text was a sonnet 'To a Librarian' who

> knew all Mines and Galleries
> And Veines and Beds of excellent Assaye:
> In that brute Rocke whereunder Learning lies
> And where ye blinde Gem waits upon ye Daye.

Tedder was about to retire at the time and Rudyard had been one of the subscribers to his portrait. According to the *Library Association Record*, 'Having surprised Mr Tedder with this ingenious mystification, the author [i.e. Rudyard], whose deftness is equal to his wit and genius, confessed that the sonnet had been written personally for Mr Tedder to be placed beneath the picture, and that the manuscript, a marvel of imitation, was his own work.'[111] On that occasion Rudyard had confessed his fake and there is no reason to believe he had any hand in 'The Old Volunteer'. Forgeries continued to intrigue him, however, as he put to good creative use in his later story 'Dayspring Mishandled'.

As for the war itself, the early months of 1918 had been chequered with reverses. Rudyard gritted his teeth and hoped that the current government could see it through. In May Charles Repington, the well-connected military correspondent, attended a lunch at Lord Rocksavage's where someone reported Rudyard saying that the nation had to back Lloyd George 'on the principle that if a man addicted to whisky drinking tried to give it up he would get delirium tremens'.[112]

Even after the first American troops arrived that month, the Allies made little progress on the Western Front. Rudyard was still wary of American intentions as articulated in President Wilson's Fourteen Points in January. He himself much preferred (because he better understood) the naked self-interest of Theodore Roosevelt's diplomacy, and he derided Wilson as an inexperienced 'schoolmaster' whose talk of national self-determination was dangerous because it gave succour to independence aspirations in Ireland and India. By way of welcome to the Americans stationed in Britain, Rudyard composed a poem called 'Ed Baker', which he thought an ideal name for the GI, along the lines of 'Tommy Atkins' for the British squaddie. The verses told how Baker's ancestors had crossed the sea to get away from Europe's troubles but had failed, and were now having to return to sort matters out. Such were deep-rooted sensitivities that Rudyard was prevailed upon not to publish the poem 'for fear it would be misconstrued as a fling at America'.[113] However, in July he went to talk to some of the newly arrived American troops at their Morn Hill rest camp in Winchester. At the end of a short message to some 7000 men in the open air, the Camp Commandant Colonel Samuel G. Jones called for three cheers and a 'tiger' – a traditional American cry: 'What's the matter with Kipling?' 'He's all right.' 'Who's all right?' 'Kipling.' Elsie was delighted to receive a gift of 'candy' from the canteen and Rudyard was impressed to have a company called to his attention in the close of the cathedral, though he could not help noticing that the Americans insisted on calling it a church. At the end of the day he was calmed by the thought that they would be 'a damn awkward crowd to tackle if excited'.[114]

A few days earlier Rudyard had been to dine at Buckingham Palace. As recently as 1911 a government minister had reported George V as disliking Rudyard's work, 'finding him coarse' and preferring the naval yarns of Captain Marryat.[115] However, the King's views had changed: in November 1917, he had requested Rudyard's help in redrafting his letters to bereaved families of servicemen. The earlier wording was considered 'very bald', according to Lord Derby at the War Office, who wanted Rudyard 'to counteract the pro-German pacifist poison which is being freely scattered in stricken homes'.[116] Now, in July 1918, Rudyard was slightly bemused to find himself on the Palace guest list, attending a dinner where there was 'nothing to drink but lemonade, ginger beer, barley & Malvern water'.[117] (The King had probably learnt of the writer's friendship with his uncle, the Duke of Connaught. Perhaps he also heard good reports from his wife's family, the Tecks, for whom Rudyard had written 'The Spies' March' for the Prince Francis of Teck Memorial Fund for the Middlesex Hospital.)

Only in August could the Kiplings start to feel cheered by news from the battle front, as the Allies steadily inched their way forward along the Somme. By now Oliver Baldwin had joined the 2nd Battalion of the Irish Guards in France and Rudyard would write to boost the morale of this 'lion heart' (as Carrie described him).[118] Even on holiday in Cornwall in September Rudyard could not let go his resentment towards Germans. Having seen launches bringing in bodies of people killed in recent submarine attacks, he told Oliver approvingly how a mob had tried to attack 'a dog-Hun and three bitches' who had lived for over a year in a boarding-house overlooking the sea. He was disappointed to learn that the Germans had fled by a back door and the two boys who perpetrated the 'riot' were fined ten shillings each.[119]

As a sign of the times, the Kiplings were delayed by a railway strike on their way home. Discussing the future peace with Landon and some friends in early October, they were still not fully convinced it would actually happen. But the end was indeed close to hand and Rudyard was ready to leap in, a couple of weeks later, with his indictment of Germany in his poem 'Justice':

> A People and their King
>   Through ancient sin grown strong,
> Because they feared no reckoning
>   Would set no bound to wrong;
> But now their hour is past,
>   And we who bore it find
> Evil Incarnate held at last
>   To answer to mankind.

According to Carrie, this stern, unforgiving message was syndicated to 200 newspapers around the world.

Early the following month Rudyard was writing uncomprehendingly to his school friend General Dunsterville who had just carried out the military operation that made his name in military circles: feinting in Stalky fashion so as to convince the Turks that he commanded a much larger army than he actually did. This had prevented the Turks from taking advantage of the disintegration of the Russian army and marching into Persia, which would have disrupted oil supplies and threatened India. Back home, Rudyard told Dunsterville, the English had been watching events 'stupefied like children at a cinema ... The last four years have slain all our faculty for emotion and there isn't a sign of jubilation anywhere. Of course Europe is back where she was in the 8th century when the Roman Empire finally smashed but our main preoccupation now is that the Hun shall be made to suffer.'[120]

At last, on 11 November, came news of the armistice. The Kiplings did not relax until it was confirmed the following day by the tolling of bells at the churches in Brightling and Burwash. But then, soon afterwards, came another realisation, encapsulated in Carrie's inelegant diary entry: 'Rud and I feel as never before what it means now the war is over to face the world to be remade without a son.'[121]

Eighteen

Waking from Dreams

1919–1925

Rudyard took six years to recover from the immediate effects of the war. Whatever image he used – whether emerging stupefied from the cinema, as he told Stalky, or 'coming out of an an-aesthetic – before things had adjusted themselves to sight and hearing'[1] (his words to his Bath doctor William Melsome), the meaning was the same: he had been through a numbing experi-ence and needed time to regain perspective and equilibrium. When, in November 1921, he was awarded a doctorate by the University of Strasbourg, he made a short address on the post-war situation which he titled 'Waking from Dreams'.

For the time being Rudyard was exhausted, both physically and mentally. He had warned against the war, he had lobbied and cajoled to improve Britain's defences, he had railed against all manner of defeatism, he had encouraged his son to make the ultimate sacrifice. Yet, in November 1918, he found himself alone, without his son John, in the middle of a still hostile world he did not understand.

Ironically, he was more famous than ever, fêted on all sides, not merely by the King, but by foreign dignitaries, war veterans, academics and society hostesses. Ironically, too, the Empire was at its zenith. Once territorial gains from the recent conflict had been confirmed at the Paris peace conference in 1919, the 'pink bits' on the two globes in his study showed more parts of the world under British sovereignty than ever before. Others might have regarded this as vindication of a twenty-year personal crusade for the imperial ideal. Rudyard, however, felt entirely out of sympathy with the forces of democracy and self-determination the war had unleashed. So far as he could see, the former had brought only social and industrial unrest, and the latter were likely to create problems for the running of the Empire, particularly in India.

He could summon little energy for a great state-of-the-nation poem. Whereas in 1902 he had raised people's sights in 'The Lesson' and apportioned blame in 'The Islanders', now he could only manage 'The Gods of the Copybook Headings', a stubborn instinctive plea for traditional nous, while 'Chant-Pagan', his lament for the returning Boer War soldier, was echoed only whimsically in 'The Scholars', which told of battle-hardened young naval officers being introduced to undergraduate life in Cambridge. He reminded his readers that these men had 'touched a knowledge outreaching speech' and 'by God, if they owe you half a crown, you owe 'em your four years' food'.

As the peace-makers sat down to business in Paris, he had more personal priorities. One way he felt he could come to terms with the war was to pursue what he now saw as a sacred task of creating fitting memorials for the men who had lost their lives. For the majority, this meant devoting time to the Imperial War Graves Commission; for his son, it required him to write a noble and enduring history of the Irish Guards in the conflict.

If there was one poem which expressed his innermost thoughts, it was the often overlooked 'Seven Watchmen', which served as the dedication to *The Years Between* – and therefore the summation of his collection of war-related verses. These few simple lines suggested that man should reject the temporal world – the seven watchmen with their visions of the glory and the power – and listen to his inner voice, 'But the Kingdom – the Kingdom is within you'. More than ever, Rudyard's post-war output was to express the struggle between the demands of the individual and society. His efforts to resolve this dilemma (partly through his

Christianised Freemasonry) provided the basis for his art. But that did not assuage his own pain.

When Dorothy Ponton, one of Elsie's pre-war governesses, returned to Bateman's as secretary in early 1919 she noticed 'insidious changes in the family'.[2] Since she did not elaborate, she might have been referring to the household management: only one member of the staff had survived from before the war. In her own role she no longer had use of Park Mill Cottage at the bottom of the garden, but had herself to find accommodation in the village.

More likely, she was pointing to the toll that the war (and John's death) had taken, individually and collectively, on the Kipling family. Rudyard's pain could be seen most clearly in his diminished physique. He had never been a large man: his height on his wartime passport was given as five foot five and three-quarter inches. Now, with his persistent stomach pains, his weight had fallen to a puny eight stone eleven and a half pounds. In addition, Miss Ponton recalled in a short privately published memoir in 1953, he had 'lost his buoyant step'.

Less obvious was the extent of Carrie's suffering. Unlike her husband, she had no outlet for her feelings in poetry, nor could she escape to London clubland. Most of the people she knew locally were part of Rudyard's circle; her only close friend was the eccentric Lady Edward Cecil, with whom she shared the bond of a lost son. Essentially, she was still an immigrant in an unwelcoming land. As a parent, with the same deep relationship to John as Rudyard's to Josephine, she could not help wondering if her son's death had been necessary – recalling how her husband had earlier, if only briefly, blamed her for their daughter's death. Dutifully, she plunged herself into her role of running the estate. But her efforts to regain some normality in her life were cruelly undermined in March 1919 when her mother died in her sleep. For over twenty years the two women had kept up a twice-weekly correspondence across the Atlantic. Now, Carrie admitted, her mother's death 'tears up all the roots I have left of my childhood, home and life'. This feeling of dislocation was all the more painful when Carrie learnt that, as she suspected, Beatty had spent all Anna Balestier's money. Carrie received the paltry sum of $3723 and some family jewellery after her mother died. On the death, in 1923, of her Aunt Emma – the childless widow of her father's brother Joseph – she received a further $9697 which had been held in trust under her rich grandfather's will.

The strain showed as Carrie's already stoutish body fleshed out, and a woman who had been plain and occasionally neurotic became matronly and demanding. Since he was going through his own grieving and had little to offer her emotionally, Rudyard's response was to let her take control. Carrie had been dominating enough before the war, but afterwards accounts of the Kiplings' behaviour invariably depicted a man who had given up his run-of-the-mill relations with the outside world to the care of his wife. Enid Bagnold, wife of Roderick Jones, provided a consensus view: 'I would have said, but nobody knows, that he and his wife had a hard time together. She seemed to feel herself the guardian of his genius, the governess of his working hours, even his hours for bed. They had death-battles on the subjects of his dogs.'[3]

Rudyard once told Herbert Baker how to have a successful marriage: 'Never justify', he observed, 'Never say I told you so.' Later he would speak to one or two close friends, such as Gwynne, about his own matrimonial difficulties. One hint was his 1924 story 'The Enemies to Each Other', a reworking of the Genesis myth about the Garden of Eden and the beginning of the battle of the sexes, from an Islamic perspective. Certain phrases seemed to reflect hard-won experience: 'when the steeds of recrimination had ceased to career across the plains of memory, and when the drum of evidence was no longer beaten by the drumstick of malevolence, and the bird of argument had taken refuge in the rocks of silence'. Rudyard was referring to this (in the absence of any credible alternative) when he told Oliver Baldwin on 4 October 1918, 'I've got a story that would blister the paper it's written on. So I can't send it you tho' I wish I could.'[4] Since Carrie's diaries made no mention of this or any other tale at the time, Rudyard must have written it and, like many of the fragmentary manuscripts which he finally pulled together in *Debits and Credits* in 1926, put it aside, taking care, in this case, not to inform Carrie. If nothing else, it projects two mates adjusting to the emotional ups and downs of their interdependency.

Rudyard might have coped better, but for the steady erosion of his own valued support systems. During the war his great friend Perceval Landon had lived at Keylands and was in regular contact with Rudyard. He was the only person whom Carrie was always happy for her husband to see. Towards the end of the war, however, Landon had decided he could no longer afford the rent on Keylands when he was away. To Rudyard's intense disappointment, Landon gave up his tenancy and based himself on a flat at the wrong end of the King's Road. Rudyard was delighted whenever his friend returned for occasional visits.

He was also affected by the deaths that continued after the armistice. At an inopportune moment in January 1919, shortly before the start of the Paris peace conference, Theodore Roosevelt died, inspiring Rudyard's poetic effusion 'Great-Heart'. Before the end of the month William Isted, the old hedger immortalised as Hobden in the *Puck* stories, passed away. In July Rudyard acted as pallbearer at the funeral of his distinguished uncle Sir Edward Poynter and then, in February 1920, came the loss that hit him hardest: the death of Aunt Georgie whose love for him had always been stronger than her aversion to his politics.

Only a few months earlier Aunt Georgie had shut up her house in Sussex and returned to London, bringing Rudyard's involvement with Rottingdean to an abrupt and unsatisfactory close. Her move was forced upon her as a result of a turbulent period in the life of her granddaughter, Josephine's great friend Angela Mackail. In order to escape her overpowering family (which revolved on the axis between Aunt Georgie in Rottingdean and John and Margaret Mackail in London), Angela had escaped into an unsuitable marriage to Jim McInnes, a Lancashire-born lieder singer of Scottish ancestry. She was only twenty-one at the time of her wedding in May 1911 and, within a short time, McInnes had become a drunken abuser, assaulting not only her, but her simple-minded sister Clare, who was Elsie's age and had often visited her at Bateman's. (Tony Gould, biographer of Angela's son, the writer Colin MacInnes, suggests that Clare was raped by her brother-in-law.) By early 1917, when her third child Mary was born, Angela was having to hide from her husband in the houses of friends such as Mary Wemyss. When McInnes came to Rottingdean to look for his wife, Phil Burne-Jones showed some spirit, for the first time in his life, by wrestling the burly baritone to the ground. The pain of Angela's messy divorce was not helped by the death of her baby daughter Mary from pneumonia in February 1918. The headstrong Angela did not wait long before jumping into marriage again in December that year – this time to an Australian army engineer, Captain George Thirkell who, perhaps thinking he was doing the right thing to remove her from the scene of such recent anguish, whisked her out to Australia as soon as he was able in January 1920. (Like another family member Hugh Poynter, 'Thirk' – initially, at least – was assisted financially by Stanley Baldwin.) The infant Mary was buried in the Burne-Jones plot in Rottingdean. But before Angela left for Australia the family decided that Aunt Georgie, who was seventy-nine in 1919, could no longer remain in North End House on her own. Since the Mackails' house in Pembroke Gardens was full with Angela and her children (until they left), Aunt Georgie had to live in West Kensington, in lodgings at 55 Holland Road. It was there that she died in February 1920. (Angela Thirkell, the name she began to write under, mentioned none of these murky details in her sunny memoir of life at *Three Houses* – the Grange, North End House and her parents' at 27 Young Street, Kensington.)

These events were watched with quiet amazement by Elsie, the third member of the Kipling family at Bateman's. The emotional extravagances of the Burne-Jones family were so different from her own parents' quiet stoicism in the wake of her brother's death.

Outwardly dutiful and pragmatic, she had something of her Macdonald grandmother's wilfulness that occasionally manifested itself in, for example, her annoyance at her father's verses 'The Female of the Species'. More than ever, now that she was an only child (albeit of reasonably mature years), she found herself bearing the emotional burden of her parents' expectations and frustrations. It was an almost impossible role to be cast into.

After the war she did her best to pick up the threads of her social life. She attended the wedding of Lady Diana Manners (the future Lady Diana Cooper), she was a bridesmaid at her cousin Margot Baldwin's wedding, her own father gave away her great friend Cecil Bailey – all in the first six months of 1919. But Elsie experienced no romance herself. When her high-spirited cousin Oliver Baldwin visited Bateman's in November 1919 it was only natural that she should take an interest in the friend who accompanied him, a tall, stiff fellow Old Etonian Irish Guards officer called George Bambridge. Rudyard was delighted to call upon the account of two more witnesses for his history, Elsie had an agreeable period before Christmas of, as her mother's diary put it, 'meeting many young Guardsmen' and Carrie admitted, the day before Oliver left, 'We all love to have him and deplore his leaving.'[5] And then there was that plaintive addition: 'A hint of a son about the house always crosses with his visits.'

Oliver himself had spent the five months since his demobilisation in June working for the fledgling Secret Intelligence Service or MI6, as a passport control officer in Boulogne.[6] Finding this work petty and bureaucratic, he decided after Christmas to go with Bambridge to North Africa. In those days Algiers rather than Tangier was the destination for louche members of the bourgeoisie looking for hashish and buggery. Oliver loved Algeria's warmth and freedom, and one can imagine his writing back to Bateman's (to both Rudyard and Elsie), telling them, as he wrote in his autobiography *The Questing Beast*, how infinitely superior French colonisation, with its lack of a colour bar, was to the British. Bambridge left after a month, bound for Morocco. Oliver stayed behind, grew a beard and moved in with a French painter, Roger Duval, who introduced him to a colony of French artists, including Etienne Dinet and Eugène Deshayes. The coded references in his book to enjoyable walks in the desert with Arab boys are clear enough.

Mediterranean sun was to be a regular lure for the Kiplings. But it provided no easy solutions for Elsie in her immediate search for romance. Carrie's friend Lady Edward Cecil did her best to help. She was surprisingly well disposed to the world: following the death of her husband in December 1918 she no longer felt inhibited about her relationship with Lord Milner. She tried to honour her late husband's memory by publishing posthumously his book, *The Leisure of an Egyptian Official*. However, this did not please other family members, who thought this gentle satire on social and political life in Cairo was inappropriate. Rudyard probably helped with editing the text, which carried (with the words slightly transposed) his admonitory epigram from earlier days: 'Here lies a fool who tried to hustle the East'.

Since her own son was dead, Lady Edward pushed forward another neighbour, Oswald Frewen, Rudyard's witness at the battle of Jutland, as a suitable match for Elsie. Young Oswald frequently visited Bateman's on his motorcycle (though he could never entice Rudyard to take a trip in his side-car). In October 1921 he found Elsie 'growing on' him. ('After tea Ma turned on the Jutland tap and I spouted while Kipling absorbed knowledge and Elsie chortled.') In February 1922 he thought Elsie was 'looking really beautiful and ... as ever, very pleasant and friendly'.[7] But nothing came of these initiatives and Elsie remained at home, unsatisfactorily sharing her life with two depressed parents.

By then, Rudyard had washed his hands of the peace-making in Paris. He had always been suspicious of President Wilson's intentions, but when he began to hear what was happening at the conference table he was disgusted at the Allies' failure to push Germany until 'the pips squeaked'. With the American President more concerned about the future of his 'baby', the League of Nations, than the details of making Germany pay, and with Britain (under the influence of John Maynard Keynes) painfully aware of the need to build up Germany's economy, it was left to Clemenceau, chief negotiator for France, the country which had suffered most in the war and the one which would bear the brunt of any future German irredentism, to press for the fullest possible reparations. Rudyard could only agree whole-heartedly.

In the immediate aftermath of the war he had still hoped for a different outcome. At the British general election in December 1918 large crowds had bayed for German blood, as Lloyd George's Liberal-Unionist coalition swept back into power with a huge majority. At that stage Rudyard believed it worth lobbying for his views in advance of the forthcoming Paris peace negotiations. He had been encouraged by the outcome of Congressional elections in the United States in November 1918 – when Republican opponents of President Wilson's wary approach to the peace had also triumphed. Although now elder statesman rather than active politician, Theodore Roosevelt was adamant that Germany should be forced to surrender unconditionally. At the end of December 1918, Rudyard was so excited to receive a letter from Roosevelt outlining his views (and the post-election American mood) that he took it to Lord Milner, the new Secretary of State for the Colonies, who was shortly to attend the peace conference as part of the British team.

With delegations from various countries congregating in London in advance of the peace talks, Rudyard was 'commanded' to attend a couple of functions for Wilson at Buckingham Palace. But the experience only confirmed his prejudice that Wilson was 'arid and first, last and all the time, a schoolmaster'.[8]

Frank Doubleday, an American more to Rudyard's taste, was also in town, combining business (as a good publisher, he hoped to sign up the best accounts of the war and its aftermath) with pleasure (he had married for a second time in November and was enjoying his honeymoon with his new wife Florence). At a dinner given by Evelyn Wrench, founder of the newly formed English Speaking Union, Doubleday met the young British army officer Colonel T. E. Lawrence, who had made his name as instigator of the Arab revolt against the Turks during the war. The two men appreciated each other's company so much that they arranged to meet again, when Effendi invited Rudyard to join them. Rudyard agreed to attend (even though he had to break a previous engagement), because he considered 'Lawrence the most romantic figure that has come out of the war'.[9] He had first encountered the desert warrior a few weeks earlier and had immediately recognised the brilliance of a young man who had 'made more Kings than Warwick the Kingmaker ... The *Arabian Nights* are tame and unconvincing beside his adventures.'[10]

Meeting in Doubleday's freezing-cold rooms at Brown's Hotel on 3 January 1919, these three men, together with Alan Bott, a young airman who had been shot down in Mesopotamia, 'divided the world and its obligations in a manner that would have made the Versailles treaty quite unnecessary had their plans worked out'.[11] Lawrence was concerned that Britain had reached a secret deal with France that would prevent his protégé, the Emir Faisal of the Hejaz, from becoming King of Syria, as he himself had promised. He wanted to meet Milner who, as Colonial Secretary, would be responsible for the post-war settlement in the Middle East.

Rudyard was particularly interested when Lawrence spoke of seeking American involvement in the Middle East. Four days later he wrote to him expressing interest in this idea, which was similar to a half-baked scheme of his own – to give Constantinople as a mandate to the United States as a token of appreciation for her role in the war.[12] Lawrence's concept was more sophisticated – to involve the United States so as to prevent Britain and France squabbling over the spoils in the Arab world. However, Roosevelt had just died and Rudyard warned his new friend that the former President was the only man who could have brought the appropriate pressure to bear. Wilson, he said, was unlikely to be of much help as his 'most human and most politic notion is to give lofty advice and return to his national fireside'.[13] However, Rudyard promised to assist as far as he could by contacting his friend Henry Cabot Lodge, who had taken over from Roosevelt as the Republican party's most vocal critic of Wilson.

Whether Rudyard ever did this is doubtful. A letter he wrote to Cabot Lodge in March 1919 was full of praise for Roosevelt, while attacking Wilson for seeking agreement in Paris for the League of Nations before dealing with Germany. Rudyard said Wilson gave 'one rather the impression of the Labourer who entered the Vineyard at the Eleventh Hour and spent the time in a lecture on the Principles of Viticulture and the Horrors of Intemperance, instead of helping to clean up the winepress of the wrath of God'.[14] Rudyard's fine phrases did little for the cause of Lawrence or the Emir Faisal, who would soon learn that Syria had been promised to France in a wartime agreement and he would have to settle for the throne of Iraq.

Nevertheless, Rudyard believed he had made a friend. In October 1919 he invited Lawrence to Bateman's, asking him to bring maps so that the two men could plan the future of the Middle East.[15] His offer was not taken up but, undeterred, he contacted Lawrence while in Oxford on Rhodes Trust business a few months later. His note to Lawrence was undated and apparently hurriedly written. It simply asked if he and the Colonel could meet, admitting it was 'a bow drawn at a venture'.[16]

Lawrence, now a Fellow of All Souls, had little time for Rudyard's political ideas which, in common with many old India hands, were predicated on a fear of the effects that Arab nationalism would have on the sub-continent. However, Lawrence did value the older man's literary abilities enough to send him an early draft of his *Seven Pillars of Wisdom* – a suggestion Rudyard had greeted with gratuitous offensiveness: 'I may as well warn you that, if you are a pro-Yid, and think that the present cheap Hell in Palestine is "statesmanship", I shall most likely turn the whole thing back in your hands and refuse to touch it.'[17]

According to one of Lawrence's biographers, Lawrence James, Rudyard did not like what he read. He balked at the king-maker's criticism of the French role in the Middle East. As a Francophile (whose ardour for France was growing rather than diminishing), Rudyard saw France as civilisation's bulwark against a revival of German militarism. He felt France had been let down at the Paris peace conference by the British and American failure to guarantee her borders against further German aggression. 'I dare say the French are pigs from certain points of view,' he told Lawrence, 'but seldom has a race been "carted" to the extent that we and the U.S. "carted" them.'[18]

Lawrence did, however, encourage Rudyard to think more deeply about the romance of the desert. Rudyard's interest in this subject had been evident in *Egypt of the Magicians* where he described the desert as 'all devil-device ... crammed with futile works, always promising something fresh round the next corner'. By 1925 Rudyard was recommending Haggard to read Charles Doughty's *Travels in Arabia Deserta*, the classic travel book that Lawrence had prevailed on Jonathan Cape to republish in 1920. Lawrence called the work 'the first and indispensable work upon the Arabs of the desert'. Rudyard appreciated its Elizabethan prose, telling Haggard, 'It's styptic, for one thing, in style and as Culpeper would say, "helps mightily against the emerods".'[19] So far as is known, he and Doughty never met, though they shared a similar view of the world: in 1920 Doughty put out a book of verse called *Mansoul*, which looked back to John Bunyan's original source as Rudyard had done in his poem 'The Holy War' three years earlier.

Lawrence himself could not make up his mind about Rudyard. He was painfully aware of the two sides to his friend's genius. He later admonished Robert Graves, who had written in lukewarm fashion about Rudyard. 'I read your "Kipling",' he observed: 'acute: but Laodicean. I'd have written both hot and cold, by turns: for he is a very wonderful fellow and a very mean fellow.'[20]

*

Away from the Middle East, Rudyard's post-war views were as predictable and as politically incorrect. It is not necessary to quote every single example of his blimpishness. Domestically, during the national railway strike in the autumn of 1919, he believed, 'In a land where all men and most women have the vote, we are in the midst of a spirited attempt to govern the English by making them uncomfortable and frightening them. Nominally, it is the Railway men and the Trade Unions who are doing it. Actually it is the Hun, the Bolshevik and the Jew of Poland chiefly.'[21] Looking abroad in January 1922, Rudyard took 'a most despondent view of the position in Ireland, Egypt and India, and even went so far as to say that it looks as though the Empire were going to fall to pieces'.[22] Searching for an explanation, Rudyard knew where to lay the blame. After browsing through the latest volume of his friend Charles Fletcher's *Introductory History of England*, he was confirmed in his 'opinion that Liberalism is the mother of Destruction the world over'.[23]

Rudyard could not see that, with the carnage on the battlefields, the great age of High Tory Imperialism had passed. His isolation from the contemporary world became clearer as a gap developed between him and younger pre-war associates. During the war, Beaverbrook had discovered a new circle of friends, such as F. E. Smith (now Lord Birkenhead) and Winston Churchill. The Kiplings' visits to Cherkley became fewer and petered out in the early 1920s, largely because of Rudyard's distaste for Beaverbrook's role in setting up the Irish Free State.

'Taffy' Gwynne could still be relied on, but he now spoke to a smaller section of society than he once did. Before the war, under his editorship, the *Morning Post* had sold over 80,000 copies a day and had posed a serious threat to the market dominance of *The Times*. By 1919 its circulation had slumped by a quarter (while *The Times* held its own). Gwynne attempted to resuscitate the paper's fortunes with a spirited campaign in support of Brigadier-General Reginald Dyer, the Indian Army officer dismissed for ordering the massacre of unarmed Punjabis in Amritsar in April

1919. The *Post*'s fund for Dyer reached the respectable figure of £26,000, including a donation from Rudyard. However, Gwynne overstepped himself when, later in the year, he published 'The Protocols of the Elders of Zion', a forged tract that attributed the ills of the world to the Jews. In his efforts to convince his proprietor Lady Bathurst, Gwynne told her that Rudyard did not think they were 'moonshine' and neither did Leo Maxse or Basil Thomson. That was because the Protocols reflected Rudyard's views entirely. In a different context Rudyard had told Haggard as recently as 4 December 1919 that 'we owe all our Russian troubles, and many others, to the machinations of the Jews'.[24]

Haggard himself was equally susceptible to lost causes and in March 1920 dragged Rudyard into signing a letter to *The Times* in support of the Liberty League, which promised to 'combat the advance of Bolshevism in the United Kingdom and throughout the Empire'. (Its original name, the Anti-Bolshevist and Freedom Defence League, did not have the right ring.) Supporters were invited to send donations to a colonel at an address in Mayfair, who promptly absconded with the money.

It all confirmed how far Rudyard had drifted from the mainstream of British life. There was a poignant moment in March 1923 when, speculating about the financial crash which would follow the election of a Labour government, both Rudyard and Haggard admitted to each other that they might just be out of touch with the times. As before the war, Rudyard had no sympathy with modern culture. In November 1919 he told André Chevrillon about 'one Einstein, nominally a Swiss, certainly a Hebrew who (the thing is so inevitable that it makes one laugh) comes forward, scientifically to show that, under certain conditions Space itself is warped and the instruments that measure it are warped also'.[25] He admitted he did not pretend to understand the mathematics, but was clear that 'Einstein's pronouncement is only another little contribution to assisting the world towards flux and disintegration'. Equally, Rudyard showed minimal interest in the works of Freud, and while he was clearly aware of developments in modern literature, he never commented on James Joyce, Virginia Woolf or E. M. Forster. When he first read Lytton Strachey's *Eminent Victorians* he thought it 'downright wicked in its heart'.[26] As Strachey's biographer Michael Holroyd has intimated, Rudyard was beginning to think about his mortality and how his own career would be treated by future chroniclers.

Rudyard's more personal preoccupations were already clear in April 1919 when he visited one of his London haunts, the exclusive literary dining coterie known simply as the Club. (Barred from election, Winston Churchill had formed the 'Other Club' with his friend F. E. Smith.) Rudyard enjoyed getting away from Sussex, with its pervasive memories; he told war stories and was reported to be on 'very good form'. However, he could not shake off his brooding introversion, for he told a fellow member, Sir William Osler, that 'he would not be surprised if in a few years the monastic life was revived – as men were seeking relief from the burdens of a hard world and turning more and more to spiritual matters'.[27]

One young man who appreciated the subtle mixture of tradition and spirituality in Rudyard's work was the American poet T. S. Eliot, who reviewed *The Years Between* in the 9 May issue of the *Athenaeum*. The content of this particular collection (Rudyard's political blasts before and during the war) held no great appeal, but Eliot, who had just delivered his early *Poems* to Leonard Woolf at the Hogarth Press, made a realistic assessment of Rudyard's place in English letters. 'Mr Kipling is a laureate without laurels. He is a neglected celebrity. The arrival of a new book of his verse is not likely to stir the slightest ripple on the surface of our conversational intelligentsia.' Eliot's acutest remark was to add, 'The mind is not yet sufficiently curious, sufficiently brave, to examine Mr Kipling,' implying that there were aspects of Rudyard's work that might take years to fathom. (As critics are belatedly noticing, Rudyard's influence was apparent in *The Waste Land*, the verses Eliot was working on at the time. Having been able as a young man to recite 'Danny Deever' from memory, Eliot looked to Rudyard – and the music-hall – for inspiration in moulding popular and classical themes.)

Recognising the unwelcome truth of Eliot's barbed comment that he was a 'neglected celebrity', Rudyard (with Carrie at his side) worked to correct this image. During the war his books had sold well: 77,087 copies of the Uniform and Pocket Editions in 1918–19, compared with 61,110 in 1912–13. With the peace, however, his sales began to drop. When in the autumn Macmillan wrote to point this out, Rudyard was annoyed. He accused his publisher of failing to promote his books, which had been 'allowed to sell themselves'. He claimed, through the mediation of A. P. Watt, that this would have been unwise with a business one third his size. 'As things stand, it is worse than unwise. For the last quarter of a century Macmillan has been in charge of a property of mine which was developed, I do not say in spite of his exertions, but certainly with the minimum of attention on his part.'[28]

So long as Rudyard was occupied with his history of the Irish Guards, his publishers had little to chew on. Macmillan had to be content with putting out a collection of his *Letters of Travel (1892–1913)*, comprising articles from his trips on his honeymoon in North America and Japan, to Canada and to Egypt. Publication, which had been postponed from before the war, was scheduled for June 1920. Hodder & Stoughton, which had stolen a march on Methuen to produce his *Collected Verse* in 1912, was allowed to publish a three-volume Inclusive Edition of his poetry in December 1919. Methuen had to deal with Leslie Cope Cornford, to whom Rudyard entrusted the additional job of compiling anthologies of both his verse and his prose. 'There will be no "passionate protests" from the author,' he promised his friend, 'whatever scheme you devise, whether that be propagandesque, picturesque, philosophical or a mixture of the lot.'[29]

Rudyard had not finished castigating his publishers. On 20 November 1920 he wrote a long letter of complaint to Watt about his American affairs.[30] Wisely, Effendi valued his personal friendship with Rudyard enough to send his assistant, Sam Everitt, to

Bateman's the following August. When the Doubleday company came up with a plan to publish Rudyard's books in Britain through its new acquisition William Heinemann,[31] Rudyard decided it was not worth jeopardising his existing arrangements with Macmillan. While Effendi was in England, Rudyard preferred to deal with him as a friend. Having taken over Heinemann following the death of the firm's founder in 1920, Doubleday moved its printing works out to a green-field site at Kingswood, near Banstead, in Surrey. When Rudyard came to view it he suggested a small ornamental pond and fountain, and later supplied water lilies and goldfish from Bateman's.

His established publishers were clearly on their mettle, however, with anxious memos winging from old Sir Frederick Macmillan, the chairman, to his son Daniel: 'Of course you cannot keep Kipling waiting and we must make a proposal ... We must be as liberal as possible as we must not forget that Hodder & Stoughton & many others would give their eyes to get R.K.'[32]

In his efforts to reach out to a new market Rudyard recalled his wartime experience of the powerful medium of cinema. From October 1920 the name Randolph Lewis frequently appeared in the Bateman's visitors' book. He was sent by Pathé Frères to help Rudyard develop screenplays for two films called *Without Benefit of Clergy* and *The Gate of the Hundred Sorrows*. Intriguingly he took over from an earlier Pathé emissary, noted in the same source as M. Gans – in fact, the young French director Abel Gance, fresh from his first success, *J'Accuse*. But Gance lost interest in Kipling material and went on to film his epic *Napoleon*. Menwhile, encouraged by Theda Bara, whose career Rudyard had tangentially helped launch, the cinema industry was going through an Orientalist phase, and Pathé chose the sexiest possible subject matter from Rudyard's oeuvre. *Without Benefit of Clergy* is a tragic tale of an Englishman's love for a Moslem girl in India, while *The Gate of the Hundred Sorrows* brings together story-lines from Rudyard's *Mother Maturin* and his poem 'The Ballad of Fisher's Boarding-House' to produce a racy saga of drug taking and prostitution. Unfortunately Pathé produced neither of these films, though it did finance an idiosyncratic low budget 'one-reeler', *The Ballad of Fisher's Boarding-House*, the first film made by Frank Capra, in 1922. In his autobiography *The Name above the Title*, Capra recalled how, in an effort at realism, he had tried to hire West Coast tarts for the film, but they would not get out of bed for the paltry fee he offered. Subsequently, in order – so he said – to stimulate further interest from the studios, Lewis sold the screenplay of *The Gate of the Hundred Sorrows* to the *New York Times* magazine. (After being used as an aide memoire for *Kim*, *Mother Maturin* was mysteriously lost, probably burnt by Carrie because it was too revealing of Rudyard's penchant for low life in India. So this *New York Times* piece on 23 April 1923 is the nearest approximation to this lost novel that anyone will ever read.)

Rudyard was predictably annoyed, though he charitably attributed this incident to the young man's inexperience. Carrie quickly contacted the family solicitor to see what rights had been infringed. (Five years later, another film-maker wanted to revive *The Gate of the Hundred Sorrows*, but was uncertain if the English censor would allow the use of 'dope' in the plot. Taking her lead clearly from her husband, Carrie told Watt, 'The dope is not dope; it is opium, but I don't suppose the dope censor would distinguish between it.'[33])

For their own entertainment, Rudyard and Carrie occasionally stole up to London to see a show – usually something undemanding such as a Gilbert and Sullivan operetta. After Aunt Georgie's funeral and the delivery of *Letters of Travel* to the press, they suddenly decided, towards the end of February 1920, to take a short trip to the Isle of Wight. Lorna Baldwin, who was staying at Bateman's, recalled Carrie putting her head round the door of Elsie's drawing-room and announcing, 'Tomorrow we are going to the Isle of Wight.' When Elsie asked why, her mother said, 'Because, according to the newspapers, the island is bathed in spring sunshine.'[34] Elsie, who had a reputation as a doom monger (she was known as 'Bird of Ill Omen', according to Lorna), predicted that this would not last. It rained for most of the journey, which was not enhanced by a puncture to the Rolls. However, when they reached Ventnor on the south of the island, the skies brightened and the Kiplings, with Elsie and Lorna, enjoyed a few days in the sun.

Having been unable to travel to America for her mother's funeral, Carrie paid her respects by visiting the Five Rocks, her brother Wolcott's old house in nearby Chale, where she, her mother and her sister Josephine had stayed in 1891. In a spirit of nostalgia Rudyard took his wife across the Solent to the scene of his own childhood unhappiness in Southsea – a memory which still preyed on his mind. At Lorne Lodge Carrie recorded that this was where Rudyard 'was so misused and forlorn and desperately unhappy as a child' and he 'talk[ed] of it all with horror'.[35] Rudyard's decision to take her there now (when he could have done so on several previous occasions) suggests a conscious effort to communicate with his grief-stricken wife by sharing part of his earlier life.

The combination of sun and intimate experience encouraged the Kiplings to stop wallowing in self-pity and to travel abroad for the first time since the war. At the beginning of the month André Chevrillon had sent him a copy of his latest book, *Marrakech dans les Palmes*, and Rudyard had replied, saying he had liked the descriptions of sights and smells, but could not understand his friend's liking for the 'barbaric music ... for I always thought that Europeans were not affected by the scales of coloured people – always excepting those imbeciles who find satisfaction in the horrors of "jazz" music which is pure nigger'. He admitted he would like to see the place. 'But travel is not for me – yet.'[36]

Just over a month later, on 16 March, he had changed his mind, as he set off for France with Carrie, again at short notice. Her diary gave no details of their movements, apart from a visit to a bullfight on 5 April and their return, via Paris, towards the end of the month. Carrie needed the change; her diary entries for early March showed someone at breaking point as a procession of ungrateful servants took their leave: on 2 March, 'Nellie Beeching, sewing maid, who has been taught everything under me, received every kindness for 16 years, comes to say since her father's death she decided it will be to her advantage to work at home. No word of thanks for all I have done for her. No sign of gratitude ... 4 [March] Cook gives notice. 6 [March] Housemaid gives notice.' Carrie may well have thrown a fit and demanded to get away from the dismal Sussex winter with its painful memories.

At the same time, after more than two years' involvement with the War Graves Commission, Rudyard wanted to see its work at first hand. Over the course of the previous year the organisation had begun the huge task of collating information, preparing cemeteries, hiring labourers and gardeners, and reburying hundreds of thousands who had died. It had to do this at a time when the front line was still devastated, relatives were beginning to converge on existing temporary graves and the press campaign against the Commission had hotted up. After Rudyard had chosen some simple words from the Book of Ecclesiasticus for an inscription, 'Their name liveth for evermore', which would grace the Lutyens-designed memorial stone in each cemetery, the cantankerous Lord Hugh Cecil questioned Rudyard's bona fides for this job since he was 'not a known religious man'.[37] With great poignancy, given the continuing uncertainty about his own son's fate, and after considerable debate, Rudyard also produced some suitable words for the headstones of unidentified graves: 'A soldier of the Great War – Known unto God'. He put on record his feeling that headstones should commemorate a man's regiment as well as other details. He took on the chairmanship of a sub-committee responsible for registering the names of all the bodies found on the battlefields. And he wrote a basic public-relations booklet, *The Graves of the Fallen*, that provided good value for Kipling collectors when published by His Majesty's Stationery Office in April 1919 at the modest price of sixpence.

However, the attacks on the War Graves Commission had continued and a vote of censure was scheduled in Parliament on

4 May 1920. A week earlier Winston Churchill, the Commission's new chairman, asked Rudyard – now buoyed with first-hand knowledge of conditions in the field – to address a meeting of one hundred and fifty MPs who had served in the war, in a committee room in the House of Commons. This helped rally support, making it easier on the day of the debate for William Burdett-Coutts, the unenterprising member for Westminster who was the Commission's main parliamentary voice, to win the debate – assisted by the emotional response to a letter he quoted from Rudyard, 'You see we shall never have any grave to go to. Our boy was missing at Loos. The ground is of course battered and mined past all hope of any trace being recovered. I wish some of the people who are making this trouble realised how more than fortunate they are to have a name on a headstone in a named place.'[38]

Rudyard's short trip abroad also gave him time to consider his forthcoming address to the Royal Society of St George on 23 April, the feast day of England's patron saint. The Society, founded in 1894, took patriotism to the point of racism. Its magazine, *The English Race*, attacked the Welsh, Scots and Jews for selling the pass at Versailles, and published charts showing how the other nations of the United Kingdom had higher rates of illegitimate births and mental illness than England. Its St George's Day dinner was a colourful occasion, with red and white roses at each table, the presence of the Grenadier Guards dressed in Tudor and Georgian uniforms, and a menu whose centre-piece was 'the roast beef of Old England' (Sussex baron, for choice) brought in to the accompaniment of fife and drum. But although Rudyard was an honorary Vice-President of the Society, he chose, as in his *Puck* stories, to stress the heterogeneity of English culture. Quoting Daniel Defoe's lines,

> A true-born Englishman's a contradiction.
> In speech an irony, in fact a fiction,
> A metaphor intended to express
> A man akin to all the Universe,

he described the Englishman as 'like a built-up gun barrel, all one temper though welded of many different materials, and he had strong powers of resistance'. Various influences, from the Romans to Democracy, had helped mould the English character, with its essential 'imperturbable tolerance'. Occasionally, when domestic conditions were inimical, the Englishman took ship for some distant land, where he could 'seek or impose the peace which the Papal Legate, or the Medieval Trade Union, or a profligate Chancellor of the Exchequer denied to him at home'. Thus was the Empire born, Rudyard told his audience, and not in a fit of absence of mind.

As always, he was claiming a special genius for the English. But for all his pride in his nationality, Rudyard never tried to make it an exclusive club. As his mother had told him thirty years earlier, and he reiterated in his poem 'The English Flag', 'And what should they know of England who only England know?' Before long he was to refine these thoughts into the deceptively light-hearted poem 'We and They', which accompanied his 1926 collection of stories *Debits and Credits*:

> All nice people, like Us, are We
> And every one else is They:
> But if you cross over the sea,
>   Instead of over the way,
> You may end by (think of it!) looking on We
>   As only a sort of They!

The St George's Day dinner proved a welcome diversion, for throughout the rest of 1920 Rudyard was plagued by uneasy reminders of the war. At the end of April he courted controversy by opening the war memorial in nearby Etchingham. This was interpreted as a snub to his own village – an impression reinforced when he later declined to participate at the unveiling of the Burwash memorial. In May he was forced to reject the initial casting of the bronze memorial he had commissioned for his son in Burwash church. At the recommendation of his friend Herbert Baker, who was occupied with War Graves Commission work, he had chosen the young sculptor Charles Wheeler for the job and arranged to use the words *Qui Ante Diem Periit* (from Henry Newbolt's 'Clifton Chapel') as an epitaph. Seeing the wreath around the inscription, Rudyard asked Wheeler to tighten the ribbon binding the laurels because 'John would not have liked a loose strap'.[39] However, he noticed a fault in the casting of the bronze, which had to be redone.

In July the Kiplings made a second battlefield tour, covering nearly 1500 miles, visiting some thirty cemeteries between Ypres, Amiens and Rouen. The highlight for them personally was their painful and fruitless attempt to discover where their son had fallen at Loos. At Arras Rudyard showed his compassion when he drove out of his way to take a photograph of an inaccessible grave for an old woman from Durham whom he had met the night before. In Rouen he was struck by the 'extraordinary beauty of the cemetery and the great care that the attendants had taken of it, and the almost heartbroken thankfulness of the relatives of the dead who were there'.[40]

There was a moment of light relief in December when Rudyard won an injunction preventing Genatosan Limited from advertising its patent food, Sanatogen, with the words from 'If–':

> If you can force your heart and nerve and sinew
>   To serve your turn long after they are gone,
> And so hold on when there is nothing in you
>   Except the Will which says to them, 'Hold on!'

The company had refused Rudyard's request to pay one hundred pounds to a charity of his choice for infringing his copyright. Its counsel, Quintin Hogg KC, tried to show that not only had Rudyard's poetry been widely quoted in all sorts of media but that Rudyard himself had lifted snatches of songs from other authors. Mr Justice Peterson was unimpressed by this argument and awarded forty shillings damages and costs.

In the new year, Rudyard's attention was turned to the Arab world. A few months earlier Lord Milner had been in Egypt trying to reach agreement with nationalist leaders before the San Remo conference in April confirmed details of the post-war settlement of the Middle East. But the Colonial Secretary had enjoyed little success and, in a widely predicted move, he resigned on 14 February 1921 to make way for Winston Churchill. Having retired from politics, Milner was at last able to marry Lady Edward Cecil, though for Carrie Kipling this proved a mixed blessing as her friend was now taken up with her duties as chatelaine of her new husband's small estate Sturry Court, on the banks of the River Stour near Canterbury.

Slightly earlier, on 23 January, Rudyard had been fascinated to meet Emir Faisal of the Hejaz at Seacox Heath, the seat of the Goschens, a respected local family of diplomats and statesmen. (The link probably came through Milner and his new wife, whose grandson Lord Hardinge of Penshurst later married into the Goschen family.) The Emir was in a delicate position as he had been unceremoniously ejected from Syria by the French and was lobbying for the throne of Iraq. According to his British 'minder' Ronald Storrs, Faisal was not impressed by Rudyard's persistent questioning about the varieties of camel in Arabia and asked if the Englishman thought he traded in these animals.[41] But, inspired to an extent by Lawrence, Rudyard was genuinely interested in the Middle East as a crucible of noble sentiments and great religions. On 1 February he was in Brighton, watching the Prince of Wales open the Indian war memorial – another personal triumph, as he had worked hard within the War Graves Commission to ensure that Moslem and Hindu sensibilities were respected.

With their appetites whetted by Lawrence, Rudyard and Carrie were encouraged to look to the Arab world for their first trip outside Europe for eight years. Algeria was an obvious choice as young Oliver Baldwin had sung its praises so highly. He himself had left North Africa in August 1920 and had travelled, via Constantinople, to Russia, where he managed to get himself incarcerated in a Bolshevik prison, suspected of supporting the Armenian independence movement.

The future of the Kiplings' trip was thrown in doubt, however, when, on 7 February 1921, less than two weeks before the planned date of departure, Rudyard needed to consult Bland-Sutton about the pain in his stomach. Priding himself on his knowledge of dentistry, the eccentric surgeon decided that his patient's problems were caused by infected teeth, all of which needed extracting immediately. Since Carrie's brother-in-law Theodore Dunham had also recommended this procedure,[42] Rudyard reluctantly agreed to an operation two days later. While under an anaesthetic, he was given 'a most thorough exam' by Bland-Sutton, who pronounced him otherwise healthy. (Only a few months earlier, in October 1920, the surgeon had subjected himself to the same ordeal.[43] For all his scientific rigour, his clinical judgement was often quirky, even suspect. He was a regular visitor to Chirk Castle, the Welsh border estate of Lord Howard de Walden, whose heir recalled an elderly great-aunt asking, 'Sir John, what is your favourite operation?' 'Circumcision, dear lady,' was the reply.[44])

Since Rudyard was not fitted with new teeth until July, he was, understandably, feeling 'very ill' when he, Carrie and Elsie climbed into the Duchess on 18 February and made their way to Marseilles, *en route* to Algiers. Before leaving home he wrote to a Frenchman who had contacted him with an extraordinary story a couple of years earlier. Maurice Hamoneau had been shot while fighting on the Western Front. His life was saved by the copy of *Kim* he was carrying in his breast pocket. The book's cover and first forty-five pages absorbed the force of a German bullet. Hamoneau was so grateful that he sent Rudyard not only the book but the Croix de Guerre he had won in the conflict (both of which were later returned). Through their sporadic correspondence Rudyard discovered a man with similar views on the world. When Hamoneau became the father of a girl in December 1920

Rudyard wrote touchingly, 'A thousand congratulations and all the good wishes in the Alliance of Civilization (one does not say "the World" since the Boche also is alive) ... Daughters are quite the nicest things that exist (I know) and I foresee that you will go in bondage to her all the days of your life.' Now he wanted Hamoneau's help in contacting the French Foreign Legion when he was in Algiers.[45]

In the North African capital, the Kiplings were joined by Oliver Baldwin's frivolous and attractive sister Lorna. While Elsie and Lorna gambolled in the grounds of the Hotel St Georges, Rudyard enjoyed observing the well-heeled English families who had fled inclement weather and political conditions at home; among them Lady Astor, 'as amazingly energetic as ever, with the figure of a girl and the volubility of a nigger revival meeting',[46] and old Mary Wyndham's grandson Guy Charteris, a keen entomologist (and future father-in-law of the writer Ian Fleming) who had identified thirty-seven different species of butterfly on the North African littoral.

Rudyard was keen to understand how his beloved France was handling its post-war colonial responsibilities. He was pleased, and a little surprised, to find the Algerians 'serenely occupied with their own affairs, into which, it appeared the French entered as not too exacting comrades'.[47] He ascribed the general state of good relations variously to Islam in North Africa being less caste-ridden and therefore more homogeneous than in Asia, to the lack of 'organised bodies of public opinion in France to advocate the claims of the ineffective in order to justify their own inefficiencies' and simply to the fanciful formula he had heard from Gustave Le Bon in his father's house in Lahore, '*C'est l'emprise morale*'. Because of his health he did not see as much of the country as he would have liked. He failed to make contact with the French Foreign Legion, whose commander was in the south sorting out a border conflict. Instead, he had to be satisfied with being escorted round Algiers by an ex-mayor, M. de Galland. His own prejudices were shown up only too readily when he was invited on board the visiting USS *Pittsburgh*: Rudyard approved of the Southern officer who called his men 'dirty niggers' and claimed to be the only person on his ship who could manage the 'coons'.[48]

However, he did appreciate the city's 'beauty of colour, mystery, darkness, blazing white minarets and gaily tiled mosque fronts'. It could have been Lahore, except for a new sensation: 'a mixture of warm dust, petrol and jasmine, and Arab. I have not smelt Arab before. He is milder than nigger but not so nice as decent Asiatic.'[49]

With Oliver Baldwin held in Armenia until the summer, Rudyard wrote to George Bambridge giving his impressions of North Africa. He also asked George, who was staying in Biarritz, to obtain photos of the Guards Cemetery at Bayonne – part of his campaign to bring all such cemeteries under the control of the Imperial War Graves Commission.

Crossing back to France, the Kiplings passed through the 'queer, quiet old portlet' of St Tropez to Cannes, which Rudyard described as 'like the third act of a music-hall review' with its 'pink and white houses, blinding sun, blinding green vegetation, roses, wistaria, irises, judas trees, even hydrangeas and rhodo-dendrons all out together; and wonderfully dressed females of surpassing beauty promenading up and down through it all'.[50] He was only sorry that the Carlton Hotel, where they stayed, had been built by a Hun company before the war and represented 'the last ideas in horrible magnificence' – a feature young Elsie and Lorna rather enjoyed. They were having a good time, as Rudyard captured in a limerick after a day trip along the coast:

> There were two young ladies of Nice
> Who drank seven cocktails apiece
> Then they tried to undress
> In the Paris express
> But were stopped by the local police.[51]

On their journey home the Kiplings decided to avoid Paris and take a more easterly route through Alsace. There they met their old friend, the former Julia Catlin from New Jersey, who had not returned to her château in Compiègne after the armistice. Instead, she had divorced her alcoholic husband Chancey Depew and married (for a third time) a French war veteran, General Emile Taufflieb, with whom she lived in Neuilly, just outside Paris, and, now that he was a senator in his native Alsace, in Strasbourg. The General took Rudyard and his party on a motor tour of the battle front at Verdun. Rudyard was overwhelmed by the sight of what the French had endured during the war, describing it as 'as terrible as anything the North has to show'.[52] Julia Taufflieb recorded him taking off his cap, passing his hand over his head and saying, 'For the first time in my life, I have come to a place where I feel that if anyone gave me another idea my head would not stand it – it would burst.'[53] Despite his holiday, Rudyard had clearly yet to recover his composure.

While they were in France, Lorna's father Stanley Baldwin was brought into the Cabinet as President of the Board of Trade. Her naïve response was, 'Now we'll have green lights on our car and be able to drive as fast as we please.' Rudyard took this as a challenge to change his own motor: in June the pre-war Rolls was sold for £1550, £200 more than he had paid, and replaced with its latest equivalent. In the face of these economics Rudyard's tongue was only partly in his cheek when he told the writer Rupert Croft-Cooke that Rolls-Royces were the only cars he could afford to run. He might have sold his seven-year-old Duchess earlier, but Carrie regarded it as a link with John and was reluctant to see it go.

On the Continent, Rudyard had been alarmed by the extent of anti-English feeling which followed the Versailles treaty, in which Lloyd George's government had refused to support Clemenceau's demands for an independent buffer state in the Rhineland or even to guarantee France's existing borders. Admittedly, there were few places in the world where Rudyard was not disappointed – Egypt, India and Ireland, where later in the year he was 'more depressed over the terms to Southern Ireland than he ever was during the war'. But ever since childhood he had developed a special affection for France. Having been schooled by his father in the lessons of the Franco-Prussian War, he understood French fears about German militarism. More than ever, in the wake of the war, he was convinced that France and Britain shared a genius for civilisation.

He soon had an opportunity to elaborate on these themes, as he had been sounded out by his friend André Chevrillon about receiving an honorary degree from the University of Paris at the Sorbonne in November. This was to coincide with the publication of Chevrillon's book *Trois Etudes de Littérature Anglaise*, containing a major essay on Rudyard, and with another degree ceremony in Strasbourg. In his address to the Sorbonne, Rudyard contrasted the charm and simplicity of French and English fairytales with the violence of German ones, with their emphasis on the werewolf, a beast which switches unpredictably between human and blood-thirsty animal. Sticking to literary references, he counselled his audience against putting its faith in grand Utopian organisations such as the League of Nations, which he likened to the Literature of Escape. At the end of the day, he stressed that France and England (always England, never Britain) had a common interest in the struggle against 'barbarism'.

He was still in Paris, being received by the Chamber of Deputies and lionised by French society, when *The Times* published a lighthearted piece in which he recalled his 'first assault' on the Sorbonne one drunken night in 1890. When Julia Taufflieb gave a reception for the Kiplings at her house in Neuilly, she hired an actor from the Comédie Française to declaim Rudyard's pre-war ode 'France'. 'For days before,' she recalled, 'I had been pursued by three French translators of that poem, each begging that his version might be the one to be read. I chose Puaux's.'[54] At the time, Rudyard must have been the most revered Englishman in France.

On New Year's Day 1922, he told Cope Cornford he had at last finished his Irish Guards history, adding that it was 'rather fine, too, in that it deals all with the Eternal Verities, complicated with awful official lies'.[55] But he soon found reasons not to be satisfied with a book he described to Miss Ponton as his 'great work ... done with agony and bloody sweat'.[56] She recalled it going through four versions, all of which needed typing. Carrie had a rule that no text could leave the office with Rudyard's writing on it. When she saw a copy about to go to Watt with her husband's autograph corrections, she refused to allow it out of the house. Miss Ponton told the story nicely: ' "But this is not the final copy," she [Carrie] remarked. Mr Kipling raised his eyes to heaven and groaned, then glanced quickly at me. "It's all right, Carrie," he said, after a pause. "I've made only a few alterations; they're quite clear." But Mrs Kipling was adamant ... He bowed wearily to her wishes, and the work was handed to me to be re-typed at high pressure.'

In early March Rudyard again thought he had finished the history, thus giving the family an excuse to book a passage on the Orient Line's s.s. *Ormuz*, bound for Gibraltar and their winter holiday in Spain, which he described warmly as 'the nearest Oriental land I know'.[57] Rudyard found some War Graves business to perform in Gibraltar, where Elsie was thrilled to dance with Prince George on the visiting liner the *Queen Elizabeth*. Carrie was in one of her filthier moods. When they reached Algeciras on 23 March she announced she was going to bed and was likely to stay there for some time. She complained she was worn out by having to arrange these continental holidays, on top of her usual duties, and could not get Rudyard to realise it.[58]

For a few days around Easter the Kiplings were joined by George Bambridge who, as far as he could be said to be living anywhere, was based in Spain. He had just been in Madeira with Oliver Baldwin, who had returned from his Russian adventures the previous July in poor physical and mental shape. To Elsie's delight, Oliver came to Bateman's to recuperate. With her girlish affection for her favourite cousin she lent him her two-seater Singer car to tour Devon. During the autumn he started a doomed relationship with Doreen Arbuthnot, whom he did not love but hoped would help him out of a rut. Although he became engaged to her in the new year, he did not stay long, having obtained a job (probably with Rudyard's help) as Special Correspondent for the *Morning Post* in South and East Africa. In the manner of the Kiplings in the old days, he sailed from Southampton in the *Kinfauns Castle* in February. His fiancée saw him off at the quayside, but Bambridge, who accompanied him as far as Madeira, remarked, 'You'll never marry her' and, as Oliver admitted in his autobiography, his friend was quite right.

With his knowledge of Spain and North Africa, George was an ideal guide to the once Moorish cities of Granada and Seville. He adapted easily to the expected role of the Kiplings' surrogate son, partly because he had been in the Irish Guards and partly because his own parents were both dead and he needed a family. His father had been private secretary to Queen Victoria's second son, the career sailor Alfred, Duke of Edinburgh, later Duke of Saxe-Coburg and Gotha. George's childhood in the hierarchic world of minor courtiers had made him diffident, courteous and remote.

On 16 April, Easter Day, he took the Kiplings to a bullfight in Seville. Rudyard had been initiated into the finer points of this ritual sport by John Bland-Sutton, who was obsessed. Before the war the surgeon had written an article, 'The Science of the Bull-Ring', for Gwynne's *Morning Post*. He once likened the role of the surgeon to that of the bullfighter.[59] As a result, whenever he was in Spain or in parts of France, Rudyard made a point of attending bullfights, storing his observations for his story 'The Bull That Thought'. More generally, he had been encouraged by Bland-Sutton to take a more scientific approach to the animal world. As a keen observer of local fauna since India, Rudyard was delighted to be elected a Fellow of the Zoological Society (one of Bland-Sutton's stamping grounds) in 1921. He found he could use the London Zoo which was off the beaten track and an ideal venue for meeting friends like Doubleday.

Bambridge appears to have introduced Rudyard to the Rinconcillo, a circle of literary friends, including the homosexual poet Federico García Lorca, who hung out at the Café Almeida in Granada's Plaza del Campillo.[60] But Rudyard was not interested in intellectual chit-chat: he was working on an important speech for King George V to deliver when visiting war graves in France and Belgium in May. A few weeks earlier, he had been taken aback by yet another attempt to 'stick him' with an honour – this time the Order of Merit, which it was thought he might accept because theoretically the award was in the King's gift. Once again he declined, preferring to keep his independence, as had True Thomas in his poem of 1894. However, he was annoyed to discover that the King's Secretary, Lord Stamfordham, leaked details of his refusal to the newspapers. Almost as a gesture of apology to Rudyard, King George agreed to alter the tenor of his forthcoming trip to the war graves and treat it as a sacred journey, for which Rudyard would write not only a speech, but an appropriately reverential poem, 'The King's Pilgrimage'.

Rudyard had only been back in England a fortnight before, on 10 May, he was heading across the Channel again in the Rolls. In Calais he picked up a passenger, the Canadian High Commissioner P. C. Larkin, who needed a lift to the ceremonies the King was to perform. Rudyard was not impressed by an 'earnest Liberal'[61] who admitted he did not like graves because they made him sad. At Vlamertinghe, over the border in Belgium, he commandeered a peasant's cottage to change into his morning dress. Carrie sat in the car while the King 'did the usual very well and seemed really moved by the graves themselves'. (The King and the other High Commissioners had come in a fleet of Rolls-Royces that Rudyard found 'nothing very splendid'.) This was a preliminary to the main ceremony two days later when George V delivered Rudyard's speech at the coastal cemetery at Terlinchtun, near Boulogne. This time the King, accompanied by Queen Mary, spoke to Carrie whose curtsies, Rudyard remarked, were 'nice to behold'.[62] When he congratulated the monarch on his 'most seemly' delivery and their conversation drifted to politicians,

Rudyard was interested to observe the King's face: the look of 'a decent man who suspects he is being carted. Rather like a frightened horse.' (As evidence of his growing friendship with the royal family Rudyard had allowed himself, a few weeks earlier, to be diverted from his work to inscribe a miniature version of 'If—' for the Lutyens-designed Doll's House which was presented to Queen Mary by her family and exhibited at the inaugural British Empire Exhibition at Wembley in 1924.)

In June George Bambridge returned to England, prior to taking up a post in the diplomatic service as honorary military attaché in Madrid in August. Again he featured prominently in family outings, taking Carrie and Elsie for a day's racing at Ascot, for example. Meanwhile Rudyard persevered with his War Graves business. He donned his old editor's hat to look through the proofs of a quick book (by somebody else) on *The King's Pilgrimage* and comment on the need for more paragraphing and better typography. He continued to work on inscriptions for various monuments and memorials as they were built. He was a founder member of the War Graves Commission Masonic lodge, to which he gave the attractive name The Builders of the Silent Cities. At the same time he was putting the final touches to his Irish Guards history, which he was finally able to say was finished on 27 July. But the effort had taken its toll: Rudyard was exhausted, and even his wife thought he looked 'yellow and shrunken, like an old man'.[63] She had difficulty hiding her concern from her husband.

In August Rudyard's listlessness called for another series of major and 'very unpleasant' medical examinations. The X-rays, which required a bismuth meal in advance, showed 'no sign of the always to be dreaded cancer'.[64] But an old ulcer was found – a large area of inflammation in the colon and lower bowel from which there had been a haemorrhage, which had caused his anaemia. Rudyard was put on a 'no solids' diet and for a while lived on milk, enemas and Epsom Salts. (This may well have been the occasion when Rudyard was examined rectally. He later joked, or so Oliver Baldwin liked to recount, 'If this is what Oscar Wilde went to prison for, he ought to have got the Victoria Cross.'[65])

Rudyard's health was not improved when, in September, a row broke out following the publication of a controversial interview with him in a New York paper. Embarrassingly, the piece was by Clare Sheridan, the tempestuous artist daughter of his neighbour Moreton Frewen. In June she had accompanied her brother Oswald to Bateman's, ostensibly to sketch Rudyard for a paper she worked for, the *New York World*. Oswald recorded in his diary how he heard Rudyard's 'remark, or rather his dismissal' of the actor Charlie Chaplin with whom Clare had recently enjoyed an affair, ' "He's the Englishman who stayed in America during the war and made a lot of money, isn't he?" he said ingenuously and sweetly! He told her all about America, too, it seems – that she came in the war 2 years 4 months and 7 days too late, botched the Versailles treaty for us, and withdrew without assisting any further. She has our gold, but we have our souls. He has a great deep contempt for America, and so have the rest of us.'[66]

Now, three months later, the *New York World* had plucked the most anti-American sentiments from this conversation and published them in a front-page story headlined 'Kipling Impeaches America's War Record'. Rudyard was quoted as saying that the United States had forced the Allies to make peace at the first opportunity, instead of fighting to the finish in Berlin, and so on. With all seriousness, he had blamed America's ills on the steamship, which allowed 800 immigrants to cross the Atlantic instead of eighty: as a result, 'America was flooded with aliens of the wrong type ... America – the real America – died in 1860.' (Coming from the author of 'The "Mary Gloster" ' and several other paeans to global seamanship, this was a ridiculous line, though he had put it in the mouth of a Mrs Burton in his pre-war story 'The Edge of the Evening' and he later expanded on it in his autobiography.)

The interview caused a predictable uproar in the United States. Since Clemenceau was there at the time, he was forced to dissociate himself from Rudyard's 'diatribe', while expressing affection for the 'great writer cruelly stricken by the war'. Because London correspondents of American newspapers were laying siege to Bateman's, Carrie had to issue a statement to the Associated Press in which Rudyard claimed, 'I did not give Mrs Sheridan an interview. I did not say the things which I see she ascribes to me, and have not discontinued the habit of saying what I wish to say over my own signature.'

In the aftermath Rudyard was still not well. As a result of further consultations, Bland-Sutton decided to perform a major operation on 15 November. According to his private surgical diary, he found 'a broad band of amentum 2 inches wide embracing the ascending colon near the hepatic flexure'[67] – or, in plain English, a thick furry deposit in Rudyard's stomach near his liver. Two days later Carrie received a telegram from the King: 'The Queen and I are distressed to hear of Mr Kipling's illness. We sincerely hope that he is making satisfactory progress and that his condition does not give you any cause for anxiety. George R.I.'

When, in the new year, Rudyard's pains did not subside, Bland-Sutton glibly stated he was not worried, ascribing the discomfort to 'an adjustment after such a long arrangement'.[68] Rudyard's ordeal at the hands of the medical profession was not over, for in Bath on 26 January 1923 he had another small operation on his eyes. After such prolonged and inconclusive probing by the doctors he might have been forgiven for feeling total 'gloom and depression',[69] and have developed a healthy scepticism about conventional medicine. In the circumstances his speech to the Royal College of Surgeons a few days later on 14 February was surprisingly tame. He spoke at a dinner following the annual Hunterian oration by the President of the College, the ubiquitous Bland-Sutton (now suitably adorned with a baronetcy). Rudyard voiced no scepticism, let alone anger, about conventional allopathic medicine. Instead he adopted an elevated quasi-mystical tone, portraying surgeons (both here and in his poem 'Doctors') as dedicated searchers after the mystery of man's divinity. As he told a fellow Freemason, he tried to enlighten his audience by introducing them to 'twin secrets' from the Craft – 'the Universal Medicine and the Nature of Man's Soul – this latter, of course, the Secret of Brahm'.[70] But he admitted that he had not managed to 'make it quite clear' (one reason, perhaps, being that his ideas were going through a stage of rapid evolution). Nevertheless, his speech contained some nice Kiplingesque touches, such as the line: 'There is no anaesthesia so complete as man's absorption in his own job'.[71] Not that supping with the nation's leading doctors did him much good personally: five days later, on 19 February, he was 'feeling below par in the afternoon' and then was 'sick after dinner, followed by fainting, giddiness and a haemorrhage of the bowels'.[72]

The following month Haggard found him 'drawn and considerably aged'.[73] During their regular wide-ranging talk, Rudyard seemed unusually interested in spiritual matters. He was now convinced that the individual human being was 'not a mere flash in the pan ... but an enduring entity that has lived elsewhere and will continue to live after death'. But this metaphysical insight did not relieve Rudyard's pain, the source of which was clear, as he wondered aloud, 'whether all those that we lost in the war, his boy John and the rest, died to bring about such a state of affairs as we see today'.[74]

Rudyard's state of mind could only improve. While in Bath at the start of the year he visited an old friend, George Saintsbury. In his late seventies, Saintsbury was a throw-back to Henley, Lang and the High Tory literary world of the 1890s. An omnivorous reader and prolific critic, he had kept in touch with Rudyard over the years – while he worked at the *Saturday Review*; as Regius Professor of Rhetoric and English Literature at Edinburgh University (the post David Masson had held when he first welcomed Rudyard's *Barrack-Room Ballads*); and now in retirement in Bath, where he wandered around his set of rooms in the Royal Crescent, looking like a medieval monk, with his black skull-cap and wispy white beard. Rudyard respected Saintsbury's judgement in 'the weightier matters of the Laws of Literature'.[75] (In 1895 he wrote from Vermont asking for a copy of the older man's *Corrected Impressions: Essays on Victorian Writers.*) Saintsbury's attitude to the world was also very similar – from his reactionary politics (Orwell once wrote of him, 'it takes a lot of guts to be openly such a skunk as that'), through his love of France, to his determination (laid down in his will) that he should have no biography. In 1920 he dedicated his vinophile *Notes on a Cellar-Book* to Rudyard, who was one of the few modern authors he could stand. Yet the two men seldom met. For nearly thirty years Saintsbury had kept an umbrella which Robert Louis Stevenson had asked him to give to Rudyard who, as recently as September 1921, had pleaded, 'One of these days I want that brolly.'[76] Saintsbury, for his part, noted in his introduction to *Notes on a Cellar-Book* that 'by some cantrip of fortune' he had never had the opportunity to drink a bottle of wine with his dedicatee.

When Rudyard called on him in February 1923, Saintsbury was working on a miniature cellar-book for Queen Mary's Doll's House. Having presumably returned the umbrella, he cracked open a bottle of Tokay and was disappointed when Rudyard pronounced that it tasted like medicinal wine. The alcohol did loosen his tongue a bit, however. In the city where Jane Austen had once lived, Rudyard discussed an idea that fascinated him: about the sense of fellowship felt by people who shared a powerful joint experience – whether fighting in war, or membership of a Masons' lodge, or even familiarity with the works of an author such as Austen. The following month he began to develop this concept into 'The Janeites', his first new story for five years. On a personal level he was expressing his regard for companionship – a basic human need that, as far back as India, he had understood was essential to the well-being of both the individual and society. Nowadays, he had a sense of this from his various clubs, but he realised that this was not enough and wrestled with ideas of community as expressed through Freemasonry and religion.

Rudyard's mood was improved by news of the Franco-Belgian occupation of the Ruhr. Having tired of Germany's failure to pay reparations, her neighbours marched across the border in an effort to exact economic retribution from her industrial heartland. Britain and America were predictably concerned that this would undermine their careful policy of nurturing Germany back to economic health. But French opinion was less tolerant and demanded action, which Rudyard applauded.

In early March, when the Kiplings paid one of their now regular visits to Buckingham Palace, King George V demonstrated his concern for Rudyard's health by insisting that he sit down. By the end of the month the author felt fit enough to sail, via Gibraltar, to the Mediterranean port of Toulon, where his chauffeur Taylor met him with the Duchess (all the Kiplings' Rollses were now called the Duchess). In Toulon, Rudyard contentedly occupied himself with a crash course in the local flora. He bought a copy of an illustrated book, *Les Noms des Fleurs* by Gaston Bonnier, a former professor of botany at the Sorbonne. Opposite the title page he wrote a hitherto unpublished poem, beginning 'The Buttercup and the Berberis...', which he described as his 'Culpeper pastiche' and which comprised a suitably metrical listing of the names of nearly one hundred plants.

Rudyard was still in Toulon, where he had just finished 'The Janeites', when on 16 April his long-awaited Irish Guards history was published – to mixed reviews. John Buchan in *The Times* liked the methodical approach of 'a man of genius who brings to his task not only a quick eye to observe and a sure hand to portray, but a rare spirit of reverence and understanding'. However, the poet Edmund Blunden, who later took on Rudyard's role as literary adviser to the War Graves Commission, dissented in the *Nation and Athenaeum*, arguing it was too dispassionate: 'Mr Kipling appears not perfectly to understand the pandemonium and nerve-strain of war.'

From Toulon the Kiplings drove on 24 April to Monte Carlo, where Rudyard worked on a speech for King George V to deliver in Rome the following month. Both the royal visit and Rudyard's text proved controversial. For Italy had a new leader, the Fascist Benito Mussolini, who seemed poised to end the cycle of political violence that had plagued it since the war. The King was criticised for bestowing the Order of the Bath on Il Duce and, even more, for voicing Rudyard's opinion that the country's political crisis had been overcome 'under the guidance of a strong statesman'.[77]

The Kiplings continued up the Route Napoléon to Aix-les-Bains, where Rudyard was cheered to find a pile of letters (including one from the now widowed Duke of Connaught) congratulating him on the publication of *The Irish Guards*. His sense of relief showed how important this five-year labour of love had been to him. Over the next few days he relaxed in the hills around Aix, even going so far as to berate himself for not having had the sense to invest money in the tourist hotel he was staying in. On 8 May, after an old French chemist had showed him a foxed botany book from 1824, his long suppressed *joie de vivre* could no longer be contained and he exclaimed, 'Praised be Allah for his men and women.'[78]

Three days later Perceval Landon came over from Lausanne where he was covering the last great post-war conference, tidying up details of the settlement between Turkey and the Allies. Rudyard had heard about this meeting, where Mussolini made his début on an international platform, from Oliver Baldwin, who had attended as part of an Armenian delegation, before going to stay with Bambridge in Madrid. (Also present had been Clare Sheridan, who so attracted the Italian leader's fancy that he invited her to Rome where he tried to seduce her.) In his role as a reporter for the *Daily Telegraph*, Landon had met Oliver and been amused at the young man's support for the Armenian cause. He told Oliver that there was nothing the British Foreign Office disliked more than Englishmen meddling with other countries or peoples.[79] (The name of Colonel Lawrence was mentioned.)

While in Aix, Rudyard met Bonar Law, who had been suffering from what was diagnosed as throat cancer and was taking extended convalescence. Rudyard was so concerned about the condition of the Prime Minister, who could hardly speak and was obviously in great pain, that he took the unusual step of cabling Beaverbrook.[80] (It was ironic that he had wished this disease on the Kaiser in his thoroughly unpleasant poem, 'A Death-Bed'.)

Nevertheless, Rudyard maintained his good humour as he and Carrie journeyed home. As usual when passing through northern France, there were pilgrimages to be made and graves to be visited: in Troyes, where Rudyard had last been during his trip to the French front in August 1915, memories 'cut like hot pokers'; in Villers-Cotterets he spoke to the mayor about erecting a memorial stone to the 1st Battalion of the Irish Guards, which had engaged there during the retreat from Mons at the start of the war. Nevertheless, at Beaune he was carefree enough to order six dozen half-bottles of Chambertin at nine francs each – to be sent to Bateman's. Along the way, he amused himself with composing 'A Song of French Roads', which applauded the French (Napoleonic, indeed) genius which had created the orderly system of *routes nationales*.

Nearing the Channel, the Duchess's magneto (or generator) broke down and Taylor, the chauffeur, had to wire the manufacturer to ensure that a new part was awaiting them at Newhaven. Even before the Kiplings reached Sussex on 23 May, Bonar Law's ill health had forced him to resign, and Stanley Baldwin had seen off the challenge of the Foreign Secretary Lord Curzon to take his place as premier. Rudyard was probably unaware that while he was away an art exhibition had opened at the Walker Galleries in New Bond Street. The show comprised paintings by Miss Flo Garrard and her cousin Captain James Garrard. (Following in the footsteps of her father, cousin James had juggled an army career – he came out of retirement to serve in the First World War – with an unsatisfactory period in the family goldsmith business, before retiring to Gloucestershire to pursue his own interests.[81]) 'Maisie', meanwhile, had pursued a moderately successful career as 'a Chelsea painter' – a description she liked to use of herself. Based at 43 Glebe Place, Chelsea, since the start of the century, she was a local character with a reputation for her fondness for cats. She had shown at the Paris Salon and the Royal Academy, but was better known for her involvement in small shows of women artists, such as the Women's International. At the Walker Galleries Flo's works, which were priced between eight and seventy-five guineas, comprised mainly landscapes executed in Ireland (County Wicklow) and St Valéry sur Somme. There was one oil of Florence, where Mabel Price's great friend Vernon Lee lived. By chance, Miss Lee published her book *The Handling of Words – And Other Studies in Literary Psychology* that year. In comparison with Meredith, Stevenson, Hardy and Henry James, she found Rudyard's work inferior and took the opportunity to emphasise the point personally: 'The origin of the faulty construction, even of the misuse of tenses, lies, I fear, in the slackness and the poverty of the thought.'

Rudyard was at least thinking seriously of literary endeavour. In late July he entered a protracted correspondence with Rider Haggard who had just published *Wisdom's Daughter*, a sequel to his earlier and better known *She*. Rudyard's enthusiasm for one of Haggard's drearier efforts indicated both the importance he attached to his chats with his friend (his only regular discussions about the craft of writing) and the extent of his striving to find a wider canvas for his own powers. Rudyard offered Haggard criticism: he felt that a woman with such knowledge of 'the Continuity of Things' as the book's heroine needed to be less arrogant. But he was referring to his own aspirations when he suggested, 'You've got the whole tragedy of the mystery of life under your hand, why not frame it in a wider setting?' (He gave Charles Reade's *The Cloister and the Hearth* as a telling example of the sort of expansive work he had in mind. Indeed he called it 'one of the greatest novels ever written'.) Clearly feeling he was dealing with sensitive material (his letter was marked 'confidential and burn after reading'), he described a scenario for a trilogy about The Wandering Jew, a rootless figure, detached from the grace of

God by his role in the crucifixion, but a keen observer of history, from St Paul's day to the nightmare of the recent war.

Rudyard told Haggard he was occupied in 'answering the demands of idle idiots and helpless imbeciles', one of whom had a plan for universal peace based on the identity of the British as one of the lost tribes of Israel.[82]

Rudyard now had to prepare for an important engagement of his own. He had been elected to become Rector of St Andrews University in Scotland. This was the sort of honour he was happy to accept and he spent part of the summer contacting people who he hoped would receive honorary degrees at his inauguration in October. Sir James Frazer declined, but among the acceptances were his cousin Stanley, the surgeon John Bland-Sutton and the poet Henry Newbolt whom he had grown to know and like – through shared involvement in wartime propaganda work and through the Club and the War Graves Commission.

Travelling north for the ceremony, Rudyard stopped in London on 27 September to meet Hansard Watt, Alick Watt's second son who dealt with his agency's non-literary properties. Together they went to the American Embassy to register a contract for a film of *Kim*. Under this agreement Rudyard was to receive $50,000 from the New York-based South Church Street Company in return for an eight-year option on *Kim*. When he returned to Brown's later that afternoon, Alick Watt turned up with a draft for the first half of this payment, which Rudyard received 'with much pleasure'.

Driving to Scotland was still an arduous and sometimes hazardous journey: having reached the George Hotel in Stamford the following evening, he had to wire ahead to Ripon for rooms for the next night; later, north of Penrith, Taylor had his cap knocked off by a sparrow (which Rudyard initially thought was a clod of mud thrown from behind a wall). At St Andrews, his rectorial address on the value of 'independence' was well received. He was able to quote Robbie Burns:

> To catch Dame Fortune's golden smile
> Assiduous wait upon her,
> And gather gold by every wile
> That's justified by honour –
> Not for to hide it in a hedge
> Nor for the train attendant,
> But for the glorious privilege
> Of being independent.[83]

After giving a short talk to the University College of Dundee a couple of days later on 12 October, he was 'chaired' to his car by students who appreciated his support for their campaign for full university status. He was feeling in particularly good humour by the time the Duchess reached Harrogate on the return journey. His car had been averaging 40–45 miles an hour, with spurts of 50–54 (so Rudyard meticulously noted in the journals of his Motor Tours). The presence of young people in Scotland had done him good. His weight had risen to nine stone seven pounds. Suddenly in mid-October he was 'very keen and stirred to fresh work and impatient to begin'.[84] A couple of days later he began to pull together some fragments of stories he had had in his notion book. On 27 October he was 'rearranging quantities of his work'.[85] In early November he revised 'A Friend of the Family', one of his wartime Masonic tales. A few days later he started on a new story, 'The Prophet and the Country', which showed conclusively that his mind had finally left the war-damaged limbo of the past five years and that his daemon, his creative unconscious, was again in full working order.

This fascinating story drew directly on his experiences on his way home from Scotland less than a month earlier. In his Motor Tours journal, he had recorded how, on the fine morning of 15 October, somewhere between Doncaster and Grantham, he passed through an area of countryside where the wind 'blew the smoke of the Black Country across the North Road'. Later he came to two level crossings with 'a system of insane police controls where licences were demanded and a filthy red-diamond label offered (by a man with a workmanlike pink tongue) to be stuck on the car as a protection against further "inspections".[86]

In the story, Rudyard reworked these images and drew on his recent experience of his car's magneto breaking down in France. Stranded by the roadside at nightfall, his narrator falls into a sort of dream, in which he comes across a caravan occupied by a fast-talking American called Tarworth who has made a film attacking prohibition as a female-inspired plot to undermine the United States. As he pokes fun at pseudo-scientific jargon about microbes and immunisation, Rudyard makes the case for the value of innate common sense in the face of the deadening effects of modern civilisation (and, particularly, his old bug-bear – modern American civilisation). When, at one moment, 'a puff of air from the woods licked through the open door of the caravan, trailing a wreath of mist with it' and Tarworth 'pushed the door home', he shut himself off from the beneficial effects of native wisdom.

Rudyard was now suggesting that the values of fellowship that he had trumpeted in 'The Janeites' needed to be complemented with the rather different (but in his mind related) British virtues of independence and individualism, as he made clear in 'The Portent', another ode from Horace's non-existent Book V, which preceded the story,

> Cease, then, to fashion State-made sin,
> Nor give thy children cause to doubt
> That Virtue springs from iron within –
> Not lead without.

In arguing that judgement and integrity come from internal values and cannot be imposed from outside, Rudyard showed why, for all his strident conservatism, he could never have become a fascist.

As dawn breaks in the story, Rudyard indulges in a lyrical (but, as ever, pithy) description of the English countryside – 'with smoking mists that changed from solid pearl to writhing opal'. A hearse comes round a corner and moves on, just as the narrator thinks about being towed to nearby Doncaster to find a new magneto.

In this way Rudyard depicted his real-life daemon being restored to order. The original manuscript of the story in Durham University made this clear. Here, as the narrator curls up in his car, expecting to spend the night on the road, he refers to the onset of sleep and 'those gates ... forever shut through which my Personal Demon used, long ago, to descend and possess'.[87] (In other words, he used to dream creatively, but no longer.) Meeting Tarworth somehow stimulates the return of his powers. He is confronted with a *doppelgänger* who represents an alternative, brutish side of his own personality. (In the context of the story he is given a psychic inoculation.) Towards the end, Rudyard *qua* narrator hears his daemon say, 'Did you think I had abandoned you? I am here.' In his published story Rudyard toned down these hints of his personal involvement. However, with its complex imagery of immunology, cinema, politics and nature, mixed with Rudyard's observations from his travels (for example, Americans coming ashore from cruise liners at Monte Carlo, and 'tankin' up' and trying to kiss everybody), 'The Prophet and the Country' showed the author back on form.[88]

Rudyard made the most of his creativeness. By mid-November he had sent four further stories to Watt for dissemination to various newspapers and magazines. At the same time he did not neglect his more formal work – writing his poem 'London Stone' to commemorate the fifth anniversary of the armistice, discussing inscriptions for further war memorials with Fabian Ware, attending meetings of the Rhodes Trust and advising on the naming of the streets and avenues at the British Empire Exhibition at Wembley. The great bard of Empire showed surprising restraint in his suggestions: visitors entered the new Wembley complex through a 'Great Circle' of gardens, passing through the East or West Quadrant to Palaces of Engineering and Industry. The individuals commemorated in the names of 'ways' or gates were Anson, Drake, Watt, Faraday, Stephenson and Arkwright.

The main dampener on the rest of the year was the defeat of Baldwin's government in the general election in December. Rudyard's cousin had fought on a platform of old-fashioned protectionism, which he believed would provide the solution to the country's deteriorating economy. For a while it seemed that domestic politics might return to the pre-war tussle between free trade and protectionism. Although the Conservatives tried to soldier on without an overall majority, Baldwin was forced to resign in January 1924, when Ramsay MacDonald became the first Labour Prime Minister.

Then, suddenly, towards the end of the month, Rudyard had a temporary recurrence of his depression. This had followed yet another offer of the Order of Merit (possibly a recommendation in Baldwin's resignation honours list). However, the cause was more directly linked to Baldwin's quick visit to Bateman's (for breakfast) on 26 January when Carrie described him as 'very clamlike'. Three days later, her husband was 'quite hopeless with depression, nerves and nerves'.[89]

What had happened was that Elsie had indicated that she wanted to leave home. At the start of the month she had uncharacteristically declined to accompany her parents to a local New Year children's party. Instead, on 2 January she went to London to dine with George Bambridge. It seems likely that the subject of marriage was broached. As an honorary attaché, Bambridge had limited means of financial support. But Elsie's father was rich: with her twenty-eighth birthday fast approaching on 2 February, she was probably so desperate to leave home that she agreed to tackle her parents about providing an adequate income for herself and thus, by extension, for Bambridge. Carrie made no mention of an engagement in her diary at this stage. But she did refer to a rearrangement of Elsie's financial settlement 'to meet the changes of the times'.[90] Elsie's trust had originally been set up in 1916 and the following June Rudyard had given his daughter an investment ledger inscribed in his own hand with a saying from Confucius (which might have served as an overall Bateman's motto), 'It is as necessary and as important to know one's own income as it is to know one's own mind.'

One reason for Baldwin's visit to Bateman's was to give his assent, as a trustee, to a change in Elsie's settlement. She could now call on an income of £3634 (in 1925), rising to £5023 in 1931[91] – not huge wealth, but more than enough to live well on at the time. Free from responsibilities of office, Baldwin is also likely to have told Rudyard the truth about his son Oliver. Rudyard no doubt knew that, after gambolling round the world, young Oliver had a profound sense of social injustice and had recently joined the Social Democratic Federation, which was affiliated to the Labour party. Just over a year earlier, after Oliver had returned from Africa, Rudyard had advised him not to flirt with Labour ('try not to make an unusual ass of yourself',[92] he said in friendly enough tones) and expressed satisfaction that his young cousin once removed had turned to Freemasonry – a calling Oliver quickly rejected 'owing to its local bourgeois outlook and starched-shirt hypocrisy',[93] opting instead for the brotherhood of Socialism. That must have been hard enough for Rudyard to take, but now he needed to be told that Oliver had come out as a homosexual and was living in Oxfordshire with his lover Johnnie Boyle. If nothing else, this information potentially had some bearing on Elsie's future, for there was a strong implication that Oliver's relationship with George Bambridge had been gay.

Women were not supposed to know about such things in the Kipling household, which explains Carrie's observation about Stanley Baldwin's reticence. Rudyard must have considered Oliver's coming out a personal betrayal. For years he had taken a stand against homosexuality. When Dunsterville's son Lionel experienced it at his school, Cranbrook, Rudyard wrote to his old friend (somewhere in Central Asia),

This is perfectly sickening. You can imagine what the old Coll.

would have been with a system of cubicles instead of the old dormitories and the masters moving about at all hours through 'em – which was what saved us. I don't think that as the world is today the thing will count against him in the future as it would have done in our time. And yet – how many men do we know who have risen to all sorts of positions who when they were kids were – not found out! I always go in *deadly* fear of the cubicle system at any public school. They had it at Wellington and Eton, as we know, is . . .[94]

His words literally trailed off the page.

Hidden in this curious outburst was a mixture of conflicting sentiments – a personal revulsion towards homosexuality, coupled with a realisation that many men he knew had practised it and, far from being harmed, had risen to high rank. His attitude reflected the fact that, while he was comfortable with the two sides of his head, he had trouble relating with conflicting elements in his sexuality.

More immediately, at the end of January he found himself wrestling with unsettling news: his daughter looked as though she would shortly leave home and Oliver Baldwin, whom he had looked on as a son, had adopted a sexual nature he disdained. What is more, Elsie appeared on the brink of marrying a man whose own sexual orientation was unclear. The combination of these pieces of information sparked Rudyard's depression. He was able to put his sour mood to good use writing one of his most profound later stories, 'The Wish House', an intriguing medico-psychological drama about an overtly physical Sussex country woman, Grace Ashcroft, who is so besotted by an erring but sick lover that she visits a medium (or 'wish house') and asks to take on her man's illness – in an effort to cure him and bring him back to her. ('I says: "Let me take everythin' bad that's in store for my man, 'Arry Mockler, for love's sake." ') However, this selfless act has consequences for her own well-being and at the end of the story the lesion on her leg is known to be cancer.

Through Mrs Ashcroft's eyes, Rudyard slyly observed modern village life – with the Saturday 'shopping' bus, the 'tractorisin' firms' and the girl who asks for her quarter pound of suet to be chopped at the butcher because she cannot be bothered to do it herself. Once again he grappled with a subject that obsessed him – the healing power of the mind. Significantly, he came closer than ever to explaining his ideas on the complicated relationship between suffering and love. He implied that, as individuals can take on another's pain, so selflessness, the state of 'grace' (as in Mrs Ashcroft's Christian name) and sacrifice (even, though he does not say it, the Crucifixion of Jesus Christ), can assume and absolve human anguish.[95] If this was not immediately obvious (little was obvious in a later Kipling story), it was clearer in the two poems that framed the tale in *Debits and Credits* – 'Late Came the God', which marvelled at woman's capacity to bear pain (a tribute to his wife's fortitude), and 'Rahere', where love transforms the 'faceless, fingerless, obscene' leper into something without 'blemish':

'Tis a motion of the Spirit that revealeth God to man.
In the shape of Love exceeding, which regards not taint or fall,
Since in perfect Love, saith Scripture, can be no excess at all.

In his autobiography Rudyard noted how a reviewer in the *Manchester Guardian* (among others) had pointed out the similarities between Mrs Ashcroft and Chaucer's Wife of Bath, particularly the 'mormal on her shinne'. He admitted 'And it looked just like that too! There was no possible answer, so, breaking my rule not to have any commerce with any paper, I wrote to the *Manchester Guardian* and gave myself "out – caught to leg".' However, the usually meticulous Rudyard was careless with his references, for it was Chaucer's Cook rather than his Wife of Bath who had this affliction. This slip showed how, occasionally, with his autodidact's eagerness to display his erudition, Rudyard could be too clever by half.

It was no coincidence that, while Rudyard was writing 'The Wish House' in February, he and Carrie were again taking the waters in Bath where she was having three more cysts removed from her head. Although he knew that his wife had suffered from these fatty extrusions since childhood, he, with his worries about cancer, must have wondered if her melancholic state would somehow turn them malignant. And, more curious, she must have read his story and understood this dimension of its meaning.

The Kiplings' concern about their own health had become an obsession. In March 1924 Rudyard wrote to Bland-Sutton prissily recording that he had not been eating uncooked fruit 'except half a grape fruit for dessert and I get as full of wind as a Zepp'.[96] Consequently he badly needed his spring holiday in the Mediterranean. Rather later than usual he, Carrie and Elsie sailed to Gibraltar, before picking up the car and, as was becoming a pleasurable habit, making their way slowly up through France. As soon as he arrived at the Hotel Reina Cristina in Algeciras, Rudyard wrote as jauntily as he could to George Bambridge in Madrid:

> My wife and daughter, maid and me,
> The Queen of Spain and Auntie B.
> Are at this dreary place again
> A-promenading in the rain.[97]

Rudyard visited the garrison at Gibraltar, where he was impressed by the fine library of some 40,000 volumes – 'mostly trash but some priceless historical stuff'[98] – and he went on board HMS *Tourmaline*, commanded by his friend Charles Fletcher's son, Alexander. Informing Fletcher approvingly how the Spaniard was being 'Mussolinied for his own good', he referred sadly to a perpetual, nagging feeling: he had visited 'my boy's battalion on the Rock. He'd have been close on 27, and might have had a company of Micks. Lucky you, with a boy in command of a 36 knot deestroyer and enjoying, so I thought, every minute of it.' Although he and the family proceeded to Madrid, he decided not to take

up Bambridge's invitation to address a meeting of 'Spanish intellectuals'[99] on this occasion.

Instead, he was struck, as he wrote to Fabian Ware on 8 April,
that when he reached France, 'where (Insh'Allah!) I hope to be at
the end of the month, I ought to go round the cemeteries again;
as my informations are out of date, and I can't tell the people who
ask me what is being done now, and what is going to be done'.[100]
However he did not 'want any of the – gravely – interested parties
with me ... I just want to slip out from Paris and look at things
for myself.'

His interest in the library in Gibraltar suggests he was research-
ing his extraordinary story 'The Eye of Allah', first mentioned in
Carrie's diary in July. At its simplest, this tells of John of Burgos,
a medieval illuminator of manuscripts, who returns to his English
monastery with a microscope, the secrets of which had been
discovered in the multi-cultural (Christian, Jewish and Moslem)
universities of Spain. However, his sophisticated abbot Stephen
de Sautré refuses to allow this innovation into his closed environment and smashes it up: he can see that his pre-enlightenment
world is not yet ready for the radical advances in knowledge that
the microscope will bring.

Rudyard examines the dilemma of people who take their
professional insights beyond their usual limits. In 'The Eye of
Allah', the artist tires of copying his illuminations and wants to
branch out into the forbidden territory of drawing devils as well
as saints. He, along with the physician Roger of Salerno and the
philosopher Roger Bacon, are all keen to extend the boundaries
of their disciplines.

Rudyard plays with the theme of going beyond established
limits in another context. Both John of Burgos and Abbot Stephen
have mistresses. John's woman is in Spain (and there is idle gossip
in the monastery that she may be a Moslem or a Jewess). Subversively, Rudyard suggests that such cross-cultural and sexual
liaisons often assist for the advancement of knowledge and understanding. However, as with Holden and his inter-racial romance

in 'Without Benefit of Clergy', and Strickland who sought to understand Indian culture through disguise and subterfuge in 'Miss Youghal's Sais', such extensions of knowledge are not to be encouraged because, if such behaviour becomes the norm, society will collapse. Thus the Raj had anathematised these social deviations, in the same way as the medieval church cannot countenance premature extension of knowledge in 1266–7 (the mostly likely dates for the story, according to the internal evidence analysed by the critic Lisa Lewis). Even though, poignantly, the Abbot Stephen's 'lady' is dying of cancer (that recurring scourge in Rudyard's stories) and the microscope might bring insights that would cure it, he cannot allow this instrument to make headway – for the overall and future benefit of the community.

At last Rudyard was managing to address a story with the moral and historical complexity he had often discussed with Haggard. Abbot Stephen has learnt to walk softly as a result of two years' captivity among the Saracens (or Moslems) in Cairo – not that he was any spy, Rudyard hurriedly assures his readers. In fact, Stephen is a medieval Kim moving stealthily between cultures, faiths and systems of belief in a manner Rudyard would have appreciated.

On the basis of Mrs Lewis's dating, John Coates has demonstrated Rudyard's familiarity with medieval philosophy.[101] In the late 1260s Thomas Aquinas was working on *Summa Theologica*, his great synthesis of Augustinian Christianity and Aristotelianism, which was the Catholic church's retort to Islamic commentators such as Averroës (or Ibn Rushd), who had rediscovered Aristotle through Arabic translations and threatened to undermine Christendom with their incisive interpretation of his works. Rudyard's story suggests that Stephen de Sautré has encountered Averroist thinking in Cairo, understands its radicalism and sees the microscope as a similar danger to his society. Even in this unfamiliar territory Rudyard does not stray far from certain perennial themes. Confronted by the pain of the soul in his complex, changing world, Abbot Stephen notes, 'There is, outside God's Grace, but one drug, and that is a man's craft, learning, or other helpful motion of his own mind.'

The story shows the influence of various individuals – T. E. Lawrence, George Saintsbury, Cardinal Gasquet (whose book *English Monastic Life* is quoted almost verbatim in places) and, in particular, the polymath Sir William Osler who, as a curator of the Bodleian Library in Oxford, had tried to acquire manuscripts by Averroës and his fellow philosophical iconoclast Avicenna. Although he had died in December 1919, Osler bequeathed the Library several priceless manuscripts, including at least one from the famed School of Salerno. He had presided over the Roger Bacon colloquium that he wanted Rudyard to address in 1914. 'The Eye of Allah' was Rudyard's belated tribute to a friend whom he had respected rather than loved.

By the summer of 1924 Rudyard's more upbeat mood had returned and he was seeing the sunny Mediterranean in a different light. In 'The Bull that Thought' he managed to transmute his experience of bullrings in southern France and Spain into one of his most cheerful late stories. This was a celebration of instinct and artistry: a tale of a lively, playful bull, with the intelligence to taunt his matador tormentors. Rudyard started it with a typical stylistic feature – an anecdote about a car trial along the long straight roads of the Camargue, thus contrasting the precision of the mechanical world with the meandering, darting, slightly cruel antics of Apis, 'the supreme artist' among bulls, who was a model for Rudyard's own creative spirit. To bring the story closer to home he linked it with his verses 'Alnaschar and the Oxen', an affectionate tribute to his own herd of Sussex cattle.

He was working on this story at Bateman's in May when Elsie informed her parents that George Bambridge was coming back from Madrid and she wanted to make their engagement official and set a date for their wedding. Now it was Carrie's turn to be cool: George was nice enough, she felt, but she did not want to lose Elsie. She realised how dependent she had become on her daughter's company, particularly after John's death. Given the money lavished on Elsie's social life, including her coming out, Carrie hoped for someone better than an 'honorary' and therefore impoverished diplomat, lacking connections. She, like Elsie, was clearly still unaware of Oliver's homosexuality. But did she have some sense that Elsie was falling into the old family trap of latching on to Bambridge simply because of his closeness to her great friend Oliver Baldwin? Elsie, in her happiness (and perhaps her keenness to escape from Bateman's) did not care. On 2 August she wrote to 'my dear old Olly', inviting him to dine with her and George as 'somehow I feel that you would bring John's special blessing with you'.[102]

In the event, the Kiplings rose to the occasion, brushed aside any concerns and, as might be expected, carried out their conventional duties as parents. They met George's nearest relation – an aunt, Mrs Louis Floersheim – who proved not only agreeable but wealthy. Unexpectedly, George had a legacy of £27,500 under the will of his late uncle Louis Floersheim, which he appears to have put into a marriage settlement that Rudyard agreed to top up so that, in addition to Elsie's own trust, it produced an annual income of £4482.[103] In addition, Rudyard bought his daughter a house in Brussels where George was due to be posted. Carrie took Elsie shopping in Paris for a wedding dress. In anticipation of the nuptials the Bateman's Rolls was refurbished by the carriage-maker Hooper.

On 22 October, over 1000 guests crammed into St Margaret's, Westminster, for the Bambridges' marriage. With his lack of musical ear, Rudyard may not have registered the Germanic nature of the three items of music before the entrance of the bride – the Overture to *Die Meistersinger*, the 'Liebestod' from *Tristan* and the Prelude to Act Three of *Lohengrin*, all by Wagner. Within forty-eight hours the newly-weds had packed their bags for Brussels and the Kiplings returned to Bateman's, where Carrie could only moan about having 'to face an empty side of our life' and for the present being 'too weary to meet it'.[104]

*

With his creative rehabilitation under way, Rudyard was in better spirits than his wife. Three days after the wedding he was back in his study or 'mould-loft' (as he called it), working on 'Fairy-Kist'. This was a psychological detective story, overlaid with Masonic and gardening references, about a man seriously disturbed (or 'fairy-kist') as a result of shell-shock, who is suspected of murder – until a group of Freemasons (in particular, a doctor) ascertain that he could not have committed the crime because of his familiarity with a story (Mrs Ewing's 'Mary's Meadow', a childhood favourite of Rudyard's) which had been read to him by a nurse while he was in hospital. More subtly than in 'A Prophet and the Country', 'Fairy-Kist' showed a man's consciousness being restored to well-being. Rudyard makes much of the fact that in his war-blasted state, Wollin was potentially susceptible to any bizarre idea – 'Jack the Ripperism or religious mania' – that he might encounter. Only through the creative imaginations of these professional men, piecing together the strands of his story as if evidence in a detective story, and assisted by the hazy, benevolent quasi-occultism of his housekeeper, can Wollin's mind be restored to wholeness. In this way Rudyard was acknowledging the mixture of expertise and magic required in the healing process. His insights reflected in part his continuing intellectual debate about the benefits of medicine, and in part his reaction to his own situation, where he was emerging from his depressed post-war state. Adopting a sophisticated psychological idea, he suggests the rediscovery of self after a breakdown requires a process of building up the frames of consciousness. While that healing, that metaphorical piecing together, is happening, a sufferer has to find what solace he can. Rudyard's own interest in plants is more understandable in the light of his reference to the disturbed Wollin gaining 'Comfort out of plants and bot'ny, and that sort of stuff'. If further evidence were required that Rudyard was alluding to himself and his own recovery from a near psychotic state, it came in the poem 'The Mother's Son' which accompanied 'Fairy-Kist' when it was published in book form:

I have a dream – a dreadful dream –
A dream that is never done.
I watch a man go out of his mind,
And he is My Mother's Son.

At the general election, a few days later on 28 October, Stanley Baldwin and the Conservatives were returned to power with a handsome majority (and some help from British intelligence, which leaked the Zinoviev letter, a Russian document allegedly stirring British workers to pro-Soviet activity). Rudyard had taken an interest, not just because he was Baldwin's cousin, but because he was linked to the consortium which had taken over the *Morning Post*, following Lady Bathurst's decision to sell this loss-making concern. The paper had been bought by a group of right-wing Conservatives, headed by the Duke of Northumberland, who had backed the National party a few years earlier. Rudyard does not appear to have put money directly into the paper, but he was soon peppering the board members with ideas. One of them, Sir Percy Bates, chairman of Cunard, told Gwynne – who was still editor – in August that he had a long letter from Rudyard (later a good friend of his) 'offering all sorts of help on subjects, titles and if we want them quotations'.[105]

Without Elsie to amuse them, the Kiplings sought diversion in social activities. On 10 December they visited William Cazalet, father of the up and coming MP Victor Cazalet, at Fairlawne, his sumptuous eighteenth-century house set in 3000 acres, near Tonbridge. There they met several fixtures of the inter-war social scene, including the writer Hugh Walpole and the portrait painter Sir John Lavery, whose gossipy wife seemed to know all about Philip Burne-Jones going to the United States to sell his father's paintings. 'I don't suppose that there will be more of that ancestor left "unexploited" than a high-class bacon factory leaves of a pig,'[106] Rudyard commented to Elsie. In London the following day he and Carrie lunched with the Duchess of Somerset, where a Mrs Wingfield was complimentary about Elsie's teas in Brussels.

(It says something about the Bambridges' sybaritic life-style and George's lack of a proper role in the Embassy that this was mentioned.) Later Rudyard went to the Athenaeum where the Archbishop of York seemed to think his son-in-law was in the air force. 'Tell that to G. and see him jump,' Rudyard informed his daughter. A few days later, invited to dinner to meet the King at Hall Barn, Lord Burnham's estate near Beaconsfield, Rudyard showed his dependency on his wife by worrying that, as he would be on his own, he might forget something when dressing for dinner.

Family members sensed the Kiplings' loneliness and did their best to keep Rudyard and Carrie entertained. Baldwin's eldest daughter, Diana Munro, had married a stockbroker who helped look after the Kiplings' investments. On a visit to Bateman's she brought news of her wayward brother Oliver, who had befriended a housekeeper at Chequers who was sympathetic to his life-style and secretly fed him every Monday evening. Lorna Howard also called in as she was looking for a house with fifteen bedrooms in the vicinity. The big family Christmas at Astley was reminiscent of those at Cherkley before the war. However, Elsie was not there – an absence that struck Carrie deeply, for she took the trouble to note in her diary that Lorna was 'almost a daughter'.[107]

Not surprisingly, the Kiplings did not wait long in the new year before embarking on their first trip to Brussels. The highlight of their visit in early February 1925 was the Bambridges' 1850s fancy-dress ball, which ended with sausages and mash at three in the morning. At least, when she came home a week or so later, Carrie could state rather melodramatically that she was happy to have 're-found' Elsie who had sometimes seemed to her to be dead.[108]

In London, Rudyard attended his first meeting of yet another club, the Beefsteak, where he had been put up for membership by Landon and Sir Frederick Macmillan. He was amused at its practice of calling every servant by the same name, Charles. After initial reservations about being forced to sit at a communal table,[109] he found it 'a very nice human little pot-house'[110] and described it as the favourite of his clubs in his autobiography. Landon had returned from a trip to China and not only wanted to rent Keylands again for a while, but was talking about travelling with the Kiplings on the Continent in the spring. 'Exciting prospect!' Rudyard enthused to Elsie.

In March the Kiplings were back on the other side of the English Channel, this time accompanied by Landon, *en route* for Rouen, Chartres and the South. Among the 11,000 graves at the Imperial War Graves Commission cemetery in Rouen, Rudyard talked with the head gardener and the local contractors. 'One never gets over the shock of this Dead Sea of arrested lives,' he told Rider Haggard, '– from VCs and Hospital Nurses to coolies of the Chinese Labour Corps. By one grave of a coolie, some pious old Frenchwoman (bet she was an old maid) had deposited a yellow porcelain crucifix!! Somehow that almost drew tears.'[111] It did not make him weep, or perhaps he could not admit that to Haggard, but it did profoundly affect him. Recalling similar cemeteries he had visited over the years, and the gardeners who meticulously tended the graves, Rudyard began the following day to write 'The Gardener', a story about Helen Turrell's search for the grave of her nephew, who had lost his life in the war and who is clearly her illegitimate son, and about the gardener who comforts her and is clearly Jesus Christ. With its social ambivalence, this was a fine and moving story about a woman who is given a glimpse of the resurrection. It was imbued with extra feeling because Rudyard began to write it after spending the day in Rouen, paying tribute to another independent woman who saw visions, Joan of Arc.

Rudyard was inspired by Landon's presence to write a sonnet celebrating the great stained-glass windows at Chartres. 'Colour, old man, is what *au fond* clinches a creed,' he told Haggard, nicely paraphrasing his poem: 'Colour and the light of God behind it. That's as near as Man will ever get.'[112] Proceeding via Rambouillet, where they briefly met a 'visibly plumped' Elsie, who was on a shopping trip to Paris, the Kiplings made their way south, stopping to visit a friend of Landon's, Princess Charlotte of Monaco, at her château outside Chartres (but she was not there), passing through Lourdes (where they kept up their religious sightseeing), before arriving in Biarritz, with its more secular comforts. 'The instant Mr L. entered the Hotel,' Rudyard noted, 'he fell into the arms of a white and fluffy woman and thereon disappeared. He admits to "knowing some people in Biarritz". *Je n'en doute pas.*'[113] Subsequently Landon left the party; with 'The Gardener' finished, Rudyard was left 'for once'[114] feeling bored.

This feeling of alienation persisted and, pathetically, Rudyard and Carrie returned to Brussels to visit the Bambridges in May. Within forty-eight hours of their arrival they heard of Lord Milner's death. They rushed home as quickly as they could, only to discover that Rider Haggard had also just died, followed by Aunt Louie Baldwin a couple of days later. Towards the end of the month Elsie visited Bateman's for the first time since her wedding. The following day Rudyard wrote to Sir Hugh Clifford, Governor of Nigeria and one of his many correspondents at the furthest reaches of Empire: 'My condolences on the approaching departure of the daughter. All sons-in-law are direct descendants of the Devil. And the nicer they are the more devilish it is.'[115] This paradoxical statement was as close as he got to condemning George Bambridge.

After the funerals, in June Lady Milner asked Rudyard to write her husband's life but, mindful of the potential pitfalls, he refused. A month later she was distressed to learn that he had resigned from the Rhodes Trust. Rudyard was opposed to the appointment of Philip Kerr, a former member of Milner's kindergarten, as secretary of the Trust. He felt that Kerr, a prominent member of the liberal and federally minded Round Table, was out of tune with Rhodes's ideas. Despite entreaties, Rudyard not only stuck to his decision but made the Trustees issue a statement explaining why he had resigned.

That summer Rudyard moved among some of the grandest people in Europe. He was invited to meet the King of Greece at Claridge's (in belated recognition of his English translation of

the Greek national anthem on the anniversary of the Battle of
Navarino in October 1918). The Queen of the Belgians consulted
him personally about her forthcoming trip to India. While in
London for a garden party at Buckingham Palace (where he
chatted with King George), he went to the theatre to see Noël
Coward's *Hay Fever*, which he found 'a really funny modern play –
with Marie Tempest at her best'.[116] In August he visited the Duke
and Duchess of Beaufort at Badminton. Having discussed the
'saintly mysteries of the pack' with a Duke obsessed with hunting,
he found Badminton exactly as he hoped it would be and Carrie
was thrilled to meet 'such a charming Duchess' (the daughter, as
it happened, of the Kiplings' royal friends the Tecks).[117]

More mundanely, he was admitted to the Stationers' Guild and
became a Freeman of the City of London. Aware of his mortality,
he began consulting people about where he should leave his
manuscripts after his death. He talked with responsible figures at
the British Museum, where the majority of his work would later
go. In the meantime he decided to send the autograph text of his
book *Traffics and Discoveries* to St Andrews University, where he
was rector. When Carrie packed this for despatch to Scotland in
October, she found herself strangely unwilling to let it go. Her
husband had always given her bound copies of his manuscripts.
This one had become a surrogate child and she clung to it pos-
sessively, as if seeking affirmation of her vital role in its gestation.

Carrie was also thinking of Elsie. George Bambridge had
proved superfluous to requirements at the British Embassy in
Brussels and was returning in the new year to Madrid where his
friend Gerald Agar-Robartes was now serving. In anticipation of
the Spanish winter, Carrie suggested that her daughter should
take advantage of the Belgian capital's reputation as a market for
furs and buy herself a suitable coat as a Christmas present. In
November the Kiplings went to Belgium to stay with the Bambridges one last time. A week after returning Rudyard caught a
cold, which developed into pneumonia. For a while he was delirious and appeared close to death. Lord Dawson, the King's

doctor, was summoned and the Bambridges came hurriedly from Brussels. By 5 December Rudyard began to pull through, though he remained feeble for several weeks. Celebration of his sixtieth birthday on 30 December was muted because of Carrie's permanent sense of loss, characterised in her pitiful comment: 'A very sad year for me with nothing ahead for the other years but the job of living.'[118]

Rudyard would have expressed himself differently. From time to time his Indian cultural heritage had a habit of reasserting itself. Since the war, he had been contemplating the old Hindu custom (about which he had written approvingly in 'The Miracle of Purun Bhagat') of the older members of the community giving up their material interests and preparing themselves for the spiritual plane. His meditations were mirrored in his writing, where his sparse late style incorporated his precepts of 'Higher Editing': for the best effect in a story, he said, 'let it by to drain as long as possible'. Not everyone was convinced: C. S. Lewis, generally an enthusiast, later commented that one needed roughage as well as nourishment in a diet. But Rudyard's approach to the world was now essentially minimalist, as he strove to make effective use of what he expected to be his last few years of life.

Nineteen

The New Conservative

1926–1931

'I have never left England any year that I can recall since the war without being held up by some dam sort of Bolshevism,' Rudyard complained to Gwynne when the General Strike prevented him from returning from his winter holiday in May 1926. 'And yet Mussolini rides the storm quite serenely.'[1] Rudyard responded with a rich man's canniness at odds with his trumpeted patriotism – sending his chauffeur Taylor home via Newhaven and Dieppe, and booking the Duchess in for a major service in Paris, where he congratulated himself he would pay for decent engineering in weak French francs, rather than for slack English workmanship in still valuable pounds.

He had spent longer than expected in the South of France, partly because he liked the colourful villa overlooking Monte Carlo where he and Carrie stayed, and partly because he needed the rest after his illness. (It was not until 28 February, thirteen weeks after his first bout of pneumonia, that he was able to dispense with a nurse.)

He put his holiday to good use collecting the various stories he had written over the previous productive couple of years. As usual, he sought to weave them into a meaningful but not too didactic structure for the book *Debits and Credits* that he planned for the autumn. Each tale was framed with a poem, the most interesting of which was 'A Legend of Truth', accompanying 'A Friend of the Family', about an Australian ex-serviceman's

unusual manner of assisting a fellow Mason in business difficulties. These verses told of two sisters, Truth and Fiction. Normally the latter held sway, glossing the 'gentle deeds' of man. But
when the stark reality of war needed recording, she made way for
her seemingly more appropriate sister. Truth did not take long to
understand that the details presented to her were 'not really half
of what occurred'. In desperation, she had to telegraph her sister:

> 'Come at once.
> Facts out of hand. Unable overtake
> Without your aid. Come back for Truth's own sake!
> Co-equal rank and powers if you agree.
> *They need us both, but you far more than me!*'

Rudyard was admitting that his painstaking efforts to relate the
history of the Irish Guards in the war had not been wholly successful. Instead, he was making claims for the ability of his more
familiar art of fiction to tell the story in the whole – a theme he
elaborated in a short speech when he was awarded the Gold Medal
of the Royal Literary Society in July. In this, Fiction became Truth's
elder sister, 'the oldest of the arts, the mother of history, biography,
philosophy . . . and, of course, politics'. He quoted the example of
Jonathan Swift, 'a man of overwhelming intellect and power
[who] goes scourged through life between the dread of insanity
and the wrath of his own soul warring with a brutal age' and who
came up with one small book, *Gulliver's Travels*, which Rudyard
described as 'like turning-down the glare of a volcano to light a
child to bed'. Again, he highlighted those at the limits of their
profession: 'writers raking the dumps of the English language for
words that shall range farther, hit harder, and explode over a
wider area than the service-pattern words in common use.'

He showed his author's regard for these basic units of communication in November when he completed some short epi-
graphs for *A Book of Words*, an appropriately named collection
of his speeches, to be published the following year. The most

poignant motto preceded 'The Uses of Reading', the talk he gave to his son John's house literary society at Wellington in 1912. It ran: 'A. "When I heard thy words, my Father, I almost fell asleep through weariness." B. "Had I foreseen that sleep, my Son, I would have put aside all else to have pleased thee alone." '² In this portentous tone, adapted from *The Greek Anthology*, a well-known eighteenth-century translation of anonymous Greek epigrams, Rudyard was apologising to his son for boring him with the poems that were quoted back to him at school. He was also regretting that he had not spent more time simply enjoying life with John.

Rudyard's daily existence was improved by his acquisition of an Aberdeen terrier, Wop, who adopted an almost permanent position on the sofa in his study. He had referred to the emotional bond between dogs and their owners in 'Garm – A Hostage' (originally published in 1899) and explored the idea of the animals' strange powers of communication in 'The Dog Hervey' in 1914. Now he wanted to state more positively that dogs were good for one's psychological health. 'The Woman in his Life', started in October 1926, was among several stories and poems Rudyard wrote on this theme over the next few years. It told how a man who has served as a sapper during the war recovered from a nervous breakdown by getting, predictably, an Aberdeen terrier. However, when this dog becomes trapped in a badger set and the man needs to rescue her, the circumstances are so similar to his war service – which involved tunnelling underground – that it threatens a recurrence of his psychosis. Only his love for the animal forces him to persevere and bring her back to the surface. Rudyard's subsequent output about dogs is often tedious for anyone who does not share his obsession. However, it offers interesting biographical insights. Its undisguised sentimentality indicates the deep reservoir of emotion beneath his conventional, rather prickly façade. (Florence Doubleday recognised this, recording how on several occasions Rudyard kissed her husband on both cheeks.³) And Rudyard was making at least some comment on his marriage in his willingness, however jokingly, to compare a dog's love with that of a woman.

Back in England in the aftermath of the General Strike, Rudyard had a newly serviced Rolls which 'pull[ed] like a cyclone',[4] running a good five miles an hour faster than before. But the engine that powered the Bateman's estate was still unreliable. Rudyard was annoyed when a kitchen maid quit because she did not like the local bus service. 'So much for the Progress of Civilisation,'[5] he complained to a friend. Further afield, in Spain, the Bambridges were already experiencing financial problems. In August Rudyard sent them £1600 which, Carrie comically noted, 'we can ill spare'.[6]

Having a close relation as Prime Minister revived Rudyard's interest in day-to-day politics. Like himself, Baldwin was struggling to make sense of the post-war maelstrom of conflicting ideologies and economic uncertainties. He felt that 'the problem of the age' was that British and other people had reached 'a political status in advance of their cultural status'[7] – or, in other words, they had the vote but lacked a mature sense of their history and way of life. As Baldwin began to articulate a sense of the traditions and 'ordered freedom' of the English, he turned to his cousin for literary and presentational advice. Contemporary political diaries, including those of Tom Jones, the deputy Cabinet Secretary, and John Davidson, later Conservative party Chairman, attest to a productive relationship between the cousins. When Jones suggested that Rudyard's prose was becoming a little too hard, Baldwin recommended he should read 'An Habitation Enforced'. He said he had done this 'over and over again'[8] – as had been evident in his famous reference (at the annual dinner of the Royal Society of St George in May 1924) to the sounds and sights of England 'since England was a land'. Rudyard would advise his cousin on the relevance of Dickens or how to appeal to the 'flapper' vote. And the exchange of views was by no means one way. Baldwin's efforts to reach his political consensus encouraged Rudyard to soften, at least temporarily, his political extremism.

With Empire and protectionism (now known as Empire free trade) back on the political agenda, Rudyard found himself treated respectfully by leading politicians, who saw him as a potential link to Downing Street. He was not impressed by the way the ambitious new Chancellor of the Exchequer, Winston Churchill, bounded up to him and Gwynne after dinner at Abe Bailey's in July 1926, 'and, for his own reasons, was very ingratiating, and told tales about the General Strike. I do not, however, much trust that gentleman.'[9] (During the strike, Gwynne had come to the government's assistance by producing the official newspaper, the *British Gazette*, which, though nominally edited by Churchill, was in fact run by Gwynne.)

Typically Rudyard distrusted Churchill's political promiscuity. (The Chancellor had recently returned to the Conservative benches after two decades as a Liberal.) Out of preference, Rudyard gravitated towards the most conservative of Stanley's colleagues. One was Sir William Joynson-Hicks, the hard-line Home Secretary, who had come into his own during the General Strike as the government's leading scourge of Bolshevik subversion. A Freemason who lived not far away in Newick, 'Jix' had made his name before the war as a champion of road and aviation issues. As well as his mainstream political duties, he was a staunch member of the Church of England who, in 1927, led the successful parliamentary battle to stall a projected revision of the prayer book. Usually loath to show his religious colours, Rudyard supported the Home Secretary's campaign, and was amused that the High Church bishops who had wanted the change had had their come-uppance because they had failed to understand the strength of English Protestantism.[10]

Joynson-Hicks was backed by another of Rudyard's ministerial friends, Lord Stanhope, the self-effacing Civil Lord of the Admiralty and scion of a distinguished political and literary family (whose great-great-aunt, the Middle Eastern traveller Lady Hester Stanhope, had been a godparent to Moberly Bell's mother). One of the youngest pre-war 'die-hard' Conservatives, Stanhope played host to an eclectic group of latter-day imperialists at Chevening, his 3600-acre seat in Kent (again within striking distance of Bateman's). Stanhope's weekend parties were usually well seeded with reactionary generals and admirals. When Sir Henry Wilson, Chief of the Imperial General Staff, received news of the signing of the Anglo-Irish treaty there in December 1921, General Sir Claud Jacob, Chief of the General Staff (and later Commander-in-Chief) in India, indicated the widespread acceptance of the domino theory to which Rudyard subscribed, by remarking, 'Well, that means we shall lose India.' Aubrey Newman, the Stanhope family biographer, went to some lengths to deny that this group constituted a Chevening 'set',[11] but it did. The Kiplings always had to go to church when they visited the house – an obligation that, from the way she noted it in her diaries, Carrie resented.

Chevening provided the leafy autumnal backdrop for a meeting between Rudyard and the Australian Prime Minister S. M. Bruce in October 1926. This gave Rudyard an opportunity to show his new practical approach to the promotion of Empire. In France earlier in the year, Gwynne had introduced him to William Morris, the car manufacturer, who was staying nearby in Menton. Rudyard now urged Morris to contact Bruce, who had impressed on him 'that the Australians do not love the Yankees, but that the Yank cars fill their requirements; whereas our manufacturers tell them what they ought to have ... It looks to me as if there were a big chance here for some one to play a large hand in the Imperial game.'[12]

Bruce was in Britain for the latest Imperial Conference which was intent on redefining the post-war constitutional relationship between Britain and its former colonies, now known as the Commonwealth. The economic depression of the 1920s had given a fillip to the idea of Empire free trade. With the backing of Leo Amery, the Colonial Secretary, a new Empire Marketing Board (EMB) was established to promote imperial commerce. Stephen Tallents, an energetic publicist who was both a Balliol man (like

Amery and Milner before him) and one-time Irish Guards officer, was hired to run it.

Since his brother Tommy had been a friend of John in the regiment, Tallents looked to Rudyard, an acknowledged master in the art of propaganda, for advice on the EMB's most ambitious project – a major feature film. Rudyard recommended that Walter Creighton, who had impressed him as producer of the pageant that accompanied the Wembley exhibition in 1924, should be responsible for the Board's cinema output.

Rudyard's dabbling in movies proved an unmitigated disaster on this occasion. He and Creighton developed a scenario for a mirthful Kiplingesque fantasy about the gathering of the ingredients for the King's Christmas plum pudding from different parts of the Empire. The idea was that the process should be seen through the eyes of a small boy. Unfortunately, the two cineastes made the mistake of starting the film with a grand meeting at Buckingham Palace of the dominions, as personified by various society ladies. Rudyard knew at least two of the actresses – Phyllis Neilson-Terry, who played the spirit of Australia, and Lady Lavery, the embodiment of the Irish Free State. Another *grande dame* taking part (as Canada) was Lady Keeble – in her day the well-known actress Lillah McCarthy, but now married to Sir Frederick Keeble, whose job as agricultural adviser to Imperial Chemical Industries suggested some early product placement.

As if this ponderous approach was not bad enough, it coincided with a period of unprecedented change in the cinema industry. For, in the autumn of 1927, the first Hollywood talking film, *The Jazz Singer*, was released. Since Creighton knew nothing about film production he was sent on a tour of film centres, including Hollywood, to learn the trade. While in Canada in October 1927, he wrote to Rudyard because he was having difficulty visualising a scene involving a horse. Rudyard, who loved showing off his cinematic know-how, suggested copying the chariot scene from Fred Niblo's action-packed epic *Ben Hur*, which he had just seen (and was to see again at Christmas). The horse should 'be shown –

like the racers in *Ben-Hur* marching four abreast, right out of the film at the beholders. Similarly the wheat laden train of rocking surging cars must make their "appeal" head on.'[13] At that stage the story-line was still unclear, for the same day Rudyard warned Tallents, 'The trouble will be to weave in some sort of linkage of a domestic and British tale to hold the beads together on a string.'[14]

By the following year the film was struggling. Shortly after hiring Creighton, Tallents had met a dynamic Scotsman called John Grierson who impressed him with his ideas for documentary films. In 1928 Grierson was allowed to direct his first short film, *Drifters*, about the British herring industry. It was immediately clear that the EMB had spawned an important new talent. Rudyard tried to revive the plum pudding project by informing King George about it. Because of his good standing, he was given permission to use Buckingham Palace for some of the filming. Later that summer, when Rudyard went to stay with the royal family at Balmoral, he was embarrassed to find that *The Times* had been pestering the King and Queen to contribute to a War Graves supplement to commemorate the tenth anniversary of the ending of the war. He reprimanded Perry Robinson at the paper for taking this liberty. Eventually the Queen agreed to contribute some comments to the supplement, but only after they had been overlooked and slightly altered by Rudyard.

Meanwhile Creighton was struggling to add a sound-track to a movie that was conceived in the age of silent films. When his offering was shown in July 1930 under the title *One Family*, it was roundly panned. For three years it had eaten up most of the EMB's film budget, or £15,740 in total. It was so awful that its commercial run lasted all of one week, taking £334 at the box-office – not enough to pay the cost of the band hired for the première.'[15] Even before the release, Rudyard was denying to Gwynne that he had worked on the screenplay. '[Creighton] used to come down from time to time and talk things over with me.' However, he hoped 'the dam thing will be a success if only for the inside views that it gives of Buck House. If the Yanks had had such a chance you can imagine the amount of money they would have spent on the get up of it. But our officials are – officials.'[16] Despite Rudyard's concern about Amery's 'ineffective'[17] leadership, the films produced by the Empire Marketing Board proved milestones in the development of British cinema. But these were the work of John Grierson, whom Tallents continued to patronise when he went to the Post Office as Director of Public Relations in 1933.

Despite this ignominious failure, the Wembley Exhibition, where Creighton had come to Rudyard's attention, acted as both show-case and catalyst for a new phase of imperialism, where technology served to emphasise the inter-connectedness of Empire, while reinforcing the superiority of British know-how and products. This was a hard-headed business-orientated extension of the pre-war attitude in which romantic enthusiasm for early motoring and air travel went hand in hand with a forward outlook towards the colonies.

As coiner of the phrase 'Transportation is civilisation', Rudyard was still fascinated with aviation. In 1919 the crew of the R–34, the first British airship to fly the Atlantic, carried a copy of *Actions and Reactions*, with its story 'With the Night Mail', which they autographed and presented to him. When *The Times* learnt that Rudyard had contributed to an Air Ministry memorandum for the first post-war Imperial Conference in 1921, the paper asked him to develop his ideas into 'one or two articles on the imperial possibilities of air transport',[18] but he declined. Two years later his futuristic concepts of air transport took a step closer to reality when the British government announced the construction of two giant airships for trans-continental flights to India, Australia, Africa and Canada. In the spirit of a decade which had witnessed Charles Lindbergh's first solo flight across the Atlantic, Rudyard penned his 'Hymn of the Triumphant Airman' in 1929. With its subtitle, 'Flying East to West at 1000 mph', this poem combined a paean to the new technology with wariness about the challenge it posed to the domain of the gods. This sense of foreboding was justified when the second of the airships, the R–101, crashed on its maiden voyage to Delhi in October 1930, killing forty-six people, including the Secretary of State for Air Lord Thomson, a nephew of Lockwood Kipling's old India colleague Sir George Birdwood.

Rudyard was on safer ground with the wireless – another technological development that he had espoused before the First World War and that was now coming into its own. Visiting Bateman's on 17 June 1926, Lady Milner found Rudyard 'looking marvellously well. The house is full of wireless sets. A wonderful portable set with which a radius of 250 miles can be covered.' F. N. Doubleday, a wireless enthusiast, had provided at least one of the sets. Rudyard recognised the medium's potential on the domestic front. A couple of years earlier, just before Christmas 1924, he had a set installed in the servants' hall, where an early outside broadcast – a forgotten drama called *Primrose* from the Winter Gardens Theatre, Bournemouth – met with approval. 'We are immensely pleased to think that we've found something that looks as if it might empty their idle times,'[19] commented Rudyard.

Appropriately, a pioneer airman provided Rudyard's link to the official world of broadcasting. Before 1914 Frederick Sykes had been known to Rudyard as head of the military wing of the Royal Flying Corps. He had risen during the war to become Chief of Air Staff (at a time when Hugh Trenchard was out of favour). He had clearly impressed the right people for in 1920 he married Bonar Law's daughter Isabel and two years later they had a son, Bonar, who became another of Rudyard's many godchildren. As a Unionist MP, Sykes was appointed in 1923 to chair a committee on the organisation of the British Broadcasting Company, as it was known. This body spawned another committee under the Earl of Crawford and Balcarres to advise on the structure of the BBC after its first licence ran out. To the annoyance of John Reith, the Company's Managing Director, Rudyard was appointed to this committee and went to its first meeting on 19 November 1925. However, he was unable to attend further meetings because of his illness, and resigned.[20] The committee's findings led to a change in the BBC's status from company to corporation, and the granting of a Royal Charter in 1926.

Rudyard's views continued to be sought by this new entity. He was 'associated' with the BBC's Advisory Committee on Spoken English, which met three times a year from April 1926 to discuss 'debatable words'. In October that year he was consulted by Eric Dunstan, who had been seconded from the BBC to become General Manager of the Indian Broadcasting Company. In November 1928 John Reith overcame his prejudice and offered Rudyard a hundred-pound fee to broadcast the first National lecture (an early more literary version of what are today known as the Reith lectures).[21] Even after Rudyard declined, claiming that he lacked experience of broadcasting and would be out of the country on the proposed date in January, Reith persisted, saying that the date could be changed and a few minutes' explanation would put him 'completely *en rapport* with the medium'.

Still Rudyard refused – he found Reith 'a portent of the New Second-rate mind in authority, the typical school-master let loose'[22] – and the job was performed by the Poet Laureate Robert Bridges, who had, coincidentally, approached Rudyard after hearing him speak at the Chamber of Shipping in February 1925 and asked if he would like to join him in composing some educational verses for children. Having committed himself to one such collaboration, Rudyard had no desire to repeat the experience. However, he showed no ill feeling towards a man who had become Poet Laureate in 1913 when many people felt he himself should have been given the job. When he was next passing through Oxford, he called on Bridges and found an aesthete with a manner 'quite as self-conscious as is good for one'. Although they talked a lot, Rudyard remembered not one word of his host's 'vague and nebulous ideas of giving school-children better ideas of life and "the State" by means of carefully written textbooks and so forth'.[23]

Rudyard viewed the education of the working classes in much the same way as he once regarded the babus in India. He described to a writer friend 'the State-aided murder by "education" of an 8

year old child on my farm, with the inherited instincts of a generation of cattle-men – the son of an artist, as you might say. He
lives on terms of perfect amity with my Sussex bull, and knows
more about the beasts than anyone except his father. He is now,
at your and my expense as taxpayers, being turned into an utterly
worthless item in a village "school". '[24] Little wonder he despised
Reith and declined his invitation to lecture to the nation. As might
be expected, Rudyard's technophilia failed to hide his distaste for
such ramifications of modern democracy.

The French also understood the range of Rudyard's political contacts. While in Paris for Christmas in 1926, he managed to see
both President Poincaré and Georges Clemenceau. Noting that
each statesman took the opportunity to make barbed comments
about the other, Rudyard was amazed at the vitality of old 'Tiger'
Clemenceau, whose recent book on Demosthenes he had enjoyed.
In the French capital he and Carrie now usually stayed with
Frances Stanley, daughter of their friend Julia Taufflieb. Frances
had married Peter Stanley,[25] an English surgeon who had worked
in the hospital at Compiègne. The young couple lived in great
style in the rue des Belles Feuilles in Paris's fashionable seventh
arrondissement.

Rudyard liked the Stanleys for their genuine interest in ideas.
He built them up into an ideal married couple – a view reflected
in Carrie's diary comment, 'Love and affection of Stanley and
Frances is so rare.'[26] The reality was slightly different. Frances was
an uncompromising woman who, after the war, had refused to
accompany her husband back to his lucrative Harley Street practice in London. She laid down that she was to travel abroad three
times a year. On these occasions they roamed the Mediterranean
littoral: Peter, who was skilled in navigation and astronomy,
exploring the Biblical lands of the Near East, Frances taking a
more particular interest in the Bedouin culture of the Arabs.
She liked to discuss her dreams, corresponding about them with
Rudyard, who described himself jocularly to her as 'almost the

greatest authority on Dreams and their meanings – next to the *Housemaid's Own Dream Book*'.[27]

From a long line of surgeons (a great-grandfather had been President of the Royal College of Surgeons and Surgeon-Extraordinary to Queen Victoria), Peter had followed the family profession in London before the war, attached both to St Bartholomew's Hospital, where he trained, and the Seamen's Hospital at Greenwich. His bravery in front-line field hospitals won him the Croix de Guerre avec Palmes, as well as two mentions in despatches. Because of his wife's determination to stay in France, he had dutifully qualified as a French doctor, and worked on the staffs of the British and American hospitals. He also helped with the orphan colony which Frances founded on the outskirts of Paris. But his medical career was unfulfilled and he spent rather too much time with his rich man's toys – his 100 mph Isotta-Fraschini sports car, which Rudyard admired, and later his 821-ton ocean-going yacht *Trenora* (after her late father's even more sumptuous vessel), which his wife bought him as a consolation.

During his few days in Paris over Christmas and the New Year, Rudyard conceived the idea for one story and was inspired to finish another. 'Aunt Ellen' was a laboured farce about the consequences of a motor accident in which an eiderdown full of presents spills out on to the road.[28] Its peripheral interest comes from the fact that it was based on a similar incident in Paris on Boxing Day. It drew on Rudyard's recent experience in its reference to an Englishman who went to Hollywood to learn about the cinema. Indeed, Lettcombe, the former colonel in the Territorials, 'whose mission, in peace, was the regeneration of our native cinema industry', is based on a mixture of Creighton and Tallents. 'He was a man of many hopes, which translated themselves into prospectuses that faded beneath the acid breath of finance. Sometimes I wrote the prospectuses, because he promised me that, when his ship came in, he would produce the supreme film of the world – the *Life of St Paul*. He said it would be easier than falling off a log, once he had launched his Pan-Imperial Life-Visions'

Association.' Better than the tale itself was its accompanying poem, 'The Playmate', which celebrates the power of the sudden amusing (or, in Rudyard's terminology, mirthful) incident to lighten one's mood.

Rudyard put more effort into polishing off 'Dayspring Mishandled', which combined several of his favourite fictional genres – hoax, revenge and academic mystery. The story tells of two writers who had turned out pulp fiction for a literary syndicate in the 1890s, when they were both rivals for the love of the mother of Vidal Benzaguen, the music-hall star in 'The Village that Voted the Earth was Flat'. One of them, Castorley, leaves journalism to make his name as a Chaucerian scholar. The other, Manallace, remains on the lower rungs of the literary profession, nursing ''Dal's mother' through a fatal illness. When the two men meet during the war, Manallace conceives a plot to blacken his old friend's reputation by forging a manuscript of an unknown tale by Chaucer. He hopes Castorley will authenticate it and then he will be able to expose him as a fraud. Castorley predictably makes much of his discovery of this new Chaucerian text (a set piece that allows Rudyard to show off his knowledge of medieval manuscripts). But he is not well and, before Manallace can reveal his old friend's gullibility, he discovers that Castorley's wife is having an affair with his doctor. Somehow guessing Manallace's game, she encourages him to hurry and expose the hoax, for she hopes this will kill off her husband. Unable to do this, Manallace decides in disgust that his best course is to help maintain Castorley's reputation. This will at least prevent the academic's wife from enjoying a successful conclusion to her adultery. As so often, Rudyard's subject was rather more worldly, even racy, than his reputation suggests.

On 29 December, the eve of his sixty-first birthday, Rudyard informed the Bambridges that his story was 'not at all a nice tale, but it came by itself'[29] and at least had a pretty title. As the self-confessed author of the spoof sonnet 'To a Librarian' in 1914, Rudyard was still exercised by the issue of literary authenticity.

Preparing his manuscripts for deposit at St Andrews University, the British Museum and elsewhere, he must have thought of the problem that would arise about verifying authorship of his own works. Mistaken claims about his Indian output had been made since the 1890s. When he learnt from *The Times* of a sale of Kipling material in 1921 he commented, 'Golly! what fools collectors are!'[30] The following year he gave short shrift to Ernest Martindell, a London barrister who produced a bibliography and supplement of his uncollected material. He later put obstacles in the way of two American bibliographers – Admiral L. H. Chandler and Flora Livingston, rare book librarian at Harvard University – but was won round by their application and scholarship.

In 1927 Jack Brooking, a tiresome, self-seeking electrical engineer, finally succeeded in setting up the Kipling Society that Rudyard had opposed for almost a decade. Brooking had inveigled himself into Rudyard's confidence twenty years earlier by sending a copy of his poems.[31] At the time he was General Manager of the St Helen's Cable and Rubber Company. Rudyard typically asked for information about electrical cabling for Bateman's and seemed happy in 1910 when Brooking claimed to have manufactured a 'flicker' or parachutist's suit that Rudyard had invented in a cod advertisement at the end of his story 'With the Night Mail'. But then the relationship soured: towards the end of the war Rudyard had sought legal advice to prevent Brooking using his verses for commercial advertising. This contretemps was forgotten because the two men shared similar right-wing political views. By November 1918 Rudyard was quietly trying to steer Brooking away from his idea of starting a Kipling Society. Brooking persevered: in 1921 he failed to summon much support; in March 1923 he claimed to have received around one hundred applications after enlisting General Dunsterville's backing, but again the idea came to nothing. In 1924 he unsuccessfully pestered Rudyard to sit for a portrait, then a photograph, of himself with Dunsterville and G. C. Beresford. 'M'Turk' was now a successful society photographer, taking portraits of celebrities such as Virginia Woolf during the week and returning to his mistress and illegitimate family in Brighton at weekends. Since Rudyard would not co-operate, Beresford produced a photo-montage of the three school friends. The following year Brooking showed his unpleasantness by trying to blackmail Rudyard, saying he had written an article which would expose his supposed idol's unwillingness to sit for a portrait of the Dusky Crew.

Rudyard did his best to avoid Brooking. However, he could not hold back the popular interest in his own life and work. As an example, Dunsterville had capitalised on his wartime exploits in a lecture which turned out to be more about his school-days as Stalky than anything else. Given his inability to manage his money (Rudyard had lent him £500 at the start of the war), it was almost inevitable that Dunsterville would continue to use his place in literary history as a source of income. In July 1925 he denied to Rudyard that he had anything to do with Brooking, who he claimed was 'repugnant'.[32] Eighteen months later, however, he had written a memoir, *Stalky's Reminiscences*, and early in 1927 he was one of the first members of the committee of the Kipling Society that Brooking finally succeeded in establishing. Within weeks, on 20 July, Rudyard was objecting to an article about his time in India in the new society's journal:

> As to your dam Society [Rudyard informed Stalky that November] how would you like to be turned into an anatomical specimen, before you were dead, and shown up on a table once a quarter? It makes one feel naked as well as ridiculous. What's worse, it loads up my already-heavy-enough-mail with all sorts of extra correspondence, silly questions, and demands for information. Seriously, old man, when a man has given all that he has to give to the public in his work, he is the keener to keep for himself the little (and it is very little) that remains.[33]

But the Society had taken root: at its height in the 1950s it boasted over one thousand members; forty years later it still had nearly seven hundred. Brooking remained a malignant influence; on the one hand expressing his admiration for the master (on whose death he moved to Burwash to live in what he himself named Rudyard Cottage); on the other showing his true feelings in his inscription on a postcard of Bateman's he sent to Beresford:

> Piles of cash, but a shrewish wife
> Poor old Ruddy, what a life![34]

Since Bland-Sutton had impressed on Rudyard that he needed, for his health's sake, to get out of Europe that winter, the Kiplings had booked a passage for Brazil on the s.s. *Andes* leaving Southampton on 27 January 1927. They refused to be delayed when, only four days before their departure, Landon died in the nursing home which Rudyard had only recently prevailed on him to enter. With its echoes of Browning's 'A Death in the Desert', Rudyard's poem 'A Song in the Desert' was a lament for a friend he had loved. He recalled Landon's candid criticism of his writing:

> If it were good – what acclaim! None other so moved me.
> If it were faulty – what shame? While he mocked me he
> loved me.

He also commemorated his friend's gifts for travel and for story-telling, and his generosity in bringing back treasures from distant places.

As with Rhodes, Rudyard was too upset to attend Landon's funeral. Within weeks he had inherited his friend's letters and papers but, sadly, they did not survive the later brutal weeding out of Rudyard's intimate correspondence by his widow Carrie and daughter Elsie.

In the circumstances, Brazil was a tonic. A quarter of a century earlier Rudyard had written in one of the *Just So Stories*[35] of his disappointment at never having seen a jaguar or an armadillo:

> Oh! I'd love to roll to Rio
> Some day before I'm old!

Now, ensconced in the Hotel Gloria in Rio de Janeiro, he confessed he was lost for words to describe a 'marvellous and unreal town ... like nothing on earth'.[36] He was not weighed down by the cultural baggage of colonisation or attitudes to Islam. Having been introduced to both the President and the Minister of Foreign Affairs, and accorded a reception at the Brazilian Academy of Letters, he found a people who were 'enormously quick-witted and adaptable, as is natural with such mixed blood'.[37] The British consul was Rider Haggard's nephew, Carrie found a long-lost cousin and it was carnival time. In his poem 'The Open Door', which accompanied a series of articles for the *Morning Post*, Rudyard wrote of England as a 'cosy little country' where one was required to shut every door because of the draughts. But in Brazil

> The Deep Verandah shows it –
> The pale Magnolia knows it –
> And the bold, white Trumpet-flower blows it: –
> There isn't any Door that need be shut!

He said the place reminded him of South Africa, but his mind was probably drifting further back to Bombay.

On the return journey the Kiplings left their ship at Lisbon and travelled by train to Biarritz, where they met Elsie. A few days later, on 21 April, they motored north to Cap Ferret, south of Bordeaux, where the Stanleys had a house (the Villa la Vigne) and Peter later kept his yacht in the nearby Bassin d'Arcachon. Rudyard was now seeing a lot of the Stanleys: he returned to stay with them in October (when he was visiting La Bassée, close to Loos, for the opening of the Indian war memorial), in December (for Christmas and the New Year) and again in the following April. From time to time Peter came to London, where he kept up his medical contacts, including John Bland-Sutton who was godfather to his eldest daughter Jane, born in 1921. In December 1927 Peter attended the Fountain Club, a dining club at St Bartholomew's Hospital, where Rudyard, as guest of honour, summarised his increasingly unorthodox views on the medical profession. Rudyard was introduced, in bantering doctors' style, as having an 'extensive and peculiar' knowledge of medicine, despite his lack of qualifications. 'By his work "Love-o'-Women" he showed himself to be an authority on the late manifestations of syphilis.' Rudyard provided a witty potted history of surgeons and physicians, but showed the direction of his own thinking when he suggested that the physicist, 'the accoucheur of new ideas', would soon 'short circuit' both these specialities.[38]

In this spirit, Rudyard was 'working hard'[39] the following month on 'Stars in their Courses' (as it was originally called), later 'Unprofessional', a complex tale about the effects of planetary influences on a woman's cancer. Harries, an amateur astronomer with a million-pound fortune (clearly drawing on Stanley), convinces his doctor friends from St Peggotty's (a mixture of St Bartholomew's and Bland-Sutton's Middlesex Hospital) to test his ideas about sidereal (or tidal) influences on living cells. (As a Freemason, Rudyard is expert at conveying the doctors' professional camaraderie.) One woman who is operated on during the flood tide gets better. Afterwards she adopts a curious trait of wishing herself dead – Rudyard's way of suggesting that one cannot escape one's destiny. Nevertheless, he managed to get his basic idea across, as articulated by Harries: 'Imagination *is* what we want. This rigid "thinking" game is hanging up research. You told me yourself the other night, it was becoming all technique and no advance.' (In a fine accompanying poem, 'The Threshold', Rudyard made a similar plea that elemental spiritual understanding should not be hijacked and overwhelmed by monotheistic religion.)

Such ideas about 'complementary' medicine were heresy in most hospitals, but John Bland-Sutton – who, for all his delight in wielding the surgeon's knife, was a true polymath, open to a variety of non-clinical disciplines – expressed his appreciation of a story which he said was as far in advance of its time as Rudyard's quasi-science fiction about flying two decades earlier.[40] Rudyard might have wanted to communicate his scepticism about modern clinical medicine in his speech (before Bland-Sutton) to the Royal College of Surgeons five years earlier. He was more successful when addressing the Royal Society of Medicine later in 1928. Referring to the example of his favourite Nicholas Culpeper, he pleaded for what would later be called 'holistic' medicine, as he argued that disease might 'depend on some breath from the motion of the universe – of the entire universe, revolving as one body (or dynamo if you choose) through infinite but occupied space'.[41] As he told Peter Stanley, he made a speech 'on the old "astrological" lines that we discussed more than a year ago. It was rather fun: but it has unchained on me every dam' astrological crank in England (with pamphlets!) and the US mail has yet to come.'[42]

Continuing his medical theme, Rudyard also penned 'The Tender Achilles', about a gaggle of doctors at St Peggotty's who trick a brilliant former colleague suffering from shell-shock back to sanity. They achieve this by performing on him a dubious operation which he is forced to tell them is wrong. The story, which was published in the London Magazine in December 1929, allowed Rudyard to display his knowledge (to which Stanley must have contributed) of surgical procedures in field hospitals during the war. He examined the phenomenon of shell-shock as fully as in 'Fairy-Kist'. Once more he looked to applied imagination as the basis for the cure. Along the way he enjoyed an elaborate joke at the expense of surgeons who, according to one of the doctors in the tale, a general practitioner, act as carpenters in the medical process, while the GP looks upon the patient as a holistic being. 'In other words,' he concluded, 'medicine and surgery is the difference between the Priest and the pew-opener.' With its punning title, suggesting the Achilles tendon, or weak point in a person's make-up, the story also dealt with Rudyard's fascination with individuals pushed to their limits – until they break – a theme reiterated in the 'Hymn to Physical Pain', the poem which accompanied the story in book form and which alluded to the physical and psychological discomfort that Rudyard was experiencing on a daily basis.

Intriguingly, Rudyard wrote another medical story that he or Carrie later destroyed. In March 1930 the *Daily Telegraph* reported he had written 'some new stories', including one that suggested it was possible to cure disease by sound. 'This story is based, if not on actual facts,' the paper reported, 'at least on a belief held by a living doctor. Each element and metal, he holds, has somewhere in the range of sound its friendly and its hostile note. To the former it responds, while the latter shatters it by its vibrations, just as a certain note of an organ will break a window ... The story, as Mr Kipling has written it, deals, I am told, with the illness of an eminent politician. A doctor is called in, and prescribes a somewhat unusual treatment. The treatment appears to be a failure, and the patient's life is despaired of, but a sudden and miraculous recovery follows. The doctor is sought, to be congratulated, but is found dead by his own hand, and the secret of his treatment remains a mystery.'[43] As a result of his own (and Carrie's) experience of physical pain, Rudyard had come a long way in his appreciation of alternative approaches to medicine, but he or his wife felt that a 'sound cure' was going too far and suppressed the idea.

Prior to that, in January 1928, he had acted as a pall-bearer at Hardy's funeral in Westminster Abbey – the occasion for a gathering of literary lions that one observer, the young author J. I. M. Stewart, likened to a Beerbohm cartoon. That March the Kiplings took a holiday in the fashionable Sicilian resort of Taormina where, appropriately, they stayed in a hotel which was once a monastery (and the rooms old monks' cells). Rudyard found the spring flowers 'beyond anything I've met – both tame and wild: and the beauty of the place (here) is unbelievable.'[44] But he could not take his mind off medical subjects. Among his fellow guests was an American dermatologist who talked about treating chlorine gas blisters with bicarbonate of soda – the sort of information Rudyard savoured and passed on to Bland-Sutton, along with the latest update on his own health.[45] He claimed he had been suffering from a splintered bone or necrosis in his lower right jaw and had treated it with iodine. Suddenly, one day, a piece of his molar came out, worn on one side by the pressure of his plate. 'You'd better go through your gums again,' he told his surgeon friend, with some relief. 'Dentists seem dam careless.'

From Naples he and Carrie experienced a choppy and uncomfortable voyage across the Mediterranean to Gibraltar. They then made their usual leisurely way up through Spain, where they saw George and Elsie in Madrid, and through France, where a visit to the Stanleys was *de rigueur*. The Bambridges introduced Rudyard to a Polish diplomat Jan Perlowski, who was not only a writer, but also a ward of Joseph Conrad's guardian Tadeusz Bobrowski. Rudyard had entertained Conrad at Bateman's in 1904 and had written to him lavishly praising *Typhoon*. Now, abandoning his usual reticence about contemporary writers, he treated Perlowski to an expert critical appraisal of Conrad, whom he found both more intense and more sincere than British writers. He himself was more adamant than Conrad that individuals were responsible for their actions. He also was clear that Conrad was not English: 'Reading him, I always have the feeling that I am reading a good translation of a foreign writer.'[46]

Once home, Rudyard paused only to order a new Rolls-Royce Phantom II Landaulette, with shagreen-lined doors and a patent cellulose finish, before settling down to write two new stories which mixed aspects of Biblical history, sailing and the Mediterranean – all subjects of interest to Peter Stanley. On 12 May Rudyard was working on what Carrie described in her diary as 'St Paul at Antioch' (later published as 'The Church that Was at Antioch'), a tale about a young Roman working in the occupied city of Antioch in the early days of Christianity, when there are still quarrels, particularly over the rituals of eating, between Christians and Jews, and between Gentile and non-Gentile Christians. St Paul and St Peter both visit the Syrian town to calm inter-racial tensions. In a scuffle the young Roman (as 'good' an imperialist as anyone in Rudyard's Indian tales) is killed, but not before imploring his uncle, the prefect of police, to be lenient with his murderers: 'Don't be hard on them . . . They don't know what they are doing.' This sympathetic reference to Christian compassion in a story about the exercise of imperial rule in an alien, multi-religious environment showed how Rudyard's thinking had developed since his Indian days. He was still, as his references to St Paul indicated, prepared to render Caesar his due, but he was beginning to argue the primacy of spiritual over temporal aspirations.

This theme was followed up on 2 June with what Carrie called a second story about Paul – clearly a reference to 'The Manner of Men', in which a sea captain (plying the same Mediterranean that Rudyard himself had just travelled) recalls the impression once made on him by one of his passengers, St Paul. The captain is convinced by the apostle that he would benefit, and his irrational fears of the sea and the void would cease, if he accepted Roman sovereignty, for this would at least provide some structure for his life. 'And Paul said to me: "Serve Caesar. You are not canvas I can cut to advantage at present. But if you serve Caesar you will be obeying at least some sort of law." '

Rudyard's fascination with St Paul, the subject of Lettcombe's putative 'supreme film' in 'Aunt Ellen', is instructive. Like himself, the apostle was a writer and ideologue born outside his native land. St Paul's evangelism provided a model for present-day political activism – a theme Baldwin took up when he spoke of party workers as 'missionaries' and 'apostles' and the British population as needing 'salvation' or 'redemption'.[47] Most of all, Rudyard identified with St Paul's desire to be 'all things to all men'. As a reclusive individual, this was the last of his ambitions. But as an artist, pushing his ideas to their limits, it was his primary goal. While ostensibly about St Paul, his poem 'At His Execution', which accompanied 'The Manner of Men', expressed the perennial dilemma of the creative man – that in adopting the voice and perspective of those around him, he loses his own:

> I was made all things to all men,
> But now my course is done –
> And now is my reward –
> Ah, Christ, when I stand at Thy Throne
> With those I have drawn to the Lord,
> Restore me my self again![48]

More down to earth were Rudyard's nautical interests. The sea had been an inspiration for over thirty years, a symbol of British courage, ingenuity and independence. Since the 1890s he had injected an almost theological spirit of purpose and romance into the business of modern seafaring in poems such as 'The "Mary Gloster"' and stories including 'Bread Upon the Waters'. Over the years he had grown close to Britain's shippers, from Sir Donald Currie at the Union Castle line to Sir Percy Bates at Cunard. (One such acquaintance came to an abrupt halt in 1931, however, after Rudyard lost £5000 he had invested in a company floated by Lord Kylsant, chairman of White Star Line, who went to prison for providing false information in a Stock Exchange prospectus.)

Rudyard was much fêted by the official world of shipping. In February 1925 he addressed five hundred members of the Chamber of Shipping of the United Kingdom, allowing him to air deeply felt views about the importance of maritime transport to Britain and her economy. In June 1927 he himself became an honorary master mariner[49] and, that December, he wrote the epitaph for the war memorial to members of the merchant navy.[50]

Through his involvement with the *Morning Post*, Bates, in particular, became a friend (though it was not until July 1935, well over a decade after they first met, that Rudyard diffidently suggested they should call each other by their Christian names). In May 1928 Bates presented him with a replica of the alphabet necklace from the *Just So Stories* (a book that contained an amusing catalogue of shipping companies in its poem beginning 'China-going P. & O.'s'). In October that year Rudyard joined Bates in Liverpool to view plans for a giant new Cunard liner *Queen Mary* and to address the Liverpool Shipbrokers' Benevolent Society. Looking for further background details for 'The Manner of Men', he called on the Cunard chairman the following year: 'I am working the ship with a jib-headed driver, almost a lateen; mainsail that is brailed, not furled close, and the sprit. What canvas would she scud under? Could she be worked jib and jigger, so to say?'[51]

At the same time he kept up his contacts with the Navy and its traditions. In June 1928 he watched the Trooping the Colour from an office in the Admiralty, where Lord Stanhope was now Civil Lord. Over dinner at Chevening the following year, Rudyard made his mark on the heritage industry by suggesting to Stanhope that the proposed new National Nautical and Naval Museum at Greenwich should adopt the simpler name the National Maritime Museum. Later, when Stanhope was the first chairman of the trustees of the Museum, Rudyard donated part of his great collection of nautical books to the institution. Around the same time he told a visitor that he had two unrealised ambitions in life – one was to build or buy a 400-ton brig and sail her round the world (thus imitating the lifestyle of his old stockbroker friend Barclay Walton) and the other was to be an archaeologist – 'for sheer gem-studded romance, no other job can touch it'.)

With his direct access to top politicians, Rudyard was not afraid to voice his concerns about domestic and social issues – areas he had sometimes glossed over. In May 1927 he quizzed Joynson-Hicks, the Home Secretary, about the police raid on the Soviet trading company Arcos, which was accused of spying. Though he learnt 'a little, not much',[52] he wrote encouragingly to his cousin Stanley that 'if the thing goes through with a clean break, it will do more to rehabilitate the Party in the country and England in the world's eye than anything that has come our way in a long time.'[53] He intervened with his cousin Stanley in June 1928 to make sure that Lord Byng, the hero of Vimy Ridge during the war, was appointed Commissioner of the Metropolitan Police. (When Byng did not want to take up the job, Rudyard had 'a good go' at him and 'spoke to him like 10 Fathers'.[54]) Later, at a time when Joynson-Hicks was conducting a puritanical crack-down on night clubs, Rudyard used his connections to inform Byng about a particularly noisy *boîte* in Albemarle Street, close to where he liked to stay at Brown's Hotel.[55] Predictably, he had told Marie Stopes, the family planning pioneer, that she could not alter the text of his poem 'If–' to reflect the aspirations of her clinics. She had wanted to give a more feminine interpretation to the last line that suggested if the protagonist kept his head and filled the unforgiving minute with sixty seconds' worth of distance won, he would 'be a Man, my son!'. But Rudyard argued that this would establish a precedent and 'we might end by sanctioning the change of every line'.[56]

Rudyard's increasingly conservative personal morality was evident when Joynson-Hicks prevailed on him to appear as a witness for the prosecution in the Crown's case against Radclyffe Hall's novel *The Well of Loneliness*.[57] Hall and her publisher Jonathan Cape had been convicted in the autumn of 1928 of putting out an obscene novel, which dealt overtly with lesbianism. Unswayed by personal connections with the family of Hall's lover Una Troubridge, Rudyard presented himself at the London Sessions on 14 December for their appeal, but was told his professional opinion would not be required. (His influence can nevertheless be discerned in the literary references to lesbianism quoted by the Attorney-General, Sir Thomas Inskip, in opening the case: one was from Juvenal and the other from Rudyard's favourite St Paul's Epistle to the Romans, Chapter 1, verses 24–8.) It was extraordinary that Rudyard, a man who had so regularly rejected official honours because he wanted to maintain his basic freedoms, should have lent his name to the state prosecution of an author. In the 1890s he had been prepared to support Aubrey

Beardsley in the controversy over the *Yellow Book*. Only four years earlier, in July 1924, when Sir Rennell Rodd started a campaign to have Lord Byron's body buried in Westminster Abbey, Rudyard suggested that when he put the poet's case, the former ambassador should 'go light (the present generation are quite expert enough in their own sins) on Byron's moral lapses' and concentrate on his prowess as a poet. Rudyard added, 'It might save some people with a taste for moral disquisitions rushing into the papers and giving us their views on his personal weaknesses. This is because I am jealous for the Poet. The man must, as always, be in the hands of Allah!'[58]

Rudyard's change of view can be attributed largely to his direct personal experience. For in October, he received from France an advertisement for a book which can only have been *The Well of Loneliness*. At the time the publisher Jonathan Cape had bowed to official threats and declined to publish the book in England. However it had arranged for copies to be printed in Paris and distributed to customers by mail order. When Rudyard received a promotion addressed to Miss Kipling, he opened it and sent it to Joynson-Hicks, adding, 'There is no "Miss Kipling" now, but I suspect that the trade is active among young girls, just the same as the smutty books of the old days used to be advertised from Belgium among Public Schools. It seems to me pretty damnable, but I don't know if your powers stretch to bringing them up with a round turn. *Mem*. The whole point of the book is that people with that particular taste should be made much of and received into general society with their "lovers". Otherwise, as you know, there is no moral.'[59] Joynson-Hicks got the point. Rudyard's letter to him was dated 11 October. Four days later the Home Secretary told the London Diocesan Council of Youth that he might have to act to 'deal with immoral and disgusting books'. On the 19th the offices of Cape and of Radclyffe Hall's main British distributor, the bookseller, Leopold Hill, were raided and copies of the newly arrived French edition of her book impounded. Summonses to appear in court soon followed. On 25 October, Rudyard informed the Home Secretary he would be happy to provide evidence against it. 'What *I* object to,' he intoned, 'is its being sent to unmarried women. That gives the whole game away.'[60] Thus, Rudyard played a direct role in the case against *The Well of Loneliness*.

Rudyard's altered opinion also stemmed from his concern at what he saw as the breakdown of established values in the countryside. He attributed a spate of country house fires directly to the practice of allowing junior maids to smoke,[61] for example. He felt that morality was being eroded by servants staying out late at dances. At the same time, the land was suffering from 'the multiplication of small Government billets of from 270£ to 550£ on which young couples marry and look forward to short hours, long holidays and a pension. We've created the white Babudom, and now we pay for it in morale as well as cash.'[62] (It was odd that Rudyard had forgotten that his own father had been just such a Babu, and that he himself had striven to get him a pension.)

Rural tensions were reflected in late August 1928 when he started his story 'Beauty Spots', a laboured revenge tale, with elements of farce, about a feud between the family of a businessman, newly arrived in the countryside, and a retired major who saw them as upstarts. In an accompanying poem, 'Neighbours', Rudyard stressed the benefits of sociability: 'he that is costive of soul toward his fellow, / ... Him food shall not fatten, him drink shall not mellow; / And his innards shall brew him perpetual strife.' He mocked himself in details about the businessman's son – whose Asian complexion was said to result from his father's cohabitation with a person of colour. (Rudyard was sometimes accused of being tarred with the same brush.) The main instrument of revenge was a white sow called Angelique (after a pig the Kiplings once kept).[63] This has led to comparisons between the story and P. G. Wodehouse's 'Lord Emsworth and the Girl Friend', which Rudyard described as 'one of the best humorous short stories in the English language'.[64] Such suggestions are valid: introduced to Wodehouse in January 1929 at his neighbours' the Cazalets, Rudyard told Elsie he had already met him at the Club and had taken an immediate liking to him.[65]

With his conventional morality and rural attitudes, Rudyard had fully adopted the English countryman's view of the world. Before the war he could not help reflecting his rootlessness in his sometimes patronising appreciation of the skills of men such as Hobden in the *Puck* stories. He now recognised the extent to which his conservatism was based on an aristocratic system of land tenure, which went hand in hand with the traditional country pursuits of the gentry. In September 1928, soon after starting 'Beauty Spots', Rudyard was writing what Carrie describes as 'a poem about foxes, stimulated by an R[oyal] S[ociety] for the P[revention] of C[ruelty] to A[nimals] agitation against hunting'.[66] This is unlikely to have been his poem 'Fox-Hunting', which did not appear for nearly five years. Since Carrie's diary records him working over the next few months on a 'dog story' ('Thy Servant a Dog') and a 'pig story' ('Beauty Spots'), the 'poem about foxes' seems to have changed into the first of these, one of several sentimental paeans to man's favourite pet that Rudyard wrote in his later years.

This tale of an Aberdeen terrier (the same breed as his own Wop and James) who wants to be a 'true sporting dog' encouraged Rudyard to quiz his country friends about hunting. Lord Bathurst, Master of the Vale of White Horse foxhounds and husband of the former owner of the *Morning Post*, fielded most of his enquiries late in 1929. Rudyard's obsession with detail was apparent in his questions about 'swine-chopping' and pack psychology. He seldom indicated more clearly his habit of placing his stories in environments he knew than when he told Bathurst, 'I have set the stage roughly much as at Cirencester [Park]',[67] the peer's seat in Gloucestershire.

While at Cirencester in May 1927, Rudyard met a local couple, the Masons. He was immediately attracted to Michael Mason, an Old Etonian explorer in the Roosevelt tradition who, when not trapping bears in Canada or shooting elephants in the Sudan, wrote books and ran his estate in Oxfordshire. Both he and Carrie liked Mason's wife Annette, despite his description of her as 'a wildish girl ... of the extreme modern type'.[68] Not that there was any other interesting company – part of the price Rudyard paid for cavorting with the aristocracy. He found them all 'of a stuffiness unimpeachable', an opinion he did not alter when he was told to talk to the Duke and Duchess of Montrose. However, the Masons became good friends of the Kiplings in the latters' declining years.

Rudyard also discussed hunting with Guy Paget, a Northamptonshire landowner whom he had met by chance at the Carlton Club at the start of the war. In 1932, Rudyard asked him to comment on 'Fox-Hunting', a rollicking, Surteesian social history of hunting in verse. Paget pointed out – apropos the lines, 'a Gentleman in Red / When all the Quorn wore woad, sir!' – that the Quorn's evening colours were indeed blue. Slightly put out, Rudyard commented, 'I *did* know that Quorn facings were blue – I don't spend all my time indoors.'[69] In return, Rudyard offered criticism of Paget's *History of the Pytchley Hunt*. Normally he declined to help others with books. But he ignored this self-denying ordinance for such friends, assisting Lord Bathurst with his limited edition *The Earl Spencer's and Mr John Warde's Hounds 1739–1825*, published in May 1932, and Michael Mason with his writings on exploration – in particular *The Paradise of Fools*, his 1936 book about the Libyan desert.

When Guy Paget expressed concern that his son Reginald had become a Socialist (after sitting at the feet of Keynes at Cambridge), Rudyard knew exactly the right metaphor to adopt: 'My father told me that if you don't pull a horse's mouth about he won't pull at you. I consulted him when I found my seven-year-old boy was getting a bit out of hand! He added: – "more things are done by judicious leaving alone than you'd think." '[70] Rudyard's laissez-faire conservatism had a long and respectable history.

*

Planning to visit Egypt and Palestine in the spring of 1929, Rudyard asked Peter Stanley for his recent experiences of 'that end of the world which is all microbes & Jews & germs'.[71] On the voyage to Alexandria in February, he and Carrie were able to devote at least part of their time to the useful joint task of preparing their accounts. (Rudyard's assessed income for the year was £38,560. His publisher, Harold Macmillan, cannot have been too far off when he told Beaverbrook's favourite, Lord Castlerosse, in 1931 that Rudyard's fortune 'must be nearly a million', though he exaggerated when he said that the *Jungle Books* alone 'had brought him in a steady £30,000 a year for years'.[72])

In Egypt, Rudyard made his way up the Nile to Assouan, retracing much the same ground as on his previous visit sixteen years earlier. The main difference was that he now took time off to visit imperial war cemeteries. This connection proved useful when he went to Jerusalem and met Colonel C. E. Hughes, the Australian in charge of war graves in the region. Hughes escorted him around the countryside, introducing him to Claude Jarvis, Governor of Sinai and an authority on Bedouin customs and law. Jarvis was impressed that Rudyard did not immediately try to quiz him about the Arab–Jewish conflict but commented simply, 'I suppose most of your troubles here are in connection with land ownership – that and smuggling.' Concluding that Rudyard must be a man of exceptional intelligence to grasp the nature of his job so quickly, Jarvis added,

> He was a great student of the Old Testament, and on the principle that there was nothing new under the sun held the view that most of the world situations of today were merely wider repetitions of those recorded in one or other books of the Bible, and that our various leaders and soldiers had their counterparts in the kings and patriarchs mentioned in Joshua, Judges and Samuel. Once when I was puzzling over the title of a book, he said, picking up the Bible, 'This is the best place to look for one,' and promptly read out half a dozen.[73]

A gesture of Rudyard's in Jerusalem showed that his fascination with the Bible sprang as much from his interest in Freemasonry as from any specific religious quest. He made a point of retrieving a piece of rock from the supposed quarries under King Solomon's Temple that he had referred to in 'Banquet Night', the poem which accompanied his overtly Masonic story 'In the Interests of the Brethren' in *Debits and Credits*. He sent this to his old Burwash friend Colonel Sutherland Harris with 'fraternal regards' and the advice that it was probably not tough enough for a lodge master's gavel-head (though Rudyard claimed to have used one piece for that purpose), but might be cut up into 'marks'. Although Sutherland Harris had moved from the immediate vicinity, he was still Rudyard's main contact with Sussex Freemasonry.

As usual, Rudyard had the knack of giving different reactions to a place to different people. After visiting the grave of Charlie Law, Bonar Law's son, a casualty in Gaza late in the war, he and Carrie both wrote to Charlie's sister Isabel who was in Bombay, where her husband Sir Frederick Sykes had been posted as governor. Rudyard told Isabel, 'This is a mad and amazing country, with three religions at each other's throats, and the Bolshie dancing in the background to see where he can get in a stab.'[74] To Henry Newbolt he wrote of Palestine as 'a most marvellous land'.[75] The synthesis of his views came in a letter to Elsie to whom he described Jerusalem as 'an indescribable muck heap, but it's the most interesting muck heap in the world'.[76] At least he had found a latter-day imperialist after his own heart in Colonel Hughes, with whom he kept regularly in touch.

While in Egypt, Rudyard met Alfred (A. E. W.) Mason, who wrote dashing adventure stories, including the often filmed *The Four Feathers* which, in its depiction of blindness set against a backdrop of a British campaign against the Mahdi in the Sudan, had obvious similarities to *The Light that Failed*. During the war, Mason had been recruited into naval intelligence by Admiral 'Blinker' Hall. His love of yachting had provided cover to nose around Mediterranean ports looking for evidence of German activity. His secret service work subsequently suggested plots for several stories.

Rudyard had several other points of contact with the rakish Mason: they had both been born in 1865, they shared a publisher (Macmillan), they had been friends of Andrew Lang and they liked ostentatiously touring on the Continent in their Rolls-Royces. Mason turned out to be close to James Mason, father of Rudyard's young explorer friend Michael who, curiously, knew him as 'Uncle Alfred', even though they were not blood relations. (The reason was that Alfred and James Mason had once been Members of Parliament together.)

Rudyard was fascinated by *The Three Gentlemen*, Alfred Mason's book in progress, which suggested elements of *Puck of Pook's Hill* in its account of a man with three lives in Rome, Elizabethan England and the present day. Rudyard advised Mason to consult *The Ring of Return*, an anthology of metempsychosis – a fashionable word for reincarnation – that included material from ancient Egypt to 'your bloody 'umble', or Rudyard himself. The volume quoted a passage from 'The Finest Story in the World', as well as a more obscure fragment from *Songs from Books* (originally based on *The Naulahka*), from which Mason used a couple of lines as the epigraph to his book:

> They will come back, come back again, as long as the red
>   Earth rolls.
> He never wasted a leaf or tree. Do you think he would
>   squander souls?

Rudyard also discussed the creative process with Mason: 'I don't envy you the last pangs of parturition. Nor that awful state of woolliness and fuzziness, when one gets so soaked in one's stuff that one can't see, think or judge.'[77] If this was an oblique comment on his current view of the world, he offset it by reading writers such as Mason, whose works he could understand – mainly romances of the type Lang once regarded as the future of English literature. Over the years Rudyard had known several similar authors, including John Buchan, E. Phillips Oppenheim, Valentine Williams and Edgar Wallace, whose *West Coast Yarns* were among the books (mainly naval tales) that he recommended to the sick King George V later in 1929.

By chance, Wallace's son-in-law Alexander Frere-Reeves ran William Heinemann, the publisher with which Rudyard remained in regular contact through his involvement with Doubleday. Frere-Reeves not only kept him informed about Doubleday's failing health, but sent him regular supplies of non-fiction. Rudyard was dismissive of D. H. Lawrence's letters, doubtless for defensive reasons ('I suppose people *must* write letters but it is not fun to have 'em collected'),[78] but he loved *From Southern Cross to Polar Star*, a travel book about 'a 10,000 mile ride from Buenos Ayres [*sic*] to Washington with a couple of Argentine horses – almost human – done by a Swiss who was a real horse master' that he told Guy Paget he had '*got* to read'.[79] In return, Rudyard gave Frere-Reeves suggestions for his 'Windmill' series of reprints – among them Thomas Amory's eighteenth-century *Life of John Buncle Esq.*, Burton's classic *Dahomey* and the Koran. Adventure and travel, animals and country pursuits, obscure classics and religion: Rudyard's reading was a reliable measure of his personal interests.

Having enjoyed an Indian summer during Stanley Baldwin's premiership, Rudyard was not amused when Ramsay MacDonald's Labour party was returned to office in a general election in late May 1929. MacDonald was committed, *inter alia*, to speeding India's progress to Dominion status, as had been recommended by the Governor-General Lord Irwin and accepted, to Rudyard's disgust, by Baldwin. After Lord Beaverbrook had stepped up his Empire free trade campaign and the Wall Street Crash in October had depleted the Kipling family fortunes, Rudyard urged Gwynne to 'get after' the new government, of which he observed, 'Not a bad record for less than 5 months, is it? One attempted revolution on the mere fact of their being in office. One real débâcle set and staged for Egypt, to come off next touring season. One hell-broth cooked up in India to spill over at about the same time ...'[80] The following week he suggested that, because of Britain's economic problems, MacDonald would soon have to begin selling off some of the nations' more distant colonies, starting with the West Indies.[81]

He was thinking of the Caribbean because that was where he and Carrie intended to go in the new year. Originally – inspired, perhaps, by A. E. W. Mason – they had thought of visiting Suakin, one of the places featured in *The Light that Failed*. But unrest in Egypt put a stop to that idea. When they sailed from Avonmouth for Kingston, Jamaica, on 6 February 1930, they were accompanied by Helen Hardinge, daughter of Lady Milner (formerly Lady Edward Cecil). Although married to the King's assistant private secretary and the mother of three children, Helen was a timid creature. Carrie probably suggested she should come as a favour to Violet Milner, who had recently returned to Great Wigsell after giving her husband's house, Sturry Court, to King's School, Canterbury, to accommodate its junior school (renamed Milner Court). Rudyard had performed the opening ceremony in October.

Carrie herself was in poor shape, racked with rheumatism and now suffering from diabetes. Over the previous couple of years her eyesight had deteriorated badly, though she left it until she was in mid-Atlantic before complaining she could neither read nor write. After five days in Kingston, the capital of Jamaica, the Kiplings left for the Titchfield Hotel in Port Antonio in the north of the island. Rudyard discovered that, along with his usual problem about noisy Yankee tourists, the whole of the island's economy (essentially its banana and sugar industries) was in the hands of the American United Fruit Company. He was just beginning to savour the countryside and its tropical associations when Carrie was laid low with stomach pains. Despite her condition, the Kiplings were determined to continue on the next stage of their journey to Bermuda. The Governor arranged for his private railway coach to bring them back to Kingston, where the Canadian National Lines pulled their ship the RMS *Lady Rodney* up at the rail terminal to accept its sick passenger.

In Hamilton, Bermuda, the Kiplings were greeted with a calypso-style poem in the local *Royal Gazette*:

> Mornin' Mis Smif – Ain't dis de j'yful day!
> Yas-sir-ee – Mister Kiplin's come to stay!
> Betchy sojers up to Prospec' is tunin' pipe an' drum,
> Singin' 'Lolly-lolly-hoo! By! Mister Kiplin's come'.

Carrie was in no mood for this celebration as she was immediately rushed to the King Edward VII Memorial Hospital, while Rudyard stayed a mile and a half away at the Hotel Bermudiana. Four days later, when Helen Hardinge left for home, her departure was welcomed: 'She has a gizzard instead of a heart,'[82] Rudyard told Elsie, as he complained about their companion's unhelpfulness during his wife's illness.

His attitude had clearly been shaped by his wife's. For, as Mrs Hardinge's letters to her mother indicated, she had little time for Carrie's histrionics. She told Lady Milner that Carrie had been an 'impossible patient' and she marvelled at Rudyard's patience with his wife. 'I'm most worried about *him*,' she wrote from Port Antonio. 'He does day and night nurse and has not been outside the annexe except for meals and that only sometimes for my sake since we arrived. He gets very little sleep and what he does, under the worst possible conditions – by her side. He hardly eats anything – I shall do something desperate about it soon!'[83] Probably Helen Hardinge had voiced her concern about the effects of Rudyard's dogged devotion on his own health, but this had only led to her being cast as a demon by Carrie, while he had meekly taken his wife's side.

At one stage Carrie seemed to be improving from what had been diagnosed as appendicitis, but she fell ill again with a bladder infection, and, with the end of the Bermuda season fast approaching and his hotel being about to close down, Rudyard moved to Inglewood, a boarding house closer to the hospital, where Carrie was eventually able to join him on 8 May.

In the meantime Rudyard worked himself into a lather about American tourists getting drunk, a sight that never failed to annoy him whether he was in Monte Carlo, Port Antonio or Hamilton. To make matters worse, though the barman at the hotel knew how to serve rum cocktails, he had no idea how to mix gin, tonic and bitters. Once he had been taught, he called the drink a 'Kipling'. Rudyard was at least able to work on his story 'A Naval Mutiny', which referred pointedly to Bermuda as Stephano's Island, after the drunkard who lays claim to Prospero's Island in *The Tempest*. His related poem 'The Coiner' provided a witty commentary on his old idea that poets draw inspiration from factual events, there are no new stories under the sun and Shakespeare probably obtained the basic information for *The Tempest* from drunken sailors who embellished a tale of being shipwrecked off the coast of Bermuda.

As soon as Carrie could travel the Kiplings caught a boat from Bermuda to Canada. In Montreal they were visited by Carrie's sister Josephine Dunham and her family. Josephine's twenty-two-year old daughter, also called Josephine, noted that her Aunt Carrie's hair had turned completely white since she had last seen her on a trip to England in 1926. As on previous visits to North America, Rudyard was pestered by journalists, who now included a new breed of newsreel cameraman. He took the telephone receiver off the hook in order to give his niece and her sister Beatrice a sanitised version of his views about the responsibilities of imperialism. Canada had developed into a mature country, free to go her own way – 'when you have grown-up children, you have to give them a latch-key'. However, India was still a child, not worthy of Dominинion status; the English were only there because the Indians wanted them. As for Ireland, he assured the girls it was still a violent and troubled place. He was appalled when they suggested it was an erudite nation. 'There are a great many bogs in Ireland,' he noted cryptically. 'You see what that means.'[84]

Back in Britain, Beaverbrook had responded to the political and economic depression by joining forces with his fellow press magnate Lord Rothermere to form the United Empire party, with the specific aim of forcing Baldwin's removal from leadership of the Conservative party. Rudyard was placed in a greater political quandary than ever: Beaverbrook, his old friend turned enemy (over Ireland) was making the right imperialist noises, but Rudyard's loyalty to his cousin was stronger – even if he did adopt something of an ostrich approach, telling Elsie in August that he could not 'make head or tail of the Beaverbrook attitude about Empire Union'.[85] His political confusion was all the more acute because Rothermere had led the press attack against the civil disobedience campaign in India, where Congress party leader Mahatma Gandhi was trying to impose his terms for the proposed Round Table conference on the country's future.

Rudyard was on more familiar ground in November when he told Gwynne that the whole Indian independence movement was a Brahmin plot, 'plus Balliol (don't forget that), *and* the envy of the unfit intelligensia of this country against the man who can and does lead and will assume leadership'.[86] He added that British administrators in India were the only barrier between the lower castes and the Brahmins, who would introduce suttee again within a year of any move to self-government. 'Meanwhile the whole dam Empire is bankrupt – and there are no two words to it.'

Beaverbrook harried Baldwin by running his own Empire Crusade candidate against the official Conservative (Duff Cooper) in a by-election in St George's, Westminster, the following March. Baldwin fought back by accusing newspaper proprietors of wanting power, 'but power without responsibility – the prerogative of the harlot throughout the ages'. Rudyard is supposed to have suggested this remark to his cousin. While there

is no definitive evidence for this, he had recently written to his
Aunt Edith Macdonald, 'If I'd been Stan I should have felt inclined
to resign and gracefully push my job over to Lord Rothermere.
Power without responsibility isn't a nice thing to watch.'[87]

While Rudyard kept up his attack on the transference of power
in India (and was to become a vice-president of the Indian
Defence League after the Government of India Bill was introduced
in November 1934), his political focus had shifted homewards.
He could have been repeating lines from twenty or so years earlier,
as he railed against the MacDonald government's willingness to
lower its military guard. In September 1929 he had published his
poem 'The English Way' in *The Legion Book*, which was put
together on behalf of the British Legion. Ostensibly about
fourteenth-century border rivalry between the English and Scots,
this reiterated an old Kipling theme about the dangers of mistaking apparent English indifference for lack of will to take up
arms. In choosing Sir Henry Percy, Shakespeare's Hotspur, as his
hero, Rudyard was paying tribute to his friend Alan Percy, the
right-wing eighth Duke of Northumberland who had helped
rescue the *Morning Post*.

Rudyard was particularly concerned about the popular anti-
war mood in the country, which he attributed partly to the sophisticated propaganda of the League of Nations and partly to official
government policy. Having been disquieted by the disarmament
conference in London in the spring of 1930, he published his
poem 'Memories' in the *Daily Telegraph* on 3 November, shortly
before Armistice Day. This attacked 'the Socialist government' for
seeking 'the eradication of memories of the Great War' (as the
subtitle of the poem put it). The verses were soon reprinted in
The Patriot, a magazine owned by the Duke of Northumberland's
Boswell Publishing Company. (The following year Rudyard was
recommending *The Patriot* to Clive Wigram, King George V's
assistant private secretary. The two men had been in correspondence about *The Secrets Behind the Revolution*, a book

about Continental Freemasonry, a force which Rudyard appeared to equate with international Jewry. 'If you want to keep up with the movement,' he advised, 'you had better (unofficially) take in *The Patriot* . . . which quotes and comments on the Jew press.')

Rudyard's plea was the more potent because, a few weeks earlier, he had braved an August storm for a very personal statement of his involvement in the War Graves Commission's work. After years of coining inscriptions and visiting graves, he (with Carrie beside him) was in France for the opening of Sir Herbert Baker's Loos Memorial at Dud Corner, one of several monuments to the missing in the war. Since John Kipling's name had not been included on Sir Reginald Blomfield's great Menin Gate at Ypres, he had to wait for the inauguration of the Loos Memorial to be commemorated. Rudyard and Carrie were so impressed by the playing of the 'Last Post' at the Menin Gate every evening that they offered to pay for a similar solemn daily sounding at Loos. Initially their commitment was for one year, but the practice continued until their deaths.

Rudyard's concern for the memory of Britain's dead and his insistence on the maintenance of the country's defences followed from his alarm at the threat of a reviving Germany. As early as August 1925 he was wary when the Bambridges returned from a visit to Germany with positive opinions about Teutonic culture and cuisine. 'We shall have to hear from the Hun in seven or eight years from now, I fear,' he warned, 'and his voice will be very loud and clear.'[88] (George Bambridge's even-handedness reflected his father's term as secretary to Prince Alfred, the seafaring Duke of Edinburgh, who returned to Germany as hereditary Duke of Saxe-Coburg and Gotha.)

Although sympathetic to Mussolini in Italy, Rudyard was appalled by the rise of Hitler's fascism in Germany and by its imitators in Britain. After Oswald Mosley broke away from the Labour party in February 1931 and Oliver Baldwin looked set to join his New party, Rudyard counselled George Bambridge against any involvement: 'If Ollie has gone in with that crowd, please put down 10 francs worth of strychnine for him on my account. He isn't worth more!' George was serving out his final diplomatic posting in Paris and was thinking of taking up a political career. A couple of weeks later Rudyard added, 'Mosley don't impress me as any dam sort of bird to go out tiger-shooting with ... The man is temperamentally a bounder and an arriviste. Have you ever listened to him all out? After all he and his lot have left the Socialist party because it did not go far enough.'[89] In addition, Rudyard felt that Mosley had no interest in protecting India. He advised his son-in-law to recognise the fact that he was a 'crusted Tory'.[90]

Rudyard was beginning to pride himself on his forecasting abilities. Preparing for another visit to Egypt that spring, Rudyard told Gwynne that if anything happened to him the *Morning Post* should print 'The City of Brass', his pre-war blast against democracy and pacifism. It should include 'annotations and political parallels, and point out how the thing has come true almost line for line'.[91] (In June, the paper printed it anyway, though without notes.)

Political prospects did not improve in August 1931 when, after internal divisions about how to deal with unemployment, the majority of the Labour party broke away from MacDonald who was forced, with his rump, to set up a National Government in coalition with Baldwin's Conservatives. Rudyard's ideological accommodation with his cousin was now being sorely tested. In August he noted disparagingly that Stanley was 'a Socialist at heart',[92] brought up in the same intellectual tradition as their Aunt Georgie.[93] Three months later, after the National Government had been confirmed in office in an election, he observed that Baldwin and MacDonald were 'of one kidney – almost like the old Nigger minstrels – "corner men" with their "brudder Bones" gags'.[94]

One positive development was the formal pact of friendship signed by Britain and France at Lausanne in June 1932. Rudyard celebrated this by publishing his short memoir *Souvenirs of France* the following year. At the same time he never lost sight of the reason why this pact was required and stepped up his attacks on the 'Huns'. He reiterated his idea of Germany as the 'Fenrys Wolf', the werewolf from Nordic mythology that veers periodically between tameness and bestiality. Noting the Germans' thrift in a proposal to dress their soldiers like British officers in June 1931, he added, 'The Wehr-Wolf [*sic*] has got tired. He's been a man for 12 years, and has got all out of mankind that he needs. At least he can't get any more – so it is time for him to change shape. In less than a year he will be clamouring for the return of his Colonies, as "necessary for his self-respect". You wait and see! And he'll get 'em!'[95]

He referred to the Fenrys Wolf on the loose in his poem 'Bonfires on the Ice', published in the *Morning Post* on 13 November 1933. The title image reflected Rudyard's alarm at contemporary political myopia. As Gwynne helpfully explained in his editorial, ' "Bonfires on the Ice", if we interpret the poem aright, are policies built upon falsehood, which cheer and deceive for a time, but in the end fall through the foundations on which they are built.' By then, after Hitler had won power in February 1933 and proceeded to lay about his opponents, Rudyard was looking remarkably percipient.

Twenty

Limits and Renewals

1931–1936

Some things never changed at Bateman's. Almost every child who visited the house was amazed by the friendliness of the gnome-like creature with bushy eyebrows whom they were encouraged to call 'Uncle Ruddy'. As throughout his life, Rudyard took trouble to communicate with young people, and, particularly, with children as if they were his equals. His niece Josephine Dunham was thrilled when he told her about his 'box dreams' (or dreams within dreams) when she came with her family in December 1931. As an added amusement, the following year Rudyard launched a yellow and green paddle-boat, 'guaranteed to make the stoutest sweat like pigs,'[1] on the garden pond. As in other areas of his life, he had the knack of giving the boat different names for different people. To Bonar Sykes, his godson in India, he called it the 'Margaret'. To Miles Huntington-Whiteley, son of Baldwin's daughter Margot, it was the 'Queen Mary'. (Born in 1929, this young cousin twice removed was Carrie's godson. She insisted that he should be christened 'John-Miles', in memory of her son, though, elsewhere, he was known simply as Miles.)

However, there were exceptions to this rosy picture. A useful corrective to the conventional view was the experience of Roderick Jones's son Timothy, who was plunged into confusion when, in a conventional discussion about school, he was asked by Rudyard, 'Do they give you extra choo [meaning homework]?' He was then offered an opportunity to fire Rudyard's revolver. When young

Timothy showed apprehension, Rudyard said exasperatedly, 'At your age I would have given anything to shoot a revolver.'[2]

Another regular visitor, Henry Feilden, the teenage great-nephew of the late 'Colonel Sahib', would often drop round to borrow a book from the Bateman's library. Bounding up to the house one day in the early 1930s, he saw Rudyard standing at the window and exchanged waves. But when he knocked at the door he was told by a maid, 'Mr Kipling is not at home.' After he pointed out that he had just seen him the maid retreated in confusion. Shortly afterwards, Carrie appeared and said that her husband would be down in a minute.

Feilden had come face to face with the other great immovable at Bateman's – Carrie. Opinions still varied widely about her. According to Sibyl Colefax, Carrie was 'a super-bossy second rate American woman ... completely without humanity, the sort of woman you could only speak to about servants'.[3] But Lady Milner genuinely liked her and later remembered Carrie as 'the only person down here I could talk openly to'.[4]

One thing was certain: Carrie was an effective protector of her husband's space. The writer Hugh Walpole witnessed her in action at Victor Cazalet's house Fairlawne in October 1928. Discussing Radclyffe Hall's controversial *Well of Loneliness* with Rudyard over lunch, he was aware of Carrie's beady eye on them, making sure that her husband was spared 'any kind of disturbance, mental, physical or spiritual. That's her job and she does it superbly.' Walpole left a sympathetic portrait of a quiet, genial man with apparently no vanity. 'He walks about the garden, his eyebrows are all that are really visible of him. His body is nothing but his eyes are terrific, lambent, kindly, gentle and exceedingly proud. Good to us all and we are all shadows to him. "Carrie", he says, turning to Mrs K., and at once you see that she is the only real person here to him – so she takes him, wraps him up in her bosom and conveys him back to their uncomfortable hard-chaired home. He is quite content.'[5]

This was certainly the public image. Walpole was probably not informed enough to recognise the other, less attractive side of Carrie's hold on her husband. She had him completely in her thrall. As her own illnesses grew worse in her later years, she seldom allowed him out of her sight. He was hardly ever permitted to spend the night away on his own. (She was determined never again to feel that alarming sense of abandonment she had suffered on several occasions in the past – as, for example, when Rudyard joined the Channel fleet on naval manoeuvres in 1901.) Her insecurity was hardly helped by John's death, and her negative reaction to Elsie's marriage reflected the same underlying problem. When Rudyard tried to resist and do what he wanted, Gwynne recalled that 'she flew into hysterical tantrums which he learned to dread and [she] threatened to commit suicide with such violence that Kipling was terrified she would do so'.[6]

Gwynne also claimed that Rudyard was prevented from visiting his house in Essex on his own. Whenever he suggested it, Carrie would say, 'Why can't you ask him here?' Rudyard was driven to writing desperate letters (which he took to the post himself), begging Gwynne to come to Bateman's because he 'was so bored and you know why'. When Gwynne did appear, he and Rudyard would go for long walks. On being asked for the latest news, Rudyard would reply, 'Same old thing. She says she will throw herself out of the window if I don't do what she tells me.'[7]

Since such sentiments are not found in his surviving letters to Gwynne, they should be treated with caution. On the other hand, there is no evidence of friction between Gwynne and the Kipling family. There was no question of settling old scores. Any letters in which opinions were expressed about Carrie must have been ruthlessly removed in the general weeding process after his death.

Elsie dutifully did as her mother had requested. But she was not insensible to the effect that Carrie's behaviour had on Rudyard's health. And in this respect her recollections were markedly similar to Gwynne's. Her father was not allowed to visit her alone. If he put his foot down, Carrie became hysterical, which 'upset him beyond measure'.[8] He was terrified that his wife would throw herself out of a window. At one stage (Elsie did not specify when) Rudyard's doctors, including Lord Dawson, recommended that he should go away on a holiday on his own. 'But they would not take the responsibility of suggesting it,' she recalled to Lord Birkenhead. 'So it was left to George and me to try and arrange things. We very nearly succeeded but at the last moment my father would not go on with the plan as he knew that my mother would upset herself (not *be* upset or *be* made ill) and so his courage failed him.'[9]

An air of tension hung over the house. Elsie put it well in her epilogue to Carrington's biography of her father: 'My mother introduced into everything she did, and even permeated the life of her family with, a sense of strain and worry amounting sometimes to hysteria.'[10] Always susceptible to hypochondria, Carrie had, by the early 1930s, added gout and glaucoma to her list of afflictions, and needed to be treated by a variety of doctors at home and abroad. As for Rudyard, his daily life was increasingly restricted by what, in more cheerful moments, he called the 'circus in my inside'.[11] At times he contemplated suicide, recalled his friend Peter Stanley, who destroyed his letters because they contained 'such suffering'.[12]

Dogs still provided some emotional outlet at Bateman's and when Wop died in December 1930 it was an occasion for a general, cathartic outpouring of grief. At his burial in his own white coffin, Carrie was 'dreadfully upset' and Miss Walford, the secretary, 'went to pieces ... and yowled – "like an ineffective cow" '.[13] At least there was better news on the literary front, with Macmillan selling close on 100,000 copies of *Thy Servant a Dog* in the three months between its publication in October and Christmas.

Carrie was confined to bed with rheumatism at the time. The King's doctor Lord Dawson was consulted and recommended that after her regular treatment in Bath in January 1931 she should go to Egypt. After asking Hughes, his friend on the spot, about suitable places, Rudyard was directed to the spa at Helouan outside Cairo. But this proved too cold in February and the

Kiplings proceeded further up the Nile 'in search of heat',[14] until they came to Assouan where they were rewarded by 'a perfect ten days... [in] the finest climate in the world'.[15] Rudyard rediscovered the delights of long glasses of gin and tonic, which he described as 'the best friend I had'. As he relaxed, he observed the bird life: the British sparrow was driving out the local finches and bee-catchers, he informed Bland-Sutton.[16] Quite what Egyptians made of Carrie, with her parallel ray lamp (which had to be directed to her limbs while iodex ointment was applied) or her twice-daily sessions of 'electric battery' was not recorded.

Back home, Rudyard acquired a new black Aberdeen terrier, Mike (short for Malachi), as a companion for James. Despite the usual staff problems (a secretary, Miss Stone, quit after only two months: 'a calamity as I have been giving her intensive training all these weeks, ... Carrie), the estate was thriving. In the autumn Rudyard sold a pair of his eighty head of cattle for fifty-four pounds. A fallen oak yielded 160 feet of first-class timber, which had to be hauled through the mud with two tractors. 'Lovely job,' he commented. 'Like Ypres.' He complained to Hughes that townspeople could not allow British farmers to be prosperous as they needed cheap food so they could afford their amusements. Nevertheless, there was a note of defiance in his comment, 'Things are dam bad, but not bloody bad.'[18]

In September the pain in Rudyard's stomach was again unbearable. After consulting with Lord Dawson, Bland-Sutton suggested another operation. As Rudyard explained to Elsie, this would '[produce] a small dimple in which J.B.S. takes great pleasure just to one side of my tummy button' and give vent to 'bottled up wind that ought to blow freely'.[19] The man scheduled to wield the knife on what was described as an 'umbilical hernia' was Alfred Webb-Johnson, who had inherited Bland-Sutton's role as top people's surgeon. However, after an interminable series of examinations and X-rays in October, he decided this invasive procedure would not be required. Rudyard was bidden to take more exercise and, once more, to cut down on his smoking.

Long periods of discomfort had taken their toll. Rudyard told Gwynne in November, 'To say that I am (mentally and morally) sick is to put it but feebly.'[20] This was, sadly, all too apparent to people he met. He had recently paid a surprise visit to Arthur Lee, a remarkable soldier whom Theodore Roosevelt described as the only Englishman, apart from Rudyard and Rider Haggard, he wanted to hear from. Lee had served as military attaché to the United States Army in Cuba and been adopted as an honorary colonel in Roosevelt's Rough Riders. A driving force in the Ministry of Munitions during the war, he had given his house, Chequers, to the nation, for the use of the Prime Minister.

Although cast in the same imperialist mould, Lord Lee of Fareham, as he now was, recognised Rudyard had 'become hopelessly reactionary and even expresse[d] his belief that the Labour Ministers take bribes of the crudest sort ~~and is~~ ~~gr~~~~...~~ ~~here is~~ equal to the worst in America! That wonderful brain of his, which used to have the most delicate and subtle perceptions, seemed to have atrophied from the time when his only son was lost at Loos, and he cannot now accept or "do with" any of the changes since the pre-War period, the spirit of which he had understood and portrayed so marvellously.' Lord Lee had just returned from India, following the long-awaited Round Table conference, which accorded the country Dominion status. In New Delhi he had stayed with the Viceroy, Lord Irwin, whom Rudyard regarded as a traitor for having sat down with Gandhi. Accordingly, Lee knew to steer well clear of this topic with his guest. 'We only just touched on India, but I could see that his feelings about the later developments there were as set and prejudiced as those of any old "Qui Hai".'[21] Younger people could see the funny side of this situation. The poet John Betjeman expressed the fashionable ennui for Rudyard's work when he wrote to his friend Camilla Russell in August 1931, 'We have invented a very good game which consists in taking the first verse of any of the more awful poems by Kipling and inventing verses in the manner and from the moral standpoint of Kipling to follow after them.' Not that Rudyard minded: at the Beefsteak one night, he blurted out to a fellow diner, the lawyer John Maude, 'I hate your generation.' When asked why, he replied, 'Because you're going to give it all away.'[22]

When Lady Milner came to stay at Bateman's for the New Year she found Rudyard on the road to recovery. On 30 December, his sixty-sixth birthday, he sat up discussing politics and – unusually – poetry. He talked about Keats, Shelley and Wordsworth, and recited a poem, 'Akbar's Bridge', which he had written in Cairo at the start of the year and which accompanied 'The Debt' in his latest collection of stories, *Limits and Renewals*, which was in the press and would be published in April 1932. (The names of Rudyard's books were often as close as he got to making a personal statement and, accordingly, he put considerable effort into them. 'I'm rather hesitating between titles,' he told his aunt Edith Macdonald on 31 December. '*That's* the difficult part of a book.'[23])

'The Debt' was an intriguing tale, based on an incident Rudyard had himself witnessed, of a former Indian soldier, a Moslem, who had seen King George V, on a visit to war graves in France, telling a sick general to put on his overcoat (or 'Baritish warrum'). The Moslem believed that as a result of this act of kindness the King would survive the illness that nearly killed him in 1929. In 'Akbar's Bridge', Rudyard provided a secular antidote to the hint of sympathetic Islamic magic in his story. While affirming the nobility of 'kingly justice', the verses reiterated an old theme: a bridge across a river is more useful to the poor than another mosque.

Lady Milner went to bed at eleven o'clock, worrying about both Kiplings. 'He looks better than he did, but still suffers acute indigestion and she is very much bothered about him.' The next day he talked to her in a more personal manner than usual. He told her – wrongly, but indicative of his real feelings – that his illness had begun fifteen years earlier (a year after John's death). 'He suffers acute pain that may seize him at any moment. He does not want to go abroad or far from a Doctor, and yet I am sure both Kiplings need a change and to get warm.'[24]

The demands of the medical profession proved stronger than

any desire to travel, though the Kiplings' period in Bath in January 1932 was designed to relieve Carrie's ailments rather than Rudyard's. He visited old literary colleagues – George Saintsbury, Dr William Melsome and Ellie Bridson – who helped him as he battled with a late story, 'Proofs of Holy Writ' – an erudite debate between Shakespeare and Ben Jonson on the craft of writing, inspired by a request to the former to help in the translation of the King James Bible. Rudyard was able to demonstrate his learning in a manner he enjoyed and, in particular, to show off his familiarity with Jacobean literature and culture.

While in Bath, he wrote a speech on social welfare reform for the Prince of Wales. This kept up his links with the royal family and helped boost the Prince's incongruous reputation as a champion of the underprivileged. But it was a hypocritical exercise, since his own thinking, as Lord Lee had noticed, was almost entirely backward-looking. His personal concerns were much better represented in February when he suggested to Geoffrey Dawson, editor of *The Times*, a series of articles on the music-hall as an early form of English propaganda.[25] He even proposed John Booth, a journalist from the literary world of the 1890s, as the right man to write on the subject. He later sent Booth a version (from memory) of 'Kafoozalum',[26] his favourite popular ballad from the halls, that he had referred to in his story 'The Maltese Cat'. As he had told Gwynne, jazz was 'on its last legs' and people were 'fed up with songs without incident'.[27] His rendering of the rollicking 'Kafoozalum' (later the basis of a bawdy rugby song) suggested there was some sound basis to his argument.

In part, Rudyard's retrospection reflected the age. The previous autumn a play had appeared on the London stage that marked a turning point in post-war consciousness. With its unashamed nostalgia, Noël Coward's *Cavalcade* turned its back on both the despondency of the immediate post-war years and the freneticism of the jazz age, and tried to evoke a wry sense of pride in British society and its enduring values. There is no specific record of the Kiplings having seen this play, but Rudyard had enjoyed Coward's works before. He certainly seemed to be well informed when Julia Taufflieb, who had definitely seen *Cavalcade*, sought his advice about producing a similar series of tableaux about France, stressing the Franco-British relationship. In her unpublished memoirs she claimed that Rudyard worked on this project with her for three days. (Again, there is no reference in Carrie's diaries.) According to Mme Taufflieb, he suggested that she should take the finished piece to the playwright Henri Bordeaux, who worked on it with a celebrated colleague, Marcel Prévost. They eventually decided that a stage version would be too costly and wanted to make a film. Rudyard continued to provide encouragement, counselling her, initially, to keep her temper 'while the film experts are making a hash of your baby' and then not to 'let 'em tarry over it too long. It will be needed and the sooner the better.' A couple of years later, in 1934, Rudyard took a more personal role in a similar project – writing three poems for the Pageant of Parliament that the failed film-maker Walter Creighton devised to boost his flagging career.

In keeping with Rudyard's mood the Bible, more than ever, was his favoured source book: for its sounds and general expansiveness as much as for anything else, a point he made to Bland-Sutton, whom he was advising on the republication of a book about Uganda. He offered a quotation from Job xxvi: 3 for the title-page – 'By his spirit he hath garnished the heavens: his hand hath formed the crooked serpent' – adding, 'There's something spacious about that which takes my fancy.'[28] Since Bland-Sutton's book was mainly about African wildlife, Rudyard remarked on man's encroachment on the animal kingdom. 'Birds, I assume, will always exist, but what will come to the big and little game as settlement extends? The same fate as overtook the buffalo in the U.S., or some extension of the game reserves and regulated control. With the advance of roads and cars, there will be no interest in going out to kill things in S. Africa.'[29] As a Fellow of the Zoological Society, he speculated that this process might lead to the creation of 'real' zoological gardens in East Africa.

*

Once Carrie's medical treatments were over the Kiplings were free to depart for Monte Carlo on 1 March 1932 at the start of an eleven-week holiday. Despite the amusement of watching millionaires with their mistresses at gaming tables, Rudyard was more interested in a dog show on the terraces below the Casino, where he tried to interpret the basic elements of French canine psychology. (All the animals were bored or nervous, he noted, except the Pekinese.) He had already started to write 'Leading Dog Malachi', later published as 'A Sea Dog', a story about a terrier on a destroyer during the war, when he met a retired rear-admiral who had served on one of the very vessels he was describing. With his attention to detail he sent him a three-page questionnaire. 'Isn't it funny that when one is dead-keen on one subject, all Earth stretches out her hands to help one?' he asked Bland-Sutton rhetorically.

Shortly before returning home he was dismayed to learn of the assassination of the French President Paul Doumer, whom he had met the previous year. Passing through Paris in early May, he found the city in a state of silent shock – a mood which tallied with his own, as he had just learnt of the death of his dog James. His general sense of foreboding was reflected in 'The Storm Cone', the latest of his brooding poems warning of the political dangers ahead, which was published in the *Morning Post* in May.

While he had been away in France he was asked to become an honorary fellow of Magdalene College, Cambridge. This was the sort of invitation he liked, particularly as Magdalene had been the alma mater of a literary hero, Samuel Pepys, whose notable collection of books was housed in the College library. The Master of the College was A. B. Ramsay, the former Eton 'beak' who had collaborated with Rudyard and others on Horace's non-existent Fifth Book during the war years. Once he became Master of Magdalene, Ramsay had regularly sought Rudyard's attendance at various dinners and lectures. Rudyard resisted until he was offered the supreme accolade, a fellowship. Then he happily cast his pro-Oxford sympathies aside and, as a non-graduate, found it greatly satisfying to be able to talk about 'my College'. Before the end of May he paid his first visit when, for his induction in the chapel, he wore a white linen surplice, with his red D. Litt. hood trailing behind his back. He celebrated by offering the college magazine some of the 'Freer Verse Horace' translations he had been making since before the war.

His association with Magdalene and Cambridge was appropriate. Despite Rudyard's angry rejection of Einstein's 'warped' experiments in 1919, his more recent references to science showed some familiarity with developments in modern physics. Cambridge University was the main British centre for research into quantum mechanics. Its professor of astronomy, A. S. Eddington, had given these new ideas wider currency in his 1927 Gifford lectures 'The Nature of the Physical World'. (The title of one of these lectures – 'Limits of Physical Knowledge' – might have been written by Rudyard.) William Empson, a Magdalene don, had translated these new scientific insights into the field of English literature in his 1930 book, *Seven Types of Ambiguity,* another title tailor-made for Rudyard. Empson subsequently lost his fellowship for disciplinary reasons (following the discovery of contraceptives in his rooms), but his mantle was taken up by another Magdalene English don, Ivor Richards, who had spent long hours debating the relationship between Science and Mysticism with his friend T. S. Eliot, and who was probably as responsible for inviting Rudyard to join the College as anyone.[30]

Rudyard's connection with Magdalene coincided with a better period in his life. One reason was that Trix's depression had lifted: when she visited Bateman's in May, Rudyard noted that 'at 64 she looks no more than a dishonest 40' and was 'as quick and as on the spot as ever'.[31] (On her part, her husband had been threatening to leave her and although she fought him, she no longer had to keep up the pretence of being a happily married woman.) Another summer visitor was Abe Bailey's son John, who brought his fiancée, Winston Churchill's daughter Diana. Rudyard was pleased for the couple, who seemed 'gaga-ly devoted', but disappointed in the young man's choice of a father-in-law.

However, he could never tell when his stomach troubles would flare up. Suffering considerable pain in September, he had to cancel a scheduled talk to the Society of Mechanical Engineers. 'Officially, I regret beyond words,' he told Lady Bland-Sutton. 'Privately, I'm as pleased as Punch.'[32] Because he was unwell, he was unable to participate in the dousing of a fire in one of the wooden cottages by the mill at the bottom of the garden. He was amused to discover the conflagration had been caused by the carter's wife putting down some smouldering ashes for her cat's litter.[33] According to Cecily Nicholson, the Bateman's secretary at the time, he wrote a story about the incident, but it has not survived.

He had recovered by early December, when he received a summons from King George, who wanted help with the Christmas Day broadcast he had finally, after much prodding, agreed to make. Rudyard did as required and was deeply touched when, on 25 December, he heard his sovereign declaiming his words to the Empire over the wireless. It was as if the 'Song of the Cities' had come true, commented Carrie.[34] The following July, Rudyard was even prepared to follow suit and make his own first broadcast, a talk to Canadian authors.

His only set-back, as he worked on proofs of his *Collected Verse* and on his *Souvenirs of France* over the holiday period, was a visit from Sir Herbert Baker, who tried to get him to agree to other artists and writers using The Woolsack in Cape Town. Although he had not been there for well over two decades, Rudyard was incensed at what he perceived as a plot to provide 'some sort of soft billet for some pet of the (Rhodes) Trustees – probably a pink Bolshie'.[35] Baker reported this 'die-hard attitude' to the Marquess of Lothian, the former Philip Kerr, who was secretary of the Trustees. He added that Rudyard had at least promised to consider the matter. But when Baker approached him again, Rudyard was implacable: 'It seems to me that – as I am in my 68th year – any matter of reversions might be left over for the little time that remains, without inconvenience.'[36] A month later Baker heard some truths (or was it simply historical revisionism?) from Sir James Macdonald, a former associate of Rhodes: 'Kipling has always been very sticky about the Woolsack. Between ourselves Rhodes latterly found him rather trying.'[37]

Rudyard was reluctant to let go of the vestiges of his relationship with Rhodes. Undoubtedly he understood that the future of France – suddenly under much greater threat following Hitler's accession to power in January 1933 – was far more important than developments in South Africa. As a show of support his *Souvenirs of France* was published in the *Daily Mail* in March (and, more or less concurrently, in translation, in the *Revue des Deux Mondes*).

As he was back in Monte Carlo, he could not attend a grand dinner to celebrate the 300th anniversary of Pepys's birth at Magdalene on 23 February. By way of apology he sent verses, 'To the Companions', that were published in *The Times*. The title caused Carrie some confusion, as she described the poem as Rudyard's 'Horace verses', mixing it up with the similarly titled Horace Book V spoof that Rudyard had published in *Debits and Credits*. As a result this newer poem was later called simply 'Samuel Pepys'.

Returning through Paris, Rudyard would normally have stayed with the Stanleys, but instead he sought accommodation at the Hotel Lancaster in the rue de Berri. The reason, as a couple of melancholy letters from Peter Stanley had indicated, was that his highly strung, demanding wife Frances had had a nervous breakdown. Details are sketchy, but family members recall that after returning from a desert trip she began acting strangely (taking her clothes off in public, for example) and had to be hospitalised. Rudyard was preoccupied with his own medical problems. As he informed Hughes,

My 'tummy' trouble came to a head in Paris as I was passing through on my way, as I thought, home. I had to lie up for five weeks there, in charge of a couple of doctors who, being French, went remorselessly to the root of the trouble. Which, as I have

> always suspected, is ulceration of sorts and of long standing. Anyhow they put me on a diet that would starve a cat, and a system of treatment almost as drastic and I am told that, in Allah's good time, I shall be reestablished.[38]

His diet consisted of potato, spaghetti and one boiled egg per day. He also had to take an unhealthy sounding cocktail of bismuth and belladonna – ten days on and twenty days off.[39] But at least his pain was temporarily relieved.

Carrie made her usual fuss about the amount of tax she and her husband had to pay in February: around half their gross income of £32,831 went in a combination of income tax and supertax, and she claimed they would have to survive on bare necessities for the rest of the year. Unsurprisingly, she still had £200 to lend to her relative Mabel Leigh in August. And, equally unsurprisingly, she demanded Mabel's diamond necklace as surety.[40] Quite how the daughter of General William Washington Gordon had been reduced to a state of relative penury was a roundabout story. When, in 1898, she married the indolent barrister, the Honourable Rowland Leigh, Mabel had had the reasonable expectation that he would inherit his father's title of Lord Leigh, along with the estate of Stoneleigh Abbey in Warwickshire. Rowland's elder brother Rupert was in his forties and seemed set for bachelorhood. However, in 1906, at the age of fifty, Rupert defied the pundits by marrying an eighteen-year-old girl who soon gave birth to an heir. By then Mabel had two children, Rowland and Margaret (known as Peggy), and her husband was doing little to support them. Rowland (junior) took to the stage and later went to Hollywood to try to make his fortune. Beautiful but impecunious, Peggy was a bridesmaid at Elsie Kipling's wedding. The night before the ceremony she was rung by Charles Graves, a journalist on 'Londoner's Log', the gossip column of Lord Beaverbrook's *Sunday Express*, who was looking for a story. The outcome was that she later married Charles, brother of the poet Robert Graves, and they were notable 'bright young things' in London society in the late 1920s. She was pretty enough to attract the attention of Beaverbrook, for whose papers she wrote as Jane Gordon.

Carrie would see Mabel from time to time. This had the unexpected bonus for Rudyard of re-introducing him to Lord Dunsany, the Irish peer who wrote finely wrought tales of fantasy. Dunsany was the nephew (by marriage) of Mabel's husband Rowland. (His wife, Beatrice, was the daughter of Rowland's sister, the Countess of Jersey, the active wife of the Governor of New South Wales when Rudyard had been in Australia in the early 1890s.) Dunsany had originally encountered Rudyard in South Africa, where he worked as an assistant press censor under Lord Stanley. When the Leighs and the Dunsanys visited Bateman's in August 1926, Mabel remarked to Carrie and Lady Beatrice, 'I haven't married a genius, as both of you have, but I assure you he can be quite as temperamental and tiresome.'[41]

Dunsany was a notable addition to Rudyard's corps of literary-inclined aristocratic correspondents. Another was Lord Gorell, the politician and poet who edited an old-fashioned literary magazine, the *Cornhill*, for John Murray. Rudyard expanded to Gorell on his disenchantment with modern aesthetics:

> This isn't a world, just now, where there is a great recognition of Beauty. Did you notice how, after the War, the men who sung dwelt, quite naturally, on the harsh line and colours of the wreckage in which they had lived for years. And their metres conformed to their scheme. Later, when they drew free of the first stresses, they pinned their themes to some small intense aspect of some small thing, long watched and intensely pored over ... The fellows who hadn't 'been there' imitated – that's my theory – and emphasised the note and structure of harshness without the authentic experiences to bite it in.[42]

Rudyard attributed the curse of modernity to changes in the 1860s and 1870s when there were the 'first mutterings against respectability ... [and] revelations of the Prussian spirit on its way to become Hitlerism'.[43]

In August 1933 the Kiplings visited Southampton for the launch of Peter Stanley's yacht the *Trenora* (the model for the industrialist Sir Bernard Docker's gin palace, the *Shamera*, which was also built by Thornycroft). With Frances well enough to attend, they spent a night on board and returned to Bateman's the next day. The experience provided an idea for Rudyard's obscure political offering 'The Pleasure Cruise', which appeared in the *Morning Post* on Armistice Day, a parallel piece to the more accessible 'Bonfires on the Ice' a couple of days later. Drawing on *Dialogues of the Dead* by Lucian, a third-century writer from Asia Minor, 'The Pleasure Cruise' told of the shades of dead soldiers returning to their homeland to make sure that their ultimate sacrifice has not been in vain. Inevitably, they discover they have been forgotten and the country's defences have been allowed to run down. They go back to the underworld, sad and disillusioned.

Since his friend Sir Archibald Montgomery-Massingberd had become Chief of the Imperial General Staff (in 1933), Rudyard was better informed about defence matters – as he lost no opportunity to impress on trusted journalistic friends. Lady Milner had taken over the direction of the *National Review* after her brother Leo had become ill in 1929. Rudyard peppered her with memos about topics to cover, including articles with titles such as 'The Return of the Wehr-Wolf'.[44] To Gwynne at the *Morning Post* he was more specific: 'Personally I shall be grateful if we are allowed 3 years: but given our present administration and our disturbing internal influences, I can't see why the [German] General Staff should not strike before that time. We aren't merely asking for it; we're imploring it; and that dam' League of Nations Union is rotting out all the schools (any proof of Hun money?) with their gas scares and horrors of war propaganda.'[45]

Having severed their connection with the Foreign Office, George and Elsie Bambridge were inspired by Rudyard's fellowship at Magdalene to lease Wimpole Hall, a magnificent largely

Georgian pile owned by the 7th Viscount Clifden. George had known and loved the place since his youth when he used to shoot there with the Agar-Robartes family. He had been at Eton with Cecil Agar-Robartes, a feckless but cultured younger son of the sixth Viscount. Through Cecil – who, appropriately, went to Magdalene – George came to know Gerald Agar-Robartes, with whom he had served as a diplomat in Madrid. After the war, Gerald had lived with the eccentric homosexual peer Lord Berners and was almost certainly gay himself. Through the accident of history, he inherited this vast Cambridgeshire mansion in 1930.

Set in 2,400 acres of land, Wimpole was a monument to gracious aristocratic living. Originally built by the local MP Sir Thomas Chicheley in the mid-seventeenth century, it had passed to Queen Anne's High Tory chief minister, Robert Harley, the first Earl of Oxford, who, in the early years of the eighteenth century, had engaged the classical architect James Gibbs to renovate it (and in particular to build a library for his well-known collection of books). Harley's heyday did not last: under the Whiggish Hanoverians, the house was acquired by George II's Lord Chancellor, Philip Yorke, the first Earl of Hardwicke, who in 1729 prosecuted the notorious warden of the Fleet prison, Thomas Bambridge, whom George may well have claimed as an ancestor. George Bambridge would certainly have warmed to the fourth Earl in this line, 'Old Blowhard', who, as well as serving as an admiral in the navy, had been Lord-in-Waiting to Queen Victoria (and later Lord Privy Seal).

However, the fifth Earl, a friend of the Prince of Wales, earned the nickname 'Champagne Charlie' because of his extravagance, mainly on the race-course. After he fell seriously into debt, his main creditor was a bank controlled by the Agar-Robartes family, which had briefly owned the house two hundred years earlier. In 1894, Lord Robartes, the chairman of the bank, acquired the house but, five years later, when he succeeded his cousin as the 6th Viscount Clifden, he decided to retain his ancestral home at Lanhydrock in Cornwall as his main seat. (Originally Cornish, the Robarteses had grown wealthy from wool and tin in the later middle ages. An earlier Lord Robartes was said to have purchased his barony from James I's favourite Lord Buckingham for £10,000 in 1625.)

The 6th Viscount had a large, reclusive and old-fashioned family. Only two of his ten children ever married. One son, John, died in infancy; another, Tommy, was killed in France at the Battle of Loos (though serving in a different regiment – the Grenadier Guards – from John Kipling). Alexander, the youngest son, also fought at Loos where he was shot and wounded in the jaw. Subsequently he became a depressive and took his own life in January 1930, a loss which is thought to have precipitated the death of his father. After extricating himself from the Foreign Office, Gerald, the new Viscount, decided to continue the practice of living at Lanhydrock.

Wimpole was therefore available for rent at £225 a quarter. Since it was eight miles from Cambridge, Rudyard was able to combine visits there and to 'his College'. He told the Bambridges that if they knocked down Wimpole's wings, they would have a lovely 'gite'.[46] But they had only taken the place for four months and, on 15 August, had to move on. In the autumn they rented Attingham Park, another vast neo-classical lodge near Shrewsbury in Shropshire. But their eight-year-old marriage was suffering under this peripatetic life-style and the Kiplings felt they had to help out. They bought Elsie a small car, and sent her and George on a cruise to Jamaica in early 1934. *En voyage* they corresponded about the next stage in the Bambridges' peregrinations. George and Elsie were thinking of taking Burgh House, a Queen Anne house in London's Hampstead. Rudyard offered to pay up to £300 in rent, but advised his daughter and son-in-law that they were living beyond their means and 'that will mean worry and strain'.[47] However, some other concern seems to have been indicated on 9 March when the Kiplings, in the South of France, received 'letters from Elsie in Jamaica [that] greatly distress us'.[48] Money probably was at the root of the matter.

Was Elsie pushing George to get a job? Did he resent the financial support of his in-laws? Or perhaps Elsie had been trying to have a baby and now realised this was no longer possible.

This would have saddened the Kiplings who were undergoing their latest round of medical treatments at the Villa l'Enchantement, a rented house at Mougins, a few miles inland from Cannes. Carrie was receiving regular massage from a thick-set Swede, while Rudyard had put his stomach in the care of a local doctor, Dr Brès, whom he liked. He was in no mood for socialising, however, turning down Somerset Maugham's invitation to meet the King of Siam, who had struggled to translate 'If–' into the Thai language. Rudyard did little work, but savoured the almond blossom and enjoyed observing the local peasantry who were largely of Italian origin and who, he claimed rather too enthusiastically, were greatly supportive of Mussolini.

Back in England, Rudyard's internal 'circus' persisted and he was restricted to a diet of Allen & Hanbury processed foods and Horlicks Malted Milk. When in August a new specialist, Sir Maurice Cassidy, said he could also eat sardines, it was a cause for rejoicing. That month the Kiplings travelled to Jersey, seeking pain relief at the clinic of Sir Herbert Barker, a controversial healer cum manipulator, who had been recommended by Peter Stanley. Rudyard did not immediately benefit from the great man's examination, which left him 'depressed and feeling sore'.[49] Carrie, on the other hand, was interested to discover that relations[50] had lived on the island, which reminded her of Bermuda – a comparison that Rudyard, in sourer mood, disdained. When he remarked that most of the population were 'nudists from Huddersfield, Batley, Dewsbury and so forth',[51] he was not only keeping up his attack on tourism but also decrying the cult of 'naturism', which was linked in his mind to popular 'left-wing' causes such as hiking and, of course, pacifism.

Peter Stanley himself was cruising the Mediterranean in the *Trenora*. In September he contacted Rudyard from off the coast of Turkey where he visited Gallipoli. When Peter sent a photograph of a local sunset, Rudyard indicated their shared interest in cosmology and religion: ' "Modern Science" says that St John got the inspiration and background of "Revelation" from the sunsets off Patmos.'[52]

The following month the Cunard liner *Queen Mary* was unveiled. Rudyard had viewed its early plans in 1928 and made suggestions for its name when it was still known as No. 534. His favourite was Magnalia – meaning 'mighty works', which he said could not be twisted into Yiddish. For its launch, he provided the Queen with a text from Ecclesiasticus. But, although he had called on Cunard's services from time to time (for example, to transport 'the Duchess' to Marseilles in 1933), he refused either to celebrate the new ship in verse or to take up an invitation to travel in it: his aversion to the United States persisted and, as he told Percy Bates, 'nothing this side of Gehenna would make me go to New York.'[53]

On the other side of the Atlantic, Mabel Leigh's son Rowland was trying to discover what the MGM studio was doing with its option to film the book *Kim*. 'I have Mabel Leigh to lunch re Rowley Leigh's cable about *Kim* from Hollywood,' wrote Carrie in her diary on 9 November 1934. This project had been in the offing since the South Church Street Company acquired an option in 1923. But Hollywood, around the time of the introduction of the talking movie, had been in an indecisive mood and unwilling to spend large sums shooting the story on location in India with native actors as Rudyard wanted. The option was taken up by MGM, whose Vice-President Irving G. Thalberg came to discuss terms in July 1931. Thalberg was interested in four projects – *Gunga Din*, *The Road to Mandalay*, *Captains Courageous* and *Kim*. Although he paid $25,000 each for options on the latter two properties, Rudyard had come to view this aspect of his business with wry scepticism. When the studio asked if he could add some sex appeal to the script of *Captains Courageous*, he provided the information that 'a happily married lady cod fish lays about 3 million eggs at one confinement.'[54]

Rudyard was happier dealing with Colonel Dick Rawlinson, a

former colleague of his son John in the Irish Guards who had been hired as military adviser and script-writer by Michael Balcon's Gaumont British Picture Corporation, which paid £2500 for an option to film *Soldiers Three* in July 1934. Rudyard complained to Bambridge in December that he was having the same problems with Gaumont as with other film companies: 'not only won't they learn, they cannot conceive any need to depart from the blood and sex standard'.[55] Ironically, the following month Rudyard had to impress upon Rawlinson, 'Dinah says "bloody" in all innocence with strict reference to M[ulvaney]'s cheek. Can you get that into their heads?'[56] (Clearly the script drew on the complete repertoire of Mulvaney stories for this referred to an encounter in 'The Courting of Dinah Shadd'.) That same month Rudyard accepted an offer of £5000 from Alexander Korda's London Film Productions for a seven-year option on 'Toomai of the Elephants'. At the same time an independent producer, Widgey Newman, was completing a version of 'Thy Servant a Dog' which, as Rudyard explained to Michael Mason, was nothing to do with his story of that name, but was a sentimental 'short', loosely based on his 1932 poem 'His Apologies'.[57]

Despite this activity, few of these projects were completed. Neither Balcon's *Soldiers Three* nor Korda's *Toomai* was ever made, while MGM's *Kim* had to wait until 1950 for an audience. However, Kipling's death in January 1936 did spark a new round of interest in filming his work. Hollywood had discovered imperial history as a source for grand epics such as *Lives of a Bengal Lancer*. In March that year contracts were signed with Reliance Pictures for a romantic *Gunga Din* and with 20th Century Fox for *Wee Willie Winkie*. These productions competed with MGM's *Captains Courageous* to become the first big-budget movie from Kipling material. With the author no longer to contend with, 20th Century Fox was able to change the sex of Wee Willie Winkie from a boy to a girl – the 1937 vehicle for Shirley Temple that Graham Greene considered was child pornography (and was served with a libel writ for saying so). MGM also turned to a child actor, Freddie Bartholomew, for its nervy, actionful *Captains Courageous*, which was nominated for an Oscar the same year. In 1939, RKO (in lieu of Reliance Pictures) produced *Gunga Din*, starring Douglas Fairbanks Jr, which drew plaudits from, among others, Bertolt Brecht. Along the way there were undistinguished versions of *Elephant Boy* by the documentary maker Robert Flaherty and Paramount's *The Light that Failed*, starring Ronald Colman. Alexander Korda returned to the fray to make the first movie of *The Jungle Book* for United Artists in 1942. The Disney cartoon version followed in 1967.

By early 1935 the Bambridges were installed in Burgh House, Hampstead, where their life centred on entertaining. Angela Thirkell's son, Graham McInnes, remembered 'the buzz of scented conversation' at a party there when he passed through London shortly after finishing university in Australia. He was introduced to Rudyard who asked after his friend 'Banjo' Paterson. When McInnes innocently suggested that the old bushwhacker poet was dead, Rudyard exploded. ' "Dead?" he said, with such vehemence that several people near us stopped talking and turned their heads with glasses half raised to their lips. "Dead?" he repeated. "That's very curious. I had a letter from him recently. Is this true?" ' After Rudyard calmed down, he laid his hand on Graham's shoulder and said, 'After all, why should you know? He isn't read nowadays.' Graham noted that he smiled, as if to say, 'Neither am I.'[58] But Rudyard was right about Paterson who did not die until 1941.

Angela Thirkell herself had returned to England from Australia at the end of 1929. Two years later she published *Three Houses*, a memoir that recalled her life at The Elms and her friendship with Josephine Kipling. Rudyard made no known comment, but the idea of a relation trading on family secrets irked him. When, in 1933, she worked on the centenary of Edward Burne-Jones's birth, he observed, 'I don't mind the heathen eating their ancestors but I draw the line at "Christians" living on 'em.'[59] Angela, for her part, felt Rudyard should have helped with this event. When she asked the artist Will Rothenstein's help in contacting Rudyard she noted, 'He is so queer that his family can't well approach him.'[60] Perhaps Oliver Baldwin felt he could do the job because, a couple of months later, he wrote a 'tipsy letter' inviting himself to Bateman's. He said he was 'fat and forty', and trying to support himself with his pen. But the Kiplings had just finished entertaining fourteen people in six days and, as Rudyard told Elsie, 'Somehow I think one Agg [Angela] is quite enough in the family.'[61]

With a general election pending in November 1935, Bambridge had at last decided to commit himself to a political career as a Member of Parliament. Over the years he had debated the political situation with his father-in-law, who had continued to steer him away from involvement with fascism. In April 1934 Rudyard had expressed scepticism about how much of this 'Blackshirt racket' was a newspaper stunt and how much genuine. (This was in the days when Oswald Mosley's British Union of Fascists was being backed by Lord Rothermere's *Daily Mail*.) Rudyard blamed the movement's rise on official ineptness. He had no real quarrel with the National Government's policies on finance or trade, but believed 'that a clear attitude (if you can imagine RM or SB having one) on Defence and India would have calmed things'.[62]

Despite Rudyard's financial backing (for family rather than political reasons, he stressed),[63] George failed to win adoption as a Conservative candidate in Eastbourne, Petersfield or Basingstoke. After he finally accepted that he was not going to be successful Carrie noted, 'George B. is fed up with politics and will not stand for parliament.'[64] Rudyard had his own views on what had happened: 'Electors don't seem to care for men with war-service.'[65]

Earlier in the year, from February until early May, the Kiplings had spent three months in the Mediterranean sunshine in Cannes. Rudyard climbed in the pine woods overlooking the sea and paid a couple of visits to Monte Carlo where he resisted the urge to gamble. To occupy his time, he became obsessed with a story about truffles and the dogs trained to root around for them in the woods of central France. He wrote to Bland-Sutton for scientific information about the truffle. The result was his story 'Teem: a Treasure Hunter', which commentators have dissected for its autobiographical detail. But the manuscript notes[66] provide little support for this view. If the tale has relevance to Rudyard's life, it is as a fable about the need for dedication to one's Art. Its most important, and debatable, line runs, 'Outside his Art an Artist must never dream!', in which Rudyard seems to admonish himself for his political interests, which have diverted him from his real vocation.

Even now, political argument tormented him, as if an addiction. On 30 April he informed Percy Bates from France that he was as 'nervous as a bag of ferrets' about the King's Jubilee celebrations the following week. His concern was trivial: that South Africa might cause problems because of its close relationship with Germany. He returned to England in time for Jubilee Day, 6 May, when he was scheduled to address a meeting of the Royal Society of St George. At this fiercely patriotic event he covered much familiar ground, but with greater foreboding than usual, arguing how incongruous it was that the pacifist idea of war as evil had developed at the same time as the growth of 'an opponent whose national life and ideals were based on a cult – a religion as it now appears – of War'. More than ever, he blamed the world's problems on the excesses of state machines: 'Today, State-controlled murder and torture, open and secret, within and outside the borders of a State, State-engineered famine, starvation and slavery are requisite; State-imposed Godlessness, or State-prescribed paganism, are commonplaces.'

He took comfort from the fact that Ramsay MacDonald's National Government was beginning to rearm, and he hoped that this had not come too late to prevent Britain drifting further and becoming one of 'those submerged races of history'. Carrie recorded that Rudyard spoke 'firmly and in good form'.[67] He followed the speech with a more personal statement of his affection for his sovereign – a poem called 'The King and the Sea', which described a man coming to terms with himself through his relationship with the ocean. Its publication coincided with the Jubilee Review of the Fleet, which Rudyard watched with Percy Bates from RMS *Berengaria* off Spithead.

Rudyard's own psychological state was described in another poem, 'Hymn of Breaking Strain', that he published without further comment in the *Daily Telegraph* and in the professional journal *The Engineer* in March. Varying slightly his 'broken spring' or 'magneto' theme, he contrasted the loads and pressures that engineers calculate with the unpredictable stresses human beings endure. He pointed to painful experience as he prayed for the 'veiled and secret power' to help anyone broken in this way to 'rise and build anew'. Despite this personal background, the phraseology also had clear Masonic connotations, as he acknowledged in referring the poem to Professor H. Haultain at the University of Toronto, one of the Canadian engineers for whom he had devised an induction ritual after the war.[68]

Carrie was also at her wits' end. 'I am so wretchedly ill that I can neither read, write or talk and all these days and many more besides I have existed, not lived,' she noted on 7 April. 'There [has] to be a smash one day.' They had returned to Bateman's to find one thousand letters – the accumulation of three months' mail. Answering them would have been difficult enough if all the staff, except the cook, had not chosen to give notice the day following the Jubilee. After some wrangling Carrie induced the secretary Miss Nicholson to stay. On 20 April she had started taking insulin, which brought some relief for her diabetes. But her condition caused Rudyard concern: 'All life is to her more of an effort than I like to see. It is the depression and the difficulty of getting through her work that is the great handicap, that distresses me.'[69]

As his talk to the Royal Society of St George suggested, Rudyard was relieved that the British government was beginning to take the German military threat seriously. His confidence was further revived when Stanley Baldwin became Prime Minister in June (swapping roles with MacDonald) – though he was less enthusiastic when MacDonald's son Malcolm was brought into the Cabinet with responsibility for the Dominions.[70]

On 1 August Rudyard started writing his autobiography, or, as Carrie coyly called it, 'his "A" '.[71] Readers expecting details of his personal life have been disappointed. The book contains no mention of Flo Garrard, Wolcott Balestier or Mrs Hill, the deaths of Josephine and John are passed over, and Carrie emerges as part of a caricature 'Committee of Ways and Means'. But as she herself noted at the time, Rudyard was attempting to deal 'with his life from the point of view of his work'. As a description of a writer's objective influences (in particular, his reading and his routine) it is exemplary. Richard Holmes aptly describes it as 'one of the provoking masterpieces among modern autobiographies' – begging important questions about the nature of such memoirs and how much a person's emotional experiences contribute to his overall view of the world. With typical precision, the title only claimed to offer 'Something of Myself'.

He worked productively on the project, and was already revising an instalment on 15 August, when he and Carrie departed from Paris on the first stage of their journey to the Czech spa town of Marienbad. He was wary about having to pass through Germany and asked Gwynne to publicise the fact that he was going to Marienbad. In Hitler's Reich he was struck by the 'brooding repression and unease in the air. A sort of darkening of the stage everywhere with music off – but I didn't like the suggestions of that music.'[72]

While taking the waters in Marienbad, he heard from Charles Allen who was running the family business in India. Charles was a son of Rudyard's old boss, but a different type from either Sir George or his own brother George Burney Allen who died in 1917. George Burney had been educated in a board school before his father became rich and had inherited the latter's tough commercial sense. Charles, the product of a second marriage, had gone to Eton and, despite manifest charm, was interested in little more than a life of ease. Before long, under his direction, the family concerns were floundering. For old times' sake, Rudyard promised to invest 25,000 Canadian dollars in an effort to keep the *Civil and Military Gazette* afloat. For the next few months he peppered Charles (known as C.T.) with memos – as in the old days – about who to approach about leaders and what to put in the paper. He was enthusiastic, for example, about plans for an agricultural supplement for the *CMG*.[73]

Perhaps he was encouraged by his own successes. For at home, despite a drought, Bateman's was thriving. Rudyard had hired a new bailiff who amazed him by his industry: 'If you tell him to do a job, he does it next day.'[74] As a result, the hedges and ditches were in good repair, poachers had been severely restricted and Rudyard was able to develop rabbits as a new cash crop, selling up to fifty at the local market each week for between one shilling and one and eightpence a head.[75] The beef trade was in recession, but the estate had produced 200 tonnes of hay and was preparing to take in an extra 250 sheep for the winter.

When Lady Milner called on 1 October, she found Rudyard in surprisingly good form, though Carrie was 'piano'. He gave his visitor a copy of what he described as 'the finest lines of poetry written during the war', some verses from A. E. Housman:

> These, in the day when heaven was falling,
> The hour when earth's foundation fled,
> Follow'd their mercenary calling
> And took their wages and are dead.
>
> Their shoulders held the sky suspended;
> They stood, and earth's foundations stay;
> What God abandon'd these defended,
> And saved the sum of things for pay.

In early December he and Carrie went to London for a reception at the French embassy followed, on the same day, by a cocktail party at the Bambridges'. He confirmed to Trix a few days later that he was feeling better and, despite the foul weather, had been 'clearing up odds and ends of things, as behoves one whose Seventieth Birthday is close upon him!'.[76] His renewed involvement with the *CMG* had brought him face to face with the realities of modern India. A once regular user of ekkas and gharries, he had been shocked to learn of a journal called the *Northern Indian Motorists Magazine*. In addition, he told his sister, he had discovered that 'the old C & M presses in the printing office are run by electric power furnished by water supplies – under the Himalayas for ought I know. These are the things, me dear, that make one feel old indeed.'

Despite these reminders, the dominant foreign issue of the moment was not India, or even Germany, but Italy's border dispute with and, in October, invasion of Abyssinia. This affair showed how imperial considerations compromised Rudyard's opinions. He had been happy enough when Britain, France and Italy met at Stresa in May to counter German rearmament. As a result, in return for Mussolini's apparent support against Hitler, Rudyard, in common with the British government, was prepared to condone Italian militarism in Africa. In addition, although he realised that the Italians were unlikely to make much headway against the 'local native with a handful of dhurra and a machine gun',[77] he was aware that they 'sit on our road to the East' and that, unless Britain provided support, they, as 'a long-memoried and vindictive Race', would hate Britain for three generations.[78]

Other factors came into his equation. The League of Nations wanted to impose sanctions on any member country (such as Italy) which violated another's borders. But Rudyard had made up his mind about the League long ago. As far as he was concerned, it was the leading propagator of the anti-war sentiment he had attacked in his speech to the Royal Society of St George. Indeed, at that very moment the League's supporters had been organising its successful so-called 'Peace Ballot' in support of sanctions. In addition Rudyard was a supporter of Mussolini. How much he really believed that Italy's strength could be harnessed in the battle against Germany is unclear. His intransigence was doubtless encouraged by Lady Milner who, as owner of the *National Review*, was courted by the Italian Ambassador Count Dino Grandi, who flattered her she was the only person in London who understood the Italian position[79] and that he had sent a copy of an article in her paper to Mussolini himself.[80] Peter Stanley may also have played a role, since his yacht ferried medical supplies to the established Italian colony of Eritrea.

Although Rudyard decided that Il Duce had a God-given right to do as he wanted in benighted Ethiopia, the British public, which had backed the Peace Ballot, did not agree. In December it was incensed to learn that the Foreign Secretary Sir Samuel Hoare had concluded a pact with his French counterpart Pierre Laval, giving Italy a virtual free hand in Ethiopia. When, on 18 December (in advance of a parliamentary debate on the subject the next day), Baldwin held a Cabinet meeting, he failed to obtain the necessary support for this deal. The pact had to be repudiated and Hoare was forced to resign.

This news had a curious effect on Rudyard. He had been in London since 16 December, staying at Brown's where he revised both his autobiography and his will. On the 18th he dined at Grillons, the latest in his growing list of clubs. On the 20th he returned home, but something (perhaps an item of gossip at Grillons) had irked him and that very day he dashed off a poem about the Hoare–Laval pact and sent it to *The Times*. The following morning he frantically contacted the paper and demanded its return. His reasons are unclear. Was he frightened of embarrassing his cousin? No record of the verses survives at *The Times*. On the 21st Carrie's diary noted simply that Rudyard had recalled the piece, 'and just hit it off in time'.[81] The irony of the affair was that, having seen the confusion surrounding sanctions against Italy, Germany felt emboldened to reoccupy the demilitarised zone of the Rhineland in March 1936.

After Christmas Rudyard returned to his autobiography. On 30 December, his seventieth birthday, he received 108 telegrams (including one from the King) and ninety letters, which Carrie dutifully dealt with the next day, her own birthday. He had been corresponding expansively with Dr Theodore Dunham, his wife's brother-in-law, about the nature of man and the universe. This gave him an opportunity to air his ideas about the influence of cosmic rays on physical reality. 'We seem to be set in a revolving universe from which we draw some sort of power – for 25,000 days or so,'[82] he said, hinting at a fixed Biblical span of life. But he gave no indication that this applied to him. Indeed, he was preparing to go to the South of France when Michael and Annette Mason came to stay on 4 January 1936, a few days before themselves setting out on a new expedition to the Red Sea Hills.

In London to discuss his will on 12 January, Rudyard was taken ill at Brown's Hotel. His ulcer had burst and at 8 a.m. the following morning he was rushed by ambulance to the Middlesex Hospital for an emergency operation. Violet Milner went to Brown's to comfort Carrie who had been up all night with her husband. She learnt that Rudyard was 'very ill though not hopelessly so'. When his heart began to cause complications, he needed a blood transfusion. On 17 January Lady Milner noted, 'Rud desperately ill. His heart is not reviving and though he disputes every inch of the way his condition has been "unchanged" all day.'[83]

Rudyard Kipling did not survive another night. Ten minutes after midnight on 18 January he died. It was his forty-fourth wedding anniversary. The following day, as he would have approved, Carrie appeared completely unruffled. When Violet Milner spoke to her on the telephone, she found Carrie 'as she always is, perfectly natural. I can't bear to think of her.'

After a ceremony at Golders Green Crematorium, Rudyard's ashes were taken to Westminster Abbey for his funeral on 23 January. By then the country had been plunged into a new round of mourning. For, two days after Rudyard, his friend King George V had followed him to the grave. It was said that the King had sent his trumpeter before him. If this meant that Rudyard's obsequies were overshadowed, no-one attending the Abbey would have guessed it. Rudyard's body was brought in by eight pallbearers – the Prime Minister Stanley Baldwin, Admiral of the Fleet Sir Roger Keyes, Field Marshal Sir Archibald Montgomery-Massingberd, Sir Fabian Ware, A. B. Ramsay, Howell Gwynne, A. S. Watt and Professor J. W. Mackail (standing in for the author Sir James Barrie who was ill). Rudyard's extraordinary role as unofficial national bard was reflected in the singing of 'Recessional' (to J. B. Dykes's setting). A poem written in self-consciously religious terms as a warning against overweening political pride had become part of the national hymn book. As the coffin was taken to its resting place in Poet's Corner, Carrie's composure finally gave way and she was observed, behind her thick black veil, to be weeping copiously.

For nearly half a century Carrie had devoted herself to her husband. As his helpmeet, she had run his home, travelled with him, attended to his business affairs and protected him against unwelcome intrusions into his privacy. Although Rudyard's genius was uniquely his own, the promotion of his name and work was a joint venture and, now that Rudyard was dead, she was not going to give up on that.

In the immediate aftermath Malcolm Muggeridge, a journalist who had worked on an Indian newspaper in the latter days of the Raj, looked back over Rudyard's work and was struck by the vitality of the verses – 'How full of contempt for what I despised – "brittle intellectuals" – and of poetic genius; how, if he praised Empire, it was not at all because he had not counted the cost (who had expressed better the wrongs of the common soldier?) but because, men being what they are, he saw it as one of the less despicable manifestations of their urge to over-run and dominate their environment.'[84]

But the prevailing critical consensus was better expressed by Sir John Squire, former editor of *London Mercury*, whom Macmillan put to trawl through Rudyard's work for a volume[85] of uncollected writings in the Sussex edition. Squire adopted the fashionable note of scepticism: 'I began to wonder if it wasn't all going to be Beetle let loose and trying to be a slick He-man – the prose even has an American Nasal Twang.' He liked the story 'A Fallen Idol' (originally printed in the unauthorised American volume *Abaft the Funnel*) and felt 'In Partibus' deserved reprinting, along with 'The Enlightenments of Pagett M.P.', which was 'sheer good history'. Otherwise he could not avoid concluding that 'Kipling was India's last dying groan'.

Rudyard's will confirmed his wife as the controller of his physical and intellectual properties – albeit in trust. He noted that he had made 'ample provision' for his daughter in her marriage settlement. So, apart from bequests of £5000 to Elsie and £1000 to George Bambridge, the remainder of his estate (worth £168,171) went to Carrie, along with Bateman's and an income from his copyrights. When the details were finalised, he still owned shares in George Allen's business (now the British India Corporation) and, separately, in the *Civil and Military Gazette*. He also held stakes in the *National Review* and Hawker Aircraft Company. Rudyard was only adamant that none of his money should be invested in either Irish or Russian securities.

Brooking, the Kipling Society Secretary, greeted the will with accustomed sourness. He commiserated with Dunsterville that there was 'not a sliver to yourself, whom he made thousands out of'. All in all, Rudyard 'had a marvellous brain', he felt, 'but his heart was mud'.[86]

This was one area where Carrie was not prepared to let anyone pry, particularly when the more personal detractors began to line up. One of the first was Oliver Baldwin, who chose an obscure meeting of elocution teachers at the London Academy of Music on 29 July to voice his opinion that his cousin had had a fearful inferiority complex, resulting from his family's rejection by social superiors while in India. This complex drove Rudyard to push his son to serve in the war, said Oliver. After John's death, Rudyard had blamed himself. 'It broke him completely. He shut up like a clam. All his creation went. He was not interested in creating anything new. All the lovely side of his nature – all the "jungle book", all the playing with children, all the love for people – went like that.' Instead, Rudyard concentrated on revenge, particularly revenge on the German people. And he looked to Oliver as his chosen instrument to carry out his revenge. Oliver's argument was riddled with inconsistencies and half-truths, which Elsie countered in a short letter to the *Daily Telegraph*, noting that Oliver had not seen her father for ten years and that his 'statements . . . and his feelings [were] of little value'.

Rudyard had already made clear his aversion to potential biographers. On one of his last visits to Bateman's before his own death in 1934, Frank Doubleday had encountered a sweating Rudyard shovelling bundles of papers into a blazing fire. When asked what he was doing, he replied, 'Well, Effendi, I was looking over old papers and I got thinking. No one's going to make a monkey out of me after I die.' He had also written a couple of short verses called 'The Appeal', which begged his readers to respect his death and 'not to question other than / The books I leave behind'.[87]

Carrie took up where he had left off. In November 1936 she wrote to Howell Gwynne, who was advising her on editing the manuscript of *Something of Myself*, 'I think the thing as it stands is too offensive, if it is not libellous, and I don't, above all things, want to have that kind of criticism of the Autobiography. I don't, in fact, want anything that people can ride off and dispute about.'[88]

In her stewardship of her husband's literary estate, she continued the job of dispersing his manuscripts (and printed works) to various libraries, including Magdalene College where she endowed a Kipling fellowship whose first incumbent was appropriately T. S. Eliot. Otherwise, all extraneous or potentially damaging material was ruthlessly disposed of. She burnt the leather notions book containing Rudyard's unfinished stories and poems, notes and ideas. She put feelers out to major dealers to let her know if any of Rudyard's letters came on the market. When she learnt that Mrs Hill, living in straitened circumstances in Baltimore, had sold her correspondence with Rudyard to a

Chicago collector, Carrie contacted the man's widow, who graciously gave her the letters – whereupon Carrie promptly put a match to them. She did not realise that copies had been made, which were later deposited in the University of Sussex.

When Trix wanted to quote her brother in a memoir she encountered difficulties. She was forced to confirm that she had written a particular verse, because the editor of *Chambers's Journal* feared Carrie's reprisals: 'Ruddy's ... relict had threatened pains and penalties if anything written in the past by Mrs Kipling's husband was published,' noted Trix. 'Truly "the sweet influence of a good woman" takes many forms.'[89]

Anyone who wanted to write about Rudyard found himself in a similar position. Even Michael Mason was rebuffed when he wanted to produce a collection of his letters from Rudyard. However, he was encouraged to publish a poem 'To the Memory of R.K.' as the epigraph to his book *The Paradise of Fools*. Mason's verses recalled the man who had been the 'delight of my childhood ... priest of my boyhood ... and

> Friend of my manhood – across the world I brought him
> Tales, ill-told, of snow and sea, forest and desert,
> Strange wild beasts and men untamed. Smiling he would
>   hear them,
> 'Child, thou art mad!' he laughed. 'Lose not thy madness.'[90]

After *Something of Myself* was published in February 1937, Carrie began to think of a biographer for Rudyard. She alighted on Hector Bolitho, a middlebrow historian who specialised in respectful royal biographies and who she felt would not be tainted by literary fashion. He found her supervision too overbearing and she turned to Taprell Dorling, who wrote sea stories under the pen-name 'Taffrail'. But he also pulled out.

When Carrie herself died in December 1939 it was a release. Elsie admitted, 'The future could have been nothing but misery and pain, so I cannot wish her back.'[91] As Rudyard had stipulated,

Bateman's was donated to the National Trust and a significant bequest was made to the Fairbridge Farm Schools – a token of respect for Rudyard's imperialism. Kingsley Fairbridge had been a Rhodes-type visionary: a South African who, after studying at Oxford University, founded farm settlements to bring assisted emigrants to Australia and Canada.

Thereafter Elsie Bambridge became the keeper of the Kipling flame. When the Bambridges' three-year lease on Burgh House was up, she used her inheritance to purchase Wimpole Hall, the house in Cambridgeshire where she and George had most enjoyed living. Surrounded by its huge expanse of parkland, fashioned variously by Charles Bridgeman, 'Capability' Brown and Humphry Repton, the Bambridges lived there in great comfort and virtual seclusion. Occasionally George travelled to London where his wife's money allowed him to indulge a passion for buying expensive works of art. When he died in December 1943 he left a mere £2717, confirming that he had never enjoyed riches on his own account.

Shortly before his death, he had met Lord Birkenhead, the literary-minded son of the former Conservative Lord Chancellor F. E. Smith, who had been a friend of Beaverbrook. Having written a biography of his own father, Birkenhead was looking for a new project. Through Bambridge he asked Elsie's permission to work on Rudyard's life. Without consulting widely she agreed, probably liking the idea that a peer should do the job. Nevertheless, after George's death she tied Birkenhead to an absurdly onerous contract, which laid down various conditions ('the author will, if requested by Mrs Bambridge to do so, visit at his own expense the United States of America') and gave her complete control of the work and its copyright.

Birkenhead presented the manuscript to Elsie in 1948. After taking advice from T. S. Eliot and others, she was not happy and wrote a long list of the book's failings: it was 'a jerky patchwork' and made no mention of Rudyard's 'great love of the Bible, English and French literature',[92] for example. When Birkenhead explained that this was only a first draft, she refused to countenance further changes. According to him, she wrote 'with growing offensiveness, culminating in a letter which one of the partners of Lewis & Lewis who acted for me described as "one of the most disgraceful he had ever seen in his professional career", a filthy letter, brutal and with the intention of wounding – not, of course that one ever could be wounded by such a person'.[93] With help (and legal advice) from his brother-in-law Lord Camrose, proprietor of the *Daily Telegraph*, Birkenhead won £3500 compensation. But he told his friend Roderick Jones, who had provided reminiscences, that Elsie was 'a vile character [who] should be added at once to the less creditable section of Mme Tussauds'.

In 1951 she found an alternative biographer in Charles Carrington, a New Zealand-born historian of the British Empire. He, like Birkenhead, was allowed access to the voluminous but now well-weeded papers at Wimpole. When his measured life of Rudyard was published in 1955 it was difficult to understand the earlier fuss. Carrington had done an appropriate job for the times in detailing Rudyard's life and works from the original sources.

Once this had been digested, the mystery of Lord Birkenhead's treatment remained. Had he unearthed some dark family secret? For over thirty years after George Bambridge's death, Elsie stayed in her vast house, alone and increasingly befuddled. When, in 1976, she died at the age of eighty, there was newspaper speculation that the truth would finally emerge. But even, perhaps especially, in death, she was not prepared to abandon the barricades. She was the last of the immediate Kipling line and, while happy to donate Wimpole Hall (like Bateman's) to the National Trust, she stipulated that the forty-five small notebooks that made up her mother's diaries should be destroyed, along with her own diaries and those of her husband.

Subsequently, resumés of Carrie's diaries, as made by both Charles Carrington and Douglas Rees (Lord Birkenhead's collaborator), have surfaced. Taking the two together, it is clear that the notebooks were largely mundane records of the Kiplings' daily lives. Certain key moments were conveniently not recorded – for example, a tricky period in Spain and France, just prior to Elsie's engagement in 1924, and a few months in 1930 around the time of the film flop *One Family*. In the first case the objective was probably to protect domestic sensibilities; in the latter, to ensure that no sense of failure besmirched Rudyard's name. Overall, Elsie must simply have objected to Lord Birkenhead's approach which, while always interesting, could be cavalier and over-reliant on quotations.

The more significant losses were Elsie and George Bambridge's private papers. For these would have indicated something of the family dynamics that, until now, have been the hidden dimension in the Kipling story.

Over the years the other players in Rudyard's life peeled away. Flo Garrard died a couple of years after him, on 31 January 1938, her 73rd birthday. An obituary in *The Times* described her as a 'vigorous painter of both portraits and landscapes' and noted her 'ruling passion' was for animals and their welfare. 'Her collection of cats was famous in Chelsea and at any mention of cruelty to animals her incisive comments on the offender delivered in a low growling voice were something to be remembered. Miss Garrard's sturdy figure and rather masculine costume – adopted for practical reasons and not from anything mannish in her temperament – gave no clue to her nature.' Flo's 'sardonic humour', which was referred to in her obituary, is evident in her extraordinary illustrated story, *Phantasmagoria*, which is one of the more inaccessible volumes in the British Library. Ostensibly by 'Silivigi', it tells of Flo's ordeal when she tried to sketch outside the Houses of Parliament and was arrested for her pains. With her sketches and commentary, it provides a lively satire on pompous authoritarianism. In April 1928 she received a useful boost to her finances: after her friend the painter John Singer Sargent's death three years earlier, his sisters had given her some of his canvases for her use. Among them she discovered two original portraits which the sisters allowed her to keep and later sell.

Rudyard's equally feisty sister Trix survived ten years longer until 1948. She entertained family and friends in Edinburgh where she liked to visit the zoo and talk to the elephants in Hindustani. For posterity she had produced several short memoirs which managed both to be interesting and to adhere to officially sanctioned guidelines. To certain people, however, she had conveyed her sense of anger at the way the Kiplings treated her. One of them, Howell Gwynne, edited the *Morning Post* until 1937 and survived a further thirteen years. Ted Hill lived on to 1952 and Violet Milner to 1958.

Over the years Rudyard's literary reputation has waxed and waned. Several times he threatened to come back into fashion, but never really made it. His robust style did not tally with the mid-century mood. He was too much a relic of the Raj and, for all his command of irony, he actually believed in his imperialism. The prejudices ranged against him were epitomised in the cowardly reaction of W. H. Auden who, in his 'New Year Letter' of 1940, ranted against 'horrible old Kipling' and suppressed the stanzas in his 'In Memory of W. B. Yeats', written only the previous year, in which he had claimed that Time had pardoned Rudyard for 'writing well'. In the 1980s, under sustained fire from Professor Edward Said and critics of 'Orientalism', Kipling studies seemed set to disappear from the academic curriculum.

But that would be to underestimate Rudyard's influence on the popular imagination. The Royal Navy used to have a warship named after him – HMS *Kipling*, which distinguished itself in May 1941 by rescuing the crew of the sinking HMS *Kelly*, the incident on which the film *In Which We Serve* is based. When Forest Lawn, the Californian funeral park satirised in Evelyn Waugh's *The Loved One*, wanted a theme for a chapel, it alighted on the Church of the Recessional, which it modelled on St Margaret's, Rottingdean. Walt Disney's 1967 version of *The Jungle Book* remains one of the most successful animated films of all time. Bags manufactured by a Belgian company under the name 'Kipling' were a sought-after fashion accessory of the late 1990s.

On the popular music scene, the Liverpool band Space went to the top of the 'indie' charts in 1996 with its idiosyncratic version of 'Female of the Species'. That same year, according to a BBC poll, 'If–' was the nation's favourite poem. Its stirring words confront tennis players about to enter the Centre Court at Wimbledon. They provided the link for BBC Television's 1998 World Cup highlights.

Predictably Rudyard has been commandeered and quoted as an influence by British politicians from Winston Churchill to Margaret Thatcher. But he is also highly regarded further afield – by Alexander Lebed, the Russian nationalist leader, for example. And his fans crop up in the most unlikely places. John Huston, whose film of *The Man Who Would Be King* provides a gritty counterbalance to the Disney vision of India, recalled his immodest friend Ernest Hemingway referring to Kipling respectfully as a greater writer than himself. When Paul Theroux visited Jorge Luis Borges in Buenos Aires, he was requested to read to the blind Argentinian writer from *Plain Tales from the Hills*. The Marxist playwright Bertolt Brecht was excited by Kipling's emphasis on the ethic of work. More surprisingly, women such as Aung San Suu Kyi and Maya Angelou have recorded their debt to Rudyard.

For all his political incorrectness, Rudyard's writing retains a universal hold. As V. S. Naipaul put it in *An Area of Darkness*, (and Salman Rushdie later said something almost identical), 'It was all there in Kipling ... no writer more honest or accurate, no writer more revealing of himself and his society.'

Bibliography

L. S. Amery, *My Political Life* (Hutchinson, 1953)

Mark Amory, *Lord Berners: The Last Eccentric* (Chatto and Windus, 1998)

Mark Amory (ed.), *The Diaries of Evelyn Waugh* (Weidenfeld & Nicolson, 1976)

Mark Amory, *Lord Dunsany* (Collins, 1972)

Christopher Andrew, *Secret Service: The Making of the British Intelligence Community* (William Heinemann, 1985)

Allen Andrews, *The Splendid Pauper* (Harrap, 1968)

Arthur R. Ankers, *The Pater* (Hawthorns Publications, 1988)

Theo Aronson, *Prince Eddy and the Homosexual Underworld* (John Murray, 1994)

Robert Baden-Powell, *Sketches in Mafeking and East Africa* (Smith Elder, 1907)

Enid Bagnold, *Autobiography* (Heinemann, 1969)

A. W. Baldwin, *The Macdonald Sisters* (Peter Davies, 1960)

Oliver Baldwin, *The Questing Beast* (Grayson & Grayson, 1932)

Dr Vaughan Bateson, *Something More of Kipling* (privately published, 1938)

Max Beerbohm, *The Poet's Corner* (Heinemann, 1904)

Harold Begbie, *Albert, Fourth Earl Grey* (Hodder & Stoughton, 1918)

S. N. Behrman, *Conversation with Max* (Hamish Hamilton, 1960)

Anne Olivier Bell (ed.), *The Diary of Virginia Woolf* (The Hogarth Press, 1978)

Mrs (Marie) Belloc Lowndes, *The Merry Wives of Westminster* (Macmillan, 1940)

Michael Bentley (ed.), *Public and Private Doctrine* (Cambridge University Press, 1993)

George C. Beresford, *Schooldays with Kipling* (Gollancz, 1936)

Dr George Birdwood, *The Industrial Arts of India* (Chapman & Hall, 1880)

Lord Birkenhead, *Rudyard Kipling* (Weidenfeld & Nicolson, 1978)

Sir John Bland-Sutton, *The Story of a Surgeon* (Methuen, 1930)

Wilfred Blunt, *Cockerell* (Hamish Hamilton, 1965)

Edward Bok, *The Americanization of Edward Bok* (Charles Scribner's Sons, 1920)

Mark Bonham Carter and Mark Pottle (eds.), *Lantern Slides: The Diaries and Letters of Violet Bonham Carter 1904–1914* (Weidenfeld & Nicolson, 1996)

Martin Booth, *The Doctor, The Detective and Arthur Conan Doyle: A Biography of Arthur Conan Doyle* (Hodder & Stoughton, 1997)

Piers Brendon, *The Motoring Century* (Bloomsbury, 1997)

Asa Briggs, *The History of Broadcasting in the United Kingdom* (Oxford University Press, 1961)

Hugh Brogan, *Mowgli's Sons* (Jonathan Cape, 1987)

Hugh Brogan, *The Penguin History of The United States of America* (Penguin, 1986)

Horatio Brown (ed.), *Letters and Papers of John Addington Symonds* (John Murray, 1923)

E. J. Buck, *Simla Past and Present* (Thacker Spink, 1904)

Georgiana Burne-Jones, *Memorials of Edward Burne-Jones* (Macmillan, 1904)

Molly Cabot, 'The Vermont Period: Rudyard Kipling in Vermont' (*English Literature in Transition*, 29/2, 1986)

Charles Carrington (ed.), *The Complete Barrack-Room Ballads of Rudyard Kipling* (Methuen, 1973)

Charles Carrington, *Kipling* (Macmillan, 1955)

Charles Carrington (ed.), *Kipling's Horace* (privately printed, 1980)

Willa Cather, *The Autobiography of S. S. McClure* (University of Nebraska Press, 1997)

Desmond Chapman-Huston, *The Lost Historian* (John Murray, 1936)

Anne Chisholm and Michael Davie, *Beaverbrook: A Life* (Hutchinson, 1992)

Susan Chitty, *Playing the Game: A Biography of Sir Henry Newbolt* (Quartet, 1997)

Alan Clark (ed.), *A Good Innings: The Private Papers of Viscount Lee of Fareham* (John Murray, 1974)

John Coates, *The Day's Work: Kipling and the Idea of Sacrifice* (Associated University Presses, 1997)

Morton Cohen (ed.), *Rudyard Kipling to Rider Haggard: The Record of a Friendship* (Hutchinson, 1965)

John Connell, *W. E. Henley* (Constable, 1949)

John Constable (ed.), *Selected Letters of I. A. Richards, CH* (Clarendon Press, 1990)

Harvey Cushing, *The Life of Sir William Osler* (Oxford University Press, 1940)

George Dangerfield, *The Strange Death of Liberal England* (Serif, 1997)

Frances Donaldson, *P. G. Wodehouse* (Weidenfeld & Nicolson, 1968)

Florence Doubleday, *Episodes in the Life of a Publisher's Wife* (privately printed, 1938)

James Doyle, *Stephen Leacock, The Sage of Orillia* (ECW Press, 1992)

Marchioness of Dufferin and Ava, *Our Viceregal Life in India* (John Murray, 1889)

Foster Rhea Dulles, *Yankees and Samurai* (Harper & Row, 1965)

Major-General L. C. Dunsterville, *Stalky's Reminiscences* (Cape, 1928)

Renee Durbach, *Kipling's South Africa* (Chameleon Press, 1988)

Max Egremont, *The Cousins* (Collins, 1977)

Edward Elgar, *The Windflower Letters: Correspondence with Alice Caroline Stuart Wortley and her Family* (Clarendon Press, 1989)

Richard Ellmann, *Oscar Wilde* (Hamish Hamilton, 1987)

A. B. Filson Young, *The Complete Motorist* (Methuen, 1904)

Penelope Fitzgerald, *Edward Burne-Jones: A Biography* (Michael Joseph, 1975)

John Flint, *Cecil Rhodes* (Hutchinson, 1974)

Newman Flower (ed.), *The Journals of Arnold Bennett* (Cassell, 1932)

John Fraser, *Sixty Years in Uniform* (Stanley Paul, 1939)

Patrick French, *The Life of Henry Norman* (Unicorn Press, 1995)

Patrick French, *Younghusband* (Harper Collins, 1994)

Ian Gibson, *Federico Garcia Lorca: A Life* (Faber, 1989)

Eliot Gilbert (ed.), *O Beloved Kids: Rudyard Kipling's Letters to his Children* (Weidenfeld & Nicolson, 1983)

Martin Gilbert, *The First World War* (Weidenfeld & Nicolson, 1994)

Martin Gilbert, *Servant of India* (Longmans, 1966)

David Gilmour, *Curzon* (John Murray, 1994)

Tony Gould, *Insider Outsider: The Life and Times of Colin MacInnes* (Chatto & Windus, 1983)

Lord Ronald Sutherland Gower, *Old Diaries* (John Murray, 1902)

Robert Graves and Alan Hodge, *The Long Weekend* (Abacus, 1995)

Roger Lancelyn Green, *Kipling and the Children* (Elek Books, 1965)

Roger Lancelyn Green, *Kipling: The Critical Heritage* (Routledge & Kegan Paul, 1971)

Roger Lancelyn Green, *A. E. W. Mason* (Max Parrish, 1952)

John Gross, *The Rise and Fall of the Man of Letters* (Penguin, 1991)

John Gross (ed.), *Rudyard Kipling: The Man, His Work and His World* (Weidenfeld & Nicolson, 1972)

Stephen Gwynn (ed.), *The Letters and Friendships of Sir Cecil Spring Rice* (Constable, 1929)

Cosmo Hamilton, *People Worth Talking About* (Robert M. McBride, NY, 1933)

General Sir Ian Hamilton, *Listening for the Drums* (Faber, 1944)

R. E. Harbord, *The Readers' Guide to Rudyard Kipling's Work* (privately printed, 1970)

Frank Harris, *Contemporary Portraits* (Methuen, 1915–24)

Duff Hart-Davis (ed.), *End of an Era: Letters & Journals of Sir Alan Lascelles from 1887 to 1920* (Hamish Hamilton, 1986)

Rupert Hart-Davies, *Hugh Walpole* (Macmillan, 1952)

Philip J. Haythornthwaite, *The Colonial Wars Source Book* (Arms & Armour, 1995)

James Hepburn, *The Author's Empty Purse* (Oxford University Press, 1968)

James Hepburn (ed.), *The Letters of Arnold Bennett* (Oxford University Press, 1986)

Joan Hichberger, *Images of the Army* (Manchester University Press, 1984)

D. S. Higgins (ed.), *The Private Diaries of Sir H. Rider Haggard* (Cassell, 1980)

Christopher Hitchens, *Blood, Class and Nostalgia* (Chatto & Windus, 1990)

Philip Hoare, *Noel Coward* (Sinclair-Stevenson, 1995)

Tonie and Valmai Holt, *My Boy Jack?* (Leo Cooper, 1998)

Peter Hopkirk, *Quest for Kim* (John Murray, 1996)

Peter Hopkirk, *The Great Game: On Secret Service in High Asia* (John Murray, 1990)

Lo Hui-Min (ed.), *The Correspondence of G. E. Morrison* (Cambridge University Press, 1976)

Ronald Hyam, *Empire and Sexuality* (Manchester University Press, 1990)

Gordon Ireland, *The Balestiers of Beechwood* (privately printed, 1948)

Lawrence James, *The Golden Warrior: The Life and Legend of Lawrence of Arabia* (Weidenfeld & Nicolson, 1990)

Lawrence James, *Raj: The Making and Unmaking of British India* (Little Brown, 1997)

Robert Rhodes James (ed.), *Memoirs of a Conservative: J. C. C. Davidson's Memoirs and Papers 1910–37* (Weidenfeld & Nicolson, 1969)

C. S. Jarvis, *Desert and Delta* (John Murray, 1938)

Tim Jeal, *Baden-Powell* (Hutchinson, 1989)

Thomas Jones, *Whitehall Diary* (Oxford University Press, 1965)

Denis Judd, *Empire* (HarperCollins, 1996)

Peter Keating, *Kipling the Poet* (Secker & Warburg, 1994)

John Keegan, *Battle at Sea* (Pimlico, 1993)

Sandra Kemp, *Kipling's Hidden Narratives* (Basil Blackwell, 1988)

Sandra Kemp and Lisa Lewis (eds), *Rudyard Kipling: Writings on Writing* (Cambridge, 1996)

Sunil Khilnani, *The Idea of India* (Hamish Hamilton, 1997)

Stephen Koss, *The Rise and Fall of the Political Press in Britain* (Fontana, 1990)

Mary Lago (ed.), *Burne-Jones Talking* (John Murray, 1982)

Richard Lamb, *Mussolini and the British* (John Murray, 1997)

Perceval Landon, *Raw Edges: Studies and Stories of These Days* (Heinemann, 1908)

Marganita Laski, *From Palm to Pine* (Sidgwick & Jackson, 1987)

T. E. Lawrence, *T. E. Lawrence to his Biographers Robert Graves and Liddell Hart* (Cassell, 1963)

Walter Lawrence, *The India We Served* (Cassell, 1928)

Hermione Lee, *Virginia Woolf* (Chatto & Windus, 1996)

Anita Leslie, *Cousin Clare* (Hutchinson, 1976)

Jeffrey D. Lewins, *Kipling and his 'Coll'* (Magdalene College Occasional Papers no. 9, 1992)

R. W. B. Lewis, *Edith Wharton: A Biography* (Harper & Row, 1975)

Philip Longworth, *The Unending Vigil* (Leo Cooper, 1976)

Andrew Lownie, *John Buchan* (Constable, 1995)

Candida Lycett-Green (ed.), *John Betjeman Letters* Vol. 1. (Methuen, 1984)

David C. McAveeney, *Kipling in Gloucester* (The Curious Traveller Press, 1996)

Fiona MacCarthy, *William Morris* (Faber, 1994)

Edith Macdonald, *Annals of the Macdonald Family* (H. Marshall, 1928)

Frederic Macdonald, *As a Tale That is Told* (Cassell, 1919)

Arthur Machen, *The Bowmen and Other Legends of the War* (Simpkin, Marshall, Hamilton, Kent, 1915)

Colin MacInnes, *Out of the Way* (Martin, Brian & O'Keefe, 1979)

Graham McInnes, *Finding a Father* (Hamish Hamilton, 1967)

Graham McInnes, *Goodbye Melbourne Town* (Hamish Hamilton, 1968)

John Marlow, *Milner: Apostle of Empire* (Hamish Hamilton, 1976)

Edward Marsh, *A Number of People* (Heinemann & Hamish Hamilton, 1939)

Peter Marsh, *Joseph Chamberlain* (Yale University Press, 1994)

Archibald Marshall and Lady Troubridge, *Lord Montagu of Beaulieu* (Macmillan, 1930)

Michael Mason, *The Paradise of Fools* (Hodder & Stoughton, 1936)

Lucy Masterman, *Life of C. F. G. Masterman* (Nicholson & Watson, 1939)

Keith Middlemas and John Barnes, *Baldwin* (Weidenfeld & Nicolson, 1969)

John Milner, *The Studios of Paris* (Yale University Press, 1988)

Partha Mitter, *Much Maligned Monsters* (University of Chicago, 1992)

B. J. Moore-Gilbert, *Kipling and Orientalism* (Croom Helm, 1986)

Charles Morgan, *The House of Macmillan 1843–1943* (Macmillan, 1943)

Elting E. Morison, *The Letters of Theodore Roosevelt* (Harvard University Press, 1951–54)

A. J. A. Morris, *The Scaremongers: The Advocacy of War and Rearmament 1896–1914* (Routledge, 1984)

Malcolm Muggeridge, *Like It Was* (Collins, 1981)

Charles Neider (ed.), *The Selected Letters of Mark Twain* (Harper and Row, 1982)

Aubrey Newman, *The Stanhopes of Chevening* (Macmillan, 1969)

Adam Nicolson, *Bateman's* (National Trust, 1996)

Harold Nicolson, *Helen's Tower* (Constable, 1937)

Harold Orel (ed.), *Kipling Interviews and Recollections* Vols 1–2 (Macmillan, 1983)

Norman Page, *A Kipling Companion* (Macmillan Press, 1984)

Thomas Pakenham, *The Boer War* (Weidenfeld & Nicolson, 1979)

Benita Parry, *Delusions and Discoveries* (Allen Lane, 1971)

A. B. Paterson, *Happy Dispatches* (Angus & Robertson, 1934)

James Pethica (ed.), *Lady Gregory's Diaries* (Colin Smythe, 1996)

Edith Catlin Phelps, *Memoir* (privately printed, no date)

John Physick, *The Victoria and Albert Museum: The History of its Building* (V&A, 1982)

Thomas Pinney (ed.), *Kipling India* (Macmillan, 1986)

Thomas Pinney, *The Kipling that Nobody Reads* (Magdalene College Occasional Papers no. 19, 1998)

Thomas Pinney (ed.), *The Letters of Rudyard Kiping* Vols 1–4 (Macmillan, 1990–)

Thomas Pinney (ed.), *Something of Myself and other Autobiographical Writings* (Cambridge University Press, 1990)

Edith Plowden, *Fond Memories* (privately printed, no date)

Dorothy Ponton, *Rudyard Kipling at Home and at Work* (privately printed, 1953)

Val Prinsep, *Imperial India: An Artist's Journals* (Chapman & Hall, 1878)

Craig Raine (ed.), *A Choice of Kipling's Prose* (Faber, 1987)

Julian Ralph, *War's Brighter Side* (C. Arthur Pearson, 1901)

Lt Col C. a Court Repington, *The First World War: Personal Experiences* (Constable, 1921)

Major-General R. C. W. Reveley Mitford, *Orient and Occident: A Journey from Lahore to Liverpool* (W. H. Allen, 1888)

Howard Rice, *Rudyard Kipling in New England* (Stephen Daye, 1936)

Harry Ricketts, *The Unforgiving Minute* (Chatto & Windus, 1999)

Edgell Rickword (ed.), *Scrutinies by Various Writers* (Wishart, 1928)

Richard Rive (ed.), *Olive Schreiner Letters* (OUP, 1988)

James C. Robertson, *The Hidden Cinema: British Film Censorship in Action 1913–1975* (Routledge, 1993)

Phil Robinson, *In My Indian Garden* (Sampson Low, 1878)

Sir Rennell Rodd, *Social and Diplomatic Memories 1902–1919* (E. Arnold, 1925)

Kenneth Rose, *The Later Cecils* (Weidenfeld & Nicolson, 1975)

Barbara Rosenbaum, *Index of English Literary Manuscripts* (Mansell, 1990)

Andrew Rutherford (ed.), *Early Verse by Rudyard Kipling 1879–1889* (Clarendon Press, 1986)

Andrew Rutherford (ed.), *Kipling's Mind and Art* (Oliver & Boyd, 1964)

Christopher St John (ed.), *Ellen Terry and Bernard Shaw: A Correspondence* (Max Reinhardt, 1949)

George Seaver, *Francis Younghusband* (John Murray, 1952)

Martin Seymour-Smith, *Rudyard Kipling* (Queen Anne Press, 1989)

Elaine Showalter, *Sexual Anarchy: Gender and Culture at the Fin de Siècle* (Viking, 1990)

Gladys Denny Shultz and Daisy Gordon Lawrence, *Lady from Savannah* (Girl Scouts of the USA, 1988)

Michael Smith, *Rudyard Kipling: The Rottingdean Years* (Brownleaf, 1989)

Diana Souhami, *The Trials of Radclyffe Hall* (Weidenfeld & Nicolson, 1998)

Margarite Steen, *William Nicholson* (Collins, 1943)

James McG. Stewart, *Rudyard Kipling: A Bibliographical Catalogue* (Dalhousie University Press and Toronto University Press, 1959)

Anthony Storr, *Churchill's Black Dog and Other Phenomena of the Human Mind* (Fontana, 1989)

Ronald Storrs, *Orientations* (Nicholson & Watson, 1937)

Margot Strickland, *Angela Thirkell: Portrait of a Lady Novelist* (Duckworth, 1977)

Matthew Sturgis, *Aubrey Beardsley* (HarperCollins, 1998)

Zoreh T. Sullivan, *Narratives of Empire* (Cambridge University Press, 1993)

Paul Swann, *The British Documentary Film Movement 1926–1946* (CUP, 1989)

Frederick Sykes, *From Many Angles* (Harrap, 1942)

Julia Taufflieb, *Memoir* (privately printed, n.d.)

Ina Taylor, *Victorian Sisters* (Weidenfeld & Nicolson, 1987)

Angela Thirkell, *Three Houses* (Oxford University Press, 1931)

Anthony Thomas, *Rhodes, The Race for Africa* (BBC Books, 1996)

Basil Thomson, *The Scene Changes* (Collins, 1939)

T. H. Thornton and J. L. Kipling, *Lahore* (1876)

Ann Thwaite, *Edmund Gosse: A Literary Landscape* (Secker & Warburg, 1984)

J. M. S. Tompkins, *The Art of Rudyard Kipling* (Methuen, 1959)

G. O. Trevelyan, *The Competition Wallah* (Macmillan, 1864)

Paul Tritton, *John Montagu of Beaulieu: Motoring Pioneer and Prophet* (Golden Eagle, 1985)

John Vincent (ed.), *The Crawford Papers* (Manchester University Press, 1984)

Arthur Waugh, *One Man's Road* (Chapman Hall, 1931)

George Webb (ed.), *The Irish Guards in the Great War* (Spellmount, 1997)

Geoffrey Wheatcroft, *The Randlords* (Weidenfeld & Nicolson, 1993)

Frederic Whyte, *William Heinemann: A Memoir* (Cape, 1928)

A. N. Wilson, *Hilaire Belloc* (Penguin, 1986)

Angus Wilson, *The Strange Ride of Rudyard Kipling* (Secker & Warburg, 1977)

Keith Wilson (ed.), *The Rasp of War* (Sidgwick & Jackson, 1988)

Oliver Woods and James Bishop, *The Story of The Times* (Michael Joseph, 1983)

Lewis D. Wugraft, *The Imperial Imagination* (Wesleyan University Press, 1983)

Zoe Yelland, *Boxwallah* (Michael Russell, 1994)

W. Arthur Young and John H. McGivering, *A Kipling Dictionary* (Macmillan, 1967)

Kenneth Young (ed.), *The Diaries of Sir Robert Bruce Lockhart* (Macmillan, 1973)

Notes

A number of principles have been followed in compiling these notes.

* Book titles are usually shortened versions of full listings in the bibliography.

* Kipling family members are designated by their initials: Rudyard Kipling (RK), his wife Carrie (CK), father Lockwood (LK), mother Alice (AK), sister Trix (TF), son John (JK), daughter Elsie (EK – later EB), and son-in-law George Bambridge (GB).

* Repositories of papers are truncated. Thus 'Berg' means the Berg Collection in the New York Public Library, 'Dunham' the Dunham family papers lodged mostly on microfilm in the libraries of both Sussex and Harvard Universities.

* I have not laboured the references to Kipling's own works. They should be self-explanatory (i.e. in the context of a particular story, any quotation will come from it, unless otherwise noted). Given the large number and variety of editions, providing page numbers etc. only causes confusion.

* Various abbreviations have been used: KJ (Kipling Journal), LOC (Library of Congress), PRO (Public Record Office), BL (British Library), RCS (Royal College of Surgeons), UNC (University of North Carolina), SOM (*Something of Myself*), n.d. (no date), n.y. (no year).

* Carrie Kipling kept a daily diary, but, on her instructions, it was burnt at her daughter Elsie's death. However, two biographers, Charles Carrington and Lord Birkenhead, read it and made extensive

notes. Their versions of the diaries are designated as 'CK diary' (Carrington) and 'Rees extracts' (Birkenhead – after Douglas Rees, his assistant, who did the copying.) Also mentioned are Rudyard Kipling's 1885 diary, his accounts of his Motor Tours in Britian and on the Continent, and his medical diaries – comprising details of his health which Carrington extracted from Carrie King's diary and other sources. The 1885 diary is held at the Houghton Library, Harvard University, while the other two sources form part of the Kipling archive at Sussex University.

* Much of Kipling's correspondence is collected in *The Letters of Rudyard Kipling*, edited by Thomas Pinney and published by the Macmillan Press, Volumes 1–4, 1990–. Where this is so, I have indicated with a †.

1: Hair of the Dog [pp. 11–28]

1. Bateson, *Something More of Kipling*.
2. RK to Dr Vaughan Bateson, 10 June 1896, quoted Bateson, op cit.
3. It was considered the Northern equivalent of the Methodists' Kingswood School, near Bristol.
4. Macdonald, *Annals of the Macdonald Family*.
5. See Fitzgerald, *Edward Burne-Jones: A Biography*.
6. Quoted Ankers, *The Pater* (but without attribution).
7. Plowden, *Fond Memories*.
8. Plowden, op. cit.
9. Quoted in A. W. Baldwin, *The Macdonald Sisters*.

2: Of No Mean City [pp. 26–68]

1. See Wugraft, *The Imperial Imagination*.
2. John Griffiths (1837–1918) had also studied at South Kensington under Godfrey Sykes. He did the decorations for the Victoria Terminus and High Court in Bombay, but was later better known as a painter.
3. *Pioneer*, 18 July 1870.

4. 'To the City of Bombay', 1894, Dedication to *The Seven Seas*.

5. 'Some Memories of my Cousin' by Florence Macdonald, KJ, July 1938.

6. LK to Edith Macdonald, 12 December 1866, Sussex.

7. *SOM*.

8. LK to Edith Macdonald, 12 December 1866, Sussex.

9. See Lee, *Virginia Woolf* for how, after advertising in *Time & Tide*, Woolf employed a Miss Rivett-Carnac as a temporary maid. According to Lee, Miss Rivett-Carnac's life story provided 'useful ammunition' for Woolf's *Three Guineas*.

10. *SOM*.

11. Alice (known as Trix) was born on 11 June 1868.

12. Hannah Macdonald's diary – quoted Thomas Pinney, 'Rudyard Kipling's first English residence', KJ, December 1985.

13. See Pinney, ibid.

14. See 'My Brother, Rudyard Kipling', KJ, December 1947.

15. LK to Edith Macdonald, quoted A. W. Baldwin, op cit.

16. Bombay Archive Volume 6, 1868 – quoted in 'John Lockwood Kipling's Contract in Bombay' (article in Kipling Society library).

17. Allen Brothers (also known as Peake Allen and Co. and the Punjab Trading Company).

18. *Pioneer*, 30 June 1873.

19. 'The Potted Princess', *St Nicholas Magazine*, January 1893.

20. *North American Review*, July 1851.

21. See Charles Eliot Norton's foreword to the American edition of *Plain Tales from the Hills*.

22. *Pioneer*, 9 May 1870.

23. 'The Brushwood Boy'.

24. PRO PMG 23 7 & 10.

25. Keegan, *The Battle at Sea*.

26. 'Baa Baa Black Sheep'.

27. See Trix Fleming, 'Some Childhood Memories of Rudyard Kipling', *Chambers's Journal*, March 1939.

28. Trix Fleming, 'Through Judy's Eyes'.

29. See RK to Edmund Gosse, 16 November 1907, BL.†

30. 'Baa Baa Black Sheep'.

31. Trix Fleming to Stanley Baldwin, 27 March 1945, Sussex, Baldwin papers.

32. Plowden, op. cit.

33. Mrs Macdonald's diary, Sussex.

34. Trix Fleming to Stanley Baldwin, 27 March 1945, Sussex, Baldwin papers.

35. Margaret Mackail's description – as recalled by Trix Fleming, Sussex, Baldwin Papers.

36. *SOM*.

37. Georgiana Burne-Jones, *Memorials of Edward Burne-Jones*.

38. Ibid.

39. See Ellmann, *Oscar Wilde*.

40. *SOM*.

41. See N. Naeem Qureshi, 'A Museum for British Lahore', *History Today*, September 1997.

42. *Pioneer*, 11 November 1877.

43. Ankers, op. cit.

44. Quoted Khilnani, *The Idea of India*.

45. Plowden, op. cit.

46. 'Baa Baa Black Sheep'.

47. Storr, *Churchill's Black Dog and Other Phenomena of the Human Mind*.

48. AK to Crom Price, 19 May 1877, collection of Lorraine Price. See also Birkenhead, *Rudyard Kipling*.

49. *Chambers's Journal*, March 1939.

50. *SOM*.

3: Dusky Crew [pp. 69–110]

1. AK to Crom Price, 19 May 1877. Collection of Lorraine Price. All further quotations in this chapter from the correspondence between Rudyard's parents and his headmaster come from the same source.

2. 'An English School', *Youth's Companion*, 19 October 1893, later *Land and Sea Tales for Scouts and Guides*.

3. *SOM*.

4. Margaret Burne-Jones to Mary Wyndham, 14 January 1878, Stanway.

5. Alice Kipling to Crom Price, 24 January 1878, quoted KJ, March 1965.

6. See Sybil Colefax papers, Bodleian Library, Oxford. The Halseys were a prominent Anglo-Indian family who owned a mill in Cawnpore, the heart of the Allen commercial empire.

7. See Birdwood, *The Industrial Arts of India.*

8. See Thornton and Kipling, *Lahore.*

9. See LK to Mrs Halsey, Colefax papers, Bodleian.

10. See notebook, Kipling papers, Sussex.

11. Beresford papers, Sussex.

12. Beresford, *Schooldays with Kipling.*

13. Beresford describes Rudyard's artistic style: 'Drawing from nature was no employment for Gigger. He could however draw wonderful grotesque figures out of his head – demons and ghouls and monsters of all sorts, with many legs and wings; he was strong on bats' or devils' wings; also fat men as bankers and misers, protuberant at the waist-line.'

14. Lisa Lewis, 'The Figure by the Fireplace', KJ, September 1989.

15. *SOM*.

16. Catherine Morris Wright, 'How "St Nicholas" got Rudyard Kipling', *Princeton University Library Chronicle*, 35 (1974).

17. See RK to Mary Mapes Dodge, 3 October 1904, Princeton.†

18. See G. C. Beresford to General Powell, 14 March 1937, India Office, Mss Eur F 172/52.

19. RK to Mrs Tavenor Perry, 25 January 1882, Huntington.†

20. See 'The United Idolaters'.

21. RK to Mrs Tavernor Perry, 9 March 1882, Sussex.

22. *SOM*.

23. RK to Edith Macdonald, January 1881, Sussex.†

24. 'The Islanders'.

25. C. H. Aukland to General Sidney Powell, 11 March 1937, India Office, Mss Eur F 172/55.

26. RK to Mrs John Tavenor Perry, 22 May 1882, Huntington.†

27. 'The Moral Reformers', *Stalky & Co.*

28. 'Argument of a Projected Poem to be Called "The Seven Nights of Creation"', Rutherford, *Early Verse*.

29. Beresford, op cit.

30. *SOM*.

31. LK to Edith Plowden, 5 October 1880, Sussex.

32. Verdicts such as Jonathan Swift: 'Died mad. Two girls ... His private amusements were "ridiculous an' trivial".'

33. This book was much admired by Browning who drew on its encounter between Fra Filippo Lippi and Pope Eugenius IV.

34. 'An English School', op. cit.

35. RK to Mrs Tavenor Perry, 22 May 1882, Huntington.†

36. USC *Chronicle*, no. 8, 20 March 1882.

37. 'From the Wings', *Schoolboy Lyrics*, 1881.

38. See the W. C. Crofts collection, illustrated in 'Kipling's College' by W. M. Carpenter.

39. RK to W. C. Crofts, 18–27 February 1886, Dalhousie.†

40. Plowden, op. cit.

41. RK to W. C. Crofts, 18–27 February 1886, Dalhousie.†

42. See PRO PMG 4 226 and 231.

43. See Oriel, 'The Passing Show', *Melbourne Argus*, 21 November 1891.

44. TF to EB, 15 January 1940, Sussex.

45. Notes by Mrs Fleming on Flo Garrard, Sussex.

46. Ibid.

47. LK to Edith Plowden, 5 October 1880, Sussex.

48. Rutherford, *Early Verse*.

49. Ibid.

50. *Schoolboy Lyrics*.

51. 'A Profession of Faith', dated 17 February 1882, Rutherford, op. cit.

52. RK to Mrs Tavenor Perry, 22 May 1882, Huntington.†

53. Rutherford, op. cit.

54. In February 1881 Phil wrote to his friend Mary Wyndham, daughter of Percy Wyndham, an important patron of his father's,

enthusing, 'I have had absolutely *the* most drivelling note from Oscar Wilde that it is possible.'

55. *The World*, 8 November 1882.

56. Georgiana Burne-Jones to AK – quoted Seymour-Smith, *Rudyard Kipling*.

57. AK to Edith Plowden, 18 December 1881, Sussex.

58. *SOM*.

59. Robert Buchanan, 'The Voice of the Hooligan', *Contemporary Review*, December 1899.

4: Punjab Sahib [pp. 113–41]

1. Trevelyan, *The Competition Wallah*.

2. RK to Edith Macdonald, 30 July 1885, LOC.†

3. See Hopkirk, *Quest for Kim*.

4. Ankers, op. cit.

5. Walter Lawrence, *The India We Served*.

6. See Notes by Mrs Fleming, Kipling Papers, Sussex.

7. LK to Edith Plowden, December 1880, Sussex.

8. TF to CK, 29 November 1936, Sussex.

9. See A. W. Baldwin, op. cit.

10. AK to Edith Plowden, 18 November 1880, Sussex.

11. TF to W. G. B. Maitland, 5 February 1938, LOC.

12. RK to Rev. George Willes, 17 November 1882, Dalhousie.†

13. *SOM*.

14. RK to Rev. George Willes, 17 November 1882, Dalhousie.†

15. See Rutherford, op cit. The version sent to Willes reads, 'More mystic than C——t's list of fines' (referring to Crofts).

16. JK to Edith Plowden, 1883, Sussex.

17. AK to Edith Plowden, 24 February 1883, Sussex.

18. RK to Cormell Price, 1 June 1883, LOC.†

19. RK to Edith Macdonald, 14–17 August 1883, LOC.†

20. 'A Beleaguered City', *CMG*, 28 January 1884.

21. *SOM*.

22. RK to Edith Macdonald, 4 February 1884, LOC.†

23. Ibid.

24. *CMG*, 27 March 1884.

25. Ibid.

26. RK to Edith Macdonald, 10–14 July 1884, LOC.†

27. Ibid., 17 September 1884.†

28. *CMG*, 26 September 1884.

29. 'Lord Ripon's Reverie', *CMG*, 15 September 1884.

30. RK to Edith Macdonald, 21 November 1884, LOC.†

31. This point is convincingly argued in Sullivan, *Narratives of Empire*.

32. In August 1885. See also RK to Margaret Burne-Jones, 27 September 1885, Sussex.†

33. RK Diary entry for 21 August 1885. The original of the Diary is in the Houghton Library, Harvard. It is reproduced in Pinney, *Something of Myself*.

34. RK to Edith Macdonald, 30 July 1885, LOC.†

35. Mrs Hill's note accompanying RK's letter to her, 8 April 1902, Sussex.†

36. RK to E. K. Robinson, 30 April 1886, Sussex.†

5: Special Correspondent [pp. 142–67]

1. See *Egypt of the Magicians*, Chapter 6.

2. LK to Edith Plowden, 16 March 1885, Sussex.

3. *CMG*, 1 April 1885.

4. See also RK to unidentified recipient, 6 March 1890, Sussex.†

5. RK to Isabella Burton, 26 October 1887, private collection.

6. *CMG*, 1 April 1885.

7. RK to Isabella Burton, 7 November 1887, private collection.

8. *CMG*, 1 April 1885.

9. *CMG*, 8 April 1885.

10. Ibid.

11. RK to Cyril F. Herford, 9 May 1896, Huntington.†

12. RK to Moberly Bell, c. 12 September 1898, LOC.†

13. See Mortimer Durand papers, SOAS.

14. LK to Edith Plowden, 16 March 1885, Sussex.

15. Walter Lawrence (1857–1940) was in the office of the Lieutenant-Governor of the Punjab. He was later Secretary to the Viceroy, Lord Curzon, and was created a Baronet. Rudyard helped him write his memoirs, *The India We Served*, in 1928.

16. Prinsep, *Imperial India.*

17. RK to W. H. Lewis, 7 December 1912, Sussex.

18. RK Diary, 30 April 1885, see Pinney (ed.), *SOM.*

19. Ibid. 5 May 1885.

20. Ibid. 6 May 1885.

21. Ibid. 8 May 1885.

22. Ibid. 10 May 1885.

23. Ibid. 12 May 1885.

24. Quoted Taylor, *Victorian Sisters.*

25. RK to Edith Macdonald, 30 July 1885, LOC.†

26. RK Diary, 1 August 1885.

27. RK to Edith Macdonald, 30 July 1885, LOC.†

28. 'The Tale of Two Suits', *Pioneer*, 15 August 1885, Rutherford, op. cit.

29. Originally published in *Pioneer*, 13 July 1885.

30. 'My First Book', originally published with the poem 'In the Neolithic Age' in *San Francisco Examiner*, 18 December 1892, and *The Idler*, December 1892, later collected in Sussex Edition.

31. A similar case of mistaken identity is found in 'Pink Dominoes', one of the *Departmental Ditties.*

32. RK to Margaret Burne-Jones, 28 November 1885, Sussex.†

33. RK to Margaret Burne-Jones, 27 September 1885, Sussex.†

34. *CMG*, 20 October 1885, quoted in Rutherford, op cit.

35. RK to Margaret Burne-Jones, 28 November 1885, Sussex.

36. See RK to Margaret Burne-Jones, 27 September and 28 November 1885, Sussex.†

37. Ibid.

38. Ibid.

39. Ibid.

40. RK to W. C. Crofts, 18–27 February 1886, Dalhousie.†

41. RK to Louisa Baldwin, 24 January 1886, LOC.†

42. *CMG*, 24 August 1886.

43. Yelland, *Boxwallah*.

44. 'The Indian Delegates', *CMG*, 21 November 1885.

6: Wit and Sex Appeal [pp. 168–201]

1. In June 1884.

2. See Roberta Mayer, 'The Aesthetics of Lockwood de Forest: India, Craft and Preservation', *Winterthur Portfolio*, Spring 1996.

3. Duchess of Connaught's diary, 22 December 1884, Royal Archives VIC Add A 15/8445.

4. *Souvenirs of France*.

5. LK to Lockwood de Forest, 29 May 1881, Harvard.

6. RK to Margaret Burne-Jones, 28 November 1885–11 January 1886, Sussex.†

7. Trix Fleming's medical notes, Sussex.

8. *CMG*, 5 January 1886.

9. *Departmental Ditties*, 1886.

10. *CMG*, 5 February 1886.

11. A two wheeled cart pulled by a single horse.

12. Reveley Mitford, *Orient and Occident*.

13. 'With the Main Guard'.

14. RK to W. C. Crofts, 18–27 February 1886, Dalhousie.†

15. RK to Margaret Burne-Jones, 27 September 1885, Sussex.†

16. RK to Margaret Burne-Jones, 25 January 1888, Sussex.†

17. See The Punjab Masonic Year Book and Calendar, 1937–8.

18. See Harry Carr, 'Kipling and the Craft', *Transactions of the Quatuor Coronati Lodge*, 77, 1964.

19. Quoted Laski, *From Palm to Pine*.

20. See Thomas Pinney, KJ, September 1997, for light on exact date of publication.

21. 'A General Summary', *Departmental Ditties*.

22. *Longman's Magazine*, October 1886.

23. RK to Margaret Burne-Jones, 3 May–24 June 1886, Sussex.†

24. LK to Edith Plowden, 27 July 1886, Sussex.

25. Ibid.

26. TF to Sir Ian Hamilton, 27 August 1942, private collection.

27. RK to Isabella Burton, 26 October 1887, private collection.

28. Ibid.

29. See RK to Isabella Burton, March 1888, private collection: 'And if ever you come across a thing as in two Chapters called "The Education of Otis Yeere" you will know that is yours also.'

30. *CMG*, 26 August 1886.

31. 'A District at Play', *CMG*, 27 August 1886.

32. According to the 1893–4 *Gazetteer of the Lahore District*, there were 'only two hotels worthy of the name', the Sindh and Punjab (Mr Nedou's) and the Charing Cross Hotel, under Mrs Kennelly.

33. E. Kay Robinson, 'Kipling in India', *McClure's Magazine*, July 1896.

34. See 'His Chance in Life'.

35. See 'The Broken-Link Handicap'.

36. 'The Bisara of Pooree'.

37. See B. J. Moore-Gilbert, *Kipling and Orientalism*.

38. *Victorian Studies*, Vol. 3, 1959–60.

39. 'Thrown Away'.

40. RK to Edith Macdonald, 4–5 December 1886, LOC.†

41. RK to Thacker Spink, 19 August 1886, Yale.

42. Ibid., 21 July 1886.

43. RK to Edith Macdonald, 4–5 December 1886, LOC.†

44. RK to Thacker Spink, 3 February 1887, Yale.

45. Buck, *Simla Past and Present*.

46. Lord Dufferin to Lady Helen Blackwood, 2 September 1887, Dufferin papers at Clandeboye.

47. RK to Mrs Maunsell, 10 June 1887, LOC.†

48. Seaver, *Francis Younghusband*.

49. Birkenhead archive.

50. RK to Thacker Spink, 23 August 1887, Yale.

51. Ibid., 3 November 1887.

52. RK to Isabella Burton, 26 October 1887, private collection.

53. Ibid., 7 November 1887.

7: Allahabad and Home [pp. 202–44]

1. RK to Isabella Burton, 19 November 1887, private collection.
2. RK to Margaret Burne-Jones, 25 January 1888, Sussex.
3. *Letters of Marque.*
4. Ibid.
5. As Zohreh Sullivan has pointed out, Kipling anticipates Freud's 1919 essay 'The Uncanny' by thirty years.
6. *Letters of Marque.*
7. *CMG*, 24 August 1886.
8. RK to Isabella Burton, 20 January 1888, private collection.
9. *SOM.*
10. *Letters of Marque.*
11. *SOM.*
12. Ibid.
13. Ibid.
14. RK to Thacker Spink, 9 January 1888, Yale.
15. RK to Isabella Burton, 20 January 1888, private collection.
16. A measure of weight that varied radically.
17. 'At Twenty-Two', *Week's News*, 18 February 1888: 'The Giridih Coal-Fields', *Pioneer*, 24 August, 6 and 20 September 1888.
18. 'City of Dreadful Night', *Pioneer*, 18 February–9 April 1888.
19. Ibid.
20. At Syracuse University (facsimile in Ballard; quoted in Rosenbaum, *Index of English Literary Manuscripts*).
21. Edmonia Hill to Caroline Taylor.
22. RK to Isabella Burton, 20 January 1888, private collection.
23. RK to Edmonia Hill, 22 June 1888, Sussex.†
24. RK to Margaret Mackail, 11 February 1889, Sussex.†
25. RK to Edmonia Hill, 22 April 1888, Sussex.†
26. Ibid., 8 May 1888.†
27. Ibid., 9 May 1888.†
28. *Pioneer*, 17 April 1888.
29. RK to Edmonia Hill, 8 May 1888, Sussex.†
30. Ibid., 19–21 May 1888.†

31. Edmonia Hill's note attached to RK's letter, 29–30 May 1888, Sussex.†

32. 'The Young Kipling', *Atlantic Monthly*, April 1936.

33. RK to Edmonia Hill, 9 July 1888, Sussex.

34. Rudyard had just rewritten this piece which was first published in the *CMG*, 28 September 1887, and then reprinted in *Week's News*, 21 April 1888 – later in *Under the Deodars*.

35. Edmonia Hill, 'The Young Kipling', *Atlantic Monthly*, 157, April 1936.

36. RK to Edmonia Hill, 8 May 1888, Sussex.†

37. Ibid., 30 April 1888.†

38. Ibid., 22 June 1888.†

39. Ibid.†

40. Ibid., 28 June 1888.†

41. Quoted A. W. Baldwin, op. cit.

42. RK to Edmonia Hill, 15 June 1888, Sussex.

43. Ibid., 25 June 1888.†

44. Ibid., 7 July 1888.†

45. Ibid., 27 June 1888.†

46. Ibid., 13 July 1888.†

47. Ibid., 9–10 July 1888.†

48. Walter Herries Pollock, *Saturday Review*, 9 June 1888. (Pollock was a friend of Andrew Lang.)

49. *Spectator*, 23 March 1889.

50. RK to Thacker Spink, 9 August 1888, Yale.

51. RK to Edmonia Hill, 22 April 1888, Sussex.†

52. RK to Thacker Spink, 26 October 1888, Yale.

53. Ibid., 5 January 1889.

54. *SOM*.

55. Alice Kipling to Lord Dufferin, 17 December 1888, PRO Northern Ireland (PRONI).

56. *Pioneer*, 26 October 1888.

57. See 'A Study of the Congress by an Eye Witness', *Pioneer*, 1 January 1889.

58. 'On the City Wall'.

59. RK to Edmonia Hill, 6 February 1889, Sussex.†
60. In LOC.
61. See Andrews, *The Splendid Pauper*. Lord Randolph's contacts when he was Secretary of State for India helped secure Frewen his job with the ex-Vizier of Hyderabad.
62. RK to Margaret Burne-Jones, 11–14 February 1889, Sussex.†
63. Hill, 'The Young Kipling', op. cit.
64. These articles were collected in *From Sea to Sea*.
65. *SOM*.
66. *CMG*, 31 July 1889.
67. Note in LOC, dated 21 June 1930.
68. *From Sea to Sea*.
69. Ibid.
70. RK to Georgiana Burne-Jones, 31 May 1889, Bancroft Library, University of California, Berkeley.†
71. *From Sea to Sea*.
72. Ibid.
73. RK to Alexander Hill, 2 July 1889, Sussex.†
74. *From Sea to Sea*.
75. Ibid.
76. RK to Edmonia Hill, 5 September 1889, Sussex.†
77. RK to Edmonia Hill, 10 September 1889, Sussex.†

8: Poet of the Music Halls [pp. 247–80]

1. See Aronson, *Prince Eddy and the Homosexual Underworld*.
2. See Chapman-Huston, *The Lost Historian – Sidney Low*.
3. *SOM*.
4. RK to unidentified recipient, 6 March 1890, Sussex.†
5. RK to Edmonia Hill and Caroline Taylor, 25 October 1889, Sussex.
6. *SOM*.
7. Ibid.
8. *CMG*, 11–15 January 1890.
9. *CMG*, 3 December 1889.
10. *SOM*.

11. RK to J. A. Symonds, 15 October 1889, Bristol.†

12. Stevenson, *Diogenes at the Savile Club.*

13. RK to Edmonia Hill and Caroline Taylor, 1 November 1889, Huntington.†

14. Gilmour, *Curzon.*

15. RK to Caroline Taylor, 2 November 1889, Sussex.†

16. RK to Edmonia Hill, 8–16 November 1889, Sussex.†

17. Ibid., 3–25 December 1889, Sussex.†

18. Ibid.

19. 24 January 1920, *The Diary of Virginia Woolf,* Volume 2, 1920–4, Penguin, 1981.

20. Belloc Lowndes, *The Merry Wives of Westminster.*

21. See Morgan, *The House of Macmillan.* His official history of the Macmillan firm states, 'There is good reason to believe, though no documents confirm it, that what brought him (Kipling) to the firm was the benign and invaluable influence of Mrs W. K. Clifford.'

22. RK to Edmonia Hill, 3–25 December 1889, Sussex.†

23. Ibid.

24. RK to Caroline Taylor, 2 January 1890, Sussex.†

25. Turnovers, Vol. IX, *CMG,* 21 February 1890.

26. RK to Edmonia Hill, 3–25 December 1889, Sussex.†

27. 8 November 1889. See RK to Edmonia Hill, 8–16 November 1889, Sussex.†

28. RK to Carrie Taylor, 2 November 1889, Sussex.†

29. RK to Edmonia Hill, 3–25 December 1889, Sussex.†

30. Mowbray Morris to Albert Baillie, 10 November 1889, quoted Hector Bolitho, *Medical News,* 31 December 1965.

31. He had worked for his brother-in-law, Alexander Strahan, who not only published Tennyson, but also founded several more popular journals, including *Argosy* and *Contemporary Review.*

32. RK to Walter Besant, 20 November 1889, Dalhousie.†

33. RK to John Addington Symonds, 15 October 1889, Bristol.†

34. RK to Edmonia Hill, 8–16 November 1889, Sussex.†

35. RK to Caroline Taylor, 9 December 1889, Sussex.†

36. RK to Edmonia Hill, 3–25 December 1889, Sussex.†

37. Ibid., February 1890.†
38. Ibid., 8–16 November 1889.†
39. Fitzgerald, op. cit.
40. *SOM*.
41. He claims to have suggested *The Times* to Rudyard after this, but RK in *SOM* says he went to *The Times* first.
42. RK to William Canton, 1 April 1890, Berg.
43. Fuzzy-Wuzzy referred to the 1884–5 Gordon relief expedition.
44. See Frank Harris *Contemporary Portraits*.
45. Carrington, *Barrack Room Ballads*.

9: Artistic Rejection [pp. 281–95]

1. RK to Alex Hill, 6–10 January 1890, Cornell (with Edmonia Hill's note).
2. Alice Kipling to Edmonia Hill, 4 March 1890, Sussex.
3. LK to RK, 2 March 1890, Sussex.
4. In the Berg Collection, NYPL.
5. RK to Edmund Gosse, 28 May 1890, British Library.†
6. See Hichberger, *Images of the Army*. ' "Art for Art's sake", in which subject matter and content were considered subordinate to painterly and evocative qualities, in part ensured that battle painting ceased to interest art critics. Where, in the years after Waterloo, "factuality" was deemed a poor alternative to a loftily conceived and executed battle scene, in the 1880s battle pictures were judged primarily as "truth", with only grudging attention to "artistic" merit. It was undoubtedly the impact of newspaper illustration which compounded this tendency to see value in battle paintings only as a record of military history.'
7. RK to Margaret Clifford, 15 August 1890, Berg.†
8. *Scots Observer*, 5 July 1890.
9. 'New Lamps for Old', originally published in *Pioneer*, 1 January 1889.
10. RK to W. E. Henley, 23 September 1890, quoted Connell, *W. E. Henley*.

11. First published *Harper's Weekly*, 23 August 1890.

12. RK to William Canton, late June 1890, Berg.†

13. In September 1890 issue of *Contemporary Review*.

10: The Family from Vermont [pp. 296–329]

1. See Dulles, *Yankees and Samurai*.

2. Rochester Historical Society, Publication Fund Series, Volume 6, 1927.

3. Wolcott Balestier to Molly Cabot, 22 February 1889, Marlboro.

4. Ibid.

5. Caroline Balestier to Josephine Balestier, 18 March 1890, Dunham.

6. See Waugh, *One Man's Road*.

7. Josephine Balestier to Caroline Balestier, 11 July 1890, Dunham.

8. Alice Kipling to Lord Dufferin, 7 February 1891, PRONI.

9. *Athenaeum*, 22 November 1890.

10. RK to W. E. Henley, September 1890, Morgan Library.†

11. 6 May 1898, note in Grolier Club *Catalogue of the Works of Rudyard Kipling*, New York, 1930.†

12. RK to the John W. Lovell Company. See *Soldiers Three*, New York, John W. Lovell, 1890.

13. Caroline Balestier to Josephine Balestier, January 1891, Dunham.

14. Ibid.

15. Wolcott Balestier to William Dean Howells, 18 February 1891, Harvard.

16. Caroline Balestier to Josephine Balestier, n.d., Dunham.

17. Ibid., 31 December 1890.

18. Caroline Balestier to Josephine Balestier, January 1891, Dunham.

19. Ibid., 30 December 1890.

20. Ibid.

21. Belloc Lowndes, op. cit.

22. RK to George Allen, c. 5 January 1891, Dalhousie.†

23. Edmund Gosse to Richard Watson Gilder, June 1891.

24. RK to Meta de Forest, 23 July 1891, Harvard.

25. From a letter from Molly Cabot to an unknown recipient,

Marlboro. Molly seemed to be on the point of coming over to London, perhaps to accompany her brother Will on a continental tour which would include a visit to their von Funcke cousins in Dresden.

26. *SOM*.

27. RK to Ethel Clifford, n.d., private collection.

28. RK to Olive Schreiner, 23 September 1891, Sussex.†

29. From 10 to 25 September 1891.

30. *The Weekly Press*, 5 November 1891.

31. *New Zealand Herald*, 30 January 1892.

32. *Melbourne Argus*, 21 November 1891.

33. 'Home', *CMG*, 5 December 1891.

34. A. P. Watt to LK, 20 November 1891, Sussex.

35. E. Marston of Sampson Low to A. P. Watt, 25 November 1891, Sussex.

36. G. M. Chesney to RK, 23 December 1891, Sussex.

37. See Molly Cabot to Grace Holbrook (Dearest Infant), 6 January 1892, Marlboro.

38. Henry James to Edmund Gosse, 10 December 1891, LOC.

39. Molly Cabot to Grace Holbrook, 6 January 1892, Marlboro.

40. RK to Cormell Price, 17 January 1892, LOC.†

41. RK to W. E. Henley, n.d.

42. Edmund Gosse to Richard Watson Gilder, 18 January 1892.

43. RK to A. P. Watt, 1892, UNC.

44. CK diary, 23 January 1892.

45. Quoted Connell, op. cit.

11: En Puissance de Femme [pp. 333–88]

1. Headings to chapters V, XVII, XVIII and XXI, *The Naulahka*.

2. *Pioneer*, 26 July 1870.

3. 'In Sight of Monadnock', *The Times*, 13 April 1892.

4. CK diary, 28 October 1893.

5. *The New York Sun* paid £25 per piece.

6. See CK's addendum to RK's letter to William Heinemann, 2 September 1892, Princeton.†

7. Kipling had already written appreciatively of the Canadian Pacific Railway on his outward journey, as recorded in 'Across a Continent', first published on 7 May 1892.

8. 'Captains Courageous', *The Times*, 3 November 1892.

9. See Catherine Morris Wright, op. cit.

10. RK to Mary Mapes Dodge, 21 October 1892, Princeton.†

11. RK to William Heinemann, 19 November 1892, Princeton.

12. Charles Carrington ignores the evidence of this 19 November 1892 letter to Heinemann when he says that 'Mowgli's Brothers' was written before 'In the Rukh'. His only evidence is Carrie's diary entry of 29 November 1892 which says that RK has finished 'Mowgli's Brothers'.

13. *SOM*.

14. *SOM*.

15. RK to W. E. Henley, 18–19 November 1893, Morgan Library.

16. 'The Law of the Jungle', *The Second Jungle Book*.

17. RK to C. E. Norton, 8 February 1895, Harvard.†

18. RK to W. E. Henley, 3 January 1893, Berg.†

19. CK diary, 31 December 1892.

20. *Windham County Recorder*, 24 March 1893.

21. *SOM*.

22. 18 February 1893 – information from Hepburn, *The Author's Empty Purse*.

23. See RK and CK to William Heinemann, 12 March 1893, Reed Archives.

24. Georgiana Burne-Jones to Mary Elcho (née Wyndham), 6 July 1893, Stanway.

25. RK to William Heinemann, 2 September 1892, Princeton.†

26. RK to Margaret Mackail, 29 January–1 February 1893, Sussex.†

27. RK to Margaret Mackail, 18 January 1893, Sussex.†

28. CK diary, 2 April 1893.

29. See Cabot, 'The Vermont Period: Rudyard Kipling in Vermont', *English Literature in Transition*, 29/2, 1986.

30. Henry James to Ariana Curtis, 14 July 1893, Henry James letters.

31. CK to Nellie Gosse, 9 December 1893, Cambridge.

32. CK to C. E. Norton, 11 February 1895, Harvard.

33. Molly Cabot to Grace Holbrook, 5 February 1894, Marlboro.

34. Edith Catlin Phelps, *Memoir.*

35. See Eileen Stamers-Smith, 'Kipling and Bermuda', KJ, March 1996.

36. Phelps, op. cit.

37. W. E. Henley to Charles Whibley, 23 April 1894, quoted Connell, op cit.

38. RK to May Catlin, 10 June 1894, Yale.

39. Ibid.

40. See CK diary, 12 February 1894.

41. Ibid., 14 May 1894.

42. RK to Stanley Baldwin, 17 April 1895, Dalhousie.†

43. Ibid.

44. See RK to Stephen Wheeler, 1 February 1897, Harvard.†

45. RK to Henry James, mid-June 1894, Harvard.†

46. RK to Charles Eliot Norton, 5 August 1895, Harvard.†

47. RK to Robert Barr, 28 July 1894, Sussex.†

48. Ibid.

49. See account in Gower, *Old Diaries.*

50. *Journal of Royal African Society,* October 1932.

51. *SOM.*

52. Gwynn (ed.) *The Letters and Friendships of Sir Cecil Spring Rice.*

53. Theodore Roosevelt to Anna Roosevelt, 10 March 1895, Morison, *Letters of Theodore Roosevelt.*

54. Ibid., 1 April 1895.

55. *SOM.*

56. So says RK in *SOM*, though in a letter to William Hallett Phillips (19 June 1895), he suggests it was Phillips who made the introduction.

57. In March 1897 Rudyard wrote to inform Langley that he had been fascinated to read an account of his aero-motor in the magazine *Modern Machinery.*

58. See Sturgis, *Aubrey Beardsley.*

59. RK to Ripley Hitchcock, 22 January 1895, Berg.†

60. CK diary, 5 April 1895.

61. Henry Adams to Sir Robert Cunliffe (Liberal Unionist MP for Flintshire), 26 November 1895.

62. RK to William Hallett Phillips, 19 June 1895, Dalhousie.†

63. RK to Lockwood de Forest, 12 April 1895, Harvard.

64. RK to Mr Wyatt, 14 June 1895, BL RP 4336, whereabouts unknown.

65. CK diary, 21 March 1895.

66. RK to Edward Bok, 25 March 1895, LOC.†

67. RK to Mary Mapes Dodge, 22 September 1894.

68. Mark Twain to RK, August 1895, quoted Neider (ed.), *The Selected Letters of Mark Twain*.

69. William Hallett Phillips to John Hay, 16 July 1895, Brown.

70. RK to Ripley Hitchcock, 26 August 1895, Berg.

71. RK to Charles Eliot Norton, 5 August 1895, Harvard.†

72. RK to Ripley Hitchcock, 26 August 1895, Berg.

73. RK to William Hallett Phillips, c. 16 May 1895, Dalhousie.†

74. Ibid., 19 June 1895.†

75. William Hallett Phillips to John Hay, 4 September 1895, Brown.

76. RK to John Hay, 4 September 1895, Brown.

77. RK to Ripley Hitchcock, 10 September 1895, Berg.

78. CK diary, 23 August 1895.

79. RK to Sarah Orne Jewett, 16 October 1895, Colby.†

80. Rees extracts, 25 September 1895.

81. *Pall Mall Gazette*, 8 December 1891.

82. RK to Robert Barr, 4 November 1894, Sussex.

83. LK to Charles Norton, 1 August 1895, Marlboro.

84. See Judd, *Empire*.

85. RK to Moberly Bell, 26 October 1895, LOC.†

86. See Keating, *Kipling the Poet*.

87. French, *The Life of Henry Norman*.

88. Quoted Cabot, op. cit.

89. RK to William Heinemann, 23 November 1895, Reed archives.

90. CK diary, 13 May 1896.

91. See A. P. Watt archive, UNC.
92. See Cabot, op. cit.

12: Sobering Down [pp. 389–433]

1. RK to James Conland, 1–6 October 1896, LOC.†
2. See RK to John Hay, 8 October 1896, Brown.†
3. *Atlantic Monthly,* January 1897.
4. RK to Ripley Hitchcock, 8 November 1896, Berg.†
5. RK to James Conland, 1–6 October 1896, LOC.†
6. Nellie Gosse to CK, 1 March 1899, Sussex.
7. Quoted Cabot, op. cit.
8. RK to Moberly Bell, 16 February 1897, LOC.
9. Ibid.
10. Edward Burne-Jones to Lady Lewis, 21 July 1896, Bodleian.
11. See Flint, *Cecil Rhodes.*
12. See *SOM.*
13. CK to Molly Cabot, 1 December 1896, quoted Cabot, op. cit.
14. *SOM.*
15. See Thomas, *Rhodes.*
16. See Rees extracts, 2 April 1897.
17. RK to James Conland, 1 June 1897, LOC.†
18. Ibid., 8–24 November 1896.†
19. Ibid., 1 June 1897.†
20. Lago (ed.), *Burne-Jones Talking,* 19 April 1897.
21. RK to Moberly Bell, 28 April 1897, LOC. (Ironically Canadians were not overjoyed with the poem. Although Rudyard made some concession to the Catholicism of the French Canadians by addressing his poem to 'Our Lady', he antagonised other Canadians by appearing to typecast their country as snow-bound. There was talk that the poem should be called 'Our Lady of the Sunshine'. See James L. Mitchell in KJ, March 1998.)
22. See RK to James Conland, 25 March 1897, LOC.†
23. Ibid.
24. RK to Herbert Baker, 13 January 1934, Sussex.

25. RK to Moberly Bell, 8 May 1897, LOC.†

26. RK to William Hallett Phillips, 29 March 1897, Harvard.†

27. CK diary, 15 June 1897.

28. RK to James Conland, 1 June 1897, LOC.†

29. RK to William Joshua Harding, 25 June 1897, LOC.†

30. 'A Fleet in Being'.

31. Morris himself had died the previous year.

32. See *Literature*, 13 April 1901.

33. *The Times*, 17 July 1897.

34. Seymour-Smith, op. cit.

35. RK to J. W. Mackail, 21 July 1897, Sussex.†

36. RK to Rider Haggard, 10 July 1897, quoted Cohen (ed.), *Rudyard Kipling to Rider Haggard*.

37. W. Caius Crutchley to RK, 28 July 1897, Watt archive, UNC.

38. RK to Crom Price, 8 September 1897, LOC.

39. Quoted in talk by Lorraine Price to Kipling Society, 23 September 1992.

40. CK to Meta de Forest, 5 December 1897, Harvard.

41. Thirkell, *Three Houses*.

42. RK to Rider Haggard, 10 July 1897, quoted Cohen (ed.), op. cit.

43. See Diary of A Voyage, BL RP 1874.

44. 'Song of the Wise Children', *The Five Nations*, 1903.

45. *SOM*.

46. See Rive (ed.), *Olive Schreiner Letters*, Vol 1.

47. RK to André Chevrillon, 14 January 1919, Sussex.†

48. RK to Mr Campbell, 1898, Cornell.

49. RK to Charles Norton, 16–17 December 1897, Harvard.†

50. RK to Charles Norton, 23 June 1898, Harvard.†

51. Ibid.

52. He blamed Mackenzie Wallace, Foreign Editor of *The Times*, for keeping 'The Truce of the Bear' out of the main paper. As he told Wynnard Hooper, he wanted Wallace's 'head in a paper-basket' because the latter's pro-Muscovite feelings had prevented his 'little Natural History poem about bears' appearing in *The Times* – quoted in KJ, September 1991, letter in possession of Shamus Wade.

53. RK to Edward White, 21 August 1903, University of Texas.†

54. See RK to William Heinemann, 25 January 1896, Reed archives.

55. See Steen, *William Nicholson*.

56. Heinemann to RK, 11 October 1897, Reed Archives.

57. RK to Louisa Baldwin, 8 October 1898, Dalhousie.†

58. See RK to Arthur Ridsdale, 23 July 1908, Baldwin papers, Sussex.

59. RK to L. C. Dunsterville, 17 February 1899, Sussex.†

60. Carrington, *Kipling*.

61. Theodore Roosevelt to H. Cabot Lodge, 12 January 1899, LOC.

62. CK to Alice Kipling, 4 February 1899, Sussex.

63. The fevered dream is reported in full in Birkenhead, *Rudyard Kipling*.

64. Lord Curzon to Queen Victoria, 23 March 1899, Royal Archives, VIC/O6/69 (albeit that RK's stories were not about Calcutta society).

65. Sally Norton to C. E. Norton, 25 March 1899, Sussex.

66. CK to Georgiana Burne-Jones, 17 March 1899, Sussex.

67. Sally Norton to C. E. Norton, 30 March 1899, Sussex.

68. Phelps, op cit.

69. See Bok, *The Americanization of Edward Bok*.

70. Blunt, *Cockerell*.

71. LK to Sally Norton, 22 July 1899, Harvard.

72. Thirkell, op. cit.

73. RK to Georgiana Burne-Jones, 6 March 1899, Sussex.

74. RK to Andrew Carnegie, 25 June 1899, LOC.†

75. RK to Lord Stamfordham, 14 October 1928, Royal Archives RS/GV/J/2203/31.

76. RK to Henry James, 19 September 1899, Harvard.†

77. Moberly Bell to L. S. Amery, quoted Pakenham, *The Boer War*.

78. CK diary, 14 October 1899.

79. Durbach, *Kipling's South Africa*.

80. 25 February 1900, quoted Pethica (ed.), *Lady Gregory's Diaries*.

81. RK to William Fraser, 8 January 1900, Dalhousie.†

13: Flannelled Fools [pp. 434–68]

1. Henry James to Anna Balestier, 30 January 1900, Harvard.
2. RK to Lockwood and Meta de Forest, 15 January 1900, Harvard.
3. RK to Moberly Bell, 22 January 1900, LOC.
4. Henry James to Anna Balestier, 30 January 1900, Harvard.
5. Amery, *My Political Life*.
6. Sir George Allen died on 4 November 1900. Just over a month later his son George Burney Allen, who took over his business, was on the same ship as the Kiplings, the s.s. *Tantallon, en route* to South Africa – presumably to see how his business was faring. (See RK to James Walker, 16 May 1901.)
7. See Pakenham, op. cit.
8. Quoted in Morris, *The Scaremongers*.
9. RK to Duchess of Sutherland, 10 October 1900, Dalhousie.†
10. RK to C. R. L. Fletcher, 10 April 1915, Sussex.†
11. KJ, April 1942, p. 13.
12. See Durbach, op. cit.
13. Ralph, *War's Brighter Side*.
14. Paterson, *Happy Dispatches*.
15. *SOM*.
16. CK diary, 26 March 1900.
17. *SOM*.
18. RK to Alfred Baldwin, 19 May 1900, Sussex. In the same letter, he expressed his anger that 'German agents are creeping up behind our army and getting orders to replace all the stuff that the Boers have smashed and wasted.'
19. RK to Dr James Conland, 24 July 1900, LOC.†
20. RK to Fabian Ware, 2 May 1900, Cornell.†
21. Quoted Durbach, op. cit.
22. RK to Henry Wilson, 16 May 1900, Bodleian.†
23. Quoted in Brendon, *The Motoring Century*.
24. *SOM*.
25. RK to Dr James Conland, 24 July 1900, LOC.†
26. See CK to Meta de Forest, 11 May 1900, Harvard.

27. See Mabel Leigh's account, Sussex 27.14 (wrongly attributed to Edward, Lord Dunsany).

28. RK to James Conland, 2 December 1900, LOC.†

29. Henry James to Grace Norton, 25 December 1897, Harvard.

30. RK to Charles Eliot Norton, 24–28 November 1899, Harvard.

31. See Margaret Feeley, 'The *Kim* that Nobody Reads', *Studies in the Novel*, Fall 1981. See also Edward Said, Introduction, *Kim*, Penguin Classics 1987.

32. Henry James to RK, 30 October 1901, Harvard.

33. CK to Sally Norton, 3 January 1901, Sussex.

34. CK to Miss Lawrence, 6 July (n.y.), LOC.

35. RK to James Conland, 2 December 1900, LOC.†

36. Georgiana Burne-Jones to Charles Eliot Norton, 12 July 1901, Harvard.

37. CK to Mrs Hancock, 14 February 1901, Morgan Library.

38. See Brogan, *Mowgli's Sons*.

39. Lo Hui-Min, *The Correspondence of G. E. Morrison*.

40. RK to Cecil Rhodes, 14 April 1901, Rhodes House Library.†

41. RK to Charles Eliot Norton, 19 May 1901, Harvard.†

42. Gwynne's diary, 3 January 1901, Bodleian.

43. Lo Hui-Min, op. cit.

44. Gwynne's diary, 6 April 1901, Bodleian.

45. RK to Charles Eliot Norton, 19 May 1901, Harvard.†

46. RK to John S. Phillips, 4 July 1901, Dr A. S. W. Rosenbach Catalogue number 36.†

47. RK to H. A. Gwynne, 23–24 August 1901, J. P. Morgan.†

48. RK to Anna Balestier, 5 July 1901, Marlboro.†

49. CK to Sally Norton, 3 January 1901, Sussex.

50. RK to H. A. Gwynne, 23–24 August 1901, J. P. Morgan.†

51. RK to Cecil Rhodes, 24 October 1901, Rhodes House Library.†

52. Lord Roberts to RK quoted KJ, December 1989.

53. RK to Rider Haggard, 28 January 1902, quoted in Cohen (ed.), op. cit.

54. G. K. Chesterton, *Bookman*, November 1902.

55. RK to Edmonia Hill, 8 April 1902, LOC.†

56. RK to H. A. Gwynne, 15 April 1902, Dalhousie.†

57. RK to Edmonia Hill, 8 April 1902, LOC.†

58. Ibid.

59. RK to H. A. Gwynne, 15 April 1902, Dalhousie.†

60. RK to Maitland Park, 11 July 1902, University of Cape Town.†

61. RK to Dr Starr Jameson, 17 June 1902, National Archives of Zimbabwe.†

62. RK to Lady Edward Cecil, 24 September 1902, Syracuse.†

63. See RK to L. Cope Cornford, 23 May 1902, LOC.

64. Written, according to CK's diary, on 5 August 1902.

65. RK to Ambrose Poynter, 23 August 1902, Birkenhead archive.

66. Rees extracts, 3 September 1902 (in RK's hand).

67. RK to L. Cope Cornford, n.d., LOC.

14: Most Wonderful Foreign Land [pp. 469–523]

1. RK to Charles Eliot Norton, 30 November–8 December 1902, Harvard.†

2. Nicolson, *Bateman's*.

3. RK to Charles Eliot Norton, 30 November–8 December 1902, Harvard.†

4. Ibid.

5. Arthur Gordon, KJ, June 1967.

6. *SOM*.

7. See Marsh, *Joseph Chamberlain*.

8. Trix Fleming in discussion at Kipling Society meeting, reported KJ, December 1937.

9. Sir Henry Newbolt to John Lane, 25 February 1898, quoted KJ, March 1980.

10. Hepburn (ed.) *Letters of Arnold Bennett*.

11. See Henry Newbolt to A. S. Watt, 3 and 11 August 1902, Watt archives, UNC.

12. RK to Colonel Sutherland Harris, 23 June 1908, Syracuse.

13. RK to Rider Haggard, received 9 November 1912, quoted Cohen (ed.), op. cit.

14. See RK to L. Cope Cornford, 2 October 1902, LOC.

15. RK to James Conland, 27 January 1903, LOC.†

16. RK to Lord Milner, 26 February 1903, Bodleian.†

17. RK to Edward White, 11 November 1902, Johns Hopkins.†

18. *The Five Nations* was published in October 1903.

19. RK to Lord Milner, 21 April 1903, Bodleian.†

20. RK to Kinsey Peile, n.d., Sussex.

21. RK to Kinsey Peile, 24 June 1903, Sussex.

22. Cosmo Hamilton, *People Worth Talking About.*

23. CK diary, 2 December 1900.

24. Beerbohm, *The Poet's Corner.*

25. RK to Edward White, 21 August 1903, University of Texas.†

26. CK diary, 27 September 1903.

27. RK to Lord Milner, 4 April 1904, Bodleian.

28. RK to Charles Eliot Norton, 18 February 1908, Harvard.†

29. Durbach, op. cit.

30. RK to Charles Hughes, 26 June 1905. However, according to Professor Thomas Pinney, referring to Partridge's *Dictionary of Slang*, the phrase did not come from Ruskin but from the *Daily News* (10 September 1885).

31. Filson Young, *The Complete Motorist.*

32. Ibid.

33. *SOM.*

34. RK to Gilbert Murray, 13 August 1902, Bodleian.†

35. RK to Aurel Stein, 1 September 1903, Bodleian.

36. RK to H. A. Gwynne, early October 1904, Dalhousie.†

37. RK to Edward Bok, 3 January 1905, Syracuse.†

38. RK to *Daily Mail*, 6 August 1904.

39. RK to Edmonia Hill, 8 March 1905, LOC.†

40. *SOM.*

41. See Raine, Introduction to *A Choice of Kipling's Prose.*

42. See Hart-Davis (ed.), *End of an Era.* Also Philip Burne-Jones to Charles Eliot Norton, 9 November 1904, Harvard.

43. See London, 'These Bones Shall Rise Again' (from *Revolution and*

Other Essays); Mencken, *My Life as Author and Editor*; St. John, *Ellen Terry and Bernard Shaw: A Correspondence.*

44. CK to Anna Balestier, 10 June 1904, Dunham papers.

45. Ibid., 8 June 1904.

46. Ibid., 19 June 1904.

47. Elsie Parker to Sara Anderson, 3 October 1904, Sussex.

48. Elsie Parker to Seymour Obermer, 3 May 1904, Sussex.

49. Elsie Parker to Sara Anderson, 3 October 1904, Sussex.

50. In April 1904 RK paid £984. 3s. 1d. in income tax.

51. RK to James Walker, 16 May 1901, Syracuse.

52. Quoted Lo Hui-Min, op. cit.

53. RK to James Conland, 7 January 1903, LOC.

54. CK to Anna Balestier, 19 June 1904, Dunham papers.

55. RK to Rider Haggard, 5 December 1904, quoted Cohen (ed.), op. cit.

56. See Watt to Macmillan, 25 January 1905, British Library.

57. CK to George Macdonald, 17 June 1903, East Sussex County Archives.

58. CK diary, 30 August 1904.

59. French, *Younghusband.*

60. RK to Mary Mapes Dodge, 3 October 1904, Princeton.†

61. Winston Churchill, 10 November 1904 (quoting Chamberlain), see Koss, *The Rise and Fall of the Political Press in Britain.*

62. Published *The Times*, 1 August 1904.

63. See Begbie, *Albert, Fourth Earl Grey.*

64. Published *The Times*, 22 July 1905.

65. RK to Edmonia Hill, 27 June 1906, LOC.†

66. RK to Mr McFie, 16 March 1906, Cornell.

67. See RK to Edward White, 3 April 1907, University of Texas.†

68. RK to Edmonia Hill, 27 June 1906, LOC.†

69. RK to R. Duckworth Ford, 3 April 1907, Sussex.

70. Ibid., 16 September 1907.†

71. RK to Lord Milner, 27 January 1908, Bodleian.†

72. RK to Lord Selborne, 17 March 1908, Bodleian.†

73. Royal Archives VIC/ADD A15/6504a.

74. See 'The Road to Quebec' in *Letters to the Family*.

75. RK to Sir Charles Crewe, 19 July 1907, East London Museum.†

76. LK to Aurel Stein, 9 March 1904, Bodleian.

77. RK to H. A. Gwynne, 15 June 1907, Dalhousie.†

78. Catlin Phelps, op. cit.

79. There had been translations from the late 1890s, and the great critic Hippolyte Taine described the author of *The Light that Failed* in 1892 as 'un homme de génie'.

80. RK to Jules Huret, 31 August 1905, King's School, Canterbury.†

81. These two tales – 'Brother Square-Toes' and 'A Priest in Spite of Himself' – possibly owe their presence in *Rewards and Fairies* to Rudyard's desire to impress Edward Bok, the American editor of *Ladies' Home Journal*, who had taken four of the earlier stories. The ruse did not work, for Bok turned down this batch.

82. RK to Hugh Thursfield, 8 November 1900, LOC.

83. Sir William Osler to Mrs Brewster, 19 July 1907, quoted KJ, June 1983.

84. RK to John Kipling, 27 June 1907, Sussex.†

85. RK to Sir William Osler, 29 June 1907, quoted KJ, June 1983.

86. Cushing, *The Life of Sir William Osler*.

87. RK to Lord Grey, 14 May 1907, Durham University.

88. Stephen Leacock to his mother, 15 January 1908, quoted in Doyle, *Stephen Leacock*.

89. RK to Cormell Price, 19 September 1907, LOC.†

90. See CK diary, 16 October 1907.

91. RK to 'Family', 29 September 1907, Sussex.†

92. *SOM*.

93. 'Values in Life', *A Book of Words*.

94. CK diary, 3 October 1907.

95. RK to H. A. Gwynne, January 1908, Dalhousie.

96. See RK to Andrew Macphail, 13–28 December 1908, National Archives of Canada.†

97. RK to Lord Milner, July 1908, Bodleian.†

98. *SOM*.

99. RK to Conan Doyle, December 1907, University of Cape Town.†

100. RK to John and Elsie Kipling, 10 December 1907, Sussex.†

101. RK to Colonel H. W. Feilden, 2 August 1910, Syracuse.†

102. The stories were initially published over a period of four and a half years – from 'Weland's Sword', the first from *Puck of Pook's Hill*, which appeared in *Ladies' Home Journal* in January 1906, to 'A Priest in Spite of Himself', the last from *Rewards and Fairies*, in *The Delineator* in August 1910. The *LHJ*, which published the first four stories from *Puck of Pook's Hill*, paid well, and Rudyard would have liked to see his later output there. But there was a trans-Atlantic mix-up over 'Weland's Sword', which *Strand* wanted to publish in its Christmas 1905 issue, but the *LHJ* was unable to alter its publishing schedule to accommodate this request. Edward Bok later admitted he had a poor response from his readers, who regularly wrote in to ask what the author meant. So after 'inquiry grew into irritation', Bok was happy not to take further stories.

103. Parnesius's family went to relax at Aquae Sulis, which has been suggested (by B. J. Moore-Gilbert in *Kipling and Orientalism*, for example) as a prototype British Simla: 'All the old gluttons sit in hot water, and talk scandal and politics', 'A Centurion of the Thirteenth' in *Puck of Pook's Hill*.

104. RK to Lord Milner, July 1908, Bodleian.†

105. MacInnes, *Out of the Way*.

106. RK to George Wyndham, referred to in Wyndham's letter to Mrs Drew (October 1906?) quoted in KJ, May 1993.

107. RK to Charles Norton, 18 February 1908, Harvard.†

108. *SOM*.

109. *A Book of Words*.†

110. RK to Lord Milner, July 1908, Bodleian.

111. RK to Lady Edward Cecil, 2 December 1908, Syracuse.

112. RK to Edward Lucas White, 5 April 1910, Texas.

113. See *Thomas*, Rhodes.

114. RK to Leo Amery, 19 June 1907, sold at Sothebys, 1998.

15: The New Jeremiah [pp. 524–53]

1. Georgiana Burne-Jones to C. E. Norton, 22 September 1907, Harvard.

2. RK to Cormell Price, 19 September 1907, LOC.†

3. RK to Charles Eliot Norton, 18 February 1908, Harvard.†

4. See RK to John Kipling, 20 October 1908, Sussex.†

5. Ibid., 6 October 1908.

6. Ibid., 16 June 1909.

7. Ibid., 18 May 1908.

8. RK to Charles Norton, 18 February 1908, Harvard.†

9. RK to Elsie Kipling, 11 June 1908, Sussex.

10. See RK to Anna Balestier, 26 November 1908, Dunham.†

11. Ibid.

12. RK to L. C. Dunsterville, 14 July 1908.

13. RK to John Kipling, 12 July 1910, Sussex.

14. RK to Lord Kitchener, 6 November 1908, Dalhousie.†

15. RK to Andrew Macphail, 26 September 1908, National Archives of Canada.†

16. Ibid., 20 November 1908.

17. RK to B. H. Walton, 24 May 1907, LOC.†

18. Watt to Macmillan, June 1907, British Library.

19. Ibid., 4 October 1909.

20. RK to Colonel H. W. Feilden, 11 March 1908, Syracuse.

21. RK to Anna Balestier, 26 November 1908, Dunham papers.†

22. RK to H. A. Gwynne, 2 January 1909, Dalhousie.†

23. RK to Louisa Baldwin, 13 January 1909, Dalhousie.†

24. RK to JK, 15–18 March 1909, Sussex.

25. RK to Lord and Lady Rodd, 4 March 1909.

26. LK to RK, 11 March 1909, copy Birkenhead archive.

27. Philip Burne-Jones to Mary Elcho, 2 March 1917, Stanway.

28. RK to B. H. Walton, (May? 1909), LOC.

29. RK to Leo Amery, 19 June 1907, sold at Sotheby's 1998.

30. Baden-Powell, *Sketches*.

31. See Brogan, *Mowgli's Sons*.

32. See *The Scout*, 23 October 1909. (The reference is from Brogan, *Mowgli's Sons*.)

33. See RK to John St Loe Strachey, 10 October 1910, House of Lords.†

34. RK to John Kipling, 20 January 1909, Sussex.

35. Baden-Powell to RK, 6 May 1909, Sussex (quoted Brogan, *Mowgli's Sons*).

36. See CK diary, 20 August 1909.

37. RK to R. D. Blumenfeld, 26 April 1910, Sussex.

38. *Daily Express*, 4 November 1911.

39. RK to Stanley Baldwin, 18 March 1911, Sussex.†

40. RK to Edward Lucas White, 13 December 1910, Texas.†

41. RK to Anna Balestier, 6 January 1910, Dunham papers.†

42. RK to Anna Balestier, (16 March 1906), Dunham papers.

43. See *SOM*.

44. RK to EK, 15 July 1908, Sussex.

45. RK to Anna Balestier, 6 January 1910, Dunham papers.†

46. RK to Dr Alfred Fröhlich, 14 February 1910, Dalhousie.

47. RK to Cormell Price, 27 January 1910, LOC.†

48. RK to John Kipling, 9 March 1910, Sussex.†

49. RK to John Kipling, 28 February 1910, Sussex.

50. RK to John Kipling, 9 March 1910, Sussex.†

51. RK to H. A. Gwynne, 13 March 1910, Sussex.

52. RK to Andrew Macphail, 5–18 April 1910, National Archives of Canada.†

53. RK to Edmonia Hill, 6 April 1910, LOC.†

54. RK to Andrew Macphail, 5–18 April 1910, National Archives of Canada.†

55. RK to JK, 20 May 1910, Sussex.†

56. RK to Andrew Macphail, 5–18 April 1910, National Archives of Canada.†

57. RK to Andrew Macphail, 4–11 August 1910, National Archives of Canada.†

58. RK to C. R. L. Fletcher, 18 May 1910, Sussex.†

59. *A History of England*.

60. RK to JK, 15 July 1910, Sussex.†

61. Ibid.

62. CK diary, 10 August 1910.

63. Watt to Macmillan, 4 October 1910, British Library.

64. RK to 'family', 15 March 1907, Sussex.

16: Max, Money and Motors [pp. 554–602]

1. LK to Aurel Stein, 30 September 1904, Bodleian.

2. See Trix Fleming and Alice Kipling's correspondence with Elkin Matthews in the Berg Collection, NYPL.

3. Indian Army List. (Technically Fleming took thirteen months' leave in July 1910 and formally retired in August 1911.)

4. CK diary, 4 November 1905.

5. RK to Louisa Baldwin, 27 October 1909, Dalhousie.

6. Rees extracts, 29 June 1903.

7. RK to Edmonia Hill, 27 June 1906, LOC.†

8. RK to Crom Price, 27 April 1910, LOC.†

9. RK to Colonel Hughes, 25 February 1935, LOC.

10. TF to J. H. C. Brooking, n.d., Birkenhead archive.

11. Ibid.

12. CK diary, 24 November 1910.

13. Rees extracts, 25 November 1910.

14. Ibid., 18 April 1911.

15. See 'The Lockwood Kiplings at Tisbury, Wiltshire' by Ralph Jackson, one time President of Tisbury Historical Society, *Hatcher Review*, Vol 2, No 16, autumn 1983.

16. TF to J. H. C. Brooking, Birkenhead archive.

17. RK to Stanley Baldwin, 18 March 1911, Sussex.†

18. Ibid.

19. RK to Colonel H. W. Feilden, 15–19 March 1911, Sussex.†

20. Ibid.

21. CK diary, 8 April 1912.

22. RK to Colonel J. Fleming, 13 March 1911, private collection.

23. TF to Brooking, Birkenhead archive.

24. RK to Stanley Baldwin, 19 January 1911, Sussex.

25. CK to Anna Balestier, 18 September 1914, Dunham papers.

26. Ireland, *The Balestiers of Beechwood.*

27. Henry James to Anna Balestier, 10 May 1911, Harvard.

28. RK to Edmonia Hill, 10 February 1911, Sussex.†

29. Max Aitken to RK, 21 December 1910, House of Lords.

30. RK to Max Aitken, 9 March 1911, House of Lords.

31. See Box 21/19 Kipling archives, Sussex.

32. RK to Lord Milner, 23 September 1911, Bodleian.†

33. CK to Lady Edward Cecil, 23 September 1911, Bodleian.

34. Milner papers, Bodleian.

35. Memo in Beaverbrook papers, House of Lords.

36. Ibid.

37. RK to George Buckle, 27 June 1911, *Times* archives.†

38. RK to H. A. Gwynne, 10 November 1911, Sussex.†

39. See Beaverbrook papers, House of Lords.

40. RK to Aitken, 15 November 1911, House of Lords.†

41. RK to Colonel H. W. Feilden, 22 October 1911, Sussex.†

42. Ibid.

43. RK to R. D. Blumenfeld, 30 October 1911, Sussex.

44. CK diary, 8 November 1911.

45. Ibid., 21 July 1910.

46. RK to H. A. Gwynne, 21 June 1910, Sussex.

47. RK to Andrew Macphail, 25 June 1910, National Archives of Canada.†

48. RK to H. A. Gwynne, 10 November 1911, Sussex.†

49. RK to Anna Balestier, 25 December 1911, Dunham papers.†

50. Ibid.

51. RK to Max Aitken, 24 June 1911, House of Lords.

52. Max Aitken to Claude Johnson, 25 June 1911, House of Lords.

53. Claude Johnson to Max Aitken, 26 June 1911, House of Lords.

54. Claude Johnson to RK, 26 June 1911, House of Lords.

55. RK to Aitken, 27 June 1911, House of Lords.

56. RK to Colonel H. W. Feilden, 16 March 1912, Sussex.†

57. Ibid., 24 March 1912.

58. See RK to Gwynne, 21 April 1912, quoted Carrington, *Kipling.*

59. RK to L. Cope Cornford, 5 April 1912 (actually dated 5 March, but clearly wrong), LOC.

60. *The Times*, 16 April 1912.

61. RK to JK, 5 May 1910, Sussex.

62. Ibid., 1 May 1912.†

63. *Near East Magazine*, 10 May 1912.

64. RK to JK, 5 June 1912, Sussex.†

65. Ibid., 6 November 1912, Sussex.

66. RK to Roderick Jones, Reuters.

67. See RK to Anna Balestier, 24 September 1912, Dunham.†

68. CK diary, 3 December 1912.

69. RK to R. Duckworth Ford, 13 December 1911, Sussex.†

70. RK to JK, 12 February 1913.

71. See KJ, June 1963, pp. 11–13.

72. See RK to J. Pierpont Morgan, 7 April 1911, Morgan Library.

73. RK to H. A. Gwynne, 14 March 1913, Sussex.†

74. CK diary, 13 March 1913.

75. RK to H. A. Gwynne, 14 March 1913, Sussex.†

76. Quoted Rose, *The Later Cecils*.

77. *Egypt of the Magicians*.

78. Ibid.

79. Quoted Cohen (ed.), op. cit., pp. 77–9.

80. *Egypt of the Magicians*.

81. Ibid.

82. Clare Mackail to Angela Mackail, 10 June 1913, private collection.

83. *SOM*.

84. Watt to Doubleday, 2 April 1912, Watt archives, UNC.

85. The Bombay Edition was initially known as the Florence edition, after the type-face Macmillan intended to use. But Rudyard preferred the plainer Riccardi, and then decided he wanted 'some quite distinctive title like the Outward Bound', as used in the de luxe edition in the United States.

86. RK to Francis Younghusband, 21 February 1914, India Office MSS Eur F 197/242.

87. RK to Nellie Doubleday, 10 May 1913, Princeton.

88. RK to Max Aitken, 9 April 1913, House of Lords.†

89. Max Aitken to RK, 13 November 1913, House of Lords.

90. RK to Max Aitken, 14 November 1913, House of Lords.†

91. CK diary, 13 June 1913.

92. Quoted Andrew, *Secret Service*.

93. Rees extracts, 1 July 1913.

94. RK to H. B. Marriott Watson, 29 October 1909, Huntington.†

95. RK to Major C. F. Massy, 27 January 1910, Syracuse.†

96. RK to JK, 17 May 1910, Sussex.

97. In his autobiography *From Many Angles* (Harrap, 1942) Sykes explicitly notes that Rudyard was 'a valued friend' around this time.

98. RK to W. H. Lewis, 7 December 1912, Sussex.

99. See RK to Max Aitken, 25 November 1912, House of Lords.

100. See RK to Blumenfeld, 28 March 1912, Sussex.

101. See RK to JK, 3 October 1913, Sussex.

102. RK to Captain W. H. Lewis, 5 December 1913, Sussex.†

103. RK to Colonel H. W. Feilden, 25 December 1913, Sussex.†

104. RK to Milner, (23 February 1914), Syracuse.†

105. RK to Gwynne, 10 March 1914, Sussex.†

106. Ibid., n.d. (1913).

107. Ibid., 26 November 1913.

108. RK to Aitken, 15 January 1914, House of Lords.†

109. See RK to Aitken, 12 February 1914, House of Lords.

110. See CK diary, 1 March 1914.

111. RK to Gwynne, 3 March 1914, Sussex.

112. RK to Captain W. H. Lewis, 1 November 1913, Sussex.

113. CK to Anna Balestier, 27 March 1914, Dunham Papers.

114. See RK to Sir James Dunlop Smith, 14 April 1914, Yale.†

115. This is stated categorically in John Monroe's biography of Lord Milner, but there is no further evidence in either Milner's papers in the Bodleian or in PRONI.

116. RK to JK, 2 March 1913, Sussex.†

117. CK diary, 25 May 1913.

118. RK to JK, 30 July 1913, Sussex.

119. RK to H. A. Gwynne, 10 March 1914, Dalhousie.†

120. Edward Marsh, *A Number of People*.

121. CK to Lady Milner, 25 May 1914, Bodleian.

122. RK to Leo Amery, 7 June 1914, Sussex.

123. RK to Colonel H. W. Feilden, 7 August 1914, Sussex.

124. RK to H. A. Gwynne, 7 August 1914, Sussex.†

17: What Stands If Freedom Fall? [pp. 605–59]

1. See Tonie and Valmai Holt, *My Boy Jack?*

2. CK to Anna Balestier, 11 September 1914, Dunham.

3. CK diary, 31 August 1914.

4. CK to Lady Milner, 2 September 1914, Bodleian.

5. Nellie Doubleday sent 200 pounds of linen.

6. CK to Anna Balestier, 7 October 1914, Dunham.

7. CK to Lady Milner, 3 September 1914, Bodleian.

8. Grey to Masterman, 14 September 1914, quoted Masterman.

9. RK to Lord Milner, 13 September 1914, Bodleian.

10. RK to Krebs, 13 September 1914, Bodleian.

11. Roosevelt to RK, 4 November 1914, LOC.

12. CK to Anna Balestier, 18 September 1914, Dunham.

13. RK to EK, 28 September 1914, Sussex.†

14. CK to Anna Balestier, 26 September 1914, Dunham.

15. See RK to Aitken, 5 November 1914, House of Lords.

16. Published by Hodder & Stoughton, January 1916.

17. RK to C. R. L. Fletcher, 10 April 1915, Sussex.†

18. Ibid.

19. Ibid.

20. See Machen, *The Bowmen & Other Legends of the War*.

21. RK to C. R. L. Fletcher, 5 May 1915, Sussex.†

22. See RK to Gwynne, 2 January 1915, Sussex.

23. RK to JK, 22 October 1914, Sussex.

24. Ibid., 4 March 1915.

25. CK to Anna Balestier, 5 August 1915, Dunham.

26. RK to Henry James, 22 July 1915, Yale.†

27. See CK to Anna Balestier, 21 April 1915, Dunham.

28. CK to Lady Edward Cecil, Tuesday (17 August 1915), Bodleian.

29. RK to CK and EK, 23 August 1915, Sussex.†

30. RK to CK, 22 August 1915, Sussex.†

31. RK to JK, 28 August 1915, Sussex.

32. JK to RK, 20 August 1915, Sussex.

33. JK to RK, 25 September 1915, Sussex.

34. CK diary, 26 September 1915. (The Rees extracts say this was 25 September which seems more likely.)

35. E. Y. Daniel to Sir Claud Schuster, 27 September 1915, Watt papers, UNC.

36. RK to Dr Curteis, 3 June 1916, Syracuse.

37. Gwynne to Lady Bathurst, 7 October 1915, quoted Wilson (ed.), *The Rasp of War*.

38. I am grateful to George Webb's foreword to *The Irish Guards in the Great War*, Spellmount, 1997, for this and several other details.

39. RK to L. C. Dunsterville, 12 November 1915, Sussex.†

40. See 'The Egg-Shell' in 'Their Lawful Occasions', first published in 1903, one of the stories in *Traffics and Discoveries*.

41. Quoted Stewart, *Rudyard Kipling: A Bibliographical Catalogue*.

42. Elgar to Lady Stuart of Wortley, 18 September 1917, quoted in Elgar, *The Windflower Letters*.

43. See Rose, op. cit.

44. RK to Max Aitken, 18 December 1915, House of Lords.

45. CK to Anna Balestier, 7 November 1915, Dunham papers.

46. RK to Max Aitken, (December 1916), House of Lords.

47. RK to André Chevrillon, 31 December 1915, Sussex.†

48. Ibid., 2 June 1916.

49. RK to Stanley Baldwin, 24 July 1916, Sussex.

50. RK to Edmonia Hill, 4 August 1915, Sussex.†

51. RK to André Chevrillon, 31 December 1921, Sussex.

52. RK to Edmonia Hill, 4 August 1915, Sussex. His comments on the soldiers at Charing Cross Station are in Vincent (ed.) *The Crawford Papers*.

53. Flower (ed.), *Journals of Arnold Bennett*, 8 June 1916.

54. Erwin Nader to RK, 27 May 1919, Sussex.

55. See Gilbert, *The First World War*.

56. RK to R. D. Blumenfeld, 27 February 1916, Sussex.

57. Julian Corbett to RK, 6 September 1915, Sussex.

58. Douglas Brownrigg to RK, 29 June 1916, Sussex.

59. Oswald Frewen diary, 2 November 1916.

60. Quoted Gilbert, *First World War*.

61. Quoted Middlemas and Barnes, *Baldwin*.

62. RK to Beaverbrook, 12 April 1917, House of Lords.

63. See Rodd, *Social and Diplomatic Memories*, pp. 213–15, for an account of how the Conclave of Cardinals which elected Benedict XV was pro-German and believed Russia responsible for the war.

64. Jones stayed from 6 to 8 January 1917. (CK diary).

65. RK to Roderick Jones, 8 February 1917, quoted Notes for Lord Birkenhead, 18 August 1945, Reuters archive.

66. RK to 'Dearests' (CK and EK), 7 May 1917, Sussex.†

67. Ibid.

68. Ibid., 10 May 1917.†

69. Ibid.

70. Rees extracts, 17 May 1917.

71. CK diary, 28 May 1917.

72. RK to Bonar Law, 2 July 1917, House of Lords.†

73. CK diary, 1 July 1917.

74. RK to Herbert Baker, 2 February 1934, Sussex. (The actual quotation from Abt Vogler runs, 'That out of those sounds he frame, not a fourth sound, but a star'.)

75. Notes on *The Years Between*, sent to F. N. Doubleday, n.d., Sussex.

76. Lisa Lewis (KJ, June 1997) notes that there were two manuscripts of 'On the Gate' and that CK may have objected to the earlier version, which was suffused with RK's war-time hate.

77. 22 May 1918, quoted Higgins.

78. Haggard's diary, 23 May 1918, quoted Cohen (ed.), op. cit.

79. RK to C. R. L. Fletcher, 29 April 1917, Sussex.†

80. Notes on *The Years Between*.

81. RK to Stanley Baldwin, 1 December 1917, Sussex.†

82. Empire Day message to New Zealand.

83. RK to Ian Colvin, 5 October 1916, Syracuse.†

84. See RK to R. D. Blumenfeld, 22 April 1918, Sussex.

85. Amory (ed.), *The Diaries of Evelyn Waugh.*

86. RK to Almroth Wright, n.d., private collection.†

87. RK to Ian Colvin, 30 September 1917, Syracuse.

88. See *The Times*, 25 May 1917.

89. RK to Ian Colvin, 17 August 1917, Syracuse.

90. Ibid., 30 September 1917.

91. CK to Anna Balestier, 30 September 1917, Dunham.

92. CK diary, 10 April 1918.

93. RK to Lord Northcliffe, 28 June 1918, LOC.

94. Rees extracts, 5 January 1917 and 31 December 1918.

95. See RK to Colonel Feilden, 1 February 1918, Sussex.†

96. Roderick Jones to RK, 10 January 1918, Sussex.

97. RK to Roderick Jones, quoted Notes by Sir Roderick Jones for Lord Birkenhead, Reuters archives.

98. RK to F. N. Doubleday, 18 March 1919, Princeton.†

99. The actual date of Beaverbrook's request is not known, but Rudyard replied on 14 February, the day before his Folkestone speech.

100. RK to Beaverbrook, 14 February 1918, House of Lords.

101. See Watt to Society of Authors, 9 November 1913 and 2 February 1916, BL.

102. See Robertson, *The Hidden Cinema: British Film Censorship in Action.*

103. *A Book of Words.*

104. RK to Herbert Baker, 22 February 1934, Sussex.

105. RK to C. R. L. Fletcher, 24 March 1918, Sussex.

106. RK to Beaverbrook, 17 April 1918, House of Lords.

107. Rees extracts, 28 March 1918.

108. Rees extracts, 11 May 1918.

109. 22 May 1918, quoted Cohen (ed.), op. cit.

110. *SOM.*

111. See *Library Association Record*, May 1914, reprinted *Library Journal*, July 1915, p. 481.

112. See Repington, *The First World War: Personal Experiences*, entry for 8 May 1918.

113. See diary of John W. Davis, University of Virginia.

114. See RK to Oliver Baldwin, 2 August 1918, LOC.†

115. Augustine Birrell to Violet Asquith, 7 September 1911, quoted Bonham Carter and Pottle (eds), *Lantern Slides*.

116. Lord Derby to RK, 21 November 1917, Sussex.

117. RK to Oliver Baldwin, 4 October 1918, Sussex.

118. CK diary, 29 May 1918.

119. RK to Oliver Baldwin, 4 October 1918, Sussex.

120. RK to Dunsterville, 2 November 1918, Sussex.†

121. Rees extracts, 11 November 1918.

18: Waking from Dreams [pp. 660–720]

1. RK to Dr W. S. Melsome, 25 November 1918, Sussex.

2. Ponton, *Rudyard Kipling at Home and at Work*.

3. Bagnold, *Autobiography*.

4. RK to Oliver Baldwin, 4 October 1918, LOC.

5. CK diary, 13 November 1919.

6. For this and subsequent details see Baldwin, *The Questing Beast*.

7. Oswald Frewen diary.

8. CK diary, 8 December 1918.

9. Quoted Doubleday, *Episodes in the Life*.

10. RK to L. C. Dunsterville, 2 November 1918, Sussex.

11. Doubleday, op. cit.

12. See RK to L. C. Dunsterville, 2 November 1918, Sussex.†

13. RK to T. E. Lawrence, 7 January 1919, Syracuse.†

14. RK to H. Cabot Lodge, 15 March 1919, Harvard.†

15. RK to T. E. Lawrence, 8 October 1919, Syracuse.†

16. Ibid., undated.

17. Ibid., 20 July 1922.

18. Ibid., 25 July 1922.

19. RK to Rider Haggard, 8 March 1925, quoted Cohen (ed.), op. cit.

20. T. E. Lawrence to Robert Graves, 22 September 1929, quoted Lawrence, *Lawrence to his Biographers*.

21. RK to André Chevrillon, 6 October 1919, Sussex.†

22. Haggard diary, 30 January 1922, quoted Higgins, *The Private Diaries of Sir H. Rider Haggard*.

23. RK to C. R. L. Fletcher, 9 June 1923, Sussex.

24. Haggard diary, 4 December 1919, quoted Higgins, op. cit.

25. RK to André Chevrillon, 10 November 1919, Sussex.†

26. RK to C. R. L. Fletcher, 12 July 1918, Sussex.

27. Quoted Cushing, *The Life of Sir William Osler*.

28. RK to A. P. Watt, 3 November 1919, BL.†

29. RK to L. Cope Cornford, 31 July 1921, LOC. (In fact, Methuen published a verse anthology, and Macmillan a prose one.)

30. CK diary, 20 November 1920.

31. See Rees extracts, 20 December 1921. Doubleday worked closely with Heinemann and, in 1921, took over the company, following the death of the founder William Heinemann.

32. Sir Frederick Macmillan to Daniel Macmillan, 10 August 1923, BL.

33. CK to Watt, 14 December 1928, NYPL.

34. See Lorna Howard, KJ, September 1988.

35. CK diary, 25 February 1920.

36. RK to Chevrillon, 7 February 1920, Sussex.

37. See Longworth, *The Unending Vigil*. (Perhaps Lord Hugh Cecil remembered that RK had looked to the same chapter of Ecclesiasticus for the school song at the beginning of *Stalky & Co.*)

38. Ibid.

39. See KJ.

40. Quoted Longworth, op. cit.

41. See Storrs, *Orientations*.

42. See Josephine Dunham to CK, n.d. (probably 1919), Sussex.

43. See RK to Lady Bland-Sutton, 11 October 1920, RCS.

44. Lord Howard de Walden to author, 1998.

45. RK to M. Hamoneau, 5 December 1920, LOC.

46. RK to Colonel Feilden, 21–22 February 1921, Sussex.

47. *Souvenirs of France.*

48. RK to Colonel Feilden, 25 February 1921, Sussex.

49. Ibid., 20 February 1921.

50. Ibid., 27 March 1921.

51. KJ, September 1988.

52. RK to Guy Paget, 7 May 1921, *Letters to Guy Paget.*

53. See Taufflieb, *Memoir.*

54. Ibid.

55. RK to Cope Cornford, (1 January 1922), LOC.

56. Ponton, op. cit.

57. RK to Michael Mason, 19 May 1932, private collection.

58. Rees extracts, 23 March 1922.

59. See Bland-Sutton's book of epigrams at the Royal College of Surgeons.

60. See Gibson, *Lorca.*

61. Motor Tours, 11 May 1922.

62. Ibid., 13 May 1922.

63. RK medical diary, 28 July 1922.

64. CK diary, 14 August 1922.

65. Oliver Baldwin to Lord Birkenhead, Birkenhead notes.

66. Oswald Frewen diary, June 1922.

67. Sir J. Bland-Sutton's surgical diary, RCS.

68. RK medical diary, 7 January 1923.

69. Ibid., 27 December 1922.

70. RK to Dr Vaughan Bateson, 30 April 1923, quoted Bateson.

71. *A Book of Words.*

72. RK medical diary, 19 February 1923.

73. 20 March 1923, quoted Cohen (ed.), op. cit.

74. Ibid.

75. *SOM.*

76. RK to Saintsbury, 20 September 1921, Sussex.

77. See Lamb, *Mussolini and the British.*

78. Motor Tours, 8 May 1923.

79. Baldwin, op. cit.

80. See Rhodes James (ed.), *Memoirs of a Conservative.*

81. Captain James Garrard left effects worth a mere £1667. 10s. 9d when he died in a nursing home in Guernsey on 11 July 1935.

82. See RK to Haggard, 30 July and 1 August 1923, quoted Cohen (ed.), op. cit.

83. Like Burns before him, Rudyard was 'Poet Laureate' of the Lodge Canongate Kilwinning No 2 (S.C.). He had joined in 1899, while in Scotland recuperating after Josephine's death. He became 'Poet Laureate' six years later.

84. CK diary, 17 October 1923.

85. Ibid., 19 October 1923.

86. Motor Tours, 15 October 1923.

87. Manuscript, Durham University.

88. See Lisa Lewis's article 'Some Links between the Stories in Kipling's "Debits and Credits", *English Literature in Transition*, 25/2, 1982, pp. 74–84. I am indebted to Mrs Lewis for bringing this to my attention.

89. CK diary, 29 January 1924.

90. Ibid., 28 January 1924.

91. See statement of accounts etc., Sussex.

92. RK to Oliver Baldwin, 26 October 1922, LOC.

93. See Baldwin, op. cit.

94. RK to Dunsterville, 11 June 1917, Sussex.

95. Sandra Kemp has suggested that RK was influenced by Roman Catholic ideas of the 'Way of Exchange'. See her notes to the Penguin edition of *Debits and Credits*.

96. RK to Bland-Sutton, 3 March 1924, RCS.

97. RK to Bambridge, 20 March 1924, Sussex.

98. RK to Fletcher, 30 March 1924, Sussex.

99. RK to Bambridge, 31 March 1924, Sussex.

100. RK to Fabian Ware, 8 April 1924, Commonwealth War Graves Commission.

101. See Coates, *The Day's Work*.

102. EK to Oliver Baldwin, 2 August 1924, private collection.

103. See Kipling papers, Sussex.

104. CK diary, 22 October 1924.

105. Sir Percy Bates to Gwynne, 20 August 1924, Bodleian.

106. RK and CK to EB, 11 December 1924, Sussex.

107. CK diary, 24 December 1924.

108. Rees extracts, 9 February 1925.

109. RK to EB, 19 February 1925, Sussex.

110. RK to Bates, 2 February 1932, Sussex.

111. RK to Haggard, 14 March 1925, quoted Cohen (ed.), op. cit.

112. Ibid.

113. Motor Tours, 24 March 1925.

114. CK diary, 27 March 1925.

115. RK to Sir Hugh Clifford, 24 May 1925, quoted *Notes and Queries*.

116. RK to EB, 24 July 1925, Sussex.

117. CK diary, 28 August 1925.

118. CK diary, 30 December 1925.

19: The New Conservative [pp. 721–62]

1. RK to Gwynne, 10 April 1926, Sussex.

2. *A Book of Words*.

3. See Doubleday, op. cit.

4. RK to EB and GB, 12 June 1926, Sussex.

5. RK to Frances Stanley, 28 May 1926, Sussex.

6. CK diary, 31 August 1926.

7. *The Times*, 2 July 1929.

8. Jones, *Whitehall Diary*.

9. RK to EB and GB, 13 July 1926, Sussex.

10. RK to Lady Joynson-Hicks, 8 January 1928, private collection.

11. See Newman, *The Stanhopes of Chevening*.

12. RK to William Morris, 23 October 1926, National Library of Australia.

13. RK to Walter Creighton, 10 October 1927, Sussex.

14. RK to Stephen Tallents, 10 October 1927.

15. Information from Swann, *The British Documentary Film Movement 1926–1946*.

16. See correspondence in Royal Archives PS/GV/PS 48756.

17. RK to Gwynne, 14 November 1929, Sussex.

18. B. K. Long to Gordon Robbins, 20 June 1921, *Times* archives.

19. RK to EB, 22 December 1924, Sussex.

20. See Briggs, *The History of Broadcasting*, Vol. 2; also CK diary, 19 November 1925, and information from BBC archives.

21. See correspondence between RK and John Reith in Kipling papers at Sussex.

22. RK to Gwynne, 11 September 1933, Sussex.

23. RK to EB, 30 August 1925, Sussex.

24. RK to Samuel Bensusan, 29 April 1932, Syracuse.

25. Confusingly, Peter Stanley's real name was Gerald (Stanley).

26. CK diary, (1) January 1927.

27. RK to Frances Stanley, 28 May 1926. Sussex.

28. For an alternative view, see Tompkins, *The Art of Rudyard Kipling*, p. 256: 'The arabesques in "Aunt Ellen" have an unexpectedness that can be found in Dickens, together with a literary allusiveness which was outside his range.'

29. RK to EB and GB, 29 December 1926, Sussex.

30. RK to Colonel Feilden, March 1921, Sussex.

31. Many of these details come from a file of correspondence between RK and J. H. C. Brooking in the Kipling Society library.

32. Dunsterville to RK, 27 July 1925, Sussex.

33. RK to Dunsterville, 20 November 1927, Sussex.

34. Brooking to Beresford, 6 October 1942, Sussex.

35. 'The Beginning of the Armadilloes'.

36. RK to EB and GB, 14 February 1927, Sussex.

37. Ibid., 22 February 1927, Sussex.

38. Records of Fountain Club, St Bartholomew Hospital archives.

39. CK diary, 30 January 1928.

40. Ibid., 24 June 1928.

41. Speech to Royal Society of Medicine, 15 November 1928, published in *Official Bulletin of RSM*, no. 49.

42. RK to Peter Stanley, 26 November 1928, Sussex.

43. *Daily Telegraph*, 7 March 1930.

44. RK to Bland-Sutton, 12 March 1928, RCS.

45. Ibid.

46. Jan Perlowski, 'O Conradzie I Kiplingu', *Przeglad Wspolczesny*, Warsaw, 1937 (quoted in KJ, June 1967).

47. Baldwin, *On England*, p. 197, quoted in Philip Williamson: 'The Doctrinal Politics of Stanley Baldwin', an essay in *Public and Private Doctrine*, edited by Michael Bentley, CUP, 1993.

48. Reading of Lettcombe's desire to make a film about St Paul, and perhaps understanding something of Rudyard's interest, the American author and script-writer Don Marquis contacted him and offered to collaborate on a real film on the apostle. Marquis, author of *Archy and Mehitabel*, was not impressed when he was fobbed off with a secretary's note: 'the son-of-a-bitch was too proud to write me direct about it ... He could have got $100,000 for nothing, and he needs the money.' (Information from Professor Tom Pinney.)

49. CK diary, 22 June 1927.

50. CK diary, 18 December 1927. There is some doubt as to RK's exact role. On 15 December he informed the Imperial War Graves Commission that he felt no need to alter the inscription Sir Henry Newbolt had written for the Merchant Navy memorial outside Trinity House at Tower Hill. However, three days later he was, according to his wife's diary, definitely working on the inscription.

51. RK to Bates, 28 August 1929, Sussex.

52. RK to EB, 25 May 1927, Sussex.

53. RK to Stanley Baldwin, 25 May 1927, Baldwin papers 162/100, Cambridge.

54. Lady Byng to Lord Stamfordham, 20 June 1928, Royal Archives, GV Ka 2176/4, quoted in Williams, *Byng of Vimy*.

55. See *Evening Standard*, 1 December 1969.

56. RK to Marie Stopes, May 1925, Sussex.

57. See Souhami, *The Trials of Radclyffe Hall*.

58. RK to Rennell Rodd.

59. RK to Joynson-Hicks, 11 October 1928, private collection.

60. Ibid., 25 October 1928.

61. See RK to Gwynne, 10 April 1926, Sussex.

62. RK to Colonel Lewin, 25 May 1932, Sussex.

63. See Josephine Dunham, 'Our Weekend at Bateman's', KJ, December 1996.

64. Quoted Donaldson, *P. G. Wodehouse.*

65. See RK to EB and GB, 22 January 1929, Sussex.

66. CK diary, 2 September 1928.

67. RK to Lord Bathurst, 24 November 1929, Leeds.

68. RK to EB, 16 June 1927, Sussex.

69. RK to Guy Paget, 30 October 1932, *Letters to Guy Paget.*

70. Ibid., 4 January 1933.

71. RK to Peter Stanley, 26 November 1928, Sussex.

72. 4 June 1931, reported Young, *The Diaries of Sir Robert Bruce Lockhart.*

73. See Jarvis, *Desert and Delta.*

74. RK to Isabel Sykes, n.d., quoted KJ, March 1996.

75. RK to Sir Henry Newbolt, 5 April 1929, LOC.

76. RK to EB, 26 March 1929, Sussex.

77. RK to A. E. W. Mason, 30 October 1931, Sussex.

78. RK to A. S. Frere-Reeves, 27 December n.y., Syracuse.

79. RK to Guy Paget, 15 January 1933, *Letters to Guy Paget.*

80. RK to Gwynne, 14 November 1929, Sussex.

81. Ibid., 21 November 1929.

82. RK to EB, 24 March 1930, quoted KJ, December 1997.

83. Helen Hardinge to Lady Milner, 1930, Violet Milner papers, Bodleian.

84. Josephine Dunham memo, Sussex.

85. RK to EB, 25 August 1930, Sussex.

86. RK to Gwynne, 26 November 1930, Sussex.

87. RK to Edith Macdonald, 9 July 1930, Sussex. Two years earlier Edith had published her memoir, *Annals of the Macdonald Family.*

88. RK to EB and GB, 24 August 1925, Sussex.

89. RK to GB, 4 March 1931, Sussex.

90. Ibid., 20 March 1931.

91. RK to Gwynne, 19 February 1931, Sussex.

92. Ibid., 26 August 1931.

93. R. A. Butler recognised this quality and said that Baldwin's

'springing from the milieu of intellectual socialists to lead ... the Conservative party had been a great stroke of fortune.' Butler to Brabourne, 19 April 1937, quoted in Williamson, 'The Doctrinal Politics of Stanley Baldwin'.

94. RK to Gwynne, November 1931, Sussex.

95. Ibid., 11 June 1931, Sussex.

20: Limits and Renewals [pp. 763–801]

1. RK to Colonel Hughes, 4 September 1930, LOC.

2. Bagnold, *Autobiography*.

3. Birkenhead archive.

4. Lady Milner's diary, 19 December 1939, Violet Milner papers, Bodleian.

5. See Hart-Davis, *Hugh Walpole*.

6. See Birkenhead archive.

7. Ibid.

8. Ibid.

9. Ibid.

10. Carrington, *Kipling*.

11. 30 December 1931, quoted RK medical diary, Sussex.

12. See Birkenhead archive.

13. RK to EB and GB, 11 December 1930, Sussex.

14. CK diary, 10–11 March 1931.

15. RK to Bland-Sutton, 24 March 1931, RCS.

16. Ibid.

17. Rees extracts, 7 August 1931.

18. RK to Hughes, 14 December 1931, LOC.

19. RK to EB, 15 September 1931, Sussex.

20. RK to Gwynne, November 1931, Sussex.

21. Lord Lee's diary, 10 September 1931, quoted Clark (ed.), *A Good Innings*.

22. See Lycett Green (ed.), *John Betjeman, Letters*, Vol.1. Betjeman to Camilla Russell, 29 August 1931. Information on John Maude from Anthony Lejeune, letter to author, 24 November 1997.

23. RK to Edith Macdonald, 31 December 1931, Sussex.

24. Lady Milner's diary, 30 and 31 December 1931, Bodleian.

25. See correspondence between RK and Geoffrey Dawson in Bodleian. Rudyard had recommended a similar article to Gwynne at the *Morning Post*, 13 September 1931, Sussex.

26. See RK to J. B. Booth, 16 May 1933, quoted KJ, March 1997.

27. RK to Gwynne, 13 September 1931, Sussex.

28. RK to Bland-Sutton, 21 December 1932, RCS.

29. Ibid., 4 February 1932.

30. Richards had two favourite books – one of which was *Kim*. See Dr Richard Luckett, introduction to Constable (ed.), *Selected Letters of I. A. Richards CH*.

31. RK to EB, 31 May 1932, Sussex.

32. RK to Lady Bland-Sutton, 3 October 1932, RCS.

33. See also CK diary, 27 May 1935.

34. CK diary, 25 December 1932.

35. RK to EB and GB, 23 December 1932, Sussex.

36. RK to Herbert Baker, 13 January 1933, copy Rhodes Trust (file 2179).

37. Herbert Baker to E. T. Millar, 13 February 1933, Rhodes Trust (file 2179).

38. RK to Hughes, 11 May 1933, Sussex.

39. See RK medical diaries, April and May 1933, Sussex.

40. See CK diary, 30 August 1933.

41. Quoted Amory, *Lord Dunsany*.

42. RK to Lord Gorell, 1 January 1933, sold at Sotheby's, July 1997.

43. Ibid.

44. See RK to Lady Milner, 11 June 1932, BL.

45. RK to Gwynne, 12 January 1934, Sussex.

46. RK to EB and GB, 17 May 1933, Sussex.

47. Ibid., 21 January 1934, Sussex.

48. CK diary, 9 March 1934.

49. RK medical diary, 28 August 1934.

50. Almost certainly Reveres rather than Balestiers.

51. RK to Peter Stanley, 9 September 1934, Sussex.

52. RK to Peter Stanley, 9 September 1934, Sussex.

53. RK to Percy Bates, 5 December 1930, Sussex.

54. *SOM*.

55. RK to GB, 3 December 1934, Sussex.

56. RK to A. R. Rawlinson, 11 January 1935, Berg.

57. See RK to Michael Mason, 23 November 1935, private collection.

58. See McInnes, *Goodbye Melbourne Town*.

59. RK to EB, 7 June 1933, Sussex.

60. Quoted Strickland, *Angela Thirkell*.

61. RK to EB, 23 August 1933, Sussex.

62. RK to GB, 29 April 1934, Sussex.

63. Ibid., 18 February 1935.

64. CK diary, 12 June 1935.

65. RK to TF, 15 December 1935, private collection.

66. This is a rare example of Rudyard's working notes for a story. It was found by Lisa Lewis in a bound book of Rudyard's short stories in Durham University Library. She believes they probably were put there after Rudyard's death in mistake for the actual story. See Kemp and Lewis, *Writings on Writing*.

67. Rees extracts, 6 May 1935.

68. RK to Professor H. Haultain, 8 November 1935, Sussex.

69. RK to Dr P. Brès, 11 May 1935, BL photocopy, Syracuse.

70. RK to Hughes, 27 July 1935, LOC.

71. CK diary, 1 August 1935.

72. RK to TF, 15 December 1935, private collection.

73. RK to Charles Allen, September to December 1935, Dalhousie.

74. RK to Hughes, 6 January 1933, LOC.

75. Ibid., 3 January 1934, LOC.

76. RK to TF, 15 December 1935, private collection.

77. RK to Hughes, 14 June 1935, LOC.

78. Ibid., 9 December 1935, LOC.

79. 3 June 1935, see Lady Milner papers, Bodleian.

80. Ibid., 4 September 1935.

81. CK diary, 21 December 1935.

82. RK to Dr Theodore Dunham, 8 January 1936, Dunham papers.

83. Lady Milner papers, Bodleian.

84. See Muggeridge, *Like It Was.*

85. In fact two volumes of uncollected writings were published, with little or no input from Squire.

86. Brooking to Dunsterville, 25 April 1936.

87. See Definitive Edition of Rudyard's poetry, published by Hodder and Stoughton in November 1940.

88. CK to Gwynne, 3 November 1936, Dalhousie.

89. TF to Julius Macdonald, 26 June 1939, private collection.

90. See Mason, *The Paradise of Fools.*

91. EB to Lady Milner, 27 December 1939, Violet Milner papers, Bodleian. (Carrie was cremated and her ashes were subsequently scattered in the garden of Bateman's.)

92. EB notes on Birkenhead's manuscript, Sussex.

93. Birkenhead to Roderick Jones, Reuters archives.

Acknowledgements

I could not have written this book without help, encouragement and advice from a large number of people – to all of whom, many thanks.

At the very beginning of my research, Peter Hopkirk gave me an extremely useful collection of books. He also put me in touch with the leading Kipling expert, Lisa Lewis, who has courteously fielded my questions, shared her insights, and read various versions of my text. Among others who have been generous with their time and knowledge are Professor Thomas Pinney and Michael Smith, secretary of the Kipling Society.

I have been helped enormously by the kindness of various individuals who have allowed me to use original manuscripts in their possession. They include Wolcott B. Dunham, Mrs Susan Eastmond, Jonathan Frewen, Lorraine Price, Helen and Betty Macdonald, Lady Juliet Townsend, the Earl and Countess Baldwin of Bewdley, Viscount Brentford, Michael Mason, Lord Montagu of Beaulieu, Lord Neidpath, Josias Cunningham, Christopher Walker, Stowe Phelps, Charles Yorke, Dr Peter Hard, the Marchioness of Dufferin and Ava.

I would also like to thank the following people who have assisted in various important ways: Fiona Campbell, Kevin Angell, Dr Philip Williamson, David Richards, Nick Wilson, Lola Armstrong, Robin Egerton, Kathleen Browne, Mary Lutyens, Count John de Salis, Nigel Clarke, Dennis Griffiths, Roberta Mayer, Dave Tansey, Peter Lewis, Patrick French, Jane Hard, John Physick, John Christian, Alison Inglis, Linda Shaughnessy, Richard and Leonée Ormond, Lord Egremont,

Melvyn Sturridge, Terry Pitt, Fred Lusted, Lieutenant-Colonel Sir John Johnstone, Dr Francis Price, Sir Martin Gilbert, Anthony Lejeune, Miles Huntington-Whiteley, Lieutenant-Colonel Lionel Landon, Lord Howard de Walden, Kiloran Russell.

In addition to those mentioned above, other people have commented on sections of the text: Andrew Huxley, Major Michael Lycett, Professor Caroline Dakers, Nigel Cross, Michael Holmsten and Tessa Schneider.

A large number of libraries and institutions have provided Kipling-related letters and other documentary material. I acknowledge their assistance and (where relevant) permission to quote from their archives.

These include Sussex University, the official repository of the Kipling papers (special thanks to Bet Inglis), Dalhousie University (Karen Smith), Beinecke Library, Yale University (Vincent Giroud), New York Public Library (Rodney Phillips and Philip Milito), Library of Congress (Rob Shields), Marlboro College (Molly Brennan), the Royal Archives by gracious permission of Her Majesty the Queen (Lady de Bellaigue), News International (Eamonn Dyas and Nick Mays), British Library (Sally Brown), Bodleian Libary (Judith Priestman), Brenthurst Library (Diana Madden), Cornell University (Lorna Knight), University of Reading (Michael Bott), University of North Carolina (Richard Shrader), Eton College (Michael Meredith), McGill University (Richard Virr), Kipling Society (Trixie Shreiber), Durham University (Elizabeth Raine), Public Record Office (Nicholas Cox), State Library of New South Wales (Warwick Hirst), Princeton University (Don Skemer), Birmingham University (Chris Penney), Portsmouth Central Library (Alan King), Reuters (John Entwistle), House of Lords Record Office on behalf of the Beaverbrook Foundation Trust (Katharine Bligh), South African Library (Jackie Loos), Brown University (Mary-Jo Kline), University of Cape Town (Lesley Hart), Rhodes House Library (Caroline Brown), Syracuse University (Terrance Keenan), Royal Society of Medicine (Claire Jackson), London Library (Alan Bell).

Reed Archives, Huntington Library, India Office, Cambridge University Library, Duke University, Columbia University, Houghton Library at Harvard University, Bristol University, Public Record Office for Northern Ireland, University of Virginia, King's School Canterbury,

National Library of Australia, National Library of Wales, Beaver College, Brattleboro Library, Boston University, School of Oriental and African Studies, Winchester College, University of Texas, Wellesley College, Trinity College Cambridge, Churchill College Cambridge, Cheltenham Ladies' College, National Library of New Zealand, Pierpont Morgan Library, Commonwealth War Graves Commission, East Sussex, West Sussex, Wiltshire and Oxfordshire Record Offices, Royal College of Surgeons, St Bartholomew's Hospital, National Maritime Museum, Victoria and Albert Museum, Athenaeum Club.

In particular, I should like to thank the following copyright holders: The National Trust for Places of Historic Interest or Natural Beauty (the Kipling copyright holder) and Macmillan Press (for material in its editions of *The Letters of Rudyard Kipling* edited by Professor Tom Pinney).

While every effort has been made to trace copyright holders, if any have inadvertently been overlooked, the publishers will be pleased to acknowledge them in future editions of this book.

At Weidenfeld & Nicolson, I have again been privileged to be edited by Ion Trewin. His assistant Rachel Leyshon was unfailingly helpful and a pleasure to work with, while Emma Baxter made light work of some difficult late changes to the text. Ilsa Yardley was a highly effective copy editor and Douglas Matthews proved more than just an indexer sans pareil.

Finally and perhaps most important has been the wonderful and loving support of Sue Greenhill.

If anyone wants to communicate with me regarding this book please do so either through my publisher or by e-mail directly to me at alycett@btinternet.com

Index